D1757022

ARTICLE 81 EC AND PUBLIC POLI

This book discusses the role of public policy in Article 81 of the EC Treaty. The Commission, and recently the Court of First Instance have said that the sole objective of Article 81 EC is consumer welfare. Many competition lawyers support this view. Writing in a crisp, plain style, Townley demonstrates that public policy considerations are still relevant in that provision. He also suggests how and where they should be considered.

The book explains how some of the most complex competition law cases can be understood and offers a framework for those fighting or deciding such cases in the future. As such, it will be of interest to European competition lawyers, both academics and practitioners; as well as students, seeking a deeper understanding of how the European competition rules work and how they interact both with European Union and Member State public policy goals. It will also help competition economists by revealing the mechanisms through which public policy considerations impact upon the consumer welfare test in European law.

Article 81 EC and Public Policy

Christopher Townley

·HART·
PUBLISHING

OXFORD AND PORTLAND, OREGON
2009

Published in North America (US and Canada) by
Hart Publishing
c/o International Specialized Book Services
920 NE 58th Avenue, Suite 300
Portland, OR 97213–3786
USA
Tel: +1 503 287 3093 or toll-free: (1) 800 944 6190
Fax: +1 503 280 8832
E-mail: orders@isbs.com
Website: http://www.isbs.com

Hart Publishing Ltd, 16C Worcester Place, Oxford, OX1 2JW
Telephone: +44 (0)1865 517530 Fax: +44 (0)1865 510710
E-mail: mail@hartpub.co.uk
Website: http://www.hartpub.co.uk

British Library Cataloguing in Publication Data
Data Available

ISBN: 978-1-84113-968-5

Typeset by Columns Design Limited, Reading, UK
Printed and bound in Great Britain by
TJ International Ltd, Padstow, Cornwall

This book is dedicated to Mr F.E. Townley (my grandad),
for his friendship, patience and wisdom.

Acknowledgements

Work on this book would never have begun had it not been for the support and enthusiasm of one of my favourite lawyers, Anna Bessant. Professors Amato, Motta, Petersmann, Ullrich and Whish all made helpful comments on the Ph.D. thesis which led to this book; Giorgio Monti's 2002 article in the area and his criticism of my work have been invaluable. Since the Ph.D., which I defended at the EUI, Florence, I have received untiring competition law and economics feedback from Giorgio Monti, James MacBeth, Liza Lovdahl Gormsen and Richard Whish. In addition, many have provided support to me (though perhaps you did not know it) both during my stay in Florence and at other times, my family and friends (particularly Aidan Maddocks, Alex Carter, Alex Waters, Amy Walker, Charlotte Maddocks, Clare Townley, dad, Dave Dyer, David Osman, Fred Houwen, Galina Cornelisse, Heli Askola, Javier San Julian Arrupe, Lorenzo Zucca, Mark Braley, Maya Daoud, Monica Ariño Gutierrez, mum, Neil Carter, Oke Odudu, Osla Fraser, Rafael Gafoor, Rob Maddocks, Ross Velton, Srdjan Cvijic, Vittorio Muschitiello and Zahid Naqvi), thank you all.

I would also like to thank my Ph.D.-funding body, the Department for Education and Skills, which was extremely generous; as well as King's College London.

But most of all, thank you to Ellie Smith, my anchor through all of this writing; you gave me so much, and made me so whole. Your leaving has torn me in two, a blue boat battered on a stormy sea. Though I will never understand, I hope that you have found what you were looking for. I always remember you; forever, suddenly.

Table of Contents

Part C: How and Where Should Public Policy Balancing be Performed in Article 81 EC?

List of Abbreviations

CFI	Court of First Instance
CMLRev	*Common Market Law Review*
Commission	European Commission
Community	European Community
Community Courts	The CFI and ECJ
Council	The Council of the European Union
CSR	Corporate Social Responsibility
CUP	Cambridge University Press
ECJ	European Court of Justice
ECLR	*European Competition Law Review*
ECMR	Council Regulation 139/2004, *On the Control of Concentrations Between Undertakings*, OJ 2004 L24/1
EEA	European Economic Area
ESCB	European System of Central Banks
EU	European Union
EU Treaty	The Treaty on European Union, as amended by the Lisbon Treaty
FEU Treaty	The Treaty Establishing the European Community, as amended by the Lisbon treaty
Institutions	The institutions of the EU including, the Commission, the Council and the Community Courts
Merger Regulation	Council Regulation 4064/89 *On the Control of Concentrations Between Undertakings*, OJ 1990 L257/13 (as corrected and amended up until 2004)
NYU	*New York University Law Review*
OECD	Organisation for Economic Co-operation and Development
OFT	Office of Fair Trading, UK
OUP	Oxford University Press
R&D	Research and development
SEA	Single European Act
SME	Small or medium-sized enterprise
Treaty	The Treaty establishing the European Community
U Pa L Rev	*University of Pennsylvania Law Review*
USA	United States of America
USD	United States Dollars

Other abbreviations have been used, but they are either defined in the text, or can be found in the Bibliography.

Table of Cases

European Commission decisions

EUROPEAN FREE TRADE AREA (EFTA)

UNITED KINGDOM UK COMPETITION APPEAL TRIBUNAL

Table of Legislation

Resolutions, Notices and Communications

NATIONAL LEGISLATION AND REPORTS

Côte d'Ivoire

International Competition Network

Mexico

The Netherlands

OECD

UNCTAD

Introduction

This book discusses public policy's place within Article 81 EC.[1] It demonstrates that both economic and non-economic goals[2] are relevant there; and suggests how and where relevant public policy goals should be considered within Article 81.[3]

Bork has famously said that:

> Antitrust policy cannot be made rational until we are able to give a firm answer to one question: What is the point of the law – what are its goals? Everything else follows from the answer we give. Is the antitrust judge to be guided by one value or by several? If by several, how is he to decide cases where a conflict in values arises? Only when the issue of goals has been settled is it possible to frame a coherent body of substantive rules.[4]

Bork's first point is that we must consider whether, in competition cases, the decision-maker should be guided 'by one value or by several' goals. An OECD report on the design and implementation of competition law and policy refers to two ends of a spectrum in the debate about competition policy's objectives.[5] At one end is the view that the sole purpose of competition policy is to maximise economic efficiency; this approach leaves no room for the direct consideration of socio-political criteria, such as environmental policy. The conflicting view is that competition policy is based on multiple values that cannot be reduced to a single economic goal. These values reflect society's wishes, culture, history, institutions and perception of itself. They cannot and should not be ignored in competition law enforcement.

---

[1]   Art 81 EC is the Community equivalent of s 1 of the Sherman Act 1890 in the USA and Ch 1 of the UK's Competition Act 1998.

[2]   In this book, 'non-economic goals' refers to all public policy objectives, with the exception of economic efficiency. Furthermore, 'non-economic goals', 'political considerations', 'non-economic values', 'non-welfare aims', 'non-efficiency goals' and 'public policy objectives', and any combination of the above, are treated as synonyms.
  Note the decision to pursue economic efficiency through competition law is itself a public policy choice and this carve-out of the non-economic definition is not intended to deny that.

[3]   This book should also interest many not focused on Art 81 EC. Community competition policy forms a whole, the different provisions pursue the same aims, see, for example, Case 6/72 *Europemballage and Continental Can v Commission* para 25. Therefore, many of my conclusions are equally applicable to Art 82 and merger analysis. Furthermore, my demonstration of how and why the Treaty should be interpreted as a systemic whole will interest readers outside of the competition law world. In this sense, I hope that it might be viewed as a bridge between competition lawyers and other Community specialists. Finally, Ch 5, in particular, on how public policy can impact within the consumer welfare test, should be of interest to economists.

[4]   Bork (1978) 50. See also Carlton (2007) 1.

[5]   The World Bank and OECD (1999) 1, 2.

Hovenkamp is a vocal exponent at the first end of this spectrum. He has, somewhat controversially, said that no-one in the mainstream United States debate:

> [W]ould any longer assert that consumer welfare should not be the central or even exclusive goal of antitrust, or that antitrust should be concerned about unemployment, inflation or other macroeconomic issues.[6]

By way of contrast, in the European Union, the Council, Commission, Community Courts and European Parliament have all repeatedly endorsed the consideration of public policy objectives within Article 81 EC; and Community competition lawyers generally recognise that public policy has been considered there.[7]

However, change is afoot. In 2004 the Commission said the '… objective of Article 81 is to protect competition on the market as a means of enhancing consumer welfare and of ensuring an efficient allocation of resources.'[8] There is a (growing) tendency among Community competition specialists to treat their topic in a highly technical way, as distinct from Community law as a whole.[9] Many now agree with the Commission that Community competition policy should pursue a unitary consumer welfare goal.[10]

One might question whether excluding the consideration of socio-political criteria from the competition assessment is the right approach. Some argue that, as the law stands, the competition rules contained in the Treaty are part of a wider system and must be interpreted in this context. Take the late Lord Slynn for instance:

> The task of the European Court is to ensure that in the interpretation and application of the EEC Treaty the law is observed. In construing particular Articles of the Treaty it is hardly surprising that the Court should have regard to the framework of the Treaty as a whole, to its general principles, to the tasks and activities which the Treaty prescribes for the Community.[11]

More particularly, in relation to Community competition policy, former Competition Commissioner van Miert has said:

> Competition policy has so long been a central Community policy that it is often forgotten that it is not an end in itself but rather one of the instruments towards the fundamental goals laid out in the Treaty – namely the establishment of a common market, the approximation of economic policy, the promotion of harmonious development and economic expansion, the increase of

---

[6] Ehlermann (1998) 13. For contrary views see, Fox (1998) 15 and Laussel and Montet (1995) 57 and the references there.

[7] See, eg, Monti (2007) ch 4; Odudu (2006) ch 7; Goyder (2003) 121–123; B&C (2008) paras 1–071–1–077; Whish (2008) 19–23; Korah (2000) s 1.3.2.; Ritter and Braun (2005) 17–19; Faull and Nikpay (2007) paras 3.12–3.22; Mercier, Mach, Gilliéron and Affolter (1999) 130–132; Ehlermann (1998) 356, 359–385, 489; Amato (1997) 114; Sauter (1997); Bouterse (1994); Frazer (1990) 616 and Verstrynge (1988) 5. For a contrary view see Schaub (1998) 9.

[8] Commission, *Article 81(3) Guidelines*, para 13. More recently, this was mirrored by the CFI in Case T–168/01 *GlaxoSmithKline Services v Commission*, esp paras 118, 273. This judgment is currently on appeal to the ECJ, in part on this issue, see Joined Cases C–501/06 etc *GlaxoSmithKline Services v Commission*. See also, the Opinion of A-G Trstenjak, Case C–209/07 *The Competition Authority v BIDS* para 56, supporting the CFI's judgment and Joined Cases C–468/06 to C–478/06 *Sot Lelos kai Sia EE and Others v GlaxoSmithKline*, esp para 65, which seems to undermine it.

[9] Baquero Cruz (2002) 1. This tendency is often reinforced by political scientists and specialists in other Community law disciplines who tend to ignore Community competition policy, Wesseling (1999a) 6, 7.

[10] See, eg recordings of the Fiesole conference in Ehlermann (2001) 302, 303, 359. See also Amato (1997) 116 and further references can be found in Ch 2 n 8.

[11] Slynn (1985) 393. Lord Slynn of Hadley was formerly a judge at the ECJ.

living standards and the bringing about of closer relationship between Member States. Competition therefore cannot be understood or applied without reference to this legal, economic, political and social context.[12]

This dispute, between those that read the competition rules in isolation and those that read the Treaty holistically, goes to the very heart of Treaty interpretation. It affects everything, from the substantive interpretation of individual provisions to the facility with which the Treaty can be applied, procedurally. Its resolution is vital for determining whether, in Article 81 cases, the Community decision-maker should be guided 'by one value or by several' goals.[13]

In the light of the paucity of recent, systematic, English language analysis in the area,[14] this book examines public policy's role in Article 81 EC and how it should be considered there. I have been helped in this task by three studies which discuss Article 81's interaction with specific public policies.[15] I hope that, by encompassing several policy heads, my approach complements these other works by revealing general trends in the role of public policy within Article 81.

Part A of the book discusses the relevance of non-economic objectives in antitrust. Chapter 1, which serves as a theoretical starting point for the discussion, asks why public policy objectives might be incorporated within a competition law and when this might be appropriate. This analysis is not made within the context of a specific legal system. However, useful as this approach is, in theory, it is less useful for helping us predict what the relevance of public policy goals ought to be in a specific legal context. Legal context is important. As Shenefield, somewhat pessimistically says:

> [A] goal of perfect convergence [in global competition policy] … is an illusion. It can never happen; and even if it could happen, it would in all probability be a bad thing. There are too many variations of country and culture to permit a uniform formulation of the law of competition to be successful everywhere and for all times.[16]

One might agree or disagree with his views on the feasibility of introducing international antitrust rules; but, it is hard to dispute that law (and more importantly legal interpretation) is founded in country and culture. As we have seen, Slynn and van Miert both agree that Article 81 must be interpreted in its Treaty context, for example.

It is an interesting debate; but, one might ask, whether it is worth spilling ink on this topic; or, does the debate about Article 81's goals makes any substantive difference? The clear answer to that question is that, of course, it does. The inclusion of non-economic objectives in Article 81 cases can significantly complicate decision-making. It can also fundamentally alter the final outcome. This is important, as it impacts upon the agreement's status under Article 81(2) EC; there are also fining, damages and reputational

---

[12]   van Miert (1993) 120. Admittedly, he may have changed his mind of late, see the implications of van Miert in Ehlermann (2001) 52.

[13]   Townley (2008) discusses whether, in the absence of government regulation, part of the solution to the UK's binge-drinking problem might be to allow supermarkets and other outlets to fix minimum prices for the sale of alcohol. I ask whether this anti-competitive solution could be justified under Art 81 EC on public health grounds.

[14]   Ehlermann (1998) 480 makes a similar point. Monti (2002) is an excellent recent exception; however, we disagree on many points.

[15]   eg Cseres (2004) consumer protection; Vedder (2003) environmental policy; and Sauter (1997) industrial policy.

[16]   Shenefield (2004) 388, 389. See also Ehlermann (1998) 484.

implications. For these reasons alone, resolving this debate is vital. However, there are additional reasons why answers are particularly keenly sought today.

First, the idea that competition is currently given too much weight in the Community legal order was a major source of conflict in the recent Lisbon Treaty negotiations. French President Sarkozy, for example, argued that more weight should be given to public policy goals in the balance.[17] The latest financial crisis has further tested the decision-makers' resolve to ignore public policy goals in the competition rules. Regardless of whether the Lisbon Treaty is implemented, the Community courts will need to deal with the fallout from these incidents.

Secondly, Regulation 1/2003 abolishes the notification regime.[18] As a result, the parties to an agreement[19] can no longer gain immunity from fines through notification.[20] More importantly, this lack of guidance reduces the certainty about the agreement's status under Article 81(2) EC. More uncertainty increases the litigation risk, which may deter parties from concluding welfare-enhancing agreements in the first place, even where acceptable under Community law.

Furthermore, Regulation 1/2003 decentralises Article 81 enforcement. The Commission can still take Article 81 decisions; however, in addition, the whole of Article 81 is now directly enforceable in the Member States' courts and competition authorities. A plethora of new bodies can now apply Article 81(3) EC, unless it is clear which objectives are relevant in Article 81, there is a risk of inconsistency and even 'wrong' decisions.

Another important reason for studying the relevance of public policy in Article 81 today is that Neelie Kroes, the current Competition Commissioner, may be replaced at the end of 2009. The Commissioner for Competition can dramatically affect, in a day to day way, the consideration of non-economic objectives by the Commission, and thus by other relevant decision-makers[21] (although I show that this should only happen within the limits that the Community courts dictate).

Article 81 has often been used as a tool for achieving Treaty objectives, such as market integration,[22] to bypass blockages in the legislative process.[23] If the Lisbon Treaty is not adopted, the recent enlargement of the Community and its impact on decision-making effectiveness may mean that more reliance is again placed on this objective, and others, in Article 81.

---

[17] Graupner (2007).

[18] Commission, *Guidance Letters Guidelines*, still allows the parties to seek informal guidance from the Commission on novel questions; however, this will not often apply, arts 7–10.

[19] For the purposes of this book I only refer to 'agreements' but, where the context allows, this also includes, by implication, 'decisions by associations of undertakings and concerted practices'. Also, I only refer to 'restriction of competition'. This expression usually includes 'prevention, restriction or distortion of competition'.

[20] Something they effectively had once their agreement had been notified. Commission, *Guidance Letters Guidelines*, art 4, emphasises the Commission practice of only imposing more than symbolic fines when '… it is established, either in horizontal instruments or in the case law that a certain behaviour constitutes an infringement'.

[21] McGowan (2000) and McGowan and Wilks (1995) 160–162. This effect could have less impact now, due to decentralisation, but the Commission still has considerable authority in relation to Community competition policy. Decentralisation may even give the Commission the time to set a more overt competition policy. It is still too early to tell.

[22] Massey (1996) 122, 123.

[23] Gerber (1994) 108.

Finally, the ECJ is currently examining an appeal from the CFI's judgment in the *Glaxo Case*, where the objectives of Community competition law were discussed.[24] This is a perfect opportunity for the superior court to consolidate and explain the often contradictory jurisprudence in this area.[25]

Given the potential impact of considering public policy goals in Community competition law, outlined above, Chapter 2 debates their relevance, specifically in Article 81 EC. It concludes that both the Treaty's structure and the presence of the policy-linking clauses[26] create the possibility of conflicts between different goals. In many cases, including recent ones, where these conflicts occurred in Article 81 analysis, public policy objectives have been considered relevant there. I argue that this position is still correct today.

This leads us to Bork's second main point. If the decision-maker is to be guided by several values, how is he (or she) to decide which values are relevant in competition law and how to resolve clashes between them? The Commission recognises these problems and has produced a series of guidelines to clarify how decentralisation will work. In particular, Commission, *Article 81(3) Guidelines*, set out its view of the substantive assessment criteria for the application of Article 81 as a whole, and Article 81(3) EC in particular.[27] As former Competition Commissioner Monti says, '… one of the major goals of our reforms is to guarantee that, after 1 May 2004, companies benefit from a high degree of legal certainty as to what is allowed and what is not under the competition rules.'[28]

These guidelines are generally helpful. However, they say nothing of how to take proper account of non-economic objectives within Article 81, except that such goals are relevant only insofar as they can be subsumed within Article 81(3)'s four conditions—not easy given the Commission's declared objective of Article 81.[29] The Commission's bare statement on goals is particularly confusing because it does not take into account recent Community Court judgments; and, it may contradict the normal approach to Treaty interpretation, explained above by Lord Slynn. The lack of clarity is exacerbated because the Commission's policy statements are out of synch with its own decision-making practice, where it considers public policy arguments.

An interesting legal point, but surely the consideration of non-economic objectives within Article 81 does not arise very often? Such is the predominant view;[30] it is also in line with worldwide antitrust developments.[31] However, an examination of formal Commission decisions under Article 81 EC shows that public policy goals have influenced many of them. I estimate that, between 1993 and 1 May 2004,[32] public policy goals were decisive

---

[24] See references in n 8.

[25] Part C makes some suggestions in this regard.

[26] There are seven policy-linking clauses in the Treaty covering various public policy areas. One example is Art 152(1) EC, which reads: 'A high level of human health protection shall be ensured in the definition and implementation of all Community policies and activities.'

[27] Commission, *Article 81(3) Guidelines*, para 3.

[28] Monti (2004) 406.

[29] Commission, *Article 81(3) Guidelines*, para 42. van Gerven (2004) 434, says the same.

[30] See eg van der Woude (2002) 55, 56; Lenz (2000) 62 and Heimler and Fattori (1998) 599.

[31] See, Ch 1, Introduction.

[32] I have only examined Commission decisions until May 2004 because since then the profile of the decisions being taken by the Commission has changed, it mainly conducts cartel investigations today, where public policy arguments are likely to be less relevant. That said, more recent Commission decisions still imply that public policy considerations might be relevant in Art 81, for example, Commission decision, *CISAC*, paras 93–99, and I consider them elsewhere in this book.

(that is, altered the result) in over 32 per cent of formal Commission Article 81(3) decisions, see the pie chart below.[33]

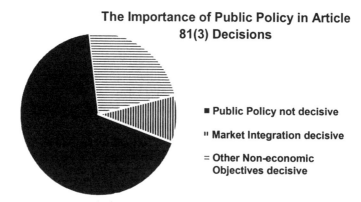

The book is in three sections. Part A, briefly explained above, considers whether non-economic objectives should be considered in antitrust and what the theoretical limits should be, in Chapter 1. Then, Chapter 2 examines Article 81 EC, in particular. It examines the Treaty, Community Court judgments and Commission practice and shows that many public policy concerns are relevant in Article 81 EC.

Chapters 1 and 2's conclusions are somewhat different. Chapter 1 argues, in a legal vacuum, that the consideration of non-welfare objectives is warranted, but only under strict conditions. Chapter 2 reveals a Treaty, and Community institutions, that more readily embrace the consideration of these objectives.

Having concluded that non-economic objectives are relevant in Article 81 appraisal, Part B discusses how and where public policy concerns are currently considered there. It also examines how important these non-economic considerations have been in the analysis. It is vital to understand what is happening today, when evaluating whether changes are needed.

I argue that non-economic objectives are considered within Article 81 EC via two mechanisms. I call the first mechanism 'mere-balancing'. Mere-balancing operates *outside* of the consumer welfare assessment. By this I mean that the decision-maker first assesses

---

[33] I include market integration as a public policy goal within this figure. Even if market integration is excluded, public policy goals were decisive in about 23% of these decisions.

As these objectives are not always discussed overtly, some subjective interpretation is required. As a result, my categorisation of some decisions may be controversial. Nevertheless, these numbers are taken from Table 1 in the Annex. Table 1's numbers are detailed and explained in Table 2 in the same Annex. Furthermore, whatever the precise numbers, the pie chart demonstrates that non-economic objectives were important in a far from negligible number of cases.

Shelkoplyas (2003) 229 and Monti (2002) 1091 suggest that the amount of public policy in Art 81 is increasing. My research does not support the idea that, of late, non-economic objectives have been decisive in Art 81 more often (either absolutely, or as a percentage of decisions) see Annex; although, market integration has been used more often in Art 81(1) of late. However, the Commission often relies on non-economic objectives in its reasoning more overtly; which might be the effect that Monti and Shelkoplyas refer to.

an agreement's effect on consumer welfare and then balances this against its impact upon relevant public policy objectives.[34] Chapters 3 and 4 deal with mere-balancing in relation to Article 81(1) and (3), respectively.

Chapter 5 argues that there is a second mechanism for considering non-economic objectives within Article 81 EC; I call this market-balancing. Market-balancing occurs *within* the consumer welfare test itself, by altering the importance of its various components.[35] For example, in the consumer welfare analysis, by placing less weight on allocative efficiency losses and more weight on dynamic efficiency gains one can encourage R&D advances, which might generate industrial policy benefits.

Part B's findings are worrying. Non-economic objectives are considered in both Article 81(1) and (3). There is no guidance, or apparent consistency, about when one paragraph is more appropriate than the other. There is no explanation of what objectives might be considered relevant and why; in fact, the very consideration of these objectives is often disguised or even denied. Nor are we told how much weight these values should be given. Even the appropriate balancing mechanism is unclear. There is much work to do, and, as explained above, answers are urgently needed.

> [S]ince the foregoing objectives will not always be in perfect harmony, there is a requirement for a careful balancing of these sometimes competing objectives in the administration of competition law, and the need for an administrative framework that ensures independent and effective decision-making in the implementation of the law.[36]

Part C reflects upon the problems raised in Parts A and B. The current system is too unclear. The Commission's recent guidelines, while aiding transparency, ignore the Treaty's fundamental premises as well as those in the Community Courts' public policy jurisprudence. This is unacceptable, not only from a constitutional perspective; but, because this conflict undermines legal certainty, which is particularly important post 1 May 2004.

Certain elements must be at the heart of any proposed clarification. First and foremost, the proposed system must respect the Treaty, unless amendments are proposed; and the fundamental tenets of the Community Courts' case law. This means that decision-makers must be able to consider relevant public policy objectives within Article 81. Secondly, undertakings, decision-makers and consumers need more legal certainty in the balancing test and transparency in the way it is conducted. Thirdly, within this framework, we need as efficient a set of competition rules as possible.

Chapter 6 discusses Article 81(1) EC; it covers three main issues. First, the concept of a 'restriction of competition' is unclear and unsatisfactory; I suggest making consumer welfare Article 81(1)'s sole goal. Secondly, I discuss mere-balancing[37] within Article 81(1) EC and argue that this should be restricted to Article 81(3); Article 81's structure will then ensure that mere-balancing's costs are more clearly defined. The point is not that, in the Community legal order, economic welfare should permanently outweigh all other objectives; however, the Community increasingly relies on the market mechanism as the basic means of wealth creation and so it is logical to organise its competition law around the

---

[34]   Mere-balancing, as a mechanism, is explained in more detail in Ch 1, Section 2.2.2.
[35]   Market-balancing, as a mechanism, is explained in more detail in Ch 1, Section 2.2.1.
[36]   Goldman and Barutciski (1998) 415. Their discussion centres on balancing long and short-term efficiency in Canadian antitrust. Nonetheless, their underlying point is relevant to balancing non-economic objectives in Community competition law too.
[37]   Balancing consumer welfare against public policy outside of the consumer welfare assessment.

welfare standard. Finally, I consider that, as it lacks the requisite transparency, market-balancing[38] should be avoided in Article 81. It is hoped that these suggestions augment clarity, while respecting the Treaty's telos.

Chapter 7 analyses Article 81(3) EC. Many public policy goals will be automatically promoted through Article 81(1)'s consumer welfare test. Nevertheless, some objectives cannot be pursued indirectly through this test; others can be pursued in part, but not to the level that the Treaty demands. Given that, in the Community legal order, public policy goals cannot be isolated from the competition provisions, I suggest considering them in Article 81(3), via mere-balancing. Chapter 7's core analysis comes in four parts, each of which discusses one of Article 81(3)'s four tests. It explains, for example, some of the implications of incorporating non-economic objectives within that provision and suggests how this might better be done. In light of this and Chapter 1's conclusions, Chapter 7 also advocates the reinterpretation of Article 81(3)(a), to incentivise the pursuit of public policy goals through more optimal policy instruments. Finally, Chapter 8 provides a framework for balancing non-economic objectives under Article 81(3)'s first test.

Before concluding this Introduction, two further issues must be highlighted. First, antitrust, particularly when non-economic objectives are considered there, involves a combination of economics, politics and law. This book has been written by a lawyer, from a legal perspective. There is, accordingly, an emphasis on the interpretation of legal texts and case law, which in part eschews other contemporary approaches influenced by sociology and political science. Secondly, this book restricts itself to a mainstream discussion of public policy under Article 81 EC. It mentions Articles 82 and the ECMR only briefly. I spotlight Article 81 EC because there is more case law than in relation to Article 82 EC. Nevertheless, my Article 81 conclusions equally apply to Article 82, because these two provisions' objectives are the same.[39] The ECMR also seems to adopt the framework I suggest for analysing Article 81.[40] Furthermore, within the field of EC antitrust law, only the general context is really discussed. Exceptions to these rules, as in force in, for example, the agricultural and transport sectors, are highlighted only insofar as the general discussion requires.[41]

---

[38]   Balancing consumer welfare against public policy inside of the consumer welfare assessment by altering the importance assigned to the different constituent parts of the test.

[39]   Case 6/72 *Europemballage and Continental Can v Commission* para 25.

[40]   Recital 23, Reg 139/2004.

[41]   Special rules relating to public undertakings and undertakings to which Member States grant special or exclusive rights, Art 86 EC, are not considered either.

Part A

Considering Public Policy Objectives in Competition Law

Introduction to Part A

Competition policy cannot be rational until we decide what its underlying objectives are. Some argue, and this is the orthodox position, that economic efficiency should be the exclusive goal of competition law. Others say that public policy objectives should also be considered in the competition analysis.

Part A approaches this debate from two perspectives. Chapter 1 poses two core, theoretical, questions in a legal vacuum; by legal vacuum I mean that the assessment is not made within the context of a specific legal system. The first question I focus on is *why* it might be apposite for competition policy to incorporate public policy objectives. I conclude that considering public policy objectives within competition law analysis is sometimes warranted. So, I ask *when* it might be appropriate to consider public policy objectives in competition policy, suggesting that this should only happen under strict conditions.

Chapter 2 changes the emphasis, examining the first '*why*' question under Community law; I specifically focus on Article 81 EC. The consensus is that public policy objectives have been considered in Article 81 in the past. However, many now assume that the influence of these objectives in European competition policy is inappropriate, recent Commission policy statements support this view. Chapter 2 challenges this position. It reveals a Treaty that demands the consideration of public policy goals within competition assessments; and Community institutions, including the Commission itself, that readily consider public policy objectives in their Article 81 cases and decisions.

Part B then examines when and where public policy goals are considered within Article 81 EC. It reveals a confusing mix of approaches and outcomes, many of which differ from those set out in Chapter 1; so, Part C suggests how, when and where public policy should be considered within Article 81.

1

Competition Policy and Public Policy Objectives in a Theoretical Framework

1 INTRODUCTION

Many scholars and practitioners believe that only economic efficiency should be relevant in competition decisions; others argue that public policy has a role to play there too. Different legal systems reflect these two positions. Competition law cannot be rationally implemented until it has been decided whether public policy objectives should be considered there, and if so when.

The OECD Global Forum on Competition and UNCTAD note that competition systems, increasingly, place greater emphasis on economic efficiency, rather than other public interest goals, such as protecting small and medium-sized enterprises or cultural goals.[1] Indeed, the shift has been so great in some jurisdictions that, for example,

---

[1] Respectively, OECD (2003) 3, 4, 12 and UNCTAD (1995) 6. See also, Ehlermann (1998) ix, 323, 347, 354.

Hovenkamp, a prominent legal scholar, argues that no one in the mainstream United States debate would any longer assert that consumer welfare should not be the central or even exclusive goal of antitrust.[2]

In the European Union, the Commission has recently said that the aim of the Community competition rules is to protect competition on the market as a means of enhancing consumer welfare and of ensuring an efficient allocation of resources.[3] Other jurisdictions have adopted a similar stance. In most jurisdictions with a competition law today, the legislation's objective is to increase economic efficiency.[4]

That said, in some jurisdictions, competition policy also pursues 'non-efficiency' objectives.[5] Canada's competition law, for example, as explained by section 1.1 of its Competition Act 1985, was promulgated:

[T]o maintain and encourage competition in Canada in order to promote the efficiency and adaptability of the Canadian economy, in order to expand opportunities for Canadian participation in world markets while at the same time recognising the role of foreign competition in Canada, in order to ensure that the small and medium-sized enterprises have an equitable opportunity to participate in the Canadian economy and in order to provide consumers with competitive prices and product choices.

The theoretical debate about antitrust's goals largely mirrors this divergence in the competition rules. Many economists believe that economic efficiency (welfare) should be the exclusive focus of competition policy.[6] A leading textbook notes that economists generally view antitrust as a set of laws designed to promote competition and, therefore, economic efficiency.[7] Other scholars believe that competition policy should also advance non-efficiency objectives.[8] In the face of this disagreement, Chapter 1 poses two core questions *why* might competition policy incorporate public policy objectives, Section 2; and, given that I believe that this is sometimes appropriate, *when* might competition policy incorporate public policy objectives, Section 3? Both questions are discussed in a legal vacuum. This is not to say that legal context is unimportant; rather, I want to explore a theoretical 'ideal' and then, in the later chapters, to examine this 'ideal' in the specific legal context of the European Union.

---

[2] See Hovenkamp in Ehlermann (1998) 12–13. See also, United States' submission to OECD (2003) 2, 5; Hovenkamp (1998) 328 and Lipsky (1998) 331. For contrary views, see Fox (1998) 15 and Laussel and Montet (1995) 57 and the references there.

[3] Commission, *Article 81(3) Guidelines*, para 33. See also, DG Competition Discussion Paper, *on Article 82 EC*, para 4 and Case T-168/01 *GlaxoSmithKline Services v Commission* esp paras 118, 273. This judgment is currently on appeal to the ECJ, in part on this issue, see Joined Cases C-501/06 etc *GlaxoSmithKline Services v Commission*. See also, the Opinion of A-G Trstenjak, Case C-209/07 *The Competition Authority v BIDS* para 56, supporting the CFI's judgment and Joined Cases C-468/06 to C-478/06 *Sot Lelos kai Sia EE and Others v GlaxoSmithKline*, particularly para 65, which seems to undermine it.

[4] UNCTAD's submission to OECD (2003) 4.

[5] UNCTAD, *Model Law on Competition* (2007) 13–15. For example, s 2 of South Africa's Competition Law 1998 states that the purpose of the Act is to promote and maintain competition in the Republic in order, amongst other things, to promote employment and advance social and economic welfare of South Africans; to enable small and medium sized enterprises to participate in the economy; and to promote a wider ownership spread, particularly in relation to historically disadvantaged persons. See also ICN, *Report on the Objectives of Unilateral Conduct Laws* (2007) 17–20, 26, 27 and Annex A; n 9 of this report explains that most respondents' unilateral conduct objectives were common to their competition regimes as a whole.

[6] Motta (2004), s 1.3; Bishop and Walker (2002) 23–27; Posner (2001) ix and Bork (1993) 89, 405.

[7] Viscusi, Vernon and Harrington (2000) 67.

[8] See eg Siragusa in Ehlermann (1998) 469–70.

These two questions (why and when) must be answered before discussing the objectives of European competition law. This is because these questions provide theoretical insights into whether (and to what extent) it is desirable to consider non-economic objectives in antitrust.

2 WHY COMPETITION POLICY MIGHT INCLUDE PUBLIC POLICY OBJECTIVES

One way of thinking about whether public policy goals should be considered in competition decisions is to conduct a thought experiment, which might go something like this: what would be the result of excluding public policy goals from competition analysis? If said exclusion raised serious difficulties one could assess whether the inclusion of public policy there would be more or less problematic. If the consideration of public policy objectives solved more problems than it created, one might be tempted to include them in competition policy decisions, at least some of the time.

Before commencing this thought experiment I need to define some terms related to economic efficiency, in particular the three welfare standards: consumer surplus, producer surplus and total surplus.[9] Consumer surplus (consumer welfare) is the aggregate measure of the surplus of all (relevant) consumers. The surplus of a specific individual consumer is given by the difference between the consumer's valuation for the good considered (or her willingness to pay for it) and the price, which effectively she has to pay for it.[10] Likewise, producer surplus (producer welfare) is the aggregate measure of the surplus made by all (relevant) producers. The surplus of an individual producer is the profit it makes from selling the good in question. Finally, total surplus (total welfare) is the sum of the consumer and the producer surpluses.

The total surplus standard theoretically increases the gains for society as a whole. Some urge its adoption as *the* competition law goal, noting that even if this produces an outcome which is 'unfair', redistribution can occur later. For example, Motta embraces the total surplus goal which he describes as a summarising measure of how efficient a given industry is as a whole. Although this measure does not address the question of how equal or unequal income is distributed, Motta argues that this can be dealt with by other measures.[11]

Others appear to go even further. Hovenkamp, for example, implies that economic standards are value-neutral.[12] He appears to assert that non-economic goals are not promoted by the consumer welfare standard (presumably he would say the same of the total welfare standard), the selection of the relevant welfare standard being '... an economic decision, not a political decision ...'[13]

To the extent that arguments such as those of Motta or Hovenkamp are true *in practice*, policies that advance total surplus (such as some competition policies) might be given a

---

[9]   See Motta (2004), s 1.3 and Bishop and Walker (2002) ch 2, for more details.
[10]   Motta (2004) 18.
[11]   Motta (2004) 18. See also, Shyam Khemani (2002) 15; Lyons (2002) 1; Bork (1993) 111; Scherer (1987) 998, 999 and Williamson (1968) 27, 28.
[12]   See references to him in p 14 in this chapter.
[13]   Ehlermann (1998) 12–13. Fox seemed to understand him to mean this; see, eg Fox (1998) 15.

special (privileged) status. This is because, so the argument goes, they make society as a whole better off (the cake is bigger). If society thinks that the wealth distribution that these rules generate is inappropriate, it can redistribute this later (ie re-cut the new bigger cake), using other tools, such as taxation, for example, to achieve other public policy goals, such as environmental or cultural goals.

This argument relies on two premises: (i) that reliance on a total welfare standard makes society 'better off', Section 2.2 argues that this is not necessarily true; and (ii) that redistribution is possible through other means, Section 2.3 argues that it is not always possible/the best solution. If either of these premises does not hold, whether the total welfare standard (and indeed all welfare standards) is value neutral becomes important. This is because a competition law based on such a welfare standard could result in outcomes which are not in the best interests of society as a whole and which one may not be able to adequately compensate for later through redistribution. Section 2.1 demonstrates that all welfare standards (including total welfare) are (in practice) distributional. As a result, it may be appropriate both to use a different (ie not total) welfare standard and to consider public policy in competition law assessments.

2.1 Welfare standards and their influence on income distribution

I have defined three welfare standards: consumer surplus, producer surplus and total surplus. Now I want to show that all three standards are distributional. This would undermine Hovenkamp's claim that the selection of the relevant standard is not a political choice, or at least shows that it has political effects; it would also damage one of the three justifications for a unitary total surplus goal, see above. To demonstrate this, I focus on three types of efficiency and how they interact within each welfare standard.

Economic orthodoxy points to a relationship between market power and three types of efficiencies (allocative, productive and dynamic; all three can be present in the three welfare standards which I have already defined). A firm has market power when it can (profitably) raise prices above the competitive level.[14] Allocative efficiency is achieved when the existing stocks of goods and productive output are allocated through the price system to those buyers who value them most.[15] Where market power increases and costs are given, prices will rise above marginal cost (the increment to total costs that results from producing an additional increment of output).[16] As a result, the producer surplus increases, producers receive higher profits,[17] and the consumer surplus falls. The increase in the producer surplus is normally less than the fall in the consumer surplus caused by the higher prices; therefore, price increases normally increase producer welfare at the expense of both consumer and total welfare.[18]

The negative effects of market power may exceed the allocative efficiency losses. This is because the existence of an opportunity to obtain monopoly profits will attract resources

---

[14]   Motta (2004), s 2.2.1 and Bishop and Walker (2002) 43–51.
[15]   Brodley (1987) 1025.
[16]   Motta (2004) 447 and Bishop and Walker (2002) 22.
[17]   Motta (2004), s 2.2.2.
[18]   This is not always the case, however. Imagine that the parties to a joint venture agreement were, through the agreement, able to significantly *cut their costs*, in relation to research and development, for example. As a result, there might be an increase in total surplus, as the parties could make larger profits; although, any price rises that the agreement facilitated would still reduce the consumer surplus: see Fishwick (1993) 56.

into efforts to obtain monopolies, and the opportunity costs of those resources are social costs of monopoly too.[19] Some of these rents do not have any social value.[20] Consumers also incur costs lobbying to counteract the firms' rent-seeking behaviour; enforcers would also face increased costs.[21]

Productive efficiency occurs when a given set of products are produced at the lowest possible cost, given *current* technology, input prices, etc.[22] There is also a relationship between market power and productive efficiency. Firms with market power often exhibit less productive efficiency because, as they are exposed to less competitive pressure, they can make less effort to use (and find) the best available technologies, to improve their products and to innovate. This means higher costs for the firms and, normally, higher prices for consumers. Productive efficiency losses can be as large as allocative efficiency losses.[23]

Under atomistic competition, firms whose production costs are above those of their rivals will (unless they cut costs) be forced out of the market.[24] Neo-classical economics offers two theories for the relationship between market power and productive efficiency. First, managers of firms with market power have less incentive to increase productivity; increasing competition reduces managerial slack, but only up to a point; Motta argues that increasing pressure in a market where there is already a lot of competition might reduce efficiency.[25] Secondly, where competition exists, more efficient firms will survive and thrive, less efficient firms are forced out of the market. So, competition increases productive efficiency by selecting the most efficient firms, those with lower prices.[26] Furthermore, where firms incur (recurrent or start-up) fixed costs, the duplication of these costs represents a dynamic (as opposed to static) efficiency loss. This highlights another trade-off with allocative efficiency. More firms means more competition, driving prices down (allocative efficiency), but may involve a loss of economies of scale (productive inefficiency).[27]

Dynamic efficiency is the extent to which a firm introduces *new* products or processes of production.[28] To some extent, firms with market power have less incentive to innovate than firms that face more competition. This is not a linear relationship however, because firms' incentives to innovate are determined not only by the existence of competition, but also by the possibility of appropriating the results of their investments.[29] Where there is strong competition, appropriability is reduced and so is the incentive to invest and innovate.[30] Dynamic efficiency losses may be even larger than allocative and productive efficiencies.[31]

---

[19]   Posner (1975) 807. See also, Scherer (1987) 1000.
[20]   Posner (1975) 811. However, some rent-seeking creates socially valuable results (Posner (1975) 811), eg advertising may increase consumer information, Motta (2004) 45.
[21]   Posner (1975) 811, 812.
[22]   Bishop and Walker (2002) 20.
[23]   ibid, 26; Neven (1998) 114; Scherer and Ross (1990) 668–72; Scherer (1987) 1002, 1018 and Brodley (1987) 1026, 1027.
[24]   Bishop and Walker (2002) 20.
[25]   Motta (2004) 47, 48.
[26]   ibid, 51.
[27]   ibid, 51, 52 and Scherer (1987) 1002, 1003.
[28]   Motta (2004), s 2.4 and Bishop and Walker (2002) 36–39.
[29]   See Scherer (1987) 1010–19.
[30]   This is because, at marginal cost, firms cannot recover their fixed costs, Motta (2004) 21. Furthermore, managerial slack affects dynamic efficiency in the same way as productive efficiency, Motta (2004) 48. There is a

I have discussed three types of efficiency and their relationship with market power. Now, in order to expose their distributional effects, I briefly analyse the relationship between the welfare standards and the three types of efficiency.[32] Consumer welfare is explicitly concerned with gains to consumers,[33] ignoring increases in producer surplus. Reductions in allocative efficiency are unacceptable, regardless of their effect on producer welfare, because consumers suffer. This is in direct contrast to the position under a producer welfare standard, which is concerned with gains to producers alone. This illustrates the main interests behind the different situations:

> An industry's producers will try to lobby in favour of more protection and less competitive pressure, while consumers and users of the industry products will have an interest in backing proposals of more competition.[34]

Increasing competition compels producers to sell closer to their marginal cost. A similar position emerges in relation to both productive and dynamic efficiencies. Consumers (and the consumer welfare standard) would generally advocate more competition. In a competitive environment, firms have an incentive to invest and innovate in both existing and future technologies. Successful investments allow them to reduce their costs (and thus their prices), undercutting other firms, forcing their less efficient rivals to exit.

However, as noted above, there comes a point where increasing competition undermines the incentive to generate both productive and dynamic efficiencies. Both current and future welfare matter;[35] so, a competition authority seeking to maximise consumer welfare will not increase competition at all costs. Under atomistic competition, maximum allocative efficiency occurs when prices equal marginal cost. If competition authorities force prices down to marginal cost, for example, by increasing short term competition, then producers have less incentive to invest and innovate; meaning that possible future welfare gains may be lost. Competition authorities need to balance the long-term need for innovation (and the future allocative benefits to be gained because of this) with the short-term allocative efficiency loss of letting prices rise above marginal cost; otherwise welfare (both consumer and total) may be undermined over time. There is disagreement about where this trade-off between short and long-term benefits lies[36] and thus, how much competition is 'good' for consumers.

Producers seeking to enhance their own welfare would also highlight the ambiguous effects of increasing competition on both dynamic and productive efficiencies. But they have an additional reason for doing so; less competition allows them to appropriate a larger share of any gains they make through innovation.

We have seen that the pursuit of the consumer welfare or producer welfare standard determines which efficiencies (and thus how much competition) the regulator considers

---

need to balance allocative competition with some ability to appropriate the results of their research, see also, Fishwick (1993) 39; Scherer and Ross (1990) ch 17 and Schumpeter (1942). Note that the extreme position adopted by Schumpeter has been refined later, see, eg Faull and Nikpay (2007) 36–40; Areeda, Solow and Hovenkamp (1995); Gual (1995) 19–21 and the references made there and Scherer (1987) 1000–02, 1014, 1019.

  [31] Neven (1998) 114; Scherer (1987) 1002, 1018 and Brodley (1987) 1026.
  [32] See also ICN, *Report on the Objectives of Unilateral Conduct Laws* (2007) 9.
  [33] Whish (2008) 4 and Brodley (1987) 1020, 1021, 1032, 1033.
  [34] Motta (2004) 43.
  [35] See ibid, 19; Faull and Nikpay (2007) 36–40 and Jorde and Teece (1992) 4.
  [36] Motta (2004) 57; Ahdar (2002) 350–53; Fels and Edwards (1998) 59–61; Fishwick (1993) 19; Brodley (1987) 1036–41 and Scherer (1987) 1011.

beneficial. This choice affects those to whom the efficiency benefits accrue and cannot be described as value neutral, absent redistribution.

Furthermore, even though the total welfare standard formally appears to be value neutral (it values consumer and producer welfare equally), *in practice*, it often leads to redistribution from consumers to producers (and their owners).[37] There are three key reasons for this. Where producer and consumer welfare are valued equally, then the interest group willing to invest the most resources (normally the producers) in any competition dispute that may arise is likely to have a disproportionate effect on the outcome.[38] The total welfare model is likely to give greater weight to producer welfare gains.[39] In addition, the producers have informational,[40] distributional[41] and timing advantages that can have an important effect on outcomes in antitrust analysis. Finally, the strength of the producers' position is reinforced by the fact that it is they that make the deals. However, these are dressed up, deals are done out of self-interest for the firms concerned.[42] This may help to explain why the consumer welfare standard is so popular, from a political perspective, as it helps tip the balance in favour of weaker/under-represented groups.[43] For these reasons, it is the welfare standard I favour.

Bork accepts that selection of the total welfare standard has income distribution effects. Nevertheless, in relation to the US antitrust system he argued that the income distribution effects of economic activity should be completely excluded from the determination of the antitrust legality of the activity. The shift in income distribution, so he argued, does not lessen total wealth, and a decision about it requires a choice between two groups that should be made by the legislature rather than by the judiciary. Bork thought that this conclusion was reinforced by the recognition that disapproval of the income redistribution could only rest upon a tenuous moral ground.[44] He went on to state that he is unable to distinguish a merger which is acceptable under the consumer welfare standard from one which is acceptable under the total welfare standard. Both increase total welfare and redistribute income (the former redistributes from sellers to purchasers and the latter redistributes from inefficient sellers to efficient sellers). If income redistribution is not counted against one, why should it be counted against the other? There seems no reason, he says.[45] In fact, Bork goes on to suggest three potential reasons, but dismisses them all.[46] First, an aversion to the deadweight loss, but Bork argues that this is misplaced, and it is

---

[37] See eg Ehlermann (1998) 1–27; Frazer (1990) 621; Fox and Sullivan (1987) 957–60; Brodley (1987) 1035, 1036 and Comanor and Smiley (1975).

[38] Neven, Papandropoulos and Seabright (1998) 19.

[39] Motta (2004) 21 and Lyons (2002) 3 and the references made there, and Buigues, Jacquemin and Sapir (1995a) xii.

[40] Motta (2004) 21 and Lyons (2002) 2, 3 and the references made there.

[41] Trebilcock (1987). An anti-competitive agreement's effect on consumers is likely to be dispersed among many of them, while it is much less dispersed for producers: see Motta (2004) 20, for an example. This makes individual consumers less likely to pursue an antitrust action, favouring producers.

[42] Not that there is necessarily anything wrong with this, but the reason for the deal is clear – to increase producer welfare, any consumer welfare benefits are normally secondary.

[43] OECD (2008) 8. As to why this is necessary see also, Amato (1997) 125 and Cseres (2007) 127, 128, 170. Lyons (2002) 2 and Farrell and Katz (2006) suggest other reasons too. Note, though, Carlton (2007) 5.

[44] Bork (1993) 111.

[45] ibid, 111.

[46] ibid, 111, 112.

not relevant for our discussion, so it is ignored here. Secondly, Bork argues that a net-efficiency standard may lead to social discontent, for example, due to increased unemployment.[47] Thirdly, Bork argues:

> If income redistribution were to be weighed against cases of net efficiency creation on the ground that consumers are generally poorer than producers (which would be a most dubious ground), then the principle would seem to require that income redistribution be weighed in favour of any economic behaviour when producers of a product had generally lower incomes than consumers [he adds that this would lead to some complex calculations]. This would justify price fixing by poorly remunerated producers.[48]

Bork assumes that it is the wealth of the producer/consumer which is important. Yet, the reason for redistribution is not that consumers are generally poorer than producers, although this may be true; it is that consumers are a different (and more important) category from producers.[49] All citizens are consumers, they are not all producers. Societies often aim to further the good of their citizens, promoting firms because of the beneficial impact this has on citizens.[50] This is true, for example, of the European Union, the Preamble to the EC Treaty affirms as the essential objective of the Member States' efforts the … constant improvement of the living and working conditions of their peoples …' This is a key reason why redistribution between producers and consumers is different from a mere redistribution between two different sets of producers and why society might be more concerned with it.[51]

As all the welfare standards considered here have redistributional effects, unless they redistribute in an ideal way, it is important to ascertain whether they make society better off and whether redistribution is possible (and effective) later.

2.2 Welfare standards and their influence on public policy

Another of the arguments necessary to justify giving a special status to competition law that solely seeks to achieve a welfare goal is that pursuit of this one goal makes society better off. Here I challenge that assertion, seeking to show that this is not always the case. I do this by highlighting the negative (and positive) impacts that the pursuit of welfare goals can have on public policy aims.

UNCTAD sees competition as a means of creating markets responsive to consumer signals and ensuring the efficient allocation of resources in the economy and efficient production with incentives for innovation. This should lead to the best possible choice of quality, the lowest prices and adequate supplies to consumers. Efficient allocation and

---

[47]   See below, Section 2.2.2.

[48]   Bork (1993) 112.

[49]   Motta (2004) 18 and Carlton (2007) 2 caution that one should not overstate the difference between consumers and producers, given that in most countries consumers are also owners of the firms either directly, as shareholders, or indirectly through pension and investment funds. This may be true, but as long as this is not all consumers it is probably safer to focus on consumers rather than the indirect proxy of producers when we strive for consumer benefits.

[50]   Intuitively Bork's argument is hard to accept and one would need a lot more reasoning to overcome this. Many theories of justice, for example, focus exclusively on people, as opposed to legal people; see, eg Rawls (1999), Part One and the references made there, particularly pp 6–36. For a practical European perspective see, eg Kroes (2007a).

[51]   Cseres (2007) 125.

utilisation of resources also lead to increased competitiveness, resulting in substantial growth and development. There is growing consensus, says UNCTAD, that competition is an essential ingredient for the enhancement and maintenance of competitiveness in the economy.[52] Likewise, the Commission says that Community policies in general '... rely on competition for their effective implementation and that enforcement of the competition rules supports the objectives pursued by these policies.'[53]

So, competition has many direct and indirect benefits. It can also have negative effects (costs) on society, or certain groups within it, which can include external costs, distributional effects and unemployment. Elements of 'market failure' arising from these welfare considerations are not generally corrected by competition policies—indeed such policies may aggravate them.[54]

The idea that competition can affect other policy goals both positively and negatively is important because the claim that total surplus makes society as a whole 'better off' is itself value-laden.[55] For example, when evaluating the concept of 'better off', one might focus on increases in surplus (welfare), or include some measure of the agreement's environmental or cultural impact. It does not seem possible to say that the total welfare standard makes 'society' better off, unless one considers the effect on wider public policy goals too. For example, would one encourage an agreement between manufacturers that would increase their total surplus by €1 million, if this were to immediately lead to the irreparable poisoning of all drinking water? If the total welfare standard does not make society better off then this would significantly weaken the claim that competition law should pursue a unitary welfare goal.

This section shows in more detail how some public policy objectives are influenced (sometimes positively, sometimes negatively) by welfare standards. It focuses on the consumer welfare standard (because this facilitates the discussion in later chapters), but similar points arise in relation to the total welfare standard, over the long term, and so it is directly relevant to the argument being analysed here.[56] The analysis is in two parts: Section 2.2.1 focuses on this issue from an 'internal' perspective. By placing more or less weight on specific elements of the consumer welfare test one can enhance (or undermine) other public policy objectives. In this way, the internal logic of the consumer welfare standard directly influences other public policy goals. Secondly, Section 2.2.2 considers the 'external' perspective. The consumer welfare standard can enhance (or undermine) other public policy objectives, not because they are directly considered within its logic, but because it indirectly impinges on them. By way of example, I examine the relationship between consumer welfare and: (i) small and medium-sized enterprises; and (ii) employment policy.

---

[52]   UNCTAD's submission to OECD (2003) 2, 3. See also, Schaub (1998) and Bishop and Walker (2002) 11.

[53]   Commission, *RCP 1991* 39. For example, see CES, *Green Paper on vertical restraints*, para 1.2. This is also supported, to some extent, by economic thinking, eg Brodley (1987) 21.

[54]   Fishwick (1993) 21–25. See also, Poiares Maduro (1999) 466–70 and ICN, *Report on the Objectives of Unilateral Conduct Laws* (2007) 21, 22.

[55]   See Arnull, Dashwood, Ross and Wyatt (2000) 540, 541 and the references made there.

[56]   Motta (2004) 18–22, argues that where consumer surplus is maximised over time it is similar to a total surplus standard. See also, Carlton (2007) 4.

2.2.1 'Internal' influences of the welfare standards

To illustrate how the internal weighting of the welfare standards' different constituent elements can impact upon public policy goals, I examine three areas of public policy: consumer protection, industrial policy and research and development (R&D). There is also a discussion about internalising externalities (ie how one can 'internalise' policy areas which would otherwise be external to the discussion by amending the things assessed in the consumer welfare standard), environmental policy is used as an example. In this book, I call attempts to achieve public policy outcomes by placing different emphasis on these constituent elements 'market-balancing'.

Various welfare standards can contribute towards certain types of consumer protection.[57] Wide definitions of consumer protection include the consumers' economic situation; for example, Article 153(1) EC states that in order to '... promote the interests of consumers ... the Community shall contribute to protecting the health, safety and *economic interests* of consumers ...'[58] (emphasis added)

The consumer welfare standard protects consumers' economic interests by helping to ensure low prices for them.[59] However, as I go on to discuss, there is a tension between achieving long and short-term consumer benefits.

As for industrial policy,[60] one of the objectives of the Canadian Competition Act 1985 is '... to expand opportunities for Canadian participation in world markets ...' In the European Union, the ECMR lists some of the criteria that should be taken into account by the Commission when deciding whether or not a merger is compatible with the Common Market. These include the structure of markets outside the European Union, article 2(1)(a); and, the development of technical and economic progress, article 2(1)(b). Both criteria imply some kind of industrial policy concern.[61]

This chapter has already hinted that welfare, especially a producer welfare standard, could be used to promote the competitiveness of industry.[62] Yet, there is disagreement about how much competition is optimal. Some advocate an interventionist approach in order to develop and strengthen national industries on the domestic and even the international stage. This might be implemented, so the argument goes, by reducing domestic firms' exposure to competition, to some extent. Traditionally, this involves, for example, controlling market-entry or capacity expansion, channelling investment or allowing firms to collude in R&D, or even later stages of distribution and marketing. In the Republic of Korea, for example, the government promoted the development of large conglomerates as a means of achieving economies of scale in mature heavy industries. One

---

[57] See also, Commission, *RCP 2001* 3, 18–21; Cseres (2004); Hovenkamp (1998) 426 and Averitt and Lande (1996–7).

[58] See also, Stuyck (2000) 399 and OECD (2008) 8.

[59] The producer welfare standard does not do this and the total welfare standard does not do it to the same extent, at least in the short term.

[60] For a more detailed analysis see Buigues, Jacquemin and Sapir (1995) and Sauter (1997).

[61] The second element may also include consumer protection goals, because it is encouraging dynamic efficiency, which in the long term, given sufficient competition, should lead to increases in allocative efficiency, see above.

[62] Commission, *RCP 1990* 13; Vickers (2004) 5; Commission, *RCP 1999* 19; COM(90) 556 5; Commission, *RCP 1991* 11, 223, 260; Press Release, IP/94/809 and Commission, *Immunity Guidelines*, paras 1, 2; Motta (2004) 29 and ch 2 and Gual (1995) 19, arguing for competition, within certain limits.

UNCTAD report states that the interaction of government policy and inter-firm rivalry stimulated the growth of technological capabilities and exports.[63]

There are strong arguments emphasising that, in general, competition has a positive effect on industrial policy. That said, at times some (especially short-term) consumer surplus standards might undermine industrial policy objectives;[64] because they can lead to sub-optimal investment in research and development, or they may fail to allow for necessary strategic or structural adjustment.[65]

We have also seen a relationship between the amount of competition and firms' investment in R&D.[66] Competition generally provides incentives for firms to innovate and invest in productive or dynamic efficiency-enhancing technology; in many industries competition is one of the main drivers of innovation and job creation.[67]

However, above a certain point, more competition undermines these incentives. In part this is because firms perceive less benefit in investing in this way, due to the reduced appropriability of their investments. Martins reports that relatively high mark-ups are found in innovation markets; concentration may be inevitable due to the large fixed costs concentrated industries have a higher R&D/turnover ratio and propensity to patent.[68]

There is a balance to be achieved, push R&D and risk reducing allocative efficiency, at least in the short term; or, focus on the short term allocative efficiency gains and risk reducing the scope for investment in R&D, as prices fall to marginal cost.[69]

Once again, the consumer surplus standard normally encourages R&D investments. However, there comes a point where this relationship does not hold and R&D investments may be threatened by increasing competition. As has been explained above, the decision about how to balance these positive and negative effects also has both consumer protection and industrial policy implications. An ambiguous effect is also noted under the producer welfare and total welfare standards.

Different welfare standards (or indeed different emphasis within these) can be used to promote different objectives. However, there are many public policy objectives that these standards simply ignore.[70] This happens when a specific objective is not included in the parties' pricing decisions:[71]

> External effects occur when an action by one party or a transaction between parties has (positive or negative) consequences for another … who is not directly involved in that action or transaction. An example of a negative external effect is the passing on of the consequences of

---

[63]   UNCTAD document TD/B/COM.2/EM/10/Rev.1 14. The efficacy of this type of industrial policy has been questioned, see Townley (2004) 132, 133, and the references made there; UNCTAD, *Corporate Policies in the Republic of Korea* and Chang and Choi (1988). The Treaty adopts a similar stance, see Art 157(3) EC. So does UNCTAD, the report cited above continued '… there have been numerous policy failures … and infant industry protection has often led to the creation of permanent infants.'

[64]   Despite claims to the contrary by the then Commissioner Bangemann, Press Release, IP/94/809.

[65]   Gual (1995) 20. More generally see Gual (1995) 18–21 and the references to Motta (2004), above.

[66]   For a more detailed analysis, see Buigues, Jacquemin and Sapir (1995).

[67]   Mario Monti (2002a) 9. See also, Commission, *RCP 2002* 19; Commission, *RCP 2001* 3; Commission, *RCP 1991* 44–46 and the Commission's reply to the European Parliament's, *Report of the XIXth Report on Competition Policy 1990*, in Commission, *RCP 1991* 223.

[68]   Martins (1996) 71.

[69]   The Commission has been explicit about this, see Commission, *Horizontal Guidelines*, paras 41, 43. See also Gual (1995) 19.

[70]   Pearson (2000) chs 2, 3, applies this to environmental considerations, for example.

[71]   For a more detailed analysis, see Nadeau (2003); Pearson (2000) and Petrakis, Sartzetakis and Xepapadeas (1999).

pollution caused by a production process to the surrounding community. An example of a positive external effect is the transfer of knowledge (education, research and development), which also benefits third parties.[72]

It is often possible to ensure that these extra costs and benefits are internalised by the parties to the agreement. This might be done by providing, for example, an appropriate compensation mechanism so that the parties to the agreement can be forced to compensate third parties for the costs that they have unilaterally imposed upon them. However, this may not always be appropriate;[73] and, sometimes, it may be beneficial for the state to force the parties to the agreement to internalise these other costs in other ways.[74] Taking environmental protection as an example, I show how this might be done.[75]

The state concerned could fine companies that emit more than X tonnes of sulphur dioxide each year, for example. One problem with this kind of regulatory solution is that it does not encourage firms to reduce their pollution below X. This is not a problem where the regulation sets the limit at the most efficient point. However, this is difficult to calculate and is likely to change in different industries and over time. Adjusting for these problems would impose significant costs on both the legislator and industry.[76]

States are increasingly turning to market-based instruments as a supplementary implementation tool. Market-based instruments are generally considered to be both more effective at reducing pollution as well as more efficient.[77] Such instruments may include taxing pollution[78] and tradable emissions vouchers.[79] These force producers to include all (or at least part) of the environmental cost of production in their price. As a result, demand moves away from environmentally 'costly' goods to those that cause less damage.

The Commission has said that if environmental considerations are internalised then competition will generate the most efficient allocation of resources possible, by prompting business to reduce costs. This will benefit both the environment and the economy in general.[80] While this may be true, as the Commission also acknowledges, its environmental policy is founded on the 'polluter pays' principle; the effectiveness of which depends in particular on the proper operation of the price mechanism, which ought to translate into costs the negative effects of a particular process on the environment, so that prices can perform their signalling function which forms the basis of the market economy.[81]

To the extent that environmental considerations have yet to be properly internalised then the market's price mechanism does not perform its proper signalling function. These Commission statements are more indications of where the Commission would like to be,

---

[72]   Dutch Ministry of Economic Affairs, *The Liberal Professions* 19. See also 41–52, 83.
[73]   Think, eg, of a situation where the costs imposed by the parties on each 'victim' are so small that a lawsuit is not a paying proposition, even where cumulatively the costs are large. Other mechanisms (eg class actions) might be more efficient in this case, see Posner (1998) ch 21.
[74]   Dutch Ministry of Economic Affairs, *The Liberal Professions* 51 and Posner (1998) 401–03.
[75]   For a more detailed analysis see Vedder (2003) chs 2, 3; Posner (1998) 410–16 and Hahn and Hester (1989) 109–53.
[76]   Posner (1998) 410, 411.
[77]   Vedder (2003) 48.
[78]   Posner (1998) 410–16.
[79]   ibid, 416 and Hahn and Hester (1989).
[80]   Commission, *RCP 1991* 54. See also, Commission, *RCP 1993*, points 163–65.
[81]   Commission, *RCP 1991* 54.

as opposed to a serious assertion that environmental considerations are fully taken into account by efficiency considerations in anything but a minority of cases.[82]

Two points need to be made as regards externalities. First, it is not always practicably possible to internalise all objectives. This might be because procedurally it is too difficult to price them or there is no agreement over the value of these policy objectives, for example. Secondly, internalising objectives in this way may have implications for other public policy objectives. For example, forcing firms to adopt expensive environmental standards may affect their international competitiveness compared to firms from jurisdictions without such obligations; which could undermine industrial policy, for example.[83] So the decision whether or not to internalise externalities (and if so, how much) is itself based on a balance between various public policy objectives.

2.2.2 'External' influences of the welfare standards

In order to understand welfare standards' influence on non-economic policy objectives from an 'external' perspective, this section examines two public policy aims: promotion of small and medium-sized enterprises and employment policy. It shows that competition can affect these policy goals in both a positive and a negative way. We must at least ensure that the harm to other policies is less than the total surplus 'gain', otherwise, we cannot be sure that society as a whole is 'better off' at all. The objective of increasing society's *economic* wealth is itself a value-laden objective. In this book, I call balancing the public policy and economic welfare impacts 'mere-balancing'.

Competition policy in many jurisdictions has been eager to come to the aid of small and medium-sized enterprises (SMEs). This was a key reason for the adoption of antitrust law in the US, for example. The Sherman Act 1890 was adopted because, amongst others, farmers and other SMEs complained about the large trust companies.[84]

Protection of SMEs has been a goal of Community competition law as well.[85] The Commission seems to have come to the view that SMEs are more dynamic and likely to contribute to innovation and growth than their larger competitors, although the economic evidence here is ambiguous.[86] A related point also arises in relation to the debate about encouraging smaller shops in our city centres, as opposed to 'soul-destroying' supermarkets.[87]

The Commission sometimes uses competition law and regulation to force prices down, sometimes a key reason for doing this is to reduce the prices of inputs for SMEs, to help them compete more effectively. Take, for example, the proposals for a regulation on international mobile roaming charges, the Commission's memo dwells heavily on the

---

[82]   However, some progress has been made as regards greenhouse gas externalities, eg, in relation to carbon trading see Commission Reg 916/2007, *for a standardised and secured system of* registries; Commission Decision, *on avoiding double counting of greenhouse gas emission reductions under the Community emissions trading scheme for project activities under the Kyoto Protocol*; Commission Reg 2216/2004, *for a standardised and secured system of registries*; European Parliament and Council Directive 2004/101, *establishing a scheme for greenhouse gas emission allowance trading within the Community* and European Parliament and Council Directive 2003/87, *establishing a scheme for greenhouse gas emission allowance trading within the Community*.

[83]   Scholz and Stähler (1999). Energy policy, for example, may also be affected: Bouterse (1994) 34, 35.

[84]   Stigler (1985).

[85]   For example, see Commission, *RCP 1985*, Pt One, Ch III.

[86]   Motta (2004) 22.

[87]   Simms, Kjell and Potts (2005).

effects on SMEs. Indeed, at one point, in response to the question 'What will be the overall impacts of the proposed EU regulation?', the Commission said:

> The proposed regulation is likely to provide a significant economic boost to businesses, particularly small and medium sized enterprises, to those persons living close to national borders who are frequently roaming to other networks …[88]

The Commission is certainly right to point out that SMEs are hurt by a lack of proper infrastructure, when other, larger firms, may be better able to overcome such problems owing to their size or through financial means, for example. Motta goes even further, saying that favourable treatment of SMEs under the competition rules does not necessarily conflict with the objectives of economic welfare if it is limited to protecting SMEs from the abuse of larger firms, or giving them an advantage to balance the financial and economic power of their larger rivals.[89]

Increased competition can also disproportionately harm SMEs. It introduces another layer of regulation, which they have to comply with; legal and other bills often absorb a higher part of SMEs' income (and key managerial time) than they do for their larger rivals, undermining their ability to compete. Furthermore, where competition is intense, and prices are forced down near marginal cost, where SMEs are so small that they are unable to achieve equivalent efficiencies of scale in production, etc, their larger rivals may be able to undercut them, forcing them out of the market. Allowing SMEs to survive encourages inefficient allocation of resources, and could contribute to higher prices (presumably this would be found to undermine consumer welfare, although choice may be enhanced). Once again though, this effect can be ambiguous. A temporary period of protection for SMEs may allow them to achieve an efficient scale of production to compete with their larger rivals, thus increasing competition in the long term.

Some also argue that pursing economic efficiency will help achieve the Community employment policy and through this increase economic and social cohesion.[90] The Commission believes that competition policy can contribute to the success of employment policy. This occurs through its effect on the structure of markets, its influence on the competitiveness of the European economy and its rate of growth and hence helps to orient the Union's macroeconomic framework towards employment. The Commission uses competition policy to open up markets in the Union, which makes a major contribution to the completion of the single market, guaranteeing more trade and faster growth.[91]

However, the pursuit of economic efficiency does not always increase employment *in the short term*. As the Commission acknowledges, more competition also leads to restructuring, with the weakest going to the wall, which inevitably results in the short term in plant closures and job losses. In such circumstances there can be no getting away from the fact that measures to promote competitiveness are in some cases, at least in the short run,

---

[88]   Commission Memo, *International Mobile Roaming Charges* (2006).

[89]   Motta (2004) 22. See also, Commission decisions, *Transocean Marine Paint Association* (1967), (1974) and (1988).

[90]   CES, *Green Paper on vertical restraints*, para 1.2 and the Commission's reply to the European Parliament's, *Report of the XIXth Report on Competition Policy 1990*, in Commission, *RCP 1991* 223, 224.

[91]   Commission, *RCP 1997* 8–9. See also, Commissioner Monti who has said '… in many industries competition is one of the main drivers of innovation and job creation.', Mario Monti (2002a) 9.

job-destroying.[92] US antitrust rules were implemented more leniently during the Great Depression in the 1930s; the idea being that price agreements would help firms to avoid bankruptcy, easing social tensions caused by unemployment. It is unclear whether this policy reduced unemployment.[93]

That said, many advocate ameliorating the short-term negative employment effects with specific employment policies that might restrict competition. Former Competition Commissioner van Miert said:

> Beyond growth-based solutions, to which competition policy can actively contribute, a social response must be found to these short-term effects because, as Mr Santer has said, Europe cannot be just an economic project. I am a firm believer in the social dialogue: not only does it meet human needs, but it fits in with a new way of thinking about economic efficiency.[94]

Many economists try to circumvent the debate about which segment of society competition policy should favour by focusing on total surplus in competition law.[95] In their view this avoids the need for interpersonal comparisons and subjective value judgments about what is fair and equitable. They often focus on total surplus hoping to ensure that 'society's pot' is bigger, so there is more wealth to share, including for any redistribution if the competitive outcome were felt unfair.[96] This ignores the harm that might be done to other relevant policy objectives by the pursuit of a welfare goal. We must at least ensure that the harm to other policies is less than the total surplus 'gain', otherwise, we cannot be sure that society as a whole is 'better off' at all. The objective of increasing society's *economic* wealth is itself a value-laden objective.[97] It emphasises material wealth. Admittedly, this is an important political objective that governments often pursue. That said, other policy goals are also significant.

2.3 Redistribution and the relevance of welfare standards' values

I now consider the last of the three arguments justifying giving a special status to competition law that solely sought to achieve a welfare goal: if the bigger cake created through that pursuit of this one goal is not fairly distributed, it can always be redistributed at a later date. I show that neo-classical economists discourage this later redistribution, which undermines reliance on it as a justification in the first place.

The welfare standards redistribute between different groups. The neo-classical economists' position assumes that even if the distribution created by the total (or consumer) surplus is considered 'unfair', a redistribution can be performed later (if this were considered necessary[98]). Commissioner Kroes advocates this approach:

> These objectives [creating and maintaining the right framework for business in Europe, in the context of a global economy; helping to develop a global level playing field; and keeping our

---

[92]   Commission, *RCP 1997* 8–9.
[93]   Motta (2004) 26, 27.
[94]   Commission, *RCP 1997* 9.
[95]   Canada may have adopted a total welfare test, other countries have too: see Mexican submission to OECD (2003) 3; Lyons (2002) 1; Shyam Khemani (2002) 14, 15; Matte (1998) 21 and Crampton (1997) 60.
[96]   Although, even those economists that advocate the total surplus standard do not avoid difficult decisions. They still need to balance short-term allocative efficiencies with productive and dynamic efficiencies, see above.
[97]   Ahdar (2002) 348–50, and references made there and Brodley (1987) 1023, 1035, 1036.
[98]   Which is not the case under Kaldor-Hicks efficiency, because the redistribution is only *hypothetical*.

markets open, using trade and competition law] are ... there to provide the right conditions for companies to innovate and prosper, and so to increase the overall size of Europe's 'cake'. More 'cake' means more cash for governments to sustain the fabric of our societies, guarantee social justice for all and protect the natural environment and our cultural heritage for generations to come. In short, you could say that the bigger the cake, the better the means to protect the well-being of our citizens.[99]

However, given the dynamic nature of business practices, the 'risk' of later redistribution would feed back into the undertakings' initial investment decisions (potentially undermining the actors' underlying incentives), meaning that the size of the cake may not grow as hoped, in any event. As a result, neo-classical economics tends to interfere at the redistribution level too, arguing that it should be kept to a minimum.[100]

Furthermore, redistribution is not always possible or convenient, in the sense that it does not provide the best solution at that time. Sometimes one cannot redistribute later, or the costs of waiting can be high: delay may make redistribution more expensive, or can even make it impossible to remedy the inequality later, such that everyone is 'better off'.

Consumer welfare is an extremely important goal that can help us achieve many public policy objectives. It can also undermine them due to market failures. Efforts to resolve these failures may cause other unforeseen (and potentially greater) costs. This may lead to important welfare reductions; so, we need to decide when public policy goals might be incorporated into competition policy.

3 WHEN COMPETITION POLICY MIGHT INCLUDE PUBLIC POLICY OBJECTIVES

Section 2 showed us that the welfare standards can all conflict with public policy goals. It also suggests that sometimes public policy goals should be taken into account in competition analysis. The next step is to decide when this should happen.

This section provides a framework for the discussion of antitrust's objectives. One cannot discuss the substantive antitrust rules until one understands the objectives that should guide decisions; in order to understand that, the theoretical framework must be applied to a specific legal system. Chapter 2 does this for Community competition policy.

Section 3 proceeds as follows: Section 3.1 describes two paths for 'resolving' conflicts: exclusion, essentially ignoring one of the conflicting policy goals; and compromise, balancing the conflicting policy goals. Section 3.2 considers some advantages and disadvantages of exclusion in more detail; Section 3.3 does the same for compromise.

3.1 Exclusion versus compromise

Imagine that two public policy objectives, A and B, pursued in a certain jurisdiction, conflict. What is meant by 'conflict'? Conflicts manifest themselves in two ways. *Only one of A or B can be achieved at the same time.* The choice is between achieving objective A and

---

[99]   Kroes (2007a).
[100]   This is the implication of Laussel and Montet (1995) 58, for example.

not achieving objective B at all, or vice versa. The conflict then becomes a question of *which* of these two policy objectives should be sacrificed. I call these first order conflicts. Alternatively, *it may be possible to achieve some of A and some of B, but not all of both.* The conflict then becomes a question of *how much* of these two policy objectives should be maximised. I call these second order conflicts. A similar situation occurs where objectives A and B could both be fully achieved, but where this is not optimal for some other reason, for example, due to our limited resources. This type of 'conflict' is included in my second order conflict definition.

First order conflicts are rarely the type of conflicts examined in this book, in part, because the objectives discussed here are divisible.[101] When this book refers to conflicts it is primarily referring to second order conflicts, unless it expressly states otherwise.

There are two ways of dealing with conflicts. We could balance objectives A and B *within* the implementing provisions, whenever they conflict. One objective might have more weight than the other in this balance, but, to some degree, both factors would be considered. Through this balance we arrive at a compromise. The decision-maker could balance both consumer welfare and other relevant policy aims when applying competition law.

Compromise is complex; the outcomes are hard to predict. The resulting lack of legal certainty discourages innovation and investment. The more competing objectives that need to be considered when an implementing provision is applied, the more complex this exercise becomes. The benefit is that this approach provides the theoretical possibility of a perfect balance in every case, called here the 'optimal balance'.[102]

Another conflict resolution strategy is to allow one of the objectives to exclude (or trump) the other. This means that, for example, whenever objective A and B conflict we only take account of one of them. When applied to competition laws, this would mean that the law would be applied solely in order to achieve, for example, consumer welfare. This would be so even where consumer welfare undermined other important goals, such as environmental policy.

Exclusion is drastic. The pursuit of consumer welfare might seriously undermine environmental considerations in a specific case, and yet, if this were the sole goal, the effect on the environment would be considered irrelevant when applying competition law (although it could be considered in an environmental law, for example).[103] That said, exclusion has the advantage of clarity and is favoured by those who see competition law as an end in itself.

Sometimes both compromise and exclusion interact; for example, when deciding whether to allow objective A or B to exclude the other, one has to balance their importance to a certain extent. Nonetheless, the two approaches are distinct.

---

[101]   Ch 8 briefly discusses this issue.

[102]   The 'optimal' or 'perfect' balance is an *end result*; as opposed to mere and market-balancing (see Part B) which are *processes*. Obviously, the 'optimal balance' can never be 'found', because there is a knowledge problem. So references in this book to 'achieving the optimal balance' should be read as getting as close to this as is possible with the resources and knowledge available to the decision-maker.

[103]   Areeda and Hovenkamp (2000), para 100b advocate this approach. The European Union accepts this as a method too, see art 3(2) and (3) of Reg 1/2003.

3.2 Exclusion

Adopting exclusion as a methodology for resolving second order conflicts has many advantages and disadvantages.

3.2.1 The advantages of exclusion

This section examines three key arguments in favour of exclusion: efficiency benefits; enhanced legal certainty and compliance costs. As regards the first of these, imagine that only two objectives (consumer welfare and environmental protection) are relevant. Exclusion means that the environmental considerations are ignored *in the competition assessment*.[104] This does not mean that environmental issues are totally ignored; they may still be pursued through, for example, specific environmental legislation.[105] Therefore, firms would still have to ensure that their arrangement complies with *both* the environmental and the competition rules. The environmental rules may mean that the most-efficient arrangement is not possible, even though it is allowed under competition law.

Many believe that the environmental, or other public policy, goals would be better dealt with outside of the competition law, from a welfare perspective. Economists tend to rank different policy instruments (such as subsidies, taxes and tariffs) according to how efficiently they achieve non-economic objectives.[106] The instruments are ranked by their relative costs. Costs arise due to the distortions that the instruments introduce into the economy. As a general proposition the optimal (or least-cost) method of doing this is to choose that policy intervention that directly impacts the constrained variable.[107]

Distorting or restricting competition to realise specific non-economic objectives is normally an inefficient way of achieving the end in question. It can be costly[108] and ineffective.[109] Economists advocate the use of optimal policy instruments; the best one to use depends on the non-economic factor being pursued.[110] As Motta explains, this does not imply that objectives or public policy considerations other than economic efficiency are not important, but simply that if a government wanted to achieve them, it should not use competition policy but resort to policy instruments that distort competition as little as possible.[111]

This seems eminently sensible as a starting point; yet, I examine three key objections. First, sometimes it is necessary to consider public policy goals within competition decisions in order to achieve these ends. Secondly, compromise is sometimes the most efficient policy. Finally, even when the consideration of public policy within competition

---

[104]   Obviously, exclusion could work the other way round and competition goals might be ignored in the public policy assessment. There is a brief discussion of this in Ch 2, Section 2.2.1; but, given the focus of this work, the main focus is on the competition assessment.

[105]   If they are not, then environmental protection is completely ignored. This means less conflicts and more efficient agreements; however, this comes at the risk of harming the environment, see below.

[106]   Bhagwati (1971) and Srinivasan (1996) and the references made there.

[107]   Bhagwati (1971) 77.

[108]   Dutch Ministry of Economic Affairs, *The Liberal Professions* 23, 46–48, 50, 67–69, 81–91; Ahdar (2002) 348; Hovenkamp (2002) 4; Jenny (1993) 218–19; Areeda & Turner (1978), para 105; Elzinga (1977) 1195, 1196; and Williamson (1969) 105–18.

[109]   OECD (2003) 4; Motta (2003), ss 1.3.1, 1.3.2 and Faull (1998) 12.

[110]   Motta (2004) 18; Ahdar (2002) 342, 343, 347; Townley (2002) and Bhagwati (1971) 78–81 discuss more efficient ways of achieving various policy goals than distorting competition.

[111]   Motta (2003) 30.

decisions is not the most efficient way to achieve these ends there are sometimes other reasons for wanting to do so, even where this is not necessary; for example, society may decide that it does not want companies just to focus on wealth creation.

Sometimes it is necessary to consider public policy within competition decisions. Some argue that objectives such as fairness, social cohesion and the protection of political democracy may occasionally require restrictions of competition if they are to be achieved.[112] Furthermore, compromise is sometimes the most efficient policy. Gual writes that:

> Imposing the cohesion restriction [Article 159 EC] might lead to the choice of non-optimal policies in trade and competition, protecting or subsidising a particular industry on the grounds of cohesion. Nevertheless, the optimality of the free-market adjustment can also be disputed. In the presence of market imperfections (for example, imperfect foresight) and/or externalities (geographically-based pecuniary externalities), adjustment support could be justified on efficiency grounds, without having to resort to distributive considerations which are best left to strict redistribution (cohesion) policies.[113]

It can also be legislatively difficult to ensure that two independent rules with different goals intersect optimally to achieve the right level of both policy aims in all cases.[114] This is especially true where achievement of one policy goal affects the achievement of another (as happens in the conflict cases we are discussing).[115] Rules prescribing the outcome between different policy conflicts may make the law workable, but are often less precise (there can be type I errors, false positives and type II errors, false negatives). Monti argues that when rules fail,[116] law is best administered by standards, which require the decision-maker to discover all relevant facts and '... to assess them in terms of the purposes or social values embodied in the standard.'[117] Standards (ie when law is guided by (potentially conflicting) policy objectives, as opposed to being made up of explicit, detailed rules) are particularly effective when there are: (a) few instances of behaviour by firms; (b) few enforcement actions; (c) the facts of individual situations vary substantially in important ways; and (d) information is easier to acquire once the firms have acted. Certainly (c) and (d) are true of the plethora of different arrangements and actions that undertakings conduct. In such cases, it is costly to try to make predictive rules, especially if most relevant circumstances are unlikely to occur.[118]

In other words, it is not always optimal to use separate rules (with separate goals) for different policies, sometimes it is better to be guided by standards, even conflicting public policy ones, within the same legal provision. Standards demand a more wide-ranging (expensive) investigation, but they can reduce (although not eliminate) the likelihood of errors (which can better achieve the 'optimal result' and may be more efficient).

Three problems with standards are (a) arbitrariness, (b) opacity and (c) a more costly legal process – it is worth asking whether the more thorough look outweighs the harm of the type I and II errors.[119] One way to achieve this is for the legislature to identify goals

---

[112]   Jenny (2000) 24. Also see Bouterse (1994) 62.
[113]   Gual (1995) 39. See also, Sandmo (2000) 11–19.
[114]   See the text around n 76, above.
[115]   See the text around n 173, above.
[116]   Monti (2007) 17.
[117]   Kennedy (1976) and Kaplow (1992).
[118]   Kaplow (1992) 562 ff.
[119]   Monti (2007) 17.

and offer examples of how to achieve balancing in practice, as guides to firms in the market place, as well as the courts.[120] One can also combine standards and rules, for example, through use of presumptions and appreciability criteria. Precedent can also be valuable here.

There are other reasons why use of the theoretically 'optimal tool' might not be considered appropriate. It may also be considered a waste of public expenditure and an unwise use of parliamentary time to create, administer and police a system that the industry is demonstrably able to produce and pay for itself (through environmental agreements, for example).[121] This is particularly so when one remembers that the effectiveness of traditional regulatory instruments for achieving environmental (and other) goals is increasingly questioned.[122] As mentioned in the discussion on corporate social responsibility (CSR),[123] agreements sometimes allow a particular goal to be achieved more effectively, cheaply and completely than legislation.[124] They may also be preferred as they are better at raising awareness on particular issues and changing behaviour in general.[125] CSR received strong European Union backing because time is of the essence in dealing with many social and environmental problems.[126]

Even when the consideration of public policy within competition decisions is not the most efficient way to achieve these ends, there are sometimes other reasons for wanting to consider public policy within competition law. For example, society may decide that it does not want companies just to focus on wealth creation. There may be a value in encouraging private actors (be they individuals or firms) to actively participate in society as 'moral' actors; perhaps taking responsibility, along with public authorities, for environmental and other public policy goals.[127]

That said, prudence is needed. Economic history suggests that government failures are more important and more frequent than market failure. Intervention in this manner should be exercised with caution.[128]

A second argument in favour of exclusion is that it enhances legal certainty,[129] which expresses the fundamental idea that those subject to the law must know what the law is so

---

[120]   Arthur (1988) 1225–28.

[121]   See, eg the views of Baroness Coussins in a debate on a bill for alcohol labelling, Hansard HL vol 679 col 1547 (18 January 2008).

[122]   Rehbinder (1997). See also, COM(2004) 394 final 2.

[123]   See Section 3.2.2, below.

[124]   COM(2001) 486 16, 17; Grimeaud (2000) 212–15; Commission, *From Cardiff to Helsinki* 2; COM(96) 561 3; Bouterse (1994) 74; Jacobs (1993/2) 43; Baldock (1992) 2–4, 18 and European Parliament Resolution A3–0170/92.

[125]   A point made in relation to voluntary environmental agreements, OECD (2003a) 10, 18, 50.

[126]   Public choice theory also highlights power and motivational difficulties that a state might face if it were to try to achieve environmental or other policy goals through alternative legislative tools. Explicitly it refers to the problems of 'capture', see Petersmann (2003) 52, and the references made there. Section 2 also discussed other rent-seeking behaviour issues. It is unclear whether these issues are best solved by compromise within competition law (which might also be tainted by 'capture') or by resolving the issue of capture at a more fundamental level, see Petersmann (2003) 52 *ff*.

[127]   Gyselen (1994) 244. See eg <http://www.berr.gov.uk/whatwedo/sectors/lowcarbon/cr-sd-wp/page50437.html> accessed 30 April 2009 and <http://ec.europa.eu/enterprise/csr/index_en.htm> accessed 24 April 2009 and David Cameron's recent comments after the credit crunch 'Business is not just about making money. It is also about acting in an ethical way and I think we need to build a more ethical capitalism in Britain as we come out of this dreadful recession.' <http://news.bbc.co.uk/1/hi/uk_politics/7808634.stm> accessed 24 April 2009.

[128]   Mavroidis (1995) 120. Although note the limits of this in the text around nn 219 and 220.

[129]   Areeda and Turner (1978), para 105 and Odudu (2006) 170–72 and the references made there.

as to be able to plan their actions accordingly.[130] In the Community legal order, for example, legal certainty is a general principle of law,[131] which requires that legal rules be clear and precise, and aims to ensure that situations and legal relationships governed by Community law remain foreseeable.[132]

Of course, there will never be absolute certainty in law; particularly, laws with a welfare goal;[133] yet, increasing legal certainty is important[134] for two main reasons.[135] First, uncertainty is the enemy of business.[136] It is vital that undertakings are aware of the legal framework within which they operate.[137] This allows them to better plan their affairs; reducing the certainty/predictability of a competition assessment '… increases the risk that firms may be breaking the law when they have been trying in good faith to abide by it.'[138] The legal consequences of breaching the competition provisions can be severe.[139] Firms' innovation and investment decisions involve business risks. They are less likely to accept these business risks in the presence of further legal risks with large sanctions.[140] Enhancing legal certainty reduces the legal risks, facilitating innovation and investment.[141] Legal certainty also reduces administrative costs and the costs imposed awaiting legal advice.[142] It may also be that economic criteria are easier for undertakings to understand; giving competition law a unitary welfare goal might provide more predictability for firms than a political balancing test. Secondly, competition policy will only receive the support of business, policy-makers and the general public when they understand it.[143] Without the support of these actors competition policy cannot be as effective;[144] in which case the efficiency benefits that competition policy delivers are less likely to be achieved.[145]

---

[130]   Tridimas (1999) 163.

[131]   Joined Cases 205/82 to 215/82 *Deutsche Milchkontor v Germany* para 30; Case T-51/89, *Tetra Pak v Commission* para 36, and the cases referred to there and Case C-63/93 *Fintan Duff v Minister for Agriculture and Food and A-G* para 20.

[132]   Case C-63/93 *Fintan Duff v Minister for Agriculture and Food and A-G* para 20.

[133]   The relationships between the wide array of market structures, organisational arrangements, transactional attributes, and contractual arrangements in a market economy and the market performance indicia of concern are imperfectly understood from both a theoretical and empirical perspective. As a result, there is always a tension between the specification of clear simple rules and their confrontation with situations where their rigid application can lead to type I or type II errors, Joskow (2002) 100.

[134]   The importance of this may change due to the procedural mechanism in different jurisdictions. The shift from a system of *ex ante* administrative exemption in the Community on 1 May 2004, for example, theoretically increases the importance of legal certainty for undertakings now that the certainty provided by a Commission decision (admittedly it was rare to get one) cannot be relied upon.

[135]   Reg 1/2003, recitals 21, 22, 38 and art 16; Commission, *Guidance Letters Guidelines*, paras 1, 2 and COM(90) 556 1.

[136]   Holmes (2000) 79, citing Jacques Bougie, CEO, Alcan Aluminium Ltd.

[137]   Edward (2002) 129; Commission, *RCP 1993* 52 and Schaub (1996) 79.

[138]   Neven, Papandropoulos and Seabright (1998) 18, 19. See also Bell (1983) 26.

[139]   In relation to contracts governed by English law, eg, see Whish (2008) 311–15. In relation to the financial penalties that can be imposed see Reg 1/2003, Ch VI.

[140]   Jenny (1993) 186 and Coarse (1960).

[141]   Reg 1/2003, recital 38.

[142]   Neven, Papandropoulos and Seabright (1998) 19. These can be important, although they are often small in relation to the benefits to the economy of competition policy, Gardner (2000). Nevertheless, the smaller they are the better, provided that this is not achieved at the expense of an even larger loss to society as a whole, COM(96) 721, para 86. For a brief indication of some business costs related to possible changes in the UK competition regime see DTI (2002) 13–15. For other benefits of legal certainty see Jebsen and Stevens (1995–6) 450, 460 and Scalia (1989) 1179.

[143]   Commission, *RCP 1993* 103.

[144]   Commission, *RCP 2002* 20–22; Commission, *RCP 1992* 15 and Commission, *RCP 1991* 11, 57.

[145]   Commission, *RCP 2001* 5.

It is worth asking whether exclusion really enhances legal certainty. Exclusion, adopting the sole consumer welfare objective in competition law, ensures that there is only one consideration *in the competition law*.[146] Where the competition rules are unclear, under-takings need only be guided by one over-arching objective, consumer welfare. They do not have to assess whether the agreement's welfare benefits outweigh other public policy goals. Predicting the balance between two objectives within one policy instrument is difficult;[147] in this sense, exclusion increases legal certainty, in relation to the competition provisions. Assume now that the other relevant policy objective is environmental policy. If this were pursued using legislation with a 'pure' environmental goal then, in cases of ambiguity within that rule, predicting the outcome of the decision would be easier too. It may be difficult for firms to ensure that their agreement complies with *both* the competition provisions and the environmental rules, but they do not have to balance the two objectives themselves.[148] As a result, exclusion seems to enhance legal certainty *overall*.[149]

Yet, predictability is not a legal system's only value,[150] the 'right' decision is important too. One should not generally ignore constitutional imperatives, just to increase legal certainty, for example;[151] especially where exclusion makes it hard or impossible to achieve other relevant goals. It is sometimes difficult to balance the relevant objectives and to predict the optimal balance.[152] Compromise, and the uncertainty this engenders, has a cost. This is an important objection but it should not be over-stated.

However, where the advantages of considering non-welfare objectives within competi-tion policy are small, then the benefits of legal certainty may make exclusion preferable.[153] Such a carve-out would not justify a rejection of compromise; but, it might limit compromise's remit and, when compromise is to be used, we might seek ways of reducing uncertainty.[154] In addition, we might seek ways of mitigating the consequences of an

---

[146]   That is not to say that the consumer welfare standard is easy to apply, see above. See also, Amato (1997) 123 and Jebsen and Stevens (1995–96) 460.

[147]   See Ch 8.

[148]   Hopefully the public authorities balanced these two objectives when they enacted both sets of rules.

[149]   Amato (1997) 122, 123 and Jacobs (1993/2) 44.

[150]   Case C-354/95 *The Queen v Minister for Agriculture, Fisheries and Food, ex p National Farmers' Union and Others*, para 58.

[151]   Frazer (1990) 622, 623.

[152]   COM(1999) 587, points 17–21 and Amato (1997) 118. Ch 8 suggests some ways of increasing the facility and the predictability of compromise as a process.

[153]   Jacobs (1992/3) 44.

[154]   One way of doing this may be through the appreciability doctrine, which would allow us to ignore objectives that the agreement affects in a non-material way. This might be combined with the promotion of these non-welfare objectives through other legislative provisions; clearer explanation of the relevant public policy goals and the weights to be ascribed to them; development of a balancing methodology, etc. Ch 8 further develops such ideas. Another idea is to only integrate policies in major legislative proposals. This was suggested with environmental impact assessments, eg, Commission, *From Cardiff to Helsinki* 5. Major pieces of legislation are likely to have a large impact in many policy areas, justifying the cost of conducting the impact assessment. That said, while decisions in competition cases are not major pieces of legislation they can have considerable effect due to their value as precedents for other decisions. As a result, this 'solution' may be less helpful in our area.

infringement for the parties concerned, where the contraventions are relatively novel, by not imposing fines.[155]

Finally, exclusion reduces firms' compliance costs. This is particularly important as more jurisdictions adopt competition laws.[156] Antitrust laws increasingly emphasise consumer welfare, rather than other public policy goals. As these rules harmonise across the globe, compliance costs decrease.[157] This is because where a contract triggers competition laws' jurisdictional tests in multiple jurisdictions, transactions are cheaper if the competition assessment is similar in all of them.[158] Fewer lawyers are needed both before and after the transaction.[159] Furthermore, as competition law converges, transactional delays and uncertainty are reduced,[160] making agreement easier to attain. This aids the development of international commerce.[161]

That said, how much difference does 'exclusion' make towards the reduction of costs? The aforementioned benefits apply to the competition assessment. However, as noted above, if, for example, there is no room for environmental considerations in the competition assessment, states are likely to implement specific environmental laws. Firms must comply with these rules in the relevant jurisdictions too.[162] This implies that exclusion may have less impact on cost reduction than one would expect, because the competition rules are just one set of rules that must be complied with, among many.

However, it should not be forgotten that competition authorities are particularly renowned for their attempts to extend the extra-jurisdictional reach of competition law.[163] Excluding environmental considerations from the competition analysis may, in fact, reduce firms' compliance costs overall, simply because, currently, competition laws often have a larger jurisdictional reach than their environmental counterparts.

3.2.2 The disadvantages of exclusion

Under exclusion, potentially important policy objectives are completely ignored. Even where they are protected with other legislation, the balance between different policy objectives is less likely to be optimal[164] and, in practice, where different policies are implemented independently insufficient attention is paid to their impact on other relevant policy objectives.

A further disadvantage of exclusion is that it limits access to an important policy tool. Many states increasingly emphasise corporate social responsibility (CSR). CSR encourages

---

[155] See, eg Case T-51/89 *Tetra Pak v Commission* para 38.

[156] Calvani (2003) 415; Whish (2008) 1 and Dabbah (2003) 1, 2.

[157] Calvani (2003) 415. See Dabbah (2003) 4–6 and the references made there, for other benefits of convergence.

[158] Value judgments are still needed when implementing a pure consumer welfare model, see above. So, there is a risk that the various jurisdictions may interpret an agreement's anti-competitive effects differently even when they try to achieve the same objective.

[159] By way of example, in its proposed merger with Honeywell, General Electric had to notify the merger in over 10 jurisdictions. The substantive legal tests were different in many of these.

[160] COM(2001) 745, para 160.

[161] Kaczorowska (2000) 124 and Jenny (1998) 29.

[162] This problem would be reduced if environmental protection (and other relevant) requirements were harmonised across the globe as well. However, there is less impetus for this than for the harmonisation of competition laws.

[163] See eg Whish (2008) ch 12 and Goyder (2003) ch 23.

[164] See the text around n 76, above.

companies, on a voluntary basis, to integrate social and environmental concerns into their business operations and their interaction with stakeholders.[165]

The move towards CSR is driven by citizens, consumers, public authorities, investors and companies themselves in response to the damage caused by economic activity to the environment and the fabric of society.[166] CSR is promoted throughout the Community and is considered important,[167] even though both the Council and the Commission recognise that it can undermine economic efficiency its objective is to ensure a balanced approach to sustainable development, which maximises synergies between economic, social and environmental dimensions.[168] Both institutions accept the need to integrate CSR into other Community (and Member State) policies to further the awareness, dissemination and adoption of such practices.[169] This should include competition policy. The Commission has called this integrated approach '... the lynch pin in the process of establishing sustainable social and economic development patterns.'[170]

Both the Commission and the Council recognise the need for firms to work together to better meet shared CSR objectives.[171] The Commission believes that co-operation agreements have three main advantages over legislation: they can promote a pro-active attitude on the part of industry, they can provide cost-effective, tailor-made solutions and allow for a quicker and smoother achievement of objectives.[172] In addition, co-operation agreements are popular with policy-makers as they provide benefits that may not be achieved otherwise. For example, with environmental agreements, there is therefore a trade-off between environmental benefits and economic costs provided by the adoption of voluntary approaches. This may be because the necessary emission abatement cannot be obtained through other policy instruments; or, if there is a relevant economic and environmental gain from achieving the emission abatement through a co-operation agreement, then the optimal strategy could be the one which favours reduced competition in the market (so one needs to check that these two policy goals are optimally aligned).[173] Furthermore, conventional regulation has various constraints and there is a belief that businesses may undertake pollution prevention efforts (and other actions with social value) under voluntary programmes that cannot be imposed upon them purely through traditional instruments.

If one cannot take environmental and social factors into account in competition policy at all, then the drive for CSR is undermined. This is because undertakings risk fines for including CSR criteria in appreciable agreements under the competition rules where this

---

[165]   COM(2002) 347 5 and COM(2001) 366, paras 8, 20–26.

[166]   COM(2002) 347 6 and COM(2001) 366, para 10.

[167]   COM(2002) 347 3. See also, Council, *on CSR* 3, 4; COM(2002) 347 4, 7, 8 and COM(2001) 366, paras 2, 6, 9, 13–19. See <http://www.euractiv.com/cgi-bin/cgint.exe?204&OIDN=2000470&-tt=cs> accessed 30 April 2009 for a list of recent Community CSR initiatives.

[168]   COM(2002) 347 20. See also, Art 2 EC; Council, *on CSR* 3 and Grimeaud (2000) 209. It is also there because the Commission believes in 'shared responsibilities', see Gyselen (1994) 244, 245.

[169]   Council, *on CSR* 3, 4; COM(2002) 347 7, 8, 18, 19 and Grimeaud (2000) 209.

[170]   Cited in Baldock (1992) 1. See also, OECD (2006) 39, 40, 44.

[171]   European Parliament and Council Directive, *on waste electrical and electronic equipment (WEEE)*, recital 20 and art 5(2)(c) explicitly envisage co-operation; Council, *on CSR* 4; COM(2002) 347 10, 12, 17; COM(2001) 366, paras 42–60 and COM(96) 561. This is supported by other academic work too: see Bouterse (1994) 40 and references made there, and Jacobs (1993/2) 43.

[172]   COM(96) 561 3. See also, OECD (2003a) 3, 4, 15, 62 and Videras (2002) 1 and references made there.

[173]   Brau and Carraro (2001) 65, 66.

undermines welfare. This is particularly ironic when the relevant institutions expressly accept that welfare is often undermined through CSR and yet still advocate its use.

That said, co-operation agreements can undermine competition on the market,[174] either: intentionally[175] or accidentally/inadvertently, leading to sub-optimal results.[176] One needs to check the institutional fine-tuning of these systems, general conclusions can be misleading or incomplete (such as always ignore public policy),[177] especially given the relative youth of the theoretical and empirical economics' sweeping rules.[178]

As a result, one should not always allow voluntary agreements, nor should public policy be excluded from the competition assessment purely on these grounds. However, some limits are appropriate, in anti-trust law one might, for example, place weight on the way that the agreement is entered into, including the presence or not of the state and the roles it adopts.[179] One might also seek to use a voluntary approach in combination with other instruments, eg regulation, to achieve maximum efficiency.[180]

3.3 Compromise

This section considers some advantages and disadvantages of compromise (balancing) as a method of conflict resolution.

3.3.1 The advantages of compromise

When compromise takes place within the competition analysis of a specific arrangement, the decision-maker considers economic efficiency as well as other relevant policy objectives. This is to ensure that the optimal balance between conflicting goals is achieved in the specific case in question. In contrast, where non-economic public policy considerations are excluded from the competition law analysis they are ignored (in the competition assessment). This means that public policy objectives, potentially of great significance, think of national security or environmental protection, could be jeopardised:

> [A] conflict between environmental policies and competition policies may occur. Indeed, the two policies may have conflicting objectives if the adoption of VAs [voluntary agreements] and the consequent environmental benefits are associated with reduced competition within the industry. In other words, if a VA is the optimal environmental policy tool to deal with a given environmental problem, an environmental regulator may prefer a concentrated industry structure in which the VA can more easily be implemented and is likely to be more effective. But a competition authority may not accept to trade-off the environmental benefits of the VA with the economic costs possibly induced by a concentrated industry.[181]

One could deal with this trade-off by ignoring the competition aspects and designing the best environmental outcome possible. Then, if there are competition problems ex post one

---

[174]   Brau and Carraro (2001) 64, 65. That said, this is not always the case, and, under certain conditions, they can even raise consumer surplus, Brau and Carraro (2001) 63.
[175]   This can help achieve, eg, environmental ends: see Videras (2002) 12 and Brau and Carraro (2001) 53.
[176]   Brau and Carraro (2001) 45.
[177]   Lehmann (2004) 444–47.
[178]   Brau and Carraro (2001) 64, 66, 67.
[179]   Videras (2002) 12, 13.
[180]   This issue is largely unexplored, Higley, Convery and Lévêque (2001) 11 and Convery and Lévêque (2001).
[181]   Brau and Carraro (2001) 65, 66.

can attack them with competition legislation. However, if the competition legislation does not consider environmental benefits then this will mean that these will be lost/diluted if the agreements are struck down. It may even mean that they never occur at all, as the parties' competition lawyers may advise them never to enter into the agreement. It may be better to take account of environmental benefits in competition law to achieve the optimal result. One might think *ex ante* and try to design the voluntary agreement so that its effects on competition are totally offset or minimised.[182]

The benefits of compromise can be great. Yet, balancing in every case is not ideal. Sometimes it is difficult/expensive to balance the relevant objectives and to predict the optimal balance.[183] This uncertainty has a cost. This is an important objection but, as we have seen, it should not be over-stated. Predictability is not a legal system's only value, the 'right' decision is important too.[184]

Another issue is that compromise allows the decision-maker to adopt a seamless approach to 'legislation'. If this were not the case then the legislator would not be neutral vis-à-vis the different regulatory or legislative techniques which States choose to pursue various policies. Neutrality of this sort has many advantages, including increased efficiency.[185]

3.3.2 The disadvantages of compromise

Compromise allows the decision-maker to achieve the optimal policy balance[186] in competition cases.[187] However, there is an argument that the objectives assigned to a competition law might be more completely achieved if they are drawn narrowly.[188] As a result, a potential downside of compromise is that it may mean that none of the conflicting objectives are satisfactorily achieved. This may be worse than adequately achieving one of them, even where the others are ignored.

Furthermore, commentators often argue that many non-economic objectives are applied arbitrarily and subjectively.[189] Why contaminate the competition policy's welfare calculations with such goals?[190] This is not so much an argument against compromise, but against the consideration of non-economic objectives.[191] Taken to an extreme this would mean that many such objectives could never be implemented. Arguably, the inclusion of these goals can undermine legal certainty, but this is not the legal system's only objective. Anyway, it is not as if welfare standards can be applied objectively either. A better response

---

[182]   Brau and Carraro (2001) 66.

[183]   COM(1999) 587, points 17–21 and Amato (1997) 118. Ch 8 suggests some ways of increasing the facility and the predictability of compromise as a process.

[184]   See the discussion in Section 3.2.1.

[185]   These are outlined in Gyselen (1994) 245–46, 250–52, 256, 257.

[186]   As mentioned above, there is a knowledge problem and so the 'optimal balance' can never be perfectly achieved. However, compromise allows the decision-maker to approach this ideal, in the sense that the test would *allow* it (ie even if this is impossible to *ensure*).

[187]   Although, this might sometimes be tempered with an appreciability doctrine, ie only consider large impacts on public policy, for example. This idea is further developed in Ch 8, Section 3.4.

[188]   Neven (1998) 8.

[189]   Schaub (1998) 126 and Hawk (1998) 355. The World Bank and OECD (1999) 1 notes the same argument.

[190]   Hovenkamp (1998) 421 and Areeda and Turner (1978), para 109a.

[191]   Although the related issue of commensurability is discussed in Ch 8, Section 2.

to these issues, rather than side-lining non-economic policies, may be strive to find more predictable and objective ways of applying them.[192]

Similarly, Areeda and Turner make a point about justiciability. They argue that considering non-economic objectives would involve the courts in political decisions for which there are no workable legal standards. This would place them in a regulatory or supervisory role for which they are ill-equipped.[193] Given this, so the argument goes, the subjective nature of balancing public policy objectives should affect the institutional structure of the decision-making body, ie it should be done by political bodies.[194]

It is difficult to balance non-economic objectives. The absence of workable legal standards is certainly a handicap.[195] However, it is believed that the reference to 'political decisions' and Areeda and Turner's conclusions are too extreme. Political decisions are made even within a 'pure' economic framework. Furthermore, courts regularly make political decisions of this nature;[196] although, I argue that it is far better when this is explicit, in the words of Justice Holmes (US Supreme Court):

> I think that judges themselves have failed adequately to recognise their duty of weighing considerations of social advantage. The duty is inevitable, and the result of the often proclaimed judicial aversion to deal with such considerations is simply to leave the very ground and foundation of judgments inarticulate, and often unconscious.[197]

Having said that, some institutional structures do seem more perfectly designed for such balancing; one example was the Commission, because there the various Commissioners from all areas have an equal say in the adoption of Commission competition decisions. Including experts from these various policy areas must help achieve the optimal balance of the relative policy goals. But one should not put the cart before the horse; institutional design should follow from the constitutional imperative of the decisions' content, not the other way round.[198]

A second, admittedly rarer, issue is that a jurisdiction may not have the legal capability to achieve the ends by other means; for example, where powers have not been granted to the relevant body in law[199] or other conflicts/difficulties which a specific legal system generates.[200] For example, in the European Union certain matters are reserved to the exclusive competence of the Member States.[201] This means that the Community cannot directly act in these areas. If the Community could not take account of relevant public policy objectives, when applying Community competition law in a way which affected an area of exclusive Member State competence, this could undermine the Member States'

---

[192] See Ch 8.

[193] Areeda and Turner (1978), para 105. See also Bork (1993) 115; Hawk (1998) 58 and Odudu (2006) 172, 173.

[194] See Ehlermann (2001) and Ehlermann (1998), for example.

[195] Ch 8 suggests a framework.

[196] eg Member States' courts balance Arts 28 and 30 EC; Poiares Maduro (1998) 16–25; and, for an interesting discussion in the area of human rights, see Hirschl (2007).

[197] Holmes (1897) 467.

[198] Ch 2, Section 3.2.1 considers the matter in more depth in a Community context.

[199] Think of the Community's limited competences in culture, public health and sport, and yet the exigencies of Arts 151(4) and 152(1) EC and the Declaration on sport, annexed to the Treaty of Amsterdam.

[200] Cappelletti (1987) 5–7, provides some examples in a European Union context.

[201] Even where the Community has the relevant competence, it has not always been given the appropriate tools to achieve the objective in the most efficient way possible, Gual (1995) 39.

ability to achieve their own goals,[202] which might not be the case where the Commission could take account of the Member States' goals in Community competition law.

This argument may seem unconvincing at first.[203] Jurisdictional obstacles are often there to check uninhibited competence. It may be more appropriate to change the competence (if this were considered necessary) as opposed to changing the substance of the legal provision.[204] That said, imposing a duty on the Commission to consider, for example, cultural policy when applying the competition rules would limit its ability to undermine the Member States' policy in this area which they have intentionally reserved to themselves.[205] Rather than taking affirmative action in a reserved area, the Community recognises a Member State interest.[206] This could have significant benefits otherwise the Member States may ignore the need for competition in their cultural legislation and the Commission may ignore cultural benefits in its competition decisions, undermining the Member States' intentions and the achievement of both policy objectives.[207]

Finally, although an objective could, theoretically, be achieved more efficiently using another policy instrument, there might be practical reasons (at least in the short term) why the best way of achieving certain ends at a given moment in time is by distorting competition. This might be because of a fear of political fallout, for example;[208] or there may be political obstacles to agreeing specific environmental legislation such as a lack of time in the legislative programme, even where a measure has universal support. As seen in the CSR discussion, agreements between undertakings may achieve a given level of, for example, environmental protection, more quickly than could be achieved by legislating.[209] It may be acceptable to allow compromise in these areas until appropriate legislation is enacted.[210]

Even where these arguments apply, one should critically examine claims that undermine competition to achieve public policy ends to see whether they could be achieved more efficiently in a different way within the required timeframe and given the powers of the

[202]   On this point and others like it, see also, Ariño (2004) 20; Jacobs (1993/2) 41, 42 and Baldock (1992) 18.
[203]   In a similar vein, Vogelaar (1994) 546 argues that voluntary environmental agreements are beneficial because legislating often demands political compromise, which often makes legislation less effective. However, this is one of the costs of democratic institutions and it is not necessarily a convincing justification for ignoring the legislature.
[204]   Monti (2002) 1092, notes the argument that the '… increase in Community policies in achieving other Treaty objectives directly … mean that the need for competition law to be deployed indirectly to achieve other Treaty aims is gone.' This is only true if the Community now has all the powers needed to achieve all relevant objectives. This is not the case: see Ch 2, Section 3.
[205]   Cunningham (2001) 136, 137.
[206]   Such a mechanism is necessary if Member States are to reserve certain policy areas to themselves. Cunningham (2001) 161 also argues that it is in line with subsidiarity.
[207]   It is likely that consistency increases where a single body is able to reconcile different policy objectives, Buigues, Jacquemin and Sapir (1995a) xvii, they also claim the same for clarity, although see the discussion above.
[208]   Some argue that this is the case for binge-drinking, eg see BMA Board of Science, *Alcohol misuse: tackling the UK epidemic*, February 2008, p 48.
[209]   This might create a moral hazard problem. If the legislator sees that the courts (or the Commission) deal with these difficult balances effectively then it may see even less need to face difficult, controversial and unpopular compromises in the future. This may lead to even more uncertainty in the long run. That said, legislators are unlikely to forego the considerable power that this moral hazard implies for long.
[210]   The Commission has suggested this approach, see, eg SEC(92) 1986 6. This issue is discussed further in Ch 7, in a Community context.

specific decision-making body.[211] The choice of undermining competition to achieve other objectives must be clear and adequately justified.[212] Remember that if competition policy incorporates different political interests it risks becoming captive to the political process, which may reduce its effectiveness.

4 CONCLUSION

Chapter 1 debates two questions: *why* might competition policy incorporate non-welfare objectives? and *when* should competition policy consider non-welfare objectives? It adopted a theoretical perspective. Only by answering these questions can we place competition policy within a judicial framework and understand how it can and should interact with other areas of law. Obviously, once we place these theoretical questions into a specific legal context there will be a dialectic such that this context may further impact upon the answers to these two questions.

The first question, '*why* might competition policy incorporate non-welfare objectives?' is relatively easy to answer. As noted above, arguments in favour of the unitary total welfare goal rely on two premises: (i) that reliance on a total welfare standard makes society 'better off'; and (ii) that redistribution is possible through other means. If either of these premises does not hold, whether the economic welfare standard adopted is value neutral becomes important. This is because a competition law based on such a standard could result in outcomes which are not in the best interests of society as a whole and which one may not be able to adequately compensate for later through redistribution.

We have seen arguments that a pure welfare goal is wealth-maximising. This is not always the case; sometimes balancing within competition law is the most efficient strategy, especially as the effectiveness of traditional regulatory instruments for achieving environmental and other goals is increasingly questioned. Even on their own welfare-enhancing (bigger cake) logic, the advocates of a sole welfare goal for competition law are not immune to challenge. This is because anyone who advocates the policy that is, simply, 'best for economic growth' or 'more efficient' must provide not only an explanation of why the favoured policy has those virtues, but also an argument of political morality that justifies the pursuit of growth or efficiency regardless of other social values.[213] I have shown that while the pursuit of economic welfare may aid the achievement of public policy goals, it can also undermine them. As the outcome is so contingent on the legal and factual context, it does not seem possible to say that pursuing a unitary welfare goal in competition law necessarily results in a bigger cake.

Competition policy often has a welfare objective, normally consumer welfare, the standard I advocate. Consumer welfare, like all other welfare goals, is value-laden. The pursuit of welfare objectives through competition policy can affect other important policy objectives, for example due to externalities; sometimes reinforcing them, sometimes

---

[211] The institutional design of the decision-maker is relevant to this discussion but is outside the scope of this work. See OECD (2003) 2, 4; Mexican submission to OECD (2003) 3–5; Monti (2002) 1093; Poiares Maduro (1999) 466, 470; Mitchell and Simmons (1994) 41–84 and Baldock (1992) 5, 18.

[212] Dutch Ministry of Economic Affairs, *The Liberal Professions* 24 and Fox (2000) 594.

[213] Murphy and Nagel (2002) 12. This statement was made in the context of tax policy, but the sentiment is equally applicable to competition policy.

undermining them. It is not always possible/efficient or appropriate to compensate for this later. As Areeda and Turner point out, welfare is not a foundational value. Although the general argument is that other values are important, they should just be dealt with in other, more efficient, ways; where, in fact, redistribution is not possible, efficient or appropriate,[214] then this sometimes risks becoming an argument for the pursuit of growth regardless of its impact on other social values. Remember too, that not only consequential-ist theories are important; deontological theories emphasise that there are other standards, independent of overall consequences, which we should value, such as individual rights (for example, property rights) and fairness. I also emphasised the importance of firms participating in society as moral actors. In other words, even if pursuing economic welfare always resulted in a bigger cake, some goals are so important that there can be benefits in getting the whole of society to contribute to them. Few prioritise welfare effects, regardless of the consequences on other policy goals.[215] Given that all of the economic welfare standards redistribute, I advocate a consumer welfare standard, which I believe generally benefits the most important segment of society. However, I also think that one sometimes needs to consider public policy goals in the competition assessment too.

   If public policy goals are incorporated into competition policy their consideration must be as rational, transparent and open as possible;[216] it is also vital that the relevance of public policy in competition policy is acknowledged upfront.[217]

   That does not mean that competition should always be compromised for non-economic policy objectives. Understanding when this might be appropriate was the reason for this chapter's second question, *when* should competition policy consider non-welfare objec-tives? This issue is extremely difficult to delimit outside of a particular legal context and so I have restricted myself to raising some general issues here. Once the context has been set, transparent guidelines explaining the methodology to be adopted in a balancing exercise are important.[218]

   It is difficult to agree when one should intervene in specific cases; but some possible filters are that there should only be public policy balancing where there is a reduction in the relevant welfare standard, which I suggest should be consumer welfare. Competition policy cannot do everything; only where there is a competition problem should one use it to achieve public policy goals.[219] Secondly, public policy balancing is less helpful where the public policy gain is not likely to be appreciable, although this assessment must include both the amount of public policy gain as well as a consideration of its importance.[220] Finally, one might also be less open to public policy balancing where the legislator has recently intervened in the specific balance, or explicitly decided not to, because it

---

[214] I accept this may create a moral hazard problem, but do not believe this to be as great as the risk if important public policy goals are effectively ignored.

[215] For a discussion, see Bird (2006), pt 1 and ch 6.

[216] ICN, *Report on the Objectives of Unilateral Conduct Laws (2007)* 36, 37; Furse (1996) 258 and Freeman (2008).

[217] Fuller (1969) 81–91, argues that there must be congruence between the law as declared and as administered.

[218] In particularly complex cases the regulator might also consider waiving any fine that might otherwise be imposed.

[219] If there is no consumer welfare loss one could still protect public policy goals using instruments specifically designed to directly protect these ends.

[220] Clearly, agreement on the definition of 'appreciability' is vital, see Ch 8, Section 3.4.

thought the current balance was appropriate.[221] In other cases, where the legal context demands it, public policy balancing should be conducted.[222] The entity performing the balancing exercise must consider, in the legal and economic context, the impact upon competition and weigh this against the impact upon other relevant public policy goal(s).[223] However, one should be sceptical about any claimed public policy effects. These should either be costed in some way, or at the least be supported by some widely accepted theoretical model.[224]

---

[221] Once again, the definition of 'recent' and 'specific balance' is important here.

[222] Note that I am not advocating a full cost-benefit analysis in every competition decision; some limits have been suggested here and Part C of this work explores them in more detail.

[223] This must take account both of the amount of harm to competition/the public policy goal as well as the importance of these goals.

[224] There is a risk that this would encourage short term thinking, as likely effects are normally easier to 'prove' in this timescale, which is why I add in the reference to 'accepted theoretical models'.

2

Competition Policy and Public Policy Objectives in a Community Law Framework

1 INTRODUCTION[1]

Given that the content of competition policy is a matter of political choice,[2] the relevance/propriety (or not) of public policy considerations in competition law[3] must be assessed in a specific legal context.

The focus is on Community competition law. I spotlight Article 81 EC because there is more case law than in relation to Article 82 EC. Nevertheless, my Article 81 conclusions equally apply to Article 82, because these two provisions' objectives are the same.[4] The ECMR also seems to adopt the framework I suggest for analysing Article 81.[5]

It is important to know whether public policy objectives should be considered within Article 81 EC; undertakings need to know whether such factors can be raised in competition proceedings and decision-makers need to know whether they can/should consider public policy issues there. Community competition policy cannot be made rational until we know what its underlying objectives are.[6]

This chapter discusses whether Article 81 EC has a unique consumer welfare goal. It argues that public policy goals must be considered within Article 81 EC today.

In fact, from a historical perspective, this is obvious. As I demonstrate below, the Council, Commission, Community Courts and European Parliament have all repeatedly endorsed the consideration of public policy objectives within Article 81 EC. Community competition lawyers generally recognise that public policy has been considered there.[7]

Nevertheless, I discuss whether public policy objectives should be relevant in Article 81 today; I do so for two key reasons. In academic discussion it is often assumed as self-evident that the influence of political considerations on competition policy is unwarranted.[8] By placing Article 81 EC in its Treaty context, Section 2.1 argues that public policy's influence is warranted there. Section 2.2 examines how the Community Courts approach the relevance of public policy considerations in competition law, they generally support its inclusion and some recent judgments confirm this view.

Secondly, the Commission now argues that the objective of Article 81 EC is to protect competition on the market as a means of enhancing consumer welfare and ensuring an efficient allocation of resources.[9] There is no room in the Commission's new world for

---

[1]   This chapter is a more detailed version of Townley (2008), which also contained a case study on how, in certain circumstances, the Community competition rules might allow supermarkets to agree minimum prices on alcohol for public health reasons.

[2]   Frazer (1990) 623.

[3]   ie Chapter 1's conclusions.

[4]   Case 6/72 *Europemballage and Continental Can v Commission* para 25.

[5]   Recital 23, Reg 139/2004.

[6]   Bork (1978) 50.

[7]   See, eg Monti (2007) ch 4; Odudu (2006) ch 7; Goyder (2003) 121–23; Monti (2002); B&C (2008), paras 1–071–1–077; Whish (2008) 19–23; Korah (2000), s 1.3.2; Ritter and Braun (2005) 17–19; Faull and Nikpay (2007), paras 3.12–3.22; Mercier, Mach, Gilliéron and Affolter (1999) 130–32; Ehlermann (1998) 356, 359–85, 489; Amato (1997) 114; Sauter (1997); Bouterse (1994); Frazer (1990) 616 and Verstrynge (1988) 5. For a contrary view see Schaub (1998) 9.

[8]   Sauter (1997) 120. See, eg Ehlermann (1998) x, 9; Wißmann (2000) 143, 144; Burrichter in Ehlermann (2001) 46; Tesauro (1998) 223; Marenco (2001) 500; Schaub (2002) 46 and Gyselen (2002a) 185–87. For contrary views see Sufrin (2006) 962–67; Monti (2002) and Amato (1997) 113–24.

[9]   See, eg Commission, *Article 81(3) Guidelines*, para 13; Commission, *Vertical Guidelines*, para 7. By way of contrast, see COM(96) 721 final, para 191.

public policy goals.[10] Many Community competition practitioners and academics support the Commission's new approach.[11] The Commission has not sought to justify its adoption of a unitary objective on theoretical grounds.[12] Its guidelines claim that they outline the current state of the case law.[13] However, as we have seen, there is general consensus that public policy goals have been considered within Article 81 EC;[14] and the Community Courts' (ECJ and CFI) judgments continue to do so today (as do many of the Commission's own Article 81(3) decisions).[15] This implies that the Commission's current policy position has changed, bringing its practice into line with the mainstream academic perspective, but clashing with the other Institutions. Given the importance of the Commission's role in the development of Community competition policy and the implications of such a 'shift' for case outcomes, this change demands careful examination, and this is Section 2.3's role.

Ten years ago, Amato said that while Community competition law's objective is not a new topic, today's context provides new and intriguing elements. Generally, we refrain from discussing the issue openly.[16] In the US, the debate over antitrust's goals involved a battle for its soul,[17] consumer welfare seems to have won. In Europe, we have never really had a fight; instead we are drawn to the embers of the American struggle.[18] Section 3 discusses some objections to the inclusion of public policy in Article 81 EC, from the academic literature; but, before we bet all on this trajectory, we should ensure that our legal constellation is governed by the same rules as theirs. A proper debate on the matter is overdue. This chapter was conceived as a step on that road.

2 IN FAVOUR OF BALANCING IN ARTICLE 81 EC

2.1 The Treaty

In order to explain why the Community Courts consider public policy goals within Article 81 EC, one needs to understand how the EC Treaty generates public policy conflicts, this

---

[10] Whish (2008) 155. According to the Commission, public policy is relevant only insofar as it can be subsumed under Art 81(3) EC's four heads (not easy given the Commission's declared objective for Art 81 EC), Commission, *Article 81(3) Guidelines*, para 42. In 1999 it said that Art 81(3) is there 'to provide a legal framework for the economic assessment of restrictive practices and not to allow the application of the competition rules to be set aside because of political considerations': Commission, *White Paper on Modernisation*, para 57, although note the logical implication of para 56. Monti suggests that when the Commission refers to 'political considerations' it means public policy ones, Monti (2002).

[11] See, eg Odudu (2006) ch 7 and Ehlermann (1998).

[12] Baquero Cruz (2002) 100–03 offers some procedural and pragmatic suggestions for why many argue for a decoupling of the competition rules from public policy goals, as well as a critique of them.

[13] Commission, *Article 81(3) Guidelines*, para 7. Admittedly, para 7 adds that the guidelines also deal with issues not covered in the case law or those open to interpretation; but, as we will see the relevance of public policy in Art 81 EC is already well-established.

[14] See n 7, above.

[15] For example, the *Wouters* Case, decided just 26 months before publication of Commission, *Article 81(3) Guidelines*. The ECJ did the same in 2006, the *Meca-Medina* Case. In 2005, the CFI considered public policy concerns in its Art 81(3) analysis, Case T-193/02, *Laurent Piau v Commission*. See also Part B of this work.

[16] Ehlermann (1998) 3. See also Ehlermann's own comments at page 480.

[17] Fox (1987).

[18] Gerber (2008) 1248, 1249, 1259, 1260.

section deals with this issue. The Treaty creates a problem of conflicts through the hierarchy of its articles and due to the presence of policy-linking clauses. Section 2.1 examines these two ways of conflict creation; then, Section 2.2 asks how the Treaty deals with the conflicts that it has created.

2.1.1 How conflicts arise in the Treaty

Conflicts between Treaty goals arise from the structure of the Treaty and through the inclusion of seven Treaty clauses, such as Article 152(1) EC,[19] which I call 'policy-linking clauses'. The Lisbon Treaty (if adopted) reinforces this view.

Some might question the need for examining the Treaty's structure and the policy-linking clauses in relation to understanding Article 81 EC's content, as opposed to merely a textual analysis of that provision, for example. However, this more holistic understanding of how conflicts are created is crucial for explaining the ECJ's methodology for solving them:

> [T]he court [ECJ] usually has recourse to three types of first-order criteria in typical hard case situations: (i) semiotic or linguistic arguments; (ii) systemic and context-establishing arguments; and (iii) teleological, functional or consequentialist arguments—and that preference is usually given to systemic functional criteria.[20]

Deciding whether public policy considerations are relevant within Article 81 EC is a hard case.[21] The citation explains that, in hard cases such as these, rather than focusing on semiotic/linguistic arguments (textual analysis), the Community courts prefer systemic arguments (for example, consideration of policy-linking clauses) and teleological ones (for example, an emphasis on Treaty structure). These preferred methodologies for *solving* hard cases also help us understand when the Community courts *see* conflicts, which is why I refer to them here.

Let us start with a teleological analysis of the EC Treaty. Unlike, for example, the competition provisions of the USA, the Community competition provisions are not in stand-alone competition legislation aimed at isolated goals, but are part of a web of inter-related Treaty articles.[22] In the Community context it is particularly important to check whether other provisions (and goals) in the Community framework impinge upon the competition articles. This means putting Article 81 in its Community context.[23]

---

[19]   Art 152(1) EC reads: 'A high level of human health protection shall be ensured in the definition and implementation of all Community policies and activities.'

[20]   Bengoetxea (1993) 233–4. See also, Arnull (2006) ch 16; Slynn (1985) 393; Case 283/81 *CILFIT v Ministero della Sanità*, paras 16–20 and Edwards (1996).

[21]   Bengoetxea (1993) 218–23 implies that arguments about the consideration of public policy in Art 81 EC would count as a hard case.

[22]   'It is easy for competition lawyers to forget that EC Competition policy stems not from a particular piece of legislation resulting from specific concerns about competition or consumer welfare, but is embedded in the founding document of a unique supranational experiment.', Sufrin (2006) 952, 953.

[23]   Verouden (2003) 530; Souty (2003) 23, 43; Hildebrand (2002) 2, 11; Baquero Cruz (2002) 5; B&C (2008), para 1–015; Korah (2000) 6; Ritter and Braun (2005) 17–19; Wesseling (2000) 18, 32; Craig and de Búrca (2008) 73, 74; Ehlermann (1998) xvi, 551; Amato (1997); Sauter (1997) 116–22; Gyselen (1994) 242; Bouterse (1994) 2, 48; van Miert (1993) 120; Schröter (1987) 657; Slynn (1985) 393 and Pescatore (1974) 41.

Article 2 EC outlines the Community's task,[24] which consists of 'ultimate aims' such as the 'harmonious, balanced and sustainable development of economic activities' and 'equality between men and women'. Article 2 contains at least nine 'ultimate aims', all broad, inter-related goals. These 'ultimate aims' are to be achieved by, amongst others, implementing the common policies and activities referred to in Articles 3 and 4.[25]

Article 3 EC provides an open list of over twenty Community activities for 'the purposes set out in Article 2'. These activities range from a common commercial policy, an internal market and a system ensuring that competition in the internal market is not distorted, to environmental protection, a common transport policy, development co-operation and strengthening consumer protection.[26] The provisions of Article 3 form part of the general principles of the common market, which are enlarged upon and applied by the later Treaty provisions. Taken in isolation, Article 3 sheds no light on the relationship between these different activities.[27] For our purposes, Article 4 EC is divided into two parts: the first paragraph says, amongst other things, that for the purposes set out in Article 2 EC, the activities of the Community shall include, as provided in the Treaty, an economic policy, '… which is based on the close co-ordination of Member States' economic policies, on the internal market and on the definition of common objectives, and conducted in accordance with the principle of an open market economy with free competition.' Article 4(2) EC expands on this.

Then come the implementing provisions. Article 2 EC explains that the mechanism for achieving its goals is by establishing a common market and by implementing common policies; in other words, the later Treaty provisions implement the Article 3 (and 4) activities which, in turn, seek to achieve the purposes set out in Article 2 EC.

This idea of hierarchy brings, buried deep within it, the seed of a problem, related to the broad nature of the Article 2 aims. This is because, the 'ultimate aims' or purposes highlighted in Article 2 may conflict with one another, sometimes one aim can only be achieved at the expense of another;[28] for example, the promotion of both a high level of employment and social protection may conflict, by improving working conditions we often increase unemployment.[29] Even if there were no conflict of this type, a society with finite resources cannot pursue all aims totally, but must prioritise a few.

In a similar vein, the Article 3 activities (there is an open list of over 20 of them) cannot be implemented blindly, but must be balanced against one another, as well as with those in Article 4, in order to reflect the Article 2 balance. For example, 'a system ensuring that

---

[24]   Art 2 EC states: 'The Community shall have as its task, by establishing a common market and an economic and monetary union and by implementing common policies or activities referred to in Articles 3 and 4, to promote throughout the Community a harmonious, balanced and sustainable development of economic activities, a high level of employment and of social protection, equality between men and women, sustainable and non-inflationary growth, a high degree of competitiveness and convergence of economic performance, a high level of protection and improvement of the quality of the environment, the raising of the standard of living and quality of life, and economic and social cohesion and solidarity among Member States.'

[25]   One must not only look to Arts 2, 3 and 4 for the objectives of the Treaty. The Preamble is another important source of information, as are the later Treaty provisions. Advocate-General Warner highlighted this in Case 97/78 *Fritz Schmalla*, p 2323. General principles of law may also be relevant, see Joined Cases 43 and 63/82 *Vereniging ter Bevordering van het Vlaamse Beokwezen, VBVB, and Vereeniging ter Bevordering van de Belangen des Boekhandels, VBBB v Commission* para 34 and the Opinion of A-G Verloren van Themaat 79, including references.

[26]   Respectively, Art 3(1)(b), (c), (g), (l), (f), (r) and (t) EC.

[27]   Bourgeois and Demaret (1995) 66.

[28]   Case 27/74 *Demag v Finanzamt Duisburg-Süd*, see the Opinion of A-G Reischl, 1056.

[29]   See *Debating the Minimum Wage*, The Economist (London 1 February 2001).

competition in the internal market is not distorted' (Article 3(1)(g)) might well conflict with 'a policy in the social sphere comprising a European Social Fund' (Article 3(1)(j)).[30]

In turn, this potential for conflict between the underlying Treaty aims (and thus activities) affects the implementing provisions, such as Article 81 EC. Somehow these implementing provisions must deal with the conflicts generated within Articles 2, 3 and 4 EC. This might be through balancing the public policy goals within each implementing provision, or by pursing only one policy goal through each implementing provision and dealing with conflicts externally to the implementing provisions. The matter is discussed further, once the policy-linking clauses have been introduced.[31]

Before turning to the policy-linking clauses, two other issues are worthy of mention. We have seen that conflicts can be generated when competing Treaty goals collide; they can also arise when Treaty values conflict with those of the Member States.[32] Secondly, the Lisbon Treaty (if ratified by all Member States) amends the Treaty of European Union[33] and the EC Treaty;[34] but, it maintains the pyramidal structure. A single set of objectives is now applicable to both Treaties and all policies.[35] Under the new structure, the Union's explicit aim is to promote peace, its values[36] and the well-being of its peoples.[37] Article 3 EU provides ways of achieving these objectives. Article 3(6) EU Treaty maintains (and makes explicit) the current hierarchy between the objectives and the implementing provisions. If anything, competition may be given less weight post-Lisbon, because references to it have been removed from Article 3 EU Treaty.[38]

We have discussed how the Treaty hierarchy might create conflicts. Conflicts are also generated through the policy-linking clauses, which demand that their objectives be considered whenever other Community policies and activities are implemented. There are seven policy-linking clauses in the Treaty. They relate to environmental protection, employment, culture, public health, consumer protection, economic and social cohesion and development policy; and all make it clear that policy area should be taken into account by the Community in the definition and implementation of its other policies and activities.[39] One such clause is Article 152(1) EC:

> A high level of human health protection shall be ensured in the definition and implementation of all Community policies and activities.

Competition policy is a Community policy; so, the policy-linking clauses' goals should be considered when competition policy is implemented, even if these goals conflict with other competition law objectives.[40] There is widespread agreement that the policy-linking

---

[30]   The *Albany* Case paras 54–60.
[31]   See below, Section 2.1.2.
[32]   Section 2.2 examines how this has worked as well.
[33]   Here referred to as the 'EU Treaty'.
[34]   Which becomes the Treaty on the Functioning of the European Union, here the 'FEU Treaty', together with the EU Treaty, 'the Treaties'.
[35]   Cremona (2008) 4.
[36]   The Union's values are human dignity, freedom, democracy, equality, the rule of law and the respect for human rights, Art 2, EU Treaty.
[37]   Art 3(1) EU Treaty.
[38]   For a discussion of this point see Graupner (2007).
[39]   Respectively, Arts 6, 127(2), 151(4), 152(1), 153(2), 159 and 178 EC. Other rules, such as Declaration 29 to the Amsterdam Treaty on sport, may try to achieve a similar end.
[40]   See, eg Commission, *Environmental State aid Guidelines* (2008) para 18. For a more detailed discussion, see Ch 2, n 55.

clauses are there to ensure that other Treaty rules, for example the free movement provisions or those relating to competition, take account of these other objectives.[41]

The requirement to take account of these policy aims (such as the environment) within Treaty policies and activities that pursue different aims (such as competition), can lead to conflicts, as defined above, that need to be dealt with in the definition and implementation of the later (implementing) Treaty articles.

The Lisbon Treaty expands the use of policy-linking clauses. An all-embracing policy-linking clause has been added, which demands consistency between the Community policies and activities, taking all of the objectives into account.[42] Furthermore, specific policy-linking clauses appear for employment, adequate social protection, social exclusion, education, training, the protection of human health, environmental protection, consumer protection and the welfare of animals.[43]

2.1.2 How the Treaty deals with conflicts

Clashes can arise between competing Treaty values, or between Treaty values and those of the Member States. Given this conclusion, I wanted to understand how these conflicts should be resolved from a Community perspective.

When discussing the Treaty's hierarchy one might argue that the competition rules, amongst them Article 81 EC, are *solely* there to create a system ensuring that competition in the internal market is not distorted.[44] This would leave other chapters in the Treaty to achieve the other Article 3 activities.[45] The (independent) achievement of these activities (by the various implementing provisions) would accomplish Article 2's purposes, as a whole. Competition policy may then be seen as an instrument aiding the attainment of the Treaty objectives (specifically one of them) while also constituting *an end in itself*.[46] This

---

[41]   General Community lawyers readily embrace this conclusion: see Vedder (2003) 3–16, 169; Wasmeier (2001); Pons (2001) 2; Wyatt and Dashwood (2000) 579; Jans (2000) 276, 277; Kapteyn and VerLoren van Themaat (1998) 128; Craig and de Búrca (2008) 651; Commentaire Mégret (1996) 12, 251 and Brittan (1992) 57. Also see in relation to Art 151(4) (cultural policy), Commission Memo, *European collecting societies* (2008); Andries and Julien-Malvy (2008) 55; Council, *Resolution on Fixed Book Prices 2*; Council, *on culture's role in the EU's development*, recital 2; Council, *Resolution on Fixed Book Prices 1* and Council, *Decision on Fixed Book Prices*; Psychogiopoulou (2006) 584, 585; Psychogiopoulou (2005) 839 and Cunningham (2001) 122, 123, 158–63. Some competition lawyers (often tentatively) agree that the policy-linking clauses mean that competition law should take non-economic objectives into account: see Monti (2002); B&C (2001), para 1–040; Faull and Nikpay (1999) paras 2.14–2.16, 2.145 (*cf* Faull and Nikpay (2007) paras 3.406–3.408) and Ehlermann (1998) xvi.
   Commentators such as Barendt and Hitchens (2000) 167 and Ariño (2004) 7, suggest that Art 151(4) EC has been interpreted more as a reminder to the Community of Member State sovereignty than as an encouragement of Community action. But if this were the limit of its remit, it would be difficult to explain policy-linking clauses related to *Community* policies, such as Art 159 EC.
[42]   Art 7 FEU Treaty.
[43]   Arts 9–13 FEU Treaty.
[44]   Art 3(1)(g) EC.
[45]   Although some might be achieved indirectly through a welfare goal, see Ch1, Section 2.2. Schaub believes this should happen in the Community, Schaub in Ehlermann (1998) 119–28.
[46]   See, eg Commission, *RCP 1996*, point 2 and Kirchner (1998) 514, 516 (although he is unclear on this point, see pp 517, 518); the Commission's arguments referred to at the start of this footnote, may also be based on this logic. See also, Lenz (2000) 44, 45, who rejects this approach. Heimler (1998) 599, proffers a slightly different argument: '[A]lthough the competition rules are enforced within the general framework of achieving the fundamental objectives of Article 2 of the Treaty … such general considerations cannot override the legal effect of single provisions.' This argument is undermined by the Community Courts' use of the teleological approach, see below.

would not eliminate conflicts; but, it would ensure that they remained 'external' to Article 81, and competition policy as a whole (and the other implementing provisions). Conflict would be dealt with by exclusion, not compromise. One example of this type of treaty interpretation can be found in Lowe's reflections on the European Convention:

> The Draft Treaty is generally positive as far as competition policy is concerned. I would highlight, in particular, the fact that 'a single market where competition is free and undistorted' figures amongst the objectives of the EU, that the legislative power to establish the competition rules necessary for the functioning of the internal market shall remain in the EU's exclusive competence and that the substantive rules of the EC Treaty on antitrust and State aid have been taken over without changes.[47]

Lowe focuses on the competition provisions' (unchanged) wording; and the continued reference amongst Community objectives to 'an internal market where competition is free and undistorted'. He sees isolated competition law provisions, pursuing a single aim, 'free and undistorted competition'; competition is an end in itself.[48] In other words, his approach to competition law comes from his method of Treaty interpretation.

If the Treaty's structure supported this argument, one would expect each Article 3 activity to have specific Treaty articles implementing it. This is the case for most of them; however, Article 3(1)(u) asks for measures in the spheres of energy, civil protection and tourism. Civil protection and tourism are not mentioned elsewhere in the Treaty; in addition, Article 3 EC is not a closed list of all Community activities. As a result, these activities can only be achieved through later Treaty provisions which *also* aim to achieve other Article 3 activities *at the same time*. This does not necessarily mean that *all* of the later Treaty provisions implement *all* of the Article 3 activities; but it does mean that *some* must implement more than one Article 3 activity. This observation is reinforced by another from Snyder, who notes that the Treaty articles on competition (those in Title VI, Chapter 1 of the Treaty) are not the only implementing provisions, which help to achieve the Article 3(1)(g) activity;[49] it also reflects Article 2 EC's call for '... a harmonious and balanced and sustainable development of economic activities ...'

So, at least some of the later Treaty provisions incorporate conflicting values; and, while there is no indication as to whether compromise is always necessary, Section One of the Treaty certainly does not rule this out.

Now I turn to the Treaty's implementing provisions, to see if more guidance can be found there. The substantive Treaty (implementing) provisions 'deal' with conflict in four ways. First, the Treaty expressly allows some values to exclude others, this is rare. For example, Article 296(1)(b) EC states that the provisions of the Treaty, including the competition rules,[50] shall not preclude any Member State from taking such measures as it considers necessary for the protection of the essential interests of its security which are

---

[47]   Lowe (2004) 3. Mr Lowe is currently the Commission's Director General of Competition, but will vacate his post at the end of 2009.

[48]   Schaub subtly tries to avoid the allegation of Community competition as an end in itself, by distinguishing between competition policy's ultimate and direct goals, see Schaub (1998). I am not sure this takes sufficient account of the Treaty's structure and policy-linking clauses.

[49]   Snyder (1990) 95–99 and Komninos (2006) 458. There is also explicit support for using the later Treaty provisions to pursue various Art 3 activities. See, eg the *Declaration on Article 175 of the Treaty establishing the European Community*, annexed to the Treaty of Nice.

[50]   See Commission, *RCP 1993*, points 324–26 and Houttuin (1994) 61.

connected with production of or trade in arms, munitions and war material. In this way, the Member State's protection of the essential interests of its security can, to a limited extent, exclude competition.[51]

Exclusion is an extreme way of settling conflicts. Normally, where the Treaty expressly uses conflict resolution, it opts for a balancing process (compromise). For example, the values pursued by Article 28 (free movement of goods) must be balanced against the policy criteria listed in Article 30 EC.[52]

Thirdly, most of the policy-linking clauses demand that the specific policy in question, such as environmental policy (Article 6 EC), be taken into account in both the 'definition and implementation' of other policies.[53] Logically, the policy-linking clauses must favour compromise.[54] Imagine that the Community has to take a decision in an area where environmental protection and consumer protection conflict, there are policy-linking causes for both of these areas, Articles 6 and 153(2) EC. These policy areas can only both be considered, as the policy-linking clauses demand, if compromise is used to resolve the conflict.[55]

The final method 'adopted' by the Treaty for dealing with conflicts is silence. We have seen that Article 28 EC deals with the free movement of goods, where there are conflicts with the objectives listed in Article 30, these must be balanced against the benefits of removing quantitative restrictions on imports and measures of equivalent effect. But the Treaty is silent about what to do when Article 28 conflicts with objectives that are not listed in Article 30 EC, such as the effectiveness of financial supervision.[56] One method would be to interpret Article 30's heads broadly, for example 'public policy' is one of them, which

---

[51] Note Art 298 EC, however.

Another example of competition values being trumped, to the extent that Art 81 has been excluded, can be seen in the Common Agricultural Policy, Art 36 EC combined with Council Reg 1184/2006, *Applying Certain Rules of Competition to Production of, and Trade in, Agricultural Products*, art 2(1).

[52] See also, eg, customs duties (Art 9) or the customs union (Art 25), Art 27 implies compromise in certain areas; Art 39(1) (free movement of workers) balances other objectives through Art 39(3) and (4); Art 43 (freedom of establishment) balances other objectives through Arts 45 and 46; Art 49 (free movement of services) balances other objectives through Art 55; Art 56 (free movement of capital) balances other objectives through Arts 58 and 59; Art 61 (visa, asylum and immigration policies) balances other objectives through Art 64; and, Art 71(1) (transport policy) balances other objectives though Art 71(2) EC.

[53] There are two exceptions Art 151(4) EC (culture) and Art 178 EC (development policy), although both demand that these policies are taken into account in action under other provisions of the Treaty.

[54] The academic literature generally assumes that the policy-linking clauses imply compromise; see Krämer (2003) 8, 19, 21; McGillivray and Holder (2001), Section IV; Grimeaud (2000) 216, 217; Ross (1995) 237; and Loman, Mortelmans, Post and Watson (1992) 195, 196.

[55] Baldock suggests that the definition/implementation distinction is procedural. Decisions with significant environmental impact can be taken at different 'levels' of the policy process; a Community action plan might define policy, but this must also be implemented by regulations, decisions, etc. Baldock argues that the definition/implementation distinction means that environmental considerations should be addressed at every stage of the policy process, Baldock (1994) 7, see also, Commentaire Mégret (1996) 251. Some support can be garnered for Baldock from the fact that the policy-linking clauses refer to both definition *and* implementation, see Ch 7.

Not everyone agrees. The wide language in these policy-linking clauses states that, eg, environmental policy should be integrated into the definition and implementation of the Community *policies and activities*. Krämer says it is doubtful whether this refers to all individual measures, Krämer (2003) 21. This is in line with the interpretation in relation to conducting impact assessments, see COM(2002) 276 final 5, 6 and also the implication from an early Council document, Council, *Guidelines for Community Cultural Action*, para 7. See also Cunningham (2001) 139, 140, 145–50 for a critique. Commentaire Mégret (1999) 12 takes the opposite view in the discussion of culture.

[56] Case 120/78 *Rewe-Zentral AG v Bundesmonopolverwaltung für Branntwein* (Cassis de Dijon) 662.

should cover most policy aims, and then to balance these against Article 28's aims; but the Community Courts have not principally adopted this strategy with Article 30; instead, they have created the mandatory requirements.[57]

Balancing is also possible in Article 81 EC. Article 81(1) prohibits, as incompatible with the common market, agreements between undertakings which may affect trade between Member States and have as their object or effect the restriction of competition within the common market. Such agreements are void, Article 81(2), unless saved by Article 81(3) EC. Article 81(3) allows for compromise.[58] We saw that Article 81 EC may not only pursue the Article 3(1)(g) values, but we are not told whether it pursues all of the Article 2, 3 and 4 values, or only some. Which objectives can be considered in Article 81(3) is open to debate; it is not phrased as widely as Article 30, for example. This is especially important with the objectives pursued by the policy-linking clauses. We have seen that these clauses demand compromise; some of their goals, for example, the human rights aspect of development policy,[59] do not fall within Article 81(3)'s natural meaning at all.[60]

Finally, it should be pointed out that the 'optimal balance' between conflicting public policy objectives changes over time.[61] In part, this is because more objectives are now considered relevant, than was the case when it were purely a European *Economic* Community. Furthermore, from time to time, the weight given to the objectives changes, for example, we saw above the impact of the addition of Article 4 EC.

Because of the way that the Treaty is structured, as well as, the policy-linking clauses, I believe that Article 81 EC should generally be read so as to incorporate other objectives, through compromise. This answers Chapter 1's first question, why might Community competition policy incorporate public policy objectives. At least, in the case of the policy-linking clauses, there is an express balancing imperative; there is also a tendency for balancing public policy goals not supported by such clauses. Article 81 allows for a balancing exercise; yet, its text does not expressly seem to incorporate all objectives. The relevance of arguments about the precise wording of the provision depends on how the Treaty is to be read.

The next section examines the Community Courts' judgments to see how they deal with these issues, particularly in relation to the competition objective and Article 81 EC. More specifically, it investigates whether (and if so, how) the Community Courts have interpreted Article 81 widely enough to incorporate other objectives, including those supported by policy-linking clauses; if not, we must solve these conflicts through exclusion.

---

[57]   See the text around n 116, above.

[58]   The Commission and the Community Courts all use the balancing method, see the *Consten and Grundig* Case 348; the *VBVB/VBBB* Case, Opinion of A-G Verloren van Themaat 88; Joined Cases 25 and 26/84 *Ford-Werke and Ford of Europe v Commission* paras 33, 34 and Commission, *Article 81(3) Guidelines*, paras 11, 33, 43. That framework is adopted here.

[59]   Art 178 EC.

[60]   See eg Ehlermann (1998) xv. Even those that describe Art 81(3)'s wording as, 'extremely broad and vague', Kirchner (1998) 516, may balk at reading cultural and development policy goals into it.

[61]   See the Opinion of A-G Jacobs in Case C-379/98 *PreussenElektra AG v Schleswag AG* paras 229–33; Green (1988) 206 and Commission, *RCP 1988*, point 2.

2.2 The Community Courts

The last section discussed whether policies might be ends in themselves; it asked whether Community competition policy, for example, solely aimed to create 'a system ensuring that competition in the internal market is not distorted', Article 3(1)(g).[62] If so, any conflicts between competition policy and other Article 3 activities would be dealt with by way of exclusion, not compromise.

The Treaty gives a strong hint as to how conflicts might be resolved, but it is informative to ask what the Community Courts think on this issue, as they ensure that the interpretation and application of the EC Treaty is observed.[63]

The ECJ accepts the hierarchical Treaty 'system' embedded in Articles 2, 3 and (now) 4 EC, as described in the last section.[64] It has held that Article 81 aims to bring about the Article 3 *activities*, and thus the *purposes* of Article 2;[65] in particular, but not exclusively, the Article 3(1)(g) activity.[66] It is unclear whether Article 81 aims to bring about *all* of the Article 3 activities, including those introduced after 1966; nevertheless, the fact that it aims at more than one means that at least *some* public policy conflicts must be resolved *within* Article 81, through balancing (compromise).[67]

To my knowledge, the Community Courts have not expressly commented upon the effect of the policy-linking clauses on Article 81.[68] However, they have considered the policy-linking clauses more generally; and the ECJ implies that they demand compromise, not exclusion.[69] This is in line with Section 2.1's argument, that the policy-linking clauses logically demand compromise. With exclusion, only one objective is achieved, the other is completely ignored; so, if the objectives must be achieved 'concomitantly', then conflicts must be resolved through compromise and not exclusion.

---

[62]   See, eg the implication in the *Échirolles* Case paras 22–24.

[63]   Art 220 EC.

[64]   Case 32/65 *Italy v Council and Commission*, 405; Joined Cases C-78/90 and C-83/90 *Compagnie commerciale v Receveur principal* paras 17, 18 and Case 240/83, *Procureur de la République v Association de défense des brûleurs d'huiles usagées* paras 12, 13, demonstrate that the ECJ accepts this idea of the hierarchy of provisions, in various Treaty areas (competition and freedom of trade). See also Ellis (1963).

[65]   This interpretation has considerable academic support: see Arnull (2006) ch 16, for an interesting discussion of how this technique has developed; Verouden (2003) 530; Vedder (2003) 169; Wyatt and Dashwood (2000) 539–42; van Miert (1999) 2; Kapteyn and VerLoren van Themaat (1998) 109–32; Sauter (1997) 120; Jebsen and Stevens (1995–6) 458–61; van Miert (1993) 120; Commentaire Mégret (1992) 8–17; van der Esch (1991) and ESC, *Opinion on the Twenty-second Competition Report* 367.

[66]   Case 32/65 *Italy v Council and Commission*, 405. Many other judgments say the same, eg Case 229/83 *Association des centres distributeurs Édouard Leclerc and Others* paras 8, 9; Case 6/72 *Europemballage Corporation and Continental Can v Commission* paras 22–25 and Case 14/68 *Walt Wilhelm v Bundeskartellamt* para 5.

[67]   For an analogous discussion in merger law see Case T-96/92 *Comité Central d'Entreprise de la Société Générale des Grandes Sources and Others v Commission* paras 28–30.

[68]   They have been given the opportunity of doing so on several occasions; eg, the French court referred to both Art 151(4) EC, the policy-linking clause relating to culture, and Council, *Decision on Fixed Book Prices 1*, in the questions that it sent to the ECJ in the *Échirolles* Case para 13. The ECJ did not refer to either and, in the end, the Art 81 issue was not relevant in the case because there was held not to be an affect on trade between Member States, para 24. A-G Alber made a similar choice, see paras 41–46 of his Opinion.

[69]   Case C-233/94 *Federal Republic of Germany v European Parliament and Council* para 48. See also, Case C-180/96 R *United Kingdom v Commission* para 63 and Case C-379/98 *PreussenElektra v Schleswag* paras 76, 81, where the ECJ explicitly relies on Art 6 EC (amongst others) to justify a discriminatory quantitative restriction (or measure of equivalent effect) due to environmental (and public health) benefits. Also see the Opinion of A-G Jacobs, paras 229–34. Dhondt (2003) 163–81, is less sure of Art 6 EC's precise role in the *PreussenElektra* judgment, but agrees that ignoring the environmental protection goal, even in measures adopted with other main goals, could lead to the invalidity of the act.

To the extent that the objective of undistorted competition conflicts with other Treaty objectives, the Community Courts imply that at least some of these conflicts, whether they arise due to the policy-linking clauses or the Treaty hierarchy, should be dealt with via compromise, within Article 81. Section 2.1 argued that the Treaty's structure supports this interpretation.

Section 2.2.2 examines the Community Courts' approach to compromise within Article 81; but, before discussing compromise, Section 2.2.1 shines the light on exclusion. Outside of the express exclusionary provisions, such as Article 296(1)(b) EC, the Community Courts are reluctant to ignore relevant public policy goals in their decision-making process. I examine the Article 81 case law to see when competition policy has been found to exclude other objectives and when it, in turn, has been excluded.

2.2.1 Exclusion

Article 81 EC's wording does not explicitly mention public policy goals. One might be tempted to focus exclusively on welfare concerns when defining restrictions of competition and the exemptions to it in Article 81, ignoring (*excluding*) public policy goals in Article 81 EC analysis. The *combination* of implementing provisions (each pursuing a unique objective) would then (hopefully) pursue all Article 3 EC activities and thus fulfil Article 2 EC's aims.[70] Conflicts in Article 2 and 3 EC's goals might lead to clashes between the implementing provisions, which would be dealt with by delimiting their scope of application. The Commission's preference now seems to be for exclusion.[71] The ECJ has, on occasion, relied on this conflict resolution strategy, although such cases are comparatively rare.

Assume that objective A conflicts with Article 81's objectives, as we understand them; we must decide whether to resolve the conflict through compromise or exclusion; in other words whether 'competitiveness' is important enough to exclude other objectives, in case of conflict. If Article 81 could exclude (ignore) other objectives, this would have an enormous impact on Article 2's balance, because Article 81 is applicable throughout most of the economy.[72]

The first example is a case where one of the parties argued that competition policy should exclude/trump other public policy goals, this is the *Échirolles* Case. Before discussing the judgment I must put 'competition' into a Treaty context. The Treaty often refers to competition or competitiveness;[73] competition is important, although it is not defined in the Treaty.[74] The ECJ also underlines the importance of competition.[75]

---

[70]   See Schaub's distinction between intermediate/ultimate objectives, Ehlermann (1998) 121.

[71]   See Section 2.3.

[72]   Faull and Nikpay (2007), para 3.03 and Joined Cases 209 to 213/84 *Ministère public v Asjes* paras 27–45.

[73]   See, amongst others, the Preamble and Arts 2, 4, 27(c), 98, 105 and 136 EC.

[74]   Art 2 EC calls for '... a high degree of competitiveness ...' See Tizzano (1998) 484 and Waelbroeck (1998) 585. Nevertheless, while this has been underlined by certain specific Treaty articles, see below, it might be advisable to include a policy-linking clause in favour of competition next time the Treaty is amended, OECD (2003) 3, 7 (although it may be difficult to persuade President Sarkozy of this at the moment). This approach has been adopted, with varying degrees of success in, eg, Canada, Costa Rica, Côte d'Ivoire and the USA: see UNCTAD document TD/B/COM.2/EM/10/Rev.1. para 34 and Côte d'Ivoire, *RCP 1996*. Komninos (2006) 458, argues that the ECJ has already gone some way down this road, see Case C-17/90 *Pinaud Wieger v Bundesanstalt für den Güterfernverkehr*, para 11. See also Bourgeois and Demaret (1995) 112, 113.

[75]   Case 6/72 *Europemballage Corporation and Continental Can v Commission* para 24. This was an Art 82 case, but the ECJ makes it clear, para 25, that its comments apply to both Arts 81 and 82 EC.

Article 4 EC, is also relevant in this context. It says that economic and monetary policies have both been introduced for the purposes set out in Article 2 EC. One of the implementing articles, Article 105(1) EC, emphasises this, saying that the primary objective of the European System of Central Banks (the 'ESCB') is price stability but, without prejudice to this objective, the ESCB shall '... support the general economic policies in the Community with a view to contributing to the achievement of the objectives of the Community as laid down in Article 2', which seems to imply some sort of balancing act. Article 4(1) and (2) EC states that these economic and monetary policies must be conducted '... in accordance with the principle of an open market economy with free competition.'[76]

One interpretation of this wording in Article 4(1) and (2) EC is that these provisions demand that an open market economy and free competition somehow take precedence over (exclude or trump) other conflicting policy objectives. However, some clues to the contrary can be found in the *Échirolles* Case, which involved Article 1 of French Law No 81–766 of 10 August 1981 (the 'Law'). The Law said, amongst other things, that the publisher or importer of a book must fix its price; and the bookseller must normally sell the book at 95–100 per cent of that price. Association du Dauphiné brought the case; attacking the sale, by Échirolles Distribution SA, operating under the name Centre Leclerc, of books discounted by more than five per cent.

The French court referred several questions to the ECJ, under Article 234 EC, essentially asking whether Articles 3(1)(c) and (g), 4, 10, 7 (now repealed), 14, 98, 99(3) and (4) EC precluded the application of national legislation such as the Law.

There had already been a reference to the ECJ on the Law. Then, the ECJ held that these were purely national systems and practices in the book trade and thus, there was no effect on trade between Member States. So, as Community law stood, Member States' obligations under Article 10 EC, in conjunction with Articles 3(1)(g) and 81, were not specific enough to preclude them from enacting legislation of the type at issue on competition in the retail prices of books, provided that such legislation complied with the other specific Treaty provisions, such as the free movement of goods.[77]

Échirolles argued[78] that the Law created a non-competition area, which was wider than it needed to be to achieve its intended objectives. It added that the ECJ's judgment in the *Leclerc* Case made specific reference to the state of Community law at that time; that judgment was given before the creation of the internal market on 1 January 1993. Échirolles added that the introduction of provisions on the internal market may mean that the above-mentioned system is incompatible with the relevant provisions of the EC Treaty. In essence, Échirolles' argument is that the optimal Treaty balance (between the various public policy objectives, including competition) shifts over time, and that Article 4 EC had shifted the balance in competition's favour.

The ECJ replied that Article 3 lays down the general principles of the common market, which are to be applied in conjunction with the later Treaty provisions (once again that idea of hierarchy). This includes, since the Single European Act (SEA), the objective of an

---

[76]   Similar language can be found in the implementing provisions, Arts 98 (economic policy) and 105(1) EC, both command the relevant actors to 'act in accordance with the principle of an open market economy with free competition, favouring an efficient allocation of resources'.
[77]   The *Leclerc* Case para 20. See also Monti (2007) 104, 105.
[78]   The *Leclerc* Case paras 17–19.

internal market, Articles 3(1)(c) and 14 EC. The ECJ found[79] that as the Law involved a purely national system[80] and as Article 81 had not been amended since that judgment (ie there must still be an effect on trade between Member States), the ECJ could not call into question its previous judgment. The ECJ continued:[81]

> As regards Articles 3a, 102a and 103 [now Articles 4, 98 and 99] of the Treaty, which refer to economic policy, the implementation of which must comply with the principle of an open market economy with free competition (Articles 3a and 102a), those provisions do not impose on the Member States clear and unconditional obligations which may be relied on by individuals before the national courts. What is involved is a general principle whose application calls for complex economic assessments which are a matter for the legislature or the national administration.
>
> The answer to the question referred to the Court must therefore be that Articles 3(c) and (g) [now Article 3(1)(c) and (g)], 3a and 5 [Article 10], the second paragraph of Article 7a [now Article 14] and Articles 102a and 103 of the Treaty do not preclude the application of national legislation requiring publishers to impose on booksellers fixed prices for the resale of books.

The ECJ held that the obligation in Articles 4 and 98 EC, in relation to economic policy, that Member States and the Community act in accordance with the principle of an open market economy with free competition, does not impose on the *Member States* obligations that can be relied on before the national courts. The ECJ added that, despite the comparatively clear language of those articles, the call for an open market economy and free competition is merely a 'general principle' which calls for complex economic assessments, ie it is an objective to be balanced. A similar conclusion probably holds for comparable wording within provisions, such as Article 105(1) EC.

The ECJ did not expressly state that when the *Community institutions* are taking decisions in this area, Articles 4 and 98 merely oblige them to balance the principle of an open market economy with free competition against other relevant objectives. It is likely that this is the case;[82] especially given the Commission's wide discretion in relation to the implementation of the competition provisions.[83]

The wording in Articles 4 and 98 highlights the importance of an open market economy and free competition; indeed it may even give 'free competition' extra weight when it is balanced against other objectives.[84] However, it should not be read as promoting the concepts of an 'open market economy and free competition' such that they trump or exclude other objectives.[85]

The competition provisions themselves support this position. Some, such as Articles 86 and 87 EC expressly incorporate other public policy objectives; others, while not explicitly

---

[79]   ibid, para 24.

[80]   ibid, para 20.

[81]   ibid, para 25, 26.

[82]   See, eg Sauter (1998) 54 and Barents (1990). For a contrary view, see Mestmäcker (2000) 409, 410, where he interprets Art 98 as binding the economic policy of both the Community and the Member States. Mestmäcker does not justify this view and it seems contrary (at least as regards the Member States) to the clear wording of the ECJ in the *Échirolles* Case.

[83]   See the Opinion of A-G Alber in the *Échirolles* Case para 41.

[84]   Streit and Mussler (1995) 24. Some argue that Arts 3, 98 and 157 EC imply that competition enjoys a higher status than industrial policy and trade policy, Bourgeois and Demaret (1995) 67.

[85]   See the Opinion of A-G Mischo in Joined cases C-49/1998, etc *Finalarte Sociedade de Construção Civil v Urlaubs- und Lohnausgleichskasse der Bauwirtschaft* para 46; the ECJ did not discuss Arts 4 and 98 in this case. See also Edward in Ehlermann (2001) 566, 567. Monti (2002) 1093; Schmid (2000) 164, 165 and Bourgeois and Demaret (1995) 67. For arguments against this view see the references in Schmid (2000) 164.

incorporating such goals, for example, Articles 81 and 82,[86] as well as the ECMR, allow for their incorporation; in Article 81 this occurs in both paragraphs (1) and (3). While this work does not discuss Article 82 or the ECMR in detail,[87] Article 82 allows for the balancing of other objectives through the notion of 'abuse';[88] the decisions under the Merger Regulation were able to take account of 'considerations of a social nature', a similar stance is likely under the ECMR.[89] Also, considered from the other direction, Articles 81, 82 and the ECMR do not expressly exclude the incorporation of the other Article 2 and 3 purposes and activities within them.

Let us then examine the problem from the other angle and discuss whether competition law should be excluded by other policy goals. Assume that an implementing provision (Article X) does not incorporate competition objectives within it. Imagine that Article X applies in a specific factual situation and the application of the competition provisions (amongst them, Article 81) is excluded. In this scenario, where Articles 81 and X would have conflicted, competition values are also excluded.

We have seen that the Community Courts consider competition to be important.[90] If they were to allow competition to be trumped (excluded) by other objectives, then this key objective would be undermined. The Treaty has provided for this only on narrowly defined grounds; unsurprisingly, the Community Courts are reluctant to allow competition to be trumped or excluded outside of these limits.[91]

Despite this, the Community Courts have, on rare occasions, allowed competition to be excluded even where the Treaty did not expressly provide for it. One example is the *Albany* Case,[92] which originated in the Netherlands. In this case, a conflict existed between Articles 81, 82 and 86 EC (the competition provisions), and the social provisions, which encourage collective bargaining, Article 136 and following.

In Dutch law, employers are often obliged to affiliate their employees to a compulsory sectoral pension fund. The Minister for Social Affairs, at the request of a group of employers' associations and trade unions deemed by the Minister to be sufficiently representative, can issue a decree requiring all groups of persons belonging to a given sector of the economy to be affiliated to a specific sectoral pension fund. In the absence of a specific request the Minister has no such power. All persons falling under the decree,

---

[86]   Subject to what I say below, Art 81 does not expressly incorporate public policy aims. However, this is not the style of the Treaty. As we have seen, the policy-linking clauses state that the Community must take account of them in its policies and activities, none of them say that they will take account of others. This must be implicit though, otherwise the effect of these provisions would be significantly reduced.

[87]   There is no need, as they have the same objectives as Art 81 EC, see above.

[88]   See the concept of 'objective justification' in cases such as Case T-30/89 *Hilti v Commission*, paras 102–19, the point was not raised on the subsequent appeal to the ECJ. See also the interpretation of Rousseva (2006) 39–42 and Verstrynge (1988) 5.

[89]   See, eg Commission decision, *Mannesmann/Vallourec/Ilva*, decided under the Merger Regulation, Banks (1997); recital 23 and arts 2 and 21 of the ECMR and Case T-96/92 *Comité Central d'Entreprise de la Société Générale des Grandes Sources v Commission* paras 28–30. Mohamed (2000) discusses the consideration of national interests in the Merger Regulation Art 2(1)(b) ECMR contains wording which is very similar to Art 81(3) EC, and that has been interpreted expansively, see below. The Merger Regulation is the old version of the ECMR, see definitions at the start of the book.

[90]   See Ch 2, n 75.

[91]   Case T-61/89 *Dansk Pelsdyravlerforening v Commission* para 54. See also, Case T-144/99 *Institute of Professional Representatives before the European Patent Office v Commission* para 67; the *Pavlov* Case and the *Asjes* Case.

[92]   See also, Case C-222/98 *Hendrik van der Woude v Stichting Beatrixoord* paras 22–27. The Community Courts sometimes use other mechanisms to exclude competition too; see, eg Townley (2007) on the concept of an undertaking.

together with their employers, must abide by the rules of the relevant sectoral pension fund, making obligations to pay the contributions legally enforceable.

The Textile Industry Trade Fund (the 'Fund') was one of these sectoral pension funds; Albany was an undertaking operating within its sector. Albany also set up its own supplementary pension plan managed by an insurance company; which was more generous than the Fund's pension. The Fund improved its pension plan, but Albany still thought its own pension plan made better provision for its employees; so, Albany asked to be exempted from the Fund, the Fund refused.

Albany refused to pay the Fund contributions for 1989, arguing that compulsory affiliation to the Fund, by virtue of which these contributions were claimed, was contrary to Articles 3(1)(g), 81, 82 and 86 EC.

In its judgment, the ECJ noted that Article 3 EC contained different activities;[93] and that Article 137 EC provides that the Commission is to promote close co-operation between Member States in the social field, particularly in matters relating to the right of association and collective bargaining between employers and workers.[94] This might lead to relations based on agreement between management and labour at the European level, Article 139 EC.[95]

The ECJ went on to emphasise,[96] that the Agreement on Social Policy[97] states that the objectives to be pursued by the Community and the Member States include improved living and working conditions, proper social protection, dialogue between management and labour, the development of human resources with a view to lasting high employment and the combating of exclusion. The ECJ noted that Article 4 of that agreement says that agreements may be concluded as a result of dialogue between management and labour at the Community level;[98] the ECJ then added:[99]

> It is beyond question that certain restrictions of competition are inherent in collective agreements between organisations representing employers and workers. However, the social policy objectives pursued by such agreements would be seriously undermined if management and labour were subject to Article 85(1) [now Article 81(1)] of the Treaty when seeking jointly to adopt measures to improve conditions of work and employment.
>
> It therefore follows from an interpretation of the provisions of the Treaty as a whole which is both effective and consistent that agreements concluded in the context of collective negotiations between management and labour in pursuit of such objectives must, by virtue of their nature and purpose, be regarded as falling outside the scope of Article 85(1) of the Treaty.

The ECJ found a conflict between the social policy objectives and the competition policy objectives, as pursued by Article 81 EC.[100] The ECJ allowed the social policy objectives, as implemented by Article 137 EC, to trump the competition law ones, as implemented by

---

[93]   The *Albany* Case para 54.
[94]   ibid, para 55.
[95]   ibid, para 56.
[96]   ibid, paras 57, 58.
[97]   Community Agreement on Social Policy with the exclusion of the UK (1992).
[98]   The *Albany* Case para 58.
[99]   ibid, paras 59, 60.
[100]   ibid, para 59.

Article 81, in collective agreements between management and labour, though not those conducted outside of such a relationship,[101] which aim to improve the conditions of work and employment.

Both the ECJ and Advocate-General Jacobs favoured exclusion over compromise.[102] The first point one might make, is that one might question whether there is even a conflict here. The ECJ thought there was one, holding that certain restrictions of competition are inherent in collective agreements between organisations representing employers and workers. However, while the Treaty facilitates collective agreements, it does not demand that they restrict competition.[103] In previous cases, such as *Åhlström Osakeyhtiö v Commission*, the ECJ has held that where a conflict is not demanded, no conflict has been created.[104] With respect, it is questionable whether collective agreements inherently include, by their nature and purpose, restrictions on competition such that trade between Member States is appreciably affected; therefore, it is arguable whether, by their very nature, the social policy objectives and the competition policy objectives actually conflict at all.

Nevertheless, the ECJ felt that the social policy objectives pursued by such agreements would be seriously undermined if management and labour were subject to Article 81(1) EC. As a result, the ECJ advocated the complete exclusion of the consideration of competition objectives, via Article 81, from this sort of agreement. But, it is questionable whether subjecting these collective agreements to competition law would seriously undermine their social policy objectives. Indeed, it seems contrary to Articles 136–145 EC to per se exclude these social rules from the ambit of competition law; Article 136 says that implementing measures should take account of the need to maintain the competitiveness of the Community economy and Article 140 EC adds that Article 136's objectives are to be achieved without prejudice to the other provisions of this Treaty,[105] which would presumably include Article 81 EC.

It is anomalous to deal with the issue in this way,[106] given the emphasis on competition in other decisions, as well as the ability to balance such considerations within Article 81 itself.[107] *Albany*'s far-reaching exemption of social law from competition law's scope is not indispensable for achieving labour policy goals and pre-empts any discussion of the

---

[101] The *Pavlov* Case paras 68–70 and the Opinion of A-G Jacobs, paras 96–99. See also the EFTA Court, E-8/00 *Landsorganisasjonen i Norge and Others v Kommunenes Sentralforbund* para 35.

[102] Komninos (2006) 470 and Komninos (2005) 16 has suggested that *Albany* is not an example of exclusion, but of compromise; the idea being that the ECJ balanced the restrictions of competition with the relevant social policy objectives. However, here the balance lay so far to the extreme, that the ECJ was justified in ignoring the restrictions of competition. I do not think this is what the ECJ is doing in *Albany*; it was prepared to remove the category of collective agreements between organisations representing employers and workers from the scope of Art 81(1) EC. If it were really balancing, one would normally expect it to do this each time afresh (although one possible counter to this would be that the ECJ merely creates a per se rule here, however, for the sake of clarity). A-G Jacobs tries to deal with the lack of balancing by re-introducing a balancing element later in his analysis, paras 190–94 of his Opinion.

[103] DG Competition makes a similar point in relation to three European Parliament and Council Directives on waste management, DG Competition Paper, *on Waste Management*, paras 48, 113, 154.

[104] Joined Cases 89/85, etc *Åhlström Osakeyhtiö v Commission* para 20.

[105] The Community Agreement on Social Policy with the exclusion of the UK (1992) makes a similar point.

[106] See the Opinion of A-G Lenz in Case C-415/93 *Union Royale Belge des Sociétés de Football Association v Jean-Marc Bosman* para 273.

[107] See Section 2.2.2 of this chapter and Part B of this work. On this point A-G Jacobs is against me, see his Opinion in the *Albany* Case para 178.

welfare effects of collective bargaining.[108] Two important Treaty objectives were at stake; instead of taking them both into account, one was ignored.

The *Albany* Case demonstrates the impact of exclusion.[109] The Community Courts have been reluctant to allow for the trumping of competition policy;[110] the Treaty seems to confirm this stance and it is clear why. Post *Albany*, undertakings can appreciably restrict competition between Member States through collective agreements between management and labour, which aim to improve the conditions of work and employment; this might even include salary levels.[111]

2.2.2 Compromise

Sometimes objectives conflict; when this happens, the Community Courts are reluctant to use exclusion, at least insofar as Article 81 EC and competition are concerned. This is probably due to the perceived importance of this policy objective, as well as to the size of Article 81's footprint; and yet, the Community Courts cannot ignore these conflicts, which implies that, in Article 81, they should be resolved through compromise. This means that Article 81 EC's objectives would go beyond competition (and Article 81 EC's wording), reflecting the broader Treaty (and Member State) goals.

One might question whether it is possible to balance all relevant values within Article 81, in light of that provision's wording. However, even where the Treaty is silent, the Community Courts have principally dealt with conflicts by way of compromise. They do this by adopting a purposive or teleological approach to Treaty interpretation, Craig and de Búrca explain that the ECJ tends to examine the whole context in which a particular provision is situated. This often involves looking at the Preamble to the Treaties as well as Article 2 EC. The ECJ gives the interpretation most likely to further what it considers that provision in its context was aimed to achieve. Often this is very far from a literal interpretation of the Treaty and may even fly in the face of the express language.[112]

This applies to the values pursued by the policy-linking clauses.[113] Neither the provisions on freedom of establishment, nor those on the freedom to provide services, expressly incorporate consumer protection objectives, yet in *Germany v European Parliament and Council* the ECJ implied consumer protection into them *as a result of the policy linking clause*, Article 153(2) EC.[114] It also applies to other (non policy-linking clause) values. The free movement of goods provisions are illuminating in this regard.[115] Against Article 28's

---

[108]   Van den Bergh and Camesasca (2000) 501–08.

[109]   See also Schechter in Ehlermann (2006) 207.

[110]   If *Albany* is an extension of the principle that the competition rules can only be derogated where the Treaty makes 'express' provision (A-G Jacobs does not treat this as an example of express provision, see his Opinion in the *Albany* Case para 179), it may be a limited one. The references to 'agreement' in Arts 137 and 139 are the only references to agreements between private parties in the whole Treaty, with the exception of Art 81.

[111]   See the *Albany* Case para 63.

[112]   Craig and de Búrca (2008) 73–76. See also, Bengoetxea (1993), n 286; Wyatt and Dashwood (2000) 197–200 and de Wilmars (1986) 16–20 and the cases cited there.

[113]   See, eg the Opinion of A-G Jacobs in Case C-379/98 *PreussenElektra v Schleswag* paras 229–333 and the ECJ judgment paras 76–81.

[114]   This issue may not have been argued before the ECJ, so the precedent value on this point is unclear.

[115]   Mortelmans (2001) 618 and Aubry-Caillaud (1998) 22, 23. It happens in other areas too, eg, Craig and de Búrca (2008) ch 19 and Snell (2002) 181–94. For a justification for the mandatory requirements, see Craig and de Búrca (2008) 705, 706.

clear wording, the Community courts have 'found' an open list of mandatory require-ments;[116] these are in addition to Article 30's express exemptions.[117] The interests protected by the mandatory requirements must be recognised in Community law;[118] but, within these limits, they are repeatedly invoked to defend even national public interests.[119] Under the right conditions, the ECJ favours balancing within Article 28 EC.[120]

Not only would balancing public policy goals within Article 81 EC reflect the ECJ's preferred strategy, it also ties in with Article 2 EC's emphasis on a 'harmonious, balanced and sustainable development of economic activities.' The Lisbon reforms, with their increased emphasis on policy linking, support this approach.[121]

Yet, when the Community Courts considered balancing within Article 81 they were confronted with a problem. Article 81 EC does not, on its face, encourage the balancing of *all* public policy objectives, in particular many of those pursued in the policy-linking clauses. The Community Courts have got round this problem by reading both Article 81(1) and (3) expansively, as I show next.

In *Wouters*, the ECJ balanced different values within Article 81(1) EC.[122] The ECJ balanced professional ethics and competition, but it did not restrict the balancing to these values and Cooke believes it likely that others could be considered there;[123] time has proved him right.[124] Many point to the similarity between judgments like *Wouters* and the mandatory requirements under Article 28 EC.[125]

In *Wouters*, the agreement at issue was the Dutch Bar Council's 1993 Regulation, prohibiting lawyers in the Netherlands from forming partnerships with non-lawyers, unless the Bar Council had given its consent. Mr Wouters, and another lawyer, wanted to enter into a partnership in a firm of accountants, but the Bar Council refused their application; so, the lawyers questioned the compatibility of this rule with Article 81. Both

---

[116]   Case 120/78 *Rewe-Zentral AG v Bundesmonopolverwaltung für Branntwein* para 8.

[117]   ie this is not done through a wide interpretation of 'public policy' in Art 30 EC.

[118]   While the Community Courts demand the 'final say' on what objectives are acceptable, Oliver (2003), para 8.37, this requirement is, in fact, unimportant. Snell (2002) 191, agrees.

[119]   See Oliver (2003), para 6.74, Ch 8 and Mortelmans (2001) 622. Amongst the mandatory requirements are: cultural policy, fairness of commercial transactions, consumer protection, environmental protection, pluralism of the media; fostering certain forms of art and social order: see Oliver (2003) ch 8; Snell (2002) 192 and Craig and de Búrca (2008) ch 19.

[120]   See, eg Cases C–34–36/95, *Konsumentombudsmannen (KO) v De Agostini (Svenska) Förlag AB and TV-Shop i Sverige AB* paras 45, 46. For further examples see Kapteyn and VerLoren van Themaat (1998) 674–9 and the references made there.

[121]   See Art 26(1) FEU Treaty, for example.

[122]   For a contrary view, Gilliams (2006) 318.
   There have been many other instances of balancing under Art 81(1) EC, Case T-144/99 *Institute of Professional Representatives before the European Patent Office v Commission* paras 62–80; the concept of 'workable competi-tion', the *Metro I* Case para 20, discussed in Bouterse (1994) 24, 25; to the notion of ancillary restraints (B&C (2008), paras 2–088, 2–112, 2–113) and, possibly, the rule of reason, B&C (2008), para 2–091. See also, Whish (2008) 124–30.

[123]   Cooke (2006) 236, 237.

[124]   See the *Meca Medina* Case (2006).

[125]   See Komninos (2006) 464, 466, 471 and the references made there; Forrester (2006) 286–90; Baquero Cruz (2002) 153; Monti (2002) s 5; Mortelmans (2001) and O'Loughlin (2003) for example. The ECJ's references to 'unfair commercial practices' in Joined Cases 100–103/80 *SA Musique Diffusion Française v Commission* paras 89, 90 intentionally echo the mandatory requirements case law. The ECJ did the same in *Wouters* para 97, although by now the mandatory requirements also apply to freedom of establishment, Snell (2002).

Advocate-General Léger and the ECJ found a restriction of competition;[126] there was also an effect on trade between Member States.[127] That should have been the end of the matter.[128] However, the ECJ took a different tack:

> However, not every agreement between undertakings or every decision of an association of undertakings which restricts the freedom of action of the parties or of one of them necessarily falls within the prohibition laid down in Article 85(1) [now Article 81(1)] of the Treaty. For the purposes of application of that provision to a particular case, account must first of all be taken of the overall context in which the decision of the association of undertakings was taken or produces its effects. More particularly, account must be taken of its objectives, which are here connected with the need to make rules relating to organisation, qualifications, professional ethics, supervision and liability, in order to ensure that the ultimate consumers of legal services and the sound administration of justice are provided with the necessary guarantees in relation to integrity and experience … It has then to be considered whether the consequential effects restrictive of competition are inherent in the pursuit of those objectives.[129]

Note that the public policy goal in *Wouters* was a Member State goal, but (in a similar way) Community goals have also been balanced within Article 81 EC. *Meca-Medina* involved challenges to anti-doping tests carried out in 1999 during the long-distance swimming World Cup, when Mr Meca-Medina and Mr Majcen tested positive for Nandrolone, a performance enhancing drug. This breached certain International Olympic Committee (the IOC) regulations and they were banned. The athletes complained to the Commission, alleging that the IOC's rules restricted competition under Article 81 EC. The Commission rejected the complaint, and this decision was ultimately reviewed by the ECJ, which held that:

> [T]he compatibility of rules with the Community rules on competition cannot be assessed in the abstract … Not every agreement between undertakings … which restricts the freedom of action of the parties or of one of them necessarily falls within … Article 81(1)… account must first of all be taken of the overall context in which the decision of the association of undertakings was taken or produces its effects and, more specifically, of its objectives. It has then to be considered whether the consequential effects restrictive of competition are inherent in the pursuit of those objectives (*Wouters and Others*, paragraph 97) and are proportionate to them.[130]

The mechanism that the ECJ follows when considering these interests is important. It balances the public policy goals against the restriction on competition,[131] using what

---

[126]   *Wouters* paras 86–94.

[127]   ibid, paras 86, 95, 96. For the discussion on the restriction of competition, see ECJ paras 86–94, and A-G para 121; and on effect on trade between Member States, see ECJ paras 86, 95, 96, and A-G para 129.

[128]   The horizontal agreement did not fall within a block exemption, nor had it been notified to the Commission (Whish (2003) 123), a condition for considering Art 81(3) at that time. Gilliams (2006) 319, says that the agreements were notified to the Commission, but only after the commencement of the disciplinary proceedings, see also Cooke (2006) 236. A-G Léger also argued, in *Wouters*, that there was no room for rule of reason balancing as he thought that this is strictly confined to a *purely competitive* balance sheet of the effects of the agreement.

[129]   The *Wouters* Case para 97. Here, the ECJ may be refining the CFI's judgment in Case T-144/99 *Institute of Professional Representatives before the EPO v Commission* paras 77–79, 90–100.

[130]   The *Meca-Medina* Case para 42.

[131]   As regards the *Wouters* Case, Forrester (2006) 291, 292; Subiotto and Snelders (2003) 12; Whish (2008) 127 and Goyder (2003) 94, 95, agree that the ECJ conducts a balancing test here. Vossestein (2002) 859 agrees that this may be the case. Alternatively, he suggests that because the rule improved the quality of legal services, it enhanced '… consumer choice and thus [was] pro-competitive.' In fact, agreements to improve the quality of

seems to be a proportionality test. This should be compared with the *Albany* Case, where the ECJ solved the conflict through exclusion.[132] It is unclear why the ECJ chose exclusion in one case and not the other.[133] I believe that balancing fits more comfortably into the EC Treaty framework and allows the optimal balance to be found.[134]

Therefore, in certain cases, one can balance non-competition objectives against a restriction of competition and conclude that the former outweigh the latter, with the consequence that there is no infringement of Article 81(1) EC.[135] This might be compared with the CFI's position in, for example, *Métropole télévision v Commission*,[136] which forbids the balancing of pro-*competitive* aspects within Article 81(1).[137]

The Community Courts also use the first condition of Article 81(3) EC to balance within Article 81. This provision allows agreements that infringe Article 81(1) to be exempted if they contribute to improving the production or distribution of goods or to promoting technical or economic progress.

It is vital to understand the way this balancing works, because Article 81 implements more of the Article 3 activities and policies than merely those in Article 3(1)(g) EC. We need to understand which public policy factors can be considered within Article 81; for example, if it were all of the Article 3 activities this would be a lot, as it is an open list.

If it were the Treaty's signatories' intention that Article 81(3) be used to balance all public policy objectives, the provision might have been more clearly written. Article 81(3)'s wording seems too narrow to include many objectives. The wording has not been altered since 1957, when the Treaty's aims and objectives were narrower than they are today.[138] However, as the relevant objectives have broadened, the Community Courts have interpreted Article 81(3) EC more widely. The Community Courts have done this in two ways: by interpreting Article 81(3)'s text, specifically its first condition, expansively; and, by moving away from the literal wording altogether and conducting a general public policy test there.

First, the Community Courts and the Advocates-General interpret Article 81(3)'s first condition widely. For example, in the *Metro I* Case,[139] where the legality of SABA's selective distribution system for electronic equipment such as radios, televisions and tape recorders was at issue, the ECJ held that the establishment of supply forecasts for a reasonable period constitutes a stabilising factor with regard to the provision of employment[140] which, since it improves the general conditions of production, especially when market conditions are unfavourable, comes within the framework of the objectives to which reference may be

services in this way often reduce consumer choice, for better or for worse: see Scarpa (2001), s C. Monti (2002) 1087, 1088 criticises this part of Vossestein (2002), on other grounds.

[132]   See Section 2.2.1 above.

[133]   See also, Vossestein (2002) 856. Monti (2002) 1086–90, may disagree. He says that *Wouters* is an example of '… national interests excluding the application of Art 81 altogether.' This is the language of exclusion. That said, Monti is unclear on this point. He also refers to a balance, page 1086, and to the free movement provisions' mandatory requirements, which comprise a balancing test, see above. Monti (2007) 111, refers to a proportionality test, while simultaneously saying 'Public policy trumps the application of competition law.'

[134]   See Section 2.1, above and Ch 1, Section 3.

[135]   Whish (2008) 127 and Forrester and Maclennan (2003) 547–51.

[136]   Case T-112/99 *Métropole télévision and Others v Commission* paras 72–78.

[137]   Although, the *Wouters* Case, appears to look at pro-competitive aspects within Art 81(1), paras 86–94. On this point, also see Subiotto and Snelders (2003) 11 and Vossestein (2002) 856–59 and Ch 6.

[138]   See Wesseling (1997) 38–47, and the references made there.

[139]   The *Metro I* Case para 43.

[140]   Since this case was decided, Art 127 EC (the employment policy-linking clause) has been added.

had pursuant to Article 81(3).[141] It is a wide interpretation of Article 81(3) EC that exempts agreements under this head, in part, because they help stabilise employment.[142] By inserting the word 'general' the ECJ is more easily able to interpret 'conditions of production' widely. The ECJ added that this agreement, which allows for the establishment of supply forecasts for a reasonable period, constitutes a stabilising factor with regard to the provision of employment '… especially when market conditions are unfavourable …' By focusing on the benefits when market conditions are unfavourable the ECJ's argument seems even more acceptable; but it does not necessarily make sense to focus upon the 'bad times', the Commission's exemption ran for four and a half years in this case; it may be better to look at the agreement's overall impact on employment over this longer time-frame. However, the effect of this wording is to allow the ECJ to interpret Article 81(3) EC yet more widely.[143]

All four categories in Article 81(3)'s first condition can be interpreted widely.[144] We have seen one interpretation of improving the 'production' of goods, but similar points can be made about 'distribution'; if agreements to promote the dissemination of television programmes fall within this head, programmes relating to the different Community cultures could benefit from an exemption, remember Article 151(4) EC. Similarly, some suggest that 'improving technical progress' allows for the exemption of agreements that improve our ability to protect the environment, such as agreements to make cleaner cars, remember Article 6 EC.[145] Research and development agreements also contribute to technical and economic progress.[146]

These judgments, widening Article 81(3)'s wording, are important. I do not believe that these citations are unconsidered statements by the courts;[147] true, the ECJ relied on two other factors (as well as employment) in *Metro I* to support the Commission's conclusion that the conditions of production were improved; nevertheless, the employment discussion was central to the judgment and cannot merely be described as *obiter*.[148] The ECJ's

---

[141] The ECJ refers to this point favourably in Joined Cases 209/78, etc *Heintz van Landewyck Sàrl v Commission* paras 176, 182. Also see Case 42/84 *Remia v Commission*, the Opinion of A-G Lenz pp 2564, 2565.

[142] Note also that the ECJ is not merely using Art 81 for the purposes of 'negative integration'. A true, creative, 'policy' head is at work here. For a discussion on 'negative integration' see Craig and de Búrca (2008) 11.

[143] Also see Bouterse (1994) ch 6, in relation to monetary policy and improving the production of goods and A-G Jacobs' Opinion in the *Albany* Case para 193.

[144] Cseres (2007) 160; Goyder (2003) 59, 119, 120; Wesseling (2001) 370; Wesseling (2000) 20, 39, 109–11; Vogelaar (1994) 543; Bouterse (1994) 26–28; Art (1994) 25, 26 and Frazer (1990) 616.

[145] See Jans (2000) 278 and Jacobs (1993/2) 53–56.

[146] See, eg Commission Regulation, *Research and development agreements*, recital 10 and the *Nungesser* Case paras 55–57. R&D is encouraged in Arts 163–73 EC. Bouterse (1994) 27, 28, even argues that economic progress has been used to achieve public health goals.

[147] For a contrary view see Gyselen (2002a) 185. He refers to Commission decisions, *Synthetic Fibres* and *Ford/Volkswagen*, discussed below, and the *Matra* Case, in support, but does not explain how they support him. See also, Komninos (2006) 461, 462 and the discussion in Wesseling (2001) 371, 372 on the related issue of which 'reality' the Community Courts have embraced.

[148] The obiter dicta/ratio decidendi distinction seems to have been accepted in Community law, see Case T-224/2000 *Archer Daniels Midland and Other v Commission* para 200. More generally on the relevance of precedent in the Community Courts' jurisprudence see Arnull (2006) ch 17.

later statement in support of its *Metro I* judgment in *Van Landewyck* was also considered.[149] Finally, in *Matra*, while the CFI does not discuss social criteria,[150] the core of its decision is based upon industrial policy grounds.[151]

So the Community Courts interpret these heads generously; but is this generously enough to allow new heads of exemption too, including those of the policy-linking clauses? Advocate-General Darmon opined that Article 81(3) exhaustively lays down the objectives which justify exemption.[152]

Despite this, the Community courts seem willing to extend these four heads. This can be seen in areas such as increasing employment,[153] public safety,[154] consumer protection,[155] economic efficiency, industrial policy, fair-trading, and the ECHR.[156] That said, the Community Courts have normally gone out of their way not to *explicitly* widen the 'interpretation' of these four heads more generally. Nevertheless, the CFI has done this on one occasion, holding:

> [I]n the context of an overall assessment, the Commission is entitled to base itself on considerations connected with the pursuit of the public interest in order to grant exemption under Article 85(3) [now Article 81(3)] of the Treaty.[157]

This is a very wide statement; it would incorporate the objectives pursued by the policy-linking clauses into the Article 81(3) test and is probably even wider than that. Other than those listed above, public policy objectives that have already been considered or may be ripe for inclusion include establishment of undertakings, freedom of intra-Community trade; protecting intellectual property rights; equality of opportunity, fair-trading and legitimate self-protection, regional policy and culture.[158]

---

[149]   Although, strictly speaking, that was obiter, because the case was ultimately decided on whether competition was eliminated. That said, the ECJ discussed including social considerations within Art 81(3) over the course of five paragraphs.

[150]   This was for procedural reasons, the CFI said the Commission had not based its decision on social reasons, para 107; not because social reasons are irrelevant in Art 81(3) EC.

[151]   The *Matra Hachette* Case paras 109, 110.

[152]   Case 45/85 *Verband der Sachversicherer v Commission*, p. 430. See also, Commission, *Article 81(3) Guidelines*, para 42 and Kjølbye (2004) 570, 571.

[153]   Arts 125–30 EC, esp Art 127(2).

[154]   Art 152 EC, esp Art 152(1).

[155]   Art 153 EC, esp Art 153(2).

[156]   See eg **economic efficiency**, Case 48/69 *Imperial Chemical Industries v Commission* para 115, which emphasises both productive and static efficiencies; **employment**, Case 42/84 *Remia v Commission* para 42; **public safety**, Joined Cases T-213/95, etc, *SCK and FNK v Commission*, the CFI appears to be alluding to this, see para 3 and para 194; **consumer protection**, see the arguments of the Plaintiff, Case 249/85 *Albako Margarinefabrik v Bundesanstalt für landwirtschaftliche Marktordnung*, p 2348 and Case C-376/92 *Metro SB-Großmärkte v Cartier*, see the Opinion of A-G Tesauro para 33, '... considerations relating to *consumer protection* ... should not be unconnected with the interpretation of Art 85 [now Art 81] of the Treaty.'; **industrial policy**, the *Matra* Case para 109; **fair trading**, Case 249/85 *Albako Margarinefabrik v Bundesanstalt für landwirtschaftliche Marktordnung* para 16 and p 2348 (although see Commission, *Article 81(3) Guidelines*, para 47) and **ECHR**, the *VBVB/VBBB* Case para 34.

[157]   Joined Cases T-528/93, etc, *Métropole Télévision v Commission* para 118. Also, see the *Glaxo* Case para 244, on appeal; the *Wouters* Case, Opinion of A-G Léger, paras 107, 113; Joined Cases 46/87, etc, *Hoechst v Commission* para 25; Case 85/87 *Dow Benelux v Commission* para 36; Case 374/87 *Orkem v Commission* para 19; Joined Cases 97 to 99/87 *Dow Chemical Ibérica v Commission* para 22 and Case 14/68 *Walt Wilhelm and Others v Bundeskartellamt* para 5. See also Whish (2008) 153–55; Monti (2002); B&C (2008), paras 3.043–3.048; Whish and Sufrin (2000) 148–50; Faull and Nikpay (1999), paras 2.129–2.153; Ehlermann (1998); Gerber (1994) 140; Bouterse (1994) and Evans (1985) 101.

[158]   See, eg **establishment of undertakings**, Case T-30/89 *Hilti v Commission* para 100, although this was an Art 82 case the ECJ has said that Arts 81, 82 and the ECMR pursue the same general objectives, Case T-22/97

The Community courts have largely followed the line that Section 2.1 argued the Treaty demands. Values promoted in the policy-linking clauses should be incorporated into (balanced within) other policy areas; a similar approach has been taken in respect to other public policy objectives, without such clauses.

However, it is not certain whether *all* objectives must be balanced in *every* decision taken under the Treaty, where they are relevant. Having said that, the emphasis on balancing competition against other objectives was reinforced by the Maastricht Treaty, which changed one of Article 2's goals from 'a harmonious development of economic activities' to 'a harmonious and balanced development of economic activities'

As demanded by Article 220 EC, the Community Courts have filled in some of the Treaty's gaps. They are generally reticent to allow decisions to be taken while relevant values are ignored; more specifically, this is also true in the area of competition policy. The Community Courts are slow to exclude competition; furthermore, while competitiveness and competition are important Treaty objectives, they do not trump other values, but must be balanced against them.

In order to allow public policy balancing within Article 81, the Community Courts (and this includes the ECJ as recently as 2006, in the *Meca Medina* Case) have construed that provision against its natural meaning. Instead of focusing on Article 81's wording, they have employed the teleological approach, as they do throughout the Treaty.[159] The Community Courts have done this in relation to both Article 81(1) and (3). Many values can now be balanced within Article 81, including those that the policy-linking clauses embrace. These values do not form a closed list. In fact, as long as there are values the ECJ/CFI recognises, even if they are Member State values, then they are likely to be balanced in Article 81 EC.[160] The Lisbon reforms emphasise the importance of balancing.[161]

Kesko v Commission para 106; **freedom of intra-Community trade**, Joined Cases 100–103/80 *SA Musique Diffusion v Commission* para 107; **protecting intellectual property rights**, Case 395/87 *Ministère public v Tournier* para 31; **fair competition**, Case 32/65 *Italy v Council and Commission*, p 405, see also Anderman (1998) 19–21; **equality of opportunity**, Case C-18/88 *Régie des télégraphes v GB-Inno-BM* para 25, this was an Art 82 case but, as seen above, Arts 81 and 82 have been held to pursue the same objectives; **fair trading**, Case 249/85 *Albako Margarinefabrik v Bundesanstalt für landwirtschaftliche Marktordnung* para 16 and p 2348; **legitimate self-protection**, Joined Cases 100–103/80 *SA Musique Diffusion v Commission* paras 89–90, not allowed in this case as the breach of Art 81 was not the only means of ensuring the undertaking's survival. At p 1946, A-G Slynn implied that the act from which the undertaking was defending itself should also not have been lawful if this defence is to be allowed; although the ECJ did not demand this in an action under Art 60(2)(b) of the ECSC Treaty, Case 16/61 *Acciaierie Ferriere v High Authority* para 303; **regional policy** (Arts 158–62 EC, esp Art 159), Case T-96/92 *Comité Central d'Entreprise v Commission* and Joined Cases C-68/94 and C-30/95 *French Republic and Others v Commission*. As noted above, the ECMR pursues similar objectives to Arts 81 and 82 of the Treaty; **monetary policy**, Bouterse (1994) ch 6; and **culture** (Art 151 EC, esp Art 151(4)), Joined Cases 209/78, etc *Heintz van Landewyck v Commission* para 135.

[159]   As Bengoetxea explained, see text around Ch 2, n 20.

[160]   Part B investigates other public policy factors.

[161]   Art 26(1) FEU Treaty. The reference to the 'Treaties' appears to emphasise that a mere textual (abstract) analysis is not enough and that, amongst other things, the aim set out in the EU Treaty should impact upon the substantive provisions, including the internal market (and competition) provisions, in the FEU Treaty. This highlights the continuing importance of the teleological approach and is supported by the presence of some enhanced policy-linking clauses. For example, an all-embracing policy-linking clause has been added, Art 7 FEU Treaty: 'The Union shall ensure consistency between its policies and activities, taking all of its objectives into account.' In fact, some argue that (post-Lisbon) competition's weight in this 'balance' is now weakened as it has been removed from the list of activities, Hervouët (2008) 12–13. See also Graupner (2007).

Having said that, the CFI introduced new ambiguity when, in *GlaxoSmithKline Services Unlimited v Commission* (2006), it held that:

[T]he objective assigned to Article 81(1) EC … is to prevent undertakings, by restricting competition between themselves or with third parties, from reducing the welfare of the final consumer of the products in question.[162]

To the extent that a provision's sole objective is to prevent undertakings from reducing the welfare of the final consumer of the products in question, then one might legitimately ask what room is left for other public policy goals. Having said that, although this quote runs contrary to the ECJ's judgment in both the *Wouters* Case (2003) and the *Meca Medina* Case (decided two months before this *Glaxo* Case), the CFI is only discussing Article 81(1) EC here; and while its later discussion of Article 81(3) emphasises the relevance of economic efficiency criteria,[163] the CFI does not explicitly hold that consumer welfare is the exclusive goal of Article 81(3) EC.

From the Community perspective, the Community Courts are right to open up Article 81 EC in this way; the Treaty obliged them to choose between exclusion and compromise, but nearly always seemed to favour the latter. The Community Courts have followed this lead; in so doing, they have been able to imply many objectives into Article 81. This approach deals with the conflicts problem in a way that takes adequate account of the policy-linking clauses, the relative importance of competition and the structure and objectives of the Treaty as a whole. It also allows the decision-maker to be clearer, it need not twist its reasoning into the straight-jacket of Article 81's concrete wording, particularly important in a multi-lingual community; this encourages open and transparent decisions.

Black letter lawyers will not agree.[164] They will argue that the Community Courts are wrong to reinterpret the Treaty in this way, that they have crossed the line between interpretation and legislation;[165] and that fundamental shifts of this order should be made by way of Treaty amendment.[166] That may be so, although the policy-linking clauses are explicit, but the Community Courts have adopted a pragmatic solution and the Member States have had adequate opportunity to amend the Treaty, if they found the Community Courts' interpretative approach unacceptable. Quite the contrary, the Council, made up of the Treaty's signatories, has constantly reaffirmed the need to take account of other policy objectives within Article 81[167] and the Member States have, through their Treaty revisions,

---

[162] Case T-168/01 *GlaxoSmithKline Services Unlimited v Commission* para 118, see also para 121. This case is currently on appeal to the ECJ on these very grounds, Cases C-501/06, 513/06, 515/06 and 519/06. See also, the Opinion of A-G Trstenjak, Case C-209/07 *The Competition Authority v BIDS* para 56, supporting the CFI's judgment and Joined Cases C-468/06 to C-478/06 *Sot Lelos kai Sia EE and Others v GlaxoSmithKline AEVE Farmakeftikon Proionton*, esp para 65, which seems to undermine it.

[163] See the *Glaxo* Case paras 247–307.

[164] See, eg the implications of Fox (1998) 478, 479.

[165] For a general critique of the Community Courts' adoption of the teleological approach: see Craig and de Búrca (1998) 86–95 and Craig and de Búrca (2008) 75, 76 and the references there.

[166] Note the more general concern of the Bundeskartellamt in this regard, in Wilks (1996) 157.

[167] The most 'anti-competitive' block exemption was Council Regulation, *Shipping Cartels*, see Townley (2004); this regulation is no longer in force. Also see the discussion on fixed book price agreements, above; Declaration 29 on sport, attached to the Treaty of Amsterdam and Council Resolution *on the development of the audiovisual sector* 5 and the Council, *Conclusions on the Contribution of Industrial Policy to European Competitiveness*, (2003). The principle has also been accepted by other Community bodies; see, eg the European Parliament and the Economic and Social Committee on the Commission's *RCP 1994*, respectively point 25 and point 3.3;

either explicitly or implicitly approved of many court decisions based on the teleological approach.[168]

As explained in the last chapter, neo-classical economists are unlikely to agree with us either; many believe that Article 81 should only have economic efficiency as an objective and that all other policy objectives, to the extent that they should be pursued at all, should be attained using a more optimal instrument; which will rarely be competition policy. But the Treaty creates conflicts and these cannot be ignored, sometimes it even demands the balancing of them in competition law. Economic orthodoxy would seldom agree that competition policy should be compromised or excluded and so these economists must believe that, to the extent that they conflict with it, competition must exclude the other objectives; thus, if these other objectives cannot be (and are not) pursued by some other instrument, they will not be taken into account at all; and yet that would be to ignore the Treaty's concrete wording, and, even worse, its underlying principles.

This chapter's introduction asked whether the influence of political considerations on competition was warranted. We have seen that, when the question is viewed within the Treaty context, public policy's influence on Article 81 *is* warranted, in fact, it is often explicitly demanded. The Community Courts (and the Lisbon reforms) exhibit a strong preference for balancing in their judgments and the policy-linking clauses demand this.[169] Nevertheless, Section 3 examines some objections to balancing; but before that, I examine the Commission's position(s).

2.3 The Commission

In (relatively) recent policy statements the Commission now says that the competition rules should not be set aside because of public policy considerations.[170] This is contrary to the structure of the Treaty, contrary to the consistent position adopted by the Community Courts and involves a fundamental reorganisation of the hierarchy of Treaty objectives.[171] Furthermore, even as the Commission's administrative practice (and this includes through guidelines) changes over time, it still has to act within the framework the ECJ prescribes for it under Article 81 EC.[172]

Nevertheless, the views of the Commission, principally those of DG Competition, are particularly important in this area, given the central role that it has been given in relation to Article 81; the Commission guides the development of Community competition policy and has been given a lot of discretion for this purpose. First, I discuss the changing position the Commission has adopted in its policy statements; and then I examine whether the views that the Commission expresses in its policy statements are reflected in its

---

Economic and Social Committee, *Opinion on the Twenty-fifth Report on Competition*, in Commission, *RCP 1996* 381, point 2.5 and European Parliament, *Resolution on the XXVIth report by the Commission on competition policy – 1996*, in Commission, *RCP 1997* 368, point 2.

[168]   Fennelly (1998) 198.

[169]   As to what the limits of this are, see Part B. Part C suggests some new limits which better fit with Ch 1's recommendations.

[170]   See references in Ch 2, nn 9, 10, above.

[171]   See Sections 2.1 and 2.2, above.

[172]   See the Opinion of A-G Kokott, Case C-95/04, *British Airways v Commission* para 28. This case involved Art 82 and not Art 81 EC, but the same principles apply.

decisions. What the Commission says in its *decisions* is particularly significant because it is these that bind the Member States' courts and competition authorities.[173]

Initially, the spotlight is thrown on 1993, the first complete year of the internal market and the year of the Treaty of Maastricht, where many policy-linking clauses were adopted. The Commission's policy statements and decisions in 1993 are compared with those of 2000/2001, when Commission notices described 'major developments' in its analysis of vertical and horizontal restraints under Article 81.[174] Finally, I re-examine these issues through 2009-tinted spectacles.

2.3.1 1993

In 1993, the Commission dedicated a whole chapter of its *Report on Competition Policy* to the incorporation of other Community policies into competition policy. It said that competition policy is an instrument which complements the Community's other policies and went on to look at the role which competition policy can play in their implementation.[175]

The Commission emphasised the fact that competition policy has something to give to environmental policy;[176] this is because of the benefit of introducing into the price mechanism the 'polluter pays' principle, internalising externalities.[177] Indeed, the Commission said that, whenever possible, integration of competitiveness and the environment requires a strategy that should be built around solutions based on the competitive functioning of markets. But environmental policy also affects competition policy. The Commission undertook to carefully examine all agreements between companies to see if they are indispensable to attain the environmental objectives. It added that in its analysis of individual cases it would have to weigh the restrictions of competition in the agreement against the environmental objectives that the agreement will help attain, in order to determine whether, under this proportionality analysis, it could approve the agreement.[178] The Commission sees these competing objectives, competition and the environment, being reconciled through a type of balancing test.

As regards its relationship with competition, cultural policy displays a similar duality to that exhibited by environmental policy in Commission, *Report on Competition Policy 1993*. The Commission said it could help preserve plurality in the media by ensuring that competition between firms is not distorted and that some firms do not try to oust others through anti-competitive practices.[179] It goes on to reconcile the concerns of cultural policy with the application of the competition rules in relation to resale price maintenance systems for books. While the Commission could not agree to publishers collectively establishing prices, pricing methods or conditions of sale, it could countenance a system where these mechanisms were individual and purely vertical.[180]

---

[173]   Reg 1/2003, recital 22 and art 16. For this reason, I believe it is appropriate to read Commission decisions as if they were judicial pronouncements, ie to seek the ratio decidendi, etc.

[174]   Rivas and Stroud (2001) 935, 942.

[175]   Commission, *RCP 1993*, point 149.

[176]   ibid, point 163.

[177]   ibid, points 164, 165.

[178]   ibid, point 170, see also point 171.

[179]   ibid, point 176.

[180]   ibid, point 177. The same applies in relation to competition policy and completion of the internal market, including social and economic cohesion, point 154; also note, COM(93) 632 28–31. Although the Commission

The Commission clearly states that competition policy interacts with the Community's other policies in two ways: the Commission uses the market mechanism to help achieve the other objectives; and, the Commission sometimes distorts competition by balancing it against other public policy ends.[181] These statements are in line with the framework provided by the Treaty and the Community Courts; they also dovetail with the Commission's approach in other policy areas.[182]

Although it is dangerous to talk of patterns in such a small sample, the same attitude seems prevalent in the decisions taken by the Commission in 1993. In the OJ 1993, 16 Article 81 decisions were reported.[183] Some were argued, and based, on economic efficiency criteria;[184] others focused on restrictions of economic freedom.[185] One decision considered economic criteria and the fact that interpenetration of the national markets was prevented through absolute territorial protection.[186] In four decisions,[187] the Commission explicitly invoked non-economic objectives in its Article 81(3) analysis; and in three of these, *Ford/Volkswagen*, *VIK-GVSt* and *EBU/Eurovision System*, non-economic objectives appear decisive; in other words, three of the sixteen decisions are based on public policy criteria.

In *Ford/Volkswagen*, the Commission considers a 'foundation agreement' between two motor vehicle manufacturers, Ford and Volkswagen, setting up a joint venture company for the development and production of a multi-purpose vehicle (MPV) in Portugal. The Commission found a restriction on competition but gave an individual exemption.[188] The Commission placed a lot of weight on the industrial policy aspects noting the establishment of a new and most modern manufacturing plant using the latest production technology,[189] as well as an advanced MPV.[190] Rationalisation of product development and

implicitly acknowledges that there is a balance between allowing some territorial protection, which might be welfare enhancing and enforcing interpenetration of markets, see Motta (2004) chs 1, 6. One sees the same attitude in relation to industrial policy, Commission, *Framework for State Aids for R&D*, para 1.4, including the encouragement of SMEs and R&D, paras 155–61.

[181]   The Commission had pointed to links between competition and other Community policies even before 1993: see Commission, *RCP 1976* 9, 10; Commission, *RCP 1979* 11; Commission, *RCP 1982* 9, 10, 12–15 and Commission, *RCP 1990* 16, 17. Sometimes the Commission went further, signalling that it was prepared to restrict competition in order to achieve other policy objectives: see *Agence Europe*, 10 November 1978; Commission, *RCP 1980* 9–11; Commission, *RCP 1982* 12–15; Commission, *RCP 1988* 16; Commission, *RCP 1991* 11, 12, 39–48; Commission, *General Report 1992* 74, 75 and Commission, *RCP 1992* 13, 47–58. While the Commission emphasised that competition was an important objective in its own right, Commission, *RCP 1991*, point 42, competition policy could not be pursued in isolation, as an end in itself, without reference to the legal, economic, political and social context, Commission, *RCP 1992* 13. This point is also discussed by Kapteyn and VerLoren van Themaat (1998) 839, 840; Bouterse (1994) 34–36, 62–66, 77 and Hornsby (1987).

[182]   See, eg *Taking the environment into account in other policies*, Commission, *General Report 1990* 214, 215; Commission, *General Report 1991* 198, 199; Commission, *General Report 1992* 4, 5, 199 and Commission, *General Report 1993* 1–5, 166, 167. The Commission believed that the policy-linking clauses demanded the balancing of, eg, environmental protection, within other policies: see Commission, *General Report 1991* 198, 199.

[183]   The number cited here (16) does not marry with the figure quoted in the Annex (5). This is because, the Annex discusses the decisions *taken* in a particular year. The figure quoted here (16) relates to those decisions that were *published* in the Official Journal in 1993, regardless of when they were taken.

[184]   eg Commission decisions *Langnese-Iglo* and *Schöller Lebensmittel*.

[185]   eg Commission decision *CNSD*; this was an Art 81(1) case.

[186]   Commission decision *Zera/Montedison*; this was an Art 81(1) case.

[187]   Commission decisions *Ford/Volkswagen*, *VIK-GVSt*, *EBU/Eurovision System* and *Fiat/Hitachi*.

[188]   Commission decision *Ford/Volkswagen*, paras 24–41.

[189]   ibid, para 25.

[190]   ibid, para 26.

manufacturing is mentioned,[191] but, on pure competition grounds, it is doubtful that this joint venture should have been cleared.[192] The emphasis is essentially on technical progress; and the environmental improvements in the product as well as its prospective low emissions and fuel consumption are also given considerable weight.[193]

The Commission also notes,[194] in relation to the indispensability of restrictions, that the project is the largest ever single foreign investment in Portugal, leading to the creation of some 15,000 jobs. This, says the Commission, helps to promote the harmonious development of the Community through reduced regional disparities as well as furthering market integration. The Commission ends:

> This would not be enough to make an exemption possible unless the conditions of Article 85(3) [now Article 81(1)] were fulfilled, but it is an element which the Commission has taken into account.

The language is unhelpful: either the Commission relied on this issue or it did not, in which case why make the point?[195] It seemed confident about incorporating the other Community policy objectives, it might have been more confident in relying on this, especially in the light of the *Remia* Case.[196] The Commission may have been nervous of explicitly basing its decision on these new Portuguese jobs, as they came at the expense of jobs in Germany.

Commission decision, *VIK-GVSt*,[197] involved a set of agreements where the German electricity generating utilities and industrial producers of electricity for in-house consumption undertook to purchase a specific amount of German coal, up to 1995, for the purposes of generating electricity. The agreements were part of an initiative to support the German coal-mining industry and were actively supported by the Federal Minister for Economic Affairs and were related to simultaneous State aid negotiations. Specifically, two agreements were considered, one between the General Association of the Coal-mining Industry (GVSt) and the Association of the German Public Electricity Supply Industry (VDEW), the other between GVSt and the Association of Industrial Producers of Electricity (VIK). The Commission found that the agreements restricted competition,[198] but granted an exemption.

Article 81(3) was fulfilled because electricity cannot easily be stored; so, electricity production and demand must be in constant equilibrium; therefore, safeguarding the procurement of primary energy sources was particularly important. The Commission went on to note that the agreements made energy sources available in the form of coal and

---

[191]   ibid, para 25.
[192]   Jones and Sufrin (2008) 275 and Amato (1997) 58–62, imply the same thing.
[193]   Commission decision, *Ford/Volkswagen*, para 26.
[194]   ibid, para 36.
[195]   On appeal, the CFI said the Commission did not rely on employment criteria. Not everyone agrees, eg, Hildebrand (2002) 240 says 'The creation of jobs in a poorly developed area was considered to be a decisive criterion to qualify for exemption.' Furthermore, the CFI's view does not lie well with the Commission's submissions in that case, see the conclusion to this chapter, nor the last 12 words of the above Commission citation.
[196]   In the appeal to the CFI the Commission gave this aspect more weight, see the *Matra* Case, below.
[197]   See also Houttuin (1994) 63–65.
[198]   Commission decision *VIK-GVSt*, para 24.

thus promote security of energy supply in the Federal Republic of Germany.[199] In fact what was at stake was not that so much, but the security of energy supply in Germany *of electricity from German coal.*

The third relevant matter is Commission decision, *EBU/Eurovision System.* This decision related to the company statutes of the European Broadcasting Union, an association of radio and television organisations; other rules governing the acquisition of television rights to sporting events; the exchange of sports programmes within the framework of Eurovision; and, contractual access to such programmes for third parties. In order to be a member of the EBU an undertaking must be within the European broadcasting area, provide a service of national importance, be at least trying to cover the whole of their national territory and must provide a mix of programmes, including a substantial proportion under their own editorial control. The EBU has 67 active members and 54 associate members (those not in the European broadcasting area), from 47 countries.

The Eurovision System (ES) is a network for the exchange of television programmes, including sport programmes, which also operates a system of joint acquisition of television rights for international sporting events. All interested members that want such rights then jointly acquire them and share the fee. Members cannot bid for rights against the ES. If two members from the same country want the rights they have to split them amongst themselves. Programmes made in the Eurovision area are produced by a member in the country concerned and are then made available to all members via the Eurovision programme exchange system. This is done free, on the understanding that it will be reciprocal. If the programme is made outside the Eurovision area, sometimes they pay a fee, shared between those that broadcast it, although sometimes reciprocity exists there too. There is also some administrative and technical co-ordination provided by the EBU's permanent staff. The EBU have agreed to grant access to Eurovision sports programmes, on conditions to be freely negotiated, but not less favourable than those agreed with the Commission.[200]

The Commission found restrictions on competition between the EBU members, sometimes countries have more than one member which would normally compete for rights; also some companies broadcast in other countries too so there would be competition there. In such a situation, competition is essentially eliminated.[201] There was also a distortion of competition regarding non-members as they cannot participate in the EBU savings,[202] allowing EBU members to strengthen their market position.[203]

In relation to Article 81(3) the Commission found several benefits and granted an exemption. Regarding the joint acquisition and sharing of the rights these reduce transaction costs and ensure that negotiations are carried out in the most competent manner (using local experts etc.), which benefits smaller members.[204] It also encourages programme co-ordination at the national level, as members negotiate to share the events, which often means more complete coverage.[205] At the international level it facilitates cross-border broadcasting, as members generally get the rights not just in their country,

---

[199]   ibid, para 31.
[200]   Commission decision *EBU/Eurovision System*, paras 36–40.
[201]   ibid, para 49.
[202]   ibid, para 50.
[203]   ibid, para 51.
[204]   ibid, para 59.
[205]   ibid, para 60.

contributing to the development of a single European broadcasting market.[206] Participation in a transnational dedicated sports channel[207] also enables EBU members to provide a broader range of sports programmes, including minority sports, giving viewers a broader choice, but also bringing money to the organisers of minority sports and contributes to the development of a single European broadcast market.[208] In relation to the exchange of the television signal the Commission said that it resulted in considerable rationalisation and cost savings, particularly helpful to smaller broadcasters; and encourages dissemination, because if an event is in a country and the local broadcaster is not interested, for example no national champion involved, it still sends the signal to others, leading to more sports programmes, especially minority ones.[209] The administrative and technical co-ordination is also very helpful,[210] providing for a reliable common network, which also leads to rationalisation etc.[211] The access rights for non members reduces the restriction on competition as well as providing a one stop shop and increasing demand for second transmissions of events.[212]

Economic considerations were important in this decision; however, this comes through most at the end of the decision. The Commission emphasises arguments relating to SMEs, cultural exchanges and the aiding of the cross-border broadcasting in this process, and they all seem to have been given a lot of weight here.

Both Commission practice and policy seem[213] in line with the Treaty, the Community Courts' case law under Article 81 and the Commission's policy statements of that time. The Commission considers many other objectives in its analysis, primarily under Article 81(3) EC; often through balancing objectives outside of the market mechanism, that is, essentially by reducing competition.

Nevertheless, there are two key weaknesses with the decisions: the Commission could be clearer about the weight of these public policy objectives in the balance and the mechanism it uses for taking these issues into account and weighing them. It could also provide more help on which types of objective are relevant, for example, is it only Treaty objectives that we should consider, or should Member States' values be considered here too?

2.3.2 2000

The Commission's policy statements reaffirmed the need to balance competition objectives with other values (within Article 81) after 1993 as well. In 1996, for example, former

---

[206] ibid, para 61.
[207] A joint venture between a consortium from EBU and News International/Sky.
[208] Commission decision, *EBU/Eurovision System*, para 62.
[209] ibid, para 63.
[210] ibid, para 64.
[211] ibid, para 65.
[212] ibid, paras 66 and 67. See also, Forrester (1998) 376.
[213] I cannot say stronger than 'seem'. The Commission votes on these competition decisions as a college, this is a closed political process. It might be that, in order to guarantee the vote of the Commissioner for research and innovation, certain extraneous words are added to the decision, highlighting the importance of innovation, as has been argued of *Ford/Volkswagen*. This might be so, even if the decision was taken solely on efficiency grounds. This is probably not what happened in the three decisions discussed here, as the heart of the exemption logic does not seem to be efficiency orientated; nevertheless, if this process takes/took place, it shows that DG Competition has not (at least at that time) 'won' the argument that Art 81 decisions should ignore non-economic objectives.

Competition Commissioner van Miert called for a balanced competition policy which pays due regard both to the pressing need for economic efficiency and to the general interest.[214]

However, by 1997 the Commission's policy statements were becoming ambiguous on this issue. Then, the Commission announced its intention to modernise Community competition law;[215] hailing its Communication on vertical restraints as an example of its innovative stance. This communication, said the Commission:

> [B]reaks with a method which was differentiated by industry and category of agreement, and has become extremely complex. *It is based on the economic analysis of the effects of vertical restraints;* exemption is to depend on the market power of the firms involved.[216] (emphasis added)

The Commission stresses a break with the past; it also emphasises that the 'new' methodology is based on economic analysis. It is not immediately clear what the Commission means by the 'new' focus on economic analysis. It may indicate, for example, that, the *only* relevant issue when analysing vertical restraints, and maybe even Article 81 as a whole, is their effect on economic factors; I call this the 'pure economic approach'.[217] On the other hand, the Commission could be referring to the fact that the 'old' system of analysis and block exemptions was very rule-based. This system differentiated between the industry, the category of agreement that was involved, the number of parties, etc.[218] Perhaps the Commission means that it will move towards economic analysis, as opposed to the straight-jacket segmented approach of old, *while maintaining the relevance of public policy objectives* within Article 81; I call this the 'mixed economic approach'.

Sometimes, the Commission's policy statements imply a mixed economic approach.[219] This would still be an important shift, as the Commission's economic analysis has often been criticised.[220] The Commission has emphasised the fact that recent judgments of the Community Courts are forcing it to apply better economic reasoning in its decisions;[221] the Commission is attempting to respond to this challenge;[222] which is welcome. Such a

---

[214]   Commission, *RCP 1996* 9. See also, Commission, *RCP 1994* 19–21, 23–26; Commission, *RCP 1995* 40, 41 and Commission, *RCP 1996* 7, 8, 17, 18, 32–34.

[215]   See the references in Commission, *RCP 1998* 20–22, for example.

[216]   Commission, *RCP 1998* 21.

[217]   Ehlermann (2000a) 549, offers a refinement of this position. He says 'It would probably be an exaggeration to assume that, according to the Commission, non-economic considerations are to be totally excluded from the balancing test required by Art 81(3). Such an interpretation would hardly be compatible with the Treaty, the Court of Justice's case law, and the Commission's own practice. However, the passage quoted [Commission, *White Paper on Modernisation*, para 57, see Ch 2, Introduction] is a clear indication that non-competition-orientated political considerations should not determine the assessment under Art 81(3). I fully subscribe to this approach.' Monti (2002) adopts a similar position. That said, if political considerations can *never* set aside economic ones (determine the assessment), then their presence in Art 81(3) is largely academic.

[218]   See, eg Verouden (2003) 526, 527 and the references made there; Bishop and Ridyard (2002) 35; van der Woude (2002) 41; Whish (2000) 889 and Nazerali and Cowan (1999) 159.

[219]   Forrester and Maclennan (2001) 380, 381. See, eg Commission Memo, *European collecting societies* (2008); Andries and Julien-Malvy (2008) 55; COM(96) 721, para 86; Commission, *RCP 1998* 19, 20; Commission, *RCP 1999* 7, 23; Commission, *RCP 2000*, point 23; Mario Monti (2003a) and Mario Monti (2003), 'In making this revision, we have shifted from a legalistic based approach to an interpretation of the rules based on sound economic principles.'

[220]   See Verouden (2003) 565 and references mentioned there; Whish (2003) 1, 2; Hildebrand (2002) 161; Whish (2000a) 889–92; Venit (1998) 567, 569 and Neven, Papandropoulos and Seabright (1998).

[221]   Commission, *Horizontal Guidelines*, para 6.

[222]   Commission, *RCP 2000*, Introduction by then Commissioner Monti.

change would also bring Community competition law more into line with other jurisdictions' competition policy; which is important where the competition rules of more than one jurisdiction apply to the same arrangement.[223] However, at times the Commission, or its representatives, have gone further, advocating a pure economic approach.[224] This is a major policy shift and would clash with both the Treaty framework and the Community Courts' interpretation of Article 81.[225] It is also at odds with the Commission's increasing acceptance, outside of DG Competition, of the need to integrate the different policy areas.[226] Even more confusingly, it is often unclear whether a pure or a mixed economic approach is advocated in some statements.[227]

If the Commission has adopted a pure economic approach, I have not seen it justify this shift, although sometimes it *implies* that Article 81, and the other competition provisions, are merely there to implement Article 3(1)(g) EC.[228] There is rarely any discussion about the significance of the policy-linking clauses in such a reading of the Treaty; however, on the rare occasions when they are highlighted, the implication is that they do mean that other objectives should be considered within Article 81 EC.[229]

It is hard to reconcile these two approaches; the fact that there is so much ambiguity on this fundamental issue from such a key actor is unacceptable. There is little discussion about this in the literature; many academics simply conflate the issues and assume that the Commission now advocates a pure economic approach, possibly tempered by the market

---

[223] A mixed economic approach would not affect the analysis in this work, except insofar as it is considered in Ch 6.

[224] Mario Monti (2002). Also see Commission, *Article 81(3) Guidelines*, paras 13, 21, 33, 42, but note 43; Reg 1/2003, recital 9; Commission, *Vertical Guidelines*, paras 7, 136 and Commission, *Horizontal Guidelines*, paras 4, 32, 102, 103, 132, 151–153, 169–170; although note paras 192–194, 197, in relation to environmental agreements and Commission, *RCP 1999*, 19; COM(98) 544, 4, 5, 22.

[225] Wesseling (1999) 421–24. See also the citation above from Ehlermann (2000a) 549 and Gerber (2008) 1247.

[226] See eg Commission, *General Report 1997* 3 (employment) and 5, 190, 191 (environment); Commission, *General Report 1998* 2 (employment), 5, 168, 169 (environment), 87, 145–47, 169–71 (industry and environment); COM(1999) 587; Commission, *General Report 1999* 3, 136–38, 143, 144, 157–59, 252 (environment); Grimeaud (2000), Section 2; Commission, *General Report 2000* 413 (in general), 3, 168–70, 191, 257 (environment), 5, 263 (development policy), 82–85 (enterprise); 182–84 (energy); 207 (public health); COM(2001) 486; Commission, *General Report 2001* 2, 3 (in general), 98–102 (enterprise), 113, 143, 189–98, 211, 287 (environment), 205–07 (energy); Commission, *General Report 2002* 24 (in general), 3 (employment and social cohesion), 106, 109–13 (enterprise), 125, 153, 230, 231 (energy), 140 (economic and social cohesion), 153, 211–15, 237 (environment), 219-222, 248, 253, 256 (public health and consumer protection); COM(2002) 276 and Commission, *General Report 2003* 155 (economic and social cohesion), 169, 186, 224–26, 229–32 (environment), 236, 239 (energy), 258 (health and consumer protection), 293, 297, 299–301 (development policy).

[227] See Commission, *Horizontal Guidelines*, para 198. Gerber (2008) 1247, 1248, argues that the new-economic approach applies to both standards and methods, for example.

[228] Case C-35/96 *Commission v Italy*, para 47 of A-G Cosmas' Opinion, the Commission is cited as saying that 'Community competition law is autonomous, not solely in relation to national law but also in relation to other rules of Community law.' Is this the implication in Commission, *RCP 1999* 11, too? Also see Commission, *RCP 1996*, point 2. That said, the Commission is not even consistent in this regard: see COM(1999) 587, point 7 and Commission, *RCP 1992* 13.

[229] The quote from Commissioner Monti from 1999, reported in Cunningham (2001) 156, 157, strongly supports the integration of cultural objectives into Art 81 because of Art 151(4) EC. See also, Commission, *RCP 2000* 39, 40, cited below.

integration objective.[230] For example, Schaub, a previous Director-General of DG Competition, takes this line: 'Political, social or environmental aspects, in my view, have no place in the direct application of competition law.'[231]

In conclusion, it is unclear whether a pure economic approach has now been adopted; the Commission may not even have made up its own mind on the issue. In the draft version of Commission, *Article 81(3) Guidelines*,[232] after accepting (in a slightly circular way) that goals pursued by other Treaty provisions could be taken into account, to the extent they fell within Article 81(3), the Commission added 'It is not, on the other hand, the role of Article 81 and the authorities enforcing this Treaty provision to allow undertakings to restrict competition in pursuit of general interest aims.'[233] In the final version of these guidelines this sentence no longer appears;[234] the Commission did not explain this change in the final version.

The resulting position is a bit of a muddle. However, *if* a shift to a pure economic approach has occurred, three points demand our attention: Why did the Commission suggest such a change? Can the Commission change competition policy like this? What has been the effect of the change on the Commission's Article 81 decisions?

As the Commission has not even conceded that a change is taking place, it has obviously not explained why it advocates this change; as a result, it is somewhat speculative to seek to explain why what is happening is happening. Having said that, it may help shed some light on the demons that the Commission is confronting here, which may be of value in making the suggestions later in this work more palatable. There are countless possibilities, but, the key ones can be grouped into three heads.[235] First, DG Competition may simply believe that it is better to have a competition policy that is not 'distorted' by public policy considerations; it is tired of the short-termism of the political interference that it receives, both from outside[236] and from within[237] the Commission. By highlighting the importance of economic factors, it may hope to reduce the amount of political interference.[238] The Ordoliberal School provides an additional explanation of why they believe this might be problematic. In their view, considering public policy goals within competition law unduly opens the door to uncontrolled private regulation of public interests, potentially undermining economic freedom.[239]

---

[230]   Venit (2003) 578, 579 and Bishop and Walker (2002), paras 1.04–1.09. Although, it is not totally consistent, see, eg Commission Memo, *European collecting societies* (2008).

[231]   Schaub (1998) 9, 10.

[232]   Draft version of Commission, *Article 81(3) Guidelines*, para 38.

[233]   This may reflect the position of Ehlermann, cited above in Ehlermann (2000a) 549. The Commission did not justify this assertion in para 38, although it cited two cases to support it, which did not seem to deal with that issue.

[234]   Commission, *Article 81(3) Guidelines*, para 42.

[235]   See also Gerber (2008).

[236]   Schaub (1998) 475–76; Jenny (1998) 25 and McGowan and Wilks (1995) 158, 159.

[237]   See a brief discussion and references in Wilks (1996) 156–57 and McGowan and Wilks (1995) 158, 160, 161.

[238]   Burnside reports the then Commissioner (Monti) for DG COMP as having said that one of his prime functions is to protect the Merger Task Force (as was) from political pressure, the same may apply to the rest of DG Competition, Burnside (2002) 110.

[239]   ie allows the establishment of seemingly legitimate private power, which is no longer controlled by the operation of competition in the market. See the views of Dieter Wolf, then President of the Bundeskartellamt, in Ehlermann (1998) 131. In this work Ch 6, Section 2.2 discusses the Ordoliberal School in more detail.

To the extent that this is the Commission's motivation, it is in line with a general trend among competition authorities to focus their interpretation of the competition rules on economic criteria, DG Competition may be following suit. Former Competition Commissioner Monti emphasised pure economic criteria;[240] the current Competition Commissioner Kroes has continued this trend.[241] There are many benefits in this approach,[242] it reduces the regulatory burden when more jurisdictions have the same test; the Commission may also believe that economic criteria are easier for undertakings to understand, reducing compliance costs, giving more predictability (legal certainty) to the competition rules than a political balancing test could ever bring; and that the key aim of competition rules is best aimed at pure efficiency criteria. Gerber also argues that, in Europe from the 1990s, there was an increasing acceptance that neo-classical economics offers better competition law goals[243] because many thought that the existing Community competition rules (with their many policy goals) actually impeded economic development in Europe.[244] Fears about the slow pace of European economic development came to the fore in the Lisbon Program's call to foster the competitiveness of European industry, which the European Council laid out in 2000.[245]

However, to my mind, this is not an acceptable reason for change. Not only does Chapter 1 argue that it may sometimes be appropriate to consider public policy criteria in competition law; but, both the Treaty and the ECJ already make it clear that many other important goals that cannot always be adequately/appropriately considered if competition policy ignores them should be embraced within Article 81.[246] We have seen other Institutions do the same. As Monti points out, challenges to EC competition policy on the basis that it is politicised miss the mark; it is *designed* to be politicised, albeit within the limits of the Community competence.[247]

Alternatively, the emphasis on economic value may be the Commission's way of establishing a mechanism through which it can assess the value of these various Treaty objectives, so that it can trade them off against each other more transparently, in a specific case. The Commission may believe that it is better to have a strong (economics-based) general rule for all. In many cases, agreements have little appreciable effect on non-economic objectives; and pursuing economic efficiency can often help achieve many other objectives simultaneously. The Commission may think that this rule is generally sufficient; and, where it is not, the Commission could, where the public interest of the Community so

---

[240] Commissioner Monti has said 'When I was appointed Competition Commissioner four years ago, one of my main objectives was an increased economic approach in the interpretation and enforcement of European competition rules.', Mario Monti (2003a).

[241] Kroes (2007).

[242] See Ch 1, Section 3.2.1.

[243] Gerber (2008), s II and p 1260. He also points out that there may have been procedural reasons for these arguments too, pp 1239, 1257, 1258; these are further discussed in Ch 2, Section 2.3.3.

[244] European economic performance lagged behind that in the US with, Hovenkamp argues, its sole economic efficiency goal, Gerber (2008) 1250, 1252, 1253. Furthermore, increasing globalisation reinforced the benefits of a common set of antitrust rules in Europe and the US, Gerber (2008) 1260.

[245] <http://consilium.europa.eu/ueDocs/cms_Data/docs/pressData/en/ec/00100-r1.en0.htm>accessed   27 April 2009. The wheels of change were also oiled through the increased communication that grew-up at this time between Community and US enforcers and scholars; providing opportunities for trans-Atlantic consensus building and for putting pressure on the Commission, Gerber (2008) 1249, 1250. Powerful private-interest groups also favoured (and lobbied for) this change, Gerber (2008) 1250, 1254, 1255.

[246] See Ch 1, Section 3.2.2 and Ch 2, Sections 2.1 and 2.2.

[247] Monti (2007) 118. See also Hawk (1988) 58.

requires, find that Article 81 EC does not apply.[248] As early as 1993 the Commission seemed to envisage that it would concentrate on agreements raising particular political, economic or legal significance for the Community, leaving cases with less of a Community public interest to the courts and competition authorities of the Member States.[249]

Finally, and somewhat provocatively, one might ask whether the Commission emphasised the importance of economic criteria to make its decentralisation initiative more palatable, ie in that it would be easier for the Member States' competition authorities and courts to implement a pure economics test consistently, without also considering public policy criteria.[250] When asked for their views, Member State judges said that they did not feel competent to make general value judgments which impact upon people who are not parties to the procedure before them.[251] However, if this is the Commission's motivation, it risks putting the cart before the horse. It is not acceptable for a change in institutional structure to demand such a reinterpretation of the Treaty provisions, as interpreted by the Community Courts.[252] To be fair to the Commission, it has said that the modernisation reforms would not alter the substantive content of Articles 81 and 82 EC;[253] and so I do not discuss procedural reform in this work.

If this is the Commission strategy, to emphasise the importance of economic criteria, at the expense of public policy ones, it risks offending those Member States, such as France and Germany, that believe that industrial policy's influence on competition law should be increased.[254] In fact such ideas may have pushed President Sarkozy to take his stand on removing 'free competition' as an objective in the new EU Treaty, though it remains in Article 4 EC, because of his desire for a more balanced 'social' Europe.[255] But France and Germany may benefit from decentralisation if the Commission overtly adopts a pure economic approach. Decentralisation could increase the politicisation (as well as rent-seeking behaviour) that DG Competition so dislikes,[256] as it brings power to the Member State level, and the parties may have more influence over national courts and competition authorities.[257]

The second question, posed above, was whether the Commission can change its application of Article 81 in this way. The Commission has a wide discretion under Article 81 EC, particularly Article 81(3) EC and it can decide what weight to give these values in the balance; which can dramatically affect their importance within Article 81. The mere

---

[248]   Reg 1/2003, recital 14 and art 10.

[249]   Commission, *1993 Co-operation Guidelines – National Courts*, paras 13–15.

[250]   Gerber (2008) 1239, 1254, 1257, 1258; Monti (2007) 21; Cseres (2007) 169; Komninos (2005) 17 and Monti (2002) 1092. This is also the implication of Jones and Sufrin (2001) 192; Hawk (1998) 324, 325 and Ehlermann (1998) xi.

[251]   See the citations and discussion on this point in Wesseling (2001) 374.

[252]   Section 3.2 in this chapter explains why.

[253]   Commission, *RCP 2002* 25.

[254]   See *Premier Forum Franco-Allemand sur la Politique de Concurrence Europeenne*, in *Bulletin Quotidien Europe*, No 8627, 21 January 2004 13 and *Bravura Nonsense* and *Creating European Business Champions*, The Economist (London 22 May 2004). See also, '*Selon des sources diplomatiques, Paris et Berlin poussent M. Durao Barroso ... de rétablir un certain équilibre au sein de la Commission, notamment au détriment de la direction de la concurrence, jugée trop libérale.*' M Barroso a été officiellement nommé président de la Commission européenne, Le Monde (Paris 29 June 2004) and *La difficile émergence de l'entreprise européenne*, Le Monde (Paris 7 July 2004).

[255]   *Sarkozy modifie le projet de Traité*, Le Soir (27 June 2007).

[256]   Lafuente (2002) 166.

[257]   Although note arts 11(6) and 16, Reg 1/2003.

fact that Article 81 has been interpreted to include public policy considerations in the past does not mean that it must always be interpreted that way.[258]

Having said that, the Commission's discretion is not absolute, the policy-linking clauses are probably directly effective, through Article 81,[259] the Commission cannot simply ignore these and other relevant Treaty objectives; it has a duty under Article 211 EC to ensure that the Treaty provisions are applied. Furthermore, the Commission must ensure that the Treaty provisions are applied within the framework provided by the Community Courts' judgments, as Advocate-General Kokott explains:

> [E]ven if its administrative practice were to change, the Commission would still have to act within the framework prescribed for it by Article 82 EC as interpreted by the Court of Justice.[260]

The Commission's policy statements from 2000, or at least the interpretation of them that would indicate a pure economic approach, suggest that the Commission has stepped outside of the Community Courts' framework; bringing it into direct conflict with the Community Courts' interpretation of Article 81 EC. The potential for such a collision of ultimate goals; the risk of further confusion, that decentralisation provides; and the central role that the Commission has in relation to Article 81's application, and Community competition policy in general, means that the third question that I posed above, what the effect of this 'change' has been on the Commission's Article 81 decisions, is of critical importance.

In the OJ 2000 there were six Commission decisions under Article 81 EC. Some were purely argued and based on economic criteria;[261] one decision seems to have been based on both economic efficiency and freedom criteria;[262] however, in three decisions, the Commission explicitly invoked non-economic objectives, which may have been decisive.[263]

The first was *GEAE/P&W*, which concerned a co-operative joint venture[264] to supply a new aircraft engine for the planned Airbus A3XX aircraft. The Commission found that it breached Article 81(1) EC; but cleared the joint venture under Article 81(3). It noted the strict performance targets of the new engine,[265] and said that co-operation would lead to a technically advanced engine, being less expensive in maintenance and cost per passenger and per mile covered and would have lower gas and noise emissions; the latter two are environmental considerations. The Commission also noted that the engine could be developed more quickly through co-operation[266] and that this would also bring substantial cost savings.[267] The promised technical advances at a reduced cost were perhaps the most important criteria. If this were the case then the agreement could have led to more *ex post*

---

[258]   Wesseling (2001) 372.

[259]   See Section 3.2.

[260]   Opinion of A-G Kokott, Case C-95/04P, *British Airways v Commission* para 28. This was an Art 82 EC case, but identical principles apply in relation to Art 81 EC. See also, Gerber (2008) 1261.

[261]   For example, Commission decisions, *Inntrepreneur* and *FETTCSA*.

[262]   Commission decision, *FEG and TU*, this was an Art 81(1) case.

[263]   Commission decisions, *GEAE/P&W*; *Eurovision* and *CECED*. *Eurovision* was successfully appealed, though not on grounds relevant to our discussion, Joined Cases T-185/00, etc *Métropole Télévision and Others v Commission* and Case C-470/02, Order of 27/09/2004, *UER /M6 and Others* (unpublished).

[264]   The case was notified on 26 September 1996, this was before the Merger Regulation was adopted.

[265]   Commission decision, *GEAE/P&W*, para 79.

[266]   It is not clear why this is relevant because there was no aircraft with the specification for this engine yet and the Commission seemed to imply, para 71, that the parties were potential competitors within the required timeframe.

[267]   Commission decision, *GEAE/P&W*, para 80

competition. This penalised Rolls Royce, the only firm with an existing engine that it could adapt, which is a lot cheaper to do. This may have been a short-term political (industrial policy) decision, based more on Airbus' need for a cheap engine (allowing it to better compete with Boeing) than anything else.

The next Commission decision of interest was *Eurovision*; which dealt with the EBU agreements that we saw in 1993. By 2000, the EBU's rules had changed, although not really for our purposes. Once again, the Commission found a restriction of competition;[268] but it granted an Article 81(3) exemption. It found an improvement in the production or distribution of goods, etc. in relation to the joint acquisition of rights, for the same reasons as before,[269] this also seems to be a cultural criterion. The Commission found that the agreement reduced transaction costs, for the same reasons as before.[270] There is some indication that the underlying issue for the Commission was either SMEs, or small countries (once again cultural). The cultural aspect seems to be the most important for the Commission, which emphasised that as a result of this joint acquisition more sporting events are broadcast by a larger number of broadcasters, this improves distribution.[271]

The Commission finds that the sharing of the Eurovision rights leads to improved distribution, for the same reason as before.[272] As regards the exchange of the Eurovision signal the Commission believed that the reciprocity and solidarity principles of the Eurovision system obliged any EBU member to produce free of charge the television signal for events taking place in its country, even if it is not itself interested in the event, in order to enable other interested EBU members to show the event. So, more sports programmes are produced and shown, improving distribution.[273] The same definitional point about distribution occurs here, as was noted above in the 1993 case.

Finally, Commission decision, *CECED*, concerns an agreement between CECED, a Brussels-based association comprising manufacturers of domestic appliances and national trade associations, and its members; companies comprising some 95 per cent of the relevant market.[274] The agreement concerned the domestic washing machines' market in the European Economic Area. The Commission found that the agreement breached Article 81(1), as the parties to the agreement bound themselves to cease producing and/or importing into the Community certain categories of washing machines on criteria relating to their energy efficiency,[275] reducing consumer choice and technical diversity.[276] The agreement, said the Commission, appreciably raised production costs,[277] which might reduce demand;[278] it will also reduce the demand for electricity.[279]

The Commission cleared the agreement under Article 81(3) EC. As the agreement was designed to reduce washing machine energy consumption, the machines that would be produced would be more technically efficient, indirectly leading to less pollution from

---

[268]   Commission decision, *Eurovision*, para 72.
[269]   ibid, para 85.
[270]   ibid, para 86.
[271]   ibid, para 87.
[272]   ibid, paras 88, 89.
[273]   ibid, para 105.
[274]   Commission decision, *CECED*, paras 8, 24.
[275]   ibid, paras 19, 20.
[276]   ibid, para 32.
[277]   ibid, para 34.
[278]   ibid, para 35.
[279]   ibid, para 36.

energy generation.[280] The Commission called this more 'economically efficient';[281] particularly remarking on the speed of these changes.[282] The Commission also underlined that R&D was likely to focus on improved energy efficiency; thus, in the long run, there would be more product differentiation on this category.[283] The Commission focuses on economic benefits to consumers; it noted a higher initial purchase price but thought that savings on electricity bills would compensate for this.[284] The Commission also emphasises collective environmental benefits; highlighting Article 174 EC, it adds that agreements like CECED's must yield economic benefits outweighing their costs and be compatible with competition rules.[285]

The Commission then looks at the economic costs of pollution. It mentions the cost of avoiding the carbon dioxide and sulphur dioxide emissions, which the energy efficiency will cause and found that the CECED agreement's societal benefits were more than seven times greater than the increased purchase costs of more energy-efficient washing machines. The Commission believed that the environmental results for society would adequately allow consumers a fair share of the benefits even if no benefits accrued to individual purchasers of machines.[286] The Commission concludes that the expected improvements to energy efficiency, the cost-benefit ratio of the standard and the return on investment for individual users suggest that the agreement will contribute significantly to technical and economic progress.[287]

The Commission's public policy statements seem to have changed dramatically since 1993; however, there does not seem to have been an equivalent change in its decision-making practice over the same period. Of course formal decisions are only a small part of DG Competition's workload, as most cases are dealt with informally;[288] but precisely because of the signalling impact of its decisions, one would expect the Commission to pay special attention to the language that it uses there.

The *GEAE/P&W* decision seems primarily based on political criteria, of a sort that do not often arise. *Eurovision* is interesting for two reasons: it is essentially the same case as the 1993 one, so it provides an interesting point of comparison, the Commission adopts a similar logic in both decisions.[289] The 2000 decision actually discusses the transaction cost and other 'economic' savings less than it did in 1993; this may be because it is more willing to rely on other policy objectives, although it could be because the Commission felt that it had already made out its case in 1993.[290] While the Commission does consider economic

---

[280]   Although the Commission noted that this would be more efficiently tackled at the stage of electricity generation, para 51, see Art 174 EC.

[281]   Commission decision, *CECED*, para 48.

[282]   ibid, para 49.

[283]   ibid, para 50.

[284]   ibid, para 52.

[285]   ibid, para 55.

[286]   ibid, para 56.

[287]   ibid, para 57.

[288]   See Commission, *RCP 2001* 53, fig 2.

[289]   Other Commission decisions also demonstrate continuity in their use of Community objectives under Art 81, eg, (i) *International Energy Agency*, OJ 1983 L376/30 and OJ 1994 L68/35 (national security and consumer protection, paras 29 and 6 respectively) and (ii) *Bayer/BP Chemicals*, OJ 1988 L150/35 and OJ 1994 L174/34 (industrial policy, paras 28–31 and 6 respectively).

[290]   Tactically, it would have been sensible for the Commission to rely more on other policy goals in 2000, considering the wide discretion it is given there and the pending appeals.

criteria, it mentions improved transaction costs;[291] however, this does not appear to be the focus of the case, which is SMEs and small countries,[292] and the cultural policy dimension. The Commission discusses improvements of distribution, not as in better modes of communication but in terms of more distribution; this is important as it may facilitate the consideration of cultural criteria in Article 81(3) in future. Article 151(4) says that the reason that the Community shall take account of cultural aspects is, in particular, to respect and promote the diversity of its cultures. Agreements that encourage/facilitate the dissemination and appreciation of this diversity are surely instrumental to this goal.[293]

The *CECED* decision is also important, because the Commission's mechanism for introducing the environmental issue is through the improvement to technical progress. It is easy to define this in terms of environmental goals and the Commission seems happy doing so,[294] it is the first thing it discusses. Then, the Commission shoehorns the point into an economic efficiency argument,[295] in a contrived way.[296] The agreement does not add new, more energy efficient machines, at least in the medium term; the paternalism that the Commission exercises in removing consumer choice (to spend more now on a machine and less later or vice versa) is incomplete, from an economic perspective, as there is no discussion about the current time value of money; nor the fact that consumers do not, in fact, seem to prefer to spend more now and pay later. The Commission then assesses the cost of cleaning up the pollution that would have been caused if the predicted number of consumers that the agreement will force to switch to the new efficient machines did not take place. It estimates this at seven times the increased purchase costs; but the polluter or consumers would not have to pay these environmental costs, because the externalities have not been internalised;[297] and even if they had been, this does not necessarily mean (indeed this is unlikely) that it would have been efficient to have no pollution.

The decision is dressed up in economics; although, environmental factors had a large impact; it is troubling that, even on this basic issue, the decision's basis is unclear. If

---

[291]   Although there does not seem to be any discussion of the effect that these systems might have on reducing revenue for firms that put on sporting events and thus reducing distribution.

[292]   To the extent that the Commission relies on the solidarity principle to show that they are able to offer a better service.

[293]   See Art 151(2) EC.

[294]   See Commission, *RCP 2000* 39, 40. The Commission says that the principle is clearly illustrated by the CECED decision where it took account of the positive contribution to the EU's environmental objectives, for the benefit of present and future generations.

[295]   Commission decision, *CECED*, para 48.

[296]   Van Gerven, with a slightly different reading of the decision, says 'Although I assume this decision meant to apply a rigorous consumer welfare standard analysis, it failed to do so …', van Gerven (2004) 430.

[297]   At para 55 of its decision, the Commission refers to the European Parliament and Council Decision, *review of 'Towards Sustainability'*, which says that environmental agreements must respect the competition rules. This is circular. Before this provision can be interpreted we must decide whether environmental considerations can be balanced within Art 81. If we adopt a pure economic approach, then only two types of environmental agreements are possible. Those that have non-appreciable restrictions and those that are efficiency enhancing (and also comply with the rest of Art 81(3)). However, if we decide that a mixed economic approach is the correct one, as the Community institutions seem to have done, then saying that environmental agreements must respect the competition rules simply begs the question, how much environmental protection is acceptable under these rules?

environmental policy is the real reason for this decision, something that DG Competition's later statements lend credence to, it would have been helpful if the Commission had explained this clearly *in the decision.*

2.3.3 Through 2009-tinted spectacles

The Commission's policy statements on the objectives of competition policy seem to have changed since 1993; today, they almost exclusively emphasise the economic (efficiency) effects of agreements.

This chapter suggested three reasons why the Commission might advocate a shift to a pure economic approach, if indeed it has. The need to convince Member States' courts and competition authorities that Article 81(3) could be applied by them was influential;[298] this is because the Commission, *White Paper on Modernisation* made the clearest call for a pure economic approach. Yet, if this were the sole motivation, then, now that Regulation 1/2003 has been adopted, one might have expected the Commission to distance itself from such a strong position;[299] indeed, we saw some evidence of this in Commission, *Article 81(3) Guidelines.*[300]

However, this is not the whole story. The Commission's language now shows that economics is its preferred tool for Article 81 analysis, and that consumer welfare is becoming its preferred goal. It has regularly underlined this in its policy statements since 2000; two examples suffice. In Commission, *Article 81(3) Guidelines* (2004) the Commission re-emphasises that the objective of Article 81 is to protect competition on the market as a means of enhancing consumer welfare and of ensuring an efficient allocation of resources.[301] It also restrictively defines the types of benefit that might justify exemption, focusing on *efficiency gains.*[302] Secondly, in a speech in 2007, the current Competition Commissioner, Neelie Kroes, said:

> Fifty years on [since the Treaty of Rome], this shared objective [ensuring competition in the internal market is not distorted] retains all its pertinence. We are still striving to keep markets open and competition undistorted. We do so out of the same sense of conviction that drove the Treaty-makers in the Fifties: *competition is the key means to increase consumer welfare, to ensure an efficient allocation of resources*, to keep market players on their toes.[303] (emphasis added)

According to Commissioner Kroes, the objective of the competition rules, including Article 81 EC, is 'enhancing consumer welfare and of ensuring an efficient allocation of resources'. It is unclear what room this framework leaves for public policy objectives; the implication is little or none. This clearly clashes with the position adopted by the EC Treaty and the Community Courts.[304] It is an extreme position for the Commission to adopt and

---

[298] On whether public policy within Art 81(3) would mean that it was not directly effective, see Komninos (2006) 457, 471 and the arguments there as well as Section 3.2, below.

[299] The Commission has said that decentralisation will not alter the substantive content of Arts 81 and 82, Commission, *RCP 2002* 25. Komninos (2006) 451–55 and Venit (2003) 546, 575–79, greet this assertion sceptically.

[300] Commission, *Article 81(3) Guidelines*, para 42.

[301] ibid, para 13.

[302] ibid, para 50.

[303] Kroes (2007).

[304] See Sections 2.1 and 2.2, above.

so, confusingly, even today we sometimes see it tempered.[305] In addition, the Commission's policy statements seem to clash with the position that the Commission itself adopted in its decisions.[306] In its decisions, the Commission considered objectives protected by the policy-linking clauses, as well as those found more generally in the Preamble and Article 2 EC, both in 1993 and 2000.

Those agreements that justify a formal Commission decision are probably more likely to require this difficult balancing of objectives, such complex cases are precisely the ones where the Commission's unique skills and knowledge make it pre-eminently qualified to intervene.[307] However, if the Commission's strategy were not to take account of public policy considerations anymore, the best place to demonstrate this transparently would be in its decisions.[308] This is even more the case since 1 May 2004, given the importance placed on Commission decisions; if decentralisation is to work properly, there must be trust between the Commission and the Member State bodies; and trust is best built upon transparent foundations, whose plans are clearly and consistently explained.

Since 2000 the Commission's Article 81 decision-making practice may be moving into line with the consumer welfare focus of its recent policy statements; for example, in *GlaxoSmithKline v Commission* (2006),[309] the Commission argued that it had carried out its original examination (in its decision), by asking whether there was a restriction of consumer welfare.[310] Nevertheless, even in Commission decisions and DG Competition comfort letters post 2000, there has still been an acceptance that public policy goals have a place in Article 81.[311]

---

[305]   See, eg Commission Memo, *European collecting societies* (2008); COM(2004) 293 18 and DG Competition Paper, *on Waste Management*, paras 1, 14, 126, obviously this is DG Competition and not the Commission as a whole.

[306]   I say 'seems to', because it does not always admit it and often tries to disguise the fact; this is criticised (in another context) in Amato (1997) 62 and Korah in Ehlermann (1998) 525–41.

[307]   Commission, *1993 Co-operation Guidelines – National Courts*, paras 13, 14.

[308]   Bouterse (1994) 33, Bouterse, citing Sporman (1968) 133, argues that one reason why the Commission actually takes a decision in this area is because they are test cases and that this '… implies that the decisions which were issued have a significance which goes beyond the facts of the relevant case.' Forrester and Norall (1993) 428, agree.

[309]   Case T-168/01 *GlaxoSmithKline Services Unlimited v Commission* para 118.

[310]   This clear Commission statement about its Art 81 analysis in this case asserts that it was based upon a consumer welfare approach. However, I am still cautious of leaping to the conclusion that there has been a positive shift in its decision-making; sometimes the Commission changes position on this issue, depending upon which side of the argument it finds itself in a specific case; compare, the Commission's arguments in the *VBVB/VBBB* Case, in order to justify its decision not to grant an exemption, with those in the *Matra* Case, where it sought to justify an apparently generous exemption decision.

[311]   See, eg Commission Memo, *European collecting societies* (2008); Andries and Julien-Malvy (2008) 55 (culture); Commission, *RCP 2002* 198–200 (smooth functioning of competition in sport) 200 (public health – the fight against doping); Commission decision, *Joint selling of the Commercial Rights of the UEFA Champions League*, para 129; Commission, *RCP 2003* 30, 195 (health and environmental benefits); Commission decision, *French beef*, (Common Agricultural Policy's objectives); Commission, *RCP 2004* 111, 112; Commission decision, *Joint selling of the media rights to the German Bundesliga* (media pluralism); and Commission, *RCP 2005* 56 (environmental benefits).

3 OBJECTIONS TO BALANCING IN ARTICLE 81 EC

Despite public policy having been considered in Article 81 EC in the past and the contextual reasons offered in Section 2 that justify such an approach, the Commission now advocates the exclusive goal of consumer welfare and an efficient allocation of resources for Article 81 EC.[312] Many Community competition practitioners support the Commission's adoption of the consumer welfare goal.[313] While most agree that public policy goals are important, they argue that they can be achieved more efficiently using other instruments.[314] In addition, ignoring public policy concerns renders Article 81 EC more justiciable and provides greater legal certainty.[315] However, since the Treaty requires public policy to be considered using the Article 81 EC instrument these arguments are not really relevant.[316] Another reason offered for removing public policy from Article 81 EC is the desire to bring Community competition law into line with the 'more sophisticated' US system. However, the different legal constellations on either side of the Atlantic make the validity of this justification questionable too.[317]

In *The Boundaries of EC Competition Law*, Odudu seeks to justify an approach to Article 81 EC that excludes public policy considerations and focuses exclusively on consumer welfare.[318] His arguments are grouped into four heads: (a) jurisdictional issues; (b) direct effect by the back door; (c) the intended relationship between Treaty provisions; and (d) legal certainty and justiciability. The first three of these arguments are considered here.[319]

3.1 Jurisdictional issues

Odudu states that Article 81 EC imposes obligations on the citizen (undertaking) rather than the state; public policy grounds can only be balanced in provisions which are aimed at states (ie they cannot be considered in Article 81 EC):

> Article 81 imposes obligations on the citizen (undertaking) rather than the state ... The possibility of balancing a range of Treaty goals *within* a single Treaty provision is specifically and exclusively designed for *Member States*, treating an infringement of the Treaty by the state more flexibly than an infringement of the Treaty by the citizen because state action has a democratic legitimacy and political accountability that private action lacks.[320]

One difficulty raised by a public/private divide is that privatisation and contracting out have transferred tasks previously performed by the state to undertakings operating in the market place. Odudu acknowledges this and refines the ideas of 'citizen' and 'state', adopting a functional (as opposed to an institutional) basis for his public/private divide.

---

[312]   See Section 2.3, above.
[313]   See above.
[314]   See Ch 1, Section 3.2.1 and Motta (2004) 30.
[315]   Odudu (2006) 170–3.
[316]   See Section 2, above.
[317]   See ibid and Hawk (1988).
[318]   Odudu (2006).
[319]   Aspects of legal certainty and justiciability were discussed in Ch 1, Section 3.
[320]   Odudu (2006) 165. See also his ch 3, s IV.A.

He allows balancing of public policy for 'state-like acts', although he argues that this should be done in the free movement provisions, rather than Article 81 EC.[321]

It is questionable whether Odudu's functional public/private divide is sustainable, in the way he uses it for the competition rules, in light of the wider Treaty context. For example, Article 86(2) EC assumes that 'state-like acts' fall within the rules on competition. The activities of undertakings entrusted with the operation of services of general economic interest (a type of public policy benefit) must fall within the competition rules, otherwise the reference to these rules in Article 86(2) EC would serve no purpose.[322]

However, simultaneously advocating a functional approach and a public/private divide creates deeper problems, both concerning the argument that state action cannot be considered within Article 81 EC, as well as for the related point that one cannot balance a range of goals within that provision. This is because of Odudu's justifications for dividing the Treaty in this way. He says that, unlike private action, state action has democratic legitimacy and political accountability. The second (related) point is that private actors are principally motivated by self-interest. Section 3.1 focuses on these points in turn.

3.1.1 Democratic legitimacy and political accountability

Some commentators suggest that the Commission should operate an identical legality standard when it assesses the compatibility of market-based or regulatory action with the Common Market. For example, some suggest that the Treaty provisions on competition and free movement should contain the same legality standard.[323] The ECJ made a similar point in its *Viking* judgment about the free movement rules and their applicability to public and private actors.[324]

Baquero Cruz accepts that certain state action can fall within the competition rules, including Article 81 EC, and that public policy goals would be relevant whether the undertaking were public or private. Nevertheless, he argues that the qualification of the undertaking as public or private may be important when assessing the legitimacy of specific anti-competitive measures.[325]

Odudu takes a different tack. He believes that, when actors (be they private or public) perform 'State-like' functions, they are more appropriately dealt with under EC public law and Article 81 EC should not apply at all.[326] *The Boundaries of EC Competition Law* focuses on the type of *activities* being performed, rather than *actors' attributes*, when allocating a matter to public (eg Article 28 EC) or private law (eg Article 81 EC). However, the functional approach undermines this justification for the public/private divide in the

---

[321]   This immediately raises the issue of what is a state-like act. For a more extensive discussion, see the arguments around n 333 below.

[322]   See the Opinion of A-G Poiares Maduro, Case C-205/03 P *FENIN v Commission* para 26.

[323]   See, eg Gyselen (1994) 242.

[324]   Case C-438/05 *International Transport Workers' Federation and Others v Viking Line ABP and Others* para 34. See also, Case C-415/93 *Union Royale Belge des Sociétés de Football Association ASBL and Others v Jean-Marc Bosman* para 86.

[325]   Baquero Cruz (2002) 88. It is unclear whether he means that the balance between goals might be different for public actors (pp 124, 156, 157) or merely that the standard of review should be less for state undertakings (pp 111, 124, 159–61).

[326]   Odudu (2006) 166.

Treaty provisions in the first place. Odudu's justification focuses on *actors' attributes* (state action has a democratic legitimacy and political accountability that private action lacks) and not their *activities*.

Under Odudu's democratic legitimacy logic it must be inappropriate to consider the actions of the Dutch Bar Council (in *Wouters*) under (to use Odudu's terminology) EC public law, rather than Article 81 EC, its actions did not have democratic legitimacy or political accountability in the Netherlands. And yet, Odudu states '… the specific rule promulgated by the association [the Dutch Bar Council] seemed more appropriately dealt with by EC public law.'[327] One could argue that, as the Netherlands permitted the Dutch Bar Council to act, this is an (indirect) state act (making it 'state-like'). But, this logic could apply to most private action. Alternatively, one might justify the Dutch Bar Council's action because the Netherlands had imposed an *obligation* on it to pursue the public interest.[328] Even if this is correct, in *Meca-Medina* the ECJ followed its *Wouters* reasoning, but there is no evidence that it demanded, or found, that the IOC was guided by a democratically accountable body.[329]

One might also question whether one wants to redesignate private action in this way, as it might lead to the non-reflexive application of other public obligations on these actors as well; which might undermine other important benefits they provide, such as innovation and efficiency.[330]

In addition, applying Odudu's democratic legitimacy logic it must also be inappropriate to assess state action of any kind under Article 81 EC, for even when the state acts like a private actor, it would still be able to point to its democratic legitimacy and political accountability. Yet, Odudu accepts that, in appropriate cases, state action should fall within Article 81 EC too.[331]

In conclusion, the existence of a public/private divide, as outlined by Odudu in relation to the competition rules, is not supported contextually. Furthermore, Odudu argues that the divide's application must be functional, as opposed to institutional, yet the 'political accountability argument' is institutional, as opposed to functional, and therefore cannot justify such a divide.

3.1.2 Private actors and self-interest

The Boundaries of EC Competition Law gives a second reason for treating public and private actors differently. It presumes that, all things being equal, those in the private sphere are self-interested[332] and that those in the public sphere operate in pursuit of the public interest:

> The presumption underpinning the need for different rules for public and private spheres is that private actors pursue self-interest whilst public actors promote the general public interest.[333]

---

[327] ibid.

[328] ibid, 51, 52.

[329] The *Meca-Medina* Case, esp paras 40–56. See also Case T-193/02 *Laurent Piau v Commission* paras 76–78.

[330] Freeman (2000) 848–58.

[331] Odudu (2006) 45–56.

[332] See the Opinion of A-G Jacobs in *Albany* paras 184, 185 and Case T-155/04 *SELEX Sistemi Integrati v Commission and Eurocontrol* para 77, on appeal, Case C-113/07 *SELEX Sistemi Integrati v Commission and Eurocontrol*.

[333] Odudu (2006) 50. Also see p 55 and some of the arguments of the interested parties in Case C-2/91 *Criminal proceedings against Meng*, p 5770.

This chapter argues that the self-interest argument is (and should be) irrelevant. Even when private actors pursue their self-interest they often simultaneously promote the general public interest. We should focus on outcomes.

The Boundaries of EC Competition Law presumes that private actors pursue their self-interest unless they act contrary to their own pecuniary interests, and thus do not 'pose the dangers normally associated with collaboration' (for example, when the entity is under an obligation to pursue the public interest).[334] In other words, at the jurisdictional stage, actors must weigh the consumer welfare reduction that their actions may engender against the public benefits,[335] to see whether one should apply Article 81 EC (one should not if the public benefits are greater) or the public law rules (such as Article 28 EC).

The first point to highlight is that the classification of 'state-like acts' is difficult.[336] It introduces a high level of complexity to the analysis at the jurisdictional stage. This means that it will be hard for actors to know in advance which rules apply to them (let alone what those rules say).[337] In addition, Odudu relies on the '... formalistic and conceptually dubious characterisation of activity as essentially private or public ...'[338]

Secondly, and as noted above, the whole exercise of removing public interest cases from Article 81 EC seems contrary to the Treaty's structure. For example, Article 86(2) EC assumes that the activities of undertakings entrusted with the operation of services of general economic interest must fall within the competition rules. Yet, such firms would not, according to Odudu, be pursuing their 'private self-interest', and thus should fall outside of Article 81 EC. He might respond that, in order to fall within the competition rules, and thus the reference to competition rules in Article 86(2) EC, the service of general economic interest (public interest) must be ancillary to some private interest, otherwise the action would not fall within the competition rules at all. However, such a notion is not supported by the Treaty, or the ECJ's case law.[339]

However, there are deeper problems; this division is at once too wide and too narrow. Too narrow because it undermines the importance of competition. Odudu is prepared to exclude all those from the competition rules that act (predominantly?) in the 'public interest'.[340] But, lest we forget, competition is, itself, in the Community public interest, and an important goal, see Articles 2 and 3 EC.[341] Can we even be confident that something is in the public interest without assessing its impact upon competition?

The ECJ took the route Odudu suggests in *Albany*, where it excluded highly anti-competitive arrangements from the remit of the Community competition rules for social

---

[334]   Odudu (2006) 51, 52.

[335]   There is not total consistency; at times Odudu equates acting contrary to one's pecuniary interest with the harm that collaboration is associated with. He also seems to equate an obligation to act in the public interest with acting against one's own self-interest. Neither seems entirely right.

[336]   Freeman (2000), s I provides many interesting examples.

[337]   It also undermines a bit Odudu's later arguments about the lack of justiciability of such an assessment *within* Art 81 itself, although, to be fair, less precision would be needed in a jurisdictional test.

[338]   Freeman (2000) 841, 842. Admittedly, this often happens in administrative law, but the lines can be more blurred than those arguing for separation imply; so it seems unhelpful to introduce the dichotomy here too.

[339]   See, eg the references to Case C-41/90 *Klaus Höfner and Fritz Elser v Macrotron*, below n 361. The appellants in the *Meca Medina* Case, specifically argued, paras 46–56, that the IOC had (in their self-interest) made stricter rules than were required to achieve the legitimate public health objective. The ECJ focused on outcomes and not intention, para 47.

[340]   Other than indirectly via, eg, Arts 3(1)(g), 10 and 81 /82 EC actions.

[341]   Case 6/72 *Europemballage Corporation and Continental Can v Commission* para 24. The ECJ's comments apply to both Arts 81 and 82 EC.

policy reasons.[342] Once Article 81 EC no longer applied, competition (which was significantly undermined in that case) was ignored.[343] Arguably, it is anomalous to deal with the issue in this way,[344] given the emphasis on competition in other decisions, as well as the ability to balance such considerations within Article 81 EC itself.[345] *Albany*'s exemption of some social law from competition law's scope is not indispensable for achieving labour policy goals (unless the idea is to eliminate competition, in which case one might have to use Article 81(1) EC) and pre-empts any discussion of the welfare effects of collective bargaining.[346] Two important Treaty objectives were at stake, instead of taking them both into account, one was ignored. The ECJ found a way of reconciling the competing public and competition interests in both *Wouters* and *Meca-Medina*.[347] It allowed the arrangement in the public interest, but only once it had investigated whether the public policy aims were at least proportionate to the restriction of competition. In other words, it balanced the two public policy goals against each other, rather than allowing one to exclude the other.

According to Odudu, if the activities are allocated correctly at the outset (to EC public or private law), there is no need to balance a range of Treaty provisions within the competition provisions.[348] This is questionable. Only by balancing *within* Article 81 EC can sufficient credence be given to competition, as well as other public policy goals. Removing arrangements such as those considered in *Wouters*, where it can be shown that actors also act in the public interest, from the ambit of the competition rules is problematic; not only because these acts may not actually achieve their intended public policy goals but it would also mean removing an important check, that competition (an important Treaty goal) has not been undermined any more than is appropriate in the circumstances.

Odudu's use of the public/private divide is also too wide, because it carries within it the presumption that action in our private interest is against the public interest.[349] This can certainly be true, but this should not be exaggerated. In order to understand why, we must return to Adam Smith, who had the following insight:

> Every individual … generally, indeed, neither intends to promote the public interest, nor knows how much he is promoting it. By preferring the support of domestic to that of foreign industry he intends only his own security; and by directing that industry in such a manner as its produce may be of the greatest value, he intends only his own gain, and he is in this, as in many other cases, led by an invisible hand to promote an end which was no part of his intention.[350]

The invisible hand can lead even those acting in pure self-interest to promote the public interest.[351] This applies to the allocation of resources in the economic sphere, but it also

---

[342] As explained in Section 2.2.1, above.

[343] This is not to argue that the result was necessarily wrong, just that competition is important and should be included in the balance. This happens when public policy is considered under Art 81 EC.

[344] See the Opinion of A-G Lenz in Case C-415/93 *Union Royale Belge des Sociétés de Football Association ASBL v Bosman* para 273.

[345] See Section 2 above. A-G Jacobs' Opinion in *Albany*, disagrees, para 178.

[346] van den Bergh and Camesasca (2000) 501–8.

[347] See Section 2.2.2, above.

[348] Odudu (2006) 165.

[349] In this he follows public choice theory, for a discussion see Freeman (2000) 844, 845.

[350] A Smith (1976 Re-print), Bk IV, Ch II.

[351] See Hildebrand (2002) 112.

applies to public policy interests.[352] While pharmaceutical firms are run for profit, in the interest of their shareholders, they provide huge public health benefits as well.[353] It might be more rewarding to explore how to harness private capacity in the service of public goals.[354]

Determining whether an entity's actions are in the public interest is a more complex exercise than merely asking whether it is a private firm, or whether it is compelled to act in the general public interest.[355] A more rigorous analysis is needed.[356] It seems more appropriate to see economic activity not as something that is anathema to public policy goals, but as something that can be compatible with them and may even promote them. One must focus on the *outcome* of the entities' activities, to assess whether or not they are in line with the EU public interest, including competition.[357] As argued above, this assessment should be carried out within Article 81 EC.

Furthermore, insisting that the parties act with these public policy goals as their aim would have a serious impact on the ability to use non-economic objectives within Article 81(3). Undertakings are normally motivated by the profit that they think that a particular strategy will generate for their shareholders, not by whether their agreements are environmentally friendly. Many neo-classical economists believe that a company's primary duty is profit maximisation.[358] In many companies, to act otherwise may even breach the directors' fiduciary duty to their shareholders. This does not mean that their agreements do not also benefit others,[359] just that this is not normally the *aim* of the agreement.

In fact, this is what the Community Courts seem to ignore the parties' aims in Article 81 EC and this chimes with a functional approach in relation to economic activity.[360] They make an objective assessment, regardless of the parties' motivations.[361] The Commission

---

[352] A-G Léger adopts similar language to that of Odudu on private actors acting in their self-interest in his Opinion in *Wouters*, para 84. But A-G Léger insists that the presence of public policy benefits is not relevant for defining the scope *ratione personae* of competition law. Instead, he says that public policy concerns can be considered within Art 81 EC where self-interest leads to relevant public benefits, para 113.

[353] Freeman (2000), s I, provides many examples of how private firms are increasingly performing traditionally public functions even where privatisation does not occur.

[354] ibid, 845.

[355] ibid, 847–49. The balance will not always lie in favour of the public interest, ie price-fixing by pharmaceutical firms will not always be justified. The Community Courts do not always accept public policy claims when raised within the competition rules. For example, in Joined Cases T–213/95 and T–18/96 *SCK and FNK v Commission* para 202, the CFI was quick to reject public safety arguments when it felt these had not been substantiated; but, it did not refuse to examine these issues if they had been properly raised.

[356] This is not to deny the need for presumptions. For example, one might assume that secret cartels are not in the public interest.

[357] As such, this is wider than Schmid (2000) 167, who suggests only allowing public policy exemptions where private agreements take over public functions.

[358] See Ch 2, Section 3.1; A Smith (1976 Re-print) 477, 478; Friedman (1962) 133 and Henderson (2001) 3.

[359] For example, think of the provision of free anti-retroviral drugs to their infected workers by Anglo American, AngloGold, De Beers, Old Mutual and Transnet, see *Strategic Caring*, The Economist (London 3 October 2002) and *Digging Deep*, The Economist (London 8 August 2002).

[360] See Section 2.2, above.

[361] See Joined Cases 29/83 and 30/83 *Compagnie Royale Asturienne des Mines SA and Rheinzink v Commission* para 29, which explains that the concept of restriction of competition is an objective, not a subjective one. This is a further hint that outcomes, rather than motivations, are what matters in Art 81 EC. Also note that, in cases such as Case C-41/90 *Klaus Höfner and Fritz Elser v Macrotron*, the Bundesanstalt were not motivated by private self-interest, but a purely public one, para 3. The *Meca Medina* Case also highlights this issue, see n 339, above; *cf* the *Verband* Case paras 58–60.

does a similar thing. Once a restriction of competition was identified in the CECED decision, the Commission discussed the environmental impact of the arrangement. If as has been claimed, the Commission took this into account in its final decision (as Article 6 EC demands),[362] then the wider Community public interest was served, regardless of whether the entities acted contrary to their own pecuniary (or wider) interests.

In conclusion, the jurisdictional arguments based on the irrelevance of public policy factors in Article 81 EC do not seem to be supported by the case law or the Treaty itself. Nor do these arguments obviate the need to consider public policy in Article 81 EC. The democratic legitimacy argument cannot be relied upon, in the way Odudu proposes, once we embrace the functional approach. Finally, the self-interest arguments seem less appropriate than a focus on outcomes.

3.2 Direct effect by the back door

Odudu argues that the teleological approach to Treaty interpretation began because there were policies that required Member State action, which was not forthcoming. According to him, the ECJ responded to this period of stagnation:

> [T]he uncontested legitimacy of competition law was used as a Trojan horse to achieve non-efficiency (and on the thesis advanced, non-competition) aims indirectly … The teleological interpretation avoids the need to implement various Community policies by applying them *inter alia* through the medium of Article 81.[363]

Odudu argues that Article 2 EC and the policy-linking clauses are incapable of direct effect. Given this, so the argument goes, it is inappropriate to use another provision (such as Article 81 EC) to indirectly create these rights and obligations. This is even more so today, as there are other routes for achieving non-competition goals.[364]

Focusing on the direct effect of the policy linking clauses and Article 2 EC may be a red-herring. Rather, the emphasis must be on Article 81 EC and whether it is capable of direct effect when public policy goals are included within it. Section 3.2 challenges Odudu's argument, first by looking at the inclusion of policies into Article 81 EC supported by policy-linking clauses; and then by discussing the consideration in Article 81 EC of other policies that are not provided for in this way.

3.2.1 Policy-linking clauses

It is worth reminding ourselves of the wording of some of these provisions. They are all slightly different, but Article 151(4) EC states:

> The Community shall take cultural aspects into account in its action under other provisions of this Treaty, in particular in order to respect and to promote the diversity of its cultures.

The intention of such a provision seems to be to ensure that cultural aspects are considered when applying Treaty provisions, such as Article 81 EC. Similarly, we have seen

---

[362]   Commission, *RCP 2000* 39, 40, and Wesseling (2001). *Cf* the *VBVB/VBBB* Case, p 48 and Commission, *Article 81(3) Guidelines*, para 47.
[363]   Odudu (2006) 167.
[364]   ibid.

that Article 152(1) EC reads: 'A high level of human health protection shall be ensured in the definition and implementation of all Community policies and activities.'

Given the apparent aim of such clauses, it is hard to agree that it is inappropriate to use other provisions (such as Article 81 EC) to take account of goals such as human health and culture.[365] The tendency is to introduce more policy-linking clauses in recent Treaty amendments,[366] so it is difficult to argue that this stance is any less appropriate today.

This view is in line with that of many Institutions. The Community Courts, for example, have justified their consideration of various public policy goals with reference to policy-linking clauses.[367] For what it is worth, this coincides with the Council's views.[368]

Some suggest that, while consideration of the policy-linking clauses' goals might be acceptable if they can be easily read into Article 81 EC's wording,[369] they should not be considered if this is not the case.[370] However, the argument of this chapter has been that these sorts of textual arguments carry less weight with the courts than systemic/teleological arguments.[371]

As an interim conclusion, one might say that the policy-linking clauses seem designed to ensure that action under the Treaty (including Article 81 EC) takes into account a plurality of relevant public policy goals, as opposed to merely competition. This remains the case today.

Nevertheless, there is still an issue of appropriateness to be discussed. Is it right that a private undertaking might have obligations placed upon it, in relation to, for example, public health concerns, when Article 81 EC does not even mention them? Articles 151(4)

---

[365]   Although note the arguments of Krämer, above n 55.

[366]   See Section 2.1.1, above.

[367]   See, eg in relation to Art 6 EC (environmental protection), see Case C-379/98 *PreussenElektra v Schleswag* paras 69–80; Joined Cases T–74/00 etc *Artegodan GmbH and Others v Commission* para 184, and more generally paras 181–95. The judgment was appealed, Case C-39/03 P *Commission v Artegodan*, but not on these grounds. See also, in relation to Art 152 EC (health policy), Case T-13/99 *Pfizer Animal Health v Council* paras 113–25. Other citations of note include Case C-233/94, *Federal Republic of Germany v European Parliament and Concil* paras 45, 48. See also, A-G Cosmas '… the last sentence of the first subpara of para 2 of Article 130r [now essentially Art 6] of the Treaty appears to impose on the Community institutions a specific and clear obligation which could be deemed to produce direct effect in the Community legal order. It expressly states that: 'Environmental protection requirements must be integrated into the definition and implementation of other Community policies.', Case C-321/95P *Stichting Greenpeace Council and Others v Commission* para 62. The ECJ was silent on the point; and the Opinion of A-G Lenz in Case C-360/92P *Publishers Association v Commission* para 60. This is also the implication of Case C-180/96 R *United Kingdom of Great Britain and Northern Ireland v Commission* para 63. See also, Dhondt (2003) 144–47; McGillivray and Holder (2001) 154; Cunningham (2001) 158–60; Stuyck (2000) 386, 387; Jans (2000) 277; Grimeaud (2000) 216, 217; Whelan (1999) 50; Bär and Kraemer (1998) 318, 319; Woods and Scholes (1997) 50, 51 and Baldock (1994) 7. Bourgeois and Demaret (1995) 73, accept this possibility in light of the Art 6 language. Krämer (2003) 21, doubts this formulation saying that environmental protection must be taken into account in all other policies, but not every individual measure. However, Community competition policy is essentially defined through the individual measures so perhaps here his argument carries less weight?

[368]   Council, *Conclusions on the Contribution of Industrial Policy to European Competitiveness*, (2003). A discussion in relation to book price fixing and the views of the Council can be found in Ch 4, Section 2.5.

[369]   For example, arrangements that improve environmental protection might be said to improve 'technical progress', Art 81(3) EC.

[370]   This seems to be the implication of Commission, *Article 81(3) Guidelines*, para 42, although note the confusion para 13 causes. This also seems to be the argument in Schweitzer (2007) 5.

[371]   The ECJ has interpreted many provisions' wording against their natural meaning so as to enable it to consider public policy goals there, eg, Case 302/86 *Commission v Denmark* paras 8–22 (Art 28 EC) and the *Wouters* Case, para 97 (Art 81 EC).

(culture), 159 (economic and social cohesion) and 178 EC (development co-operation) are directed at the Community, the other policy-linking clauses are written in the passive tense.

In fact, it does seem appropriate to place obligations on undertakings, particularly given the explicit nature of the policy-linking clauses. To this end, this chapter develops two arguments. First, it provides examples of the ECJ imposing obligations on private individuals when the relevant Treaty provisions did not explicitly place obligations upon them, which is more in line with regulatory neutrality. Secondly, it focuses more tightly on the key issue here, the direct effect of Article 81 EC.

In relation to the first argument, in *Defrenne* an air hostess (Ms Defrenne) sued her employer (the company, SABENA) for sexual discrimination. She relied upon Article 141 EC, which is explicitly directed at Member States.[372] SABENA, it was held, was obliged to act in accordance with Article 141 EC. One could argue that *Defrenne* solves the debate about whether a Treaty obligation imposed on a Member State can also impose obligations on private individuals. However, in that case, SABENA was a company owned by the Belgian state. Did the nature of the respondent (ie a state company) sway the ECJ? In fact, this does not seem to have happened. Parts of the judgment seem aimed at all undertakings, whether or not they are state owned.[373] In addition, the ECJ's reasoning is also based on the improvement of the living and working conditions of the peoples of the Community,[374] in which case it matters not whether their employers are state-owned.

A similar point was made by the ECJ in its recent *Viking* judgment. This concerned actual or threatened collective union action liable to deter Viking from re-flagging one of its vessels from the Finnish flag to that of another Member State with less employment protection. The ECJ held that since working conditions in the different Member States are governed sometimes by provisions laid down by law or regulation and sometimes by collective agreements and other acts concluded or adopted by private persons, limiting application of the prohibitions laid down by Articles 39, 43 and 49 EC (which are implicitly aimed at Member States) to acts of a public authority would risk creating inequality in its application.[375] Furthermore, in *Viking* the issue arose about whether this principle was of general application, or it only arose here because the trade union was doing 'state-like acts'. The ECJ made it clear that this is not limited to private bodies exercising a regulatory task or having quasi-legislative powers.[376] At least as regards Treaty provisions, an explicit obligation on private individuals in the article relied upon seems

---

[372]   Case 43/75 *Gabrielle Defrenne v SABENA*. Clearly, Art 141 EC (and Art 28 EC, which we discuss below in *Viking*) is itself directly effective, so Odudu might argue that they are not precisely analogous. Nevertheless, they are relevant; see the discussion on Reg 1/2003, below.

[373]   Case 43/75 *Gabrielle Defrenne v SABENA* paras 9, 38, 39.

[374]   ibid, paras 10, 11.

[375]   Case C-438/05 *International Transport Workers' Federation and Others v Viking Line ABP and Others* para 34. In fact, the *ECMR*, recital 22, is more explicit, talking of a 'principle of non-discrimination between the public and the private sectors.'

[376]   Case C-438/05 *International Transport Workers' Federation and Others v Viking Line ABP and Others* paras 63–65 and Case C-281/98, *Roman Angonese v Cassa di Risparmio di Bolzano* paras 31–36, although this may be limited to direct discrimination by private parties, Dashwood (2008) 531. For some other possible limits, see Barnard (2008) 473, 474, Dashwood (2008) 527–33, 536, 539.

unnecessary;[377] although there are some limits to this, ie there is not yet horizontal direct effect for all private action.[378] Even vis-à-vis directives, where the obligations argument has been more successfully raised in relation to horizontal direct effect,[379] the Community Courts have used various strategies to ensure that relevant objectives are considered where possible.[380]

In any event, and this is the second strand of the argument, it is important to remember the issue at stake, which is whether public policy considerations should be considered within Article 81 EC. If Odudu's argument, that public policy considerations cannot be considered within a directly effective Article 81(3) EC, is correct, the solution cannot be to ignore public policy within Article 81 EC, but to conclude that that provision is not directly effective. Let me explain this thinking.

Normally, public policy arguments have been raised in Article 81(3) EC, as opposed to Article 81(1) EC.[381] Regulation 1/2003 allows the Commission to make Article 81 EC decisions.[382] The Commission is obliged to take account of the Treaty, Article 218 EC, including the policy-linking clauses.[383]

In *Artegodan* (an Article 230 EC case), for example, some pharmaceutical firms brought actions for annulment against three Commission decisions, withdrawing marketing authorisations for some medicinal products which these firms had in the EU. The Commission decisions were based on Directive 75/319. The criteria for withdrawal are set out in Articles 11 and 21 of the directive and include public health grounds. The Commission argued that where there is scientific uncertainty, as there was here, the relevant authority had to make its assessment in accordance with the precautionary principle. The CFI agreed:

> [T]he precautionary principle can be defined as a general principle of Community law requiring the competent authorities to take appropriate measures to prevent specific potential risks to public health, safety and the environment, by giving precedence to the requirements related to the protection of those interests over economic interests. Since the Community institutions are responsible, in all their spheres of activity, for the protection of public health, safety and the environment, the precautionary principle can be regarded as an autonomous principle stemming from the abovementioned Treaty provisions [Articles 3(1)(p), 6, 152(1), 153, 174(1) and (2) EC].[384]

---

[377]   See also, the cases in n 367 above. In fact, although the case law is not yet wholly consistent, this has happened on many occasions, see, eg Case 36/74, *Walrave and Koch v AUCI* 1418–19 and Case C-415/93 *Union Royale Belge des Sociétés de Football Association ASBL v Bosman*, pp 5063–66. For many other examples see Baquero Cruz (2002) 108–16.

[378]   See the references cited in n 376, above.

[379]   See, eg Case C-201/02 *The Queen v Secretary of State for Transport, Local Government and the Regions* paras 56, 57.

[380]   See Craig and de Búrca (2008) 287–03.

[381]   Art 81(3) EC seems to be the best place for public policy arguments, see Part C, but the point is also relevant for their consideration under Art 81(1) EC.

[382]   Reg 1/2003, arts 4, 7, 10.

[383]   There seems no room for arguments about direct effect in Art 230 EC actions. Direct effect is historically explicable as a means of ensuring the effectiveness of Community law in the national systems of the Member States, see Kapteyn and VerLoren van Themaat (1998) 545 and the references made there.

[384]   Joined Cases T–74/00 etc *Artegodan GmbH and Others v Commission* para 184. See more generally, paras 181–95. The judgment was appealed, but not on these grounds: Case C-39/03 P *Commission v Artegodan GmbH and Others*. See also, in relation to Art 152 EC (health policy), Case T-13/99 *Pfizer Animal Health v Council*, paras 113–25 and the cases in n 367, above.

The Commission must take account of the policy-linking clauses, as well as the teleological approach in its decisions, otherwise it risks sanction by the Community Courts.[385] If the arrangement does not achieve the right balance, then the Community Courts could declare any Commission decision allowing the arrangement void, Article 230 EC. The alternative would be for the parties to renegotiate the arrangement until it was such that a Commission decision allowing it could not be successfully challenged.

Regulation 1/2003 allows for the Member States' courts and competition authorities to apply Articles 81 and 82 EC in their entirety.[386] When national courts take Article 81 EC decisions they cannot take decisions which are already the subject of a Commission decision and are counter to the Commission's position;[387] they must also avoid giving decisions which would run counter to a decision contemplated by the Commission.[388] This is in line with the Member States' courts' obligations under Article 10 EC.[389] Given that the Commission is bound to apply the policy-linking clauses in its Article 81 EC decisions, so must the Member States' courts (as they had to in *Defrenne*) and the national competition authorities.[390]

Under Regulation 17 the Commission had exclusive competence to consider Article 81(3) EC, subject to an Article 230 EC action to the CFI/ECJ.[391] The Commission sees the decentralisation of Article 81 EC enforcement as a key part of its modernisation agenda;[392] and seems to believe that it is vital that Article 81(3) EC is directly effective if decentralisation is to work. In 1999, the Commission started to try to alter the substantive scope of Article 81 EC, arguing that public policy criteria had no place within it.[393] This was probably intended to make Article 81(3) EC more amenable to direct effect, ie to make it more clear, precise and unconditional.[394]

A Council regulation cannot make a Treaty provision directly effective if it is not;[395] nor can it alter the substantive scope of Article 81(1) or (3) EC.[396] There is some debate about whether Article 81(3) EC is directly effective; some say it is not[397] and others say it is.[398] I

---

[385]   Reg 1/2003, recital 33. See also, Kapteyn and VerLoren van Themaat (1998) 1085; Psychogiopoulou (2006) 585; Winter (2003) 4–13; Komninos (2005) 17; Jacobs (1993/2) 48 and Dhondt (2003) 176, 177.

[386]   Recital 4 and arts 1, 5, 6, Reg 1/2003. Semmelmann (2008) 45, 46, argues that these provisions do not allow the regular importation of non-economic goals into Art 81 EC. If true, I believe that Reg 1/2003 is ultra vires, for the reasons set out below.

[387]   Reg 1/2003 art 16(1).

[388]   See also recitals 17–22, 38 and arts 3, 11, 15, 16.

[389]   Case C-344/98 *Masterfoods v HB Ice Cream* paras 49–60.

[390]   See Winter (2003) 16, 17.

Dhondt argues that there may be an obligation for Member States to protect the environment, via Arts 3(l), 6 and 10 EC: Dhondt (2003) 36, 37.

[391]   Reg 17, art 9(1).

[392]   Wesseling (2001) 357.

[393]   Apparently in favour, Semmelmann (2008) 39–46.

[394]   See n 9, above which shows the change in the Commission's policy statements on the relevance of public policy in Art 81, between 1996 and 2004.

[395]   Case 127/73 *Belgische Radio en Televisie v SV SABAM and NV Fonior* paras 16, 17 and Case 48/72 *Brasserie de Haecht v Wilkin-Janssen* para 6. See also Mestmäcker (2001) 227–32; Wesseling (2001) 368 and Gustafsson (2000) 170–2.

[396]   *Société Technique Minière* p 248, this only refers to Art 81(1), but the same applies to 81(3) EC.

[397]   See, eg Mestmäcker (2001) 229–32; Siragusa in Ehlermann (2001) 44; Gustafsson (2000) 164–72 and Wesseling (1999) 424, 425.

[398]   See, eg Marenco (2001) 145; Tesauro in Ehlermann (2001) 37, 263 and Forrester and Norall (1984) 20.

believe that Article 81(3) is probably directly effective.[399] However, if for some reason the Community Courts found that it were not possible for the national courts to apply public policy requirements within their Article 81 EC judgments, when the Commission had to, then this would mean that Article 81(3) EC is not directly effective. The Commission does not have the power to alter the substantive content of Article 81 EC in order to make it more amenable to direct effect. If Article 81(3) EC is not directly effective, rather than trying to amend the substantive scope of Article 81(3) EC until it is, the proper route is to declare the provisions in Regulation 1/2003[400] which declare Article 81(3) EC directly effective, to be at fault; they must give way in the face of a higher Treaty norm.[401]

If Article 81(3) EC is not directly effective, one may have to return to some sort of prior notification system instead, that is, what took place under Regulation 17.[402] In fact, a meeting of the full Commission seems like an ideal environment in which to balance competing public policy goals within Article 81 EC, given the different portfolios that the Commissioners represent.[403]

In light of the explicit wording of the policy-linking clauses, as well as the importance of the goals they promote in the hierarchy of Treaty objectives, the public policy objectives they pursue should be considered in Article 81 EC decisions. This remains the case today. It may be that this balancing exercise is not sufficiently clear and precise to be directly effective (although this seems unlikely) but this merely means that the provisions in Regulation 1/2003 declaring Article 81(3) EC to be directly effective, would be *ultra vires*; it does not mean that public policy should be ignored in the Article 81 EC assessment.

3.2.2 Articles 2–4 EC

Odudu argues that as Articles 2–4 EC are incapable of direct effect it is inappropriate to use another provision (such as Article 81 EC) to indirectly create these rights and obligations. I disagree.

Techniques to aid in the interpretation of unclear provisions (for example, the meaning of 'restriction of competition' in Article 81(1) EC) are particularly important in international treaties with many original languages. The ECJ used the teleological approach to help it with this in 1966;[404] it was still necessary for the CFI to revert to this technique in 2006.[405]

---

[399] Whether the consideration of public policy goals within Art 81 EC means there is so much discretion that that provision cannot be directly effective does not seem in line with many other provisions that are directly effective where public policy has been considered; see, eg, Art 81(1) EC, *Wouters*. Arts 28 and 30 (free movement of goods) and 39 EC (free movement of workers) are also directly effective. This is despite the fact that between Arts 28 and 30 and Arts 39(1) and (3) EC there needs to be a balancing of the free movement 'right' and various policy areas, such as public security and public health. A similar point arises in relation to the mandatory requirements, See, eg Case C-379/98 *PreussenElektra v Schleswag* paras 69–80; see the comments of Tesauro and Marenco on this issue Ehlermann (2001) 37–9. See also, Schweitzer (2007) 10 (although she believes the legal framework in these cases (and Art 86(2) EC) has been comparatively clearly circumscribed, in a similar vein, Gilliams (2006) 326); Idot (2003) 294–97; Winter (2003) 18, 19; Dhondt (2003), 178 and Commission, *Environmental State aid Guidelines* (2008), para 18.

[400] Reg 1/2003 recital 4 and arts 1, 5, 6.

[401] Baquero Cruz (2002) 63, 64.

[402] See Schweitzer (2007) 11–15 for other suggestions.

[403] Ellis (1963) 271–8 and COM(96) 721 final, para 191.

[404] The *Consten Grundig* Case pp 345, 346.

[405] Case T-168/01 *GlaxoSmithKline Services v Commission*, esp para 91 *ff.*

The Community Courts regularly use Articles 2–4 EC, to help them interpret other Treaty provisions too. For example, in *Defrenne* the ECJ held that the question of the direct effect of Article 141 EC '… must be considered in the light of the nature of the principle of equal pay, the aim of this provision and its place in the scheme of the Treaty'.[406]

The ECJ goes on to examine, amongst other things, the Preamble of the Treaty, in order to shed light on the later Treaty provisions. The ECJ does a similar thing with Article 2 EC, interpreting the implementing provisions through that lens.[407] In fact, this is what the teleological approach demands. This technique is used even though Articles 2–4 EC are not directly effective.[408]

But Ododu's claim about the 'inappropriateness of using Article 81 EC to indirectly create rights and obligations that are not themselves directly effective' may be a bigger one. Is the point that the teleological approach is itself wrong? The teleological approach has been criticised before, although many embrace it.[409]

Lack of space prevents a detailed analysis of this issue. Section 2 explains why conflicts will arise in Treaty interpretation. These must be dealt with somehow. The removal of the teleological approach would involve a radical shift in the Community Courts' main strategy for legal reasoning in hard cases. It would also create significant difficulties in a multi-lingual organisation such as the European Union.[410]

A key argument used for the removal of the teleological approach is that, while it may be acceptable in times of political stagnation, it is inappropriate when the impasse created by legislative inertia is repaired.[411] But this assumes that the only justification for this methodological approach is an impasse; yet, there are many other reasons for public policy balancing in Article 81 EC, such as ensuring that firms participate in society as moral actors, limits on legislative time, achieving a better balance, etc.[412]

A second assumption is that (today) we are in a normalised environment, so the teleological approach is no longer necessary. True, legislation can be more easily adopted to achieve environmental and other public policy goals than before. But, for example, expansion of the European Union causes other legislative delays. If it was appropriate to use the teleological approach when delays were experienced in the past, it may be acceptable to do the same today. Indeed, some might even question whether there can ever be a normalised environment. They believe that our journey towards an 'ever closer union of the peoples' is never ending, or at least that we have not got there yet.[413] The teleological approach is an important method of transport.

---

[406] Case 43/75 *Gabrielle Defrenne v SABENA*, para 7.

[407] See also, Case C-9/99 *Échirolles Distribution v Association du Dauphiné* para 22; the Opinion of A-G Alber paras 25–28, 32–34, stating that Arts 3 and 4 '… have direct legal effect only in conjunction with those [implementing] provisions.' It might also be said that the ECJ does a similar thing with the policy-linking clause (Art 6 EC) in Case C-379/98 *PreussenElektra v Schleswag*.

[408] Ododu notes that Art 2 EC cannot in and of itself impose legal obligations on Member States or confer rights on individuals: Case 126/86 *Fernando Zaera v INSS* para 11. See also, Case C-339/89 *Alsthom Atlantique v Compagnie de construction mécanique Sulzer* paras 8, 9.

[409] See Craig and de Búrca (2008) 74, for further references.

[410] Bobek (2008) 9, 10.

[411] Rasmussen (1986) 62–4 and Ododu (2006) 167.

[412] See also, Cappelletti (1987).

[413] *How Divided Europe Came Together*, BBC News, 23/3/2007 <http://news.bbc.co.uk/go/pr/fr/-/1/hi/world/europe/6483585.stm> accessed 27 April 2009; Hartley (1996) 107–9 and Mancini and Keeling (1994) 186.

Furthermore, if the teleological approach were removed,[414] it may be difficult to justify reliance on principles developed using the teleological approach in past decisions. Many of the founding principles of Community law are based upon a combination of a teleological and contextual approach, not least of which include supremacy and direct effect itself.[415] Odudu might argue that where provisions relate to Member States then the approach is possible, but the functional approach seems inconsistent with such arguments.

In conclusion, the teleological approach helps the Community Courts infuse Treaty provisions with meaning even today. This (indirectly) creates both rights and obligations for private actors, even where the provisions themselves are not directly effective. This approach is imperative in the Community legal order. Once again, it may be (although this chapter does not embrace such a position) that this means that Article 81 EC itself is not directly effective in its entirety; but this would imply that Regulation 1/2003 is at fault, not the consideration of public policy goals within Article 81(3) EC.

3.2.3 Reflections

Ultimately, there seems to be a deeper issue at stake here. This is whether decision-makers should go about their business in a joined up way, considering a variety of goals within Article 81 EC (and other Treaty articles), or only one goal. At the extreme, this is a conflict between achieving the perfect Treaty balance (with the effects this has on legal certainty), or being clear and transparent, but not achieving precisely what is wanted in the one decision.[416]

The Treaty and many Institutions have already decided that they would prefer an integrated approach. This does not mean that competition provisions are used to achieve everything; there are limits to the notion. It is perfectly respectable to take a normative stance against this, but such a position requires re-writing the Treaty and over-turning one of the most fundamental principles of Community law. A fundamental constitutional shift of this nature demands a full public debate.

The Treaty has many objectives. These include economic and social cohesion, environmental protection, public health, consumer protection, industrial policy and culture.

Regardless of whether Articles 2–4 EC are directly effective, it is appropriate to interpret the later (implementing) Treaty articles in the light of them. There is still a need for teleological interpretation; in particular, in an ever expanding European Union, based on subsidiarity, where powers are constantly shifting. This approach is also in line with Article 2 EC's plea for '… a harmonious and balanced and sustainable development of economic activities …' The argument is even stronger with the policy-linking clauses; and, it should not be forgotten that the tendency to insert policy-linking clauses is increasing with each Treaty amendment.

It is unlikely that we will see the Community Courts reversing their teleological approach, in relation to competition law, anytime soon. Even if the teleological approach were abandoned, the policy-linking clauses still explicitly demand the consideration of seven public policy areas within, amongst others, competition policy, and the Lisbon Treaty goes even further.

---

[414]   Section 2.1.1 pointed to evidence of the teleological approach being enshrined within the Lisbon Treaty.
[415]   Respectively, Case 6/64 *Costa Flaminio v ENEL* and the *van Gend en Loos* Case. See also Case C-438/05 *International Transport Workers' Federation and Others v Viking Line ABP and Others* para 58.
[416]   See Ch 1, Section 3.

If this means that Article 81 EC is not directly effective, then this has repercussions for Regulation 1/2003. But we should not put the cart before the horse, seeking to overturn fundamental Community norms in light of secondary legislation.

3.3 The intended relationship between Treaty provisions

Competition is important in the Community legal order. The circumstances in which Article 81 EC can be sacrificed for other socially desirable goals must be expressly stated and clearly specified.[417] The Treaty does so only on narrowly defined grounds. There have been many Community Court cases where one of the parties argued that competition law should not apply to their area of activity (for example, insurance, patent agents or co-operatives) because of the disruption it would cause. Unsurprisingly, the Community Courts have proved reluctant to allow competition to be trumped (excluded) outside of these limits.[418] Odudu argues:

> It should … be recalled that where the Treaty intended to remove certain activities from the ambit of the competition rules, it made an express derogation to that effect.[419] The circumstances in which Article 81 can be sacrificed for some other socially desirable goal must be expressly stated and clearly specified … In enacting Article 86(2) EC there is recognition of 'a point to which the Treaty rules, particularly competition law, can be excluded.[420] Article 36 EC and Article 296(1)(b) EC also provide express derogation, allowing Article 81 to be trumped in pursuit of other goals. If it were legitimate to balance competing goals within Article 81 these provisions would be otiose.[421]

I largely agree with this quotation up until the last sentence. A distinction must be made between balancing and exclusion/trumping. Articles 36,[422] 86(2) and 296(1)(b) EC allow for the Article 81 EC to be *excluded* (ignored), under certain limited circumstances. Article 81 EC cannot be applied within these limited areas. But this is quite different from what was suggested above, when discussing *balancing* public policy goals within Article 81 EC (where they are *balanced* against the competition benefits (and losses)). To be clear, competition is not excluded in balancing, it is taken into account.[423] Therefore, the statement that balancing within Article 81 EC makes Articles 36, 86(2) and 296(1)(b) EC otiose, may go too far.

Having said that, it is extremely difficult to balance competition and the various public policy goals within Article 81 EC.[424] Part of the problem is that the Treaty does not give

---

[417]   Odudu (2006) 169.

[418]   Although they have allowed competition to be excluded; one example is the *Albany* Case.

[419]   Case T-61/89 *Dansk Pelsdyravlerforening v Commission* para 54. See also, Case T-144/99 *Institute of Professional Representatives before the European Patent Office v Commission* para 67 and Joined Cases 209–213/84 *Ministère public v Lucas Asjes* paras 40–42.

[420]   Auricchio (2001) 78.

[421]   Odudu (2006) 169. Odudu also makes some points about conflicts between Member State goals and Community goals; and between Community goals. Please also see Ch 7.

[422]   In combination with Council Regulation (EC) 1184/2006, *applying certain rules of competition to the production of, and trade in, agricultural products*, [2006] OJ L214/7.

[423]   Art 81(3)(b) EC emphasises that the undertakings concerned must not be afforded the possibility of eliminating competition in respect of a substantial part of the products in question.

[424]   Although the ECJ and national courts constantly do this, eg, with the free movement rules.

much guidance on the weight of the different policies within it and how conflicts between them should be resolved. This issue is discussed elsewhere.[425]

4 CONCLUSION

This chapter set out to answer two questions: in a Community context, is the influence of public policy objectives within Article 81 warranted? and, given its continued importance under Regulation 1/2003, what is the Commission's view about the place of such objectives within that provision?

Both the structure of the Treaty and the presence of the policy-linking clauses create the possibility of conflicts in Community law; these conflicts change over time, as does the 'optimal balance' between different objectives. The Treaty normally prefers compromise, but sometimes it is silent. The Community Courts have had to fill these gaps; while doing so, they had to choose between exclusion and compromise. In the vast majority of cases, including those related to Article 81 EC, they have chosen compromise; this was the case in the past, as it is today.

The Community Courts have facilitated the work of Article 81 decision-makers by interpreting Article 81(3) very widely. All Community public interest issues can probably now be taken into account there and certainly the objectives set out in the policy-linking clauses. This allows the decision-maker to aim at an 'optimal balance' of the relevant objectives in each case. In a Community context, this is the right approach to take.

Monti argues that what is missing from Community competition law is an authoritative statement on competition policy's role. He contrasts this with section 1 of Canada's Competition Act, cited in Chapter 1.[426] However, if the Treaty hierarchy and the policy-linking clauses impact upon Article 81's interpretation, as I suggest, then Article 2 EC and the Preamble to the Treaty already contain an authoritative statement on the role of Community competition policy, or at least its goals. Monti is certainly right, however, to point to a lack of clarity (and consistency) in this area; certainly the list of policy objectives is not closed, and the balance between them changes over time.

These problems are exacerbated, because the Commission does not always accept the relevance of public policy at all; it creates a lot of ambiguity by publicly implying (in many policy statements) that such concerns are irrelevant in Article 81 decision-making (although it is not consistent here). The Commission is not able to make such a policy change alone, as it is bound by the Treaty and the Community Courts' judgments. Even more confusingly, in practice, the Commission generally follows the Community Courts' lead in its Article 81 decisions, often considering public policy objectives.

Section 3 discussed some objections to including public policy within Article 81 EC. First, *the jurisdictional argument*—the claim that there is a public/private divide in the Treaty and that public policy can only be considered in relation to state acts because states have democratic legitimacy and so act in the public interest. This position is incompatible

---

[425] See Ch 8, pointing out that, eg, Arts 2–4 EC and the policy-linking clauses provide some (limited) assistance in this regard. For an interesting attempt at dealing with similar conflicts, see the UK's Communications Act 2003 s 3.

[426] Monti (2007) 19.

with a functional approach to the definition of an undertaking. I have more faith (than Odudu) that private actors act in the public interest and I place more emphasis on outcomes. Also discussed is the idea of *direct effect through the back door*—the argument that it is inappropriate to create rights and obligations for private actors through Article 81 EC, for provisions (such as Article 2 EC and the policy-linking clauses) which Odudu believes are not directly effective. This view is contrary to the Community Courts' teleological approach and I disagree with it. Even if I were incorrect on this issue, the result should be that Article 81 EC is not directly effective and not that public policy should be irrelevant there. Also advanced is the argument of *the intended relationship between Treaty provisions*—a series of Treaty provisions have explicitly excluded the application of Article 81 EC in certain areas. The Community Courts have been reluctant to extend these areas. Some argue that these explicit Treaty provisions would be otiose if public policy goals were considered within Article 81 EC. I disagree, there is a difference between *ignoring* competition in these tightly defined areas and considering competition and *balancing* it against public policy goals.

The Treaty has many objectives; these include economic and social cohesion, environmental protection, public health, consumer protection, industrial policy and culture. Competition lawyers often focus solely on their area, forgetting the context of the rules that they apply.[427] This is a mistake.[428] In the words of former Competition Commissioner van Miert:

> Competition policy has so long been a central Community policy that it is often forgotten that it is not an end in itself but rather one of the instruments towards the fundamental goals laid out in the Treaty—namely the establishment of a common market, the approximation of economic policy, the promotion of harmonious development and economic expansion, the increase of living standards and the bringing about of closer relationship between Member States. Competition therefore cannot be understood or applied without reference to this legal, economic, political and social context.[429]

The Treaty tries to achieve its aims using a variety of tools; one of these, an important one, is competition law; but, as with all systems of governance, conflicts arise between objectives.[430] The Treaty itself balances competition considerations against other basic goals both within and without the Treaty provisions on competition. The highest court of appeal in this system, the ECJ, regularly hears cases in all areas of the Treaty. The ECJ seeks to 'find' a system for the Treaty, taking into account, where relevant, non-economic rules and objectives too;[431] as competition lawyers we must do the same.

---

[427]   Gerber (1994) 99, 100.

[428]   Bengoetxea, MacCormick, and Moral Soriano (2001) 47. See also the *Albany* Case para 60 and van der Esch (1991).

[429]   van Miert (1993) 120.

[430]   Toggenburg (2003) 10.

[431]   Judge Edwards talking about the ECJ's method of legal reasoning, Edward (1996) 66–67.

Conclusion of Part A

Part A asked whether antitrust laws should consider public policy objectives outside of welfare. It did this from two perspectives. Chapter 1 was a theoretical analysis in a legal vacuum, asking whether it is rational to consider non-economic objectives within competition policy. Chapter 2 changed the emphasis, examining the question within the context of a specific legal system, Community competition law's Article 81 EC.

Chapter 1 asked why competition policy might incorporate non-welfare objectives. This was relatively easy to answer. Competition laws often have a welfare objective. I showed that all welfare standards are value-laden and advocated the consumer welfare standard. However, I went on to demonstrate that a competition law's pursuit of consumer welfare can affect public policy objectives. I argued that allowing competition policy to take account of these interactions means that a better balance can be attained overall. Nevertheless, if public policy goals are incorporated into competition policy it is vital that the relevance of public policy in competition policy is acknowledged upfront and it is incumbent on the regulators to make balancing as rational, transparent and open as possible.

Given this conclusion, a second issue arose, when should competition policy consider non-welfare objectives? While, it is difficult to agree abstract theoretical limits on when one should intervene in specific cases, I suggested some possible filters.

Let us start with tests for when public policy issues should not be considered in the competition assessment. I suggest three. First, one should only balance public policy where there is a reduction in consumer welfare. In other words, only where there is a competition problem should one use competition law to achieve public policy goals. Secondly, where the agreement's qualitative and/or quantitative impact on public policy goals is not appreciable then it should be ignored. Finally, one might also be less open to public policy balancing where the legislator has recently intervened in the specific balance, or explicitly decided not to, because it thought the current balance was appropriate.

In other cases, where the legal context demands it, public policy balancing should take place. There, the entity performing the balancing exercise must consider, in the legal and economic context, the impact upon competition and weigh this against the impact upon other relevant public policy goal(s). However, one should be sceptical about any claimed public policy effects. I argued that these should either be costed in some way, or at the least be supported by some widely accepted theoretical model.

Nevertheless, Chapter 2 shows why these limits may not be appropriate in a Community competition law context. Both the structure of the Treaty and the presence of (an ever-increasing number of) policy-linking clauses create the possibility of conflicts in Community law. The Treaty normally prefers compromise (balancing) to resolve these, but sometimes it is silent. The Community Courts have had to fill the gaps. When the Community Courts construe particular Treaty articles they have regard to the framework of the Treaty as a whole, to its general principles and to the tasks and activities which the Treaty prescribes for the Community. In the vast majority of cases, including those related to Article 81, the Community Courts have also chosen compromise to resolve these conflicts. Article 81 (and competition policy as a whole) is not an end in itself but rather one of the instruments for achieving the Treaty's fundamental goals. Community competition provisions cannot be understood or applied without reference to this legal, economic, political and social context. The Community Courts interpret Article 81 broadly and many public interest issues can now be considered within it. This includes those protected by the policy-linking clauses, as well as those promoted in the Preamble, Article 2 EC, etc. The European Parliament and the Council have explicitly supported this approach.

Against this trend, the Commission has created ambiguity by implying that public policy concerns are irrelevant in Article 81 decision-making. It is not able to make such a policy change as it is bound by the Treaty and the Community Courts' judgments. That said, in practice, the Commission seems to be following the Community Courts' lead in its decisions and often considers public policy goals there.

Chapter 1 and 2's conclusions are somewhat different. Chapter 1 argues that the consideration of non-welfare objectives is warranted, but only under strict conditions. Chapter 2 reveals a Treaty and Community institutions that more readily embrace the balancing of these objectives within competition law.[1]

There are many reasons why Community competition law does not correspond to Chapter 1's theoretical framework. Briefly put, the Treaty was designed, and has since been amended, by politicians. They must 'sell' this 'product' to their heterogeneous constituencies:

> The policy-makers try to maximise their election or re-election probabilities. This fundamental objective implies satisfying powerful interest groups, but also keeping an eye on the general interest, or at least the perception that the majority of voters could have of the major decisions.[2]

The short-term benefits of this approach are more apparent than the long-term costs. Furthermore, legislators often balance competing objectives when legislating. They may not recognise the potential costs involved. There may also be a touch of political expediency in allowing politicians to promote many policy goals while sheltering under the umbrella of 'promoting competition'. Finally, for political reasons it would have been very difficult for the administrators of Community competition policy, the Community Courts and the Commission, to ignore other policies.[3]

The 'attacks' on the consideration of multiple objectives within competition policy have been largely influenced by neo-classical economists.[4] Their arguments often ignore the legal context into which these rules must be placed. The Commission and the Community Courts do not have this luxury. They are bound by the system that the politicians built. Perhaps another factor is at play as well? Competition laws (and the consumer welfare

---

[1]   The discussion about the other limits of the balance confirms this, Ch 4, Section 3 and Part C.

[2]   Laussel and Montet (1995) 57.

[3]   Buigues, Jacquemin and Sapir (1995a) xii and Laussel and Montet (1995) 50.

[4]   For example, Gual (1995) 23, writes that the policy-linking clauses, particularly Art 159 EC on economic and social cohesion '… provides a major source of inefficiencies in EC policy-making, to the extent that this equity or redistribution mandate constrains the formulation of policies in all domains and gives rise to the inefficient use of policy instruments.' See also page 39 of the same chapter.

imperative) can affect many policy objectives. This effect is reciprocal. It is easy to implement an appreciability doctrine where these affects are small. However, outside of this, balancing disparate policy goals through different pieces of legislation is extremely difficult because it is hard to develop general rules which achieve an optimal balance in all areas. The neo-classical economists' recommendations often ignore these difficulties. Although legal certainty is undermined, where important objectives are at stake it is often easier to find the optimal balance on a case-by-case basis.[5] Easier, at least for the politicians. But, as I have said, they design the system.

Given this divergence, what solutions can be found? There is some flexibility within the Community competition law system and Part C of this book suggests ways of incorporating Chapter 1's policy recommendations within the Community legal order, to the extent that this is possible. Unless the Treaty is to be fundamentally re-written little more can be done. Before making these recommendations, it would be helpful to examine how and where these policy objectives are currently considered in Article 81. This is Part B's role.

---

[5] This is aided by the use of impact assessments which seek to ensure that the effects on different policy areas are correctly assessed, see Ch 8.

Part B

How and Where is Public Policy Balancing Performed in Article 81 EC?

Introduction to Part B

This book has three objectives. Part A argued that, while not perfectly in line with economic theory, the Treaty, as interpreted by the Community Courts, demands that non-economic objectives should be considered within Article 81 EC. This is supported by both the Council and the European Parliament. Recent Treaty amendments increase the need for this balancing.

Chapter 2 showed the Commission recently stating that consumer welfare is the sole goal of Article 81. This presumably leaves little room for public policy goals that do not also bring efficiency benefits. However, Chapter 2 demonstrated that both the Treaty and the Community Courts demand the inclusion of public policy benefits in Article 81 EC; and that, despite what it says in its guidelines, the Commission has often considered public policy in its Article 81 decisions too. Given this fact, and the fact that Commission, *Article 81(3) Guidelines*, claim not to alter Article 81's substantive scope (as indeed they could not), then I assume that the Commission's recent statements do not in fact change the substance of Article 81.

As public policy goals are relevant in Article 81 EC, one naturally asks where they should be considered and how this will occur. It is Part B's job, and this book's second objective, to analyse how and where non-economic objectives have been considered within Article 81; as well as where the balance lies between different objectives within that provision.

I argue that non-economic objectives are considered within Article 81 EC via two mechanisms. I call the first mechanism 'mere-balancing'. Mere-balancing operates *outside* of the consumer welfare assessment. By this I mean that the decision-maker first assesses an agreement's effect on consumer welfare and then balances this against its impact upon relevant public policy objectives.[1] Chapters 3 and 4 deal with mere-balancing in relation to Article 81(1) and (3), respectively.[2]

Chapter 5 argues that there is a second mechanism for considering non-economic objectives within Article 81 EC; I call this market-balancing. Market-balancing occurs *within* the consumer welfare test itself, by altering the importance of its various components.[3] For example, in the consumer welfare analysis, by placing less weight on allocative efficiency losses and more weight on dynamic efficiency gains one can encourage R&D advances, which might generate industrial policy benefits.

---

[1] Mere-balancing, as a mechanism, is explained in more detail on Ch 1, Section 2.2.2.

[2] Chs 3 and 4 consider a selection of Treaty objectives. Each discussion starts with a brief analysis of the specific objectives under consideration. A brief discussion is sufficient because this book analyses the balancing mechanism in general, rather than specific policies in particular. For those who require more detailed explanations of such policies: see Moussis (2003) and Collège d'Europe (1998), as well as the references that can be found there and in the relevant chapters below.

[3] Market-balancing, as a mechanism, is explained in more detail on Ch 1, Section 2.2.1.

There are four main reasons why I focus on how and where non-economic objectives have been considered within Article 81, as well as where the balance lies between different objectives within that provision. First, to further show that non-economic objectives are relevant within Article 81.[4]

Secondly, former Commissioner Monti, rightly to my mind, regularly emphasised the need for greater transparency in Community competition law.[5] Transparency is related to legal certainty. Balancing is a complex process, but decision-makers can make it more transparent by explaining where balancing takes place, how it is conducted and what the limits of the balance are. Transparency is important for undertakings.[6] It is also vital to provide clear guidelines for the Member States' courts and competition authorities which can now apply Article 81 in its entirety.[7] The shear quantity of decisions where public policy has been considered underlines the need for making this process as transparent as possible, including explaining any limits to the balance.

Thirdly, I also wanted to expose some other public policy balancing mechanisms. The idea that mere-balancing has taken place within Article 81(3) EC is reasonably uncontroversial. However, there is relatively little discussion about this within Article 81(1). This is important because of the different burden of proof under these two provisions;[8] as well as the further cumulative tests that one needs to get through under Article 81(3), which are not present in Article 81(1) EC. In other words, not only does mere-balancing occur in places where we are not accustomed to look for it; but the outcome of this balance may be affected by where mere-balancing takes place. As a result, I wanted to shed more light on balancing within Article 81(1). Furthermore, there is also little or no discussion about market-balancing as a concept in the legal literature. I seek to shine the light on this practice too.[9]

Finally, this book's third objective is to suggest how and where the balancing process *should* best be conducted, Part C does this. I split this issue out from the discussion of how Article 81 is currently interpreted in order to increase the transparency of my critique. As a result, Part B's discussion of how and where the balance is conducted is relatively descriptive. That said, it highlights many issues which must be considered in Part C and provides analysis to support the later debate.

---

[4] The details provided in Part B reinforce Ch 2's arguments in this regard.
[5] See, eg Commission, *RCP 2000* 8, 9.
[6] Ch 1, Section 3.2.1.
[7] Reg 1/2003, art 3(1).
[8] ibid art 2.
[9] Many of the cases, decisions and policy statements discussed in Part B are older than I might like. This is because, post modernisation, the Commission has changed the direction of its policy announcements in relation to the relevance of public policy in Art 81 EC, see Ch 2, Section 2.3. Furthermore, the way that the Commission now chooses what decisions to take means that it is principally focusing on cartel cases of late, where public policy arguments tend not to be raised. However, we have seen that recent Community Court judgments show that public policy is still relevant in Art 81 and even recent Commission decisions refer to it on occasion.

3

How the Balance is Implemented – Mere-Balancing in Article 81(1) EC

1 INTRODUCTION

Chapter 2 argued that public policy considerations are relevant in Article 81 EC. This begs the question of where these issues are considered within this article and how they are taken into account. This chapter focuses on public policy balancing/compromise in Article 81(1), specifically mere-balancing. Mere-balancing is, essentially, balancing public policy goals outside of the economic efficiency assessment.[1]

Some believe that if public policy balancing takes place, it should occur within Article 81(3) EC. Faull and Nikpay state, for example, that while public policy goals are considered under Article 81 they will only be relevant to policy considerations arising under Article 81(3), as they do not have any impact on the notion of restriction of competition for the purposes of Article 81(1).[2] The Commission seems to agree.[3]

---

[1] See Ch 1, Section 2.2. Ch 4 deals with mere-balancing in Art 81(3) EC and Ch 5 discusses market (internal) balancing throughout Art 81.

[2] Faull and Nikpay (2007), para 3.12, the focus there is cultural and environmental considerations, but their point probably covers other public policy goals too. See also, Whish (2008) 130, who hints at this; Vedder (2003) 157, 158; Monti (2002) 1059–62, 1069 *ff*; Hawk (2001) 304; Deckert (2000) 178, 179, for a brief summary of views; Forrester (1998) 380; Siragusa (1997) 285 and Vogelaar (1994) 531, 535, 543, 545.

[3] Commission, *Article 81(3) Guidelines*, para 42 says that goals pursued by other Treaty provisions can be taken into account to the extent that they can be subsumed under the four conditions of Art 81(3). Nothing is said about their consideration in Art 81(1) EC, even the *Wouters* Case is ignored there.

By way of contrast, Section 2 below shows that the Community Courts and the Commission also consider non-welfare objectives within Article 81(1) EC. The focus then shifts to two related issues: Section 3.1 looks at the limits of balancing within Article 81(1) and compares these limits with those in Article 81(3).[4] If compromise has different limits under Article 81(1), to those under Article 81(3), then it matters where balancing takes place. Secondly, and related to the last point, Section 3.2 asks why balancing occurs in Article 81(1) when Article 81(3) seems more appropriate.

Chapter 3 cannot provide definitive answers to these questions, due to the paucity of relevant decisions and the lack of clarity within those that exist. Nevertheless, it hopes to provide a helpful step on the road to transparency.[5]

2 COMPROMISE WITHIN ARTICLE 81(1) EC

The Community Courts and the Commission have considered non-welfare goals within Article 81(1) EC. Recent precedents confirm that this is still correct today. For example, in *Wouters* (2003) the ECJ balanced the proper practice of the legal profession against a restriction of competition.[6] Similarly, in *Meca-Medina* (2006), the ECJ considered equal chances for athletes, athletes' health, the integrity and objectivity of competitive sport and ethical values in its Article 81(1) assessment.[7]

Section 2.1 discusses the use of non-welfare goals in Article 81(1) by focusing on the market integration goal; Section 2.2 deals with environmental protection. Market integration and environmental protection have been selected as they illustrate several points of interest; in addition, the case law is more developed for them than for other factors.[8]

2.1 Market integration

Section 2.1.1 asks what market integration means and investigates why it is pursued and Section 2.1.2 asks the same of economic efficiency.[9] Understanding why these objectives are pursued helps one assess when (if) conflicts arise between them and to better deal with them when (if) they do. Finally, Section 2.1.3 analyses the Article 81(1) EC balance between market integration and economic efficiency. Where agreements restrict market

---

[4] For example, can one eliminate competition in the Art 81(1) balance, something which Art 81(3) EC expressly forbids.

[5] Ch 6 makes some policy recommendations based upon the observations made here.

[6] The *Wouters* Case (2003) is a decision of the ECJ's Grand Chamber, and so it is probably wrong to dismiss Art 81(1) balancing merely as an unconsidered whim, Forrester and Siragusa in Ehlermann (2006), respectively at pp 182 and 202, and Gilliams (2006) 322.

[7] Commission, *Article 81(3) Guidelines*, do not refer to the *Wouters* Case in this context at all; nor do they refer to *Meca Medina*, but that is unsurprising as the guidelines came out before that judgment.

[8] Other public policy goals have also been balanced within Art 81(1) EC. These include: (a) the dignity and rules of conduct of representatives before the European Patent Office, Case T-144/99, *IPRs before the EPO v Commission*; and (b) the integrity of UEFA club competitions, Commission Communication, *UEFA rule on 'integrity'* (1999), para 10.

[9] I assume that some form of economic efficiency is considered in Art 81(1), the *Glaxo* Case para 118, now on appeal. There is a lot of debate about what this might be, see, eg Odudu (2006) ch 5, but this is not important for the present discussion.

integration, as defined by the Community Courts, they risk breaching Article 81(1). In the light of the recent *Glaxo* Case, I start by discussing whether there is a conflict between economic efficiency and market integration at all. I believe that they do conflict, so I go on to ask whether an agreement which restricts market integration can be 'saved' within Article 81(1) if it enhances economic efficiency.[10]

2.1.1 Market integration

This section has three aims. It underlines the importance of market integration; it makes explicit the confusion about why market integration is pursued; and it highlights the formalism with which the market integration criterion is applied. All three issues help us understand when conflicts exist between market integration and other relevant goals and what weight market integration might have in case of conflict.

The Treaty's Preamble resolves to eliminate the barriers dividing Europe. The Commission has called market integration an objective of Community competition policy.[11] The Community Courts also consider market integration important. In the *Consten and Grundig* Case, a German television manufacturer, Grundig, promised Consten that neither it, nor any of Grundig's other distributors, would sell either directly or indirectly in France. Grundig made this promise to encourage Consten to become its French distributor. The ECJ held that such a clause breached Article 81 EC:

> [A]n agreement between producer and distributor which might tend to restore the national divisions in trade between Member States might be such as to frustrate the most fundamental objectives of the Community. The Treaty, whose preamble and content aim at abolishing the barriers between States, and which in several provisions gives evidence of a stern attitude with regard to their reappearance, could not allow undertakings to reconstruct such barriers. Article 85(1) [now Article 81(1)] is designed to pursue this aim …[12]

Market integration has been a key Article 81(1) objective,[13] but I want to understand why it is being pursued. This should help assessing whether conflicts exist between market integration and other Article 81 objectives. Moreover, where they do conflict, it will help me to gauge where the balance should lie between the conflicting goals.

Market integration helps achieve the single market. Prohibitions on imports and exports jeopardise the freedom of intra-Community trade, a fundamental Treaty principle, and they prevent the attainment of a single market.[14] Five reasons have recently been given for pursuit of the single market.[15] Some say it helps integrate the Member States'

---

[10]   If they cannot be 'saved' within Art 81(1), then balancing can take place in Art 81(3). Ch 4 considers this kind of balancing between Art 81(1) and (3). This chapter focuses on the balance *within* Art 81(1) EC.

[11]   Commission, *Vertical Guidelines*, para 7; although the later Commission, *Article 81(3) Guidelines*, para 13 undermine the idea of market integration as a separate goal.

[12]   The *Consten and Grundig* Case, p 340. The Community Courts have reaffirmed this on numerous occasions, eg, Case 8/72 *Vereeniging van Cementhandelaren v Commission* para 29; Case T-9/92 *Automobiles Peugeot and Peugeot v Commission* para 42 and Case C-551/03 P *General Motors v Commission* paras 64–80.

[13]   For example, Wesseling (2000) ch 4; B&C (2008), para 1–074 and Ehlermann (1998).

[14]   Joined Cases 100–103/80 *SA Musique Diffusion Française v Commission* para 107. See also, Commission, *RCP 1994*, point 10 and *Rapport des Chefs de Délégation aux Ministre des Affaires étrangères* 16.

[15]   The single market is unlikely to be an aim in and of itself, Collège d'Europe (1998) 91.

markets;[16] others that it promotes economic freedom.[17] Some believe that either economic efficiency, or the development of trade, justifies the market integration goal; for example, the CFI held in the recent *Glaxo* Case:

> While it has been accepted since then [the *Consten and Grundig* Case] that parallel trade must be given a certain protection, *it is therefore not as such but*, as the Court of Justice held, *in so far as it favours the development of trade, on the one hand, and the strengthening of competition*, on the other hand ... that is to say, *in this second respect*, in so far as it gives final consumers the advantages of effective competition in terms of supply or price ... Consequently, while it is accepted that an agreement intended to limit parallel trade must in principle be considered to have as its object the restriction of competition, that applies in so far as the agreement may be presumed to deprive final consumers of those advantages.[18] (emphasis added)

Market integration has also been touted as a way of achieving consumer protection goals.[19] The Commission argues that barriers to economic integration in the Community are particularly heinous because they shield an entire Community industry from exposure to effective competition and because they make the European consumer pay the price for cosy industry arrangements.[20] These views are increasingly common in Commission decisions and notices.[21] Indeed, the Commission has even started to talk of a consumer *right* to buy anywhere in Europe.[22]

So, the Institutions are inconsistent in their justifications for pursuing the single market. Market integration is variously justified as increasing the integration of national markets, economic freedom, development of trade, economic efficiency and consumer protection. These goals sometimes overlap, but they can conflict.[23] This makes it hard to know whether/when there is a conflict between market integration and other objectives and what the outcome of the balance might be. This lack of clarity is still important today, despite the arguments of some,[24] the single market objective remains relevant while new states queue to join the EU.[25]

Furthermore, whatever the underlying rationale for pursuing it, market integration has often been applied formalistically, without assessing the arrangement's actual effect on the underlying goal (whichever goal(s) are relevant), in the legal and economic context.[26] In the *Consten and Grundig* Case, Advocate-General Roemer emphasised the possibility that

---

[16]   Joined Cases C-468/06 to C-478/06 *Sot Lelos kai Sia EE v GlaxoSmithKline* para 65.

[17]   Monti (2002) 1063.

[18]   The *Glaxo* Case para 121. This judgment is currently on appeal to the ECJ, see Joined Cases C-501/06 etc *GlaxoSmithKline Services v Commission*. The grounds have not all been clearly explained, see OJ 2007 C42/11–13, but the ECJ may deem it appropriate to pronounce on Art 81's goals.

[19]   Joined Cases C-468/06 to C-478/06 *Sot Lelos kai Sia EE v GlaxoSmithKline*, esp para 68.

[20]   Commission, *RCP 1991* 15.

[21]   Commission, *RCP 1992* 50; Commission, *Vertical Guidelines*, para 103(iv) and Commission decision, *Distribution System of Ford Werke AG*, para 43.

[22]   Commission, *RCP 1999*, point 53. See also, Verouden (2003) 530; Commission, *RCP 2000*, point 93 and Commission decisions, *VW*, para 189, and *Opel*, para 160.

[23]   See, eg Motta (2004) 23.

[24]   See Shelkoplyas (2003) 228; Wesseling (1998) 485; Amato (1997) 52; Pera and Todino (1996) 129; Forrester (1994) 460, 461 and Verstrynge (1984) 677.

[25]   Whish (2008) 22, 23. See also, Jones (2004) 18, 49; Monti (2002) 1092; Van den Bergh (2002) 36; Gerber (2001) 122 and Ehlermann (1998) x. The Commission and the Community Courts still turn to market integration in order to try to achieve/maintain the single market; see, eg Commission, *Vertical Guidelines*, para 7; Case T-77/92 *Parker Pen v Commission* and Case C-551/03 P *General Motors v Commission* paras 67–70.

[26]   Wesseling (2000) 87, 97, 98; Korah (1997) 5 and Korah (1986) 93, 94.

the *suppression* of the sole distributorship could reduce the supply of Grundig products on the French market and consequently produce an unfavourable influence on the conditions of competition existing there.[27] Prohibiting absolute territorial protection, he argued, might stand in the way of the integration of the various national markets.[28] In its judgment in this case the ECJ seems to object, in principle, to absolute territorial protection under Article 81(1).[29] The ECJ seemed to want to stop barriers to trade above all. It did not discuss Advocate-General Roemer's point that this might reduce market integration, nor did it accept that reductions in economic efficiency were relevant. Furthermore, this formalism cannot be more readily understood in light of the other objectives, such as consumer protection, that market integration might promote. Imposing such an obligation might undermine the supply of some goods into certain territories, surely undermining consumer protection, broadly defined.[30]

2.1.2 Economic efficiency

Economic efficiency is an important objective in Community competition law; the Commission has even called consumer welfare, Article 81's primary objective.[31] Many ECJ judgments hint at consumer welfare's importance in Article 81(1),[32] even if this has not always been the only relevant goal.[33] The CFI's recent judgment in the *Glaxo* Case explicitly highlights a consumer welfare goal, which suggests that even if economic freedom was relevant in the past, the CFI has a different view today.[34]

2.1.3 The balance

This section analyses the Article 81(1) EC balance between market integration and economic efficiency. Where agreements restrict market integration, as defined by the Community Courts, they risk breaching Article 81(1). In the light of the recent *Glaxo* Case, I start by discussing whether there is a conflict between economic efficiency and market integration at all. I believe that they do conflict (and they have certainly been treated in this way in the past), so I go on to ask whether an agreement which restricts market integration can be 'saved' within Article 81(1) if it enhances economic efficiency. I illustrate the balancing exercise by focusing on two types of territorial protection.

---

[27] The *Consten and Grundig* Case, pp 359 and 360–61, respectively.

[28] See also, Neven (1998) 117 and Heimler (1998) 335.

[29] This is not the same as a per se approach for the whole of Art 81 EC, because even if absolute territorial protection is an object restriction under Art 81(1), it can still be exempted under Art 81(3).

[30] See Art 153(1) EC.

[31] Commission, *Vertical Guidelines*, para 7. See also the other sources in Ch 1, n 3.

[32] For example, Case C-250/92 *Gøttrup-Klim Grovvareforening v Dansk Landbrugs Grovvareselskab*; Case 161/84 *Pronuptia de Paris v Irmgard Schillgalis*; Case 258/78 *Nungesser and Eisele v Commission* and Case C-234/89 *Delimitis v Henninger Bräu*. See also Odudu (2006) ch 5 and the references made there.

[33] Even some recent Community Court judgments imply that economic freedom, rather than economic efficiency, is the correct basis for intervention in Art 81(1); and that while economic efficiency concerns can properly be raised in the Art 81(3) analysis, they should not be considered within Art 81(1) EC at all, the *Meca-Medina* Case (2006) paras 42–45; the *Métropole Télévision* Case paras 74–78 and Case T-65/98, *Van den Bergh Foods v Commission* para 107. I assume this is what these cases say, although there is some debate on the issue, see Ch 6.

[34] See the text around Ch 2, n 18. Some argue that only part of the efficiency analysis is relevant in Art 81(1) EC; eg Commission, *Article 81(3) Guidelines*, paras 21–23, 32, 33, 48–72 and Odudu (2006) chs 5 and 6. I do not consider this argument here, see Ch 6, Section 2.3.

The first question is whether market integration and economic efficiency conflict. We saw above that, in the *Glaxo* Case, the CFI recently held that parallel trade must be protected, in so far as it favours the development of trade, on the one hand, and the strengthening of competition, on the other hand. That is to say, in this second respect, in so far as it gives final consumers the advantages of effective competition in terms of supply or price.[35] In other words, if the CFI's view is correct, agreements to limit parallel trade are only problematic insofar as they undermine consumer welfare.[36] If this is the right interpretation today,[37] then market integration and consumer welfare do not conflict, so they should not be balanced within Article 81(1) EC.

This would be a radical change. My own view is that, if it decides to pronounce on the issue in the *Glaxo* appeal, the ECJ is unlikely to find that consumer welfare is the only Article 81(1) goal, overturning its existing case law.[38] Market integration may often overlap, but does not always overlap, with consumer welfare.[39] The ECJ has consistently held that agreements which isolate national markets and preclude all cross-border trade automatically offend Article 81(1) EC.[40] In this way, the single market objective has had a special influence on the interpretation of what amounts to a restriction of competition for the purposes of Article 81(1).[41] I believe that the ECJ will find that market integration is a separate and additional Article 81(1) goal.[42]

On the assumption that a conflict remains between market integration and consumer welfare, I will now investigate where the balance lies between them. Pre *Glaxo* (2006), any attempt to impose absolute territorial protection through an agreement that appreciably[43] affects trade between Member States, was held to restrict competition for the purposes of Article 81(1) EC, however achieved.[44] For example, in *Tretorn and others*[45] agreements

---

[35]   The *Glaxo* Case para 121.

[36]   ibid, para 118 and Jones and Sufrin (2007) 231.

[37]   It should be pointed out, however, that the CFI's reference in *Glaxo* to 'development of trade' is unclear. It may add a second objective to Art 81(1), which could conflict with the consumer welfare goal. Although this seems unlikely in the light of the *Glaxo* Case para 118; some support for this position can be garnered from the more recent ECJ judgment in Joined Cases C-468/06 to C-478/06 *Sot Lelos kai Sia EE v GlaxoSmithKline* paras 65–68; also see the argument of A-G Jacobs para 70.

[38]   The *Glaxo* Case is currently on appeal. The grounds have not all been clearly explained, see OJ 2007 C42/11–13, but the ECJ may deem it appropriate to pronounce on Art 81 EC's goals.

[39]   Motta (2004) 23, shows that an absolute prohibition on absolute territorial protection would not always be justified on economic efficiency, consumer protection or integrationist grounds.

[40]   For example, Case 161/84 *Pronuptia de Paris v Irmgard Schillgalis*; Case T-77/92 *Parker Pen v Commission* and Case C-234/89 *Delimitis v Henninger Bräu*.

[41]   Jones and Sufrin (2007) 231.

[42]   Some support for this view can be garnered from the more recent ECJ judgment in Joined Cases C-468/06 to C-478/06 *Sot Lelos kai Sia EE v GlaxoSmithKline* paras 65–68; also see the Opinion of A-G Jacobs para 70 and the references to 'development of trade' in the *Glaxo* Case para 118.

[43]   See Case 5/69 *Franz Völk v Établissements J. Vervaecke*.

[44]   See references in n 40 above and Jones and Sufrin (2007) 225–33.

Some might argue that Case 27/87 *Erauw-Jacquery v La Hesbignonne Société Coopérative* and Case 306/96 *Javico International and Javico v YSL Parfums* undermine this statement. In *Erauw-Jacquery* the ECJ allowed absolute territorial protection. However, without this the licensor would not have been able to control the quality of his product, something that was essential on the facts. The overlap between competition law and intellectual property rights is a complex one and is not discussed in this work. The ECJ did not consider the more interesting clause (i) that the French court asked it to analyse, which dealt more directly with territorial protection as discussed in this chapter *Javico* involved absolute territorial protection from licensees in Russia and the Ukraine. At para 19 the ECJ held that these restrictions '… must be construed not as being intended to exclude parallel imports and marketing of the contractual product within the Community …'

[45]   Commission decision, *Tretorn* appeal dismissed, Case T-49/95 *Van Megan v Commission*.

between Tretorn, an undertaking that manufactured tennis balls, and some of its exclusive distributors were considered. The Commission found that since 1987 Tretorn had set up, in concert with its exclusive distributors, both inside and outside the Community, an export ban in its exclusive distribution system.[46] The Commission found that this system breached Article 81(1), given that the general export ban and the barriers had the direct object and effect of restricting competition. This, in turn, said the Commission, constitutes an obstruction of the achievement of a fundamental objective of the Treaty, the integration of the common market.[47]

To my knowledge there has not been a case where absolute territorial protection was accepted under Article 81(1) EC.[48] Incorporating (appreciable) absolute territorial protection into agreements is, in effect, a per se (object) violation of Article 81(1) EC.[49] This applies even where the methods used to achieve such a territorial restriction are indirect, such as charging different prices according to the territory for which the goods are being delivered[50] or a refusal to grant discounts for these goods.[51] For these extreme market partitioning arrangements, the balance is heavily tilted in favour of ensuring market integration, however formulaically this is interpreted.

In the face of this strong approach, parties rarely argue that economic efficiency benefits justify absolute territorial protection within Article 81(1) EC. One might expect such submissions to become more regular in the future, however.[52] In the *Glaxo* Case, the parties argued that their attempts to block parallel imports of pharmaceutical products into the UK were justified because, amongst other things, they produced (dynamic) efficiency gains. They made this argument under both Article 81(1) and (3).

Because of the way it thinks that Article 81 works, the Commission only dealt with the issues under Article 81(3) EC.[53] The CFI took a different tack. It emphasised the

---

[46]   ibid, paras 13, 16–21.

[47]   ibid, para 51. See also, eg Case 22/71 *Béguelin Import v GL Import Export* para 12 and Case T-77/92 *Parker Pen v Commission* para 37.

[48]   One possible exception to this is the *Coditel* Case para 16, where the ECJ (in an unclear section of the judgment) in effect permitted absolute territorial protection in favour of licensees to exhibit a cinema film. The ECJ's reasoning seems to be based on economic efficiency, cultural and industrial policy grounds. At paras 17–20 it held that an exclusive licence might not infringe Art 81(1) EC where there was evidence of unreasonable exploitation. However, it has been argued that this case is limited to the special circumstances of film exhibitions, B&C (2008), para 2–090, and may even turn on its own facts. Nevertheless, Anderman (1998) 70, seems to read this case as establishing a general principal. See also, the discussion on Case 27/87 *Erauw-Jacquery v La Hesbignonne Société Coopérative* and Case 306/96 *Javico International and Javico v YSL Parfums*, Ch 3, n 44 above.

[49]   See the *European Night Services* Case para 136; Case 161/84 *Pronuptia de Paris v Irmgard Schillgalis*; Case T-77/92 *Parker Pen v Commission*; Case C-234/89 *Delimitis v Henninger Bräu* and Manzini (2002) 398, 399. Obviously, such restrictions can still, theoretically, be exempted under Art 81(3) EC and so absolute territorial protection is not a per se violation of Art 81 as a whole.

[50]   See, eg Commission decision, *The Distillers Company Limited*, s 2; appeal dismissed, Case 30/78 *Distillers Company v Commission*.

[51]   See, eg Commission decision, *Sperry New Holland*, para 55.

[52]   Commission, *Article 81(3) Guidelines*, para 18(2) does not necessarily rule this out. Commission, *Vertical Guidelines*, para 119(10), may even encourage it under certain limited conditions. Thanks to Giorgio Monti for this comment.

[53]   The Commission believes that any efficiency benefits of absolute territorial protection should only be considered within Art 81(3), Commission, *Article 81(3) Guidelines*, paras 21–23, 32, 33, 48–72. On the facts, the Commission found that the agreement did not enhance economic efficiency so no balancing exercise was undertaken even in Art 81(3). On the general merits of such economic arguments by pharmaceutical companies see Rey and Venit (2004) 160–77. After its judgment in Case T-41/96 *Bayer v Commission* the CFI may now demand a proper economic analysis as to whether the territorial protection is welfare reducing, see Rey and Venit (2004) 175.

well-established principle that all restrictions, even object restrictions such as absolute territorial protection, should be examined in their legal and economic context.[54] Previously, with the exception of the issue of appreciability, a provision's classification as an object restriction,[55] meant that it was unnecessary to show that the agreement had anti-competitive effects.[56] Although lip service was paid to the need to investigate in the legal and economic context, the reality was that, when there was absolute territorial protection, the parties could only argue efficiency benefits under Article 81(3), where the burden of proof would be on them. By emphasising the need to examine all restrictions in their legal and economic context, the CFI in *Glaxo* opened the door to efficiency justifications for absolute territorial protection within Article 81(1).[57] It went on to find that due to the legal and economic context, the absolute territorial protection at stake in the *Glaxo* Case was not an object restriction, going on to examine its effects, and finding that they restricted competition.[58]

This development has not been well received. Whish, for example, describes this part of the CFI's judgment as 'surprising'; adding that it was the specific and unusual conditions in which pharmaceutical products are bought and sold that led the CFI to this conclusion.[59] Whish may be right, but given the CFI's reliance on the *Consten and Grundig* Case when making these arguments,[60] the judgment could have a dramatic impact if it demands that one check object infringements' legal and economic context more thoroughly than before. I suspect that the ECJ will overturn this part of the CFI's judgment on appeal, returning to a per se stance against absolute territorial protection *under Article 81(1)*, rather than allow balancing with economic efficiency to occur there.[61]

Absolute territorial protection is an extreme form of territorial protection. There are more limited forms. In *Société Technique Minière*, decided two weeks before the *Consten and Grundig* Case, the ECJ considered an agreement where a French company, STM, had been given an exclusive right to sell certain machines in France that had been manufactured by a German firm, MU. STM had agreed not to sell competing machines and in return had been given an exclusive territory. Parallel imports were not restricted, nor were passive sales.[62] The ECJ held that the competition in question must be understood within the actual context in which it would occur in the absence of the agreement in dispute. In particular, it doubted whether there was an interference with competition if the agreement

---

[54]   See the *Glaxo* Case paras 109, 110, 117 and the references made there.

[55]   Whish (2008) 118 calls 'object restrictions' particularly pernicious types of agreement that are overwhelmingly likely to harm consumer welfare.

[56]   See the *Consten and Grundig* Case, p 342 and *Société Technique Minière*, p 249.

[57]   This aspect of the judgment is now on appeal, Joined Cases C-501/06 etc. *GlaxoSmithKline Services v Commission*.

[58]   The *Glaxo* Case paras 171–95.

[59]   Whish (2008) 117, 121; although he does not argue this due to market integration concerns. Whish believes that it is the consumer welfare effects of object infringements that are pernicious, Whish (2008) 118, although note his pp 22, 23. See also, the *Glaxo* Case para 147 and Jones and Sufrin (2007) 231–33.

[60]   The *Glaxo* Case paras 111, 112, 119–21; although note paras 115, 116.

[61]   It may be that the CFI took this stance in the *Glaxo* Case because it believes that the market integration goal is only relevant insofar as it achieves consumer welfare benefits, see above. As a result, if the ECJ overturns this view on appeal, it is possible (though not certain) that balancing the market integration loss caused by absolute territorial protection with any consumer welfare benefits achieved will be confined to Art 81(3) EC again for this reason as well.

[62]   The judgment is not clear on this point but this is the position many take, see, eg B&C (2008), para 2–070 and it is followed here.

seemed really necessary for the penetration of a new area by an undertaking.[63] The ECJ added that agreements offering an exclusive right of sale did not, by their very nature, restrict competition within Article 81(1) EC.[64] So, unless the territorial protection is absolute, the agreement's effects should be taken into account as well.

In *Société Technique Minière*, the ECJ spent some time discussing what features might be considered important within the actual context.[65] These were elements such as the nature and quantity, limited or otherwise, of the products covered by the agreement, the position and importance of the parties on the market for the products concerned, the isolated nature of the disputed agreement and the severity of the clauses intended to protect the exclusive dealership. The reason for investigating all these factors in this case was to assess whether the agreement was really necessary for the penetration of a new area.[66] Despite this relaxation in the test, these, more limited, types of territorial protection have only been allowed under Article 81(1) on a few occasions.

There is logic to this relaxation in terms of the balance. As such clauses undermine market integration less than those seeking absolute territorial protection (qualitatively), it is easier to justify them where they promote economic efficiency.

In the second example of a justification for restricting market integration, the *Nungesser* Case, the ECJ was more generous. The case concerned an agreement between the French national agricultural research institute (INRA) and Mr Eisele, trading as Nungesser. INRA exclusively assigned, to Mr Eisele, the right to produce and sell, in Germany, certain maize seeds it had developed. INRA undertook to prevent its seeds being exported to Germany, except via Mr Eisele. As in the *Consten and Grundig* Case, the ECJ held that absolute territorial protection was contrary to Article 81(1) EC.[67] However, the ECJ added that:

[I]n the case of a licence of breeders' rights over hybrid maize seeds newly developed in one Member State, an undertaking established in another Member State which was not certain that it would not encounter competition from other licensees for the territory granted to it, or from the owner of the right himself, might be deterred from accepting the risk of cultivating and marketing that product; such a result would be damaging to the dissemination of a new technology and would prejudice competition in the Community between the new product and similar existing products.

Having regard to the specific nature of the products in question, the Court concludes that, in a case such as the present, the grant of an open exclusive licence, that is to say a licence which does not affect the position of third parties such as parallel importers and licensees for other territories, is not in itself incompatible with Article 85(1) [now Article 81(1)] of the Treaty.[68]

This judgment implies that economic efficiency arguments (here in the form of dynamic efficiencies), here raised in the context of increasing competition by encouraging a new entrant, *combined with* the benefits of innovation, may be enough to outweigh the market integration objective where only open exclusive licences are used, ie licences that allow for

---

[63] *Société Technique Minière*, p 250.
[64] ibid, 251.
[65] ibid, 250.
[66] In both the *Consten and Grundig* Case, pp 342, 343 and the *Pronuptia* Case para 24, the ECJ refers to the fact that there the product/trade mark is already widely known when it finds that Art 81(1) EC has been breached and thus there was no penetration of a new area with a new product.
[67] The *Nungesser* Case para 61.
[68] The *Nungesser* Case para 57, 58.

parallel trade between territories.[69] The issue of passive sales was not explicitly raised in the case and so it is not clear where the ECJ stood on them.

Where there is no absolute territorial protection, the balance in favour of introducing new products, as opposed to introducing old products onto new geographical markets, is tilted slightly further in favour of economic efficiency. In *Société Technique Minière*, the ECJ held that the restriction on active sales had to be really necessary for the penetration of the new area. In the *Nungesser* Case, the ECJ says that, for new products, restrictions on active sales can be justified where the licensee was not certain that it would not encounter competition from other licensees or the licensor, and because of this might be deterred from accepting the risk of cultivating and marketing the product. The Commission's *Vertical Guidelines* adopt this logic, saying that the case in favour of exclusive distribution is strongest for '... new products, for complex products, for products whose qualities are difficult to judge before consumption ... or of which the qualities are difficult to judge even after consumption ...'[70] It is possible that, based on this more limited justification, the market integration/economic efficiency balance will allow open exclusive licenses for these sorts of products too.

One might ask whether the *Nungesser* Case went too far against market integration. That case is often argued to turn on the specific facts of plant breeders' rights. Korah points out that some 16 years after the *Nungesser* Case the Commission had never applied this precedent in any of its decisions.[71] Of late the Commission has attempted to clarify the position here too:

> [V]ertical restraints linked to opening up new product or geographic markets in general do not restrict competition. This rule holds, irrespective of the market share of the company, for two years after the first putting on the market of the product. It applies to all non-hardcore vertical restraints and, in the case of a new geographic market, to restrictions on active and passive sales imposed on the direct buyers of the supplier located in other markets to intermediaries in the new market. In the case of genuine testing of a new product in a limited territory or with a limited customer group, the distributors appointed to sell the new product on the test market can be restricted in their active selling outside the test market for a maximum period of one year without being caught by Article 81(1).[72]

This citation appears to give more protection to restrictions on market integration for entering new geographic markets with old products, than for entering new markets with new products. Perhaps the Commission favoured those entering new geographic markets because of the market integration dimension; although such a stance does not seem to be in line with the case law discussed above, nor is it necessarily in line with economic theory.

---

[69] In the *Pronuptia* Case para 24, the ECJ found that a certain amount of territorial protection which was not, on its face, absolute, breached Art 81(1) EC. This may have been because the products in question were of a well known brand. It has also been suggested that the ECJ felt that the exclusivity enjoyed by the franchisee coupled with the location clause preventing a franchisee from opening a second shop, might give rise to *de facto* absolute territorial protection, B&C (2001), para 2–093.

[70] Commission, *Vertical Guidelines*, para 174. See also, the *Old Technology Transfer Block Exemption*, recital 10, as interpreted in Monti (2002) 1064. Commission, *Article 81(3) Guidelines*, para 18(2) may be trying to collapse the distinction.

[71] Korah, in Ehlermann (1998) 528. Although there is sometimes some discussion of the principle, see, eg Commission decision, *Velcro/Aplix*, pp 27–31.

[72] Commission, *Vertical Guidelines*, para 119. This is generous language. However, while it is clear that active and passive sales can be prevented, independent parallel importers can never be restrained, therefore, this position is not contrary to the *Consten and Grundig* Case, pp 342, 343, such that Consten could benefit from absolute territorial protection. For the opposite view see Monti (2002) 1068. Bishop and Ridyard (2002) 35, 37 and Peeperkorn (2002) 38, 39, provide a general critique of balancing these objectives under the guidelines.

In conclusion, a balance seems to be taking place. The negative effects that absolute territorial protection has on the market integration objective can not be justified on economic efficiency grounds. As the restrictions on market integration lessen, the Community Courts are increasingly prepared to look at economic efficiency benefits and find that these outweigh the restrictions on market integration. Market integration and economic efficiency are important Community objectives, both in their own right and because of the other objectives they can promote.[73]

This does not explain the complete prohibition on absolute territorial protection. One reason for this absolute prohibition within Article 81(1) may be that the Commission and the Community Courts are saying that these restrictions, by their very nature, have the potential of restricting competition. These are restrictions which in light of the objectives pursued by the Community competition rules have such a high potential of negative effects on competition that it is unnecessary for the purposes of applying Article 81(1) to demonstrate any actual effects on the market. This presumption is based on the serious nature of the restriction and on experience showing that they are likely to produce negative effects on the market and to jeopardise the objectives pursued by the Community competition rules.[74] Under this logic, some efficient agreements would fall within Article 81(1) EC. These would be few and far between. Therefore, the opportunity costs of this happening would be outweighed by the fact that the Commission would not have to go to the trouble and expense of investigating every case. This could enhance clarity and certainty, saving costs and enhancing welfare over the long-term.[75] Furthermore, if the party relying on the clause could show that absolute territorial protection was efficiency enhancing in that case, it could rely on Article 81(3) EC, as long as all four conditions are fulfilled.

Yet, the CFI may now be prepared, on occasion, to ignore this absolute rule within Article 81(1). This may be because it is now more persuaded of the welfare benefits that absolute territorial protection can bestow; in fact, the Commission now says that this should be the case unless there are restrictions on inter-brand competition. Perhaps more efficient agreements fall within Article 81(1) than was previously thought. If the utility of the absolute rule within Article 81(1) falls in this way, it may no longer be appropriate.

Another possible reason for allowing absolute territorial protection sometimes could be that the balance has actually shifted. Some argue that, as the single market nears completion, market integration may diminish in importance.[76] Perhaps, economic efficiency is increasing in importance; some argue that it is (and should be) a fundamental objective in and of itself.[77] Efficient markets also help achieve many other objectives, such as consumer protection. As these other objectives increase in importance, so too must a policy that promotes them.

A third possible reason why this absolute rule may be crumbling is more fundamental. Perhaps there is no conflict between economic efficiency and market integration at all.

---

[73] See Ch 1, Section 2.
[74] Commission, *Article 81(3) Guidelines*, para 21.
[75] See, eg Easterbrook (1992) 129–30 and Easterbrook (1984) 39.
[76] Although I argued that I did not think that this was the case: see nn 24 and 25 above.
[77] See nn 9 and 11 above.

Consider the underlying rationale for the market integration objective. Market integration, as defined, may be an end in itself. Alternatively, it may be being used as an aid to achieve consumer protection goals. If this were true, then pursuing market integration, essentially removing barriers to inter-State trade, could still conflict with economic efficiency. However, market integration has also been described as a means of enhancing economic efficiency.[78] To the extent that this is a shift in the reasons for pursuing it (or that the reasons become more widely accepted) there should be a corresponding shift in the balance. If market integration is only there to support economic efficiency then there will no longer be a conflict and there is no need to balance at all. On this basis, there seems little reason to prohibit absolute territorial protection unless it is welfare reducing.[79]

Even if conflict still exists, the pendulum may shift towards economic efficiency for the reasons set out above. It is unclear how the case law will develop in this area. The Commission may not be receptive to allowing absolute territorial protection in product areas where it feels that the single market has yet to be achieved, especially since the expansion of the European Union.

2.2 Environmental Protection

Section 2.2.2 examines how environmental considerations may have influenced some of the Commission's Article 81(1) decisions. Before doing that I discuss the environmental protection objective and what it promotes, Section 2.2.1. Economic efficiency has already been discussed, Section 2.1.2.

2.2.1 Environmental protection[80]

Article 174(1) EC directs that Community environmental policy shall contribute to preserving, protecting and improving the quality of the environment; protecting human health; prudent and rational utilisation of natural resources and promoting measures at international level to deal with regional or worldwide environmental problems.

Environmental protection is already an important Community law principle and its importance is increasing.[81] It is a well-developed policy in its own right. The Treaty of Maastricht demanded a 'high' level of environmental protection. The Commission has called environmental policy, as embodied in Article 174 EC, a 'fundamental policy of the Community.'[82] Improving environmental protection can also further other goals. For example, the Commission points to a link between environmental protection requirements, employment policy[83] and industrial policy.[84]

---

[78]   See the discussion of the *Glaxo* Case, above.

[79]   There could still be a place for per se rules. However, in light of the developments in the Commission's economic thinking, see above, the justifications for a per se rule may no longer be made out.

[80]   For a more detailed analysis of Community environmental protection see Jans and Vedder (2008); Krämer (2006); Vedder (2003); McGillivray and Holder (2001); Jans (2000) and Grimeaud (2000).

[81]   Demetriou and Higgins (2003) 196, 197.

[82]   Commission, *RCP 1992* 52.

[83]   COM(2000) 576 10. See also, Press Release IP/03/430.

[84]   This is not a linear relationship. There may come a time where increasing environmental protection undermines industrial policy; see, eg Council Resolution, *on the automobile industry*, recitals 1, 6 and paras 4, 5 and Council Resolution, *strengthening Community industry*, para 3.

Article 6 EC is an environmental policy-linking clause, which states that '[e]nvironmental protection requirements must be integrated into the definition and implementation of the Community policies and activities referred to in Article 3, in particular with a view to promoting sustainable development.'[85] Environmental protection is based on the precautionary principle, preventive action, the idea that environmental damage should be rectified at source, and the idea that the polluter should pay.[86]

The Commission has referred to environmental issues within its Article 81(1) analysis for some time.[87] These references have become more frequent,[88] although Commission, *Article 81(3) Guidelines* only refer to the possibility of considering public policy considerations within Article 81(3) EC.[89]

2.2.2 The balance[90]

Environmental protection and economic efficiency (or, as the case may be, economic freedom) sometimes conflict. What I want to understand is whether, in case of conflict, an agreement's environmental impact affects the appraisal of a restriction of competition under Article 81(1) EC; and, if so, where the balance lies between these objectives.

The Commission's *Horizontal Guidelines* explain how to assess the compatibility of environmental agreements with Article 81(1).[91] Irrespective of the parties' market shares, the Commission says that some environmental agreements are unlikely to fall within Article 81(1).[92] For example, there will be no restriction of competition unless a precise individual obligation is placed on the parties or if they are loosely committed to attaining a sector-wide environmental target. In this latter case the assessment focuses on what discretion the parties have as to the means that are technically and economically available to them to attain the environmental objective agreed upon. The more varied such means, the less appreciable the potential restrictive effects.[93] However, where environmental agreements appreciably[94] restrict the parties' ability to devise the characteristics of their products or the way in which they produce them, they may be able to influence each

---

[85]   Ch 2 discusses policy-linking clauses in more detail.

[86]   Art 174(2) EC.

[87]   See, eg Commission decision *D'Iteren motor oils*, and Commission, *RCP 1990* 81. Environmental considerations also feature prominently in Art 81(3) EC, see Ch 4.

[88]   See, eg *ACEA*, Commission, *RCP 1998*, point 131 and page 151; *CEMEP*, Commission Press Release IP/00/508; Commission decisions *Eco-Emballages* and *DSD and others* and Commission Press Release, IP/07/1332.

[89]   Commission, *Article 81(3) Guidelines*, para 42. Note that Reg 1/2003, recital 22 and art 16, oblige Member States' courts and competition authorities to follow Commission decisions when they apply Arts 81 and 82 EC. Commission notices need not be followed; see, eg Commission, *Article 81(3) Guidelines*, para 4. It is unclear how the national authorities will interpret Commission (post modernisation) substantive changes made in guidelines where they conflict with the Commission's earlier decision-making practice. There may be a tendency to place more weight on earlier Commission decisions, especially where they reflect Community Court case law, such as *Wouters* and *Meca Medina*.

[90]   Also see Jans and Vedder (2008) 270–74.

[91]   For some time the Commission had underlined the importance of agreements between private parties to achieve environmental ends, and increasingly favoured them, see London (2003) 268–71.

[92]   Commission, *Horizontal Guidelines*, para 176.

[93]   ibid, para 177. See also, Jans and Vedder (2008) 272.

[94]   But not where product and production diversity in the relevant market, is not appreciably affected, Commission, *Horizontal Guidelines*, para 178. Where some categories of a product are banned or phased out from the market, restrictions cannot be deemed appreciable insofar as their share is minor in the relevant geographic market or, in the case of Community-wide markets, in all Member States, para 178.

other's production or sales.[95] This may breach Article 81(1) EC, if the agreements cover a major share of an industry at national or EC level.[96]

A comparison can be made with how agreements on technical and other standards are dealt with under Article 81(1) EC.[97] Although the texts are very similar the Commission, *Horizontal Guidelines* split out the guidance on 'agreements on standards' and 'environmental agreements';[98] implying a difference in approach in these two areas.

Some agreements on standards breach Article 81(1). In order to fall outside Article 81(1) EC the standards must be objectively justified.[99] In at least two matters the Commission noted that the environmental agreements were in line with the Community's strategy to reduce CO_2 emissions.[100] This implies that the environment can be an objective justification and is relevant under Article 81(1).[101]

However, when environmental agreements are involved this seems to affect the Commission's decision-making, more than for mere technical or other standards. Under the normal (standards) case law, the parties to an agreement may set standards but they must be free to decide whether or not to apply them. The Commission considers this discretion important.[102] By way of contrast, in the environmental field the Commission allows agreements to be slightly more restrictive. I believe this is because it is balancing the restriction against environmental concerns.[103]

In *ACEA*, for example, the Association of European Automobile Manufacturers undertook, on behalf of its members, to reduce CO_2 emissions from passenger cars by setting a reduction target of 25 per cent by 2008.[104] This was a cumulative reduction target for all ACEA's members; each member set its own level. The Commission found that this would encourage ACEA's members to develop and introduce new CO_2-efficient technologies independently and in competition with one another.[105] Accordingly, it decided that ACEA's voluntary agreement did not constitute a restriction of competition and was not caught by Article 81(1).[106]

---

[95]   Or where they reduce/substantially affect the output of third parties, either as suppliers or purchasers.

[96]   Commission, *Horizontal Guidelines*, paras 181, 182. This should not be the case where the importance of environmental performance is marginal for influencing purchase decisions, para 178.

[97]   Standardisation agreements can have an industrial policy rationale, Rosenthal (1990) 326. This is not discussed in this chapter, but their inclusion in the guidelines (as well as elsewhere) may evidence the consideration of yet another policy objective in Art 81(1).

[98]   Commission, *Horizontal Guidelines*, ss 6 and 7, respectively; although note paras 192–94 do refer to environmental benefits as 'economic benefits'.

[99]   This is not absolutely clear from the case law but the implication is there, see, eg Commission Notice, *Retel*, para 9. See also, B&C (2008), para 5–140.

[100]   *ACEA*, Commission, *RCP 1998*, point 131 and p 151 and *CEMEP*, discussed in Commission Press Release IP/00/508.

[101]   The fact that the environmental benefits are emphasised in the Commission's *Competition Policy Newsletter* gives some credence to this point, see Martínez-López (2000) 24, 25.

[102]   See, eg Commission decision, *VVVF*, p 24 and Commission, *Horizontal Guidelines*, para 167. For an exception see Commission Notice, *Pasta manufacturers*, para 3(a).

[103]   See also, Jans and Vedder (2008) 273, 274.

[104]   *ACEA* – COM(1998), para 5(3).

[105]   The Commission also found that this collective effort by the European automotive industry would enable a significant reduction in CO_2 emissions to be achieved in line with EU policy, see *ACEA* – COM(1998) 2, 3, where the Commission said that the ACEA commitment was consistent with the Community's strategy on CO_2 emissions from cars.

[106]   See also, *JAMA/KAMA*, Commission, *RCP 1999* 160–61 and *CEMEP*, cited above.

The Commission has said that environmental agreements, which impose targets on individual firms, restrict competition within the meaning of Article 81(1) EC.[107] The fact that the parties to the ACEA agreement were free to set their own levels seems to have prevented a finding of a breach of Article 81(1). This is in line with the normal standards case law.

However, in order to judge whether there is a restriction of competition one must examine the arrangement in its legal and economic context. What one should really ask is, do these general environmental targets, *in fact*, have an effect on each undertaking's product range and thus on consumer choice. As the Commission accepts, this is most likely where: (i) the agreement covers a significant part of the products on the relevant market; and (ii) the agreement is likely to have a binding impact on each manufacturer.

In relation to the first point, in *ACEA*, the agreement must have covered a large part of the market; the Commission called it a 'first critical step'.[108] No percentages are given, but this should certainly be the case today, because a similar agreement has now been concluded with JAMA and KAMA. The Commission has also said that it will try to make similar agreements with the other major groups of non-ACEA manufacturers present on the EU market.[109] Each time it does this more of the market is covered. Furthermore, these agreements affect a large proportion of new motorcars. It is not entirely clear, but the implication is that, in 1998, no European manufacturers sold cars with the low levels of pollution promised in the ACEA agreement.[110] In which case, the agreement probably affects all new cars manufactured by the parties for sale in the EU.

In relation to the second point, in *ACEA*, the manufacturers likely intended these targets, in effect, to bind each and every one of them. The targets set are ambitious. It is unlikely that any one manufacturer can do much better than the target, allowing other manufacturers to make less effort. In addition, the Commission said that if the targets are not met then it will legislate instead.[111] As a result, in fact, all manufacturers must try to attain the environmental levels set for all or most of the relevant cars that they produce.

It could be argued that CO_2 emissions do not affect customer choice and so do not have an appreciable effect on competition. Even if that were so when the ACEA agreement was signed, which is doubtful, it is highly unlikely to be the case at the end of its term,[112] it lasted for 10 years.[113]

Most, if not all, of the manufacturers must meet the target for most, if not all, of the cars that they produce for sale in the EU, if the agreement's environmental commitments are to be achieved. They will all be trying to do so because of the threat of legislation if they fail. These commitments probably apply to all of the new cars manufactured by a substantial

---

[107]   See, eg *EACEM*, which was closed by comfort letter; Commission, *RCP 1998*, point 130 and p 155 and Commission, *Horizontal Guidelines*, para 190.

[108]   *ACEA* – COM(1998) 3, 8.

[109]   ibid, 7, 8.

[110]   ibid, para 3(1).

[111]   ibid, 2, 5, 6. The OECD points out that such threats seem to contribute significantly to target improvement, OECD (2003a) 11, 15.

[112]   See, eg websites such as <www.autoindustry.co.uk> accessed 27 April 2009. The number of references to fuel efficiency (related to CO_2 emissions) in car advertisements also belies this notion.

[113]   *ACEA* – COM(1998) 7.

part of the industry. This would normally be considered a restriction on competition. The fact that it relates to an environmental commitment may have affected the Article 81(1) balance.[114]

On the assumption that there is a balance, there have been too few cases to confidently assess where it might lie. However, the Commission's decisions suggest that the importance of environmental protection, within Article 81(1) EC, has changed over time. Environmental considerations were not considered there until the 1990s. Their growing influence within this provision roughly matches environmental protection's growing influence within the Treaty as a whole.[115] However, where environmental considerations are balanced against economic efficiency it is not clear that their influence should be increasing. This is because while environmental protection is becoming increasingly important in the Community legal order, economic efficiency is also becoming increasingly important, both in and of itself, and because it helps achieve other objectives that have been inserted into the Treaty over time.[116] Secondly, the negative welfare effect of the environmental restrictions in *ACEA* was probably quite important. The 'wrong' compromise (ie not the optimal balance) may be established if a structured balancing process is not carried out. The environmental benefits could be over-valued, because environmental damage would not be rectified at any cost.[117] On the other hand, the welfare costs may be underestimated if they are not properly assessed because efficient markets have many non-welfare benefits. More explicit reasoning is needed in Article 81 decisions to clarify these issues.

3 TWO RELATED QUESTIONS

Section 3 discusses the two related questions, highlighted in this chapter's Introduction. Section 3.1 asks whether there are limits to Article 81(1)'s balance; and, Section 3.2 asks why balancing takes place within Article 81(1) as well as Article 81(3).

---

[114] Similar points can also be made in relation to the *VOTOB* and *CEMEP* agreements. In *VOTOB*, six independent operators offering tank storage facilities in the Netherlands to third parties agreed an agenda with the Dutch government to reduce vapour emissions from their tanks over a 10-year period. The Commission attacked a later decision by the undertakings to levy a uniform environmental charge to cover, in part, the cost of investment to reduce these emissions, Commission, *RCP 1992*, points 177–86. The restriction in competition as a result of the voluntary agreement to reduce emissions itself would typically breach Art 81(1)(b) EC, Vogelaar (1994) 545. Although there was no formal decision, the Commission held that it did not fall within Art 81(1) at all, Vogelaar (1994) 551. For a different reading of *VOTOB*, see Vedder (2003) 157.

In *CEMEP* the parties to the agreement accounted for some 80% of Community sales and made a significant commitment, agreeing to reduce their joint sales of the least efficient category three motors by some 50%. These motors currently account for 70% of Community sales. The Commission argued that competition did not take place on the basis of efficiency in this industry. This is hard to believe as the buyers are sophisticated industry operators and energy efficiency is generally considered to be highly important for motors. Nevertheless, even if this is true then it is unlikely to be so by the time the agreement expires, some three years later. Furthermore, the parties also agreed to classify all of the motors covered by the agreement into one of three levels of energy efficiency. This will likely introduce competition on that criterion to the extent that it did not exist before. Why then, was a phasing-out commitment also considered necessary? If it was not necessary then should the agreement have been allowed to escape Art 81(1) EC?

[115] See Ch 4, Section 2.3.

[116] See Ch 1, Section 2.

[117] See Ch 8, Section 4.

3.1 The limits to Article 81(1) EC's balance

Section 2 argued that policy objectives are balanced within Article 81(1) EC. A related issue is the limits to this balance. Assume that the optimal balance has been achieved between the two relevant policy objectives in a particular case; can our enquiry stop there, or must other questions be asked. By way of example, when the optimal balance has been assessed under Article 81(3)'s first test, three other tests must also be fulfilled before exemption can be granted.[118] No equivalent additional tests are listed in Article 81(1), which may mean that only the optimal balance is relevant there. In which case, public policy goals may more easily 'win the balance' in Article 81(1), rather than that in Article 81(3). This would make it important where we conduct the balance.[119]

Due to the paucity of case law and decisions one cannot be certain. In some matters, for example, *ACEA*, no other tests were imposed. This may be because the Commission claimed not to be balancing there. Other cases suggest that merely establishing that the optimal balance has been achieved is insufficient. For example, in *Société Technique Minière*, the ECJ held that:

> The competition in question must be understood within the actual context in which it would occur in the absence of the agreement in dispute. In particular it may be doubted whether there is an interference with competition if the said agreement seems really necessary for the penetration of a new area by an undertaking.[120]

As discussed above, in the *Nungesser* Case, the ECJ appeared to change the test somewhat. It held that an undertaking established in another Member State which was not certain that it would not encounter competition from other licensees for the territory granted to it, or from the owner of the right himself, might be deterred from accepting the risk of cultivating and marketing that product; such a result would be damaging to the dissemination of a new technology and would prejudice competition in the Community between the new product and similar existing products.[121] It is unclear from the judgment whether the difference in language is considered and relates to the specific objectives being weighed in the balance; or, whether the *Nungesser* Case is intended to relax the earlier test.

Post *Nungesser*, the Community Courts have reverted to the test outlined in *Société Technique Minière*.[122] The Commission has adopted this test too.[123] Increasingly, the *Nungesser* Case looks like an aberration. In Commission Communication, *UEFA rule on 'integrity'*, which was not a formal decision, for example, the Commission was prepared to allow an agreement which contributed to legitimate objectives. However:

> In order to establish whether this preliminary conclusion can be upheld or not, the Commission has to know if such restrictions are limited to what is necessary to preserve the integrity of the

---

[118] The *Matra* Case para 85.

[119] See Section 3.2, below.

[120] *Société Technique Minière*, p 250.

[121] The *Nungesser* Case, para 57.

[122] Case T-144/99 *Institute of Professional Representatives before the EPO v Commission*, paras 78, 79 and the *Gøttrup-Klim* Case para 35.

[123] Commission, *RCP 1992*, point 177. Admittedly, it is unclear which part of Art 81 the Commission is referring to here; it could have been Art 81(3) EC, point 77 may imply that environmental issues are irrelevant in Art 81(1). However, this is unlikely, see the earlier reference to Jans (2000) in Section 2 and, as noted above, environmental issues seem relevant in *VOTOB* – See, eg DG Competition Paper, *on Waste Management*, para 59. Also see the original Commission decision, *EPI Code of Conduct* and Commission, *RCP 1999* 159, 160.

UEFA club competitions and to ensure the uncertainty as to results. In other words, the Commission must confirm whether there are or not less restrictive means to achieve the same objective.[124]

There is some evidence that, in addition to falling within the optimal balance, public policy objectives can only be accepted within Article 81(1) where the restrictions on competition are necessary to achieve the objective. This reflects Article 81(3)(a)'s reference to 'indispensable'.

There is more recent support for this position from the ECJ. In *Wouters* the ECJ balanced public policy objectives within Article 81(1) EC.[125] Rules needed to ensure the proper practice of the legal profession were weighed against a restriction on competition, using what seems to be a proportionality test.[126]

De Búrca reports the three parts of the proportionality test as: (1) was the measure a useful, suitable, or effective means of achieving a legitimate aim or objective?; (2) was there a means of achieving that aim which would be less restrictive of the other interest, in our case competition?; (3) Does the measure have an excessive or disproportionate effect on the other interest?[127]

Let's briefly examine the ECJ's analysis in the *Wouters* Case. The ECJ found a restriction of competition.[128] This was the first interest in the balance. Then, the ECJ determined what the interests protected by the Bar Council rules were.[129] Next, it found that the 1993 Regulations were agreed with these interests in mind.[130] Following that, the ECJ held that the 1993 Regulation could reasonably be considered necessary to achieve that objective in the Netherlands.[131] This is the first part of the proportionality test. Then, the ECJ held that the second part of the proportionality test was fulfilled. The ECJ's judgment here is quite weak. It found that the Bar of the Netherlands is entitled to consider that the objectives pursued by the 1993 Regulation cannot be attained by less restrictive means.[132] Finally, the ECJ held '… it does not appear that the effects restrictive of competition such as those resulting for members of the Bar practising in the Netherlands from a regulation such as the 1993 Regulation go beyond what is necessary in order to ensure the proper practice of the legal profession …'[133] This is the final part of the proportionality test. As a result, the ECJ concluded that the Dutch Bar Council's rule did not infringe Article 81(1) EC.[134]

---

[124]   Commission Communication, *UEFA rule on 'integrity'*, para 10.

[125]   See Ch 2, Section 2.2.2 for a more detailed discussion, including of the facts.

[126]   See Siragusa in Ehlermann (2006) 203; Forrester (2006) 291, 292 and Baquero Cruz (2002) 152, 153.

[127]   De Búrca (1993). See also, Barnard (2004) 79, 80.

[128]   The *Wouters* Case para 97.

[129]   ibid, para 97.

[130]   ibid, para 105. See also the ECJ's judgment in the *Meca-Medina* Case para 43.

[131]   The *Wouters* Case para 107. See also the ECJ's judgment in the *Meca-Medina* Case para 44 *ff*.

[132]   The *Wouters* Case para 108. See also the ECJ's judgment in the *Meca-Medina* Case para 47 *ff*. This seems to give the undertaking(s) a lot of discretion, Siragusa in Ehlermann (2006) 203, 584–86 and Gilliams (2006) 328–30.

[133]   The *Wouters* Case para 109. See also the ECJ's judgment in the *Meca-Medina* Case para 42.

[134]   The *Wouters* Case para 110. See also the ECJ's judgment in the *Meca-Medina* Case para 55 and COM(2007) 391 14.

One might ask whether the 'full-blown' proportionality test used in the *Wouters* Case is the same as the earlier 'necessity' assessment discussed above.[135] The proportionality test has two parts that have not been explicitly discussed in the case law seen above. First, it asks whether the measure is a useful, suitable, or effective means of achieving a legitimate aim or objective. This is not normally explicitly argued in the proportionality test either because it is normally fulfilled (otherwise the body would have acted irrationally). Secondly, the proportionality test also asks whether the measure has an excessive or disproportionate effect on the other interest. This is the direct balancing of interests, weighing environmental protection against economic efficiency, for example. Section 2 argued that such balancing takes place in Article 81(1) EC. So, the balancing exercise within Article 81(1) closely follows the proportionality test.[136]

There is no evidence of the parties having to discuss whether competition has been eliminated, nor have we seen any debate here on whether customers got a fair share of the resulting benefit, as Article 81(3) demands. This means that the public policy balance may be easier to apply and that public policy goals may have more impact when considered in the Article 81(1) balance.[137]

Some imply that there are different limits to the Article 81(1) balancing test. Whish, for example, believes that there is a link between the test that the Community Courts and Commission use here and the ancillary restraints doctrine.[138] Whish distinguishes between two types of 'ancillarity'. He classifies cases, such as *Société Technique Minière* and the *Nungesser* Case, as instances of commercial ancillarity. In these judgments the restrictions, which fell outside Article 81(1), were ancillary to a legitimate commercial operation. Whish distinguishes commercial ancillarity from judgments, such as *Wouters*, which he argues are based on regulatory ancillarity. He means that the restriction was not necessary for the execution of a commercial transaction but rather was necessary in order to ensure a regulatory outcome; to ensure that the ultimate customers of legal services and the sound administration of justice were provided with the necessary guarantees in relation to integrity and experience.[139]

---

[135]   We might also ask whether the ECJ in the *Wouters* Case applies the same test but to a different standard. It seems to have accepted the national assessments very readily. The interests in the *Wouters* Case were national. Perhaps it was prepared to give the national authorities more leeway because of this? Ch 7, Section 2.2 discusses this point further.

[136]   This is unsurprising as the proportionality test features prominently in Community law, Craig and de Búrca (2008) 544–46 and De Búrca (1993).

[137]   Whish (2003) 123.

[138]   Whish (2008) 126–30. Nazzini (2006) 521–27 offers a further refinement of Whish's argument. See also, the Opinion of A-G Trstenjak in Case C-209/07 *The Competition Authority v BIDS*, para 54; Gyselen in Ehlermann (2006) 214; Weatherill (2006) 656 and Vossestein (2002) 858. More generally on ancillary restraints, Goyder (2003) 100–102; B&C (2008), paras 2–112 and 2–113 and Faull and Nikpay (1999), paras 3.181–3.213.

[139]   Forrester (2006) 290, 291, suggests the inclusion of other factors in the Art 81(1) test, such as non-discrimination and the majoritarian rule. However, these are merely suggestions and there is no evidence of them being applied so far.

If this is correct, it would potentially add[140] two restrictions to the Article 81(1) balance.[141] First, balancing within Article 81(1) would only take place to achieve a regulatory end.[142] This might limit the types of objective that could be balanced within Article 81(1) EC. Secondly, the restraint must be directly related, as well as necessary, to the implementation of a main operation.

One might question whether making a link with the ancillary restraints doctrine is either helpful or appropriate. It may not be helpful because the ancillary restraints doctrine is itself extremely imprecise, to the extent that Faull and Nikpay write that it begs more questions than it answers and is exceedingly difficult to apply.[143]

Linking *Wouters*, and cases like it,[144] to the ancillary restraints doctrine may also be inappropriate. This is because Whish's categories of commercial restraints and regulatory restraints appear to be based on fundamentally different logic.[145] In the CFI's words:

> If it is established that a restriction is directly related and necessary to achieving a main operation, the compatibility of that restriction with the competition rules must be examined with that of the main operation.
> Thus, if the main operation does not fall within the scope of the prohibition laid down in Article 85(1) [now Article 81(1)] of the Treaty, the same holds for the restrictions directly related and necessary for that operation … If, on the other hand, the main operation is a restriction within the meaning of Article 85(1) but benefits from an exemption under Article 85(3) [now Article 81(3)] of the Treaty, that exemption also covers those ancillary restrictions.[146]

Therefore, under the ancillary restraints doctrine, it appears that the main operation must be examined under Article 81(1) EC. If it falls outside that provision then any restrictions of competition that are directly related to and necessary for achieving the main aim are also safe. The ECJ in *Wouters* and *Meca-Medina* did not assess whether the restraint was

---

[140]   I say 'potentially add' because Whish (2008) 126, says that the 'commercial ancillarity' that he refers to is a broader concept than the 'ancillary restraints doctrine' considered in Case T-112/99 *Métropole télévision v Commission*. I follow the CFI because it sought to explain the previous case law. Whish does not explain how his concept of ancillary restraints is broader than this. It may be that, in line with Whish (2001) 100, 101 – the last edition of this book where he discusses the issue – he believes that the 'true' ancillary restraints test is whether the restrictions which seek to achieve a legitimate purpose are proportionate. This is more like the test in *Wouters*, than that in *Métropole télévision*. That said, some of my arguments against using this doctrine apply to this stance too.

[141]   Case T-112/99 *Métropole télévision v Commission* para 104.

[142]   Whish suggests that, in principle, *Wouters'* reasoning could be applied to any regulatory rule *adopted for the protection of consumers*. This argument is probably based on para 97 of the judgment (that is the only place where 'consumers' is mentioned). However, as we have seen above, the rule may already be even wider than that, indeed this is also the implication of para 97 (which talks of ensuring '… that the ultimate consumers of legal services and the sound administration of justice are provided with the necessary guarantees …'). The Commission may have been balancing environmental requirements within Art 81(1) in *VOTOB*, although, as stated above, this is unclear. In *VOTOB* the Commission looked at the benefit for society as a whole. Furthermore, as we saw above, Commission, *Article 81(3) Guidelines*, para 18(2), state '… a prohibition imposed on all distributors not to sell to certain categories of end users may not be restrictive of competition if such restraint is objectively necessary for reasons of safety or health related to the dangerous nature of the product in question.' The examination of the effects is not limited to consumers.

[143]   Faull and Nikpay (1999), paras 2.90–2.93 and Faull and Nikpay (2007), para 3.213. See also, Korah (2000) 63, 64. For example, matters such as Case 161/84 *Pronuptia v Irmgard Schillgalis*, especially para 24, imply that this doctrine does not apply to all restraints.

[144]   See n 8 above.

[145]   See also, Monti (2002) 1087, 1088.

[146]   Case T-112/99 *Métropole télévision v Commission* paras 115, 116. See also, Commission, *Article 81(3) Guidelines*, para 28.

directly related to the legitimate (non-restrictive) aim[147] and, crucially, it did not assess the legitimate aim itself under Article 81(1) EC.[148] Furthermore, as Whish accepts,[149] the ECJ in *Wouters* performed a balancing exercise; yet, the CFI specifically rules that this does not take place in relation to ancillary restraints.[150] It may be more helpful to view *Wouters*, and cases like it, as examples of balancing within Article 81(1) EC, unrelated to the ancillary restraints doctrine.

3.2 Why does balancing take place within Article 81(1) as well as Article 81(3)?

Some balancing occurs in Article 81(1). I have demonstrated that the outcome of the public policy balance may be different when this is performed in Article 81(1), to what it would be under Article 81(3) EC. If this is so, it is important to understand when public policy balancing should take place under these different paragraphs.

The Community Courts and the Commission have not, to my knowledge, given any indication of why they chose to balance under Article 81(1) EC in certain cases, rather than Article 81(3).

The academic literature tries to explain why public policy balancing is taking place in Article 81(1). Here, I critique suggestions by Whish, Schweitzer and Monti. In fact, I have already discussed the first of these, that *Wouters* is an example of regulatory ancillarity.[151] I remain unpersuaded by this theory.[152]

Schweitzer writes that public policy considerations have led the ECJ to exclude certain restraints from Article 81(1) EC in a limited number of cases. She calls these acts of self-regulation by collective bodies, where the restraints of the freedom to compete are justified by a legitimate objective and inherent in the organisation and proper conduct of the regulated activity.[153] In this limited carve-out, Schweitzer argues that where self-regulation by professional associations is regarded as legitimate in principle with a view to an act of state-delegation or the nature of a given activity, the ECJ controls this self-regulatory activity according to the same criteria that it would apply to Member State regulation itself.[154]

This argument is hard to accept and would be hard to enforce in practice. In the *Meca-Medina* Case the ECJ was asked whether some (ultimately the International Olympic Committee) rules, dealing with doping in sport, breached Articles 81 and 82 EC. When

---

[147] The ECJ assessed whether the restriction was a useful, suitable, or effective means of achieving the legitimate aim: the proper practice of the legal profession or the health and fairness benefits. It was even prepared to accept that there was not a means of achieving that aim which would be less restrictive of competition, ie that it was 'necessary'.

[148] Gilliams (2006) 318.

[149] Whish (2008) 127.

[150] Case T-112/99 *Métropole télévision v Commission* para 107. Also see paras 108–12 and Commission, *Article 81(3) Guidelines*, para 30.

[151] By this Whish means that where restrictions are necessary in order to ensure a regulatory outcome, to ensure that the ultimate customers of legal services and the sound administration of justice were provided with the necessary guarantees in relation to integrity and experience, this may mean that Art 81(1) EC does not apply.

[152] See Section 3.1, above.

[153] Schweitzer (2007) 3, 4. See also, Gilliams (2006) 322, 323 and Cooke (2006) 236. Schweitzer also refers to *Albany* as a second type of exception. Ch 2, Section 2.2.1 discussed this case.

[154] Schweitzer (2007) 3.

making its assessment, the ECJ did not focus on the idea that this was a regulated activity[155] of a Member State;[156] instead, its focus was on the agreement's objectives.[157] Furthermore, the ECJ strives to situate this case as merely taking account of the overall context in which the rules were adopted; something which must be done for all agreements.[158] In fact, many of the agreements that have been analysed under Article 81(3) EC were made by professional associations;[159] making it hard to believe that this criteria is the dividing line when deciding where to examine public policy arguments in Article 81.[160]

Monti offers another explanation. He suggests that Community public policy goals must be weighed under Article 81(3), while national public interests can be considered in Article 81(1) EC; he calls this a European rule of reason.[161]

I am not persuaded by this theory either. However, before delving more deeply into his argument, some theoretical background is needed. For the most part, I have discussed what are known as horizontal conflicts, conflicts between different policy goals pursued by the Community. Monti's suggestion concerns diagonal conflicts; ie conflicts between Community law and *national* policies in different areas. These are not mere vertical conflicts, where Community law would prevail.[162] Instead, at issue are conflicts between Community law in one area of competence, in this case Article 81 EC, and agreements which reflect national law/policy in a different area of competence; where the Member States have exclusive competence, or there is a parallel or shared competence not yet occupied by the Community.[163]

---

[155] To be fair to Schweitzer, in Case T-193/02, *Laurent Piau v Commission*, paras 76, 77, the CFI highlights the fact that FIFA is a private law body which had not been delegated any power by a public authority. However, these arguments by the applicant seem to relate to the free movement of services part of his case, para 58. The CFI did not think them relevant for the Art 81 discussion, para 78; it is hard to see why, if these issues are as central as Schweitzer believes them to be.

[156] Cooke in Ehlermann (2006) 204 argues that *Wouters* is not necessarily limited to the professions. He suggests that it may apply more generally, wherever a Member State can make a genuine and legitimate justification for having some inherent restraint in order to guarantee the achievement of a greater public interest. However, in *Meca Medina* the ECJ breaks any link with the need for Member State involvement.

[157] The *Meca Medina* Case paras 40–55 and the *Wouters* Case para 97. In *Wouters*, the issue of regulated activity was discussed, but in relation to whether there was an agreement between undertakings or a decision of an association of undertakings paras 54–64.

[158] The *Meca Medina* Case paras 42, 43, 47.

[159] See, eg Joined Cases T-213/95, etc *SCK and FNK v Commission*; Case T-193/02, *Laurent Piau v Commission* and Commission decision, *CECED*.

[160] Furthermore, the scope of the free movement and competition rules is different, which also undermines Schweitzer's 'same criteria' claim. In *Meca Medina*, the CFI found that these were purely sporting rules and thus fell outside of Arts 39 and 49 EC. As a result, it also concluded that the rules had nothing to do with the economic relationships of competition, with the results that they did not fall within the scope of Arts 81 and 82 either, Case T-313/02 *Meca Medina and Majcen v Commission* para 42. On appeal, the ECJ explicitly said that, in holding that rules could thus be excluded straightaway from the scope of Arts 81 and 82 solely on the ground that they were regarded as purely sporting with regard to the application of Arts 39 and 49, without any need to determine first whether the rules fulfilled the specific requirements of Arts 81 and 82, the CFI made an error of law, the *Meca Medina* Case para 33. In other words, the remit of these two sets of provisions is different, it seems too strong to argue that the ECJ controls this self-regulatory activity under Art 81 according to the same criteria that it would apply to Member State regulation itself.

[161] Monti (2002) 1083–90 and Monti (2007) 110–13.

[162] Conflicts between Community law and national policies in the same area, eg competition policy. See Craig and de Búrca (2008) ch 10.

[163] See Deckert (2000) 181, 182.

Diagonal conflicts can be politically sensitive; objectives that Member States hold dear could be at stake.[164] The Court has always had to strike a balance between the protection of the legitimate prerogatives of the Member States and those of the Community.[165] It is untenable to ignore policy goals, for the sole reason that they do not fall within Community competence,[166] or are not mentioned in the Treaty. This would promote Community interests to the exclusion of those of the Member States.

Having said that, there may be a limit as to which Member State objectives can be raised here. They may need to be justified in accordance with the Treaty's Article 2 principles, or even those in the Preamble. Back in 1965, the ECJ held that:

> While the Treaty's primary object is to eliminate by this means [either use of Article 81(1) or through the application of Article 81(3)'s first provision] the obstacles to the free movement of goods within the Common Market and to confirm and safeguard the unity of that market, it also permits the Community authorities to carry out certain positive, though indirect, action with a view to promoting a harmonious development of economic activities within the whole Community, in accordance with Article 2 of the Treaty.[167]

Monti believes that where a Member State can request that national interests justify the non-application of Community law, the Treaty has made *express provision* and the range of domestic policy considerations is fully circumscribed.[168] As there is not express reference to national public interests embedded in Article 81, they cannot be considered when exempting an agreement under Article 81(3) EC.[169] However, Monti sees, in the *Wouters* Case, a mechanism for balancing national interests with competition law in Article 81(1) EC.[170]

Assuming that the statement that one needs an express reference to national public interests within Article 81 EC before they can be considered within Article 81(3) EC, were correct; it is difficult to understand why an express reference to national public interests is necessary when public policy goals are balanced in Article 81(3) and not when this happens in Article 81(1) EC.[171]

Secondly, I have seen no explicit support for the idea, in the Treaty or the Community Courts' judgments, that one needs an express reference to national public interests within Article 81 EC before they can be considered there. There are several examples of national public policies being considered in Article 81(3) EC; although I can find no explicit consideration of why this was acceptable.[172]

---

[164]   See, eg Case C-438/05 *International Transport Workers' Federation and others v Viking Line ABP and Others* paras 39–41, involves a clash between the right to strike and freedom of establishment.

[165]   Rodríguez Iglesias and Baquero Cruz (2003) 74. See also, Boch (2003) 47 and Handoll (1994) 234. Art 4(2) EU Treaty expressly guarantees that the Union will respect the national identities of its Member States.

[166]   Schmid (2000) 163 and Monti (2002) 1086, 1089.

[167]   Case 14/68 *Walt Wilhelm and Others v Bundeskartellamt* para 5.

[168]   Monti (2002) 1083, 1084. Monti points out that this is contrary to the views of two Advocates-General, who have supported the use of Art 81(3) EC to safeguard national interests. But he argues that their logic is based on cases that were pursuing the Community public interest, A-G Jacobs in his Opinions in the *Albany* Case para 193 and the *Pavlov* Case para 90 and A-G Léger in the *Wouters* Case para 107.

[169]   Monti (2002) 1083, 1084. See also Evans (1985) 101.

[170]   Monti (2002) 1086–90.

[171]   It may be different where the national interests exclude the application of Art 81 EC altogether, as in the application of Art 296(1)(b) EC. However, as Ch 2, Sections 2.1.2 and 2.2.2 explain, this is quite different from the balancing that takes place in *Wouters*, although note Ch 2, n 133.

[172]   See Ch 4, Sections 2 and 3. Monti (2002), n 116, refers to Case C-360/92P *Publishers Association v Commission*, where the ECJ requested the Commission to consider cultural (national) policy reasons advanced by

Thirdly, it is unclear what Monti means by '… the Treaty has made express provision …' where national interests justify the non-application of the full force of Community law. He refers to two Treaty provisions to support him, Articles 30 and 86(2) EC. Both provide defences based on national interests;[173] neither expressly says that these are *national* interests.[174] The ECJ seems prepared to imply the fact that, for example, the public security exemption refers to national public security, which was not necessarily the case. Furthermore, the ECJ has considered several goals to be mandatory requirements, under the free movement provisions, when there was no express provision for this in the Treaty. These goals include interests pursued by the Community and interests that Monti calls national.[175] In other words, national interests justifying the non-application of Community law are considered even absent express Treaty provision, both in Articles 81(1) and (3) EC.

Nor, to look at the matter from the other direction, can interests pursued by the Community only be raised in Article 81(3) EC. In *Wouters*, for example, the ECJ draws support from the mandatory requirements case law, applying it in Article 81.[176] Yet, as Barnard notes,[177] the mandatory requirements are often based on *Community* policies identified in the Treaty.[178] In other words, the balancing that takes place in Articles 28, 59 (and, by analogy from *Wouters*, in Article 81(1)) EC can involve policies pursued by the Community, as well as national ones.[179]

---

the UK courts to justify a restriction of competition. Monti does not think that the ECJ addressed the point about whether Art 81(3) EC could be used for national interests fully in that case. Presumably, he means that the ECJ did not explicitly dwell on the point that culture is a national policy interest. This is true, but nor did it in *Wouters*.

[173] In relation to Art 30 EC, Case 34/79, *Regina v Henn and Darby* para 15. For Art 86(2) EC see Case C-202/88 *France v Commission* para 12; Case C-157/94 *Commission v Netherlands* para 39 and Commission Communication, *Services of General Interest*, para 22.

[174] Other exemption provisions that deal with national interests, such as Art 39(4) EC, do not make specific reference to this fact either, for some relevant cases, see Case 152/73 *Sotgiu v Deutsche Bundespost*; Case 149/79 *Commission v Belgium*; Case 307/84 *Commission v France* and Case C-4/91 *Annegret Bleis v Ministère de l'Éducation Nationale*.

[175] Monti (2002) 1086. In Case C-3/95 *Reisbüro Broede v Gerd Sandker*, eg, the German law pursued two goals, consumer protection and the sound administration of justice: (a) Consumer protection is an interest pursued both by the Community, Art 153 EC was added by the Treaty of Maastricht 1992, so this was also true when the ECJ decided *Reisbüro Broede*. In fact, consumer protection was an interest pursued by the Community long before 1992, for more information see sources in Ch 4, n 91; and (b) by the Member States, eg Germany through this law, which is also true of other interests the mandatory requirements pursue, see examples in Ch 2, n 119.

Reisbüro Broede also undermines Monti's point that the list of domestic policy considerations are fully circumscribed, see reference in n 168 above; as the Treaty does not mention administration of justice.

[176] Monti (2002) 1087, 1088.

[177] Barnard (2004) 108, 109.

[178] In fact, in *Wouters* the ECJ specifically referred to the Art 59 EC (freedom to provide services) case, Case C-3/95 *Reisbüro Broede v Gerd Sandker*. At issue there was a German law, which potentially restricted the freedom to provide services. The German law was intended to protect the recipients of the services in question against the harm which they could suffer as a result of legal advice given to them by persons who did not possess the necessary professional or personal qualifications and, to safeguard the proper administration of justice, paras 31, 36–39. In other words, this law's goals were consumer protection and the sound administration of justice. The ECJ seemed to accept that these were both appropriate objectives for mandatory requirements; yet, consumer protection is a policy pursued by the Community, Art 153 EC.

[179] Furthermore, in the *Meca-Medina* Case, the ECJ accepted policy objectives principally based on public health criteria as justifications under Art 81(1) EC, see n 8 above; public health is a goal pursued by the Community, see Art 152 EC. Section 2, above, also showed that market integration and environmental protection, both Community policies, have been considered in Art 81(1).

So, I do not agree with Monti's arguments here. To my mind, there is not convincing evidence that the decision to use Article 81(1) or (3) EC, when balancing public policy interests, is linked to whether or not that policy comes from the national or Community level.[180]

Another objection to Monti's suggestion is that it divides public policy into two categories, that of the Member States and that of the Community.[181] Yet, the distinction is not always so clear-cut; for example, the Treaty was signed in order to achieve Member States' policy goals in the long term. In addition, even if one could distinguish between Member State and Community objectives in the short term, it is unclear how one would go about doing this. Monti appears to assume that there are only two categories of competence, those where Member States have exclusive competence, and those where the Community has exclusive competence. However, there are many areas of mixed competence.[182] Policy objectives in areas of mixed competence may be hard to define as either Member State or Community aims; making it unclear where they should be considered. How would we decide this? Would it depend upon who raised the issue, for example; or on whether the Community had acted? This problem could become contentious. Yet, dispute is unnecessary under the Treaty. Better, surely, to consider all objectives in one place and eliminate this controversy altogether?

This begs the question why some public policy goals were considered in Article 81(1) EC. Whish writes that, if it were not for the procedural difficulties, analysis of the policy objectives under Article 81(3) would seem to be the natural way to proceed, given the bifurcated structure of Article 81.[183] The procedural backdrop that Whish refers to is that prior to the modernisation of the Article 81 and 82 EC procedural process in 2004. The 'agreements' at issue in *Wouters*,[184] *Albany*[185] and *Meca-Medina* had not been notified to the Commission; so, they would have been void if Article 81(1) had been breached.[186] This would have caused a lot of uncertainty in relation to these and other, similar, rules.[187] By balancing in Article 81(1), the ECJ ignored the letter of the Treaty, but ensured that the

---

[180]   See also, Gyselen in Ehlermann (2006) 198.
Monti may be making a weaker claim, that one can only have a defence if there is a specific exemption provision. Perhaps, but then Art 81(3) EC provides an explicit example of an exemption provision. It may be possible for the Community Courts to assume that this provision could apply to national interests where relevant. They have already interpreted it widely in relation to other Community interests.

[181]   Ch 7, Section 2, argues that considering Member State interests in Art 81(1) may also give them too much weight vis-à-vis Community interests.

[182]   See Arnull, Dashwood, Ross and Wyatt et al. (2006) 92 and Craig and de Búrca (2008) ch 3. The FEU Treaty lists many more areas of shared competence, see Art 4, than those of exclusive competence, see Art 3.

[183]   Whish (2003) 123 and Whish (2008) 129, 130. By way of contrast, see Ehlermann (2006) 210 and Cooke (2006) 236.

[184]   Forrester (2006) 278.

[185]   Ch 2, Section 2.2.1 argues that there was no public policy balancing within Art 81(1) in *Albany*; although note Ch 2, n 102.

[186]   Art 81(2) EC. They were horizontal agreements and did not fall within a block exemption. See Reg 17, art 9(1) and Case *NV L'Oréal v De Nieuwe* para 13. On what 'void' means in this context see Whish (2008) 309–12 and B&C (2008), para 1–019.

[187]   Deards (2002) 624, 625.

referring court could achieve the 'right' result (or at least consider all relevant values[188]) when it decided the case at hand. Perhaps for this reason the ECJ has been prepared to balance under Article 81(1), *in extremis*.[189]

Now that those procedural rules are no longer in place, the notification regime has gone and the whole of Article 81 is directly applicable,[190] one might argue that there should be no more cases like *Wouters*, and thus no more balancing within Article 81(1).

However, some disagree. Ehlermann, for example, argues that *Wouters* might be there to preserve the 'virginity' of Article 81(3) from public policy considerations.[191] Yet, I have argued that public policy is regularly considered there.[192] The Commission casts some doubt on the idea that *Wouters* may be a thing of the past.[193] In at least two matters,[194] it was prepared to balance non-welfare objectives under Article 81(1) when it could have used Article 81(3) EC.[195] In addition, the Commission's *Article 81(3) Guidelines*, written in light of the new procedural rules, speak of the consideration of health and other issues within Article 81(1), under certain circumstances.[196]

It remains to be seen whether *Wouters* and cases like it, will be repeated in matters started after 1 May 2004.[197] If so, then this should further strengthen the position of non-welfare objectives within the Treaty, compared to that of competition. If this does happen, then a clear explanation of why and when it is appropriate to use Article 81(1) for mere-balancing, as opposed to Article 81(3) EC, is needed.

4 CONCLUSION

In *Métropole télévision* the CFI holds that the pro and anti-competitive effects of an agreement cannot be balanced within Article 81(1). The rejection of a 'narrow' rule of reason in Community law implies that non-economic objectives cannot be balanced there

---

[188]   The *Wouters* Case was decided at the same time as the Enron scandal, where accountants were found to have ignored standards of conduct, Forrester (2006) 277 and Gilliams (2006) 333. Perhaps the legal profession sought to distance itself from this.

[189]   Joliet argues that Community competition law has a tendency to interpret substantive law provisions in light of the procedural regulation, rather than adjusting the procedural framework to reflect the substantive rules, Joliet (1967) 174.

[190]   Reg 1/2003, arts 1, 5, 6.

[191]   Ehlermann (2006) 210. See also, Gilliams (2006) 319, 320 and Cooke (2006) 236.

[192]   Ch 6, Section 3, argues that public policy considerations are better dealt with under Art 81(3) than 81(1) EC.

[193]   So do others, eg Forrester (2006) 285–94, implies that the *Wouters* Case will have descendants. See also, Case C-415/93 *Union Royale Belge des Sociétés de Football Association ASBL and Others v Jean-Marc Bosman* para 77.

[194]   Commission Communication, *UEFA rule on 'integrity'* and Commission decision, *EPI Code of Conduct*.

[195]   The 'precedent' value of these matters can be disputed. The UEFA matter did not go to a final decision. Perhaps the basis for the reasoning would have changed if it had? Commission decision, *EPI Code of Conduct* was a final decision. However, the Commission received the parties' notification very late (it was sent in reply to a statement of objections: see paras 1 and 2 of the decision). Because exemption decisions could only apply from the moment of notification, Reg 17, arts 4(1) and 6(1), the agreements would have been void before then. This effect, which no longer holds after 1 May 2004, may have 'forced' the Commission to balance within Art 81(1) in way that it would no longer do today. On appeal, the CFI also accepted balancing in Art 81(1), see above. It could have been motivated by the same reasons.

[196]   Commission, *Article 81(3) Guidelines*, para 18(2).

[197]   Ch 6, Section 3.2 explains why mere-balancing should not take place within Art 81(1) EC.

either.[198] This view has been embraced by the academic community and coincides with the Commission's explicit views on the topic.[199]

Having said that, *Métropole télévision* was immediately followed by the ECJ's judgment in *Wouters* and two years later by *Meca-Medina*. There the ECJ balanced the restriction of competition against public policy goals and found that, as a result, Article 81(1) was inapplicable. The Commission too may have changed its mind. This came across in its submissions in *Wouters*,[200] as well as its *Article 81(3) Guidelines*.[201] Although there is considerable doubt about whether non-economic objectives can be balanced within Article 81(1) there is reason to believe that this is possible. Section 2's first objective was to reinforce this point. Clarity could be significantly enhanced if the Community Courts and the Commission explicitly acknowledged this possibility.

A second issue should be highlighted here. The objectives that have been discussed in Article 81(1), both market integration and environmental protection, operated in quite different ways. The market integration goal has acted to make an agreement that would not have been found to restrict competition fall within Article 81(1) EC.[202] Environmental protection on the other hand, appears to have made an agreement that would have restricted competition fall outside Article 81(1).

When conducting an Article 81(1) balance, one must show that the restriction achieves the optimal balance and is necessary to achieve the public policy objective. Some factors such as environmental protection do not seem to have much weight; nevertheless, the balance shifts when there are environmental repercussions. Furthermore, compromise within Article 81(1) has sometimes had a serious impact. In *Wouters*, the objective of protecting the proper practice of the legal profession outweighed a restriction of competition, limiting production and technical development, that is expressly mentioned in Article 81(1)(b) EC.[203] A clearer explanation of where the optimal balance lies between the relevant public policy objectives, as well as an explanation of why this is so, so this can be extrapolated out for other conflicts, would be welcomed.[204]

There is no evidence of the parties having to discuss whether competition has been eliminated, nor have we seen debate here on whether customers got a fair share of the resulting benefit, as Article 81(3) demands. This means that the public policy balance may be easier to apply and that public policy goals may have more impact in the Article 81(1) balance. It would be helpful for the Community Courts to explain when it is appropriate to balance under Article 81(1), as opposed to Article 81(3) EC and to confirm whether Article 81(3)'s four cumulative conditions must also be fulfilled when balancing under Article 81(1) EC, or whether the two conditions set out above can be ignored there.

Drawing more concrete conclusions is hard, due to the lack of clarity in the cases. However, the Community Courts and the Commission should explain which objectives

---

[198]   See, eg Case Nos 1035/1/1/04 and 1041/2/1/04 *The Racecourse Association and Others v OFT* para 167 and Nazzini (2006) 505 *ff*.

[199]   See, eg Commission, *RCP 1992*, point 77 and SEC(92) 1986, Ch D(iii). Although, Jans (2000) 275, 276, suggests that these statements merely indicate that the competition rules apply to environmental agreements.

[200]   As reported by A-G Léger, at p 1607 of his Opinion.

[201]   Commission, *Article 81(3) Guidelines*, para 18(2); although, Commission, *Article 81(3) Guidelines* are silent on balancing within Art 81(1), as per *Wouters*.

[202]   Ch 6, Section 3.2 discusses the pros and cons of this approach.

[203]   The *Wouters* Case, para 90.

[204]   This is particularly important as London says that there is not even agreement between DG COMP and DG Environment about where the balance is in environmental cases, London (2003) 271.

can be balanced within Article 81(1). The content of each policy objective must also be clearly stated.[205] This helps us to ascertain why the objective is being pursued; and the importance of the objective, both in relation to its own qualitative import, but also because its weight may be enhanced if it also contributes to the achievement of other relevant objectives.

I now turn to the balancing under Article 81(3) EC. Chapter 4 examines mere-balancing there; then, Chapter 5 investigates a second method that the Commission uses to weigh different objectives, market-balancing.

---

[205] See, eg the Commission's comments in COM(90) 556 1.

4

How the Balance is Implemented –
Mere-Balancing in Article 81(3) EC

1 INTRODUCTION

Public policy considerations are relevant in Article 81 EC.[1] This begs the question of where these issues are considered and how they are taken into account. This chapter focuses on public policy balancing in Article 81(3), specifically mere-balancing.[2]

Once it has been established that Article 81(1) has been infringed[3] then the agreement can be examined under Article 81(3) EC.[4] Public policy objectives may be (and have been) considered under Article 81(3). The CFI has emphasised that:

> [I]n the context of an overall assessment, the Commission is entitled to base itself on considerations connected with the pursuit of the public interest in order to grant exemption under Article 85(3) [now Article 81(3)] of the Treaty.[5]

---

[1] See Ch 2.

[2] Mere-balancing (external balancing) is essentially balancing public policy goals outside of the economic efficiency assessment, see Ch 1, Section 2.2. Ch 3 dealt with mere-balancing in Art 81(1) EC and Ch 5 discusses market (internal) balancing throughout Art 81.

[3] In order for Art 81(3) EC to be considered, it must normally have been shown that Art 81(1) has been infringed, Case T-328/03 *O2 (Germany) GmbH & Co OHG v Commission* para 96 and Commission, *Article 81(3) Guidelines*, para 40.

[4] Commission, *Article 81(3) Guidelines*, para 11.

[5] Joined Cases T-528/93 etc *Métropole Télévision v Commission* para 118. See other references in Ch 2, n 157.

As the public interest is relevant in Article 81(3) EC, one needs to know how to consider it and any limits that there might be in the balancing process. Section 2's analysis of mere-balancing under Article 81(3)'s first test[6] focuses on the first of these issues through an examination of various public policy objectives. The seven objectives I discuss were selected because I consider them representative of the way the balance is conducted; because they illustrate several points of interest; and, in addition, the case law is more developed for them than for other factors. Section 3 then examines the limits of public policy balancing under Article 81(3) EC. Monti suggests some strict limits to the balance, which I argue are not to be found in the case law or in principle.

Once again, explaining how public policy balancing works should provide greater legal certainty to undertakings and help the Member States' courts and competition authorities to apply Article 81 in an open and consistent manner. Unfortunately, this chapter cannot provide definitive guidance, due to the paucity of relevant decisions, and the lack of clarity within those that exist. Nevertheless, it hopes to provide a helpful step on the road to transparency.[7]

2 COMPROMISE WITHIN ARTICLE 81(3) EC

One needs to know how to take the public interest into account in Article 81(3) EC. Section 2 focuses on this issue via an examination of seven public policy objectives: economic efficiency, Section 2.1; market integration, Section 2.2; environmental protection, Section 2.3; consumer protection, Section 2.4; culture, Section 2.5; industrial policy, Section 2.6; and security of the energy supply, Section 2.7.[8]

2.1 Economic efficiency

While there is some debate about the relevance of economic efficiency in an Article 81(1) analysis; there is no such discussion in relation to Article 81 as a whole. Although there are no references to the concept in the Community Courts' Article 81 jurisprudence[9] the concept regularly occurs in academic writing, as well as in Commission regulations and notices.[10]

Economic efficiency carries a lot of weight and is used in both a positive and a negative sense within Article 81(3)'s balance; ie agreements that enhance it are given extra weight in the balance, while those which reduce or undermine economic efficiency are less likely to be exempted and may even carry negative weight in the balance with public policy. Other chapters deal with economic efficiency in detail,[11] so, it is not discussed further here.

---

[6] Ch 7 considers the presence of non-economic objectives within Art 81(3)'s other tests.

[7] Ch 7 makes some policy recommendations based upon the observations made here.

[8] Other public policy goals have been balanced within Art 81(3) EC, see Ch 2, nn 156 and 158.

[9] With the exception of the *Matra* Case para 89, where the CFI merely summarises the parties' arguments and the *Glaxo* Case, where the CFI refers to consumer welfare, although this is on appeal.

[10] See, eg the *New Motor Vehicle Block Exemption*, recitals 4–6; the *Vertical Restraints Block Exemption*, recitals 5–7, 13; Commission, *Horizontal Guidelines*, paras 10, 27–29 and Commission, *Article 81(3) Guidelines*, paras 13, 33.

[11] See Ch 1, the rest of Ch 4 and Ch 5.

2.2 Market integration

This section deals with Article 81(3)'s market integration/economic efficiency balance. Chapter 3 discussed the goals of both the economic efficiency and market integration objectives, arguing that it is unclear what market integration means and why it is pursued. The same lack of clarity is present in Article 81(3) EC. Nevertheless, market integration weighs heavily in the balance.[12]

In order to investigate where the balance lies in the conflict between market integration and economic efficiency I look first at absolute territorial protection; then, I examine two weaker forms of territorial protection, restrictions on passive and active sales. I discuss the balance between economic efficiency and market integration, assuming that the former is the appropriate test under Article 81(1) and that the latter goal is, in these cases, raised under Article 81(3) EC.[13]

Under Article 81(3) EC, attempts to impose absolute territorial protection through an agreement that appreciably affects trade between Member States will not normally be exempted and fines will likely be imposed.[14] For example, the *Vertical Restraints Block Exemption*[15] lists passive sales restrictions as hardcore restraints, preventing agreements containing absolute territorial protection from falling within it. Nor is absolute territorial protection acceptable under the *New Technology Transfer Block Exemption*.[16] This was also the case under Article 81(1) EC.[17]

In Commission decision, *Glaxo Wellcome*,[18] Glaxo argued that it should be allowed to impose absolute territorial protection as this would increase consumer welfare, and contribute towards public health, industrial policy, economic and social cohesion and competitiveness improvements.[19] The Commission did not accept this on the facts. However, it did consider the argument in detail and, while its decision is slightly unclear

---

[12]   Other objectives are also balanced against market integration within Art 81(3), eg culture; Section 2 examines these later.

[13]   I assume that consumer welfare (a type of economic efficiency) is the relevant test under Art 81(1) EC, based on Case T-168/01 *GlaxoSmithKline Services v Commission* para 118; the CFI's judgment is now on appeal to the ECJ, Cases C-501/06, 513/06, 515/06 and 519/06 on, amongst other things, this point. Ch 6 discusses the notion of a restriction of competition in some detail, but even recent cases give some support to the idea that it may not be (part of) a consumer welfare test, eg the ECJ's *Meca-Medina* Case (2006) paras 42–45. I also assume that there is a conflict between economic efficiency and market integration, contrary to the CFI's argument in the *Glaxo* Case paras 119–21, because I am unpersuaded by the CFI's reading of the *Consten and Grundig* Case, see Ch 2, Section 2.2.2; this point is also on appeal. If either of these assumptions are incorrect then there is either no balance taking place here, or it is of a different nature to the one I assume, in which case one should proceed to Section 2.3.

[14]   The sole exception that I can find, and it relates only to indirect restrictions on exports to achieve absolute territorial protection, is Commission decision, *Transocean Marine Paint Association* (1967) 14. This is an early exception to the general rule. Later Commission exemptions of this agreement did not allow absolute territorial protection, Commission decisions, *Transocean Marine Paint Association* (1974) 20; *Transocean Marine Paint Association* (1980), para 7 and *Transocean Marine Paint Association* (1988), para 15. Commission decision, *Sicasov*, is not an exception to this rule as the purchasers in the relevant territory could export, see below.

[15]   The *Vertical Restraints Block Exemption*, recital 10 and art 4(b).

[16]   *New Technology Transfer Block Exemption*, art 4.

[17]   See Ch 3, Section 2.1.

[18]   Which was successfully appealed, Case T-168/01 *GlaxoSmithKline Services v Commission*; note the CFI's judgment is now on appeal to the ECJ, Cases C-501/06, 513/06, 515/06 and 519/06.

[19]   Commission decision, *Glaxo Wellcome*, paras 89–99.

on this point,[20] it might have allowed absolute territorial protection, if it had been persuaded that this was justified on the facts.[21]

As with Article 81(1), it is unclear whether economic arguments, such as Glaxo's, will prevail. This is because we do not know why market integration is pursued. In 1996, the Commission explained its position in the following way:

> Market integration has also been promoted by current policy which ensures that distribution systems can never establish absolute territorial protection. Thus, even though the pro-competitive gains from granting territorial exclusivity are permitted, vertical agreements must still leave open the possibility of alternative sources of supply. Markets cannot be sealed off to prevent intermediaries exploiting price differences.[22]

As we saw in relation to Article 81(1), there are several potential justifications for such a statement. Market integration may be justified on economic efficiency grounds, with the Commission merely creating a presumption that absolute territorial protection nearly always undermines economic efficiency. Alternatively, the absolute territorial protection prohibition may not be exclusively based on an efficiency rationale; it might, for example, be based on consumer protection, development of trade or integrationist grounds.[23]

An absolute prohibition on absolute territorial protection is hard to justify under either head. In the *Matra* Case, the CFI held that, in principle, no anti-competitive practice can exist which, whatever the extent of its effects on a given market, cannot be exempted, provided that all the conditions laid down in Article 81(3) EC are satisfied.[24] This means that, unlike under Article 81(1) EC, irrebuttable presumptions are unacceptable under Article 81(3), unless they never achieve the optimal balance, which is not the case for absolute territorial protection.[25]

More recently the Commission's policy statements have become more explicitly economic.[26] While the Commission seems convinced that absolute territorial protection is generally not efficient it seems open to persuasion in a specific case.

Absolute territorial protection is an extreme. Restrictions on both active and passive sales are possible under Article 81(3) EC. This is not surprising because, to the extent that this is a balancing exercise, the less market integration is undermined, as formally defined, then the easier it should be to outweigh it.

Restrictions on passive sales can be more readily restricted under Article 81(3) EC than under Article 81(1).[27] This is partly because the Commission is more willing to accept a

---

[20]   ibid, paras 124, 152 and p 186.

[21]   Although such hope has been voiced before, Gyselen (1984) 649, 650.

[22]   COM(96) 721, Executive Summary VII, para 26. See also, Executive Summary VI; Case 27/77 *Tepea v Commission* para 57.

[23]   See Ch 3, Section 2.1.

[24]   The *Matra* Case para 85. Also see Commission decision, *Glaxo Wellcome*, para 153 and the *Glaxo* Case paras 233, 234.

[25]   Motta (2004) 23, shows that an absolute prohibition on absolute territorial protection would not always be justified on economic efficiency, consumer protection or integrationist grounds.

[26]   The Commission, *Vertical Guidelines* emphasise an economic approach and do not prohibit absolute territorial protection per se and Commission, *Article 81(3) Guidelines* imply that market integration is there to achieve welfare ends, para 13. In addition, in its discussion of the guideline's first condition, s 3.2, the Commission focuses exclusively on efficiency issues; see also para 21. The CFI is even more explicit in the *Glaxo* Case: see references in n 13 above. The ECJ's judgment in the appeal should clarify these points. Ideally, the ECJ will explain why the market integration goal exists; if it follows the CFI, then there will be no conflict between economic efficiency and market integration.

[27]   See, eg Commission, *Technology Transfer Guidelines*, para 101.

wider range of economic efficiency arguments under Article 81(3).[28] One may be able to get an individual exemption, for example, if exemption is necessary to encourage the distributor to bear the costs of entering a new product or geographic market.[29] This is on the condition that the actors do not have too much market power in relation to customers and competitors.[30] Furthermore, under Commission, *New Technology Transfer Block Exemption*,[31] the licensor can restrict his or her ability to make passive sales into a licensee's territory.[32] Restrictions on passive sales by licensees into an exclusive territory reserved for the licensor are also possible;[33] as are those into other licensees' territories.[34] These restrictions on passive sales between a licensee and its licensor are allowed because, up to the market share threshold, such restraints, where restrictive of competition, are presumed to promote pro-competitive dissemination of technology and integration of such technology into the licensee's production assets.[35]

As one might expect, exemption is even more likely for active sales restrictions, where there are no passive sales restrictions.[36] Active sales bans are allowed under the *Vertical Restraints Block Exemption*, where the restriction does not limit sales by the buyer's customers.[37] While the Commission does not explain why the balance should shift in favour of economic efficiency in this way, in a similar provision in an old block exemption, the Commission relied on economic efficiency arguments.[38] Active sales can be restricted under Commission, *New Technology Transfer Block Exemption* even more easily than passive sales.[39]

One example of the ease of justifying territorial protection under Article 81(3), as opposed to Article 81(1) EC, can be found in Commission decision, *Sicasov*. Under the

---

[28]   This tendency may increase in the shadow of the *Métropole télévision* and *Glaxo* Cases, see Chs 3 and 6.

[29]   See the examples cited in Commission, *Vertical Guidelines*, para 174.

[30]   See the examples cited ibid, para 163.

[31]   Commission, *Vertical Guidelines*, para 50, explain that passive sales restrictions takes one outside of the *Vertical Restraints Block Exemption*, art 4(b). The exceptions to this principle in art 4(b)–(d) are special cases, mainly related to selective distribution and are not exactly on point, although they do also relate to exclusive distribution.

[32]   Commission, *Technology Transfer Guidelines*, para 99, up to the market share threshold of 30%. On market share thresholds see Commission, *New Technology Transfer Block Exemption*, art 3.

[33]   Commission, *New Technology Transfer Block Exemption*, art 4(2)(b)(i).

[34]   Where the territory has been allocated by the licensor to another licensee and this is the first two years that this other licensee is selling the contract products in that territory, art 4(2)(b)(ii). Non-reciprocal passive sales restrictions are also possible, even where the parties are competing undertakings, Commission, *New Technology Transfer Block Exemption*, art 4(1)(c)(iv).

[35]   Commission, *Technology Transfer Guidelines*, para 100. Similar reasons are given for allowing the restriction between licensees too, see para 101.

[36]   Some applaud the difference in approach to active and passive sales. They say that the main justification for territorial protection is to prevent free riders. As '… the most effective way for the free rider to use the marketing efforts of another is through active sales …', allowing active sales and preventing passive sales makes sense, Monti (2002) 1067. While this view holds under the *Vertical Restraints Block Exemption*, passive sales are allowed under Commission, *New Technology Transfer Block Exemption*, precisely because of the free rider argument, see Commission, *Technology Transfer Guidelines*, para 101. It is not clear that the distinction between the Commission's approach to active and passive sales is based purely on this reading of the free rider problem, but rather on a balance between policy objectives.

[37]   Art 4(b). As long as the other provisions of the block exemption are adhered to, eg the market share of the supplier must not exceed 30% of the relevant market: art 2(1).

[38]   *Exclusive Distribution Block Exemption*, recitals 5 and 6. *Vertical Restraints Block Exemption* replaced this exemption. Commission, *Vertical Guidelines*, paras 161–63 use similar arguments.

[39]   See Commission, *New Technology Transfer Block Exemption*, art 4(2)(b).

agreement, Sicasov groups together the breeders of plant varieties protected in France.[40] It is the only company in France to do this.[41] Among other things, Sicasov's role is to manage the plant varieties entrusted to it by its breeders. These breeders may give Sicasov the right to grant non-exclusive multiplication and sales licences or an exclusive production and sales concession.[42]

The Commission considered an obligation on licence holders not to export certified seeds directly from France for four years, from the variety's registration in the common catalogue. The Commission said that this prevented licence holders both from conducting an active sales policy outside France and from meeting unsolicited demands from customers in other Member States. The only way that seeds could be exported is via a third party established in France.[43] This made purchases more difficult and less advantageous than those made direct from licence holders; reducing competition in the other Member States, in breach of Article 81(1).[44]

The Commission then looked at Article 81(3) and applied, by analogy, the *Old Technology Transfer Block Exemption*.[45] The Commission felt that the prohibition on exporting certified seeds contributed to improving production and distribution and promoting technical and economic progress. The arrangement facilitated the dissemination of new varieties in Member States other than France by encouraging undertakings in those Member States to accept the risks involved in producing and/or marketing new varieties selected by the French breeders. Those firms, said the Commission, would be more inclined to disseminate new varieties if they could be certain that they would not have to contend with direct exports from France during the launch period. So, French breeders should have the right to protect their licence holders and distributors (in Member States other than France) against direct competition from French licence holders by imposing on the latter contractual clauses prohibiting them from exporting certified seeds. Secondly, the export prohibition improves the organisation of the production and distribution of seeds in France by encouraging French licence holders to concentrate their efforts on French territory with a view to providing user farmers with regular and adequate supplies.[46]

These benefits, said the Commission, will be preserved as parallel exports from France are allowed.[47] The Commission also noted that the *Old Technology Transfer Block Exemption* allowed for the prohibition of active and passive sales;[48] which, is the same under its replacement.

Note that *Sicasov* was not cleared under Article 81(1) EC, which seems strange in the light of the similarities between the arguments used by the Commission in favour of exemption here and those used by the ECJ in favour of negative clearance in *Nungesser*.[49]

---

[40]   Commission decision, *Sicasov*, para 1.
[41]   ibid, para 3.
[42]   ibid, para 2.
[43]   ibid, para 62.
[44]   ibid, para 63.
[45]   ibid, paras 70–73.
[46]   ibid, para 74.
[47]   ibid, para 75.
[48]   ibid, para 74.
[49]   See Ch 3, Section 2.1.

This is less important since 1 May 2004, given the procedural changes, although it is still relevant for certain purposes, such as the burden of proof and which tests must be considered.[50]

Before concluding this part, I would like to highlight one more point. Market integration is largely used as a negative factor to block what would otherwise be an acceptable agreement. Because of this it is not normally examined alone in Article 81(3), but rather in relation to another factor which it is being balanced against, such as environmental protection. However, there are hints that the beneficial effects that an agreement allegedly has on market integration has, on occasion, been successfully argued in order to *support* an exemption which might otherwise not have been allowed, ie market integration can have positive weight in the balance too.[51]

In conclusion, market integration is, to a large extent, being treated as formulaically as it was under Article 81(1) EC. There still seems to be an absolute ban on absolute territorial protection. This makes little sense from either an economic or an integrationist perspective, especially where there is strong inter-brand competition. It is not even clear, although hopefully the ECJ's judgment in *Glaxo* will clarify this, whether the ban is based on a balancing on the merits, between market integration and consumer welfare; or, whether it is merely there to provide clarity (a per se rule) because of the belief that absolute territorial protection nearly always undermines consumer welfare. In any event, irrebuttable per se rules in Article 81(3) are wrong in law.

On the assumption that market integration and consumer welfare can conflict,[52] the Commission seems more prepared to accept economic integration arguments outside of absolute territorial protection. One can see the balance shifting as market integration, as formally defined, is infringed less and less. No satisfactory attempt is made to explain the weighting or to justify this shift.

Market integration is given more weight under Article 81(1) than Article 81(3) EC. Commission decision, *Sicasov* shows that the Commission is willing to accept economic efficiency arguments within the framework of Article 81(3) to a degree that it is not willing to do in Article 81(1) EC. This may be because not all economic efficiency arguments are acceptable under Article 81(1) EC, post *Métropole télévision*.

Market integration has long been, and continues to be,[53] an important Treaty objective, providing both positive and negative weight in the balance. At one level at least, clarity is present with respect to absolute territorial protection, but it is difficult to understand the rationale for the Commission's position. As regards the rest, neither clarity nor justifications abound. The time has come to explain why market integration is important, whether

[50]   Reg 1/2003, art 2; the issue is further discussed in Ch 6's Introduction. See Ch 3, Section 3 for a discussion of the latter point.

[51]   One possible example of this can be found in a Commission comfort letter, *BDO Binder International*. There the Commission held that an agreement between an international network of accountancy firms fell within Art 81(1) because it made it more likely that the parties would refer the case to the 'right' firm geographically rather than doing it themselves, although they were allowed to do the work themselves if they wanted to under the agreement. However, the Commission found that Art 81(3) was applicable. The Art 81(1) interests were outweighed by the increased ability to compete on an international scale with larger competitors and of increased cross-border co-operation, Commission, *RCP 1991* 335 and Press Release IP/91/602. See also, Commission decisions, *Banque Nationale de Paris – Dresdner Bank*, para 18 and *EBU/Eurovision*, para 61. Without denying the relevance of industrial policy in *BDO*, market integration seems to have a lot of positive weight in the balance as well.

[52]   Which is something that I believe that the ECJ hints at in Joined Cases C-468/06 to C-478/06 *Sot Lelos kai Sia EE and Others v GlaxoSmithKline AEVE Farmakeftikon Proionton*.

[53]   See Ch 3, Section 2.1.

it conflicts with economic efficiency and to place this all within a formal balancing mechanism. Hopefully, the ECJ's judgment in *Glaxo* will go some way to doing just that.

2.3 Environmental protection

The Commission has said that improving the environment contributes to improving production or distribution or to promoting economic or technical progress.[54] While it is not exclusively the case, most environmental agreements are weighed in the balance against economic efficiency. These two objectives can conflict, where the environmental considerations have not been internalised.[55]

Environmental protection has been considered within Article 81(3) EC in Commission decisions from as far back as 1983.[56] However, in the early decisions, made at around the time that environmental protection's policy-linking clause was added by the Single European Act 1987,[57] environmental protection was probably a marginal consideration; by which I mean that its inclusion does not seem to have had much influence on the outcome of the balance. Nevertheless, environmental protection has become increasingly important since then.[58] The Maastricht Treaty 1992 inserted environmental protection into both Articles 2 and 3 EC. In addition, the Treaty now demanded a high level of environmental protection.[59] Furthermore, the policy-linking clause's wording was strengthened; no longer was environmental policy merely a 'component of other policies', it had to be 'integrated into the definition and implementation' of these other policies.

Environmental protection's growing importance in Article 81's balance is in line with its increasing influence in the Treaty as a whole.[60] Shortly before the Maastricht Treaty's changes entered into effect, the Commission mentioned environmental protection within

---

[54]   Commission, *RCP 1995*, point 85. See also, Jans and Vedder (2008) 274–76 and Gyselen (1994) 255, 256. Commission, *Horizontal Guidelines*, para 193, explains 'Environmental agreements caught by Art 81(1) may attain economic benefits which ... outweigh their negative effects on competition. To fulfil this condition, there must be net benefits in terms of reduced environmental pressure resulting from the agreement, as compared to a baseline where no action is taken. In other words, the expected economic benefits must outweigh the costs.' The Commission only refers to 'economic benefits'. What about the environment? In fact, the Commission goes on to refer to Art 174(3) EC and European Parliament and Council Decision, *Review of 'Towards Sustainability'*, art 7(d). These discuss the need to assess the costs and benefits of taking action, as well as developing economic evaluation techniques for doing so. So it seems that, when the Commission refers to 'economic benefits' in para 193, it means 'net benefits in terms of reduced environmental pressure resulting from the agreement'.

Based on Commission, *Horizontal Guidelines*, para 193, Komninos (2006) 461, implies that 'economic benefits' means that the Commission only takes account of non-economic objectives which '... have economic parameters and can always be measured as such.' See also Semmelmann (2008) 31–46. Commission decision, *MasterCard*, para 695, appears to support this. Ch 8 discusses the benefits of a common meter. Nevertheless, it also emphasises that these meters have limits. Decision-making cannot become a simple sum and Komninos is probably going too far. The Commission emphasises the need to develop economic evaluation techniques. However, non-economic objectives can be considered within Art 81 even where this has not been done. In relation to impact assessments more generally the Commission, after explaining that it was desirable to quantify economic, social and environmental impacts in monetary terms, emphasised that impacts that cannot be expressed in quantitative or monetary terms should not be seen as less important, COM(2002) 276 16.

[55]   ie priced into the economic assessment, Ch 1, Section 2.2.2.

[56]   Commission decisions, *Carbon Gas Technologie*, para 1 of the Art 81(3) discussion and *BBC/Brown Boveri*, para 23.

[57]   Then Art 130r(2) EC, now Art 6 EC.

[58]   Monti (2002) 1073–75, 1078 and Monti (2007) 92, 93 agrees.

[59]   Then Art 130r(2) EC, now Art 174(2) EC.

[60]   For a more detailed discussion of the growing importance of environmental policy in the Treaty see Wasmeier (2001) 160, 161 and Vogelaar (1994) 530–34.

its Article 81(3) analysis in at least three further decisions,[61] there was also a 1994 decision which considered it[62] and another in 2001.[63] I will show that it has been considered in other decisions since then; although there is no indication that environmental protection has had decisive weight in these decisions. In other words, arguably, the environmental factor alone has not yet warranted exemption in a formal Commission decision.

The Commission has tried to show the limit of the weight of environmental protection in the balance. I examine some express policy statements the Commission has made on this issue. Then I spotlight two matters that the Commission adjudicated upon which raise environmental issues; highlighting some interesting points that they raise, including the fact that the Commission ignored its own policy statements.

In 1995 the Commission said that environmental protection considerations will not normally justify the closure of national markets, squeezing products out of the market and price fixing.[64] It is unclear whether environmental protection can outweigh other restrictions on competition; the implication is that it could.

The Commission has also explained how to assess environmental protection's weight in the balance, saying that the agreement's:

[C]osts include the effects of lessened competition along with compliance costs for economic operators and/or effects on third parties. The benefits might be assessed in two stages. Where consumers individually have a positive rate of return from the agreement under reasonable payback periods, there is no need for the aggregate environmental benefits to be objectively established. Otherwise, a cost-benefit analysis may be necessary to assess whether net benefits for consumers in general are likely under reasonable assumptions.[65]

There is some confusion in the language, because this citation is probably discussing two Article 81(3) tests, the optimal balance (test one) and that consumers must get a fair share of the resulting benefit (test two).[66] These are not easy to separate out.

As regards environmental costs, the Commission considers effects on third parties, as well as the parties to the agreement and their customers. This is particularly important in relation to environmental issues; because, as externalities,[67] they are not adequately priced by the parties as they ignore the costs for third parties, which can be great. In relation to the benefits side of the balance, the position is less clear. The Commission refers to two stages. First, it asks whether consumers individually have a positive rate of return under reasonable payback periods.[68] If this test is not fulfilled,[69] then one must also check whether net benefits for consumers in general are likely. The first point is that if consumers as individuals do not benefit, then it is unlikely that consumers (collectively) will benefit either. This implies that the reference to 'net benefits for consumers in

---

[61]   Commission decisions, *Assurpol*, para 38; *Ford/Volkswagen*, para 26 and *Exxon/Shell*, para 68.
[62]   Commission decision, *Philips-Osram*, paras 25–27.
[63]   As reported in Case T-289/01 *Der Grüne Punkt – DSD v Commission* para 38.
[64]   Commission, *RCP 1995*, point 85.
[65]   Commission, *Horizontal Guidelines*, point 194.
[66]   Commission, *Horizontal Guidelines*, paras 32–34. The same occurred in Commission decision, *CECED*, paras 47–57 and *Visa International – Multilateral Interchange Fee*, paras 74–95. See also, Vedder (2003) 165–70.
[67]   See Ch 1, Section 2.2.2.
[68]   *EACEM* probably falls within this head, see the following discussion.
[69]   Although in Commission decision, *CECED*, paras 47–57, the Commission discussed both individual and collective effects. There the agreement fulfilled both categories. This seems unnecessary under the Commission, *Horizontal Guidelines*, as they now stand.

general' refers not to *consumers of the relevant products* but to society at large.[70] The Commission seems shy of admitting to the task of balancing public and private benefits. However, by assessing the benefits, for society as a whole, rather than the actual consumers of the product, the Commission makes it even easier to include non-welfare objectives in the balance.[71] It is similar to adopting a welfare approach for economic efficiency that is not based on a partial equilibrium analysis.[72] This distinction became more prominent in Commission decision, *CECED*, which I will argue adopts this wider interpretation of 'consumer'.[73]

Now I want to examine the balance. Where the environmental externality has not been internalised, environmental protection and economic efficiency can conflict. In one matter, the Commission approved an agreement between the European Association of Consumer Electronics Manufacturers (EACEM) and sixteen of its members, all major manufacturers of television sets and video cassette recorders.[74] This was a voluntary commitment to reduce the electricity consumption of their equipment in stand-by mode. The participating manufacturers undertook to meet certain targets on power use. This sort of co-ordinated action, said the Commission, falls within Article 81(1) EC.

The Commission exempted the agreement under Article 81(3) EC finding that the scheme's energy-saving and environmental benefits represented technical and economic progress.[75] The maximum cost per unit of reducing the standby power use of a television or video recorder was estimated at ECU 3. No individual firm in the industry felt able to introduce lower power use in its products; margins are low in the industry and the firms feared that consumers would not be prepared to pay in advance for power savings, although they would save money in the long term. The consumer electronics industry therefore devised the voluntary scheme in consultation with the Commission. This reduction in energy consumption, said DG Competition, will have a significant impact in terms of the management of energy resources, reductions in CO_2 emissions and, accordingly, measures to counter global warming.

Environmental benefits flow from this agreement. Furthermore, DG Competition may have focused exclusively on these benefits to justify exemption. Not only that, but the reason the consumer electronics industry gives for needing the agreement, the fact that these energy savings will push up the purchase price by about ECU 3 and that consumers would not be prepared to accept this, implies that environmental protection has been accepted in the face of static economic efficiency losses. Neither they nor the Commission feel able to trust consumers to take account of the reduced operating costs of this equipment in their purchasing decisions.[76]

---

[70]   Martínez-López (2002) 52 and Monti (2007) 92. Some argue that this does not properly reflect Art 81(3)'s meaning, Komninos (2006) 459.

[71]   The Commission adopted a similar argument in Press Release, IP/94/151.

[72]   Ch 5, Section 4 explains the partial equilibrium approach.

[73]   Although it should be stressed once more that the Commission has merged Art 81(3)'s first and second tests here and the issue is unclear. Furthermore, one may question whether Commission, *Horizontal Guidelines*, para 194 should present the individual and society assessments as alternative, as opposed to cumulative, tests. This may undermine Art 81(3)'s second test, see Ch 7.

[74]   Commission, *RCP 1998*, point 130 and p 152; approval came by comfort letter. Also see the Commission's position in *Spa Monopole/GDB*, reported in Commission, *RCP 1993*, point 240.

[75]   A DG XVII (Energy) report said that the energy savings could amount to 3.2 TWh per year from 2005.

[76]   See also, Commission decision, *CECED*, para 12.

Nevertheless, this voluntary agreement has not altered the balance that much. Although static allocative efficiency is reduced by the agreement, the effect should not be great because there is no agreement on price, nor is there agreement on which technology to adopt. I do not have access to the Commission's data or reasoning, but it may be that the Commission decided the matter purely on economic grounds, that is, that the lifetime cost would fall. Despite this, and if only due to the environmental reasoning used, I believe that the matter is an important step towards the use of environmental protection as a key justification for exemption.

EACEM should be compared with Commission decision, *CECED*, which came only two years later. *CECED* is, to my knowledge, the first formal Commission decision giving environmental protection significant importance in the balancing process.[77] It concerned an agreement between CECED, a Brussels-based association comprising manufacturers of domestic appliances and national trade associations, and its members. These companies made up some 95 per cent of the relevant market. The agreement concerned the market for domestic washing machines in the EEA and a decision not to import or produce machines below a certain environmental standard.

The Commission found that the agreement breached Article 81(1) as the parties to the agreement bound themselves to cease producing and/or importing into the Community certain categories of washing machines on criteria relating to their energy efficiency, reducing consumer choice and technical diversity. The Commission believed that the agreement would appreciably raise production costs, probably also reducing demand. It would also reduce the demand for electricity.

Despite this, the Commission cleared the agreement under Article 81(3) EC. The Commission raises two potential benefits. First, while these machines would cost more initially, money would be saved on electricity bills over their lifecycle. The weight of this argument is reduced, because new energy-efficient machines were unlikely in the medium term. Secondly, the Commission notes the costs of otherwise avoiding the CO_2 and SO_2 emissions which the energy efficiency prevents; these savings would be seven times greater than the additional consumer costs. However, these savings cannot be taken into account in an economic efficiency analysis (at least a partial equilibrium approach) because these costs are externalities.[78] Therefore, the benefits can only be those of society, as opposed to the individual consumers concerned.

In conclusion, environmental protection is now an important element in the Article 81(3) balance[79] and the importance of the Commission decision, *CECED*, should not be overlooked. The parties agreed to limit production, in direct contravention of Article 81(1)(b) EC.[80] A horizontal agreement this extensive is likely to result in the elimination of a significant amount of cheaper goods from the Community. This is likely to push up

---

[77]   Some believe that Commission decision, *CECED* was only decided on environmental grounds; see, eg van Gerven (2004) 430 and Lenz (2000) 65–71. Although, a lot of emphasis was placed on these considerations, other objectives were probably also relevant. In fact, to my mind, no formal Commission decision has been exempted, based on environmental factors alone. Vedder (2003) 162–69; Monti (2002) 1073–75 and Vogelaar (1994) 547 are ambiguous about what weight they believe environmental protection has been given here, so far.

[78]   Ch 8 argues that invoking environmental considerations in this way is inappropriate.

[79]   Whish and Sufrin (2000) 149, agree that environmental protection is given significant weight under Art 81(3). There are many other examples of environmental protection being considered in the balance, eg Commission, *RCP 1998*, points 133, 134 and pp 152, 153; Commission, *RCP 2000* 148; Commission, *RCP 2001* 36; Press Release, IP/01/850; Commission decision, *DSD and others* and Press Release, IP/01/1279.

[80]   Also see the Commission, *Horizontal Guidelines*, para 2.

prices. Speculative dynamic efficiency gains have been chosen at the expense of concrete (at least short term) allocative efficiency losses.[81] Not only that, but the environmental problem has not even been attacked at source.[82]

Environmental protection was the Commission's inspiration in *CECED*.[83] What is debatable is whether environmental protection considerations have yet outweighed economic efficiency in the balance. This seems unlikely. In *CECED* the Commission tried to cloak environmental criteria in economic language, by emphasising that the lifecycle costs had fallen.[84]

Nevertheless, environmental considerations will be increasingly important in Article 81(3) in the future, as they were under Article 81(1). First of all, this seems to be the political will of the Member States.[85] Secondly, perhaps because of this the way that the Commission conducts the balance, it may now be easier to take account of factors such as environmental protection.[86] Thirdly, there is evidence to suggest that the Commission is becoming increasingly confident in its use of environmental protection in the balance; or at least the increasingly ready to rely upon it there.[87] Fourthly, the two basic justifications that the Commission uses in *EACEM* and *CECED* are essentially the same: (a) while the agreement will increase the initial purchase price of the good, this will be compensated for by reduced electricity bills; (b) there will also be huge benefits to the environment. However, in *EACEM*, the focus was very much on (a), which makes the environmental and economic efficiency conflict disappear. In *CECED*, while the Commission found that customers would make savings over the lifecycle of the washing machine,[88] it seems to put the greater emphasis on the greater benefits to society as a whole (b);[89] perhaps because the first set of benefits would not occur in the short term. This is also a sign of the Commission's growing confidence in environmental protection criteria. Finally, in *EACEM* there was only a comfort letter; in *CECED* the Commission adopted a decision. An increasingly confident Commission is prepared to risk an appeal on an environmental point.

---

[81] See the Commission, *Horizontal Guidelines*, para 32.

[82] Contrary to Art 174(2) EC, ie the real problem is the effects of electricity generation/use. As the Commission accepts, this issue could be more efficiently reduced by looking at generators and not washing machines, Commission decision, *CECED*, paras 51, 55.

[83] See Commission, *RCP 2000*, point 97.

[84] *cf* Monti (2007) 93. In a more recent decision, Commission decision, *ARGEV, ARO*, a recycling scheme was cleared under 81(3) EC, but this also seems to have been done purely on economic considerations.

[85] See the *Declaration on Article 175 of the Treaty*, attached to the Treaty of Nice.

[86] For example, the Commission looks at the benefits to society as a whole, rather than just those 'directly affected' by the agreement.

[87] For example, in Commission decision, *CECED* the parties agreed to cease producing/importing certain goods into the Community. As they make up some 95% of the relevant market this is likely to effectively squeeze such goods out of the Community altogether. This is a significant amount of goods, some 10% of washing machines sold in the Community at the date of the agreement, paras 13 and 66. This is in direct contravention of the Commission's own statements in this regard in 1995, see above. This implies that the balance may have shifted. The Commission may have also relaxed its original position in relation to agreements on prices and closure of national markets to foreign operators, see Commission decision, *Eco-Emballages* and *Biffpack, Difpak and Wastepack*, in Commission, *RCP 2000* 148.

[88] Commission decision, *CECED*, para 52.

[89] ibid, paras 47–51.

It is entirely appropriate to give environmental protection more weight.[90] Nevertheless, it should not be forgotten that, in the examples discussed, environmental protection is competing against economic efficiency. Here economic efficiency must, at the very least, be contributing towards the Community's consumer protection, employment and industrial policies. These have increased in power and importance too. There is a risk that the lack of structure in the Commission's balancing analysis may have led it to conduct an incomplete assessment, not giving enough weight to these other objectives.

2.4 Consumer protection[91]

Consumer protection has not been expressly invoked many times within Article 81(3)'s balance.[92] This part considers agreements where consumer protection conflicts with economic efficiency; first, I briefly examine the consumer protection head itself.

Consumer protection has been defined extremely widely. The concept includes:

> [P]rotecting the health, safety and economic interests of consumers, as well as … promoting their right to information, education and to organise themselves in order to safeguard their interests.[93]

Lane writes that while consumer protection has been recognised as a legitimate objective of Community law, capable of justifying barriers to the free movement of goods the ECJ has always given priority to the requirements of the common/internal market.[94] Since then, Article 153(2) EC, consumer protection's policy-linking clause, has been inserted into the Treaty, by the Treaty of Amsterdam; it demands that consumer protection requirements shall be taken into account in defining and implementing other Community policies and activities.

In 1994, Advocate-General Tesauro argued that consumer protection considerations should not be unconnected with the interpretation of Article 81 EC.[95] Consumer protection has, at times, been given positive weight in the Article 81(3) balance, although only in conjunction with other factors;[96] here, I consider a decision where it was given negative weight.[97]

My analysis here focuses on Commission decision, *Grundig's EC distribution system*. There, the Commission (re)affirmed an Article 81(3) exemption of an agreement between

---

[90]   Art 174(2) EC now demands a high level of environmental protection, environmental policy also has a policy-linking clause, Art 6.

[91]   For a more detailed analysis of Community consumer protection see Cseres (2004); Stuyck (2000); Weatherill (1997); Reich (1997); Averitt and Lande (1996–7); Lonbay (1996) and Reich and Woodroffe (1994).

[92]   One reason may be that the second Art 81(3) test says that agreements must allow consumers a fair share of the resulting benefit; Ch 7, Section 3 discusses this provision. Perhaps consumer protection issues are concentrated there. Sometimes the Commission collapses Art 81(3)'s first two tests into the same discussion, see n 66 above.

[93]   Art 153(1) EC.

[94]   Lane (1993) 959, 960.

[95]   Case C-376/92 *Metro SB-Großmärkte v Cartier*, para 33. Although A-G Tesauro clearly refers to the whole of Art 81 in this quote the context of these comments implies that he is only really discussing Art 81(1) EC, see paras 29 and 41 in particular. Consumer protection has not been considered much within Art 81(1), unless one includes market integration here, see Ch 3, Section 2.1.

[96]   See, eg Commission decision, *CECED*, paras 47–57 and Haracoglou (2006), s 4.3.2.1.

[97]   See also Haracoglou (2006), s 4.3.2.2. Monti (2007) 94, makes a similar argument in relation to environmental protection.

one of Europe's largest manufacturers of consumer electronics products equipment and its selective distributors. The matter illustrates consumer protection's inclusion with negative weight in the balance.

The agreement in *Grundig's EC distribution system* contained two clauses that the Commission found restrictive of competition; an obligation on wholesalers and retailers to stock the entire range of Grundig products and an obligation on retailers to display a representative selection of these products.[98] The Commission said that these restrictions were justified by the nature of the products.[99] It exempted the agreement. This is the end of the matter as far as the official decision is concerned, consumer protection was not discussed. However, when discussing this decision in its *Report on Competition Policy*, the Commission explained its decision by saying that, in the interests of better consumer protection, it had asked Grundig to amend its warranty terms[100] so that, even where a defective item was purchased in another Member State, a consumer could have it repaired under warranty in the Member State in which he lived. To that end, said the Commission, Grundig intends to introduce a uniform, Europe-wide, contractual comprehensive warranty and has begun building up an appropriate network of repair shops. It has undertaken, pending completion of the network, to honour all cross-border warranty claims on an *ex gratia* basis.[101]

The implication here is that, in the form originally notified to the Commission, the agreement undermined consumer welfare. Faulty Grundig goods could only be repaired under warranty in the Member State in which they were originally purchased. It seems that, originally, the Commission found at least three problems; without the guarantee issue, the agreement would have been justified under Article 81(3) on the basis of pure economic efficiency criteria.[102] The fact that Grundig agreed to amend the agreement implies that without this change the exemption would not have been granted.[103]

The Commission is prepared to rely on consumer protection, although it has not got to the stage of relying exclusively on this in a decision as yet.[104] The growing influence of consumer protection can be explained by the extra weight the Treaty now gives it. Consumer protection was inserted into the Treaty as an Article 3 activity (as well as given its own article demanding a high level of protection) by the Maastricht Treaty 1992, which came into force in November 1993; just in time for the *Grundig's EC distribution system* decision, in December 1993. Thus the basis for relying on consumer protection is certainly there. However, consumer protection is often better achieved by focusing on consumer welfare.[105] This may mean that there should not be a conflict between these objectives at all. Even if this is not the case here, efficient markets bring with them many other benefits,

---

[98]   Commission decision, *Grundig's EC distribution system*, para 35.

[99]   ibid, paras 36–41.

[100]   Gyselen (2002a) 189, 190, believes that a similar negotiation occurred in Commission decision, *Ford/Volkswagen*.

[101]   Commission, *RCP 1993*, point 243.

[102]   Commission decision, *Grundig's EC distribution system*, para 36.

[103]   This could be because consumer protection has negative weight in Art 81(3), or because it helps make a restriction of competition under Art 81(1) EC. A similar clause to this one was found restrictive in Case 31/85 *ETA Fabriques d'Ébauches v DK Investment*, but this was based on market integration and not consumer protection grounds.

[104]   Note the comments in this regard in Commission decision, *Grundig's EC distribution system*, para 19, as opposed to the operative part.

[105]   As Ch 1, Section 2.1 points out.

including many favoured within the Treaty; which means that economic efficiency should have a lot of weight. A proper balancing system would expressly take account of this.

On the other hand, before the Commission introduces consumer protection issues as a separate head into the balance, it should show that they are not already internalised by consumers. Although many of these buyers will not be sophisticated, these products are often expensive and one might have expected purchasers to ensure that the warranty covered them, or at least take this issue into account when they considered the original purchase of the product. Presumably, purchasers from parallel importers get the product cheaper than those that buy directly through Grundig's distribution network; so the consumer protection benefit may already be priced in by them.

Another point relates to the value of the policy-linking clauses. Consumer protection's policy-linking clause was not added until the Treaty of Amsterdam in 1997. Chapter 7 argues that the policy-linking clauses have an important legal certainty function. They help litigants force the Commission to take account of these objectives in its decisions. It may also be that the consumer protection policy-linking clause gives the Commission the confidence to rely exclusively on this Treaty objective in its future decisions. As we will see when we look at the security of energy supply head, policy-linking clauses may be helpful, but are not necessary, in this regard.

In conclusion, consumer protection can be dealt with outside of the specific balance with which this section deals.[106] However, on occasion it has been considered within our framework. Consumer protection seems able to display either positive or negative weight in the balance. And, in at least one case, consumer protection was given significant weight in the balance. Indeed, it was given so much weight that it would have prevented the exemption of an agreement that was otherwise acceptable on economic efficiency grounds.

2.5 Culture[107]

Cultural issues have been raised in several cases. This has generated a need to balance cultural policy against two other distinct Treaty objectives, market integration and economic efficiency.[108] Lane says that the real threat to, especially the less widespread cultures, is often the homogenisation that is a necessary product of the Treaty and the internal market.[109] Indeed, culture has been defined as resistance to the transformation of certain traditional values.[110] To the extent that economic efficiency leads to market integration, there may be a conflict between it and cultural objectives too.[111]

Community action shall be aimed at:

---

[106]   See Ch 5, Section 2.
[107]   For other analyses of culture within the Community see Psychogiopoulou (2005); Tunney (2001); Bouterse (1994) and Loman, Mortelmans, Post and Watson (1992). The Institutions also have other tactics for avoiding conflicts here, see Ch 2, Section 2.
[108]   Fleming (2002) 751.
[109]   Lane (1993) 954.
[110]   Fukuyama (1992) 215.
[111]   Although this need not always be the case, see Commission decisions, *EBU/Eurovision System* and *Eurovision*.

[I]mprovement of the knowledge and dissemination of the culture and history of the European peoples; conservation and safeguarding of cultural heritage of European significance; non-commercial cultural exchanges; artistic and literary creation, including in the audiovisual sector.[112]

Article 151(1) EC says that the Community shall contribute to the flowering of the cultures of the Member States, while respecting their national and regional diversity and at the same time bringing the common cultural heritage to the fore.[113] There is also a policy-linking clause for culture; which stresses that 'The Community shall take cultural aspects into account in its action under other provisions of this Treaty, in particular in order to respect and to promote the diversity of its cultures.'[114]

Cultural issues have been discussed in several cases before the Community Courts, both implicitly[115] and explicitly.[116] There have been many 'cultural battles' in the context of the free movement provisions.[117] Article 30 EC allows restrictions on the free movement of goods for the protection of national treasures possessing artistic, historic or archaeological value. Lane writes that close scrutiny of the free movement cases shows that the Community Courts are ill inclined to place the interests of cultural protection over those of the internal market.[118] Nevertheless, the ECJ may have paid heed to Article 151(4) EC, which had just been added by the Maastricht Treaty, in the *Keck and Mithouard* Case.[119] This judgment paved the way for cultural 'exceptions' to Article 28.

Cultural arguments have also been raised under Article 81(3) EC[120] and the Commission maintains that:

Protection of culture is ... a concern that has always been borne in mind in applying the competition rules that effect businesses. Although culture is not mentioned by name in Articles 85 and 86 [now Articles 81 and 82 EC], the Commission takes account of the cultural dimension when investigating cases in the light of those provisions. Yet the aim is not to frame a policy on

---

[112]   Art 151(2) EC; it is unclear what is meant by cultural protection, Tunney (2001) 173–76.

[113]   There is a lot of confusion about exactly what is being promoted. Culture is not defined—see above—but it seems that one can take account of Community (what is this?), national and regional cultures. Tunney notes that the word 'flowering' is '... certainly different to preservation and conservation, and suggests a commitment to dynamism.', Tunney (2001) 175.

[114]   Art 151(4) EC. A-G La Pergola said of this provision, '... culture is regarded, in the Treaty, as a, so to speak, 'transversal' value, which potentially touches upon every sector of activity within the Community.', Case C-42/97 *European Parliament v Council*, 880. For other reasons to consider culture (UNESCO Convention on the Protection and Promotion of the Diversity of Cultural Expressions and the Charter of Fundamental Rights) see Craufurd Smith (2008) 38, 39.

[115]   Although it was not raised specifically in the case, the refusal to allow Germany to continue to apply its Beer Purity Laws in Case 178/84 *Commission v Germany* was considered an important attack on their culture.

[116]   Case C-180/89 *Commission v Italy* esp para 20 and Joined Cases 60 and 61/84 *Cinéthèque v Fédération nationale des cinémas français* paras 16, 22, 24.

[117]   For example, Case C-159/90 *Society for the Protection of the Unborn Children Ireland Ltd. v Grogan*.

[118]   Lane (1993) 954–56.

[119]   Case C-267 and 268/91 *Criminal proceedings against Bernard Keck and Daniel Mithouard*.

[120]   The *Coöperatieve Stremsel* Case 861–62, the French Government appears to use cultural arguments in part; the *Coditel* Case, 3391, the respondents used a purposive cultural argument; the *VBVB and VBBB* Case; possibly, Case T-66/89 *Publishers Association v Commission*, as the case turned on indispensability, apparently accepting the underlying cultural point, para 72; and the *Échirolles* Case, A-G Alber argues that at 151(4) means that '... the Community has to take cultural aspects into account in ... the field of competition ...', para 41. France and Norway appear to agree, see para 15 of the Opinion. See also, Monti (2007) 103–10.

culture or to make value judgments in applying the provisions, but rather to assess business practices with due regard to the repercussions they could have on the Community's cultural policy.[121]

As it did in relation to environmental policy, the Commission seeks to disguise the fact that balancing these values demands political decisions. While competition law is certainly not the only, or necessarily the best, tool through which to pursue one's cultural policy,[122] the Commission cannot avoid making 'value judgments' when applying the cultural provisions in Article 81. Indeed, 'assessing business practices with due regard to the repercussions they could have on the Community's cultural policy' means precisely weighing the benefit of these business practices against the cultural effects.

The principal area of tension is in relation to resale price maintenance agreements for books. Such systems are often characterised by the fact that a publisher, often in accord with other publishers, fixes a resale price for the books that he or she publishes and seeks to ensure that this is followed at the point of retail sale.[123] Such clauses are normally looked at in a negative light, because they restrict competition.[124] I will show that, in principle, the Commission seems prepared to place cultural considerations in the balance; however, it is becoming increasingly wary of accepting that agreements that undermine economic efficiency generate cultural benefits. Nevertheless, when it sees a conflict, the Commission gives cultural concerns a lot of weight in the balance, despite the fact that the Treaty does not demand a high level of cultural protection.

In 1993, the Commission accepted that a conflict between culture and market integration/economic efficiency exists and sought to find a balance between these objectives. Then, it was prepared to regard resale price maintenance arrangements for books as compatible with the competition rules provided that they were individual and purely vertical.[125] This is an important European competition rule that is potentially being breached. The ECJ has said that price competition is so important that it can never be eliminated.[126] Here, the Commission is prepared to restrict competition for cultural aims. This could have a serious affect on the degree of price competition.

However, the Council does not believe that the Commission's balance has gone far enough. This has led to some tension between these institutions. In fact, a Council decision, from 1997, addressed this specific issue. The Council highlighted Article 152 EC, as well as the dual character of books as the bearers of cultural values and as merchandise; strongly emphasising the importance of a balanced assessment of the cultural and economic aspects of book. Then it went on to acknowledge the importance attached by a number of Member States to fixed book prices as a means of maintaining and promoting the diversity and broad accessibility of books, in the consumer's cultural interest. It

---

[121]   Commission, *RCP 1993*, point 175. See also points 176, 177 and the implication from Commission Memo, *European collecting societies* (2008); Andries and Julien-Malvy (2008) 55 and Commission decision, *Joint selling of the commercial rights of the UEFA Champions League* [2003] para 129.

[122]   See Ch 1, Section 3.2.1.

[123]   See, eg the *VBVB and VBBB* Case para 6.

[124]   See Commission, *Vertical Guidelines*, paras 47, 111, 112.

[125]   In other words, while the Commission could not agree to prices, pricing methods or conditions of sale being established collectively by all publishers, it was prepared to countenance a system whereby an individual publisher lays down the conditions of sale and retail prices of his books in the bookshops. In taking this stance, the Commission sought to afford some protection to publishers of books produced in smaller print runs, Commission, *RCP 1993*, point 177.

[126]   The *Metro I* Case para 21.

pointed out that the national authorities of those Member States have accepted the restriction of competition entailed by fixed book prices on the grounds of general cultural importance. The Council adds that it considers:

> ... that the inclusion in the Treaty of Article 128(4) [now Article 151(4)] has created a new situation, the consequences of which must be clarified with respect to the application of Community competition rules to cross-border fixed book prices ...[127]

The Council asks the Commission to study the significance of Article 151(4) for the implementation of Article 81 EC that may concern cross-border fixed book prices. The Commission should indicate, if appropriate, the ways to enable fixed book-price regulations/agreements within homogeneous linguistic areas to be applied, and submit its conclusions to the Council. The Council appears to ask the Commission to accept horizontal as well as vertical retail price maintenance agreements.

The next step in the saga came in 1997, when the Commission commissioned a study investigating whether systems of retail price maintenance for books have the positive impact on the market which their proponents believe. The study concluded that, as far as the alleged advantages of book retail price maintenance are concerned, namely to further title production, to prevent concentration in publishing, to guarantee a wide network of retail outlets and to keep prices down for the consumer, countries with retail price maintenance have no substantial advantage, if any, over countries without.[128] This suggests that, at least in the area of retail price maintenance for books, there is no conflict between cultural policy and market integration/economic efficiency. In which case, one would expect the Commission to change its 1993 policy as well.

The Commission study's findings were contradicted by a later European Parliament study.[129] It is unclear what will the Council (and the European Parliament) will do next or how this factual dispute will be resolved.

In conclusion, three points should be highlighted. First, the content of the cultural objective has not been properly debated, nor is the interaction between the objectives fully explained. There is ambiguity as to exactly what Article 151 EC means by cultural protection. Even within that provision there is a potential conflict between 'conservation and safeguarding' (presumably, the Member States' cultures) and the 'need to improve the knowledge of and dissemination of Member State cultures'. While fixed book prices may have been thought to achieve the former there is no discussion about how they affected the latter. This is particularly important because the dissemination of Member State cultures

---

[127] Council, *Decision on Fixed Book Prices*. Also see European Parliament Resolution, *on book prices in Germany and Austria* and Council, *Resolution on Fixed Book Prices 2*. For similar sentiments in relation to the cultural and other aspects of sports, see Council Declaration, *on the specific characteristics of sport and its social function in Europe* (2000).

[128] This study is not public. Nevertheless, Commission, *RCP 1997* 361, describes it.

In Press Release, IP/98/30, in relation to a matter where the Commission had released a statement of objections, it noted, under the improvement of production or distribution in Art 81(3) EC, that 'It is not at all clear that the profits generated by the system of fixed prices are in fact being ploughed back into the production of less popular books with a higher cultural value. And in countries where fixed prices have been abolished, such as Sweden, Belgium, Finland and the United Kingdom, the production and distribution of books have not been damaged.' See also, OFT, *An Evaluation of the Impact upon Productivity of Ending Resale Price Maintenance on Books* (2008).

[129] European Parliament Resolution, *on common book price-fixing across borders*, which, on the basis of Art 95 EC, has issued a report containing a draft directive on the fixing of book prices, European Parliament, *Report on Book Price Fixing Directive*.

may coincide with the market integration objective.[130] Not only that, but these agreements undermine economic efficiency, at least in the allocative sense.

Secondly, cultural issues have been balanced against important Treaty objectives, namely market integration and economic efficiency. The Commission was unprepared to accept horizontal resale price maintenance. However, for cultural reasons, it was prepared to exempt certain restrictions of competition, namely vertical resale price maintenance between publishers and booksellers; which it would probably not otherwise have accepted.[131] This gives cultural objectives a lot of weight. This is particularly important because, while cultural considerations have always been present in the Treaty, culture as a general heading on its own, and its policy-linking clause, were only introduced by the Maastricht Treaty. Furthermore, the Treaty does not demand a high level of cultural protection. Sometimes, in order to protect a specific value, it must take priority over others that are normally considered more important.

Finally, the 1997 Commission study suggests that the Council and the Member States are incorrect in their assertion that resale price maintenance for books furthers cultural aims in the way that they suggest. The Commission is less likely to tolerate exceptional distortions of competition in this area in future. This may lead to the revocation, at least in practice, of the Commission's 1993 statement, cited above. However, it must be underlined that this is not because the balance has shifted between cultural and other values. Rather, the Commission increasingly believes that there is no conflict between these values in this area.[132] It now seems to accept that the positive advantages that it believed flowed from book resale price maintenance have been shown not to flow at all. Indeed, the Commission now seems to think that price competition is the best way to achieve the distribution of books in line with cultural demands.

2.6 Industrial policy[133]

The Community's industrial policy is largely non-interventionist. Despite this, industrial policy has often been raised in the Article 81(3) balance, often via pleas to sanction EU firms' efforts to increase their R&D knowledge or expenditure. When it is raised there, industrial policy has been given positive weight. The early cases often involved the restructuring of entire industries.[134] Industrial policy has also been considered alongside other Treaty objectives as a tool to promote Community industry outside of a general

---

[130] Commission decision, *EBU/Eurovision System*.

[131] See Commission, *Vertical Guidelines*, paras 47, 111, 112 and the *Vertical Block Exemption Regulation*, recital 10 and art 4(a). Exemption for vertical resale price maintenance is only granted exceptionally, B&C (2008), para 6–084 and Commission decision, *Nathan-Bricolux*, paras 110, 111.

[132] Although, if a conflict were found then a recent Commission decision implied that cultural issues would be considered in Art 81 EC, see Commission decision, *CISAC*.

[133] For a more detailed analysis of industrial policy within the Community see Amato (1997); Sauter (1997) and Buigues, Jacquemin and Sapir (1995).

[134] Restructuring has been dealt with in detail elsewhere and is only referred to in passing here; see Commission decisions, *Synthetic Fibres* and *Stichting Baksteen*, as well as Commission, *RCP 1993*, points 82, 84, 85(i), 88, 89, 158; European Parliament, *Resolution on the Twenty-fourth Competition Report*, para 15; Hornsby (1987); Bouterse (1994) ch 5 and Monti (2007) 95. These issues still arise today, see Case C-209/07 *The Competition Authority v BIDS*.

restructuring.[135] When this has happened, industrial policy has been an important factor in the Article 81(3) balance. Section 2.6 briefly examines the industrial policy head before investigating the balance in more detail.

Article 157(1) EC says:

> The Community and the Member States shall ensure that the conditions necessary for the competitiveness of the Community's industry exist. For that purpose, in accordance with a system of open and competitive markets, their action shall be aimed at: speeding up the adjustment of industry to structural changes; encouraging an environment favourable to initiative and to the development of undertakings throughout the Community, particularly small and medium-sized undertakings; encouraging an environment favourable to co-operation between undertakings; fostering better exploitation of the industrial potential of policies of innovation, research and technological development.

Community industrial policy is not (any longer[136]) principally[137] aimed at the creation of 'national' giants.[138] Rather, the Commission seeks to create a favourable business-friendly working environment.[139] Importantly, Article 157(3) EC, inserted in 1992, adds:

> This Title shall not provide a basis for the introduction by the Community of any measure which could lead to a distortion of competition.

This is the only time that the Treaty makes such a statement. It is an attempt to rule out the use of industrial policy in the Article 81(3) balancing exercise,[140] although possibly not in an Article 81(1) balance.[141] The Commission has largely ignored Article 81(3)[142] and industrial policy still affects the Article 81(3) balance; although possibly less than it did before 1992. Whenever it has been considered, industrial policy has been an important,[143] if not the dominant factor[144] in the Article 81(3) exemption. In fact, it is one of the most heavily used objectives in the Article 81(3) balance.[145]

---

[135]   Roth (2006).

[136]   Amato (1997) 44, 45, 58–64.

[137]   Although the Commission's attitude in this area cannot be described as a pure liberal-market philosophy, see Marques (2000) 49–56 and chs 3–5.

[138]   Kroes (2008).

[139]   See COM(90) 556, esp pp 5 *ff*; COM(93) 700 and Commission, *RCP 1993*, points 156–61; *RCP 1994*, points 14, 17, as well as Monti (2002) 1072.

[140]   Sauter (1997) 110.

[141]   If industrial policy were included in an Art 81(1) balance and industrial policy 'won' then one may conclude that there was not a restriction of competition at all. As a result, Title XVI of the Treaty would not have provided a basis for a measure leading to a distortion (or restriction) of competition. Note however that, when the ECJ balanced under Art 81(1) in the *Wouters* Case, it found a restriction of competition, but decided that it was justified and so held that Art 81(1) was not breached. The fact that it actually found a restriction of competition in that case may undermine this argument.

[142]   Bourgeois and Demaret (1995) 85, 92–95, 106; Commission, *RCP 1984*, point 42 and *RCP 1993*, point 158. This is ironic. It was the competition services of the Commission that pressed for the provision, Sauter (1997) 112.

[143]   Examples include, Commission decisions, *Carbon Gas Technologie*, para 1 of the 81(3) discussion and *BBC/Brown Boveri*, para 23.

[144]   Examples include, Commission decisions, *Optical Fibres*, paras 59–61; *Olivetti/Canon*, para 54; *BDO Binder International*, reported in Commission, *RCP 1991* 335; *Philips-Thomson-Sagem*, reported in Commission, *RCP 1993*, point 215; *Exxon/Shell*, para 67; *Lufthansa/SAS*, reported in Commission, *RCP 1996* 120, 121 and Commission decision, *GEAE/P&W*. Also see Commission Notice, *GEC-Siemens/Plessey*, paras 20–22, 27–29.

[145]   See, eg the *Matra* Case, discussed below, and Commission, *RCP 1993*, point 158.

Industrial policy also impacts on other public policy goals. The Commission stresses that both efficient markets and innovation are necessary for industrial progress.[146] As well as contributing to industrial policy, increasing R&D should raise the standard of living and employment;[147] however, at a certain point the pursuit of R&D may undermine economic efficiency[148] and thus industrial policy. The European Parliament and Council also point to a link between R&D and environmental protection.[149]

In order to explore the balance in relation to industrial policy I focus on two matters, the *Matra* Case and Commission decision, *BT-MCI*. These show that it is hard to split out mere and market balancing in relation to industrial policy.[150] In addition, they seem to show that Article 157(3) EC is largely ignored in relation to Article 81(3).

Industrial policy is considered within Article 81(3) in the *Matra* Case. This CFI judgment was an appeal from Commission decision, *Ford/Volkswagen*;[151] which considered an agreement between Ford and Volkswagen to build a manufacturing plant for MPVs in Portugal. Ford was the fifth largest supplier in the Community passenger car market (11.6 per cent), Volkswagen was described as a leading supplier (15.5 per cent). The joint venture would develop, engineer and manufacture the MPV. Ford and Volkswagen would distribute them separately under their own brand names.

The joint venture involved an investment of USD 2.9 billion, should last for about 10 years and would take place on a green-field site in Portugal. The parties sought an individual exemption on the grounds that the MPV market is low volume and neither party was an important supplier in this market.[152] The vehicle would be produced in a new and modern plant and the joint venture would have positive effects on the infrastructure and employment in one of the Community's poorest regions.

The Commission found a breach of Article 81(1) because Ford and VW were important competitors in the European and world car markets and in view of their financial, technical and research capacities, either company was, in principle, capable of producing a MPV on its own.[153] The Commission also felt that the joint venture would involve a substantial sharing of technical and other know how which could affect their behaviour on neighbouring market segments.[154] The Commission saw these as serious reductions in economic efficiency both on the relevant market, as well as other markets, in the long and short term.

However, the Commission granted an individual exemption. It emphasised the fact that through co-operation the parties should be able to produce an advanced vehicle designed

---

[146]   COM(96) 463 8(iii). See also, Commission, *RCP 1991*, points 47–50; Kroes (2008) and Hildebrand (2002) 18.

[147]   COM(90) 556 3–5; COM(93) 632 29, 30 and Commission, *RCP 1997* 138.

[148]   See Ch 1, Section 2.1.

[149]   See European Parliament and Council Decision, *review of 'Towards Sustainability'*, recital 20, arts 2, 3(1)(f) and 8.

[150]   In mere-balancing, public policy considerations are balanced against economic efficiency (externally). Market-balancing is where public policy goals are attained through manipulating the efficiency assessment itself. Ch 1, Section 2.2 explains the distinction in more detail.

[151]   Discussed in Ch 2, Section 2.3.1.

[152]   Ford had about 1% and VW essentially had no share. Renault dominated the market, 54.7%.

[153]   Commission decision, *Ford/Volkswagen*, para 19.

[154]   ibid, para 21, although para 38 contradicts this somewhat.

to meet the requirements of European consumers. Co-operation will also lead to a rationalisation of the manufacturing process, enabling both parties to combine their know how in many areas.[155]

On appeal, the CFI noted that the agreement would lead to a factory in Portugal. In addition, this was the first application by a European car manufacturer of the enhanced form of manufacturing process recommended in 1990 by the most authoritative research-ers in the field of technological development. The CFI held that an optimisation of the manufacturing process of that kind fell within Article 81(3) EC's first test.[156]

It is hard, though not impossible, for the CFI to adopt this position unless it reads Article 81(3) in terms of *Community* industrial policy.[157] There was no technical progress on a worldwide scale, as better manufacturing processes already existed outside Europe.

Not only is industrial policy the dominant, if not the only, factor[158] to be considered under Article 81(3) EC; but, the Commission granted an exemption on this ground in the face of serious restrictions of competition, and allocative efficiency in particular.[159] The CFI accepted this. This is despite the direct wording of Article 157(3) EC.

Other decisions make the same point. For example, Commission decision, *BT-MCI*.[160] Under the agreement in *BT-MCI*, British Telecom (BT) was due to take a 20 per cent stake in MCI, becoming the largest single shareholder, although it could not gain control. Newco (N) would be created, a joint venture company, to provide enhanced and value-added global telecommunications services to large companies. The parties would contribute their existing non-correspondent international network facilities to N.[161] N would initially focus on providing enhanced services, including data services, intelligent network services, global outsourcing services, etc. These services were to be global in nature.[162] The Commission found that the current set of national monopolies had not been able to achieve this adequately. Up until then telecom operators had co-operated to link their respective networks, customers were billed separately and in different countries, creating language and other problems.[163] BT and MCI hoped to take advantage of the liberalisation process and new technology to provide a better service.[164]

The Commission found that the relevant geographic market was global.[165] There were some competitors;[166] buyers were sophisticated and would only switch to N if it is cost-effective; they have a lot of bargaining power.[167]

The Commission found that both BT and MCI had the financial and technological capacities to enter the relevant market on their own. On top of that, N's creation means

---

[155] ibid, paras 24, 25.

[156] The *Matra* Case para 109.

[157] ie if it is sufficient that the agreement leads to the improvement of production or distribution in Europe, and/or leads to technical progress here. This position is corroborated at ibid, para 110.

[158] No express efficiency arguments are raised except that production and development costs may fall. Even then no analysis is provided explaining why the reduction in competition caused by the elimination of one competitor will not increase prices.

[159] Commission decision, *Ford/Volkswagen*, paras 20, 21. *cf* Monti (2007) 96.

[160] See also, Commission decision, *Atlas*.

[161] Commission decision, *BT-MCI*, para 2.

[162] ibid, para 6.

[163] ibid, para 7.

[164] ibid, paras 8–10.

[165] ibid, para 15.

[166] ibid, para 17.

[167] ibid, para 18.

that they will probably not develop a competing set of products. The Commission found that: (i) the appointment of BT as exclusive distributor of N within the EEA; (ii) the obligation on the parties to get all global products from N; (iii) the non-compete provision as regards the activities of N; and (iv) the 'loss of rights provision' as regards MCI's activities within the EEA meant that the agreement fell within Article 81(1) EC.[168]

Nevertheless, the Commission found that N would provide cost savings which should generate competition between those seeking to supply it basic telecom transmission capacity. N will create a whole new network, which was considered to be a real advantage over the 'national systems plus' approach used up until then. The Commission said that the combination of BT and MCI technologies would allow N to offer new services more quickly, cheaply and of a more advanced nature than either parent could offer alone. In addition, and *as a related consequence*, MCI technology, said to be one of the best in the world, would be made available to N's European customers. This would allow the Community's most important companies to achieve better telecom performance at the international level, which could enable them to better withstand global competition.[169]

It is more difficult to classify the Commission's arguments in this decision. It is a matter of emphasis. The Commission may have looked to productive efficiencies and then examined some of their consequences; or, it might have developed its industrial policy argument and then tried to achieve it any which way. The second suggestion seems more accurate. First, there is not a proper discussion of productive efficiencies and how these will be affected by the lessening of competition in the longer term. There is, debatably, no discussion of dynamic efficiencies at all, although the fact that N will be able to create a new kind of network may undermine this point somewhat. Secondly, there is the relevance of the words 'as a related consequence'. These are suspicious and imply, in the context in which they are used, that the argument is used because of its consequence, that is, to get MCI technology in the EU. This seems important to the Commission not only because it will help BT, this is implicit; but, it will also help Community businesses to better withstand global competition. Note that it does not say respond to; 'withstand' has a defensive connotation. One might argue that the second point here (the 'related consequence' point) is an economic efficiency (in the form of, total welfare) argument. Once again this is a matter of emphasis. Yet, the emphasis is on industrial policy per se, rather than achieving this through encouraging R&D and other goals through market-based mechanisms. The welfare discussion is non-existent. In any event it is difficult to understand the Commission's logic as N will also be supplying non-Community companies and it is hard to see why the improvement would accrue more strongly to Community undertakings. This is made particularly difficult because the Commission did not split up its arguments into cause (greater competition) and effect (more competitive EU companies). Rather it has mixed everything together, market and industrial policy points, in order to achieve an ultimate goal.

It seems that industrial policy was one of, if not, the decisive Commission objectives in *BT-MCI*. This is even clearer in *Matra*.[170] Industrial policy, in the sense in which it is being

---

[168] ibid, paras 45–48.
[169] ibid, para 53.
[170] A similar position can be seen in various block exemption regulations, eg Commission, *Specialisation Agreements Block Exemption* and comments in Amato (1997) 63, 64; and, Commission, *Motor Vehicle Block Exemption* and comments in Wesseling (2000) 40 and Lukoff (1986).

used here, conflicts with economic efficiency. The Commission and the CFI were not seeking productive efficiency improvements per se. They were encouraging them because of the advantages they would bring, *in Europe*, to European firms.

Furthermore, in *Ford/Volkswagen*, and apparently[171] contrary to the express wording of Article 157(3) EC, the Commission allowed industrial policy to outweigh a serious restriction on competition.[172] Industrial policy must, at times, have a lot of weight in the balance. Indeed, the weight that it has been given is even more spectacular given that, in matters such as these, the pursuit of economic efficiency also has an industrial policy component. At least over the long-term, many economists would agree that the best form of industrial policy is the pursuit of economic efficiency and efficient markets.[173] The Commission has accepted this;[174] Article 157(3) appears to do the same; and yet, in the balance, industrial policy wins. The point is not discussed by either the CFI, or the Commission in its decision.

One might, then, ask whether the CFI and the Commission went too far. What is the gain that the Commission and the CFI were seeking to achieve in, for example, *Matra?* Not, the 15,000 jobs, according to the CFI, so I can exclude them. Volkswagen's experience of using an advanced factory was one of the gains. This will mean more profits for Volkswagen, should they go into the balance? It also means more experience for European employees working in such an advanced factory. The lack of clarity of the content of the industrial policy goal makes such questions difficult to answer. And yet, they need to be answerable if we are to have a rational policy.[175]

The Commission has also used the efficiency test itself to encourage industrial development. As we saw in *BT-MCI*, the difference is often a matter of emphasis.[176] Did the Commission base its decision on economic efficiency grounds or more explicitly on industrial policy grounds; perhaps I misinterpreted the Commission in my reading of this decision? In a sense, this does not matter, as it supports my underlying point that more clarity is needed when implementing the public policy balance.

2.7 Security of energy supply

In essence, security issues normally either relate to the security of the Community's energy supply, or, to that of a particular Member State. They have not been raised very often within Article 81 EC.

I focus on Commission decisions where this issue has been raised. It is important because this goal has been given a lot of weight in the balance, despite the fact that there is no explicit reference to it anywhere in the Treaty. In addition, this is a place where Member

---

[171] This argument is not watertight because Art 157(3) EC says that this title, ie Title XVI, cannot justify distortions of competition. It does not actually say that distortions of competition cannot be justified for industrial policy reasons. However, such an interpretation may undermine Art 157(3)'s purpose.

[172] Commission decision, *Ford/Volkswagen* may also have been influenced by the employment and economic and social cohesion points mentioned later in the decision, see also, Wesseling (1997) 39; Faull and Nikpay (1999), para 2.131 and Amato (1997) 61. However, the CFI did not agree, the *Matra* Case, paras 105–08, 139, see also Faull and Nikpay (2007), para 3.407.

[173] This was highlighted in Ch 1, Section 2.2.

[174] See above, and eg, Commission, *RCP 1991*, point 3 and COM(94) 319 3, 33.

[175] Ch 8 develops these and other related issues.

[176] There is a similarity between the cases discussed here and those discussed in Ch 5, see the discussion in Ch 5, n 43 about the difficulty of distinguishing between mere and market-balancing sometimes.

State interests seem to be weighed; and, where the Member States were themselves often heavily involved in lobbying in favour of the exemption.

Protecting the security of supply of certain important goods is sometimes given a lot of weight in the balance; this was the case, for example, in the *International Energy Agency* decisions.[177] The facts in brief, the International Energy Agency (IEA) tries to respond to oil supply disruptions by ensuring the availability of oil stocks for use in emergencies, and by restraining demand and allocating available supplies among some 23 countries on an equitable basis according to an allocation process. The oil companies have agreed to co-operate with one another in the framework of the International Energy Programme and in the operation of the IEA's emergency oil allocation system. The Commission found this to be a concerted practice as it had the object and effect of taking into account and balancing allocation rights and obligations. This means in some cases directing oil to destinations where it would not have gone had the IEA system not been activated. The Commission added that there might also be an effect on market conditions from the information exchange that the oil companies operate within the framework of the IEA.

Despite this, the Commission granted an individual exemption, saying that the changes aim at improving the reallocation process and that the concerted practice improves the distribution of goods and promotes technical progress by reducing the inconvenience and sharing the difficulties in the case of supply disruptions. As was made clear in the 1983 decision, this could not be achieved by the market alone.[178]

In times of crisis serious damage could be caused by disruptions to the oil supply. The Commission seems to have weighed the advantages of the market against the need for the security of supply in times of crisis. Security of supply carries a lot of weight in the balance; sufficient that, in times of crisis, it completely outweighs the market mechanism. This is another example of an interest being taken into account by the Commission, and given heavy weight in the balance, without the need for a policy-linking clause.

The Commission is also prepared to consider security of supply in the balance outside of times of emergency. In at least two cases, the Commission gives weight to arguments that the agreements concerned would reduce the Community's dependence on the supply of oil from non-Community sources.

Commission decision, *Carbon Gas Technologie* involved an agreement between three Community undertakings to set up a joint subsidiary, CGT, with one third of the shares each. CGT was there to develop, to an industrial standard, a combined pressure gasification process using run-of-mine coal, which has been summarily upgraded, and to commercially exploit this process. The German companies would make all their current and future know how available to CGT free of charge. There was also a five-year non-compete provision if they left the joint venture.[179] The Commission said that both clauses restricted competition.[180]

---

[177] Commission decisions, *International Energy Agency* (1994) and *International Energy Agency* (1983). See also, Bourgeois and Demaret (1995) 95.

[178] Commission decision, *International Energy Agency* (1983), para 6.

[179] Commission decision, *Carbon Gas Technologie*, 17.

[180] ibid, 19.

The Commission conducted an Article 81(3) analysis, in the course of which it discussed several Treaty objectives, including industrial policy and environmental protection. While these policy considerations were important in this case, the first objective that the Commission discusses, and the one that it seems to give the most weight, was security of supply:

> Since 1973, the importation of crude oil into the Community has, as regards availability and prices, been subject to recurrent or constant pressures. Even so, crude oil still accounts for almost 49% of the Community's primary energy consumption. Under these circumstances, it is essential that the degree of dependence on this source of energy be reduced and the pattern of the Community's energy supplies diversified through the harnessing of alternative energy sources, and in particular those available in the Community itself. In the search for greater diversification and self-sufficiency and hence greater stability of energy supplies in the Community, coal gasification in particular creates favourable conditions through improved exploitation of Community coal deposits.

The Commission acknowledged that each of the parties could have developed the technology alone. However, in an attempt to accelerate the development and production of this technology the Commission allowed short-term gains to prevail over the longer-term benefits of competition, even though competing technologies were being developed world-wide.

This exemption decision is certainly more generous than the Commission's *R&D Block Exemption*, which followed just two years afterwards. This regulation required discussion of the market shares of the parties and limits on the time of co-operation, under certain conditions, neither of which was discussed by the Commission here.[181]

The Commission is generous towards horizontal cartels in Commission decision, *Carbon Gas Technologie*. However, due to the fact that it involved, in part, an R&D agreement, one cannot be certain of the weight given to these security of supply issues. Industrial policy seems to have carried some weight too. Furthermore, the Commission obliquely points to dynamic efficiency issues in the decision.[182]

In the light of this it was interesting to see what the Commission would do if R&D and Community industrial policy were not at issue. In fact, just such a case has arisen in relation to the consideration of national security issues under Article 81(3). Once again this arose in the context of security of energy supply. The matter is Commission decision, *Jahrhundertvertrag* and *VIK-GVSt*. This decision involved a set of agreements where German electricity generating utilities and industrial producers of electricity for in-house consumption (auto-generators) agreed to purchase a specific amount of German coal for electricity generation. The agreements essentially form part of an overall plan to support the German coal-mining industry and were promoted by the Federal Ministry for Economic Affairs. The Jahrhundertvertrag is only applicable to companies within the former territory of the Federal Republic of Germany before unification.[183] Two agreements form the basis of the Jahrhundertvertrag. Both were concluded in 1980: (i) the Supplementary Agreement on the sale of German coal up to 1995, between the General Association of the German Coalmining Industry (GVSt) and the Association of the

---

[181] Commission, *R&D Block Exemption*, art 3.
[182] The Commission took a similar position in Commission decision, *BBC/Brown Boveri*, para 23.
[183] Commission decision, *Jahrhundertvertrag* and *VIK-GVSt*, para 1.

German Public Electricity Supply Industry (VDEW) (the *GVSt/VDEW Agreement*); and (ii) the Supplementary Agreement on the sale of German coal to industrial producers of electricity up to 1995, between GVSt and the Association of Industrial Producers of Electricity (VIK) (the *GVSt/VIK Agreement*).[184]

The GVSt/VDEW Agreement replaced an earlier agreement (1977) between the parties. It lays down the arrangements for German coal-purchasing by the electricity supply companies between 1981 and 1996. The companies undertake to purchase and supply a fixed amount of coal, broken down into five-year time-frames. These commitments can be transferred to a limited extent.[185] Prices are fixed by the Federal Minister for Economic Affairs.[186] The GVSt/VIK Agreement also replaced an earlier agreement (1977) between the parties. The parties agree (and did) to prevail upon their members to conclude individual contracts on coal procurement up to the end of 1995.[187] There is an annual average delivery amount provided for in the agreement and individual supply agreements were concluded on the basis of these amounts.[188] The price clause is similar to the GVSt/VDEW Agreement.[189]

The Commission noted that coal production in Germany had fallen over the last few decades and that price levels were a good deal higher than on the world market.[190] This meant that German coal needed state aids.[191]

The Commission found two restrictions of competition in the VDEW agreement. First, it committed the parties to long term purchases of German coal. The Commission found that the arrangement was exclusive, '… restricting competition between the electricity supply companies for primary energy sources.' This means they have jointly deprived themselves of using other coal or other sources of power, for example, nuclear. Secondly, the purchasing commitment also means that to the extent that electricity is generated from the coal so purchased, electricity imports from other Member States are precluded.[192] The Commission also appears to find a restriction of competition in the GVSt/VIK Agreement, but it is not clear why.[193]

Nevertheless, the Commission exempted both agreements. They improve electricity generation and coal production as they provide certainty. Electricity cannot be stored so production and demand must be in constant equilibrium. Therefore, it is particularly important to safeguard the procurement of primary energy resources. The agreements do this for coal, in Germany.[194]

Commission decision, *Jahrhundertvertrag* and *VIK-GVSt* is interesting for many reasons. First, a Member State interest, as opposed to a Community interest, is taken into account in Article 81.[195] Secondly, the Commission's argument is strange. While it might be true to say that long term contracts were needed at this time of instability, it is hard to

---

[184]   ibid, para 2.
[185]   ibid, paras 5, 6.
[186]   ibid, para 7.
[187]   ibid, para 8.
[188]   ibid, para 9.
[189]   ibid, para 10.
[190]   ibid, para 12.
[191]   ibid, para 15.
[192]   ibid, para 24.
[193]   ibid, para 27.
[194]   ibid, para 31.
[195]   Ch 7, Section 2 discusses this in more detail.

believe as these contracts had been in place since 1977 and there is no mention of other Member States using them. Stability of electricity supply could just as well have been achieved through the purchase of non-German coal. Thirdly, the political nature of this case should not be underestimated. The German government was involved to a very high degree. This seems less a case of preserving electricity supply than protecting German mines and employment.[196]

Nevertheless, just imagine that, on the facts, the Commission is right and these agreements did promote the security of energy in Germany; the second issue I wanted to analyse was what weight the Commission gave this criterion in the balance. In fact, it was given enormous weight. Agreements theoretically based on this objective have been allowed to undermine both economic efficiency and market integration; by sealing off the German market as they reduce the demand for electricity generated outside Germany, even that produced in other Member States. Perhaps the Commission did not base its decision exclusively on national security considerations. However, the fact that it is prepared to give that impression implies that it is comfortable with this balance. This means that it could decide this way again in other decisions.

Third, one also needs to examine where the Commission felt it got the power to consider this interest. It is not even referred to in the Treaty; although it might be considered necessary to achieve the Article 2 EC balance. There are no relevant policy-linking clauses, no demands for a high or low level of consideration. It has come from nowhere and is allowed to outweigh fundamental Article 81 objectives, economic efficiency and market integration.[197]

The Community recognises the importance of a secure supply of energy.[198] The Commission is prepared to distort competition to ensure this security in times of need, but also to encourage technologies that are likely to reduce Europeans' reliance on oil imports. Even without the associated industrial policy and R&D considerations, the Commission may, in certain circumstances, undermine important Treaty objectives, such as economic efficiency and market integration, in order to achieve this end in the future. Once again, clarity could have been enhanced by the use of a clear theoretical framework for the balancing.

3 THE BALANCE

Some kind of balance is taking place. The next step is to assess what the Article 81(3) balance is in each area. Due to a lack of clarity in the decision-making process, this is hard. This section starts by examining some limits to the balance that the Commission has made explicit. It argues that all are problematic. So, I ask whether it is possible to induce the

---

[196] GVSt argued in this matter that the agreements were necessary as part of Germany's strategy for safeguarding energy, preserving a national source of supply independent of the international commodity markets; and that they were necessary for the prevention of social strife, speeding up the loss of jobs in this industry '… might result in tensions in the regions concerned that would be difficult to control.' Commission decision, *Jahrhundertvertrag*, para 19. Although these social arguments were not raised in the decision, they may have been decisive in the political importance of this case for Germany.

[197] Although, a combination of political and economic factors have pushed the Commission to allow for the protection of national interests in other periods too, see Wesseling (2000) 36–41.

[198] See COM(95) 682, s 4.3.1.

limits to the balance from the case law. I discuss a set of arguments put forward by Monti in his seminal article on the matter;[199] but I argue that there is little support in the case law for the limits he finds. I conclude that, as yet, public policy goals, where accepted as relevant, have always been given more weight than competition in the Article 81(3) balance.

In some cases the Commission has explicitly said where the balance is. However, it is rarely so clear; I have only found three examples. First, in relation to the balance between market integration and economic efficiency, I argued that there is a per se rule against absolute territorial protection. Here the balance is unsatisfactory. Although there are clear statements on where the balance is, they are not justified by explanations about why it is there and indeed whether there is a conflict at all.[200] The Commission also defined the limits of the balance in relation to cultural criteria; however, it has never implemented this balance in the case law and may now have changed its mind about the existence of a conflict at all. Finally, the Commission provided examples of certain restrictions on competition with environmental benefits that would not be tolerated. Yet, in later cases, it ignored the limits it first imposed; it is unclear why. Perhaps environmental protection has some special status in the balance; or the cases I discussed were exceptions to the general rule, which remains unchanged. I have found no open discussion shedding light on this area. These attempts to explicitly delimit the balance are all mired in controversy.

Given the frailty of the explicit guidance on the limits of the balance, perhaps I can create a rule through induction from the case law. To do this one needs cases on both sides of the balance, ie cases where, for example, environmental protection outweighs economic efficiency and cases where economic efficiency outweighs environmental protection. However, thus far, there are not enough cases to generate a clear idea of where the balance lies. In part, this is due to the lack of clear reasoning in the decisions. More importantly, as I explain below, when accepted as relevant, there is a complete absence of any cases where these non-economic objectives have 'lost'.

So, perhaps I can enlist an ally in this difficult task. One naturally thinks of Monti in relation to this matter, as he has been influential when it comes to explaining the limits of the balance. But even here I find no succour; as I now explain, I do not believe that his position is supported in the case law.[201]

Monti argues that there are three 'core' Article 81 values, economic freedom, economic efficiency and market integration.[202] He describes how they interact.[203] Then, he discusses other public policy goals that are also considered in Article 81(3) EC, making it clear that he does not provide an exhaustive list; he looks at employment, industrial policy, environmental policy and consumer protection. Monti concludes that there is a consistent

---

[199] Monti (2002).

[200] There is some confusion here of late, as the CFI in the *Glaxo* Case says that there is not even a conflict between market integration and economic efficiency as the former is there to achieve the latter. I assume this is incorrect in the light of the *Consten and Grundig* Case, but the ECJ's judgment should clarify this on appeal.

[201] In fact, Monti (2007) 116, 117, may abandon the idea of any current limits.

[202] The limits of the balance are rarely discussed in the English literature, Monti (2002) 1058. Nevertheless, Monti's views are often accepted, See, eg Ariño (2004) 13 and Bouterse (1994) 104. A-G Verloren Van Themaat, seems to adopt a similar position to Monti in the *VBVB/VBBB* Case, 89, (although he may merely be referring to the subjective motivations of the parties here) but he does not explain why the Treaty or the case law supports his conclusions.

[203] Monti (2002) s 2.4.

approach when non-competition factors are analysed, they are combined with the agreement's contribution to the core values in Article 81.[204] Monti then refines this point, saying that the core values are never undermined, but a reduction in competition (for him, economic freedom) is tolerated when this contributes to the achievement of a Community objective, provided that the agreement also improves efficiency.[205]

When examining this argument, I follow the three steps that he uses, as described in the last paragraph. First, Monti seeks justification for the special status of the core policies in the case law. He argues that non-core objectives are only examined if efficiencies are first established.[206] In Commission decision, *Continental/Michelin*,[207] the Commission found that it could not rely on its *R&D Block Exemption* and said:

> The Commission must therefore examine whether the agreement may be granted an exemption by individual decision, such a decision having to take account *not only of the criteria specified in Article 85(3)* [now Article 81(3)], *but also in particular of world competition and the particular circumstances prevailing in the manufacture of high-technology products.*[208] (emphasis added)

Monti's argument focuses on the part in italics. He reads this as saying that one looks first at the Article 81(3) criteria. One does not consider industrial policy at this stage. If the agreement fulfils Article 81(3), then one can look at additional criteria, such as industrial policy.[209] Alternatively, and this is what I believe the Commission is saying, the Commission may cite industrial policy (taking account of world competition and the other factors mentioned in the underlined segment) as a particular kind of objective that can go into the Article 81(3) balance. When the Commission is saying that one does not 'only take account' of the criteria specified in Article 81(3) EC, it may mean that one can take account of other objectives within the balance, even if they are not explicitly mentioned there.[210]

In order for Monti's reading of this passage to be correct, the agreement must fulfil the Article 81(3) criteria first. Only then can industrial policy criteria be examined. However, if Article 81(3) has been fulfilled, then there is no reason to look any further. Article 81(3)'s

---

[204]   Monti (2002) 1077, 1078; see also Faull & Nikpay (1999), para 2.15. As Monti believes that economic freedom is considered in the Art 81(1) analysis, he probably means that the first provision of Art 81(3) demands that the agreement enhance either economic efficiency or market integration. This is unclear however, see next footnote, where he only refers to economic efficiency.

[205]   Monti (2002) 1078. See also, Komninos (2005) 8–10. This more restrictive reading is also in line with a point Monti makes earlier in the same paper, where he argues that in the language of 'neo-classical economics' Art 81(3)'s first condition's wording refers to allocative, productive or dynamic efficiencies, Monti (2002) 1063.

[206]   Monti (2002) 1071, 1072. He only attempts to demonstrate this for industrial policy.

[207]   Monti relies on four Commission matters to support him, Commission decisions, *Optical Fibres; Olivetti/Canon* and *Continental/Michelin* and Commission Notice, *GEC-Siemens/Plessey*. I do not agree that *Optical Fibres*, *Olivetti/Canon* or *GEC-Siemens/Plessey* imply that efficiency requirements are needed; although present in those cases, the Commission does not say that without efficiency savings the parties would have lost. This leaves only Commission decision, *Continental/Michelin*, which I focus on here.

[208]   Commission decision, *Continental/Michelin*, para 21.

[209]   Monti (2002) 1073.

[210]   The Commission made the same point in the *Matra* Case para 96.

four conditions are exhaustive; when they are met the exception is applicable and may not be made dependant on any other condition.[211]

Persuading the Commission that an exemption should be provided is probably easier if there are efficiency reasons in favour of the agreement. However, I have provided examples of cases where the Commission granted exemptions based on, in the words of Monti, non-core Treaty objectives, where economic efficiency (let alone other core values) was not even discussed, for example culture,[212] industrial policy[213] and national security.[214] This was sometimes even the case when the Commission thought that economic efficiency would be undermined, for example, consumer protection.[215] There is no evidence that the core values must be combined with the other Treaty objectives. In fact, I argued that security of the energy supply is not even mentioned in the Treaty and so it is debateable whether this is a Treaty value at all.

To my mind, and this relates to the second part of his argument, Monti has not adequately demonstrated that the core values cannot be undermined by a 'non-core' value either. There are many examples of 'non-core' policies justifying exemption on their own.

One can even go further. In most cases it is not yet possible to see a balance at all.[216] I argued above that in order to establish where the balance is there have to be sufficient cases on both sides of the balance to allow us to pinpoint it. This is not yet possible for a very surprising reason. To my knowledge there are no Commission decisions[217] where non-economic efficiency objectives have been raised,[218] and where the Commission accepted that they were in fact relevant, where these objectives did not win, ie tilt the balance in their favour.[219] This is true in relation to all the objectives that I have investigated; see for example environmental protection,[220] culture,[221] public health,[222] consumer protection[223] and industrial policy.[224]

---

[211]   The *Glaxo* Case para 234; the *Remia* Case para 57; the *Matra* Case para 104 and Commission, *Article 81(3) Guidelines*, para 42. See also, Ch 7.

[212]   Where the Commission is prepared to allow vertical resale price maintenance, not on efficiency grounds, these are never discussed as a benefit, but as a way of reconciling cultural concerns with the competition rules, Commission, *RCP 1993*, point 177.

[213]   Industrial policy considerations outweighed a serious restriction of competition, the *Matra* Case.

[214]   Where the Commission seemed prepared to allow national security considerations to justify what appear to be anti-competitive agreements, Commission decision, *Jahrhundertvertrag* and *VIK-GVSt.*

[215]   Exemption seems to have been refused on consumer protection grounds for an agreement that would have had positive economic efficiency effects, Commission decision, *Grundig's EC distribution system.*

[216]   Rosenthal had a similar view almost 20 years ago, see Rosenthal (1990) 298. For a similar, and more recent view, in the area of environmental protection, see London (2003) 277; although note her attempts at divining the rules for recycling schemes p 276.

[217]   There are the Commission's express statements on these issues, as illustrated above. However, these are obviously non-binding and, in practice, the Commission does not follow them itself, see above. Furthermore, note that the discussion here only considers Art 81(3)'s first test, exemption has been prohibited under Art 81(3)'s other three tests in relation to non-economic objectives.

[218]   A possible question mark must be raised here in respect of market integration; because it is unclear what this policy means, see Chs 1 and 3. Under certain interpretations, however, one can also say that market integration always wins too.

[219]   It may be that, in some cases, the Commission forced the parties to renegotiate in the notification process, see, eg Korah (1987). See below for notes on some cases where there was a clear discussion of the Commission's reasons for such changes. For a contrary view, see Komninos (2006) 468.

[220]   For example, the Commission insisted on changes in several agreements. In Commission decision, *Ansac*, the Commission refused to allow an exemption based on environmental arguments. However, this was because, para 23, they were irrelevant. The Commission also insisted on changes in Commission decision, *Assurpol*, para 1. The reasons for these changes are not explained in the decision. *Spa Monopole/GDB*, reported in Commission, *RCP 1993*, point 240, but here the Commission's reasoning seems to have related to an elimination of

In my opinion, Monti's view underestimates the value of public policy objectives in the Treaty system as a whole and thus their weight in the balance. I do not believe that the case law and decision-making practice of the Community Courts and the Commission support him.

However, there are two further criticisms of Monti's view, based on principle. They are related to his justification for treating economic freedom, efficiency and market integration as core Article 81 aims. Monti argues that because core factors are directly referred to in the text of Article 81 (competition and efficiency) or are central to the Community's task (market integration) then, *prima facie*, they should have more weight than other factors.[225] However, neither Article 81, nor the Treaty as a whole, expressly refers to either

---

competition, rather than the wrong balance. In Commission decision, *Exxon/Shell*, paras 37–39, the Commission insisted on changes to the agreements but this was because the restrictions were not indispensable to achieve the Art 81(3) objectives. In Commission decision *Eco-Emballages*, paras 60–62, the Commission insisted on changes without explaining why these clauses would not have been exempted under Art 81(3) EC.

[221]   In relation to culture, the *VBVB and VBBB* Case paras 54–60, the ECJ merely found that the applicants had not shown on the merits that their agreement would contribute to technical or economic progress under Art 81(3). The underlying Commission decision, *Re VBBB and VBVB Agreement*, found the same, paras 48–53. For a contrary opinion see Loman, Mortelmans, Post and Watson (1992) 105 and, possibly, Bouterse (1994) 104, which suggest that cultural arguments did not 'win' in the balance. Neither source explains why they believe this. In the *Leclerc* Case, the Art 81 issue was not relevant because there was not an affect on trade between Member States, para 20. In Commission decision, *Publishers Association – Net Book Agreement* paras 70 *ff* and the subsequent appeals, Case T-66/89. *Publishers Association v Commission*, paras 71–118 and Case C-360/92P *Publishers Association v Commission*, paras 35–49, exemption was not granted because the restrictions were not indispensable. The Commission insisted on changes to the agreement in Commission decision, *EBU/Eurovision System*, paras 41–44, but the reason for this is not clear in the decision. In *KVB – Hanselsreglement*, the Commission concluded that there was no effect on inter State trade, Press Release IP/99/668. In *German/Austrian Book Arrangements: Sammelrevers* the agreement did not apply to inter State trade, Press Release, IP/02/461. Finally, in the *Échirolles* Case, the Art 81 issue was irrelevant because there no affect on trade, para 24.

[222]   In relation to public health, some exemptions have been refused. In Commission decision, *Grohe's distribution system*, refusal was based on indispensability grounds, paras 20 *ff*, see also Commission decision, *Ideal-Standard's distribution system*, paras 19 *ff*. The Commission also insisted upon certain amendments in Commission decision, *Pasteur Mérieux-Merck*, para 3. These appear to have been in order to restore competition to an appropriate level, see eg paras 102–13, but I question whether this decision was really about public health anyway, in many ways it looks like a pure economic analysis. The Commission also insisted that the duration of the co-operation be shortened in Commission decision, *Asahi/Saint-Gobain*, paras 12, 30, 31, but this was on indispensability grounds.

[223]   In Joined Cases 209 to 215 and 218/78 *Heintz van Landewyck v Commission*, para 185, the ECJ held that '… it may be seriously doubted whether the benefits in relation to distribution arising from the recommendation are likely sufficiently to compensate for the stringent restrictions which it imposes on competition in respect of sales terms allowed the trade to justify the conclusion that it contributes to improving the distribution of cigarettes within the meaning of Art 85(3) [now Art 81(3)].' This does not undermine my argument for two reasons. First, at the beginning of para 185 the ECJ explains that this conclusion came as a result of its previous discussion. This discussion related to the necessity of the restrictions for achieving the desired social aim, Art 81(3)(a). At para 184 the ECJ found that the restrictions were not necessary to achieve the social aim. As a result, it is not surprising that the social aims were not 'likely sufficiently to compensate for the stringent restrictions'. In other words, the ECJ's comments probably do not relate to the optimal balance. Secondly, the ECJ makes it clear at para 186] that its comments are obiter dicta because the restrictions also eliminated competition.

[224]   In relation to industrial policy, Commission decision, *Optical Fibres*, paras 2–4, 57, 58, 61–72, the Commission insisted on an amendment to the agreement as originally notified, but this seems to have been because the restrictions were not deemed indispensable. The fact that Corning was a US entity may also have had an impact on the Commission. In Commission decision, *Banque Nationale de Paris/Dresdner Bank*, para 15, the Commission insisted on an amendment to the agreement, but that seems to have been because they were worried about eliminating potential competition.

[225]   Monti (2002) 1070. Faull and Nikpay (1999), para 2.15, justify their opinion that environmental considerations alone cannot outweigh a restriction of competition by saying that the Treaty does not promote environmental protection over competition and because there are other ways of protecting the environment. In relation to the first point, Ch 2 argued there was no *permanent* priority of any Treaty objective over any other.

economic freedom or efficiency. There is still enormous debate about what a 'restriction on competition' actually is.[226] Article 81(3)'s first condition does not expressly refer to economic efficiency either.[227] Those drafting the Treaty could have been specific and used the terms economic efficiency and freedom if they had agreed that they should have been considered in specific paragraphs. They did not. However, even if 'economic progress' were read as economic efficiency, to my mind, Monti's point is undermined because 'improving the production or distribution of goods or … promoting technical or economic progress' contains four separate heads. It is clear from the Treaty language that any one of these is sufficient[228] to justify exemption. As one of the heads makes specific reference to 'economic progress', by implication the other heads refer to something different. This is particularly the case as these heads are interpreted broadly.[229] In response to this, one might say that all four of Article 81(3)'s first condition's heads refer to economic efficiency.[230] However, it is far from clear that these heads only refer to economic efficiency.[231] To the extent that that they do not refer exclusively to economic efficiency, it is hard to understand how they can be read as demanding its presence in every case.

In any event, and this is the most important point, strict reliance on Article 81's wording is not in line with the Community Courts' method of Treaty interpretation. Monti understands this. He believes that the approach he advocates respects the primacy of the core aims of Article 81 while giving appropriate weight to the significance of other Community policies.[232] Yet, one might question this. Before being exempted under Article 81(3), agreements must fulfil three other tests. These are designed to ensure that sufficient weight is given to competition and consumer interests. Adding an additional requirement into Article 81(3)'s first condition seems excessive. It also undermines Article 81(3)'s structure. Furthermore, Monti's position does not properly reflect the teleological method of interpretation. Instead of placing emphasis on a provision's actual wording, in hard conflict cases such as these, stress is normally placed upon its structure and place within the Treaty hierarchy. Provisions must be interpreted in light of the Treaty as a whole.[233]

That does not mean that *sometimes* one cannot triumph over another. If this were never the case then we could not resolve conflicts between objectives. If correct, this undermines their argument. As regards their second point, the Treaty's structure and the policy-linking clauses indicate that its drafters did not follow this logic. The Community Courts have not mentioned such a criterion to my knowledge. Ch 7 discusses how one might be introduced.

[226] See Ch 6, Section 2.1.

[227] Bouterse (1994) 127, 128. Though see the arguments of, eg Odudu (2006) chs 2, 5, 6.

[228] If there is sufficient quantity to outweigh the Art 81(1) restriction and the other three Art 81(3) conditions are fulfilled.

[229] See Ch 2, Section 2.2. Furthermore, if objectives such as market integration and economic efficiency are core values, why does the Treaty, in Monti's view, relegate them to mere exemption status? Monti believes that they are irrelevant under Art 81(1) EC. Furthermore, unless one considers why certain Treaty objectives are pursued then one cannot assess their weight in the balance. The justifications for market integration have changed. Its centrality to the Community's task was altered in the transition from an economic to a broader Treaty framework, Ch 3, Section 2.1.1.

[230] See the reference above to Monti (2002) 1063. *cf* Odudu (2006) chs 5, 6.

[231] Monti (2007) 90, 91 and Frazer (1990) 616.

[232] Monti (2002) 1071.

[233] See Ch 2, Section 2.

This is different from Monti's insistence on the primacy of Article 81's core aims. There is little evidence to show that the Treaty *permanently* prioritises[234] any objectives in the way Monti advocates.[235]

The Community Courts have never held that Article 81(3)'s first condition demands that some economic efficiency be present. Quite the contrary; the CFI has said that many public interest objectives can be considered there; it probably based its assessment entirely on industrial policy grounds, in cases such as the *Matra* Case, for example.

Market integration, economic freedom and economic efficiency are important Community objectives. They are key in Community competition law and are often relevant. The Treaty does not *permanently* prioritise other non-economic objectives over these values,[236] even where there is a policy-linking clause.[237] That does not mean that non-economic policy objectives cannot *occasionally* override these 'core' objectives. The Community Courts interpret each Treaty article in light of the Treaty as a whole. This is due to the structure of the Treaty itself, as well as the presence of several policy-linking clauses.[238] This understanding of the Treaty, which is dominant in Community law, is incompatible with Monti's view that certain core values *always* trump non-core values, and can *never* be trumped by them, unless the non-core value is accompanied by another core value. I do not believe that the Treaty as a whole prioritises these three objectives (or any others) to the extent that Monti suggests;[239] nor, I have argued, does the Community Courts' case law[240] or the Commission's decisions support him. Politically, it is inconceivable that the 'core' objectives could always ride roughshod over everything else. This is because there are times when public policy considerations are more important than economic efficiency.

To recap, no objectives can permanently trump other relevant objectives in the balance.[241] Outside of this extreme, the Treaty, the Community Courts' case law and Commission decisions do not yet provide much help about where the balance normally lies, because there are no decisions where non-economic objectives are 'beaten'. The important factors, when deciding whether an objective will justify exemption, remain unclear. Those drafting the Treaty tried to give some guidance by including certain objectives within Articles 2 and 3 EC. They also inserted policy-linking clauses; within some of those they demand that 'a high level of protection' be achieved, in others they did not. None of these distinctions are reflected in the case law, thus far. Environmental protection must be given a high level of protection and has not unambiguously outweighed economic efficiency in a decision to date. Consumer protection need not be achieved to a high level and yet it has outweighed economic efficiency too. Furthermore,

---

[234] Although Monti's core objectives are important in the Treaty hierarchy of values.

[235] See Ch 2, Section 2. This is not to say that the competition provisions do not emphasise, eg, economic efficiency more than, eg, the Treaty provisions relating to environmental protection, which in turn emphasise environmental protection more than the competition provisions. Indeed, I argue for just such an emphasis in Ch 6, Section 3.2. However, this is different from arguing, as Monti does, that certain objectives *permanently* trump other objectives within Art 81.

[236] There are some limited exceptions to this broad statement, see Ch 2, Section 2.1.

[237] In relation to environmental protection, eg, see Jans (2000) 18, 19 and Krämer (2000) 15.

[238] See Ch 2, Section 2.

[239] Amato argues that the Maastricht Treaty affirms competition as an autonomous and fundamental principle, Amato (1997) 45. Perhaps, but as the ECJ explained in the *Échirolles* Case, see Ch 2, this does not impose unconditional obligations on Member States, nor I argued there, on the Community as a whole.

[240] See Amato (1997) 62, 114; Jebsen and Stevens (1995–6) 513 and Ch 2, Section 2.2.

[241] This is not to ignore other parts of Art 81(3)'s test which might do this, such as Art 81(3)(b) EC.

the Treaty specifically states that Title XVI, *Industrial Policy*, should not provide a basis for distorting competition. And yet, industrial policy is one of the objectives that appears most regularly in Article 81(3) discussions. Another strong Article 81 objective, security of energy supply, barely features in the Treaty and has no policy-linking clause at all. Nor, does the fact that certain Treaty objectives are areas of exclusive Member State competence seem to have made the Commission 'more generous' about weighing these issues in the balance. Indeed, the only clear constant seems to be that over time the Commission becomes increasingly bold about relying on these 'non-economic' objectives, despite its policy statements.

The Commission should take account of the various objectives in the Article 81(3) balance in light of the importance given to these objectives in the Treaty. Objectives like environmental protection should be given a high weight in the balance, objectives like culture, should normally be given less weight. Those amending the Treaty could give the Commission more help in this regard. They could define the weight to be given to economic efficiency, for example, as well as that of the non-economic objectives, more clearly. They could also explain why certain objectives are being pursued, such as market integration. This would help establish when conflicts occur.[242]

The result of these suggestions may be to achieve the balance that Monti suggests. One cannot be sure until the greater transparency advocated above has been achieved. It is likely, however, that the non-core values should be given more weight than he suggests. It is implausible that, wherever the balance is finally set, there will be no exceptions to the general rule under the exigencies of a specific case.

Non-economic Treaty objectives are relevant in Article 81 analysis. As time goes on the Commission and Member States' authorities will become more accustomed to relying on these objectives. This does not mean that these objectives will always win. Time will teach the decision-makers to be more thorough in their balancing analysis. They will likely take more account of the Treaty's wording. In this way we will see a true balance emerging; one that is clear, not because balancing is easy, but because the foundations of this balance will have been exposed to the light.[243]

4 CONCLUSION

The Commission considers non-economic objectives, both Community and Member State interests, within Article 81(3) EC. These objectives have been used alone, as well as in combination with other objectives, both economic and non-economic. Sometimes they have had a decisive impact on the Article 81(3) balance.

The balancing process is, as yet, unrefined. The content of each objective must be more clearly explained, as well as why it is being pursued.[244] Nor have we seen a proper analysis of their weight in the specific case, for example, we do not know the effect of a

---

[242] Ch 8 discusses this in more detail.
[243] Mortelmans (2001) 648, also criticises the Commission for failing to provide sufficient help in how to take account of these non-economic objectives. Part C provides guidance here.
[244] Bourgeois and Demaret (1995) 113, 114.

policy-linking clause, or a 'high level' appellation. Legal certainty is promoted by explaining what you consider and how you consider it.[245]

Many policy objectives have had a significant impact on the balance. In relation to environmental protection, the Commission has begun to explain how to assess an agreement's costs and benefits. There is a long way to go. Cultural considerations undermined price competition to a certain degree; the need to maintain the security of the energy supply seemed even more intrusive. Consumer protection and industrial policy both reduced economic efficiency in the short and medium term, undermining the fundamental parameters of competition in some industries and ignoring Article 157(3) EC. This has happened in relation to national as well as Community interests.[246]

Most objectives have only been given positive weight in the balance. However, as the Commission becomes more open about the balance itself, there is some evidence that it is weighing a multiplicity of factors, some of which it gives positive and some of which have negative weight; see for example both market integration and consumer protection. This may signify the birth of a full-blown public interest assessment.

There is also some evidence that the balance is changing over time, see market integration, environmental protection and consumer protection. This is understandable as the Treaty's optimal balance is changing too. However, until the objectives are properly defined and their weight correctly apportioned, then these, quite proper, changes merely increase the test's lack of transparency.

Furthermore, the outcome of the balance seems to change between Article 81(1) and (3) EC. Certain objectives, such as economic efficiency, seem to be given more weight in the latter provision; but, if this is so, when should this happen and why.[247] That said, some objectives have been given a lot of weight in Article 81(1) too. In light of Section 3, it may be better not to generalise conclusions about policy objective's actual weight in relation to Article 81(3)'s balance here. One thing is certain though. Absolute per se rules, while acceptable under Article 81(1), cannot be tolerated under Article 81(3) EC; which also means that no objective can be given permanent priority in the balance.

The final point relates to the distribution of power in the balancing process. Subject to the Community Courts, the Commission remains central, even after 1 May 2004. It has been sensitive when considering certain Member State objectives within Article 81(3). Yet, the Council and the European Parliament remained impotent in their attempts to force the Commission to change the weight it ascribed to cultural policy in the Article 81(3) balance.[248]

Part C offers recommendations to deal with all of these issues; but before embarking on that exercise, Chapter 5 examines the second method of balancing used in Article 81 EC, market-balancing.

---

[245]   Ch 8 provides a framework for this.

[246]   Monti (2007) 103 argues that national policies cannot be raised under Art 81(3) EC, it is not clear why he thinks this. See also his pages 110–13. Ch 3's Introduction discussed the *Meca-Medina* Case, where public policy concerns, including public health issues, were raised in Art 81(1) EC. This seems to be an example of public policy concerns (which are *not necessarily national*, see Art 152 EC) being raised under Art 81(1) EC. Many of the cultural and security of energy supply cases discussed here seem to raise *national* public policy concerns within the Art 81(3) discussion.

[247]   This reflects Ch 3, Section 3.2's point about when balancing should occur in Art 81(3), as opposed to Art 81(1), something that I have still not been able to find a case law discussion of.

[248]   Although I commend the Commission's insistence on evidence to support the cultural claim, Ch 7 advocates a more sensitive stance in relation to diagonal conflicts of this type.

5

How the Balance is Implemented – Market-Balancing in Article 81 EC

1 INTRODUCTION

Public policy considerations are relevant in Article 81 EC.[1] This begs the question of where these issues are considered and how they are taken into account. Chapters 3 and 4 dealt with mere-balancing in Article 81(1) and (3), respectively. Mere-balancing, which I also call 'external balancing',[2] is essentially balancing public policy goals *outside of* the economic efficiency assessment.

This chapter studies a different mechanism for the consideration of public policy goals, market-balancing.[3] Here, some public policy objectives are accommodated *within* the economic efficiency test itself.[4] Chapter 5 shows how the Commission does this by highlighting three 'components' of the economic efficiency analysis and explaining how they affect the welfare assessment and impact upon public policy goals.[5]

The first 'component' is the tension between producer and consumer interests. Economic efficiency is not a value neutral concept.[6] Producer welfare and consumer welfare models can conflict. In general, proponents of consumer welfare want more competition, compelling producers to sell close to marginal cost. Allocative efficiency losses are unacceptable because consumers suffer. This is in direct contrast to the position under a producer welfare standard, which focuses on producer gains. Section 2 discusses this tension in Community competition law. The Commission normally pursues consumer

---

[1] See Ch 2.
[2] See Ch 1, Section 2.2.
[3] ibid.
[4] See also, Frazer (1990) 620–23.
[5] Other public policy goals can also be considered where externalities are internalised, see Ch 1, Section 2.2.2 and Monti (2007) 93.
[6] See Ch 1, Section 2, for more details on the economic concepts discussed in Ch 5.

welfare; however, where there are important gains to Community producers, especially those in difficulty, it sometimes considers the producers' welfare.

Secondly, a tension emerges in relation to both productive and dynamic efficiencies on the one hand, and allocative efficiencies on the other. The consumer welfare standard advocates more competition. This forces firms to invest and innovate, enabling them to reduce their costs (and thus their prices), forcing out their less efficient rivals. However, at a certain point, increasing competition undermines the incentive to invest and innovate. Competition authorities applying a consumer welfare model must balance the long-term need for innovation (and the future allocative consumers benefits to be gained as a result) with the short-term allocative efficiency loss of letting prices rise above marginal cost, to pay for this investment. Producers, seeking to enhance their own welfare, highlight these ambiguous effects of increasing competition on both dynamic and productive efficiencies even under a pure consumer welfare standard. But they have an additional reason for doing so. Less short-term competition may reduce their incentives to innovate, but it also means that they can appropriate a larger share of any gains they make through such innovation. So, an emphasis on productive and dynamic efficiencies, rather than short term allocative ones, can also help producers, Section 3. In the long term, the right level of R&D should also bring substantial consumer benefits,[7] but this is not always uppermost in the Commission's mind.[8]

Finally, Section 4 examines the Commission's use of product and geographic markets outside of the markets directly at issue in the proceedings. This does not directly aid the Commission's pursuit of any public policy objectives; however, such an approach widens the search for the agreements' effects, which can allow more public policy objectives to be considered in the discussion. Section 5 concludes.

2 CONSUMER (OR PRODUCER) WELFARE

The decision to pursue consumer welfare or producer welfare depends on a value judgment. Put simply, one either prioritises the interests of consumers or producers.[9] A consumer welfare standard, for example, could simultaneously enhance consumer protection, and undermine industrial policy. As a result, producer welfare and consumer welfare models can conflict. In general, proponents of consumer welfare want more competition, compelling producers to sell close to marginal cost. Allocative efficiency losses are unacceptable because consumers suffer. This is in direct contrast to the position under a producer welfare standard, which focuses on producer gains.

This section discusses the tension between consumers and producers in Community competition law. The Commission normally pursues consumer welfare; however, where there are important gains to Community producers, especially those in difficulty, it sometimes considers the producers' welfare.

---

[7]   See Ch 1, Section 2.2.1.

[8]   Geradin (2006) 315, 316, points towards these tensions too.

[9]   In fact, as Section 3 highlights, the issue can be more complex as increasing R&D, something that a producer welfare focus may achieve, can also lead to long term consumer welfare gains, also see Ch 1, Section 2.

The CFI has explicitly embraced the consumer welfare standard.[10] In *Glaxo*, it held that, in effect, the objective assigned to Article 81 EC,[11] is to prevent undertakings, by restricting competition with themselves or with third parties, from reducing the welfare of the final consumer of the products in question. The Commission agrees, believing that the aim of the Community competition rules is to protect competition on the market *as a means of enhancing consumer welfare.*[12]

If the Commission adopts the consumer welfare standard, supporting Community consumer protection goals,[13] then producer welfare gains would be irrelevant in its analysis;[14] yet, as I show, this is not always the case. This may be another example of a gap between the Commission's policy statements and its decision-making practice.

[10]   The ECJ has not explicitly invoked consumer welfare as a goal; however, it has impliedly rejected the producer welfare model. In the *Consten and Grundig* Case, 348, it held that, for the purposes of Art 81(3)'s first test, improvements did not mean those accruing to the parties, but objective advantages. In certain cases, the ECJ could be interpreted as saying that total welfare is the appropriate test, but this is almost certainly incorrect. Some doubt is raised by judgments such as Joined Cases 46/87 and 227/88, *Hoechst v Commission* para 25, where the ECJ said that the function of, amongst others, Arts 3(1)(g) and 81 was to prevent competition from being distorted to the detriment of the public interest, individual undertakings and consumers. One might see this as a total surplus test, but this is not necessarily the case. Reich (1997) 127, eg, says that this passage tells us that competition law serves many purposes, one of which is the increase of consumer welfare. While this is not inconsistent with a total welfare test (which aggregates producer and consumer welfare, Ch 1), I am reluctant to place more emphasis on this passage, in light of a relatively clear and consistent message from the *Consten and Grundig* line of cases, see B&C (2008), para 3–020.

[11]   Case T-168/01 *GlaxoSmithKline Services v Commission* para 171; note that this case is currently on appeal to the ECJ on these very grounds, Cases C-501/06, 513/06, 515/06 and 519/06. See also, the Opinion of A-G Trstenjak, Case C-209/07 *The Competition Authority v BIDS* para 56, supporting the CFI's judgment. Sadly, para 118 of the CFI's *Glaxo* judgment generates some confusion, it implies that the objective of Art 81(1) EC is consumer welfare, which makes the scope of Art 81(3) unclear. Ch 6, Section 2.3 discusses this point further.

Art 81(3)'s first test *does not* adopt a consumer welfare standard. That said, Art 81(3)'s second test insists that consumers must get a fair share of the agreement's resulting benefit. Ch 4 showed the Commission combining the first and second tests in its Art 81(3) analysis. Even where this is not the case, some believe that the second test influences the rest of the Commission's Art 81(3) assessment such that a consumer welfare standard is, ultimately, demanded, see, eg Commission decision, *MasterCard*, para 693; Schaub (2002) 33 and Heimler and Fattori (1998) 598–600.

To the extent that Art 81(3)'s first two tests are combined, one would expect to see a test that favours consumer protection *even more* than under a 'pure' consumer welfare standard. This is because, under the consumer welfare standard, producer welfare increases are irrelevant, see Ch 1, Section 2.1. Even if a producer welfare gain from a particular agreement were large, as long as there were some consumer welfare gain, the transaction would be allowed. This is not the position under Art 81(3)'s second test, where consumers must get a *fair share* of any benefit. This implies that, in the scenario just outlined, Community law would insist that producers pass on not merely some (and not all of it either), but a fair share, of their welfare gain to consumers. Let's call this a 'consumer welfare plus' standard.

Sometimes, the Commission may follow this 'consumer welfare plus' standard; Commission decision, *Grundig's EC distribution system*, discussed in Ch 4, Section 2.4 could be an example of this. However, this approach is not normally in evidence and is not considered further here. Furthermore, the Commission has expressly said (without justifying its view) that the net effect of the agreement must at least be neutral from the point of view of those consumers directly or likely affected by the agreement, Commission, *Article 81(3) Guidelines*, para 85, which further implies a consumer welfare standard.

[12]   See references in Ch 1, n 3. One group of economic commentators has said that the promotion of consumer welfare is one of the main goals of the Commission's competition policy, Neven, Papandropoulos and Seabright (1998) 12. See also, Van den Bergh (2002) 42 and Bishop and Walker (2002), para 2.22.

[13]   This could also support other public policy goals too. For example, when choice is emphasised in the consumer welfare standard (normally price is emphasised) then this may encourage the presence of SMEs, price, health and safety and innovation, Commission decision, *DaimlerChrysler*, para 7.

[14]   Unless there was sufficient competition to force the producers to pass on benefits to consumers.

Turning first to legal scholars' views, in 1998, Forrester said that there was little trace of real concern for the welfare of consumers as the direct beneficiaries of Community competition policy. There is, however, more concern for citizens as indirect beneficiaries, residing in a healthy economy.[15]

The Commission often highlights producer needs/benefits in its analysis.[16] Even if the standard is formally a consumer welfare one, many Commission decisions show a readiness to accept minor, speculative and unquantified consumer benefits;[17] particularly where this might benefit Community industry,[18] and especially in high technology industries, where the Commission believes that Community undertakings are being left behind by those from abroad.[19]

In fact, some Commission decisions may even hint at a producer welfare standard. Take, for example, Commission decision, *Iridium*, which involved a joint venture agreement to provide global digital wireless communications services. The agreement included pricing 'guidelines' for gateway operators. In 1997, the Commission found that the principle of uniform prices seemed appropriate to fulfil customers' needs.[20] It is probably not the Commission's view that customers must tolerate consciously parallel rate fixing as the price to pay for making European industry competitive.[21] Furthermore, it is probably going too far to argue that a pure producer welfare standard has been adopted here; after all, the Commission explains its acceptance of horizontal price-fixing with reference to consumers; although its reasoning on the link is not so convincing.[22] But, as we have seen, some weight is given to producer gains.

Even if the Commission does not implement a producer welfare standard (or even a total surplus), sometimes it gives the impression of coming close. One example of this is Commission decision, *Olivetti/Canon*.[23] The Commission examined a joint venture agreement, between Olivetti (Italian) and Canon (Japanese), to develop, design and manufacture copying machines, printers and fax machines. The agreement was exempted, because the Commission felt that, in order to compete efficiently, producers needed the latest technology, requiring large R&D investments.[24] The joint venture enabled the parties to spread these costs over more products. Community industrial policy was also aided by

---

[15] Forrester (1998) 369. Others may agree, Buigues, Jacquemin and Sapir state that, in general, lax Community competition policy was designed to boost profit margins, providing a breathing space for Community producers, Buigues, Jacquemin and Sapir (1995a) xx. See also, Cseres (2004) 235 and Laussel and Montet (1995) 62, 63.

[16] See Commission, *Horizontal Guidelines*; Commission, *RCP 1994* 23–26; Commission, *RCP 1993* 90–92; Commission, *RCP 1992* 44, 45.

[17] Reich (1997) 133–37. Neven, Papandropoulos and Seabright (1998) 104–06, also report that efficiencies are rarely quantified or given a serious hearing. In Commission decision, *Philips/Osram*, the parties quantified the efficiency benefits, para 26. That said, the Commission seems to have accepted their figures uncritically.

[18] Forrester (1998) 369, suggests that the explanation for Commission decision, *Iridium* may simply be that the Commission considers that the consumer welfare criterion is not very important when considering high-technology alliances, especially when these will create European networks.

[19] See Neven, Papandropoulos and Seabright (1998) 13, 14.

[20] Commission decision, *Iridium*, para 42.

[21] Forrester (1998) 369, agrees that such an accusation is probably unfair.

[22] The Commission said that consumers would be moving in different areas of the world but will want to receive a single bill. These guidelines help achieve the coherence of the system, which aids this process, Commission decision, *Iridium*, para 42.

[23] Also see, eg Commission decisions, *BPCL/ICI*, para 35; *Pasteur Mérieux-Merck*, paras 82–90; Forrester (1998) 369, 370; Reich (1997) 133–37; Bouterse (1994) ch 5 (restructuring of industry) and the *Metro I* Case para 47.

[24] Commission decision, *Olivetti/Canon*, para 54.

Canon's know how transfer to the Italian firm, which the Commission said should contribute to improving the technological patterns of EU industry. When it came to assessing customer benefits,[25] the Commission briefly said that they would benefit from new products and lower prices.[26]

If the Commission were always pursuing a pure consumer welfare model one would expect less emphasis on producer welfare gains, unless it had checked that there was sufficient competition to force the producers to pass on benefits to consumers. There is no emphasis on the consumers' *fair share*, as outlined above. That is not to say that the Commission ignores consumers or has adopted a producer welfare model. Indeed, this is improbable. However, by playing with the welfare advantages that accrue to producers (as well as consumers) and by readily accepting that producer benefits will be passed on to consumers, in certain cases, the Commission can give great weight to industrial policy arguments within its economic efficiency test in Article 81.

This generosity to producers may be coming to an end. Commission, *Article 81(3) Guidelines*, demands more details of what efficiencies are produced and their quantification.[27] It also says that one cannot simply presume that residual competition will ensure that consumers receive a fair share of the resulting benefit. It is, as yet, unclear how much this will affect the Commission's application of Article 81 in practice.[28]

3 PRODUCTIVE AND DYNAMIC (OR ALLOCATIVE) EFFICIENCIES

This section examines another tension, that in relation to both productive and dynamic efficiencies on the one hand, and allocative efficiencies on the other. The consumer welfare standard advocates more competition. This forces firms to invest and innovate, enabling them to reduce their costs (and thus their prices), forcing out their less efficient rivals. However, at a certain point, increasing competition undermines the incentive to invest and innovate. Competition authorities applying a consumer welfare model must balance the long-term need for innovation (and the future allocative benefits to be gained by consumers as a result) with the short-term allocative efficiency loss of letting prices rise above marginal cost, to pay for this investment. Producers, seeking to enhance their own welfare, highlight these ambiguous effects of increasing competition on both dynamic and productive efficiencies even under a pure consumer welfare standard. But they have an additional reason for doing so. Less short-term competition may reduce their incentives to innovate, but it also means that they can appropriate a larger share of any gains they make through such innovation. So, an emphasis on productive and dynamic efficiencies, rather

---

[25] ibid, para 55.

[26] It made little apparent effort to check that this was true, nor to quantify these benefits, to ensure they outweighed clear restrictions on competition.

[27] Commission, *Article 81(3) Guidelines*, paras 51, 56–72, 92–101.

[28] The CFI and the Commission clashed on this issue in Case T-168/01 *GlaxoSmithKline Services v Commission*, paras 220, 228, 253–303; note that this case is currently on appeal to the ECJ on these very grounds, Cases C-501/06, C-513/06, C-515/06 and C-519/06.

than short term allocative ones, can also help producers. In the long term, the right level of R&D should also bring substantial consumer benefits,[29] but this is not always uppermost in the Commission's mind.[30]

These tensions are important because dynamic and productive efficiencies can often exceed allocative ones.[31] Articles 163 and 164 EC support some promotion of R&D through co-operation between undertakings. The Commission[32] promotes R&D co-operation through its economic efficiency test.[33] It hopes to achieve its industrial policy goals through such means[34] and also to increase employment,[35] there are also prospective consumer protection gains to be made. It does this both within Article 81(1) and (3) EC.[36]

The Commission promotes R&D through its economic efficiency test by emphasising dynamic, as opposed to (static) allocative, efficiencies.[37] It acknowledges that there can be a trade-off between these different efficiencies:

> Cooperation in R&D may reduce duplicative, unnecessary costs, lead to significant cross fertilisation of ideas and experience and thus result in products and technologies being developed more rapidly than would otherwise be the case. As a general rule, R&D cooperation tends to increase overall R&D activities …
>
> Under certain circumstances, however, R&D agreements may cause competition problems such as restrictive effects on prices, output, innovation, or variety or quality of goods.[38]

So the Commission has a choice: push R&D and risk reducing allocative efficiency; or focus on allocative efficiency gains and risk reducing the scope for investment in R&D, as prices fall to marginal cost. However, the issue is more complex than that as consumers may favour a reduction in allocative efficiency in order to achieve dynamic efficiencies. This is because, in the long term, in a competitive industry, producers should be forced to pass any cost savings (which can be much greater than the short term allocative losses[39]) on to consumers.[40] The Commission often adopts a long-term view of when the benefits might accrue.[41] Furthermore, the Commission believes that Europe needs to 'catch up', technologically.[42] As I show, it is often prepared to accept short term allocative efficiency

---

[29] See Ch 1, Section 2.2.

[30] Geradin (2006) 315, 316, points towards these tensions too.

[31] See Ch 1, Section 2.1 and technological competition is becoming increasingly important, Pitofsky (1998) 333.

[32] Often encouraged by others, see, eg European Parliament, *Resolution on the Twenty-fourth Competition Report*, para 16.

[33] See, eg Neven, Papandropoulos and Seabright (1998) ch 4; Commission, *RCP 1991* 44, 45 and Commission, *RCP 1985* 11–15.

[34] See Forrester (1998) 373–76, 380.

[35] See Ch 1, Section 2.1; COM(2003) 96, 2 and Commission decision, *Synthetic Fibres*, para 37. More generally see Commission, *RCP 1993* 21–26; COM(93) 700, chs 2, 4, 5, 8; COM(94) 319 and Commission, *RCP 1995* 31–35.

[36] In relation to Art 81(1) see Commission decisions, *Iridium* and *Elopak/Metal Box-Odin*, for example. There are many examples of this within Art 81(3): see eg Commission decision, *Ford/Volkswagen*, discussed below.

[37] See Ch 1, Section 2.

[38] Commission, *Horizontal Guidelines*, paras 41, 43. See also, the *Glaxo* Case paras 180, 194, 220.

[39] See Ch 1, Section 2. One of competition's most important benefits is to drive productivity growth through innovation, Porter (2001) 922.

[40] Obviously, similar difficulties arise elsewhere; in relation to Canada see Goldman and Barutciski (1998) 388, 414, 415.

[41] Forrester (1998) 369 and Bouterse (1994) ch 5.

[42] Temple Lang (1996) 551, 552 and Korah (1987) 18, 19.

losses, where it believes that they will lead to R&D increases, and ultimately, long term allocative efficiency gains, boosting both industrial and consumer policy.

Examples of the Commission's attitude are hard to substantiate, for two reasons. First, there is a lack of clear, explicit, reasoning by the Commission, as well as a general absence of thorough economic analysis. Secondly, there is often just a difference of emphasis that would lead one to place a case in this section rather than in Chapter 4's section on industrial policy, or Section 2 above.[43]

The Commission often advocates very high levels of R&D[44] and the attainment of these efficiencies within as short a time frame as possible.[45] This can often only be achieved through research and development agreements, as opposed to by single firms. The Commission considers the possibility of dynamic efficiencies so important that it is often prepared to accept quite major reductions in static allocative efficiencies, in the hope that they will produce greater allocative efficiencies over the longer term.[46]

Commission decision, *Ford/Volkswagen*, may well be an example of this.[47] This decision deals with an agreement between Ford and Volkswagen to develop, engineer and manufacture an MPV. Ford and Volkswagen would distribute them separately under their own brand names. The Commission found a breach of Article 81(1), noting serious restrictions on competition in the relevant market and in others, principally as a result of allocative efficiency losses. Nevertheless, it was prepared to grant an individual exemption, emphasising that through co-operation the parties should be able to produce an advanced vehicle designed to meet the requirements of European consumers.[48] These are dynamic efficiency gains. Co-operation would also lead to a rationalisation of the manufacturing process, enabling both parties to combine their know-how in many areas, generating dynamic as well as productive efficiency gains.

The Commission has considered quite speculative gains in some cases, allowing it to rely on dynamic efficiency predictions even where they have not been clearly substantiated.[49] One example is Commission decision, *BPCL/ICI*. BPCL and ICI agreed the mutual sale of certain production units, technical know-how and goodwill for polyvinyl chloride (PVC) and low-density polyethylene (LDPE). BPCL also decided to close some PVC and chlorine wedge production units, while ICI would close some of its LDPE and ethylene production units. They also agreed to change the capacity rights in a jointly owned ethylene cracker as well as other supply agreements between BPCL and ICI for polyethylene and ethylene. The Commission found a breach of Article 81(1).

---

[43]   This is not always easy to detect, see, eg Sullivan and Grimes (2000) 205 and Monti (2007) 121. I have placed the cases where I think that the centre of gravity in the reasoning lies. That said, sometimes the Commission's reasoning bridges my artificial categorisations and so some cases appear in more than one section.

[44]   See *ACEA* and Commission decision, *CECED*, discussed in Chs 3 and 4, respectively.

[45]   For example, Commission decisions, *ENI/Montedison*, para 31 and *GEAE/P&W*, paras 74–83.

[46]   Neven, Papandropoulos and Seabright (1998) 13 and Commission decision, *GEAE/P&W*, paras 74–83.

[47]   Other possible examples are Commission decisions, *Synthetic Fibres*, paras 34–35, para 24 seems to accept that there will be some, though not 'abnormally sharp', price rises; *BT/MCI*, paras 34–42; *ENI/Montedison*, paras 22–31, para 33 accepts that there will not be short-term price cuts; and *Bayer/BP Chemicals*, OJ 1988 L150/34 paras 18–30, para 34 seems to accept that there will be short-term price rises. See also, the views of A-G Trstenjak in his Opinion in Case C-209/07 *The Competition Authority v BIDS* para 55–57.

[48]   Commission decision, *Ford/Volkswagen*, paras 24, 25.

[49]   Neven, Papandropoulos and Seabright (1998) 104–06 and Commission decision, *GEAE/P&W*, para 80.

In its Article 81(3) EC analysis the Commission balanced an important loss of allocative efficiency[50] against various productive efficiency increases as well an extremely speculative dynamic efficiency gain, the release of funds from reducing losses that could be used for R&D.[51]

The Commission seems to go even further in its analysis in *Olivetti/Canon*. There Olivetti and Canon proposed a joint venture to develop, design and manufacture copying machine products, laser beam printer products and facsimile products. The Commission found a restriction on competition but agreed to exempt the agreement. It was prepared to allow a reduction in allocative efficiency[52] in order to allow the parties to increase their research and development expenditure:

> [O]n all the markets involved, and in which the parties are competing, the technology is fast-moving and the degree of competition high. In order to compete efficiently, the undertakings on those markets have to offer products which are the result of the most up-to-date technology, at competitive prices. Up-to-date technologies, however, require large investments in research and development. The expansion of production in the EEC which is the effect of the joint venture enables the parties to spread the costs of these investments over a larger number of products: otherwise the costs of those products would be too high for producers to be able to sell them at a competitive price. The joint venture is therefore apt to avoid duplication in costs of development. Research does not fall directly within the scope of the joint venture. However, by virtue of the obligation on the partners to communicate to the JVC the continuing flow of their expertise, and on Canon the improvements of the research carried out independently, this research is tightly linked to the activity of the joint venture. Research will also be stimulated by avoiding the duplication of its costs.[53]

The Commission also relies on productive efficiency gains in order to implement its industrial policy aims here.[54] The focus on productive efficiency arguments is one way of justifying the restructuring decisions in relation to the various Community industries.[55] This mechanism works in very much the same way as described in relation to dynamic efficiency. Indeed, productive and dynamic efficiency are often both discussed in the same case to justify the reduction in allocative efficiency.[56] This can, at times, come dangerously close to negating competition as the main process of economic organisation.[57]

The emphasis on high levels of R&D and the acceptance of quite speculative productive and dynamic efficiency gains by the Commission, have skewed its analysis away from allocative efficiency questions, at least in the short term. This is not to say that allocative efficiency is unimportant to the Commission; or that this emphasis offers no benefits to consumers. However, by distorting its analysis the Commission incorporates industrial

---

[50] Commission decision, *BPCL/ICI*, para 36.2, although the Commission claimed that price rises did not occur as a result of the agreement, but would have occurred anyway.

[51] Commission decision, *BPCL/ICI*, para 35.

[52] Commission decision, *Olivetti/Canon*, para 42.

[53] Commission decision, *Olivetti/Canon*, para 54. Other examples may include Commission decisions, *BT-MCI* and *Atlas*, which were also discussed in Ch 4, Section 2.6.

[54] Forrester (1998) 364 and Amato (1997) 115.

[55] Case T-328/03 *O2 (Germany) GmbH & Co. OHG v Commission*, paras 112, 113; Commission decisions, *Synthetic Fibres* and *Stichting Baksteen*, as well as Commission, *RCP 1993*, points 82, 84, 85(i), 88, 89, 158; European Parliament, *Resolution on the Twenty-fourth Competition Report*, para 15; Bouterse (1994) ch 5 and Monti (2002) 1072.

[56] See, eg Commission decisions, *BPCL/ICI*, para 35 and *Bayer/BP Chemicals*, OJ 1988 L150/34 paras 27, 30, as well as the cases cited above.

[57] Wesseling (2000) 39; Amato (1997) 62, 114 and Streit and Mussler (1995) 25.

policy, environmental and employment objectives within the market-balancing mechanism,[58] while promoting long term consumer protection goals.[59] Having said that, if its real focus were consumer welfare one would expect more discussion of how and when consumers would receive the producer benefits.

It is unclear whether Commission, *Article 81(3) Guidelines*, indicate a toughening of this stance.[60] The wording seems to demand a more thorough and explicit quantification of efficiencies, but this is more difficult for productive and dynamic efficiencies.[61] However, there is sometimes a discrepancy between policy statements and practice.

This leads to another issue, that of where the balance lies between allocative and dynamic and productive efficiencies. This is extremely difficult to assess, due to a lack of clarity in the case law. One could argue that allocative efficiency considerations cannot be completely ignored in favour of dynamic and productive efficiency gains. The ECJ said in *Metro I* that price competition is so important that it can never be eliminated.[62] However, such a position would not lie easily with that of the CFI in *Matra*,[63] holding that, in theory, any restriction on competition that complied with the four Article 81(3) tests could be exempted.[64]

This lack of clarity makes even a tentative discussion of where the balance is foolhardy.[65] It may be that the Commission is more ruled by political considerations in these cases, but an explanation of the underlying principles it follows is vital. More clarity is needed, as well as an urgent need for the Commission to analyse the effects that its previous decisions have had on competition. As one commentator puts it, the technology outcomes of co-operative R&D arrangements initiated in Europe during the 1980s have proved disappointing so far.[66]

A more structured, formal, efficiency analysis (and the enhanced certainty this generates) is more likely to ensure concrete gains to European firms.[67]

---

[58]   Schaub (1996) 76–78. This tendency may even increase, COM(2003) 226 23. See also, Streit and Mussler (1995) 25.

[59]   A longer-term consumer welfare perspective may also mean that other relevant objectives, eg environmental considerations could be considered more readily, Wasmeier (2001) 163; Commission decision, *GEAE/P&W*, paras 79, 80 and COM(93) 632 42.

[60]   See n 27 above and the Commission's arguments in the *Glaxo* Case para 228 and Commission decision, *MasterCard*, paras 689–92. Contrast this with the CFI's arguments in the *Glaxo* Case, around para 274. The ECJ's judgment on appeal is eagerly awaited, Case C-168/01 P.

[61]   Some argue that a comparison of efficiencies and anti-competitive results is not workable on a case-by-case basis, see the summary of the literature provided in Fisher and Lande (1983) 1657–59. Other commentators are, to varying degrees, more optimistic, please see OECD (1988) 41 and Areeda (1992) 37.

[62]   The *Metro I* Case para 21.

[63]   The *Matra* Case para 85. See also Commission decision, *Glaxo Wellcome*, para 153, now under appeal: Case C-168/01 P.

[64]   Note that Art 81(3)(b) only says that competition should not be eliminated. This is not necessarily solely price competition, but might also include, eg, R&D competition.

[65]   Commission, *Article 81(3) Guidelines*, paras 102–04, provide no new objective techniques for assessing this.

[66]   Paragraph 17, UNCTAD document TD/B/COM.2/EM/10/Rev.1. Also see Scherer (1992) 1,416–1,433. In part, this may be as a result of Community trade policy, see Gual (1995) 38, 39.

[67]   That is not to say that a good test will ensure that such gains are made. The failure of the R&D could be for reasons other than the competition related issues, including the parties' incompetence, for example. One might also point to the straight-jacket effect of many block exemptions and the problems this has caused, although this is less of a problem in the more recent regulations.

4 PARTIAL (OR TOTAL) EQUILIBRIUM

This section examines the Commission's use of product and geographic markets outside of the markets directly at issue in the proceedings. This does not directly aid the Commission's pursuit of any public policy objectives; however, such an approach widens the search for the agreements' effects, which allows a more holistic consideration of an arrangement's impact on public policy objectives.

An agreement may generate costs or benefits outside of its relevant product and geographic markets. Take liner-shipping conferences, for example. These are horizontal price-fixing cartels between shipping companies. The Commission defines the relevant market in such cases as liner trade services between, for example, the Community and the coast of West Africa.[68] These cartels can lead to higher prices for shipping goods on the routes where they operate. This increases the cost of importing and exporting goods to Africa, for example, and thus affects the price of all shipped products too. These goods make up a different product market from the relevant service market in these cases. They may also have different geographic markets. Where shipping costs make up a large share of the value of these products, increases in these costs can significantly affect the quantity of the goods sold. If one solely focuses on the relevant market then the effects on the shipped goods would be ignored. By broadening our investigation and examining the agreement's effects on other markets a more complete picture can be built up of its costs and benefits; making it easier to consider environmental, developmental and other public policy goals which can arise in different markets. I call this more complete investigation the 'total equilibrium approach'.

There are other advantages of examining all the effects of an agreement. First, a partial equilibrium assessment (one that only considers the effects on the relevant market) singles out a product or group of products, ignoring the way they interact with the rest of the economy. One of the weaknesses of this type of assessment is that the consumer welfare measurements it provides within that market are only valid if consumers spend a small fraction of their total income on the goods in question.[69] Where this is not the case, think of housing, for example, ignoring the way this market interacts with the rest of the economy distorts our assessment of welfare effects.

Secondly, a total equilibrium method could help reduce the beggar-thy-neighbour attitude of many legislators. For example, in relation to export cartels, the US ignores the effects on consumers outside its jurisdiction.[70] Export cartels' negative effects are not ignored because of the use of the partial equilibrium approach. That said, such a framework does not force us to consider the global consequences of the anti-competitive behaviour to the extent that a total equilibrium approach does.

Outlawing export cartels in particular and adopting the total equilibrium approach should also lead to a more co-operative relationship between competition authorities worldwide. This is because, to the extent this approach were followed in other jurisdictions

---

[68]   See Commission decision, *Cewal, Cowac and Ukwal*, paras 12, 13.
[69]   Motta (2004) 18, 19 and Tirole (1988) 7–12.
[70]   See Motta (2004) 29 and Hovenkamp (1998) 429, 430.

too, the risk of conflicting decisions would be reduced.[71] This should help reduce political tensions and increase co-operation between antitrust agencies worldwide.

Finally, a total equilibrium approach would give the Community more credence when persuading developing countries to enact clear and transparent competition legislation. This is because it can reduce the appearance of bias, and the impact of industrial policy on the assessment.[72]

Nevertheless, stepping outside of the partial equilibrium framework can dramatically increase political and evidentiary problems. For example, should the regulator approve a cartel which increases economic welfare worldwide, but results in a net decrease in economic welfare within its jurisdiction? This might be difficult, politically.[73] On the evidentiary front, such a change would place parties under an obligation to investigate the benefit, or otherwise, of a specific action in markets potentially unrelated to their own. This could be very time-consuming, as well as costly. For the decision-maker too, a total equilibrium approach poses huge evidentiary problems. It could potentially increase the competition authorities' reliance on jurisdictions outside of their own. This may make evidence gathering more difficult.[74] That is not to say that these problems do not exist already. The extra-territorial application of antitrust is well known and sometimes political tensions can arise as a result of decisions.[75] That said, these tensions and difficulties would increase under a total equilibrium approach.

There is obviously a tension between the partial equilibrium framework and the wider total equilibrium approach. The latter gives a more complete picture of the agreement's effects, the former is quicker and easier for both the parties involved and the decision-maker to apply. As a result, it may be that pursuit of a second-best solution (a partial equilibrium framework) is better, and perhaps even more efficient, than a total equilibrium one.[76]

The Commission has not consistently preferred either method. Sometimes it implies that the effects of an agreement outside of the relevant product market are irrelevant.[77] In other cases it has, often with the approval of the Advocates-General,[78] investigated the agreement's effects on different product markets.[79]

---

[71]   See, eg the Air Products and Air Liquide merger, which looked like it would be blocked in the US and was allowed in the EU (Commission merger decision, *Air Liquide/BOC*)) due to the different effects in EU and US-related geographic markets.

[72]   Townley (2004) 130–31.

[73]   Ross (1996–97) 644–52.

[74]   Townley (2004) 134.

[75]   Think of Commission merger decisions, *Boeing/McDonnell Douglas* and *General Electric/Honeywell*.

[76]   That this is sometimes, although not always, the case, see Verhoef and Nijkamp (2003).

[77]   See, eg the *Matra* Case, Matra states, para 64, that the decision allows the Founders the possibility of co-ordinating their behaviour in markets other than the MPV markets. The Commission implies this is irrelevant, para 73, as does Ford, para 81.

[78]   See, eg the Opinion of A-G Roemer in Case 32/65 *Italy v Council and Commission*, 419.

[79]   A-G Warner notes this in Case 61/80 *Coöperatieve Stremsel- en Kleurselfabriek v Commission*, 878. See also, Commission decisions, *TAA*, paras 294–96, 302, 303, 312; *Bayer/BP Chemicals*, OJ 1988 L150/34 paras 32–34; *Continental/Michelin*, para 27; *KSB/Goulds/Lowera/ITT*, para 27; *P&I Clubs* (1999), para 108; *TPS*, para 114; as well as Commission, *RCP 1990* 31 and Crampton (1997) 60.

Similar confusion exists in relation to the geographic markets to be considered. The Commission has looked at different relevant geographic markets in some cases,[80] although it does not normally do so.

More recently, the Commission has sought to resolve this issue; coming out strongly in favour of the partial equilibrium approach:

> The assessment under Article 81(3) of benefits flowing from restrictive agreements is in principle made within the confines of each relevant market to which the agreement relates. The Community competition rules have as their objective the protection of competition on the market and cannot be detached from this objective. Moreover, the condition that consumers … must receive a fair share of the benefits implies in general that efficiencies generated by the restrictive agreement within a relevant market must be sufficient to outweigh the anti-competitive effects produced by the agreement within that same relevant market [footnote A]. Negative effects on consumers in one geographic market or product market cannot normally be balanced against and compensated by positive effects for consumers in another unrelated geographic market or product market.[81]

The Commission starts from the premise that the competition assessment must be made separately for each relevant market. This conclusion is based on two justifications. First, Community competition law has as its objective the protection of competition on the market; and, secondly, that the condition that consumers must receive a fair share of the resulting benefit confirms this approach.

Taking these points in turn, it is unclear what the Commission's first statement means. Nor does the Commission justify it. Community competition law's objectives can only be understood in the context of the whole Treaty.[82] The Treaty's Preamble and Article 2, emphasise the need to strengthen the unity of the Community's economies and to confirm the solidarity which binds us with those overseas. This does not support the Commission's statement. If anything, it leans towards considering the global effects of Community policies, although, in truth, there is little clear support for this either.[83] Likewise, Article 3(1)(g) and Article 81(3)'s first condition do not, to my mind, expressly or impliedly restrict the analysis to the relevant market.

The Commission may be worried that positive effects on one market might coincide with the elimination of competition on the relevant market. This could cause significant harm. However, if this were its fear, Article 81(3)'s fourth condition would allow it to block the agreement. Furthermore, imagine that an agreement is pro-competitive when examined from a partial equilibrium perspective, ie on the relevant market. At the same time, it might significantly harm, or even eliminate competition in another market. If the Commission were able to move outside of a partial equilibrium then it could prevent this, unless it felt this prevented the achievement of Article 81(3)'s first test. The total equilibrium approach gives the Commission more flexibility to assess the economic welfare (and other) effects as a whole.

---

[80] For example, in Commission decision, *Glaxo Wellcome* (now under appeal Case C-168/01 P), the Commission defines the relevant geographic market as national, para 114, and yet when it is discussing the welfare effects it looks across the whole EU and not just at the UK and Spain, paras 184–86.

[81] Commission, *Article 81(3) Guidelines*, para 43.

[82] See Ch 2, Section 2.1.

[83] Some might be found in Art 177 EC, see below.

The Community Courts' judgments do not necessarily support the Commission's position either. The Commission relies on two judgments. Neither of them expressly considers the issue. At footnote A of the last quotation, above, the Commission said:

> The test is market specific, see to that effect Case T-131/99, *Shaw*, [2002] ECR II-2023, paragraph 163, where the Court of First Instance held that the assessment under Article 81(3) had to be made within the same analytical framework as that used for assessing the restrictive effects, and Case C-360/92 P, *Publishers Association*, [1995] ECR I-23, paragraph 29, where in a case where the relevant market was wider than national the Court of Justice held that in the application of Article 81(3) it was not correct only to consider the effects on the national territory.

The Commission's reliance on *Shaw* seems unjustified. The matter concerned a series of beer supply agreements between Whitbread plc and its tenants. These breached Article 81(1), in part because of the cumulative effect of Whitbread's network and other similar networks of agreements.[84] Nevertheless, the Commission exempted the agreements, holding that beer supply agreements of the type at issue generally lead to improvements in distribution.[85] However, in this case, the tied lessees paid relatively high prices for Whitbread products, and the Commission thought that these might undermine the improvement in distribution.[86] Whitbread argued that its relationship with its lessees should not only be judged by reference to the prices they pay, but the whole business relationship should be taken into account to see if the lessee could 'survive'. The Commission accepted this, finding that overall there had been an improvement in distribution.[87]

The applicants before the CFI were two of Whitbread's tenants. They argued that the Commission should not have exempted the agreements. Although it is unclear from the judgment, they appear to have argued that, when deciding on an individual exemption, the Commission should assess the existence of countervailing benefits at the individual level, rather than to Whitbread's lessees as a group. The CFI disagreed:

> The disputed assessment of the countervailing benefits was made in the context of the examination of the grant of an individual exemption, after the finding that Whitbread's network of agreements makes a substantial contribution to foreclosure of the market in question. That assessment therefore had to be made within the same analytical framework, that of the effect of the notified agreements on the functioning of the market, and hence on the situation of the tied lessees taken as a whole, not on each lessee considered in isolation.[88]

The CFI's reference to making the Article 81(3) assessment within the same *analytical framework* as the Article 81(1) conclusions merely refers to the fact that the network of agreements was relevant in this case. One should look at the overall impact of all the notified agreements, in their economic context, as opposed to examining the impact on individual members of the group in isolation.[89] The CFI does not mention whether considerations outside of the relevant market are pertinent.

The Commission's reference to the *Publishers' Association* Case, can also be criticised. This case involved a fixed book agreement in the UK and Ireland. The CFI had previously

---

[84] Commission decision, *Whitbread*, paras 106–38.
[85] ibid, paras 150–54.
[86] ibid, paras 155–63.
[87] ibid, paras 164–70.
[88] Case T-131/99, *Shaw* para 163.
[89] The Commission even makes this point when citing *Shaw* in, Commission, *Article 81(3) Guidelines*, para 87.

held that the Publishers' Association, established in the UK, when arguing in favour of an exemption for their agreement, was not entitled to rely on any negative effects that might be felt in Ireland. In other words, the CFI had said, do not look at the relevant geographic market (the UK and Ireland), just look at the UK. The ECJ corrected this position by holding that nothing in Article 81(3) makes it:

> [S]ubject to the condition that those benefits should occur only on the territory of the Member State or States in which the undertakings who are parties to the agreement are established and not in the territory of other Member States. Such an interpretation is incompatible with the fundamental objectives of the Community and with the very concepts of common market and single market.

The ECJ's point is that one cannot look smaller than the relevant market. To do so would make no sense in economic theory, because the relevant geographic market is the area on which competition takes place.[90] The ECJ does not say that one cannot look at other markets as well. Having said that, it does not say that one can.

So, it seems that there is a stalemate. However, in *CGM v Commission*, the CFI, expressly advocated looking outside the partial equilibrium, at least in relation to the relevant product/service market:[91]

> [R]egard should naturally be had to the advantages arising from the agreement in question, not only for the relevant market ... but also, in appropriate cases, for every other market on which the agreement in question might have beneficial effects, and even, in a more general sense, for any service the quality or efficiency of which might be improved by the existence of that agreement ... Article 85(3) [now Article 81(3)] of the Treaty envisage[s] exemption in favour of, amongst others, agreements which contribute to promoting technical or economic progress, without requiring a specific link with the relevant market.[92]

CGM v Commission concerned intermodal transport services encompassing a bundle of, inter alia, inland and maritime transportation provided to shipping companies across the Community. The restrictions at issue related to inland transport services, which were held to constitute a separate market, whereas the benefits were claimed to occur in relation to maritime transport services.

The Commission refers to *CGM v Commission* too, defining the case as a limited exception to its general rule:

> [W]here two markets are related, efficiencies achieved on separate markets can be taken into account provided that the group of consumers affected by the restriction and benefiting from the efficiency gains are substantially the same.[93]

[90] Vickers (2003a) 99, 100.

[91] Lugard and Hancher (2004) 418, 419, reach similar conclusions.

[92] Case T-86/95 *Compagnie Générale Maritime v Commission* para 343. Also see the *Glaxo* Case para 248. The CFI's judgment in Joined Cases T-39/92 and T-40/92 *Groupement des Cartes Bancaires 'CB' and Europay International v Commission* paras 101–05, could imply that one should only look at the effects on the relevant product market. However, this is probably an incorrect interpretation of *Cartes Bancaires*. The statements could also be read as a criticism of the Commission for not defining the relevant product market correctly, it had proposed two alternatives.

[93] Commission, *Article 81(3) Guidelines*, para 43, n B. There is also a hint of this in the *Glaxo* Case para 251, although it is possible that the final consumers in these markets will not be the same.

The Commission argues that *CGM v Commission* does not undermine its point because both product markets (inland transport services and maritime transport services) had the same consumers.

There is no reason to interpret the CFI's judgment in this narrow way. The CFI does not expressly make such a link. In fact, the wording in its judgment is much wider.[94] The CFI even goes so far as to say that one should look at the effects *without requiring **a specific link** with the relevant market.* This seems contrary to the Commission's position, because the Commission appears to argue that a specific link (that both product markets have the same consumers) is necessary.[95]

To recap, the Commission argues that only the effects on the specific relevant product and geographic markets can be considered. It extends this to allow the effects in other related markets to be considered as long as they involve substantially the same consumers.[96] The Commission justifies this by saying that the Community competition rules must protect competition on the market; as well as by reference to the Community Courts' case law; and the effect on consumers. There are no explicit Community Court judgments supporting the Commission's position, indeed those that there are tend in the opposite direction.

A key part of the Commission's argument seems to be that consumers must get a fair share of the benefit. This is Article 81(3)'s second test. As a result, the Commission seeks to limit the benefits that can be considered in Article 81(3)'s first test. It is unclear why the wording of the second test should delimit the first. The Commission does not explain. Furthermore, even if a link between the two tests were made, a delimitation, in the terms the Commission advocates, would not necessarily follow.[97]

Linking Article 81(3)'s first two tests is wrong.[98] The Community Courts have stated that there are four separate tests under Article 81(3) EC, not three. The first test establishes that society benefits from the restriction of competition, through the various relevant objectives such as increased employment and environmental policy. The second test ensures that consumers get a fair share of the benefits. In any event, collapsing the two tests does not demonstrate that only the relevant market is relevant because the definition of consumer in Article 81(3)'s second test is not restricted to the parties' customers and this can include other markets. In law, there is no need to read the CFI's judgments in *CGM v Commission* and *CMA CGM v Commission* against their natural wording and in the restrictive manner proposed by the Commission. In fact, to do so may be positively harmful and could undermine economic welfare, for the reasons set out above.[99]

---

[94]   See quote attached to n 92 above.

[95]   The Commission also relies on Case T-213/00 *CMA CGM v Commission*. However, the same comments apply to that case as to *CGM v Commission*. In fact, at para 227 of *CMA CGM v Commission*, the CFI repeats para 343 from *CGM v Commission*, referred to above. It also rephrases it emphasising that one can consider the effects on '… any market on which the agreement in question might have beneficial effects …'

[96]   Note that the Commission and the CFI only refer to the consideration of benefits in other markets. My application of the total equilibrium standard is wider than both of them because I also advocate the consideration of costs in other markets. Thanks to Giorgio Monti for this comment.

[97]   Ch 7, Section 3, demonstrates that although the definition of 'consumer' is not certain in the case law, there are many cases where the consumer considered is not a customer of the parties. Sometimes the consumer is a user of a derived product of the parties', ie something on a different product market, such as the purchaser of African textiles. The Commission admits as much, Commission, *Article 81(3) Guidelines*, para 43.   ·

[98]   Monti (2002) 1076, 1077. See also, Ch 7.

[99]   It may also effect the consideration of other relevant objectives, see Ch 6, Section 2.3.

Furthermore, in relation to developing countries, the Commission may even be obliged to adopt a total equilibrium approach. Article 177(1) EC says that Community development policy shall foster, amongst other things, the smooth and gradual integration of developing countries into the world economy as well as the campaign against poverty in developing countries. Article 178 EC instructs the Community to take account of the objectives referred to in Article 177 in the policies that it implements which are likely to affect developing countries.[100] As far as possible, Article 81 EC should be interpreted in line with Articles 177(1) and 178 EC in a way that is both effective and so that both provisions are consistent with each other.[101]

The relationship between Community competition policy and development is complex.[102] However, by way of example, there is evidence to show that shipping cartels, see above, increase transport costs, reduce trade volumes and slow growth. This could affect the integration of developing countries into the world economy, as well as the campaign against poverty in these countries, see Article 177(1) EC.[103] However, if the Commission and the Community Courts considered the competitive effects of agreements that fall within Article 81(1) on product and geographic markets other than just the 'relevant' ones, then an agreement's effects on development and other policies could be more easily considered. Decisions that were pro-competitive, not just for the EU but for these developing countries could to be (relatively) quickly imposed, speeding up the integration of developing countries into the world economy, in line with the Treaty.

The more widely the Commission can cast its net in the search for an agreement's effects (both positive and negative) the more complete a picture it can draw up on how relevant Treaty objectives have been infringed. This applies to welfare as it applies to other objectives. It may well be that an agreement's direct effects are innocuous on some objectives. However, the knock-on effects on others could be tremendous.[104] Ideally, the Commission would be able to take such effects into account, ie on all product and geographic markets.[105] Having said that, the difficulties of collating evidence for a total equilibrium analysis may mean that pursuit of a second-best solution (a partial equilibrium framework) is better, and perhaps even more efficient, than a total equilibrium one. Nevertheless, Chapter 6 shows that a partial equilibrium analysis may mean that important public policy effects are ignored and so it favours a restricted total equilibrium approach.

One could argue that Article 3(1)(g) EC only refers to distortions of competition in the Common Market. However, and without forgetting the existence of the jurisdictional test of an 'effect on trade between Member States', I do not think that prevents analysis of

---

[100]   Furthermore, where distortions to competition arise in one of the ACP (a group of 78 African, Caribbean and Pacific countries) signatories to the Cotonou Agreement of 23 June 2000 (which came into force 1 April 2003 and was revised in June 2005), the duty to take into account the affect of Community antitrust decisions is reinforced, see Art 45(2) of that agreement.

[101]   For a general exposition of this principle see Case C-67/96 *Albany International v Stichting Bedrijfspensioenfonds Texielindustrie*, para 60.

[102]   See Townley (2004) 128–34, and the documents referred to there.

[103]   Furthermore, where it affects them, such legislation does not lead to the elimination of distortions to sound competition in the ACP countries, Art 45(2) Cotonou Agreement.

[104]   Often environmental effects are indirect for example.

[105]   Chs 4 and 7 demonstrate that some of the Treaty objectives that must also be considered within Art 81 demand a more global approach. Adopting a total equilibrium model in relation to economic efficiency would make the treatment of all relevant objectives more consistent.

extra-Community effects, once an effect has been found within the EU. First, as shown above, markets are interlinked, so affects abroad can distort competition within the EU. Furthermore, Article 81 is not merely there to implement Article 3(1)(g).[106]

5 CONCLUSION

I have tentatively pointed to three ways in which welfare analysis can be 'distorted' in order to achieve public policy objectives, or to facilitate their consideration. These are: consumer welfare (or producer welfare); productive and dynamic efficiencies (at the expense of allocative efficiencies); and total, over a partial, equilibrium approach. I say tentatively, because the Commission is rarely explicit about what it is trying to do; normally fails to quantify any costs or benefits that it considers; and, seldom places its analysis within a wider framework, which would allow us to more readily understand what it is seeking to achieve, or to predict its assessment in future cases.

The Commission has explicitly adopted a consumer welfare approach in its policy statements. This does not reflect the wording under Article 81(3) EC,[107] as the consumer welfare approach only demands that an agreement be neutral from a consumer perspective, as opposed to demanding that consumers get a fair share of the agreement's benefit. The Commission's decisions also refer to consumer benefits arising from the agreement, implying that the consumer welfare standard is being applied there too. That said, the Commission often pays a lot of attention to the effects on Community industry and, particularly when Community undertakings benefit from the agreement, the Commission readily finds relevant consumer benefits. In this way, industrial policy creeps into its efficiency assessment, at least to some extent.

Furthermore, the Commission particularly encourages R&D activities by Community undertakings. This is probably because of the industrial policy and employment benefits that it believes they bring. By readily accepting short term, and sometimes substantial, allocative efficiency losses to achieve these ends the Commission hopes to increase R&D spending in the European Union. It has often accepted quite speculative dynamic and productive efficiency gains in its decisions. Once again it fails to quantify the costs and benefits of these agreements, making industrial policy considerations easier to accept.

The Commission, *Article 81(3) Guidelines*, seem to be an attempt to put things on a more formal footing. They demand explicit listing and quantification of all purported efficiency gains. This would certainly be an improvement, bringing greater transparency to the Commission's assessment. However, it is insufficient. The Commission must set up a more formal, structured, method of welfare analysis, properly explaining when short-term allocative efficiency can be compromised for long-term gain, for example. A more precise definition of competition is also imperative.[108]

The Commission favours a partial equilibrium approach. However, there are many advantages to the total equilibrium analysis. It allows us to make a more global welfare

---

[106] See Ch 2. Other relevant (non-economic) objectives often require analysis of extra-Community effects, see Ch 6, Section 2.3.

[107] And even less that of Art 81(1) EC.

[108] Neven (1998) 114, 117.

assessment, encourages co-operation between antitrust agencies, should improve consistency between them and may make it easier to further other Community objectives, such as development policy, in a pro-market manner. The Commission bases itself on two cases, which do not seem to support the points it attributes to them. In addition, its position flies in the face of two clear CFI judgments rejecting the partial equilibrium.[109]

[109] Some limits may need to be placed upon what effects should be considered relevant in the antitrust analysis after the CFI judgments. Some suggestions are made in Ch 6. We urgently need clear guidance on this issue.

Conclusion of Part B

In 2002, Schaub claimed that 'Community competition law is now a mature and fully-fledged system of law, which pursues the same aims and covers the same phenomena as most other competition law regimes.'[1]

Many other jurisdictions' competition law regimes have an exclusive consumer welfare goal. Whilst Community competition law has a consumer welfare goal, the foundations on which the Community system is based also demand the consideration of non-economic objectives within Article 81. These public policy objectives sometimes clash with consumer welfare. As a result, it is not at all clear that Community competition law pursues the same aims as other regimes.

This leads us to Schaub's other claim, that Community competition law is now a mature and fully-fledged system of law. Part B raised many issues related to how to resolve the conflicts between consumer welfare and public policy. It demonstrates that often, even basic answers remain elusive; which does not make it sound like a mature legal system.

Community competition policy must become more transparent.[2] More clarity is needed about which public policy objectives can properly be considered within Article 81. For example, should Member State objectives have been raised there, or should only Community goals be considered.[3] Secondly, why each objective is being pursued should be explored; as this will help us decide whether the relevant goals conflict at all and, if they do, help us predict their weight in the balance.

In an effort to provide more transparency, Part B asked three questions: how are public policy objectives balanced in Article 81; where does this happen; and what are the limits of this balance? In relation to the first question, two balancing methods are discussed, mere and market-balancing. You will remember that, market-balancing is conducted inside, and mere-balancing is conducted outside of the consumer welfare assessment. The Commission has used (and still uses) both methodologies, regularly.

Mere balancing was discussed in Chapters 3 and 4, in relation to Article 81(1) and (3) respectively. While it is less common within Article 81(1), there is evidence that it takes place there. It is unclear why this is happening when Article 81(3) seems more appropriate. Chapters 3 and 4 raise other issues that must also be resolved before mere-balancing can make any claim to maturity; such as the fact that it seems easier to consider public policy goals within Article 81(1).

---

[1] Schaub (2002) 38. See also, Faull (1991) and Verstrynge (1988) 2.
[2] See, eg Korah in Ehlermann (1998) 525–41. For a contrary view, see Faull (1998) 15 'On the few occasions that we [the Commission] pursue goals other than efficiency under Art 85(3) [now Art 81(3)], our proceedings are transparent ...'
[3] See the discussion in Ch 7, Section 2.

Even as regards mere-balancing within Article 81(3), which is less controversial, Chapter 4 shows that fundamental questions remain unanswered. The Commission rarely even discusses whether it is taking a specific objective into account at all. I suggested that it should be more specific in its decisions about how and why it has decided a case in a certain way.[4] Also, the way that the Commission decides often means that political issues (highly relevant in the cases discussed) lead it away from a pure consumer welfare goal.[5] This could be more clearly reflected and explained in the final decision. The mechanism that the Commission adopts when balancing is also unclear and thus hard to repeat, for undertakings, their lawyers, or the Member States' courts and competition authorities.[6] Furthermore, the limits of the Article 81(3) balance are also uncertain. On the few occasions that the Commission has explicitly defined this, it did not follow itself when specific matters came before it. It does not explain why. Furthermore, Chapter 4 showed that, where they are accepted as relevant in a given case, non-economic objectives have never 'lost' to the economic efficiency goal.[7] This is contrary to the 'perceived wisdom' in this area. The Commission could better explain the determinants of an objective's weight in the balance; the limits of the balance; and, how these limits change over time. Instead of merely providing brief conclusions,[8] decisions should make the trade-offs explicit and explain why they were resolved in the way they were.[9]

There is even confusion about what methodology to use to consider public policy goals, Chapter 5 outlines a second method through which these goals are considered within the consumer welfare analysis itself. Three avenues were highlighted. First, the Commission seems to temper its consumer welfare goal, for industrial policy purposes. The second avenue was to weigh short-term allocative efficiency losses against potential long-term allocative efficiency gains through encouraging R&D. Finally, I investigated the Commission's advocacy of the partial equilibrium framework; which affects the facility with which public policy goals can be considered in Article 81.

Before ending this part, I want to make one more point. Where the parties to an agreement act in accordance with a specific Community law, DG Competition is more willing to consider non-economic objectives.[10] While it is not necessary to have prior Community support, it clearly helps.[11] It also seems beneficial to get another of the Commission's Directorate-Generals to support the agreement in question.[12] The Commission is a political body, and political pressures can and do affect it. One might expect a reduction of this effect where Article 81 decisions are taken by Member State courts and competition authorities, as they are theoretically more independent of other Community actors; however, this is far from certain as they might be exposed to other political pressures themselves. In any event, for some time after 1 May 2004, these bodies are likely

---

[4]   See the discussion about Commission decision, *Grundig's EC distribution system*.

[5]   Monti (2002) 1070.

[6]   Ch 8 suggests a more transparent balancing mechanism.

[7]   That is not to say that there are no 'external' checks on the balance. Ch 7 discusses Art 81(3)'s other three tests and how they interact with this balance.

[8]   Ehlermann (1998) and Korah in Ehlermann (1998) 526.

[9]   Lipsky (1998) 332 and Forrester (1998) 360, 382.

[10]   For example, in Commission decisions, *Eco-Emballages* and *DSD and others*, the parties were acting in compliance with certain Community environmental legislation.

[11]   Commission, *Vertical Guidelines*, para 179.

[12]   This occurred in relation to both the *ACEA* and the *CEMEP* matters. Also, *VOTOB*, got the agreement of the Dutch Government, see Ch 3.

to be extremely diffident to the opinions of Community institutions in relation to Community competition law and the resolution of conflicts within it.

In conclusion, in relation to conflict resolution between competing objectives within Article 81, the citation of Schaub at the beginning of this conclusion seems over confident.[13] The Treaty provides a different nest of values from other competition law systems. These values, and the web in which they find themselves, cannot be ignored. A mature system of law would explain how they should be taken into account; where this should happen and what the limits of this balancing process are. Community law is far from clear on any of these points. In this regard, Community competition policy is more like a teenager. It is aware of many values; it knows that they must be taken into account and even does this sometimes; but, it does so reluctantly and outside of a mature over-arching value framework.

Regulation 1/2003 further formalises the Commission's leadership role in relation to Articles 81 and 82 EC. The reforms that this regulation has brought give the Commission more time to resolve fundamental competition problems, such as conflict resolution. The Commission's leadership role brings with it a responsibility. It must be as clear and transparent as possible and explain how and where to resolve conflicts in Article 81, as well as what the limits of these conflicts are, taking account of the Community legal order. Part B shows that there is much work to do.

Part C makes some suggestions in this regard. But, ultimately, the Community Courts must ensure that the Commission lives up to its responsibilities.[14] To quote Lord Justice Woolf in relation to the English legal system:

> Appeals serve two purposes: the private purpose, which is to do justice in particular cases by correcting wrong decisions, and the public purpose, which is to ensure public confidence in the administration of justice by making such corrections and to clarify and develop the law and to set precedents.[15]

In relation to the consideration of non-economic objectives within Article 81 this means that the Community Courts must openly declare that this is possible, as well as explaining where this should be done. They must force the Commission to clarify its balancing mechanism and to show how it applies this in its decisions, providing the reasons that Article 253 EC demands.[16] Only then may Community competition policy truly claim to have come of age.

---

[13]   See also, Whish and Sufrin (2000) 146–49 and Gerber (1994) 143.

[14]   See Korah in Ehlermann (1998) 529–41.

[15]   Lord Woolf, *Final Report on Access to Civil Justice*, ch 14. For similar points in relation to Art 234 references and appeals to the Community Courts, see Evans (1983) 591.

[16]   Case T-95/94, *Chambre Syndicale Nationale des Entreprises de Transport de Fonds et Valeurs and Brink's France v Commission* para 52, explains the need for reasoning in Commission competition decisions.

Part C

How and Where Should Public Policy Balancing Be Performed in Article 81 EC?

Introduction to Part C

Many argue that non-economic objectives have no place within competition policy. They see competition policy as economic policy and do not want it to be complicated and 'polluted' by non-economic considerations. More legitimately, they argue that competition policy cannot do everything. Non-economic objectives are important, but can often be achieved more efficiently using other mechanisms.

So much for economic theory; but, the legal context is also important. Chapter 2 showed that, in the Community legal order, the Treaty's policy-linking clauses demand the consideration of seven public policy goals in, amongst others, Article 81 EC. More generally, the Community Courts see the Treaty as a whole; they interpret it as a system for achieving Article 2 EC's underlying aims. This has led them to consider many other public policy goals within Article 81 EC as well. This approach chimes with the will of both the Council and the European Parliament.

Part B showed how this is currently done. The first mechanism, mere-balancing,[1] takes place in both Article 81(1) and 81(3) EC. Public policy goals have been given a lot of weight in the balance; however, it is still unclear where balancing should take place within Article 81; when it should occur; and, there is little consistency about how to balance across the various public policy heads. Chapter 5 describes a second balancing mechanism, market-balancing[2] and unpicks several case law examples.

Part C reflects upon the problems raised in the first two parts of this book and suggests a path through the maze.

The current system is too unclear. The Commission's recent guidelines declare that consumer welfare is Article 81's sole goal. While they aid transparency, these guidelines ignore the Treaty's fundamental premises as well as those in the Community Courts' public policy jurisprudence. This is unacceptable, not only from a constitutional perspective; but, because this conflict undermines legal certainty, something that is particularly important post 1 May 2004.

Certain elements must be at the heart of any proposed clarification. First and foremost, the proposed system must respect the Treaty, unless amendments are proposed; and the fundamental tenets of the Community Courts' case law. This means that decision-makers must be able to consider relevant public policy objectives within Article 81. Secondly, undertakings, decision-makers and consumers need more legal certainty in the balancing

---

[1] Mere-balancing operates *outside* of the consumer welfare assessment; the decision-maker first assesses an agreement's effect on consumer welfare and then balances this against its impact upon relevant public policy objectives. Ch 1, Section 2.2.2 explains mere-balancing in more detail.

[2] Market-balancing occurs *within* the consumer welfare test itself, by altering the importance of its various components. Market-balancing is explained in more detail on Ch 1, Section 2.2.1.

test and transparency in the way it is conducted. Thirdly, within this framework, we need as efficient a set of competition rules as possible.

Chapter 6 discusses Article 81(1) EC; it covers three main issues. First, the concept of a 'restriction of competition' is unclear and unsatisfactory; I suggest making consumer welfare Article 81(1)'s sole goal. Secondly, I discuss mere-balancing within Article 81(1) EC and argue that this should be restricted to Article 81(3); Article 81's structure will then ensure that mere-balancing's costs are more clearly defined. The point is not that, in the Community legal order, welfare should permanently outweigh all other objectives; however, the Community increasingly relies on the market mechanism as the basic means of wealth creation and so it is logical to organise EU competition law around an economic welfare standard. Finally, I consider that, as it lacks the requisite transparency, market-balancing should be avoided in Article 81. It is hoped that these suggestions augment clarity, while respecting the Treaty's telos.

Chapter 7 analyses Article 81(3) EC. Many public policy goals will be automatically promoted through Article 81(1)'s consumer welfare test. Nevertheless, some objectives cannot be pursued indirectly through this test; others can be pursued in part, but not to the level that the Treaty demands. Given that, in the Community legal order, public policy goals cannot be isolated from the competition provisions, I suggest considering them in Article 81(3), via mere-balancing. Chapter 7's core analysis comes in four parts, each of which discusses one of Article 81(3)'s four tests. It explains some of the implications of incorporating non-economic objectives within that provision and suggests how this might better be done. Then, Chapter 8 provides a framework for balancing non-economic objectives under Article 81(3)'s first test.

Non-economic objectives must be considered within Article 81 EC. Part C offers some foundations for their consideration there and points the way to future demands that these objectives will place upon us. It does this in light of Chapter 1's theoretical insights, although it takes care to restrict the analysis to that acceptable in the Community legal order.

6

How and Where Should Public Policy Balancing be Performed in Article 81(1) EC?

1 INTRODUCTION

Competition is an important principle within the Community legal order. The Treaty refers to it many times. In particular, Article 81(1) EC prohibits as incompatible with the common market, agreements between undertakings which may affect trade between Member States and which have as their object or effect the prevention, restriction or distortion of competition within the common market. Nevertheless, non-economic goals are also important in the Community legal order and are relevant in Article 81.[1]

This chapter wrestles with two issues. Section 2 asks what 'prevention, restriction or distortion of competition' means. The expression is unclear in the Treaty and the case law and academic writing provide little assistance. I discuss various ways of defining a 'restriction of competition', taking account of Article 81's purpose. I conclude that, today, it is best defined as an appreciable restriction of consumer welfare.

Section 3 then discusses the relevance of public policy considerations within Article 81(1). Section 3.1 examines market-balancing; ie considering public policy objectives *within* the economic efficiency test itself.[2] I argue that this is too opaque and should not

---

[1]   See Ch 2 and Part B.
[2]   See Ch 1, Section 2.2 and Ch 5.

happen. Then, Section 3.2 considers mere-balancing in Article 81(1) EC; ie balancing public policy goals outside of the economic efficiency assessment.[3] I suggest that this be restricted to Article 81(3).

One might ask whether these issues are of anything other than academic interest today. Korah, for example, has said that Regulation 1/2003 effectively ends the bifurcation of Article 81(1) and (3) EC. She argues that whether the market analysis is carried out under Article 81(1) or (3) will no longer matter once courts and national authorities can proceed to analysis under Article 81(3). As a result, Korah believes that the wide scope historically given to Article 81(1) will cease to be important.[4]

Korah is right in that now the whole of Article 81 can be applied by the same decision-maker, in the same forum, the bifurcation of this provision may be less important.[5] However, to my mind, Regulation 1/2003 does not mean that the wide reach historically given to Article 81(1) is irrelevant; nor does it remove the need to clearly define the provision's scope; or, obviate the problems caused by public policy balancing there.

Article 81(1) EC's reach is still important. Agreements that fall within Article 81(1) are void, unless they can be exempted under Article 81(3);[6] there may also be fines and a reputational risk for the undertakings involved. If Article 81(1) is read widely, then a balancing of consumer welfare or public policy objectives under Article 81(3) is necessary, more often; balancing is expensive to conduct and the outcome is hard to predict. This discourages investment[7] and encourages litigation, to upset the parties' bargain.[8] The problem is exacerbated due to ambiguity about what Article 81(1) refers to; for example, a 'restriction of competition' has not been clearly defined and, public policy balancing (sometimes) takes place there, but we do not know why or when this should happen. Article 81's burden of proof is also relevant.[9] Regulation 1/2003, assigns the burden of proof to a different party under Article 81(1), the party alleging the infringement and Article 81(3), the party claiming the benefit of this provision. Therefore, knowing where arguments can be raised matters. As a result, it is still important to apply Article 81(1) with intellectual rigour today.[10]

One could even argue that these issues are more import to undertakings since 1 May 2004. Once an agreement had been notified to the Commission under Regulation 17 there was normally immunity from fines; yet, notification is no longer possible under Regulation 1/2003. Furthermore, there is likely to be much more competition enforcement today as Member States' courts and competition authorities, as well as individuals, are encouraged to use Article 81. As a result, undertakings are potentially open to more attack with less protection. Of course there is now no need to notify, which saves costs; they can also take advantage of Article 81(3) more easily, so undertakings are not necessarily worse off. I merely seek to show that they are still exposed and that this is exacerbated by the ambiguity about Article 81(1) EC's scope.

---

[3]   Ch 3, Section 2 observed that mere-balancing probably occurs in Art 81(1) EC.

[4]   Korah (2000) 189, see also 361; Gyselen (2002a) 197; Gavalda and Parleani (2002) 333 and other references at Komninos (2005), n 10.

[5]   Korah and O'Sullivan (2002) 120; Venit (2003) 575 and Albors-Llorens (2002) 72, 73.

[6]   See Ch 3, Section 3.1, which argues that the public policy balance may be easier to achieve if performed in Article 81(1) rather than 81(3).

[7]   Siragusa (1998) 543, 544; Venit (1998) 567, 568 and Hawk (1995) 983.

[8]   Forrester (2001) 45.

[9]   Komninos (2005) 3, 4, where he also attacks Korah's position with other arguments.

[10]   Whish (2003) 107; although in Whish (2008) 114, he dilutes this view.

2 PREVENTION, RESTRICTION OR DISTORTION OF COMPETITION

This section asks what Article 81(1) EC means by '… prevention, restriction or distortion of competition …' Section 2.1 argues that neither the Treaty, nor the Community Courts, nor the Commission have defined the term with sufficient clarity (or consistency) such that it can be readily applied by undertakings. This is unacceptable. Companies are entitled to expect an adequate level of predictability and consistent application of the rules allowing them to properly assess how these rules will be applied.[11]

As a result, the remainder of Section 2 focuses on finding appropriate guiding principles that properly balance, in the Community context, legal certainty with the flexibility required for governing an economy in a state of constant flux. Section 2.2 asks whether economic freedom is an appropriate foundation for such rules; and concludes that it is not. Section 2.3 advocates a consumer welfare standard.[12]

Throughout this discussion, remember that Article 81 should be interpreted in light of the Treaty's objectives as a whole and that these objectives change over time. As a result, Article 81's interpretation may change over time too.

2.1 'Restriction … of competition' is currently unclear

Much of the Treaty's wording is open-textured[13] and, despite its emphasis upon the term (which appears 32 times), nowhere does it define 'competition',[14] let alone a 'restriction of competition'.[15] This is hardly surprising given the dynamics of the object being regulated here, an economy that is in a constant state of flux.[16]

Some believe that wording such as 'restriction of competition' is incapable of manipulation. It has a meaning that simply needs to be made clear.[17] This is unlikely.[18] As with any broad and simply stated legal rule, a number of approaches can be consistent with the wording of Article 81(1) EC. The issue is which approach is, taking into account the purpose of the provision, most appropriate.[19]

As the Treaty does not provide more clarification, I turn to the statements and decisions of the Commission and the Community Courts; and examine how the academic literature

---

[11]   Mario Monti in Ehlermann (2001) 9. See also, Marenco (1999) 1231.

[12]   The notion of 'competition' is further discussed in Ch 7, Section 5, in relation to Art 81(3) EC. Similar problems emerge there to those under Art 81(1).

[13]   Baquero Cruz (2002) 10.

[14]   Souty (2003) 16, 55.

[15]   Art 81(1)(a)–(e) EC provides examples of restrictions of competition, such as directly or indirectly fixing purchase or selling prices or sharing markets or sources of supply. However, these examples are insufficient to explain the numerous intricacies involved in understanding how Art 81 works, Whish (2008) 113. See also, Verouden (2003) 529, 530.

[16]   See Möschel (1991) 7.

[17]   Marenco (1999) 1218.

[18]   Indeed, Bork (1993) 58–61, distinguishes at least five definitions of 'competition'. See also, Areeda and Hovenkamp (2000), para 100a. Furthermore, Forrester (2001) 91–93, writes that when (in 1958) the British Embassy in Paris asked about Art 81 and 82's remit '… neither the Member States nor the Commission were able to respond to the UK's questions about how the competition rules would affect executed agreements.'

[19]   Bright (1995) 506. See also, Hildebrand (2002) 183; Gerber (1998) 345, 385–87; Joerges (1997) 10 and Schröter (1987) 691.

has interpreted a restriction of competition.[20] Neither the Community Courts, nor the Commission have defined 'restriction of competition' with sufficient clarity (or consistency) such that it can be adequately applied by undertakings, or the Member States' courts and competition authorities.[21] I examine this point; not, at this stage, to 'find' a definition of 'restriction of competition', but merely to highlight the ambiguity in its interpretation. In the rest of Section 2, where I search for 'meaning' for this term, I will then ensure that my suggestions 'fit' within Article 81(1) EC's range of possibilities.

In 1997, Whish said that although the debate about what is meant by a 'restriction of competition' under Article 81(1) had been with us for 30 years, he did not believe that we were any closer to an acceptable solution to this central conundrum of EC competition law.[22] In 2006, Odudu wrote that an acceptable solution still eludes us because consensus on the function that this term is supposed to serve is lacking.[23]

I discuss four different interpretations of 'restriction of competition' from the academic literature. These are: the Ordoliberal concept of economic freedom; market integration; consumer welfare; and allocative efficiency. The point of this exercise is to show that there is still a lack of clarity as to what precisely a 'restriction of competition' means.[24]

Following the Ordoliberal tradition,[25] Monti argues that a 'restriction of competition' under Article 81(1) EC is an undue restriction of the economic freedom of the parties or a restriction on other market participants.[26] Monti believes that recent case law supports this interpretation of Article 81(1) EC.[27]

Monti relies on two recent cases when making this argument.[28] The first, *Métropole télévision*, was an appeal from Commission decision, *TPS*. It involved an agreement to create Télévision par satellite (TPS) whose object was to devise, develop and broadcast, in digital mode by satellite, a range of television programmes and services, against payment, to French speaking television viewers in Europe. TPS was a partnership between six major companies. Some were active in the television sector, others in the telecommunication and cable distribution sectors.

One of the grounds for appeal was that the Commission should have applied Article 81(1) EC in the light of a rule of reason, rather than an abstract rule. In the applicants' view, cases such as *Nungesser* and *Coditel*[29] confirm the existence of a rule of reason under Article 81(1). They argued that, under this rule, an anti-competitive practice falls outside

---

[20]   This is not an easy task, particularly in light of the balancing process taking place within Art 81(1), see Ch 3.

[21]   See also, Commentaire Mégret (1997) 171.

[22]   Ehlermann (1998) 461.

[23]   Odudu (2006) 97.

[24]   This is so, despite the fact that there is increasingly a consensus (to which I do not subscribe, see Ch 2) that the objective of Art 81 should be consumer welfare, see Ch 2, nn 9, 11.

[25]   The Ordoliberal tradition is briefly discussed in Section 2.2, below.

[26]   Monti (2002) 1061. See also, Venit (2003) 548; Lenaerts (2002) 32, 33; Schröter (1987) 667–70 and Jacquemin and de Jong (1977) 198, 199. Of the five, only Monti and Schröter justify their view with reference to the Community Courts' case law or Commission statements and decisions, see below.

[27]   Monti (2002) 1061. See also, Vossestein (2002) 857 and Faull and Nikpay (1999) 86, 87.

[28]   Case T-112/99 *Métropole télévision (M6) v Commission* paras 76, 77 and the *Wouters* Case, para 97. Also see the more recent *Meca Medina* Case (2006), paras 40–45; Case 86/82 *Hasselblad v Commission* para 46 and other references in Schröter (1987) 667–69.

[29]   The *Nungesser* Case and Case 262/81 *Coditel SA, Compagnie Générale pour la Diffusion de la Télévision, and Others v Ciné-Vog Films* para 20.

the scope of the prohibition in Article 81(1) if it has more positive than negative effects on competition on a given market.[30]

The CFI disagreed. It held that a rule of reason had not been confirmed by the Community Courts. The CFI accepted that some of the Community Courts' judgments have favoured a more flexible approach to interpretation under Article 81(1).[31] However, the CFI added:

> Those judgments [Case 56/65 *Société Technique Minière v Maschinenbau Ulm* [1966]; the *Nungesser* Case; the *Coditel* Case; the *Pronuptia* Case; the *Gøttrup-Klim* Case [31]–[35]; Case C-399/93 *H.G. Oude Luttikhuis v Verenigde Coöperatieve* [1995] and the *European Night Services* Case] cannot … be interpreted as establishing the existence of a rule of reason in Community competition law. They are, rather, part of a broader trend in the case-law according to which it is not necessary to hold, wholly abstractly and without drawing any distinction, that any agreement restricting the freedom of action of one or more of the parties is necessarily caught by the prohibition laid down in Article 85(1) [now Article 81(1)] of the Treaty. In assessing the applicability of Article 85(1) to an agreement, account should be taken of the actual conditions in which it functions, in particular the economic context in which the undertakings operate, the products or services covered by the agreement and the actual structure of the market concerned …[32]

In the next paragraph, the CFI continued:

> That interpretation … makes it possible to prevent the prohibition in Article 85(1) from extending wholly abstractly and without distinction to all agreements whose effect is to restrict the freedom of action of one or more of the parties.

Monti might argue that the CFI makes three points here. First, the notion of restriction of competition seems to be related to the issue of restricting freedom of action. Secondly, for the purposes of Article 81(1), a restriction of competition cannot be defined in the abstract as every restriction of the parties' freedom of action. Finally, account should be taken of the actual conditions in which the agreement functions.[33]

Monti assumes that the Community Courts are saying that a restriction of competition is a restriction of economic freedom (restriction of freedom of action) and that the reference to 'context' is merely there to show that Article 81(1) should not be applied in the abstract to all restrictions of economic freedom, but just to 'undue' restrictions.

Yet, many disagree that the jurisprudence unambiguously points this way. Summing up the conclusions of a group of competition law experts, Whish says that several Community Court judgments eschew the confusion between restrictions of competition and restrictions of conduct.[34] This implies that economic freedom was/is not (always) relevant under Article 81(1) EC.[35]

The ECJ gives a famous example of another Article 81 EC goal in the *Consten and Grundig* Case, abolishing the barriers between Member States (market integration):

---

[30]   Case T-112/99 *Métropole télévision (M6) v Commission* para 68.
[31]   ibid, paras 72, 75.
[32]   ibid, para 76.
[33]   The second case that Monti relies upon uses similar terminology, the *Wouters* Case, para 97.
[34]   Whish (1998) 499. Admittedly, this statement was made before either *Wouters* or *Métropole television*.
[35]   Although it is unclear, Whish's observation seems to be based on the line of cases starting with Case 56/65 *Société Technique Minière v Maschinenbau Ulm*.

[A]n agreement between producer and distributor which might tend to restore the national divisions in trade between Member States might be such as to frustrate the most fundamental objections of the Community. The Treaty, whose preamble and content aim at abolishing the barriers between states, and which in several provisions gives evidence of a stern attitude with regard to their reappearance, could not allow undertakings to reconstruct such barriers. Article 85(1) [now Article 81(1)] is designed to pursue this aim.[36]

Market integration has been a key Article 81 objective for some time;[37] note the Commission's early emphasis on vertical restraints, for example.[38]

This leads us to question whether Monti is right in assuming that the discussion of restriction of competition in *Métropole télévision* necessarily embraces economic freedom as an Article 81(1) EC goal. The Community Courts may be saying, for example, that a restriction of competition should not be determined by asking whether or not there is a restriction of economic freedom (ie whether or not the agreement restricts economic freedom is irrelevant). Instead, one should ask whether there has been a restriction of competition by examining the context in which the agreement actually operates.

If this interpretation is correct, all the CFI has said, in *Métropole television*, about goals is that economic freedom is not an Article 81 goal, assuming that this is what freedom of action means. One would then need to search for an alternative. We have seen that one such goal may be market integration. Another possibility is that Article 81(1) EC incorporates a consumer welfare test. Although it is a hotly debated topic,[39] many authors,[40] as well as the Commission,[41] argue that the Commission and the Community Courts have already applied a consumer welfare test within Article 81(1), at least some of the time.[42] There is recent support for this position in the *Glaxo* Case (2006), where the CFI held that:

[T]he objective assigned to Article 81(1) EC, which constitutes a fundamental provision indispensable for the achievement of the missions entrusted to the Community, in particular for the

---

[36]   The *Consten and Grundig* Case, 340. See also, Art 3(1)(c) EC.

[37]   The CFI argues that the ECJ is making a consumer welfare argument here, the *Glaxo* Case para 120. There is some evidence of this kind of thinking in *Consten and Grundig*. In that case the ECJ provides four reasons why Art 81 applies to vertical agreements. Twice it did this by reference to Art 81's goals. At p 339, the ECJ explains that it was worried about vertical restraints because through them '... the parties might seek, by preventing or limiting the competition of third parties in respect of the products, to create or guarantee for their benefit an unjustified advantage at the expense of the consumer or user, contrary to the general aims of Art 85 [now Art 81 EC].' However, I do not agree with the CFI in the *Glaxo* Case that the ECJ *only* relied on a consumer welfare goal, as the ECJ gave market integration as an alternative and additional reason for including vertical restraints in Art 81's remit, see quote in main text. Many other authors also interpret the *Consten and Grundig* Case as referring to market integration, see, eg Whish (2008) 22, 23 and Ehlermann (1992).

[38]   See also Commission, *White Paper on Modernisation*, paras 8, 45 and Commission, *RCP 1999*, point 3.

[39]   See Whish and Sufrin (1987) 20–36; Verstrynge (1988) 8; Korah (1986) 98–103 (although she thinks that there should be such a goal, Korah (1981)); Manzini (2002) 395–97 and Manzini (2003) 287/II-296/II, as well as the references in all these papers.

[40]   Forrester and Norall (1984) 38–40; Venit (1986) 217, 218; Korah (1990) 1018; Hawk (1995) 982, 983; Riley (1998) 483, 484, 491; Hildebrand (2002) ch IV and Souty (2003) 56, 61.

[41]   See Commission, *White Paper on Modernisation*, para 57. See also, the Opinion of A-G Jacobs in *Wouters* para 103.

[42]   Some argue that this tendency is increasing, see Faull (1998) 506; Heimler and Fattori (1998) 596 and Ritter, Braun, and Rawlinson (2000) 16; others treat this assertion more sceptically, see Whish (1998) 499 and Uitermark (1996) 9–11, or at least '... the Commission should look more rigorously into the economic aspects of the matter.'

functioning of the internal market … is to prevent undertakings, by restricting competition between themselves or with third parties, from reducing the welfare of the final consumer of the products in question.[43]

Odudu suggests a fourth alternative. He believes that a restriction of competition can always and only be said to exist when collusion causes allocative inefficiency. To his mind, a restriction of competition as a substantive element in Article 81(1) EC and allocative inefficiency are synonymous.[44]

This is a fundamental disagreement. The underlying motivation for the Community Courts' interpretation of Article 81(1) remains unclear, even in recent jurisprudence. In the past, economic freedom has been considered. It is unclear whether the Community Courts have abandoned this standard, there are some signs that they have not (*Meca Medina* (2006)).[45] If economic freedom has been abandoned, there is little clarity as to the new standard. It may be market integration (*Sot Lelos kai Sia EE* (2008));[46] consumer welfare (*Glaxo* (2006));[47] merely allocative efficiency; or, something else.

This ambiguity gives the Commission (and the Member States' courts and competition authorities) an enormous amount of freedom. Unsurprisingly, a clearer position has not emerged from them either.[48] Sometimes almost every restriction in agreements between significant players requires an exemption.[49] On other occasions the Commission interprets 'restrictions of competition' as '*undue* restrictions of economic freedom'.[50] That said, it too is inconsistent.[51] Commission, *Article 81(3) Guidelines*, does not define 'competition'

---

[43] Case T-168/01 *GlaxoSmithKline Services v Commission* para 118; however, para 171 may be interpreted as meaning that the objective of the whole of Art 81 is consumer welfare, which is in line with Commission, *Article 81(3) Guidelines*, para 33, although note para 21. This judgment is currently on appeal to the ECJ, in part on this issue, see Joined Cases C-501/06 etc. *GlaxoSmithKline Services v Commission*. See also the Opinion of A-G Trstenjak, Case C-209/07 *The Competition Authority v BIDS* para 56, supporting the CFI's judgment and Joined Cases C-468/06 to C-478/06 *Sot Lelos kai Sia EE and Others v GlaxoSmithKline* esp para 65, which may undermine it.

[44] Odudu (2006) 98, see more generally, the whole of his ch 5. Also, Roth (2006) 47.

[45] The *Meca Medina* Case (2006), paras 40–45.

[46] Market integration might be seen as one of many goals, n 37 above and Joined Cases C-468/06 to C-478/06 *Sot Lelos kai Sia EE and Others v GlaxoSmithKline* esp para 65 and the Opinion of A-G Jacobs in that case para 70. Alternatively, the CFI and Commission now argue that market integration is only relevant insofar as it enhances consumer welfare, see respectively the *Glaxo* Case para 121 and Commission, *Article 81(3) Guidelines*, para 13.

[47] Case T-168/01 *GlaxoSmithKline Services v Commission* para 118. Kroes (2007) argues that there has always been a consumer welfare standard, *cf* Lowe (2007).

[48] See, eg Bright (1995) 506, 507.

[49] Venit (2003) 574. See also Verouden (2003) 532; Lenaerts (2002) 32; Fox (2001) 127; Hawk and Denaeijer (2001) 129; Hawk (1995) 975 and Waelbroeck (1987a) 693.

[50] See eg the Commission's arguments in Case 86/82 *Hasselblad v Commission* para 42. This reflects Commission decision, *Hasselblad*, para 59. See also, Commission decision, *ACEC-Berliet*, para II(1); Commission decision, *Woodpulp*, para 133; Commission, *RCP 1991*, point 83 and p 334 and the Commission's position in matters such as the *Coditel* Case, 3389 and the *Nungesser* Case, 2035, 2036.

[51] See eg Commission decisions, *LH/SAS*, paras 52–61; *Fenex*, paras 59–64; *Banque Nationale de Paris/ Dresdner Bank* paras 15, 16; *EATA*; *FETTCSA*, here the Commission solely seems to focus on efficiency in Art 81(1) EC, all the language is economics-based, paras 132–39 and Commission decision, *SAS Maersk Air etc,* para 72(a). See also, eg, Wesseling (2000) 90; Commission, *RCP 1992* 19; Commission, *Vertical Guidelines*, para 7 and Commission, *Horizontal Guidelines*, paras 7, 19, 20, 24, 25, 197. 'Reading the *Annual Reports on Competition Policy* leads to the disappointing conclusion that the Commission actually has no definition at all or does not use its concept of competition in a consistent way. One finds: 'normal competition', 'undistorted competition', 'workable competition', 'effective competition', 'healthy competition', 'efficiency', 'real competition'; and these terms are all used in the general part of the Reports where the Commission reflects upon its own work.', Uitermark (1996) 6, 7. See also, Bright (1995) 506–13.

either; it states that the objective of the whole of Article 81 is consumer welfare; but the Commission insists that a full economic efficiency analysis should not be conducted under Article 81(1) EC,[52] leaving it unclear what precisely Article 81(1) is aimed at, although the implication here is that it must be some part of a consumer welfare assessment.[53]

This part has not sought to define what a 'restriction of competition' is. Instead, it shows that even in relation to the most recent case law, there remains significant disagreement on how to define the concept. The relevant actors continue to use multiple definitions.

Perhaps more clarity can be attained if we could at least explain what a restriction of competition *is not*. I have shown Monti assert that economic freedom is the basis for Article 81(1). Relying on *Métropole télévision*, he also argues that 'restriction of competition' cannot be read as economic inefficiency, or even, allocative efficiency.[54]

Even here, one can legitimately question whether the CFI in *Métropole télévision* was unambiguous. Monti relied on the CFI judgment where it held:

> It must … be emphasised that such an approach [ie examining the agreement under the actual conditions in which it functions] does not mean that it is necessary to weigh the pro and anti-competitive effects of an agreement when determining whether the prohibition laid down in Article 85(1) [now Article 81(1)] of the Treaty applies.
>
> In the light of the foregoing, it must be held that, contrary to the applicants' submission, in the contested decision the Commission correctly applied Article 85(1) of the Treaty to the exclusivity clause and the clause relating to the special-interest channels inasmuch as it was not obliged to weigh the pro and anti-competitive aspects of those agreements outside the specific framework of Article 85(3) [now Article 81(3)] of the Treaty.[55]

Weighing the pro and anti-competitive effects should take place, said the CFI, in Article 81(3) EC. The CFI made an equally opaque statement in *Van den Bergh Foods*.[56] The ECJ in *Wouters* and *Meca Medina* did not expressly consider this point, although in both cases it performs some Article 81(1) (public policy) balancing.[57]

As a preliminary issue, one might question the precedent value of *Métropole télévision* and *Van den Bergh Foods*. First, as I discuss below, the relevant passages are unclear. Secondly, both cases were decided by only three judges, not the full court. It is unusual that the CFI would appoint three judges to decide upon, what Odudu rightly calls,[58] '… the

---

[52]   See, eg Commission, *White Paper on Modernisation*, para 57. This is also the implication of Commission, *Article 81(3) Guidelines*, para 11.

[53]   Given that the goal it cites for the whole of Art 81 is consumer welfare, Commission, *Article 81(3) Guidelines*, para 13.

[54]   Monti (2002) 1062.

[55]   Case T-112/99 *Métropole télévision (M6) v Commission* para 77 (only the second part is relevant to this point; the first part of para 77 is cited above), para 78.

[56]   Case T-65/98, *Van den Bergh Foods Ltd v Commission* para 107.

[57]   See Ch 3.

[58]   Odudu (2002) 102 and Odudu (2001) 261.

most controversial issue in EC competition law.'[59] The ECJ did not refer to *Métropole télévision* in *Wouters* and *Meca Medina*[60] and may overrule it.[61]

Nevertheless, an examination of the last two paragraphs cited from *Métropole télévision* in a little more detail makes at least two interpretations possible. First, they may mean that the pro and anti-competitive considerations are balanced in Article 81(3) *and are not considered in Article 81(1) at all.* This must mean that something else is relevant in Article 81(1) EC, for example, economic freedom. This is Monti's argument. However, these paragraphs could equally be understood as saying that the anti-competitive effects should be assessed under Article 81(1) and the pro-competitive effects balanced against them under Article 81(3) EC. Manzini and Verouden make this point,[62] and it is essentially the argument that Odudu relies on.[63]

First let us examine what Monti, Manzini and Odudu agree on. They assume that the CFI's references to 'pro and anti-competitive' are shorthand for economic welfare. It is not certain that they are right. Nowhere in *Métropole télévision* does the CFI refer to either 'welfare' or 'efficiency', let alone assimilate them to 'competitive'.[64] If Monti, Manzini and Odudu are wrong, then pro- and anti-competitive effects may refer to non-welfare issues.[65] This could mean that efficiency is relevant in Article 81(1) after all.[66]

In any event, from this point on Monti, Manzini, Verouden and Odudu disagree. This is unsurprising as it is unclear where the line between pro and anti-competitive effects

---

[59]   Tesauro, a previous A-G at the ECJ, in Ehlermann (2001) 300, argued, in relation to a different case, 'I do not know if one judgment only can make case law. It is one judgment, only one. I have been reading the judgments of the European Court of Justice for many years now and I always tried to wait until there are three judgments on the same matter … otherwise there can be surprises.' In the same book at p 305, David Edward, who has been a judge at both the CFI and ECJ, agreed with these comments. He added 'Remember that, in order to determine who is to decide a case, the Court uses the following broad principles: (a) if the case raises a major issue of principle, it will be brought before the plenary; (b) if it is a simple question of technical interpretation, like … a simple question of applying existing jurisprudence, it goes to a chamber of three: and (c) in-between there is the chamber of five, whose basic assignment is that it may develop existing jurisprudence, but not create new jurisprudence.'

[60]   'The reader of the Court's judgments will be struck by the fact that previous decisions are often only cited by the Court where they support its argument. Authorities which point the other way are sometimes not mentioned at all', Arnull, Dashwood, Ross and Wyatt (2000) 201, 202. Judgment in the *Van den Bergh Foods* Case was handed down after the *Wouters* judgment and A-G Léger's Opinion in *Wouters* was written before the *Métropole télévision* judgment.

[61]   Korah (2002) 25, asks this rhetorically; see also, UK Competition Appeal Tribunal Case Nos 1035/1/1/04 and 1041/2/1/04, *The Racecourse Association and Others v OFT* paras 161–67 and Nazzini (2006) 505 *ff.* For a contrary view see Manzini (2002) 397. It is possible to distinguish *Métropole television* and *Wouters*, this can produce rather odd results. One could say, eg, that all objectives can be balanced within Art 81(1) EC (*Wouters* and *Meca Medina*) except analysis of the pro-competitive effects, or, possibly all of the efficiency analysis (*Métropole télévision*). Monti (2002), s 5.2 suggests another alternative, see Ch 3, Section 3.2.

[62]   Manzini (2002) 396 and Verouden (2003) 538–40, 565, 566. See also, van Gerven (2004) 426, 427.

[63]   Odudu (2002) 103–05 and Odudu (2006) ch 5.

[64]   The same can be said in relation to 'welfare' in *Van den Bergh Foods*. The CFI refers to efficiency there, but not so as to definitively answer this issue. The word 'efficiency' appears four times in the judgment. It was always used to report arguments of the parties, as opposed to the CFI's thinking. Even then it was used ambiguously, paras 120, 132, 140, 148.

[65]   The CFI's references to the rule of reason do not clarify the debate. There are many versions of the rule of reason, each balancing different things, Manzini (2002), n 24; Ehlermann (2001) 134–37; Black (1997) 145 and Hawk (1987) 738. The CFI may have been referring to one of these and not the others. For example, it has been argued that in the *Wouters* Case the ECJ conducted a rule of reason by putting the administration of justice into the balance, O'Loughlin (2003) 67, 68.

[66]   If we also agree that Monti's interpretation of *Métropole télévision*, paras 76 and 77 is wrong, ie that Art 81(1) does not relate to restrictions on economic freedom, but something different.

should be drawn.[67] Odudu believes that the CFI uses 'anti-competitive' to mean that the task demanded by Article 81(1) is '... to determine whether the agreement has the object or effect of *allocative inefficiency*.'[68] He argues that pro-competitive advantages (essentially productive efficiency[69]) should be considered in Article 81(3) EC. Monti, remember, believes that any efficiency issues (gains or losses) should be dealt with under Article 81(3) EC. Manzini implies that 'anti-competitive' is anything that undermines economic welfare and 'pro-competitive' are things that enhance it. He implies that the former can be considered in Article 81(1), the later should be assessed under Article 81(3) EC.[70] Finally, Verouden argues that there is a European rule of reason and that this mainly focuses on the functioning of the producer's distribution system (regulating intrabrand competition), rather than on competition in the market place as such (promoting interbrand competition).[71]

In many ways the lack of clarity is unsurprising. 'Restriction of competition' is not defined in the Treaty. Its content is not self-evident and needs to be fleshed out in the case law. This is not easy. Remember that the provision must be viewed in light of the Treaty as a whole and that the relevant objectives themselves have often not been clearly developed. They also conflict and change over time. In addition, the creation of the CFI necessarily reduces the ECJ's control over developments in the system. No longer is there one judicial voice, there are two. Furthermore, the Commission's growing power, authority and confidence contributes to the erosion of the leadership that the ECJ has shown in the past.[72] This is not even to mention the role of the Member States' courts and competition authorities.

It is not necessarily relevant for my purposes whether the authors are individually right or wrong. I merely want to show that even the recent jurisprudence is unclear. One can argue that some of these alternatives are more likely than others, read in light of other Community Court cases, see below. The modernisation process appears to assume that the competition system's goals are well defined and thus that those who will make decisions in the modified system can easily identify and follow them. The history of competition law in Europe suggests otherwise.[73]

It is unacceptable that Article 81(1)'s underlying principles remain so opaque. While these might change over time, clear rules could still be produced as and when these changes occur. These could then be applied more consistently, openly and transparently by all relevant decision-makers. In the words of Black:

---

[67]   Bishop (2001) 60.

[68]   Odudu (2002) 103 and Odudu (2006) ch 5.

[69]   Odudu describes pro-competitive effects as productive efficiency benefits, Odudu (2002) 104 and Odudu (2006) ch 6. These terms are explained in Ch 1.

[70]   Manzini (2002) 395–97, 399. See also, Lugard and Hancher (2004) 411. I say 'implies' because Manzini argues that anti-competitive issues fall within Art 81(1) and pro-competitive are considered in Art 81(3). Therefore, it seems like he is discussing two sides of the same coin. However, in his conclusion, Manzini refers to '... restricting the freedom of action of one or more of the parties ...' p 399.

[71]   Verouden (2003) 540. Hildebrand (2002) 220, 221 offers yet another test.

[72]   Gerber (1998) 375. See also pp 388, 389.

[73]   Wesseling (2001) 362 and Gerber (2001) 125.

It remains a scandal of competition law on both sides of the Atlantic that there is no consensus as to the kind of competition the law is intended to promote: different decisions give precedence to different kinds.[74]

As a result, Sections 2.2 and 2.3 discuss how a 'restriction of competition', for the purposes of Article 81(1) EC, should now be defined. As stated above, the 'right' definition must combine the need for legal certainty with the flexibility required for governing an economy in a state of constant flux. The definition must also take proper account of the Treaty's overall aims and fit within Article 81(1) EC. Section 2.2 considers basing Article 81(1) upon an economic freedom approach. Section 2.3 concludes that a consumer welfare approach would be more appropriate today.

2.2 Economic freedom

Many believe that the Ordoliberal School has had a profound influence on Community competition law.[75] 'Restriction of competition' has sometimes been interpreted as a restriction of economic freedom. We have just seen Monti argue that it should continue to form the basis of the Article 81(1) test. Sections 2.2.1 and 2.2.2 respectively investigate the arguments in favour and against this goal. Ultimately, I disagree with Monti;[76] but, let me briefly start by outlining the Ordoliberal School's origins and what it stands for.[77]

As the National Socialists were taking power in Germany in 1933, three academics met at the University of Freiburg in Germany and discovered that they had similar readings of the failings of Weimar and similar views of what to do about it.[78] They believed that the lack of a dependable legal framework had led to the economic and political disintegration of Germany. In their view, the core of the problem lay in the inability of the legal system to prevent the creation and misuse of private economic power.[79]

The Freiburg School followed earlier conceptions of liberalism in considering a competitive economic system necessary for a prosperous, free and equitable society. It was convinced that such a society could only develop once the market was embedded in a constitutional framework.[80] This framework[81] was designed to structure the relationship between the government and the individual along clear lines. It determined the kind of economic order the state is committed to pursue, and established a system of principles

---

[74] Black (1997) 146. This is not to say that everything in Art 81 EC is unclear, but much, especially the key concept of 'competition', remains this way, Hawk and Denaeijer (2001) 139.

[75] See, eg the references to freedom in Commission, *RCP 1971* 11; Commission, *RCP 1985* 11; Lowe (2007); Komninos (2005) 2; Verouden (2003) 534, 538; Monti (2002) 1060; Hildebrand (2002) 159, 165; Gerber (2001) 123 and Möschel (1989) 142. For example, Gerber (1998) 343, argues that the German negotiators of the Treaty were imbued with the Ordoliberal orthodoxies. Furthermore, Walter Hallstein, the first President of the Commission and Hans von der Groeben, one of the drafters of the Spaak Report and the first Commissioner for DG COMP are both associated with the Freiburg school, Verouden (2003) 535 and Hildebrand (2002) 161. Others disagree about economic freedom's early influence, see Akman (2007) and Kroes (2007).

[76] I suggest adopting a consumer welfare standard in Art 81(1) EC, see Section 2.3, below.

[77] For a more detailed analysis of the origins and views of this school see Gerber (1998); Möschel (1989); Peacock and Willgerodt (1989) and Peacock and Willgerodt (1989a) and the references made there. The brief account provided here relies heavily on these sources.

[78] Gerber (1998) 233.

[79] Hildebrand (2002) 158 and Gerber (1998) 235.

[80] Verouden (2003) 535; Gerber (1998) 232 and Möschel (1989) 154.

[81] Which would include a property rights system, a monetary system, the organisation of markets, freedom of contract, etc, Möschel (1989) 154.

which bound economic policy. For the Ordoliberals it was not enough to protect the individual from the power of government. They thought that private economic power had helped to destroy the social and political institutions during the Weimar period. They emphasised the need to protect society from the misuse of such power too.[82] In other words, Ordoliberals considered a coherent legal framework as essential to guarantee individual freedoms and economic progress.[83]

As a result, the Ordoliberals focused on the role of the economy in society. To them, the essence of the transaction economy was economic competition, as this allowed the system to function effectively. Economic competition meant a system in which no firm in a market was able to coerce conduct by other firms there.[84] Legal principles dealt with the acquisition and exercise of economic power.[85] Ordoliberals embed competition policy in the economic order to prevent those with private economic power from destroying the basis of private autonomy and ultimately jeopardising political liberties; economic power, they felt, had a tendency to turn into political power.[86] The state must provide a basic level of legal security by ensuring that the law was knowable, dependable and not subject to manipulation.[87] Ordoliberals are hostile to the inclusion of public policy issues within competition law; they believe it unduly opens the door to uncontrolled private regulation of public interests (ie allows the establishment of seemingly legitimate private power, which is no longer controlled by the operation of competition in the market).[88]

In brief, competition policy was the cornerstone of the economic constitution. Ordoliberal competition policy's goal is to protect individual economic freedom of action as a value in itself; or vice versa, the restraint of undue economic power. Economic efficiency is not an objective of Ordoliberal competition policy, although it is sometimes an unintended consequence of it.[89]

2.2.1 In favour of economic freedom

In theory, an economic freedom standard within Article 81 EC could have important benefits. Four reasons are normally given for favouring the Ordoliberal definition of a restriction of competition within Article *81(1)*.[90] First, there is the historical argument, that the economic freedom concept is what influenced the drafting of Article 81. Secondly, some argue that the Ordoliberal definition conforms most closely to Article 81 EC's

---

[82]   Gerber (1998) 240.
[83]   Sauter (1998) 46.
[84]   Hildebrand (2000) 158, 159; Gerber (1998) 244, 245 and Möschel (1989), n 16.
[85]   Hildebrand (2000) 158.
[86]   Gerber (1998) 250, 251; Amato (1997) 2, 3 and Möschel (1989) 151, 152.
[87]   Gerber (1998) 248.
[88]   See the views of Dieter Wolf, then President of the *Bundeskartellamt*, in Ehlermann (1998) 131.
[89]   Lovdahl Gormsen (2007) 333, citing Franz Böhm; Gerber (1998) 251 and Möschel (1989) 146.
[90]   Some economists, such as Adam Smith, von Hayek and Amartya Sen, emphasise the many benefits of competition as a discovery process, limiting abuses of power, safeguarding individual choice, etc. Many would be achieved under a consumer welfare standard too. Others argue that the text and direct applicability of Art 81(1) support the interpretation of this provision as a restriction of freedom (rivalry) of market participants. It will be no surprise that I am unpersuaded by the textual argument. Not only is this not a key method of Treaty interpretation (see the text following Ch 2, n 20), but there are many different interpretations of the word 'competition', n 18 above. Furthermore, I believe that even Art 81(3) is probably directly effective, Ch 2, n 399, and there is little doubt that an efficiency test has been performed there.

structure. Thirdly, there is a procedural argument. Finally, there is the 'constitutional' argument.[91] I examine each of these in turn.

The Historical Argument

Monti refers to the historical argument: 'Ordoliberal ideas influenced the drafting of the competition provisions in the EC Treaty.'[92] Gerber argues that the German negotiators of the Treaty were imbued with Ordoliberal orthodoxies.[93]

Even on the assumption that Ordoliberal ideas were influential in this way,[94] it does not mean that the concept of a 'restriction of competition', for the purposes of Article 81(1) EC, should be interpreted in line with Ordoliberal thinking. The Community Courts are the interpreters of the Treaty and its limits.[95] They prefer a teleological approach, based on an interpretation of the Treaty's *current* objectives;[96] and rarely adopt an historical-purposive approach to the interpretation of the Treaty, even when the drafters' intention is clear,[97] which it is not here.[98]

Marenco argues that it would be dangerous to ignore the history of the competition provisions.[99] In this case, it would be dangerous not to. I believe that there are three reasons why we should not adopt a historical approach in the interpretation of Article 81(1) EC. First, the Treaty's *travaux préparatoires* were deliberately never published,[100] although they can be accessed in the Florence archives. This implies that, even if they were a source that could be used, an historical interpretation is contrary to the founders' wishes.

Secondly, as noted above, 'restriction of competition' is an open concept. It does not necessarily relate to economic freedom. American antitrust scholars also influenced the drafting of the ECSC Treaty's and the German competition provisions, upon which Article

---

[91]   In order to justify the use of economic freedom within Art 81(1), it is sometimes also argued that somehow the 'European way' is different and we demand fairness on top of efficiency. See, eg Commission, *RCP 1979* 9, 10 and Commission, *RCP 1985* 11. Specifically what is meant by fairness is rarely articulated, Korah (2000) 11. Furthermore, one might ask, even if this is a relevant Art 81 goal, whether distorting competition policy is the best way of achieving such an end; there are many other, more efficient, ways of implementing notions of fairness, see Motta (2004) 24–26 and Townley (2002). I do not discuss the issue further here.

[92]   Monti (2002) 1060. Although he acknowledges, on the same page, that Art 81 '... is not a replica of Ordoliberal thought, but its structure bears the imprint of this political philosophy.'

[93]   Gerber (1998) 343 and Gerber (1994a) 73.

[94]   Though important in Germany, the prevalence of economic freedom was not universally accepted even there. For example, in the *Consten and Grundig* Case, p 342, the German Government argued that the Commission, '... before declaring Art 85(1) [now Art 81(1)] to be applicable, should, by basing itself upon the 'rule of reason', have considered the economic effects of the disputed contract upon competition between the different makes.' See also Akman (2007), in relation to Art 82 EC.

[95]   Art 220 EC. See also, Craig and de Búrca (2008) 72–76.

[96]   Case 283/81, *CILFIT v Ministero della Sanità* paras 13–21, esp 20.

[97]   See Ch 2, Section 2.2. For example, in one case, Belgium invoked an argument based upon the Member States' intention at the time the Treaty was drafted. The ECJ ignored the argument but the Commission summed up the position by saying 'As historical interpretation plays hardly any part in Community law it would be futile to refer to the intentions of the authors of the Treaty ...', Case 149/79, *Commission v Belgium*, 3890. See also the Opinion of A-G Mayras in Case 2/74, *Jean Reyners v Belgium*, 665, 666 and Craig and de Búrca (2008) 73, 74. Similar arguments were raised by the parties in relation to the notion of 'agreement' in Art 81(1) EC, see Case T-1/89 *Rhône-Poulenc SA v Commission*, 928. A-G Vesterdorf did not support their plea, pp 928, 929 and, once again, the CFI ignored the historical argument para 121. See also, Forrester in Ehlermann (2001) 78.

[98]   See the text around n 18 above.

[99]   Marenco (1999) 1244.

[100]   Craig and de Búrca (2008) 73 and Ellis (1963) 248.

81 is based.[101] 'Restriction of competition' could equally refer to efficiency criteria. If the 'founding fathers' uniquely intended to incorporate economic freedom into Article 81(1) they could have done so explicitly. They did not. Presumably, this was because they were not so singularly motivated. Perhaps, although it was influential, there was not a clear consensus that economic freedom should form the basis of the Community competition provisions.[102]

Finally, the continuous process of integration, and the transition from the European Economic Community to the European Union, reduces the relevance of the Member States' original intentions in 1957.[103] The Treaty and its objectives have fundamentally changed.[104] As an integral part of this system, the competition provisions must do so too.[105] In light of these arguments, I do not find the historical argument persuasive.

The Structural Argument

This is really a negative kind of argument: economic efficiency cannot be the relevant criterion under Article 81(1), so economic freedom must be. This ignores the fact that other criteria might be relevant under Article 81(1).[106] Even if one takes the argument at face value, it is unclear whether it works. The CFI suggests it might:

> Article 85 [now Article 81] of the Treaty expressly provides, in its third paragraph, for the possibility of exempting agreements that restrict competition where they satisfy a number of conditions ... It is only in the precise framework of that provision that the pro and anti-competitive aspects of a restriction may be weighed ... Article 85(3) of the Treaty would lose much of its effectiveness if such an examination had to be carried out already under Article 85(1) of the Treaty.[107]

The Commission agrees with the CFI in *Métropole television*. It says that one cannot cast Article 81(3) EC aside in this way without a Treaty change. It thinks that it would be paradoxical to introduce a rule of reason into Article 81(1) EC, because Article 81(3) contains all the elements of such a rule. It would also be dangerous to introduce a rule of reason without the Community Courts' backing;[108] and would divert Article 81(3) EC from its true purpose '... to provide a legal framework for the economic assessment of restrictive practices and not to allow application of the competition rules to be set aside

---

[101]   Jones (2004) 12; Goyder (2003) 21; Marenco (1999) 1220–29, 1238; Gerber (1998) 337–42; Gerber (1987) 86 and Graupner (1965) 8, 9.

[102]   Remember that in 1958 the Member States told the United Kingdom that it was for the ECJ to interpret Arts 81 and 82 EC: see n 19 above.

[103]   Lenz (2000) 37, citing Ackermann (1997a) 59.

[104]   Weiler (1991).

[105]   Ch 2, Section 2.

[106]   See Section 2.1, above.

[107]   Case T-112/99 *Métropole télévision (M6) v Commission* para 74. This argument was also used (although not developed) by the CFI in Case T-65/98, *Van den Bergh Foods Ltd. v Commission* para 107. That case also cited Case C-235/92P *Montecatini v Commission* para 133; Case T-14/89 *Montedipe v Commission* para 265 and Case T-148/89 *Tréfilunion v Commission* para 109; arguing that they made the same point. While they each cast doubt on the applicability of the rule of reason in the specific circumstances of the case, they do not seem to state, as a general rule, that it does not exist in Art 81(1) EC.

[108]   As the Community Courts have the final say on Treaty interpretation this is, in a certain sense, correct. However, in reality, what is 'dangerous', in the sense it is used by the Commission, is to interpret the Treaty incorrectly. In a similar vein, it would also be 'dangerous' to rely on the fact that there is *not* an economic rule of reason in Art 81(1), if this proved to be wrong. The Commission does not hesitate to do this, even though it acknowledges that the Community Courts have used an economic rule of reason before, see above.

because of political considerations.'[109] However, as we will see, there are many advantages to conducting an economic efficiency analysis under Article 81(1) EC and interpreting Article 81(3) as a non-economic rule of reason, see below.

Monti explains why the CFI in *Métropole television* denies a rule of reason:

> From a neo-classical perspective, the inclusion of Article 81(3) makes no economic sense: if an agreement's anticompetitive harms are outweighed by its pro-competitive benefits, then the agreement does not restrict competition at all. Conversely if an agreement's pro-competitive effects (for example in terms of productive efficiency) are outweighed by the risks generated by too much market power (which would reduce consumer welfare) then the agreement as a whole is anticompetitive. Therefore, Article 81(3) is futile – an agreement either promotes competition (and is thereby lawful) or suppresses competition (and is thereby unlawful) – the weighing of the pro and anti competitive aspects of an agreement can be carried out under the first paragraph of Article 81 ... Accordingly, the neo-classical definition of competition does not fit within the structure of Article 81.[110]

The first point that needs to be made is that it is uncertain whether these passages from *Métropole television* really mean that no efficiency analysis can take place in Article 81(1) EC. I have shown that this statement is controversial.[111]

Furthermore, arguments can be made against the CFI's position. Conducting the economic analysis under Article 81(1) does not necessarily make Article 81(3) EC redundant.[112] This would only be true if *only* economic considerations were relevant there. However, as Monti admits in the same paper, other objectives can be (and are) considered under Article 81(3);[113] providing that provision with plenty of 'effect'.[114]

Perhaps a more subtle point is being made. 'improving the production or distribution of goods or ... promoting technical or economic progress' in Article 81(3) may *demand* that some economic efficiency assessment is performed in that paragraph. In other words, perhaps the Article 81(3) criteria *necessarily* (at least in part) relate to economic efficiency in some form.[115] Monti seems to make this point.[116] If this were true, then one could say

---

[109] Commission, *White Paper on Modernisation*, para 57. See also, Odudu (2006) 141; Marenco (1999) 1240 and Waelbroeck (1987a) 723.

[110] Monti (2002) 1060, 1061. See also Cseres (2004) 229; Manzini (2002) 395 and Commission, *White Paper on Modernisation*, para 57.

[111] See Section 2.1. Also see Odudu (2006) 141, 142, where he interprets *Métropole télévision* in a fundamentally different way to Monti.
In any event, even if conducting a full economic efficiency test in Art 81(1) EC would deprive Art 81(3) of much of its effectiveness, this is not necessarily a strong argument, Case C-415/93 *Union Royale Belge des Sociétés de Football Association v Jean-Marc Bosman*, Opinion of A-G Lenz para 265.

[112] Wesseling (2000) 102–05, 112; Wesseling (1999) 421–24; Ehlermann (1998); Korah in (1987) Fordham Corporate Law Institute 731 and Forrester and Norall (1984) 41. See also, the Opinion of A-G Léger, Case C-309/99 *JCJ Wouters v Algemene Raad van de Nederlandse Orde van Advocaten*, paras 104–08. In fact, in response to the Commission's argument, that justifications linked to public policy issues should be considered under Art 81(1) EC, A-G Léger said para 107, 'Such an interpretation is liable to negate a great part of the effectiveness of Arts 85(3) and 90(2) [now Arts 81(3) and 86(2)] of the Treaty.'

[113] See also Chs 2–5.

[114] It is certainly possible that if only non-economic considerations are relevant under Art 81(3) then it will be used less often. This is because in most cases only efficiency issues are raised. In this sense the CFI might be right to say that Art 81(3) would lose much of its effectiveness. But this is not really the point. It is submitted that their point is only really relevant if *only* economic arguments can be used there.

[115] This is probably the argument of Waelbroeck in Ehlermann (1998) 485, although he does not develop it. See also Waelbroeck (1987a) 723.

[116] See Ch 3, Section 3.

that if the economic analysis had already been performed in Article 81(1), Article 81(3) would become superfluous.

Productive and dynamic efficiency gains have been considered in Article 81(3) EC.[117] Odudu argues that it is problematic to consider productive and dynamic efficiencies under Article 81(1), thus assuming that this must occur under Article 81(3); the importance of these efficiencies demands that they be considered somewhere.[118]

However, productive and dynamic efficiencies have also been considered in Article 81(1) EC[119] and even Odudu admits that it remains controversial what exactly remains to be considered under Article 81(3) EC.[120] We have seen that other, non-efficiency criteria, have been considered in Article 81(3) EC, for example.[121]

It is difficult to place much credence on the structural argument either. Conducting the efficiency analysis under Article 81(1) does not mean that Article 81(3) would be cast aside, non-economic considerations could still be (and are) looked at there.

The Procedural Argument

In 1957, when the Treaty was first adopted, Germany and France were the only Community countries that had a competition law.[122] The acceptance of the competitive economy was not free from dispute.[123] By imposing a wide interpretation on Article 81(1) (by adopting an economic freedom test rather than economic efficiency),[124] the Commission deliberately took control of the application of Article 81 and its development.[125] Under Regulation 17, only the Commission could apply Article 81(3), subject to review by the Community Courts.

The Commission's approach had some logic.[126] At least initially, control was considered important. Antitrust rules called for fundamental, indeed revolutionary, changes in centuries old habits of thoughts and patterns of conduct.[127] The Commission needed to gain experience of how the market functioned. Furthermore, antitrust rules were not well understood by European firms at the time.[128] It was thought that exemption discussions with the Commission would give businesses a lot more certainty.[129] Placing a sole decision-maker in charge of Article 81 should also have ensured a more uniform interpretation and coherent application.[130]

Such arguments imply that the Treaty should be interpreted in light of secondary Community legislation. This is incorrect. Relative competences within Article 81 should

---

[117]   Odudu (2006) 140, 141 and Geradin (2006) 319.
[118]   Odudu (2006) 137–39, 142.
[119]   ibid, 139.
[120]   ibid, 137.
[121]   See Chs 2 and 4.
[122]   Graupner (1965) 9.
[123]   Amato (1997) 43.
[124]   Hawk (1995) and Forrester and Norall (1984).
[125]   Korah (1990) 1015; Bright (1995) 514–16; Amato (1997) 118; Siragusa (1997) 276; Bergès-Sennou (2002) 438 and Komninos (2006) 452, 453.
[126]   Schaub (2001) 50.
[127]   Forrester and Norall (1984) 12, 13, 19; Marenco (1999) 1220 and van Miert (1999) 1.
[128]   Press Release IP/04/411 and Siragusa (1997) 276.
[129]   See Forrester and Norall (1984) 18–22 and Korah (1986) 94.
[130]   van Miert (1997) 36.

not have governed the article's substantive interpretation.[131] In any event, Regulation 1/2003 has fundamentally altered Regulation 17. Today, the Commission, as well as Member States' courts and competition authorities have jurisdiction to interpret Article 81 in its entirety. The whole provision is probably directly applicable.[132] As a result, the procedural argument no longer has, if it ever had, merit.

The Constitutional Argument

The constitutional argument, in brief, is that economic freedom has the status of a fundamental right in the Community legal order. This right must be protected, amongst others, through the competition provisions, particularly Articles 81 and 82 EC. If Article 81 is to protect economic freedom, then it must be considered within Article 81(1).[133]

In Community law circles it is generally accepted that the Treaty, as interpreted by the Community Courts,[134] forms the constitution of the EU.[135] The ECJ agrees.[136] The Treaty offers individuals enforceable constitutional guarantees[137] even against democratic decisions, whether taken at Community or national level.[138]

There are many types of constitution. The Ordoliberals have long understood both the German and the European Union as political systems based upon an Ordoliberal economic constitution.[139] As I showed above, the Ordoliberals considered a coherent legal framework essential to guarantee individual freedoms and economic progress. Remember that, for the Ordoliberals, the economic constitution indicates the legal structure that determines the type of economic system a state will pursue. It sets out a related system of principles that bind economic policy. The state then guarantees this economic order by enforcing the economic constitution. Sauter writes that:

> The state is constrained to observe the economic constitution, as it incorporates justiciable criteria. These constraints can take various forms, such as clear objectives for state policy, limits on its competence, limits on the instruments of state action, and, especially, individual rights that are directly enforceable.[140]

---

[131] See Ch 2, Section 3.2; Case 48/72 *SA Brasserie de Haecht v the spouses Wilkin-Janssen* para 6; Baquero Cruz (2002) 56, 57, and the references made there and Mestmäcker (2000) 414–16: 'Art 83 regulations are to give effect to the principles enshrined in the competition rules. They cannot change these principles nor can they modify the Treaty.'

[132] At least this is the claim of Reg 1/2003, recital 4 and art 1; it is also my personal view, see Ch 2, Section 3.2.

[133] If economic freedom could only be considered under Art 81(3) EC, then this value would only be relevant when Art 81(1) were breached. If, eg, Art 81(1) were held to promote economic efficiency, then an individual right (economic freedom) would be permanently undermined by something akin to a utilitarian majoritarian value (economic efficiency); fundamentally diminishing the right's value.

[134] Craig and de Búrca (1998) 163–65 and Petersmann (1991) 256.

[135] See, eg Joerges (2002) 9 and Weiler (1997). Not everyone shares the view that the Treaty is a constitutional document. The German Constitutional court, eg, refutes the idea that the Treaty is anything other than an international agreement between sovereign states, see Joerges (2002), s 2.2.2; Sauter (1998) 36, 37 and Zuleeg (1997). Nevertheless, I ignore this issue in the present discussion, because, even on the assumption that the German Constitutional court is right, the resulting arguments do not undermine the change I advocate.

[136] Opinion 1/91 *Opinion delivered pursuant to the second subpara of Article 228(1) of the Treaty*, para 21.

[137] Constitutionalism denotes the basic idea of limited government under the rule of law, Case 294/83 *Parti Ecologiste 'Les Verts' v European Parliament* para 23 and Petersmann (1991) 252.

[138] Sauter (1998) 31.

[139] ibid, 47 and Chalmers (1995) 56.

[140] Sauter (1998) 47.

If the Community legal order is based on an Ordoliberal economic constitution, this would be important.[141] Remember that, for Ordoliberals, competition law is a key part of this economic constitution. Competition has a value in its own right, which goes far beyond mere efficiency criteria. The economic constitution serves, first, to guarantee the basic equality of individuals as economic subjects; second, to back up the private law society by public authority; and third, to protect civil liberties. Under the Ordoliberal economic constitution, economic rights and freedoms enjoy equal status to traditional political rights and freedoms, and may be enforced against majoritarian decisions.[142]

Here lies the difficulty. If the Community is based upon an Ordoliberal economic constitution, then competition law (including Article 81) is a key part of that order. If one accepts that the concept of a 'restriction of competition' under Article 81(1) EC refers to economic freedom; this would be a right of higher rank, protected under this constitutional order.[143] Changing the interpretation of a 'restriction of competition' to mean economic efficiency might mean that a fundamental right (economic freedom) is replaced by a utilitarian rule (economic efficiency).[144] Such a modification would involve a fundamental change in the constitutional order. Even if this were possible, such a change would need to be justified at the constitutional level.[145]

This line of argument need only concern us if the European Union is based upon an Ordoliberal economic constitution. Fundamental rights form an integral part of the general principles of Community law.[146] The first issue to assess is whether economic freedom is one of them. Some believe that such an enquiry should start by reference to national law; if economic freedom is a fundamental right in Germany,[147] it must have this status in the EU legal order too. For example, Advocate-General Warner has said:

> [A] fundamental right recognised and protected by the Constitution of any Member State must be recognised and protected also in Community law. The reason lies in the fact that, as has often been held by the Court … Community law owes its very existence to a partial transfer of sovereignty by each of the Member States to the Community. No Member State can … be held to have included in that transfer power for the Community to legislate in infringement of rights

---

[141] ibid, 47.

[142] ibid, 47, 48. See also Chalmers (1995) 57.

[143] Coppel and O'Neill (1992) 682.

[144] Baquero Cruz (2002) 1.

[145] ie not just in some Commission guidelines, such as Commission, *Article 81(3) Guidelines*, para 7 of which claims not to be changing the existing case law.

[146] Craig and de Búrca (2008) ch 11; Coppel and O'Neill (1992) 670–72 and Petersmann (1991) 257.

[147] The same would apply if economic freedom were protected in another Member State, too. However, I restrict my enquiry to Germany because the Ordoliberal tradition is rarely followed outside Germany, Joerges (2002) 6 and Sauter (1998) 49. Attempts by authors such as Gerber to show that competition law in Europe is based primarily on ideas developed by European thinkers show little more than that the Member States (outside Germany) have often implemented competition laws with similar wording to Arts 81 and 82 EC, see Gerber (1998) 401–16. In support of his case, Gerber only examines Sweden, Italy and France. He looks at the wording, but fails to examine the substance (and background), of their competition provisions. This was a mistake. 'However similarly competition rules may have been worded by the Community and by national legislators, their application may result in divergent decisions as it has to follow the different objectives underlying apparently similar rules.', Ullrich (1996) 182. For example, the Italian equivalent of Art 81(1) is an economic efficiency test, see Siragusa (1998) 470, 565, 566 and Laudati (1998) 396–401. Wesseling (2000) 105, agrees, and suggests that the French law does the same. Drahos (2001) chs 4 and 5, describes considerable convergence between the European competition regime and that of Germany and Austria; and has similar, though weaker, conclusions vis-à-vis Dutch competition law.

protected by its own Constitution. To hold otherwise would involve attributing to a Member State the capacity, when ratifying the Treaty, the power to flout its own Constitution, which seems to me impossible.[148]

However, this starting point is unconvincing for two reasons. First, while Ordoliberals argue that economic freedom should be entrenched as a constitutional principle, it is uncertain whether economic freedom is a fundamental right in German Constitutional law.[149] More fundamentally, even if economic freedom were so protected in Germany, the Community Courts have never gone so far as to accept Advocate-General Warner's argument.[150] Indeed, they approach the issue quite differently:

> Recourse to the legal rules or concepts of national law in order to judge the validity of measures adopted by the institutions of the Community would have an adverse effect on the uniformity and efficacy of Community law. The validity of such measures can only be judged in the light of Community law. In fact, the law stemming from the Treaty, an independent source of law, cannot because of its very nature be overridden by rules of national law, however framed, without being deprived of its character as Community law and without the legal basis of the Community itself being called in question. Therefore the validity of a Community measure or its effect within a Member State cannot be affected by allegations that it runs counter to either fundamental rights as formulated by the Constitution of that state or the principles of a national constitutional structure.
>
> However, an examination should be made as to whether or not any analogous guarantee inherent in Community law has been disregarded. In fact, respect for fundamental rights forms an integral part of the general principles of law protected by the Court of Justice. The protection of such rights, whilst inspired by the constitutional traditions common to the Member States, must be ensured within the framework of the structure and objectives of the Community.[151]

This is hardly surprising, given that the Community constitutes a new legal order.[152] As a result, I need to examine this Community legal order directly;[153] asking whether economic freedom has been given a higher constitutional status by the ECJ such that Article 81(1) must refer to this concept.

To my mind, the ECJ has probably not given economic freedom a higher constitutional status. Although the ECJ calls 'freedom of competition' a general principle of Community law,[154] it has not defined the concept and it has actually said that references to 'freedom of competition' in Articles 4, 98 and 105 EC cannot be invoked by individuals against the Member States.[155] Therefore, and this is the second point, one would have to find this

---

[148]   The Opinion of A-G Warner in Case 7/76 *IRCA v Amministrazione delle Finanze dello Stato*, 1237.

[149]   See, eg Michalowski and Woods (1999); Sauter (1998) 48, 49 and the views of the Bundeskartellamt in ICN, *Report on the Objectives of Unilateral Conduct Laws (2007)* 15. Although, German Constitutional law guarantees a general right to liberty, which may be applicable in this respect, see Alexy (2002) ch 7; thanks to Ernst-Ulrich Petersmann for this comment.

[150]   Hartley (2004) 299; Joerges (1997) 4 and Joerges (2002) 5, 11.

[151]   Case 11/70 *Internationale Handelsgesellschaft v Einfuhr- und Vorratsstelle für Getreide und Futtermittel* paras 3, 4. A similar point is made in relation to Art 81, Case 14/68 *Walt Wilhelm and Others v Bundeskartellamt*, paras 3–7. It is possible that Case 4/73 *Nold Kohlen v Commission* para 13 goes further than this.

[152]   The *van Gend en Loos* Case.

[153]   Schröter (1987) 646.

[154]   Case 240/83 *Procureur de la République v Association de défense des brûleurs d'huiles usagées* para 9, see quote below.

[155]   This also undermines the possibility of a 'general right to liberty' in the Community legal order, as there is in, eg, Germany, see above.

'higher constitutional principle' embedded within one of the operational Treaty provisions, such as Article 81(1). However, the case law is unclear about whether a 'restriction of competition' is a restriction of economic freedom.[156] Furthermore, even if a 'restriction of competition' had been interpreted in this way, the Community Courts (and the Commission) have not injected this concept with a higher constitutional status; instead, it is treated as a policy objective to be balanced against all others. Finally, as the ultimate arbiters on the interpretation of the EC Treaty, the Community Courts can change their view of the fundamental status of economic freedom over time. These points should be considered in more detail.

The ECJ held in *Procureur de la République v Association de défense des brûleurs d'huiles usagées* that:

> [T]he principles of freedom of movement of goods and freedom of competition, together with freedom of trade as a fundamental right, are general principles of Community law of which the Court ensures observance.[157]

As a result, Coppel and O'Neill,[158] argue that the ECJ has elevated the free market freedoms guaranteed in the Community to fundamental rights status.[159] Presumably, in their view, the same would apply to freedom of competition.[160] They saw this as controversial.[161]

These freedoms are certainly important in the Community legal order. That said, when one penetrates the rhetoric, it is hard to believe that they have been given fundamental rights status.[162] First, the ECJ has held that when the Treaty, in Articles 4, 98 and 105, states that Community economic policy must comply with the principle of 'an open market economy with free competition', this does not impose clear and unconditional obligations on the Member States which can be relied upon by individuals.[163] Rather these are general principles, calling for complex economic assessments. They are objectives to be weighed in

---

[156]   See Section 2.1, above.

[157]   Case 240/83 *Procureur de la République v Association de défense des brûleurs d'huiles usagées* para 9. See also, the Preamble of the Charter of Fundamental Rights of the European Union 2000.

[158]   Coppel and O'Neill (1992) 689–91.

[159]   The problem arose as originally, the EC Treaty did not refer to basic fundamental rights. However, in Case 29/69 *Stauder v City of Ulm* para 7, the ECJ confirmed that fundamental rights are an integral part of the general principles of Community law. These might be found in the European Convention of Human Rights, or other sources, Case 36/75 *Rutili v Minister for the Interior* and Case 155/79 *AM & S Europe Ltd v Commission*.

[160]   Petersmann (2003) 62. Note that a more recent ECJ judgment may hint that free competition is not of a similar rank to the free movement provisions, Case C-438/05 *International Transport Workers' Federation and Others v Viking Line ABP and Others* paras 48–55.

[161]   Coppel and O'Neill saw such an elevation of these freedoms as controversial, for once this happens other 'conventional' fundamental rights will have the same status as these freedoms and can no longer act as a bulwark against them. As a result, 'The invocation of the idea of fundamental rights by the European Court does not set essential limits to lawful executive action, because executive action which has as its object the promotion of the four market freedoms [as well as, I suggest, using their logic, the freedom of competition] is itself, in the vocabulary of the European Court, instantiating a fundamental right.', Coppel and O'Neill (1992) 690. However, this could be beneficial. Petersmann argues, eg, that '... the everyday experience of most citizens is that their standard of living and their possibilities in life depend largely on their individual opportunities to produce and consume goods and services of their own choice; for that reason, the EC tradition of regulating economic freedoms and policies at the constitutional level should be maintained.', Petersmann (1995) 1155. In this view these very rights become the bulwark against state and individual power.

[162]   Case C-438/05 *International Transport Workers' Federation and Others v Viking Line ABP and Others*, paras 44–47 and the Opinion of A-G Poiares Maduro paras 24–26.

[163]   See Ch 2's discussion of the *Échirolles* Case. Sauter (1998) 40, 41, calls 'free competition' a political, as opposed to a legal, principle. See also, Arnull, Dashwood, Ross and Wyatt et al. (2006) 90.

the balance, not privileged 'trumps' that can be invoked by individuals.[164] The implication being that the reference to free competition in Article 4 does not establish an Ordoliberal constitution. It is widely accepted that freedom of competition can be balanced against the pursuit of other legitimate Community objectives.[165] The same principles are likely to apply to Community measures too.[166]

Furthermore, even if it could be argued that competition has been given such a status, the content of this 'right' remains undefined. Unless it can be shown that *freedom of competition equates to economic freedom* then economic freedom's privileged hierarchical status remains in doubt. Some seem to make this argument.[167] However, it is far from clear that the Treaty has promoted economic freedom to the level of a Constitutional principle in its own right.[168]

That does not get us all the way. It may be that freedom of competition cannot be invoked through Article 4 EC, etc. Yet, perhaps a fundamental right to economic freedom could be found in the operative provisions of the Treaty, perhaps Article 81, for example? This is the second part of my argument.

However, we have already seen that a 'restriction of competition', for the purposes of Article 81(1), has not been consistently interpreted as a restriction of economic freedom.[169] As a result, it is hard to argue that that provision promotes this 'fundamental right'. Furthermore, even if a restriction of competition, for the purposes of Article 81(1), had been interpreted as economic freedom, the Community Courts (and the Commission) have not provided it with fundamental rights status. Dworkin explains that rights must have:

> [A] certain threshold weight against collective goals in general … for example …[they] cannot be defeated by appeal to any of the ordinary routine goals of political administration, but only by a goal of special urgency …[if this is not the case] the putative right adds nothing and there is no point to recognising it as a right at all.[170]

Weiler and Lockhart argue that one should not confuse this lexographical similarity (the use of the word 'right' in relation to the four freedoms and competition) in *Procureur de la*

---

[164]   Case C-438/05 *International Transport Workers' Federation and Others v Viking Line ABP and Others*, paras 44–47 and the Opinion of A-G Poiares Maduro paras 24–26. See also, Petersmann (1995) 1154, refers to an earlier article he wrote about the '… EC's 'economic constitution' and the still inadequate constitutionalisation of the EC's agricultural, competition, industrial and anti-dumping policies…' see Petersmann, '*Grundprobleme des Wirtschaftsverfassung der EG*', (1993) *Aussenwirtschaft*, 389–424.

[165]   Sauter (1998) 63 and Poiares Maduro (1999) 454, the ECJ has '… to my knowledge never struck down Council legislation for violation of such economic rights and freedoms.' This does not necessarily decide the issue. Rights can sometimes be undermined. See also his Opinion in Case C-438/05 *International Transport Workers' Federation and Others v Viking Line ABP and Others*, paras 24–26. However, 'competition' has not been given a fundamental rights status through Art 81, see below.

[166]   See Ch 2, Section 2. This is implicitly accepted by Petersmann (1991). At page 258, he calls the market freedoms and competition policy '… the primary objective of the EEC Treaty …' He does not expressly say they have constitutional status in the Treaty, although Sauter (1998) 45, interprets him in this way. That said, Petersmann argues that the Community Courts should treat the market freedoms and competition policy as fundamental rights of EC citizens against the Community institutions, pp 266–70. The implication being that they do not as yet do that.

[167]   See the references in Sauter (1998), n 59.

[168]   Demetriou and Higgins (2003) make a similar point in relation to the free movement provisions.

[169]   Section 2.1, above. However, in relation to Art 82 see Case 322/81 *NV Nederlandsche Banden Industrie Michelin v Commission* para 113; but *cf* Akman (2007).

[170]   Dworkin (1977) 92.

République v Association de défense des brûleurs d'huiles usagées.[171] They argue that it is going too far to claim that the ECJ has elevated these freedoms to the status of fundamental rights, which is not to say that they are not extremely important Community principles.

In general, the jurisprudence on market freedoms is rather flexible in yielding to non-protectionist competing values far less grave than human rights.[172] This can be seen in *Procureur de la République v Association de défense des brûleurs d'huiles usagées* where the ECJ held:

> [I]t should be observed that the principle of freedom of trade is not to be viewed in absolute terms but is subject to certain limits justified by the objectives of general interest pursued by the Community provided that the rights in question are not substantially impaired.[173]

My argument here is not yet watertight, because even fundamental rights give way to utilitarian necessities on occasion.[174] However, the flexibility that Weiler and Lockhart point to undermines the claim to a 'fundamental rights' status for these concepts.[175] The same can be seen with respect to 'restrictions of competition' under Article 81(1).

In fact, several peculiarities in the way Article 81(1) EC is applied belie the notion that it protects a fundamental human right in the Community legal order. Restrictions of competition have been balanced against other values within Article 81(1) EC;[176] restrictions of competition are often allowed because they are not appreciable; and, the Community Courts have balanced restrictions of competition against the Article 81(3) values.[177] In fact, there are no Commission decisions where non-economic objectives had been raised, under Article 81(3), and where the Commission accepted that these arguments were in fact relevant, where these non-economic objectives did not win, ie tilt the balance in their favour (and against a restriction of competition).[178] One might say that competition can never be eliminated, Article 81(3)(b), but this protection falls far short of that given to fundamental rights.[179] Furthermore, when discussing Article 81(1) one normally resorts to shorthand and only mentions 'restrictions of competition'. However, the provision also refers to 'prevention, restriction or distortion of competition'.[180] Normally these concepts are dealt with in the same way. However, on occasion, the Commission has said that distortions do not only occur when existing competition is *diminished* by an agreement. Article 81(1) EC can also be breached when competition is *increased or intensified*.[181] The Ordoliberals believe that market power should be diffused

---

[171]   Case 240/83 *Procureur de la République v Association de défense des brûleurs d'huiles usagées* para 9.

[172]   Weiler and Lockhart (1995) 596. More generally see pp 593–96; Chalmers (1995) 70, 71 and Frazer (1990) 612–15.

[173]   Case 240/83 *Procureur de la République v Association de défense des brûleurs d'huiles usagées* para 12.

[174]   Dworkin (1977) 92. See, eg the European Convention, Pt I, Title II.

[175]   In fact, Sauter (1998) 41, calls free competition a political, as opposed to a legal, right.

[176]   See Chs 2, 3, 5 and 6, Section 2.1.

[177]   See Chs 2, 4 and 5. Even advocates of the individual freedom standard agree that this must be balanced against consumer welfare considerations, eg, Schröter (1987) 659.

[178]   See Ch 4, Section 3. Some may reject this reading of the balance. However, even Monti's reading of Art 81(3)'s first test, see Ch 4, undermines the idea that economic freedom has 'fundamental rights status' in Art 81(1) EC.

[179]   See also Frazer (1990) 615.

[180]   Although Art 3(1)(g) EC only refers to distortions of competition.

[181]   Barack (1981) 136 and Smit and Herzog (1976), Vol 2, s 85.26, para 3–122. The ECJ in Case 262/81 *Coditel SA, Compagnie Générale pour la Diffusion de la Télévision, and Others v Ciné-Vog Films SA and Others*, para 20,

as far as possible. If 'competition' for the purposes of Article 81(1) were considered a fundamental right, there would be no place for a concept such as distortion.[182] If 'restriction of competition' meant restriction of economic freedom and this had been given fundamental rights status within the Community legal order, one would not expect to find derogation so easy to achieve.

Furthermore, even if economic freedom had been given fundamental status in the past, this does not prevent later changes in the hierarchy of EU norms, as long as the right process is adopted for change. This might be through Community Courts case law;[183] or through Treaty reform. For example, the Lisbon Treaty, if adopted, removes the reference to free competition from Article 3 EU Treaty, further undermining its status.[184]

In conclusion, economic freedom has, at times, been promoted as a relevant value under Article 81 EC. It seems unlikely that it has the status of a fundamental right in the Community legal order. Even if it has, there is currently little evidence to show that it must be protected as such within Article 81(1). Furthermore, even if economic freedom has been given such status in the past, this will change if the Lisbon Treaty is adopted.

That is not to say that the economic freedom concept is worthless.[185] It is not.[186] But it does mean that its claim to Article 81(1) holds much less weight. If it does not have true constitutional status then changes to Article 81(1)'s interpretation (if indeed this is a change) need less justification. It is merely a value to be balanced against others. Section 2.2.2 provides positive reasons against employing economic freedom in Article 81(1) EC.

2.2.2 *Against economic freedom*

Article 81(1) has been given a broad interpretation.[187] Many point to a formalistic approach focusing on restrictions of economic freedom; which they criticise. Hawk, for example, complains that economic freedom: (a) fails to generate precise, operable, legal rules; (b) can undermine economic efficiency analysis, which he claims provides a suitable analytical framework; (c) favours traders/competitors over consumers and consumer welfare; and, (d) captures totally innocuous contract provisions under Article 81(1) EC which have no anti-competitive effects in an economic sense.[188] These problems are exacerbated because, as the internal market is increasingly realised, more and more agreements affect trade between Member States, and thus fall within Article 81's jurisdictional threshold.

---

may also distinguish between restriction and distortion. By way of contrast, see the views of A-G Trstenjak in his Opinion in Case C-209/07 *The Competition Authority v BIDS* para 53.

[182] My proposal for a consumer welfare standard in Art 81(1) EC also suffers from the 'distortion' point.

[183] For a contrary view see Zäch (2008), slide 35.

[184] For a discussion of this point see Graupner (2007).

[185] There are certain textual, contextual and functional arguments in favour of economic freedom. One should be careful about relying on such arguments however. The Vienna Convention's guide to Treaty interpretation is inappropriate in the Community legal order, which has its own rules of interpretation, see Ch 2, Section 2. Nevertheless, Section 2.3, below, discusses the textual and functional arguments. The contextual ones have been dealt with in Section 2.2.1. Briefly put, the ECJ held that 'free competition' did not create individual rights that could be relied on. As a result, it is improbable that the Community legal order incorporates a general right to liberty which can be relied on either.

[186] Sen (2002), esp chs 9, 17, 20–22, emphasises a similar concept; Amato (1997) 1–4; Schröter (1987) 667–70 and Petersmann (1991).

[187] See, eg Venit (2003) 548, 549; Fox (2001) 23; Bishop (2001) 56, 58; Forrester (2001) 76; Ehlermann (1998) xiv and Hawk (1995) s 2.

[188] Hawk (1995) 978.

Assume that a 'restriction of competition' under Article 81(1) can be equated with a restriction of economic freedom, which is far from clear.[189] Before one can criticise this practice, one must understand why economic freedom is being pursued. There are, essentially, two schools of thought.[190] Some believe that economic freedom is used to assess whether there is a reduction in allocative efficiency. Such people may not agree with Hawk's four-point critique, in fact, but at least they would accept that his points are relevant. The second group argue that facilitating market access is essential in its own right, even if this undermines economic efficiency; think of the Ordoliberal School, for example. For these people much of Hawk's critique is simply misplaced. By distinguishing between these two camps, I hope to inject a little more clarity into the critique of the 'economic freedom' standard.

Marenco falls into the first camp. He argues that one must assess restrictions of economic freedom under Article 81(1) EC. For Marenco, economic freedom is not a value in itself.[191] Economic freedom is merely a legal concept that helps us to assess whether an agreement tends to reduce allocative efficiency.[192] Having said that, he accepts that the legal concept (economic freedom) and the economic concept (economic efficiency) are not one and the same.[193] Some restrictions of economic freedom are actually efficiency enhancing.[194] In order to determine whether this is the case, he turns to Article 81(3), to perform an economic efficiency analysis.[195]

For Marenco, economic freedom is a legal rule through which one can assess economic efficiency benefits. It is not a perfect rule, but it is more than adequate. Hawk disagrees. First, he criticises economic freedom because it does not provide precise, operable rules.[196] This is important; because those in the first camp principally advocate economic freedom as a good, easily applicable, approximation of the economic efficiency standard.

All contracts restrict economic freedom. If all contracts restricted competition, the rule would be clear, but it would be inoperable, and the social costs of consistently implementing it would be unimaginably high.[197] In fact, the Ordoliberal notion of economic freedom is not merely about restricting freedom of contract. It is an effects-orientated enquiry with restrictions of this nature being just a starting point. That said, it is normally agreed that there must be some limit to the notion.[198] Monti argued that only 'undue' restrictions of economic freedom were relevant, for example.[199]

The problem is that the devil is in the detail and the precise delimitation of 'undue'. The concept is far from obvious. It is difficult to construct logically consistent limits to the

---

[189]   See Section 2.1, above.
[190]   Zäch (2008), slide 35, seems to fall into both schools.
[191]   Marenco (1999) 1243.
[192]   ibid, 1229, 1230. See also, 1243 and Commission, *RCP 1971* 11, the last para might be read as encouraging economic freedom for efficiency ends.
[193]   Marenco (1999) 1239, 1240.
[194]   ibid, 1238.
[195]   ibid, 1238. Although he accepts that sometimes the Community Courts do some of this analysis under Art 81(1), Marenco (1999) 1240.
[196]   See also, Riley (1998) 483; Korah (1998), n 1 and Schaub (1998) 474.
[197]   Areeda and Hovenkamp (2000) 101 and Bork (1993) 59.
[198]   See above; Hawk (1995) 978 and Bork (1993) 59.
[199]   See Section 2.1, above.

notion.[200] Schaub argues that '… the term 'freedom' provides little guidance, as the once heated debates in Germany and the US some decades ago showed.'[201]

The Commission has made many attempts to define the limits of economic freedom, for the purposes of Article 81(1). Most have come to naught or been abandoned due to lack of agreement.[202] The Commission's latest attempt is more helpful but does not go far enough;[203] nor is it a concept with which businesses are familiar.[204] Hawk believes that it is impossible to limit economic freedom in a logically consistent way. Such is the difficulty that, at times, almost every restriction in agreements between significant players seems to require an exemption. In practice, the decision-maker has a lot of discretion.[205] Therefore, one might question whether the economic freedom concept is a useful proxy for economic efficiency, in that it does not seem easy for decision-makers to apply (or for undertakings to predict the outcome). Hawk goes further, arguing that economic efficiency, unlike economic freedom, provides a framework of precise operable rules which companies and decision-makers can apply.[206]

Furthermore, Hawk points to a tension between economic freedom and economic efficiency: points (b) to (d) above. In this sense, Hawk disagrees with Marenco, in that he does not think that the economic freedom concept essentially reflects economic efficiency. This goes to the heart of the issue too. If the economic freedom concept produces fundamentally different results from those which would be achieved through application of an economic efficiency standard, then it is not a good proxy.

Hawk's argument comes in two parts. First, he argues that economic freedom is a much wider concept. According to Hawk, it captures many totally innocuous agreements, from an economic efficiency perspective. This point depends somewhat on how one delimits economic freedom and which efficiency standard is used.[207] But there is much support for Hawk's view from both jurists and neo-classical economists, when a consumer welfare

---

[200] Marenco argues that one must distinguish between restrictions which necessarily result from every contract and those which are imposed on future contracts. For example, '… *si une entreprise achète tous ses besoins en aluminium pour dix ans à venir par un contrat qui précise la quantité et le prix, soit de façon précise, soit par référence aux cours qui seront cotés par le London Metal Exchange au moment de la livraison annuelle, on est en présence d'un exercice de la liberté des entreprises. Si en revanche l'acheteur s'engage à acheter ses besoins chaque année pour dix ans auprès du même vendeur, les termes du contrat devant être négociés les 1ᵉʳ octobre, il s'agira d'une restriction de la liberté entrepreneuriale de l'acheteur en violation de l'interdiction des ententes.*', Marenco (1999) 1237, 1238. However, this distinction is unconvincing if economic freedom is there to assess economic efficiency, as neither of these methods is, in and of itself, less efficient than the other. Nor does it reflect the Art 81(1) case law; think of the *Nungesser* Case, for example.

[201] Schaub (1998) 124. Hildebrand (2002) 159, 160, agrees that the issue of economic freedom's limits has caused heated debate in Germany. See also, Hawk (1995) 979, on the failure to establish clear rules here.

[202] Luc Gyselen, then of DG COMP, while participating in the Competition Law Workshop, European University Institute, 6/7 June 2003. See also Schaub (1998) 474.

[203] Commission, *Article 81(3) Guidelines*, paras 13–31. First, these guidelines do not provide an underlying objective to guide Art 81(1) analysis in case of ambiguity. Lugard and Hancher (2004) 411, write that '… the concept of a "restriction of competition" remains in some cases difficult to grasp as a result of a lack of a clear, quantifiable standard by which agreements are judged.' Secondly, although the account of how to apply the provision is quite detailed, it does not capture the entire Art 81(1) analysis, see Kjølbye (2004) 568.

[204] Whish and Sufrin (1987) 4 note this argument.

[205] Waelbroeck (1987a) 693, points to controversy as a result of this discretion.

[206] This is discussed in Section 2.3, below.

[207] Möschel (1991) 14, for example argues that '… there is no difference between an antitrust law orientated toward protection of competition [by which he means economic freedom] or one orientated toward promotion of economic efficiency [by which he means static and dynamic consumer welfare].' See also his page 20 and Cooter (1987). To the extent that Möschel is right, an economic efficiency standard could still be preferable if it offers more predictable rules, see Section 2.3, below.

standard is adopted.[208] Secondly, Hawk says that the economic freedom notion tends to favour traders/competitors over consumers and consumer welfare, and thus often undermines economic efficiency.[209] There is some evidence for this too.[210]

Marenco argues that one cannot apply the economic efficiency standard, as it is too unclear; instead, one must translate it into a legal rule, such as economic freedom. He believes that use of economic freedom enhances legal security.[211] Marenco accepts that economic freedom does not capture all efficiencies. However, he sees it as an important (and clear) legal rule that captures most of them. Divergences can later be corrected through an efficiency analysis in Article 81(3).

However, it is hard to accept his logic; first, because the economic freedom notion is itself unclear (see above). This means that its application is difficult and controversial. Secondly, Marenco accepts economic efficiency analysis under Article 81(3) EC in any event, so he must accept that such an analysis is possible, undermining the need for a proxy.[212]

The economic freedom proxy is hard to apply. Clear rules can be made, but these seem disproportionate to the efficiency aim,[213] even undermining it at times. They capture many benign agreements within Article 81(1) only to exempt them under Article 81(3) EC. Given these problems, it might make sense to start with an efficiency analysis in Article 81(1). This should result in a more accurate efficiency assessment. But there is another important result of defining a restriction of competition within Article 81(1) EC as economic freedom. As discussed in the introduction to this chapter, use of a wide concept there substantially increases undertakings' costs. This was evident under Regulation 17, as only the Commission could apply Article 81(3) EC. However, even under the new regime a wide, uncertain, Article 81(1) can significantly increase costs, undermining economic progress for everyone in the Community.

I said above that there were two camps in favour of using economic freedom. Marenco fell into the first of these, believing that economic freedom was useful as an indirect measure of economic efficiency. The second camp sees economic freedom as a value in itself. The Ordoliberal School, for example, believe that facilitating market access is essential, even if this undermines economic efficiency.[214]

---

[208]   See, eg Bishop and Walker (2002), para 5.02; Bishop (2001) 58; Neven, Papandropoulos and Seabright (1998) 37; Siragusa (1998) 544; Heimler and Fattori (1998) 595 and Hawk (1995) 981. Venit (1998) 575, points out that, due to the uncertainty caused by the economic freedom concept, it is often interpreted even more widely than it should be, as undertakings err on the side of caution.

[209]   Hawk (1995) 978.

[210]   See, eg Motta (2004), s 1.3.1.3 and Kühn (1997) 137–43. Hawk may be reading the economic freedom concept too narrowly. He says that it favours traders/competitors over consumers and consumer welfare. In fact, economic freedom also favours consumers and their access to market. For example, the idea that, consumers have a 'right' to purchase goods anywhere in the Community would probably be supported by those in favour of economic freedom. However, Hawk is correct when he says that this is not a majoritarian rule. He is also correct that this 'rights-based approach' can undermine consumer welfare, as Motta (2004) and Kühn (1997) explain. As to the relevance of this argument, see the discussion from n 214 below.

[211]   '[C]e critère [economic efficiency] est également dangereux pour la sécurité juridique, car les entreprises n'auraient pas de point de référence.', Marenco (1999) 1239.

[212]   Marenco (1999) 1240.

[213]   See Bright (1995) 509–13, 518.

[214]   Wolf is in the second camp, although he believes that the pursuit of economic freedom, while justified in its own right, largely reflects economic efficiency concerns. When it does not, he argues that Art 81(3) can be used, Wolf (1998) 131. Schaub (1998) 124 also discusses this.

Most of Hawk's critique focuses on explaining how economic freedom is incompatible with economic efficiency, favouring competitors over consumers, see points (b) to (d) above. To those that see the protection of economic freedom as a value in itself, this is of little relevance. However, I have argued that the main arguments in favour of using economic freedom within Article 81(1) EC were unpersuasive.[215] Nevertheless, there are some good arguments in favour of this value. If it is promoted in the Community legal order, then this fact alone may justify its presence within Article 81(1).

The point of departure is to ask what weight economic freedom is given in the Community legal order. In my view, economic freedom is not a particularly important Treaty value today. It is not mentioned in Articles 2, 3 and 4 EC, or anywhere else. True, Article 6 of the Treaty on European Union speaks of 'liberty', as does the European Convention. Furthermore, Article 3(1)(g) talks of undistorted competition and Articles 4, 98 and 105 EC all promote '… an open market economy with free competition …' But it is far from clear that these concepts refer to 'economic freedom'.[216] The Community Courts have never explicitly equated them, for example. Furthermore, as we saw above, they have said that many of these references cannot be relied upon by any individual against the Member States. The recent Commission, *Article 81(3) Guidelines* do not mention economic freedom when they discuss Article 81(1) EC. Quite the contrary, they emphasise that 'The objective of Article 81 is to protect competition on the market as a means of enhancing consumer welfare and of ensuring an efficient allocation of resources.'[217]

The lack of emphasis on economic freedom is not particularly surprising. As noted above, the Ordoliberal School, which strongly supports this notion, has principally been influential in Germany. Nevertheless, the Community Courts and the Commission have both hinted at an economic freedom test in the past, see above. As a result, it would be foolhardy to assume that the concept had no value in the Community legal order, even though the Commission increasingly emphasises an economic approach and many believe that this would bring it more in line with the Community Courts' position.

Having said that, even if economic freedom were given a lot of weight under the Treaty, then the fact that it can significantly undermine consumer welfare (a majoritarian goal) is still relevant, given that economic freedom does not have fundamental rights status. Not everyone is an entrepreneur, seeking to enter the market.[218] By way of contrast, a consumer welfare test theoretically benefits us all over time.[219] In the absence of clear guidance in the Treaty to the contrary, it seems more in line with the Article 2 EC task of 'raising the

---

[215] See Section 2.2.1, above.

[216] For example, Petersmann (2003) 62, suggests that 'free competition' refers to economic freedom, while Niels and ten Kate (2004) 11, assume it refers to economic efficiency.

[217] Commission, *Article 81(3) Guidelines*, para 13. In my view one cannot place too much weight on this statement however, because it does not accurately reflect Art 81's objectives given its position within the Treaty, see Ch 2. Having said that, it implies that the Commission no longer interprets 'restrictions of competition' as 'restrictions of economic freedom' either.

[218] Which is not to say we only benefit from values which we use, see Sen (2002) 624–26. We saw that economic freedom sometimes also applies to consumers, see above, which undermines this point somewhat.

[219] Areeda and Hovenkamp (2000) 101, 102.

standard of living and quality of life'[220] to define 'competition' as something that benefits the many, rather than the few.[221]

One might argue that using economic freedom within Article 81(1) EC does not really undermine economic efficiency. Those in favour of economic freedom in its own right are not saying that efficiency considerations are irrelevant. They merely consign them to Article 81(3). But this approach can still cause significant problems. Remember that economic freedom fails to generate precise, operable, rules. Even post Regulation 17 a wide, uncertain, Article 81(1) creates costs for undertakings, and ultimately consumers, see above.

But the arguments against formally adopting an economic freedom standard in Article 81(1) EC do not stop there. Three other issues should be mentioned. First, as we saw in Chapter 1, most competition rules are now based on an economic efficiency test. Basing Community competition law on the economic freedom standard runs counter to this trend. Different standards make co-operation between those enforcing Article 81 and extra-Community competition authorities more difficult.[222] This is particularly important in this new era of antitrust law, which is called upon to keep open world, and not just national, markets.[223] Co-operation with extra-Community competition authorities becomes more difficult because it is more difficult for these authorities to understand what the Community standard is. Therefore, it is harder for them to provide assistance in a multi-jurisdictional investigation. It is also hard to avoid the suspicion that the Community standard somehow discriminates in favour of Community undertakings,[224] regardless of whether this is true. This may make these extra-Community agencies less co-operative than they would otherwise be. Different competition law goals in different jurisdictions also mean that undertakings whose agreements fall within Article 81 and an extra-Community competition regime must comply with both sets of rules.[225] This burden principally falls on Community undertakings, generating economic costs for them and the Community, particularly in relation to technology transfer, industrial co-operation, effective distribution systems and economic progress.[226]

---

[220] The Preamble also says that the essential objective of the Member States' efforts through the Treaty is '… the constant improvement of the living and working conditions of their peoples …' See also, Art 153 EC, consumer protection.

[221] Petersmann (2003) 52, 53 and Areeda and Hovenkamp (2000) 101, 102, also argue that it is fairer. However, their solutions are quite different. Petersmann suggests placing personal liberties beyond majoritarian interests through a rights-based approach. Areeda and Hovenkamp suggest the adoption of the majoritarian interests, a consumer welfare standard. Petersmann rejects this approach, because of the problem of 'capture' and its implications for political markets, Petersmann (2003) 52, 53. The link between political and economic markets is questionable however, Areeda and Hovenkamp (2000) 103, 104. Capture can perhaps be dealt with more efficiently through other means, see, eg Motta (2004) 20, 21. In any event, a consumer welfare standard already tilts the scales in favour of small interest groups, reducing the chance of capture, see Lyons (2002) and Neven and Röller (2000).

[222] Mario Monti (2001); Marsden (2000); Schaub (1998) 127, 128 and Laudati (1998) 384.

One might say that as I advocate considering public policy in Art 81(3) EC, this will remain the same. However, I think that a clear consumer welfare test in Art 81(1), will at least allow for transparency when comparing the results of this assessment (or gathering evidence) in other regimes and then we can just argue that our system has an extra dimension too, which could be analysed separately.

[223] Amato (1997) 126.

[224] This is the implication of Ostry (1993) 267.

[225] Mario Monti (2001).

[226] See Ch 1; Kaczorowska (2000); Laudati (1998) 384, 385; Bright (1995) 520 and Addy (1993) 301. This is also the implication of Venit (2003) 569.

Secondly, an economic freedom standard can undermine other Treaty objectives. In Chapter 1 we saw how it could undermine market integration, for example. Furthermore, insofar as it undermines economic efficiency, economic freedom could undermine all the other objectives that the efficiency standard tends to promote indirectly.[227]

Finally, the fact that economic freedom is hard to define complicates the application of Article 81(3) as well. Competition must not be eliminated, Article 81(3)(b), surely 'competition' used here must refer to economic freedom if it has that meaning under Article 81(1) EC. Furthermore, it is hard to weigh the objectives which fall within Article 81(3)'s first test, against the restriction of economic freedom under Article 81(1), when the latter notion is unclear. The decision-maker must balance an amorphous concept (economic freedom) against other Treaty objectives.[228] When an undefined entity must be weighed in the balance the outcome can be very hard to predict.[229] This may, in part, explain the lack of clarity so far in the Commission decisions. The introduction to this chapter discussed the costs of this lack of transparency.

In conclusion, if economic freedom is used as a proxy for economic efficiency then it should be replaced. It often undermines the very goal it seeks to promote and does not provide clear, operable rules, which are easy to implement. If economic freedom is promoted as a value in itself, its relevance for Article 81(1) is harder to judge and depends on the importance that the concept is given in the Treaty. Despite the difficulties with the definition of a relevant restriction on economic freedom, if defining 'restriction on competition' in this way helped achieve an important Treaty objective then the uncertainty (and costs) that this causes may still be worthwhile. However, economic freedom is not given much weight in the Community legal order today. Furthermore, it undermines majoritarian goals, such as consumer welfare, which better reflect the Treaty aims; it threatens co-operation with extra-Community competition authorities; it undermines other Treaty objectives; and, it imposes significant costs on Community undertakings and consumers alike. As a result, if economic freedom is to be considered at all (and we may decide that it is simply too uncertain a criterion to apply, however beneficial its aim), it may be better to relegate it to Article 81(3) EC.

2.3 Consumer welfare

I have argued that economic freedom is not (any longer/if ever) a good basis for Article 81(1) EC. Considering the values that the Treaty, as interpreted by the Community Courts, promotes today, we need another concept that better serves as a basis for Article 81(1). Section 2.3 argues that consumer welfare is such a goal.

First, the advantages of a consumer welfare objective are discussed, there are many; then, I check that this goal 'fits' in the Community legal order. Next, some potential disadvantages of selecting consumer welfare are examined, such as the impact on legal certainty and I try to further define what sort of consumer welfare test is appropriate.

---

[227]   See Ch 1, Section 2.2.

[228]   I define 'economic freedom' in line with the Ordoliberal School; whose definition is, to be fair, quite clear; however, the application of this notion, in practice, is not, Section 2.2.2, below.

[229]   It would be exceedingly difficult, if not impossible, to construct rational criteria to govern conflicts between economic freedom and efficiency, Areeda and Hovenkamp (2000) 108, 109.

Jenny claims that the key advantages of a consumer welfare standard are: larger social benefits; more consistent and predictable enforcement; and, simplicity of enforcement.[230] The social benefits of an economic efficiency standard are legion. The quest for efficiency is about avoiding or reducing waste. In a world in which not all human wants are currently satisfied and the resources available to us are both scarce and finite, a failure to make the best possible use of resources and avoid waste would be unfortunate. Inefficiencies involve costs in the form of lower output, and hence less employment opportunities and reduced standards of living for society.[231]

As to which efficiency standard is most appropriate, I agree with the Commission, the CFI and countless others who embrace consumer welfare.[232] I prefer this to a total, or a producer, welfare standard because it ensures that benefits accrue to consumers, and we are all consumers.[233] A consumer welfare approach within Article 81(1) helps achieve other public policy goals too. The Commission hopes to promote greater R&D, industrial policy, consumer protection, employment and market integration through its economic efficiency focus.[234] It is particularly efficacious to use, where possible, market forces to achieve public policy aims. If a policy runs against market forces and competition, it not only has less chance of success, but is also unlikely to benefit consumers.[235] Promoting the welfare assessment to centre stage reinforces the message, not only because of the beneficial effect of harnessing this mechanism, but because it forces us to reflect on the costs of attempting to undermine it.[236]

I believe that there are two other advantages of defining a 'restriction of competition' under Article 81(1) EC, as (an appreciable) restriction of consumer welfare. The first point is that competition systems are increasingly placing greater emphasis on the economic efficiency test, and the consumer welfare test in particular.[237] Following this lead in the EU would have many benefits, such as improving and facilitating co-operation between competition authorities and reducing the regulatory burden for Community undertakings.[238] Secondly, adopting a consumer welfare test within Article 81(1) EC will narrow its

---

[230] Jenny (1993) 197. He also mentions political stability. There is less room for politically motivated interventions in antitrust decisions where there is a lot of transparency in the system (so that such interventions would be obvious) and, probably, that economic welfare is the only goal of competition policy (so that it would be clear that such intervention would be wrong). In the Community legal order many objectives, outside of economic welfare are relevant. Nevertheless, the issue of transparency is important and is discussed in relation to the predictability point and also in Section 3, below.

[231] Massey (1996) 95. Also see, eg Korah (2000) 9, 10; Whish (2008) 3–7 and B&C (2008), para 1–072.

[232] See, eg the references in Ch 1, nn 3, 43 and Ch 2, nn 9–11.

[233] See Ch 1, Section 2's general discussion on the benefits of the consumer welfare standard.

[234] For example, in relation to: **industrial policy**, Commission, *Framework for State Aids for R&D*, para 1.4; **cultural policy**, Commission, *RCP 1993*, points 175, 176; **consumer protection**, Commission, *RCP 1994*, Introduction; **environmental policy**, Commission, *RCP 1993*, points 163–65; **economic and social cohesion**, Commission, *RCP 1993*, point 154 and Brittan (1992) 65–66; **commercial policy**, Commission, *RCP 1993*, points 180, 181 and, to a certain extent, **economic freedom**, Neumann (2001) 183; Fels and Edwards (1998) 55–58 and Möschel (1991) 15, 16. See also, Areeda and Hovenkamp (2000) 4 and Areeda and Turner (1978) 13.

However, Ch 1, Section 2.2 noted that, while this is true in the long-term, there are often short term conflicts. Furthermore, some policies often/always conflict with a consumer welfare approach.

[235] For example, in technology policy, whilst some co-operation in research may be desirable, elimination of effective competition would take away the main spur to innovate, Commission, *RCP 1990* 16.

[236] See Section 3, below.

[237] Ch 1, Introduction.

[238] Cseres (2007) 123. This would be even more so if all jurisdictions adopted a total equilibrium model, see the discussion below and Ch 5, Section 4. See also Fox (1998a) 8, 11, 12.

scope. This means fewer agreements will fall within the provision; reducing Community undertakings' compliance costs.[239]

However, Schröter warns us not to adopt general terms from other legal systems unless they 'fit' in our legal order too.[240] He was worried that the adoption of an American rule of reason (consumer welfare test) within Article 81(1) EC would be inappropriate in our legal order.[241] This is an important point. Given that (like economic freedom) consumer welfare is not mentioned in the Treaty, the question of 'fit' is not obvious. However, I believe that a consumer welfare approach in Article 81(1) EC would comply with the Community legal order.[242] Article 81(1)'s reference to a 'restriction of competition' is wide enough to cover many approaches;[243] including a consumer welfare test,[244] especially given the Community Courts' teleological interpretative approach.[245] Looking at the Treaty's goals, the Preamble, for example, gives, as the essential objective of the Member States' efforts the '… constant improvement of the living and working conditions of their peoples …' A majoritarian goal (such as consumer welfare) is also in line with Articles 2[246] and 153 EC. Contrary to *Metropole*, I believe that dealing with consumer welfare in Article 81(1) would leave something to discuss in Article 81(3), ie public policy.[247]

Manzini argues that adopting a consumer welfare test in Article 81(1) EC undermines Article 81(1)(a)-(e)'s explicit wording. He believes that these provisions rule out an economic balancing act there. In his view, they demand an examination of the agreement's specific effects, regardless of whether this has positive welfare effects.[248] However, I am not sure that the Treaty lists these five examples because such acts are wrong *in themselves*. These acts may be seen as wrong *because of the effects that they are likely to have*, for example on economic welfare. In other words, they are examples of types of restriction that are normally welfare reducing and thus can normally (but are not always) be presumed 'wrong' in a per se fashion.[249] This response is justified because, in the Community legal order, the ECJ has held that the first principle of interpretation is to look at the ordinary meaning of the word in its context and in light of the objectives of the

---

[239]   Not through a relaxation in the desire for competition, however; but through a redefinition of the test, so that it better focuses on the agreements that matter, Ehlermann (2001) 285.

[240]   Schröter (1987) 645. This is certainly right, see Ch 2.

[241]   There are many types of rule of reason, see Section 2. For the purpose of this discussion I take a wide definition, assuming it to be a full consumer welfare analysis.

[242]   Schröter (1987) 691, 692, concluded that it would not be appropriate. His arguments were based on: (1) the divergences in the Member States' legal traditions; (2) the lack of legal security that such a change would entail; and, (3) the fact that the Commission alone could, at that time, decide Art 81(3) issues. However, since Reg 1/2003, the whole of Art 81 is directly applicable and effective in the Member States' courts and competition authorities. As a result, the risks to homogenous enforcement that he points to in (1) and (3) would arise in any event, as he accepts an efficiency analysis under Art 81(3) EC. The lack of legal certainty, point (2), is discussed below.

[243]   See Section 2.1, above.

[244]   See, eg Siragusa (1998) 470, 547, 565, 566; Siragusa (1997) 284, 285; Hawk (1995) 987 and Schröter (1987) 691, 736.

[245]   Ch 2, Section 2. Even if consumer welfare has not been a consistent Art 81(1) objective (although for a contrary view see Nazzini (2006) 505–17), both the Commission and the Community Courts have interpreted it in that way in the past, Section 2.1, above. Although note Case C-209/07 *The Competition Authority v BIDS* para 21.

[246]   OECD (2005) 14.

[247]   See the discussion at Section 2.1, above and Section 3.2, below.

[248]   Manzini (2002) 394–95. See also, Case T-14/89, *Montedipe v Commission* para 265. Others also argue that Art 81 as a whole focuses on anti-competitive *conduct*, whereas in Arts 82 and 87 EC, eg, the *results* of the actions are expressed as a separate criterion.

[249]   See also the *Glaxo* Case paras 115–22.

Treaty.[250] In other words, Treaty provisions are interpreted in light of the effect that certain conduct has *on the achievement of the Treaty's objectives*. This implies that one should not focus merely on the conduct itself.[251]

Within a consumer welfare framework, Odudu argues that a 'restriction of competition' under Article 81(1) EC means allocative inefficiency.[252] Article 81's wording provides some support for this view,[253] although it is inconclusive. However, a provision's actual wording, while important, is not the key issue when it comes to Treaty interpretation;[254] the Community Courts' case law does not overwhelmingly support Odudu either.[255] Furthermore, splitting out the allocative efficiency analysis does not make much sense, from an economic perspective. Verifying whether an agreement reduces efficiency is not very meaningful without examining possible pro-competitive effects as well, be they allocative or dynamic.[256] It also leads to confusion as to what is relevant at each stage of analysis.[257] The Commission has accepted this.[258] Examining all efficiency issues together brings the 'restriction of competition' concept under Article 81(1) closer to the mainstream economic notion of consumer welfare; improving the focus and clarity of analysis there. These benefits justify emphasising a teleological approach, rather than focusing on Article

---

[250]   Ch 2, Section 2 and Case 53/81 *Levin v Staatssecretaris van Justitie*, para 9.

[251]   The approach to the notion of lack of appreciability provides one example of this kind of thinking; one might also think of the ancillary restraints doctrine as extended to Art 81 agreements, see, eg Case 42/84 *Remia v Commission*. The Community Courts and the Commission read into Art 81 the idea that the five examples in Art 81(1) are only relevant in the event that agreements that breach them have a certain effect. See, eg the *De Minimis Notice* and Case 5/69 *Franz Völk v Établissements J. Vervaecke* paras 5, 7. See also Bright (1995) 508, 509, who, commenting on the previous case, said 'Very probably what is being sought is a reduction in competition that has a consequence for the satisfactory operation of the market.' In other words, an agreement between two SMEs that, for example, led to price discrimination, Art 81(1)(d) EC, may well fall within this 'exception' because it is not perceived as having an important welfare effect. Thus, it would fall outside Art 81(1). Admittedly, the Commission's *De Minimis Notice* does not apply where certain hardcore restraints are included within an agreement, para 11. However, this list does not contain all the items in Art 81(1)'s list. Furthermore, the *de minimis* doctrine can still apply even where there is a hardcore restraint. See Case 5/69 *Franz Völk v Établissements J Vervaecke* paras 5, 7, 'Thus an exclusive dealing agreement, even with absolute territorial protection, may, having regard to the weak position of the persons concerned on the market in the products in question in the area covered by the absolute protection, escape the prohibition laid down in Art 85(1) [now Art 81(1)].' See also, Case 1/71 *Société Anonyme Cadillon v Firma Höss*, para 9 and Case 306/96 *Javico International and Javico v Yves Saint Laurent Parfums* para 17. Agreements between SMEs are just as capable of price discriminating as those of any other economic actors; but this is a problem only insofar as it leads to economic welfare effects. A similar comment could be made in relation to the *Nungesser* Case and Art 81(1)(c) EC.

[252]   See Section 2.1, above.

[253]   Neven (1998) 112.

[254]   See Ch 2, Section 2.

[255]   Although, in general, allocative efficiencies are emphasised in Art 81(1) analysis, Neven (1998) 117 and Ch 3 argue that cases such as *Nungesser* seem to consider productive and dynamic efficiencies within Art 81(1) EC. Odudu (2006) 139, accepts this; see also, Commission, *Article 81(3) Guidelines*, para 18(2) and Kjølbye (2004) 567–69. Furthermore, in some Commission decisions, such as Commission decision, *CECED*, the Commission emphasises allocative efficiency gains in its Art 81(3) analysis.

[256]   Verouden (2003) 528, 572, 574, 575; Venit (2003) 575; Gyselen (2002a) 197; Bishop and Walker (2002), para 5.05 and Hawk (1995) 987.

[257]   See Fox and Bishop in Ehlermann (2001), respectively 23 and 51. The economic analysis has nearly always been split between Art 81(1) and 81(3) in the past. As such it is unsurprising that the precise dividing line between these provisions has been a recurring question, both in the literature and the Community Courts' case law, Verouden (2003) 528, 575.

[258]   '[T]he current division between para 1 and para 3 in implementing Art 85 [now Art 81] is artificial and runs counter to the integral nature of Art 85, which requires economic analysis of the overall impact of restrictive practices', Commission, *White Paper on Modernisation*, para 49. Although, Commission, *Article 81(3) Guidelines*, provide some support for Odudu's thesis.

81's (inconclusive) wording, as per Odudu. This is particularly so, as public policy is relevant within Article 81 and it is better to keep that analysis separate from the consumer welfare assessment; I suggest restricting this to Article 81(3) EC.[259]

Jenny's second claim for a welfare approach,[260] is that it provides a more consistent and predictable enforcement mechanism.[261] Whish and Sufrin were not convinced, arguing that the form-based Article 81(1) EC test was more certain.[262] I agree: in fact, a consumer welfare standard may reduce legal certainty, by which I mean the predictability of outcome.[263] Legal certainty is certainly important;[264] however, it is not the only aim of a legal system, one has to ensure that it achieves the right goals too. I argue that there are ways of ensuring that we do that with the consumer welfare standard, while achieving an acceptable degree of certainty for undertakings and enforcers.

First, it will markedly increase legal certainty to clarify Article 81(1)'s goal. It would also help certainty for another reason, a consumer welfare test would be narrower than the old form-based test; so, fewer arrangements would fall within Article 81(1) to start with, which means that Article 81(3) will be needed less often.[265]

However, I agree with Whish and Sufrin when they question the predictability of outcome that a consumer welfare test generates. There is clearly a tension between economics and legal certainty in competition law.[266] Hawk and Denaeijer write:

> At the centre of the debate lies the inherent tension between flexibility and certainty in competition laws. A degree of legal certainty is necessary to maintain the *état de droit* and to enable businesses to operate. But competition laws, more than many if not most other sets of legal rules, must be flexible to reflect changes in economic thinking and market conditions.[267]

That is not to say that those that worry about a lack of certainty are wrong to highlight this weakness of the welfare notion. Three issues must be confronted; they also tie in with Jenny's third point about simplicity of enforcement:[268] (i) does microeconomic theory work?; (ii) do the relevant actors understand microeconomic theory?; and (iii) is it feasible for the relevant actors to apply microeconomic theory in every case?

The first problem to confront is whether microeconomic theory works, ie can it explain real-world interactions. Some argue that the impact of a single firm's conduct on consumer welfare in the future cannot be known, von Hayek talks of a 'pretence of knowledge', for example.[269] This is less often a problem for Article 81 as the analysis is normally *ex post*. In general, however, although not everyone would agree,[270] the answer is

---

[259] See Section 3, below.

[260] See the text at n 230 above.

[261] Hawk (1995) 978, made a similar claim in Section 2.2.2, above.

[262] Whish and Sufrin (1987) 20, 37.

[263] Joliet (1967) 189–90. See also, Jenny (2000) 26–31 and Bishop in Ehlermann (2001) 16. Against this view see The World Bank and OECD (1999) 5.

[264] Brodley (1987) and Joskow (2002) 99.

[265] See n 239 above.

[266] Hawk in Ehlermann (2001) 25.

[267] Hawk and Denaeijer (2001) 130. See also, Forrester (2001) 102, 103 and Bishop (2001) 55.

[268] See the text at n 230 above.

[269] See, eg Zäch (2008), slide 41.

[270] See, eg Ginsburg (1991) 26–29; Armentano (1990); Lutz (1989) 159, 160 and Hildebrand (2002) 106, 121, although at page 161 she contradicts herself, saying '... economic theory has developed over the years and provides today an analytical model, which is maybe suited for the specific situation of European competition law.'

that microeconomic theory explains the world we live in pretty well.[271] It provides a coherent set of answers to most of the central questions that antitrust considers[272] which, has wide, though admittedly not universal,[273] acceptance.[274] True, there is a lack of agreement in relation to some of the precise relationships between competition and innovation, the policy implications of entry barriers and whether vertical integration is harmful. But the great majority of these differences only impact at the margins of antitrust enforcement, as opposed to at the centre. Nearly all of the economic issues relevant to antitrust policy lie at the core.[275]

The next issue is, even if microeconomic theory generally works, do the relevant actors understand it? Here too, the answer is a qualified yes. When undertakings enter into agreements they assess the agreements' effect on prices and quality. Therefore, the sorts of questions that the consumer welfare test provokes are understood by business.[276] The same can be said of consumers. Furthermore, Venit argues that the Commission has a wealth of experience in economic analysis, now that this has become the norm in major merger decisions.[277] The Member States' courts and competition authorities also have relevant experience now, although this is obviously less in the newer Member States.[278]

But, even those that accept what has been said thus far might say that reliance on a consumer welfare standard places a heavy burden on the decision-maker. Uitermark agrees. Competition is complex and he warns against ready-made answers. In his view, '… each individual case should be judged on its own merits, using all economic insights that are presently available.'[279]

However, courts and competition authorities have neither the knowledge nor the time to conduct a full cost benefit analysis in every case.[280] Even if such analysis were possible, it is not practicable.[281] This is one of competition policy's main challenges.[282] But the problem should not be exaggerated.[283] Lawyers' concern for legal certainty can be mitigated by the development of an integrated, step-by-step approach to decision-making.[284] This should involve the use of presumptions,[285] negative block clearances,[286]

---

[271] It was the overwhelming view of the participants to Ehlermann (1998) that consumer welfare is an appropriate standard for Community competition law, for example.

[272] Areeda and Hovenkamp (2000) 116.

[273] See references in Jenny (2000) 27, for example.

[274] Verouden (2003) 538; Areeda and Hovenkamp (2000) 116, 117 and Scherer (1992a) 501–09.

[275] Areeda and Hovenkamp (2000) 116–18.

[276] That is not to argue that every corner store actually carries out an economic welfare analysis before pricing the carrots it will sell, but, implicitly, this is essentially what they do and so the concepts are relatively easily understood.

[277] Venit (2003) 551, 552 and Venit (1998) 569.

[278] As Gyselen points out, the Member States' courts are often called upon to conduct economic analysis already '… there is no fundamental *conceptual* difference between the economic assessments [we suggest under Art 81(1), although he was discussing them under Art 81(3) … and those to be undertaken under the directly applicable provisions of Art 81(1), Art 82 or Art 86(2) EC. Nor does the degree of complexity involved in these assessments differ', Gyselen (2002a) 183.

[279] Uitermark (1996) 13. See also Bishop in Ehlermann (2001) 17.

[280] See Petersmann (2003) 52; Jenny (2000) and Easterbrook (1992) 119–29. On, eg, the difficulties of calculating marginal cost, see Motta (2004) 116 and Brodley (1987) 1028–32. See also, Geradin (2006) 336.

[281] Korah (2002) 24; Jenny (2000) 28 and Korah (1981) 348, 349.

[282] Faull (1998) 503, 505.

[283] Gyselen (2002a) and Korah (1998) 487.

[284] Van den Bergh (2002) 51 and Korah (1998) 487.

[285] Faull (1998) 489.

[286] Siragusa (1998) 555–57.

per se rules[287] and market share filters.[288] The *De Minimis Notice* and the *Vertical Restraints Block Exemption* already employ market share filters, for example, and the Community Courts support their use. Economists would have to advise on the use of per se rules. The examples of conduct listed in Article 81(1)(a)-(e) EC are already effectively treated as such (at least within Article 81(1)), and might be extended, if appropriate.[289] Finally, more efforts might be made to increase the expertise in economics available to the decision-makers.[290] These measures are not perfect,[291] but they enhance certainty while providing flexibility, and can be more efficient in the long term.[292] This should reduce compliance costs; which is also important.[293]

Adoption of a consumer welfare standard does create some difficulties.[294] Nevertheless, one must not lose sight of the potential benefits. One must also seek the right blend of flexibility and certainty. I do not think that economic freedom can provide this.[295] Consumer welfare is not perfect, but it is better than most other concepts.[296] It also has relative success in other jurisdictions, such as the US. Interestingly, Hawk and Denaeijer write that despite considerable uncertainty with the US rule of reason, the 'European concern (obsession?) with legal certainty is largely absent in the United States where intellectual efforts are devoted toward formulations of a less costly and more predictable rule of reason rather than calls for more per se rules ...'[297]

---

[287] Hawk and Denaeijer (2001) 132–34; Heimler and Fattori (1998) 597; Hawk (1995) 988; Easterbrook (1992) 129–32 and Williams (1989) 23. Manzini (2002) 398, 399, points out that the ECJ in the *Matra* Case para 85, held that, in principle, no anti-competitive practice could exist which could not be exempted, *as long as it complied with the Article 81(3) criteria.* He took this as an argument against per se economic rules, saying that agreements can always be exempted under Art 81(3) EC. But this is wholly dependent on what the ECJ analyses under Art 81(1) EC and what Art 81(3)'s criteria refer to. If all economic analysis is done under Art 81(1), then the agreement can be exempted under Art 81(3), even it fell foul of a per se rule. However, it would be in line with the case law to say that an exemption could not be considered on economic grounds, but, eg, environmental protection, or whatever factors were considered relevant under Art 81(3) EC.

[288] Jenny (2000) 28, 29; Hawk (1995) 978, 979, 987–88 and Easterbrook (1992) 130. Recently, Monti (2004) 407, has said that today '... market power is a crucial element to take into account in applying Art 81.'

[289] As, under this suggestion, welfare analysis would no longer be considered under Art 81(3) EC, these rules might be better seen as presumptions that the party relying on Art 81(1) can use, but which could be rebutted under certain conditions. Although Easterbrook (1992) 129, 130 questions even this 'Even proof that a practice saves customers "millions of dollars" every year does not justify case-by-case inquiry, once the practice is located in a group likely to be harmful.'

[290] Williams (1989) 23.

[291] For example, in relation to the difficulty of defining market power, see Jenny (2000) 29 and Schroeder (1997).

[292] Easterbrook (1992) 129–30.

[293] Moussis (2000) 287.

[294] Another problem that those in favour of economic freedom highlight is that, from a liberal perspective, competition rules also protect competition as a discovery procedure and as a mechanism for limiting abuses of power, ie protection of competition as a process. However, the same can be said of welfare analysis, unless one takes an extremely short-term perspective. Ch 1 emphasises that competition must be seen as a dynamic (and not a static) mechanism. If short-term gains are delivered and these will eliminate competitors in the long-term, then welfare will likely be undermined in the long-term too.

[295] I define 'economic freedom' in line with the Ordoliberal School; whose definition is, to be fair, quite clear; however, the application of this notion, in practice, is not, Section 2.2.2, above.

[296] '[N]otwithstanding their vagueness, economic standards provide more legal certainty than populist and other elements, as well as the possibility of *ex post* empirical assessment.', Castañeda (1998) 51 and 'Modern competition theory and case law have provided better tools [than the economic freedom test] based on the assumption that the protection of a system of workable competition is at issue.', Schaub (1998) 124.

[297] Hawk and Denaeijer (2001) 137.

In conclusion, adopting consumer welfare as the Article 81(1) objective, as opposed to economic freedom, could, depending upon the statements of the Community Courts and the Commission, help clarify the application of this paragraph. To the extent that ambiguity persisted, at least it would be in the name of an important objective that, in the long term, would help us achieve other Treaty objectives too.

Nevertheless, there is much work to be done. Chapter 5 found little underlying consistency uniting the Commission's economic analysis. This lessens the Commission's chance of achieving the aims it seeks; makes it harder for the disparate decision-makers to know what they should be trying to achieve; and, makes the outcome of disputes less predictable for undertakings. These all have societal costs. I have argued that a consumer welfare standard is appropriate, but even within this, what balance should the Commission pursue between static allocative efficiency and, for example, dynamic efficiencies;[298] and, what about a partial equilibrium or a total equilibrium model.[299] Finally, there is the issue of where and how to take account of public policy within Article 81.

The Commission must provide rules for how the trade-offs between different efficiencies should be made and over what timeframe.[300] This is a highly complex task and further discussion of this point is outside the scope of this work.[301]

Chapter 5 noted that the Commission favours a partial equilibrium over a total equilibrium model. That chapter also noted that pursuit of a second-best solution (a partial equilibrium framework) may be better, and perhaps even more efficient, than a total equilibrium one, due to the evidentiary problems with collating the necessary data. Contrary to the Commission's position, I argue here for a total equilibrium approach; believing that this would be more in line with the approach demanded in relation to the assessment of other Treaty objectives within Article 81.

Some Treaty objectives, such as environmental protection and public health, often concern worldwide problems requiring worldwide solutions. It would be artificial and ineffective to disregard any effects (or contributory factors) outside of our borders. It might also breach the Treaty. Article 152(1) EC says:

> Community action ... shall be directed towards improving public health, preventing human illness and diseases, and obviating sources of danger to human health. Such action shall cover the fight against the major health scourges, by promoting research into their causes, their transmission and their prevention, as well as health information and education.

---

[298]   Within these, which 'school' of economic thought is best, Hildebrand (2002) Ch III; Hildebrand (2002a); Van den Bergh and Camesasca (2001) ch 1 and Furse (1996) 250–54.

[299]   Duhamel and Townley (2003) discuss other variants of these tests.

[300]   Something that has been neglected in the US as well: Brodley (1987) 1021.

[301]   Ch 5 points to the lack of clarity in Commission decisions in this area. True, it is hard to be clear on where the balance lies between long term (prospective) and short term (often relatively clear) allocative benefits, see, eg Hovenkamp (1986) 1018. Two things will considerably improve the current position. First, the selection and implementation of a clear underlying objective, see above. Secondly, greater insistence on the quantification of benefits. Ch 5 indicated that Commission, *Article 81(3) Guidelines* go some way towards demanding more precision in this regard. This is to be welcomed; see also, Commission decision, *MasterCard*. Ch 8 provides further guidance for this framework. However, there is a risk that this will focus the assessment on allocative benefits because: (a) these are easier to establish; and (b) they occur sooner. Given the importance of productive and dynamic efficiencies, care should be taken not to swing the pendulum too far back the other way.

There is no reference to the fact that only the health of those in the Community is relevant.[302] The idea that an international dimension to public health is important is supported in the Treaty, Article 152(3) says that the:

> Community and the Member States shall foster co-operation with third countries and the competent international organizations in the sphere of public health.[303]

Indeed, some Community action is already aimed at improving public health in other countries.[304] Secondly, it is clear that R&D has a key role to play here, and that often means that undertakings should get involved.

Even if it were only the public health of those in the Community that is important, this does not necessarily mean that an approach that only focuses on the EU is best.[305] For example, in relation to SARS, the Community found it necessary to co-operate with, amongst others, China, in order to better protect the health of those within the Community. Research and development activities outside of the Community could also benefit those suffering from SARS, or other diseases, within it.[306]

It may be that an agreement between pharmaceutical firms could help achieve these aims. As well as the economic effects of such an agreement, its effect on public health worldwide should be considered in the Article 81 analysis. To hold otherwise risks undermining the objectives the Community is bound to embrace.

A similar position emerges in relation to environmental policy. Article 174(1) EC specifically says that the Community policy on the environment:

> [S]hall contribute to pursuit of the following objectives: preserving, protecting and improving the quality of the environment; protecting human health; prudent and rational utilisation of natural resources; promoting measures *at international level to deal with regional or worldwide environmental problems* (emphasis added).

It is clear that acting alone the Community cannot do much to counteract global warming or the depletion of the ozone layer. Environmental policy must have an international dimension, see also Article 174(4) EC.[307] This international dimension is also important when environmental policy is incorporated into Article 81. Exclusively looking at effects within the Community is a nonsense and ineffective.[308]

There are other Treaty objectives, such as development policy, which, by definition, require an extra-Community analysis. Article 177(1) is very wide:

> Community policy in the sphere of development cooperation … shall foster: the sustainable economic and social development of the developing countries, and more particularly the most disadvantaged among them; the smooth and gradual integration of the developing countries into the world economy; the campaign against poverty in the developing countries.

---

[302]   A similar point applies in relation to consumer protection. Although, the Treaty refers to the '… the living and working condition of their peoples …': see the Preamble.

[303]   See also documents such as, Press Release, IP/03/1091.

[304]   See COM(2000) 585. See also recommendations for the future, such as, Press Release, IP/03/1091.

[305]   See Press Release, IP/03/1091.

[306]   See Extraordinary Council meeting, *Employment, Social Policy, Health and Consumer Affairs* (2003).

[307]   Collège d'Europe (1998) 226.

[308]   The same might easily be said of the security of the fuel supply in other countries. If there were another oil shock, for example, this could affect their ability to sell the Community the things it needs and to buy from the Community. This would affect the Community's industrial policy.

The boundaries of such a policy are extremely unclear. Does social and economic development include a cultural policy for developing countries?[309] Surely, it would include consumer protection policies;[310] environmental protection;[311] industrial policy; public health[312] and research and development aimed at helping these countries,[313] wherever it was undertaken. The Commission has underlined that:

> Today, there is a wide consensus that poverty cannot be defined merely as the lack of income and financial resources but should be recognised as a multi-faceted concept. This new definition includes deprivation of basic capabilities and encompasses non-monetary factors such as the lack of access to education, health, natural resources, employment, land and credit, political participation, services and infrastructure. It also covers the risk dimension and the notion of vulnerability. Reducing poverty therefore implies addressing these economic, political, social, environmental and institutional dimensions.[314]

The Commission has said that the private sector is a key actor in the development process.[315] It has also said that competition policy should take account of development policy.[316] These effects too must be taken into account in an Article 81 analysis.

There are some Treaty objectives, such as culture and economic and social cohesion, that less readily lend themselves to an analysis of effects outside of the Community (which may be important, depending on the relevant geographic market). Environmental policy, public health, security of energy supply and development policy all seem to require such an approach. As regards objectives such as research and development, and possibly consumer protection, they may only occasionally require an analysis of effects outside the relevant market.

That said, there must be some limits on the effects that need to be considered; otherwise the necessary investigation will be too costly, time-consuming and difficult for the relevant undertakings (and the decision-makers) to perform, especially as they will often have no experience of the problems in other sectors of the economy. There are mechanisms for reducing such problems without returning to the partial equilibrium framework (where the relevant market is less than worldwide), however. Article 81's jurisdictional test (affect on trade between Member States) already restricts which agreements fall within Article 81(1) in the first place.[317] This reduces the cases that can be considered. Evidentiary problems may be limited through rules, such that costs or benefits in other markets could only be considered if they are above a certain magnitude, for example.[318] Secondly, regulators might limit their investigation to the effects on markets closely related to the relevant markets. This approach has already been adopted, to a certain extent, by the

---

[309]   COM(2000) 212, pp 6, 23.

[310]   ibid, 13.

[311]   COM(99) 499 and Council Report, *The Integration of Environment into Economic and Development Co-operation* and SEC(92) 1986 6.

[312]   See, eg COM(2002) 129.

[313]   COM(2000) 212 pp 6, 10.

[314]   ibid, 16.

[315]   ibid, s 3.4.

[316]   ibid, 13. See also Art 178 EC.

[317]   See, eg Cases 89/85, etc *Åhlström v Commission* paras 16–18. Case T-102/96 *Gencor v Commission* para 90 is wider, but this was a merger case.

[318]   See, eg the position in Canada, Sanderson (1996–97) 631, 632.

Commission in its competition reviews.[319] Finally, while one should not artificially reduce the relevant geographic market to one's jurisdiction, when investigating the effect on total equilibrium, one might only assess the effects, or even only the direct effects, within that area.[320] If the total equilibrium approach is used, I suggest adopting the first of these measures, the last two undermine many of the reasons for adopting a total equilibrium approach in the first place. However, these changes would not be sufficient. It is also important to clearly lay down how these rules will work, so that parties can better assess their transactions and thus save costs.[321]

Finally, there is the issue of how public policy goals should interact with the consumer welfare test. Section 3 argues that the Commission should not substantially distort its consumer welfare analysis for industrial policy or other aims through market-balancing. This is because it is difficult to make the balance predictable and transparent, and the relevant objectives can be achieved through other means. However, as Article 81(3) has been deemed appropriate for the consideration of other (public policy) issues, ie it would not become an empty provision,[322] I ultimately advocate combining all the economic efficiency analysis within Article 81(1) and then balancing this with public policy goals in Article 81(3), using mere-balancing.

3 THE RELEVANCE OF PUBLIC POLICY OBJECTIVES IN ARTICLE 81(1) EC

Part B showed that public policy goals have regularly been raised throughout Article 81 EC. Chapter 2 argued that they must still be considered there today. This is because of the seven policy-linking clauses; the structure of the Treaty;[323] and the Community Courts' teleological method of Treaty interpretation.[324] In fact, the trend is for this holistic approach to the achievement of policy objectives to increase with each Treaty amendment.

There are three mechanisms for achieving a public policy balance in Article 81. In market-balancing (internal balancing), public policy objectives are considered *within* the economic efficiency test itself, by 'distorting' the weight given to its different elements.[325] Mere-balancing (external balancing), on the other hand, balances public policy goals outside of the economic efficiency assessment.[326] Finally, a welfare objective could achieve/facilitate the pursuit of other public policy goals when the costs of these goals are internalised within the economic welfare calculation.[327] Section 3's aim is to explain which of these three mechanisms is preferable.

---

[319] See, eg the form for notifying mergers, Form CO, Commission Regulation, *On Merger Notifications and Time-limits*, Annex A, ss 6–9.

[320] See, eg the comments of Wood (1999) 15.

[321] Ch 8 discusses these issues further.

[322] Chs 2 and 4.

[323] Ch 2, Section 2.1.

[324] Ch 2, Section 2.2.

[325] See Ch 1, Section 2.2 and the practical application of this in Ch 5.

[326] See Ch 1, Section 2.2, and the practical application of this in Chs 3, mere-balancing in Art 81(1) EC, and 4, mere-balancing in Art 81(3) EC.

[327] See Ch 1, Section 2.2.1. This is different from market-balancing; here the internalised public policy goal is a normal cost; in market-balancing the consumer welfare test itself is distorted by placing extra weight on one or more of the elements within it.

If public policy goals are incorporated into competition policy, as I argue they must be, it is incumbent on the regulators to make this process rational, transparent and open. First, it is vital that the relevance of public policy in competition policy is acknowledged upfront; secondly, we need to know how and where public policy will be considered.[328]

In general the Commission emphasises market solutions first, which explains its efforts to internalise environmental externalities, for example.[329] This is because, in most areas, if a policy runs against market forces and competition, it not only has less chance of success; but, is also less likely to benefit consumers.[330] The more that public policy objectives are achieved through market forces, the harder it is to justify balancing outside of this mechanism; because this will not only undermine consumer welfare, but might also undercut the public policy goals that it indirectly promotes.

The Commission has sometimes implied that only where it is clear that market forces have failed will it consider using mere or market-balancing.[331] Market forces cannot always achieve the objectives of the European Union.[332] To the extent that market forces do not (or cannot, within the requisite time) produce the optimal balance,[333] one must consider using mere or market-balancing to protect the public policy goal. I argue that one should only use mere-balancing for this, to the exclusion of market-balancing.

3.1 Market-balancing

Chapter 5 tentatively pointed to three ways in which welfare analysis can be 'distorted' in order to achieve public policy objectives, or to facilitate their consideration, ie three types of market-balancing. These are: through use of a consumer welfare or producer welfare goal; by focusing on productive and dynamic efficiencies, at the expense of allocative efficiencies, or vice versa; and through use of either a total, or a partial, equilibrium approach.

---

[328]   Ch 1, Conclusion.

[329]   In relation to environmental protection, see Commission, *RCP 1991* 54 and SEC(92) 1986.

[330]   Commission, *RCP 1990* 16. This is in line with a general trend towards market-based solutions, Colin Mayer, Financial Times (London 28 August 2002) 9.

[331]   An example of this can be seen in Commission decision, *Synthetic Fibres*; see also, SEC(92) 1986 and Commission decision, *ENI/Montedison*, para 29. That said, sometimes the Commission has been more willing to intervene, see Commission decision, *BPCL/ICI*, para 35.

[332]   European Parliament, *Resolution of the European Parliament on the Twenty-fifth Competition Report of the European Commission*, in Commission, *RCP 1996* 357, point B. Also see ESC, *Opinion on the Commission's industrial policy communication*, para 3.2.2; Commission, *RCP 1993*, points 2, 163, 164; European Parliament, *Resolution on the Twenty-second Competition Report of the Commission*, in Commission, *RCP 1993*, Annex I, para 12; Commission decision, *Olivetti/Canon*, para 56 and Snowball and Antrobus (2001).

[333]   With the possible exception of industrial policy; in Commission, *RCP 1991*, regarding the link between competition and industrial policy, the Commission said, at point 11, 'When in its 1990 communication on industrial policy the Commission opted clearly for a system of open and competitive markets, it reaffirmed the role to be played by competition policy in boosting the competitiveness of Community industry ... The new Art 130 [now Art 157] to be inserted into the EEC Treaty pursuant to the Maastricht Treaty on European Union confirms this approach: it states that the objective of ensuring "that the conditions necessary for the competitiveness of the Community's industry exist" must not lead to the introduction "of any measure which could lead to a distortion of competition".' See also, the Commission, *RCP 1994*, point 14. Nevertheless, the Commission uses a mere-balancing test in relation to industrial policy too, in contravention of the Treaty, see Ch 4, Section 2.6. As I pointed out in Chs 1 and 5, the idea that the Commission could merely implement value-neutral economic rules is wrong.

I say tentatively, because the Commission is rarely explicit about what it is trying to do; normally fails to quantify any costs or benefits that it considers; and, seldom places its analysis within a wider framework, which would allow us to intuit what it is seeking to achieve, or to predict its assessment in future cases. The Commission, *Article 81(3) Guidelines*, seem to be an attempt to put things on a more formal footing. They demand explicit listing and quantification of all purported efficiency gains. This would certainly be an improvement, bringing greater transparency to the assessment. However, it is insufficient. The Commission must set up a more formal, structured, method of economic welfare analysis, properly explaining when short-term allocative efficiency can be compromised for long-term gain, for example.

The Commission has now explicitly adopted a consumer welfare approach in its policy statements. Definition of a goal is a distinct improvement and should significantly enhance legal certainty. However, because of the relevance of public policy criteria, consumer welfare cannot be the sole goal of Article 81 EC. I believe that consumer welfare should be Article 81(1)'s goal, instead of that of Article 81 as a whole.[334] In practice though and despite this explicit consumer welfare goal, the Commission often pays attention to the effects on Community industry and, particularly when Community undertakings benefit from the agreement, the Commission readily finds relevant consumer benefits, perhaps more readily than would otherwise be the case.[335] In this way, industrial policy considerations sometimes creep into the efficiency assessment;[336] in an inappropriate fashion, significantly undermining transparency and thus, predictability.[337] Legal certainty is particularly important, post-modernisation.[338] If industrial policy should be considered in Article 81 EC,[339] then I believe that this should occur explicitly in Article 81(3) EC, using mere-balancing.[340]

Furthermore, the Commission particularly encourages R&D activities by Community undertakings. This is probably because of the industrial policy and employment benefits that it believes they bring.[341] By readily accepting short term, and sometimes substantial, allocative efficiency losses to achieve these ends the Commission hopes to increase R&D spending in the European Union. It has often accepted quite speculative dynamic and productive efficiency gains in its decisions. Once again it fails to quantify the costs and benefits of these agreements, making industrial policy considerations easier to accept. I do not think that the consumer welfare test should be distorted in this way for Community undertakings, the impact on legal certainty is too great. As I have just said, if industrial policy should be considered in Article 81 EC, then I believe that this should happen explicitly in Article 81(3) EC, using mere-balancing.

The Commission favours a partial equilibrium approach. However, there are many advantages to the total equilibrium analysis. It allows us to make a more global welfare

---

[334]   See Sections 2.3 above and 3.2 below.
[335]   Ch 5, Section 2.
[336]   Most of the sources I relied on in Ch 5 are pre-modernisation. The Commission may do this less today, there have been too few relevant post-modernisations on this point to be sure. Note though that, for example, Commission, *Horizontal Guidelines* highlight producer benefits/needs in their analysis.
[337]   I also think that it is legally inadvisable, because it may be contrary to Art 157(3) EC.
[338]   See Section 2.3, above.
[339]   See the discussion around Ch 4, n 171.
[340]   See Section 3.2, below.
[341]   Ch 5, Section 3.

assessment, encourages co-operation between antitrust agencies, should improve consistency between them and may make it easier to further other policy objectives, such as
development policy, in a pro-market manner. The Commission's position flies in the face
of two clear CFI judgments. I have argued that, within certain limits, a total equilibrium
approach is more satisfactory.[342]

The Commission, and, in its shadow, the Member States' courts and competition
authorities, have great scope for including public policy objectives within its Article 81
analysis. Internalising externalities is normally the best way of doing this. Where this does
not work, or does not work within the requisite timeframe, then another mechanism is
needed.[343] The power to balance brings with it a responsibility. If the inclusion of public
policy goals within competition policy is not to undermine the market mechanism then
the Commission must be as clear and transparent as possible. Section 3.2 argues that
mere-balancing is the next best methodology for this.

3.2 Mere-balancing

Part B showed conflicting Treaty goals being balanced in both Articles 81(1) and 81(3) EC.
There seemed no consistency in when and where the objectives were invoked.[344] Komninos
suggests that:

> Article 81 EC *as a whole* should be balanced against public interest concerns. In this sense, the
> non-economic norm (in *Wouters* the protection of the legal profession's independence) is not
> brought *into the substance of Article 81 EC* (in its first or in its third paragraph), thus blurring its
> purity, but it is taken into account at a preceding stage, leading to an exception from the ambit of
> Article 81 EC as a whole, subject to a control of proportionality.[345]

As I explain below, I think that the implication of this suggestion, that the public policy
and consumer welfare assessments be kept separate, is attractive. The problem is that what
Komninos suggests does not seem to be possible at law. When one applies Article 81, there
is not a step where one can weigh the provision *as a whole* against public policy objectives.
One must first apply Article 81(1) EC and then, if necessary, Article 81(3).[346]

Unless they are internalised, non-economic objectives should only be considered in
Article 81(3) EC, via mere-balancing with a consumer welfare goal in Article 81(1).[347] I do
not think that mere-balancing public policy goals should occur within Article 81(1). As I
will explain, mere-balancing in Article 81(1) reduces consumer welfare, decreases transparency, undermines the Commission's corporate social responsibility initiatives and
ignores Article 81's structure.[348] Furthermore, this is unnecessary; there is no need for
mere-balancing within Article 81(1), when this can be done in Article 81(3) EC.

---

[342]   See Section 2.3, the text around Ch 6, n 301.
[343]   Ch 1, Conclusion.
[344]   Deckert (2000) 176.
[345]   Komninos (2006) 465–67. See also Komninos (2005) 10–14.
[346]   See Idot (2001) 336. Schmid (2000) 166, 167 also considers this and rejects it.
[347]   This does not mean that an *Albany* style analysis should never take place within Art 81(1) EC; although
this should be kept to a minimum. Remember that, in the *Albany* Case, see Ch 2, Section 2.2.1 the ECJ did not
balance competing objectives, but said that Art 81(1) did not apply to certain types of agreements. This meant
that the rule's important competition effects could not be considered.
[348]   See also my discussion of exclusion, Ch 1, Section 3.2. My rejection of mere-balancing in Art 81(1) is not
a rejection of compromise, because this can, and should, take place within Art 81(3) EC, see Ch 7.

Delegation theory tells us that the objectives assigned to a competition law might be more completely achieved if drawn narrowly. Increases in consumer welfare are most likely where this is the only objective considered, which is what I argue should be the case within Article 81(1) EC. Consumer welfare's benefits have been discussed extensively.[349] This goal also helps reinforce the market mechanism.

Secondly, if only one objective needed to be considered in the Article 81(1) analysis, then the application of the provision would be more transparent. Increasing transparency is important. It helps to reveal the non-economic objectives' costs; and, improve legal predictability for relevant bodies.

Thirdly, whenever non-economic objectives are achieved at the expense of consumer welfare there is a cost. This does not mean that resolving the balance in that way is necessarily wrong.[350] However, in order to assess whether or not to promote a conflicting non-economic objective, one must know the costs and benefits of this. Using Article 81's structure to clearly separate the economic and non-economic considerations forces the decision-maker to demonstrate and justify the sacrifices, judgments and trade-offs it favours.[351] Knowing the cost of political intervention is important.[352] It increases account-ability,[353] which should force a better articulation of the competing policies.[354]

Transparency also means increased legal predictability for undertakings.[355] Mere-balancing within Article 81(1) EC reduces the clarity of the provision, making it less certain whether, or not, Article 81(1) EC applies in a given situation.[356] Even if the Commission and the Community Courts made every effort to explain their reasoning (which they do not[357]) the outcome of the balance would always be in doubt.[358] I have already emphasised the importance of clarity to business and to the economy as a whole;[359] it helps undertakings plan for the future. But, there is another benefit, which would also apply to consumers or others who might make use of the antitrust laws; increased clarity reduces frivolous litigation. Ambiguity makes starting aggressive litigation on competition grounds easier.[360] Those that want to claim that an agreement (or clause) is void under Article 81(2) EC have more (potential) grounds of attack. Those that wish to defend the agreement have more (potential) grounds for defence, regardless of the merits of the case. This increases litigation risks (also making what litigation there is more lengthy and complex),[361] augmenting business (and consumer) uncertainty and costs. Welfare is

---

[349]   See Ch 1 and Section 2.3, above.

[350]   Indeed, my proposed reservation of Art 81(3) for balancing non-economic objectives sends a clear message that, in certain circumstances, this is permissible.

[351]   Lipsky (1998) 458 and Ginsburg (1991) 25.

[352]   Wolf (1998) 132; Möschel (1991) 12 and Ginsburg (1991) 25. The desire for transparency and account-ability in the decision-making process has been cited as the reason for the Community Courts' application of Arts 81 and 82 (in conjunction with Arts 3(1)(g) and 10 EC) to Member States, see Möschel (1991) 12.

[353]   Neven (1998) 22.

[354]   This, in turn, strengthens the position of the voter, Kirchner (1998) 522.

[355]   Schmid (2000) 166.

[356]   See Ch 3. Few would have predicted the ECJ's decision in the *Wouters* Case. I read this as the implication in Forrester (2006) 289, 290, for example.

[357]   See Part B.

[358]   Jebsen and Stevens (1995–6) 460. On the lack of clarity in a mere-balancing approach in general see also, Baxter (1983) 621, and the references cited there, as well as Ch 1. Chs 7 and 8 advise on how to improve predictability within mere-balancing.

[359]   See Ch 2 and Section 2.3, above.

[360]   Riley (1998) 485.

[361]   Korah (2002) 25.

further reduced.[362] This could, amongst other things, undermine the Treaty's aim of raising the standard of living, Article 2.

Restricting Article 81(1) to a pure consumer welfare analysis also supports the Community's stance on corporate social responsibility for undertakings.[363] A key part of the Commission and Council's strategy in this area is to encourage firms, *on a voluntary basis*, to co-operate, within the law's limits. If other objectives are relevant within Article 81(1) EC, then where undertakings sought to co-operate so as to increase economic welfare, they could be *forced* to implement other Treaty goals, such as development policy.[364] This runs contrary to the CSR initiative as a voluntary scheme. Co-operation becomes less attractive, which could reduce the other benefits to be gained through encouraging these kinds of agreements.[365]

These benefits are important, but they would not be decisive if removing the consideration of non-economic objectives to Article 81(3) would undermine the aims of the Treaty. It does not. There is no need for mere-balancing in Article 81(1) EC; indeed Article 81(3) is the best place for it, as I will now demonstrate.

Since Regulation 1/2003,[366] there is no practical need for mere-balancing in Article 81(1) EC. Many objectives have been considered in Article 81(3).[367] Where an agreement restricts competition (reduces consumer welfare), then it could still be exempted if it fulfils Article 81(3). In addition, exempting agreements due to policy considerations under Article 81(3), better reflects Article 81's structure.[368] Although in practice they have sometimes wavered, the Community Courts[369] and the Commission[370] generally agree that, in theory, mere-balancing is better conducted under Article 81(3) EC. Legal scholars tend to support this view.[371]

Wesseling points out that such a change would make clearing an arrangement on public policy grounds harder; the agreement would have to fulfil all four Article 81(3) conditions,

---

[362] These reductions can be important, although they are small in relation to the benefits to the economy of competition policy, Gardner (2000). The smaller they are the better, provided that this is not achieved at the expense of an even larger loss to society as a whole, COM(96) 721, para 86.

[363] See Ch 1, Section 3.2.

[364] The same could apply, eg, if they had an environmental agreement that did not appreciably restrict competition.

[365] See Ch 1, Section 3.2. One could make the same point in relation to any legislation that 'forced' firms to comply with, eg, environmental goals. However, the issue is different here as Art 81(1) only applies where there is some form of co-operation, which is the basis of CSR too.

[366] Ch 2 suggested that one reason lying behind the ECJ's *Wouters* and *Albany* judgments may have been the procedural repercussions of finding restrictions of competition in the underlying agreements which had not been exempted, they would have been void under Art 81(2) EC. Agreements can no longer be notified to the Commission and these procedural problems no longer arise.

[367] See Chs 2 and 4. Monti (2002), s 5.2, argues that Member States' objectives cannot be considered in Art 81(3) EC; however, Ch 4, Section 3 disagrees.

[368] See Ch 3, Section 3.2 and Schmid (2000) 166. Furthermore, Art 157(3) EC implies that public policy balancing should take place in Art 81(3), although not for industrial policy.

[369] Case T-112/99 *Métropole Télévision (M6) and Others v Commission* para 74 and the *Wouters* Case, see the Opinion of A-G Léger paras 100–08. Although Jans (2000) 275, says that it is unclear what the Community Courts will say after the *Albany* Case. The same might be said of the *Wouters* Case too, see Vossestein (2002) 858, 859.

[370] See Commission decision, *Joint selling of the commercial rights of the UEFA Champions League*, paras 129–31; the *Albany* Case, see the reference to the submissions of the Commission, para 175 of the Opinion of A-G Jacobs and Commission, *RCP 1992*, point 77.

[371] See Ch 3; Fox and Hawk in Ehlermann (2001), respectively pages 23 and 50; Siragusa in Ehlermann (1998) 469, 486; Hawk (1995) and Ellis (1963) 272–76, makes a similar point. Some Community competition authorities interpret their equivalent of Art 81 in this way too, see Section 2.

as opposed to just outweighing the restriction of competition.[372] Wesseling makes an important observation, but it should not be exaggerated. Some of these tests have been introduced into Article 81(1), when mere-balancing there.[373] Nevertheless, Wesseling is right insofar as Article 81(3)'s clear articulation of four conditions may make exemption more difficult;[374] but this could be positive, given the importance of the consumer welfare test.[375] At the very least, it forces those conducting the balance to consider the effect on consumers, as well as the effect on competition.

There is one situation in which it potentially makes a great deal of difference whether mere-balancing takes place under Article 81(1) or 81(3) EC. Consider an agreement that would not have been considered restrictive of competition, for the purposes of Article 81(1) EC (for us this means that consumer welfare is not appreciably restricted), except for the fact that it infringed some other Treaty objective. This sort of (negative) mere-balancing is not normally performed within Article 81(1), although protection of SMEs[376] and the market integration objectives sometimes operate in this fashion.[377] If mere-balancing were prevented in respect of this kind of 'negative' objective the Treaty's aims might not be fully achieved;[378] imagine an agreement that did not reduce consumer welfare, but was particularly destructive to the environment, for example. If the agreement were cleared under Article 81(1), one might ask whether this complies with the Commission's obligation to ensure a high level of environmental protection in its definition and implementation of Community policies.

In other words, in the Treaty context, does restricting balancing to Article 81(3) sufficiently accommodate the need for compromise, or does it give competition too much

---

[372]   Wesseling (2000) 106, 107.

[373]   Ch 3, Section 3.1 showed that when balancing takes place in Art 81(1) an indispensability test is often implied. Indeed, in the *Wouters* Case and the *Meca-Medina* Case the ECJ used a full-blown proportionality test. Furthermore, we have seen that Art 81(3)'s *fair share to consumers* test is used to justify a consumer welfare test there. If consumer welfare were already relevant within Art 81(1), then all Art 81(3)'s four tests would be present within the first para, except that competition could be eliminated. Practically, this may make little difference as it is unlikely that the Community Courts or the Commission would allow competition to be eliminated often, even when balancing under Art 81(1) EC, Ch 2, Section 2.2.1.

[374]   Commission, *Article 81(3) Guidelines*, reinforce this approach. They seem to place a heavy burden of proof on the parties wishing to benefit from Art 81(3), while narrowing Art 81(1)'s interpretation, see Geradin (2006) 331.

[375]   This argument reflects Ch 1, Section 3.2.1's point about competition law not being the most efficient instrument to promote many non-economic objectives. However, it does not abandon compromise altogether, as Art 81(3) EC can be used for this.

[376]   Although more recent versions of the *de minimis* notices have introduced a market share test too. Agreements between firms are not merely exempted where the undertakings that enter into them are small. The market share test, see the *De Minimis Notice*, para 7, is analysing something else as well, ie the agreement's impact on the market, see the *De Minimis Notice*, para 1. If consumer welfare became the declared objective of Art 81(1) an appreciability test would still be relevant.

[377]   Whish and Sufrin (1987) 37, argue that those in favour of '... the rule of reason fail to give due consideration to the significance of single market integration.' Marsden (2000) implies the same thing. However, Chs 1 and 3: (1) suggested that the market integration objective may be there to enhance economic efficiency, see also the cases cited in Ch 1, n 3; and, (2) noted that the market integration objective, as currently pursued, may actually undermine market integration in ways that a welfare standard would not. Nevertheless, Whish and Sufrin's point is worth pursuing because it may be that market integration is not solely there to achieve efficiency aims. Furthermore, other objectives may also be considered within Art 81(1) which may conflict with competition, think of the *Wouters* Case, discussed in Ch 2, although that was not an example of 'negative mere-balancing'.

[378]   Ehlermann (1998) 4, notes this problem in relation to the international harmonisation of competition laws.

weight?[379] The answer is probably not, for four reasons.[380] First, I suggest defining a restriction of competition as an appreciable restriction of consumer welfare. Consumer welfare and the public interest overlap to a large degree.[381] Externalities can be internalised. Even where this has not been done, many other objectives are directly and indirectly promoted through the consumer welfare concept. As a result, the standard I suggest actually incorporates many relevant objectives within it and so reduces the problem of conflict, at least in the long term.

Secondly, agreements that cause no competition problems, but cause environmental damage, for example, can be dealt with through environmental legislation. Article 81 is not a blank cheque to legislate in all areas. The absence of environmental legislation cannot be used as an excuse for pursuing environmental policy through competition law. It is up to the Council and the European Parliament to adopt environmental legislation. Allowing the Commission (or a Member State court, for example) to bypass them in this way would undermine the separation of powers under the Treaty[382] and risks distorting the competition rules from their true purpose, possibly a *détournement de pouvoir*.[383] [384]

Furthermore, administrative action (and business decisions) would become impossible if every decision had to take account of its effect on every relevant objective. This cannot be the intention of the Treaty. In any event, most agreements between undertakings that restrict competition are found to fall outside Article 81(1) EC. Normally this is either because they do not fulfil Article 81's jurisdictional tests or because they do not appreciably restrict competition. These minor agreements would likely cause little environmental damage or consumer harm.[385] The benefits of balancing under Article 81(1) EC would not be great in most of these cases.

Finally, in the rare cases where non-economic objectives are significantly undermined by such an agreement, these objectives are normally more effectively protected through direct legislation that does not distort competition.[386] Allowing mere-balancing within

---

[379] One might also comment that interpreting a restriction of competition as a restriction of consumer welfare (instead of economic freedom) means that Art 81(1) is interpreted more narrowly, see Section 2. As a result, it applies to fewer agreements. Therefore, there is less opportunity to invoke other policy objectives (eg within Art 81(3)) in relation to agreements. However, if arguments like this held sway, we could be forced to apply Art 81(1) to all agreements. The fact that the Community Courts accept an appreciability test implies that this need not be so.

[380] Vogelaar (1994) 542, 543, argues that environmental considerations can only be raised under Art 81(3) EC '... since the test of Art 85(1) [now Art 81(1)] is a strictly legal and economic one ...' He cites two cases to support this, including Case 5/69 *Franz Völk v Établissements J. Vervaecke*. But this is a circular argument and depends on the definition of 'restriction of competition'. Furthermore, he is not supported by the later case law, think of the *Wouters* Case.

[381] See Ch 1, Section 2 and Howe (1998) 450.

[382] Vedder (2003) 158.

[383] Détournement de pouvoir, a concept derived from French administrative law, is also known as 'misuse of power', see Art 230 EC. It covers the idea that a Community institution has adopted a measure with the exclusive or main purpose of achieving an end other than that stated, or evading a procedure specifically prescribed by the Treaty for dealing with the circumstances of that case, see Case C-84/94 *United Kingdom v Council (re Working Time Directive)* and Craig and de Búrca (2008) 568, 569.

[384] This is in line with my theoretical position, see Ch 1, Section 4.

[385] Ch 8 discusses application of the appreciability doctrine to non-economic Treaty objectives.

[386] Monti (2002) 1092, points out that '... increased activism by the EC in other policy areas reduces the need for competition law to intervene to achieve other goals ...'

Article 81(1) EC may even undermine the very objectives that we seek to promote; because it reduces the Member States' incentives to deal with problems using optimal instruments.[387]

One might add that if mere-balancing takes place in Article 81(1), what is left to be considered in Article 81(3)?[388] Some may suggest, in light of *Métropole télévision*, that economic efficiency should be considered under Article 81(3) EC. It would be a topsy-turvy world where a competition law only considered economic efficiency as being a justification for otherwise unacceptable agreements.

I believe that Article 81(1) should only be about consumer welfare; mere-balancing of public policy goals can take place, but only in Article 81(3). A clear Article 81(1) test has many benefits. Negative mere-balancing (where there is no consumer welfare loss, but a restriction is found for other public policy reasons) is not normally performed within Article 81(1) EC and so outlawing it should have little practical import; except perhaps for a market integration goal, where this was not in line with consumer welfare. It is likely that market integration can be more effectively protected using instruments designed for this purpose, rather than restricting competition. Where there are restrictions of competition then market integration can be considered in Article 81(3).[389] This seems the right result, given the importance of consumer welfare, the public policy goals it also promotes; the Treaty structure and its goals.

4 CONCLUSION

Former Commissioner Monti has said that companies can reasonably expect '... an adequate level of predictability and consistent application of the rules that allows them properly to assess how the rules will be applied.'[390] Part B showed that Article 81 falls far short of this standard; and this is unacceptable.

There are two main problems with the way in which Article 81(1) EC is implemented, as far as the consideration of non-economic objectives within Article 81 is concerned. The first relates to the imprecise definition of a restriction of competition. The second relates to the lack of clarity generated by mere-balancing within Article 81(1) and market-balancing throughout Article 81.[391] Regulation 1/2003 does not mean that the wide reach historically given to 81(1) ceases to be important. Nor does it remove the need to clearly define Article 81(1)'s scope; or, obviate the problems caused by balancing in that provision. In fact, these issues have, arguably, become more important.

---

[387] See Ch 1. One cannot rely too heavily on this argument, otherwise the policy-linking clauses would be of no value; it would also allow us to forbid balancing under Art 81(3) EC. However, it is relevant insofar as it shows that the non-economic objective can often be (better) protected by other means. Therefore, critical damage can still be prevented.

[388] One option could be that Art 81(1) is a 'quick check' and Art 81(3) is a more thorough look, like Phase I and II under the ECMR. However, there is no support for this in Art 81. Paras 1 and 3 seem designed to deal with different issues, Whish (1998) 464, 500, particularly in light of Art 81(3)(b) EC.

[389] Ch 7, Section 2.1 argues for negative balancing in Art 81(3) EC, which reduces, but does not eliminate, the impact of removing negative balancing from Art 81(1).

[390] Mario Monti in Ehlermann (2001) 9.

[391] See Chs 3 and 5, respectively.

Chapter 6 is not suggesting that we become hostages to clarity. Chapter 2 showed that many objectives should be balanced within Article 81; this is not a science. The compromise requirement does not mean, however, that all policy objectives need to be directly considered all of the time and at every stage of the proceedings. This would create too much uncertainty and involve too much cost for insufficient return.

Section 2 argues that the notion of a restriction on economic freedom is unclear; that many of the arguments in favour of economic freedom are unpersuasive; and, that this definition has many negative consequences. It suggests adopting a consumer welfare test. Section 3 adds that there is no need for market-balancing and no need for mere-balancing within Article 81(1). Furthermore, the benefits of performing the mere-balance in Article 81(3) instead suggest that it is better done there. Article 81(3) EC is discussed in Chapter 7.

The position of the ECJ on these two issues is uncertain. It has not responded to the CFI's *Métropole télévision* judgment and we do not know whether the *Wouters* Case and the *Meca Medina* Case were motivated by the procedural problems discussed in Chapters 2 and 3, which no longer exist. A clear decision by the Community Courts, and the *Glaxo* Case gives the ECJ this opportunity, to follow Chapter 6's proposals would provide some much needed clarity while giving adequate protection to relevant non-economic objectives. This would benefit undertakings throughout the Community and beyond, as long as Chapter 7's recommendations are also taken into account.

7

How and Where Should Public Policy Balancing be Performed in Article 81(3) EC?

1 INTRODUCTION

This chapter examines Article 81(3) EC. The Commission is optimistic about legal certainty in Article 81 as a whole:

> Undertakings … at present enjoy a satisfactory level of legal certainty thanks to the set of clear rules that have been developed and refined through more than 30 years of Commission decision-making practice and Court of Justice case law and by the many different kinds of general instruments that have been adopted …[1]

More cautiously, former Commissioner Monti has said that the analytical framework for applying Article 81(3) has not been explained in any kind of detail. The real purpose of Commission, *Article 81(3) Guidelines* is to remedy this by focusing on Article 81(3).[2]

In setting out the analytical framework for the application of both Article 81(1) and (3) EC, Commission, *Article 81(3) Guidelines* are a useful aid to national courts, competition authorities and firms.[3] However, they do not clarify the role of public policy goals at all, except to say that 'Goals pursued by other Treaty provisions can be taken into account to

---

[1]   Commission, *White Paper on Modernisation*, para 51.
[2]   Monti (2004) 459.
[3]   Lugard and Hancher (2004) 420.

the extent that they can be subsumed under the four conditions of Article 81(3)'.[4] This is circular and unhelpful. We have seen that many non-economic objectives have been (and should be) considered within Article 81(3) EC. This has been done without reference to this recently espoused Commission test. There is now uncertainty as to public policy's proper place within Article 81(3).[5]

Uncertainty about public policy's role in Article 81(3) may lead to less application of non-economic objectives there, as well as a less Communautaire application of them when they are invoked, undermining the Treaty's aims. The Commission seeks the consistent application of Community law via a variety of mechanisms in Regulation 1/2003. However, this is unlikely to be achieved unless non-economic objectives' role is directly confronted and accurately laid out for the plethora of decision-makers.

Part C of this book provides a framework for the consideration of non-economic goals within Article 81. Chapters 7 and 8 try to fill the gaps left by the Commission, *Article 81(3) Guidelines*, in relation to the consideration of non-economic objectives within Article 81(3) EC. This is particularly important because the decision-maker has a wide margin of discretion when implementing all four Article 81(3) tests.[6]

Some suggest that Member States' competition authorities, and particularly their courts, are not appropriate fora for the consideration of public policy in Article 81(3) of the type I believe the Treaty demands; others worry about the inconsistent decisions that the public policy dimension may generate from so many decision-makers. The Commission's response is to deny/limit the relevance of public policy in Article 81,[7] contrary to the Community Courts' case law. Monti, rightly in my view, points to an additional risk that the Commission, which in its own decisions has often given great weight to public policy criteria,[8] might end up removing cases from the Member States when matters of public policy are under discussion that it believes should be considered. It would then grant an exemption on the basis of say employment considerations, which the Member States' authorities may be reluctant to take given the Commission's policy exhortations that Article 81(3) relates only to consumer welfare. This could lead to the chaotic situation where the Commission grants Article 81(3) exemptions according to a different set of standards from the Member States.[9] This is a real danger, but for the Commission to act in this way would not be an appropriate solution either, if the Commission's workload is to remain manageable. Many agreements that fall within Article 81(1) EC already raise non-economic issues. The Commission has already considered such issues in a far from negligible proportion of the decisions that it has taken. This proportion is likely to rise,

---

[4]   Commission, *Article 81(3) Guidelines*, para 42. There is also a passing reference to safety and health concerns in para 18(2), but this is equally cryptic and relates to Art 81(1) EC. Whish (2008) 155, says that it is absolutely clear that these guidelines intend Art 81(3) only to include economic efficiency concerns.

[5]   van Gerven (2004) 421; Lugard and Hancher (2004) 418; Whish (2008) 155 and Ritter, Braun and Rawlinson (2000) 118. This problem is exacerbated by the Commission's inconsistency with respect to the relevance of the non-economic criteria, see Ch 2, Section 2.3.

[6]   Joined Cases 25 and 26/84 *Ford-Werke and Ford of Europe v Commission*, 2734; Goyder (2003) 120; de Roux and Voillemot (1976) 95 and Alexander (1973) 16.

[7]   This is an inappropriate response, before the Commission can do this the Treaty must be changed, to make it clear that non-economic objectives are irrelevant there. If the plethora of decision-makers create such problems here then Reg 1/2003 should be found ultra vires, see Ch 2, Section 3.2.

[8]   See the Introduction to this book; Ch 2, Section 3 and Part B.

[9]   Monti (2002) 1095.

once it is clear that non-economic factors are relevant. The best response is to make every effort to explain how and where non-economic considerations can be taken into account.

Chapter 6 proposed making consumer welfare the sole Article 81(1) EC goal. This chapter defines what can be considered in Article 81(3). Many public policy goals are automatically promoted through the consumer welfare objective.[10] Nevertheless, some objectives cannot be pursued indirectly through this mechanism; others can be pursued in part, but not completely. That leaves room for the consideration of public policy goals in Article 81(3), via a mere-balancing test.[11]

The Commission argues that Treaty ends should be achieved via the most appropriate means, taking account of the costs of each 'solution'. Chapter 6 suggested that mere-balancing should only occur within Article 81(3) EC. Article 81's structure will then ensure that mere-balancing's costs are more clearly defined. The point is not that, in the Community legal order, economic welfare should permanently outweigh all other objectives;[12] however, the Community increasingly relies on the market mechanism as the basic means of wealth creation and so it is logical to organise EU competition law around the welfare standard.[13]

Chapter 7's core analysis comes in four parts, each of which discusses one of Article 81(3)'s four cumulative[14] tests. Section 2 deals with the first Article 81(3) test, involving a public interest balance. Section 3 analyses Article 81(3)'s second test, that consumers must get a fair share of the agreement's resulting benefit. Section 4 focuses on Article 81(3)(a) and Section 5 on Article 81(3)(b) EC. Section 6 concludes.

One final issue must be briefly considered before the main analysis starts. The use of the word 'may' in Article 81(3) EC gives the decision-maker a lot of discretion. Some believe that this allows new, additional, tests to be introduced into Article 81(3). Perhaps specific public policy issues could be consigned to these?[15] However, this is probably contrary to the CFI's holding in the *Matra* Case:

> [I]n principle, no anti-competitive practice can exist which, whatever the extent of its effects on a given market, cannot be exempted, provided that all the conditions laid down in Article 85(3) [now Article 81(3)] of the Treaty are satisfied …[16]

It is unlikely that the Member States' courts and competition authorities would ignore such statements. In any event, adding more tests to Article 81(3) is unnecessary because public policy can be adequately considered there, as it is currently interpreted. The addition of a

---

[10]   See Ch 1, Section 2.2 and Ch 6, Section 3.2.

[11]   See Ch 6, Section 3.2.

[12]   See Ch 2, Sections 2 and 3.

[13]   Where this is not the case agreements can be excluded from Art 81(1)'s remit altogether, see the *Albany* Case, although this is generally not a good mechanism, see Ch 2, Section 2.2.

[14]   See references to cases in Commission, *Article 81(3) Guidelines*, para 42.

[15]   See, eg Jacobs (1993/2) 58 and Alexander (1973) 16.

[16]   The *Matra* Case para 85. Wils (2004) 671, reads the *Matra* Case in this way, for example. Although admittedly, it is unclear whether this paragraph covers this issue, because the CFI was pronouncing on a somewhat different point. Nevertheless, Commission, *Article 81(3) Guidelines* take a decisive stand 'The four conditions of Art 81(3) are … exhaustive. When they are met the exception is applicable and may not be made dependant on any other condition.', Commission, *Article 81(3) Guidelines*, para 42.

new condition would merely add confusion as to its limits. It would also set a difficult precedent for Treaty interpretation in other areas.[17]

2 THE FIRST TEST:
BALANCING IN THE PUBLIC INTEREST

Article 81(3)'s first condition says that Article 81(1) EC may be declared inapplicable for agreements that contribute '… to improving the production or distribution of goods or to improving technical or economic progress …' According to the Commission, this requires an assessment of the positive economic effects of restrictive agreements.[18] However, I have shown that Article 81(3)'s first test is interpreted more widely than that. Many objectives have been considered there. Indeed, the CFI has held that:

> [I]n the context of an overall assessment, the Commission is entitled to base itself on considerations connected with the pursuit of the public interest in order to grant exemption under Article 85(3) [now Article 81(3)] of the Treaty.[19]

I have argued that a consumer welfare assessment should be conducted in Article 81(1) EC. This leaves Article 81(3) for the separate assessment of the agreement's public policy implications. Many objectives are considered within Article 81(3)'s first test and this should continue. However, the decision-maker (and particularly the Commission, which has a lot of influence here) must explain which objectives may be relevant, as well as the content and weight of these aims.[20] Predictability is now particularly important in relation to Article 81(3), because Member States' courts and competition authorities are applying it for the first time and undertakings no longer have the protection of the notification regime.[21]

Section 2 examines two issues of relevance when balancing in Article 81(3)'s first condition.[22] Section 2.1 asks what sort of balancing test is required. Section 2.2 discusses whose objectives can and should be considered within the balance.[23]

---

[17] Monti (2002), makes a slightly different argument, that adding a fifth test, he calls this Art 81(4) EC, would add political clarity on the issue of whether public policy should be considered in Art 81. I also believe this is unnecessary, as I think we have already seen overwhelming political support for the consideration of public policy goals in Art 81(3) from all Institutions, see Ch 2.

[18] Commission, *Article 81(3) Guidelines*, para 32. In line with his argument that Art 81(1) EC concerned allocative efficiencies, Odudu argues that Art 81(3) is about productive and dynamic efficiencies, see Ch 6, Section 2.2.1.

[19] Joined Cases T-528/93, etc, *Métropole Télévision v Commission* para 118. See Ch 2, Sections 2 and 3 and Ch 4 for other references. Many Commission decisions, as well as Community Court judgments, show that the application of Art 81(3) is 'not pure law or economics, but policy', Sauter (1997) 114.

[20] Siragusa in Ehlermann (2001) 43.

[21] See Ch 6, Introduction.

[22] Ch 2, Section 3.1 also argued that the parties' aims when entering into an agreement should be irrelevant; so, even if their goal was solely profit maximisation, any relevant public policy effects could also be considered as appropriate.

[23] In addition, the rest of Ch 7 discusses certain limits to this test and Ch 8 provides guidance on how to inject more clarity and predictability into the balancing *process*.

2.1 The balancing test

Article 81(3) EC allows restrictive agreements whose objective benefits[24] outweigh a restriction of competition, under Article 81(1). This balance is currently assessed in an ad hoc way and needs to be placed on a more formal footing.

The first step is to explain how the balancing test should be conducted. Three different contexts exist in which balancing might occur: where there is no restriction of competition; where there is a restriction of competition and the agreement has a positive impact on the public interest; and where there is a restriction of competition and the agreement has both positive and negative public interest impacts.

In relation to the first of these situations, Chapter 6 said that agreements that do not restrict competition, but cause environmental damage, for example, should be dealt with through environmental legislation and not competition law. To use competition law to achieve public policy goals in this instance would be a *détournement de pouvoir* (misuse of power).[25]

However, where there is a restriction of competition, *advantages*, due to benefits from non-economic objectives that the agreement generates, such as environmental protection, can be considered in Article 81(3).[26] Furthermore, these objective benefits can be combined.[27] To find otherwise would mean ignoring the Treaty's structure, as interpreted by the Community Courts and would overlook the policy-linking clauses' express wording; they demand the consideration of many non-economic policies within, amongst others, Article 81.[28] There is no *détournement de pouvoir* here because a competition problem exists and the Treaty's structure tends to support a full balancing exercise.[29]

The third situation to consider is whether *disadvantages*, due to the way in which the agreement undermines non-economic objectives, such as environmental protection and culture, should also be considered in the balance. Imagine an agreement that restricts competition, but also contributes to economic and social cohesion within the Community. Can the fact that the same agreement also prejudices environmental protection (ie causes negative environmental effects) be weighed in the balance?

I believe that negative effects should also be considered in the Article 81(3) balance. Considerable prejudice could be done to the pursuit of public policy objectives if negative impacts are ignored.[30] This is despite the fact that a full balancing process complicates the

---

[24] Improvements to the parties are not relevant here, see the *Consten and Grundig* Case 13 of the case summary and Commission, *Article 81(3) Guidelines*, para 49. Nor need they be benefits to consumers; Commission, *Article 81(3) Guidelines*, para 46, distinguishes between objective and consumer benefits. In essence, the agreement must produce a general positive effect, Case T-131/99 *Michael Shaw and Timothy Falla v Commission* para 163.

[25] Ch 6, Section 3.

[26] See Chs 2, 4; Monti (2002) and Bouterse (1994) 26–28, 126–29.

[27] In Commission decision, *Ford/Volkswagen*, the Commission probably took account of industrial policy, employment, environmental and economic and social cohesion arguments in Art 81(3), although this is open to debate, see Ch 4, Section 2.6. Many other examples exist, see Ch 4, esp Section 2.3 and Vedder (2003) 162–64.

[28] Ch 2, Section 2.

[29] Otherwise Art 81(3) would not be relevant, because Art 81(1) would not have been breached. Ch 8 provides a framework within which various objectives can be combined.

[30] There is other academic support for this view. Jacobs argues that there must be a conscious decision that '… the benefits of the measure in question are able to outweigh the harm to the environment.', Jacobs (1993/2) 58. Admittedly, Jacobs believes that this requires the insertion of a fifth Art 81(3) condition, whereas I suggest weighing the requirement within Art 81(3)'s first test. See also, Jans (2000) 277 and Vedder (2003) 186, 187.

decision-making exercise under Article 81(3) EC, reducing its predictability for undertakings.[31] Once again, I do not think that there is a *détournement de pouvoir* in this situation because a competition problem exists; especially as the Treaty's structure tends to support a full balancing exercise.[32]

The fact that Article 81(3)'s first test only refers to 'improvements', may undermine my argument. This could be read as excluding the consideration of negative factors; although that need not be the case, if one reads it as meaning 'overall improvements' once the agreement's advantages and disadvantages have been taken together as a whole. I can also find little direct support for negative balancing from the Community Courts.[33] Nevertheless, one might say that in Article 81(1) the Community Courts already conduct this sort of negative balance, think of the relevance of market integration there in the *Consten and Grundig* Case, for example.[34] Furthermore, some of the policy-linking clauses may demand the consideration of negative effects. Article 6 EC, for example, says that:

> Environmental protection requirements must be integrated into the definition and implementation of the Community policies [including competition policy]... in particular with a view to promoting sustainable development.[35]

This provision does not distinguish between the positive and negative effects on the environment.[36] Nevertheless, its structure implies that negative effects are important.[37] In fact, the Commission has already given at least two objectives, market integration and consumer protection, 'negative weight' in the balance.[38]

---

[31] These problems can be reduced through use of a more predictable balancing *process*, Ch 8 provides a framework for this.

[32] However, a decision which balances positive and negative factors in this way must not pretend to set down *a general rule*, eg that no agreement can be exempted that does not contribute X amount to the environment. That said, Art 81(3) decisions would not contravene the Treaty's constitutional framework where it is clear that they merely seek to balance the requisite factors *in the case at hand*, Vedder (2003) 187, 188.

[33] For example, in *Métropole Télévision* Case para 118, the CFI said that the Commission was entitled to base itself on considerations connected with the pursuit of the public interest *in order to grant* exemption under Art 81(3) EC. It does not say the Commission can base itself on public interest considerations to *refuse* exemption. This might be read as only applying to the positive aspect of such objectives.

[34] If one ignores the CFI's argument in the *Glaxo* Case, para 120, that a pure consumer welfare test was being applied there.

[35] A similar position arises in the other policy linking clauses, see Arts 127(2), 153(2), 159, 178 EC. Arguably, some of these clauses are even clearer. For example, Art 151(4) says that cultural policy must be taken into account '... in particular in order *to respect* **and** *to promote* the diversity of its cultures.' (emphasis added) Art 152(1) says that Community policy in the area of health will be directed towards '... improving public health ... and obviating sources of danger to human health.'

[36] Nor does the Community Courts' and Commission's insistence that Art 81 should be interpreted in light of the Treaty structure as a whole, see Case 14/68 *Walt Wilhelm v Bundeskartellamt*, para 5 and Commission, *RCP 1997* 10.

[37] Furthermore, provisions such as Art 174(2) EC, establishing the polluter pays principle in environmental policy, would be undermined if the parties to an agreement could profit without regard to any environmental harm that they might cause.

[38] See Ch 4, Sections 2.2 and 2.4. It also insists on the assessment of 'all relevant positive and negative impacts' in impact analysis, see, eg COM(2002) 276 15. Although, the Commission, *Horizontal Guidelines* do not consider the possibility of negative weight when discussing environmental protection, for example.

2.2 The objectives in the balance

Many goals are considered within Article 81(3) EC;[39] including both Community and national public interests.[40] There is not a closed list of relevant public policy goals and they develop over time. Section 2.2 discusses three issues: where public policy goals should be considered within Article 81; who should decide how much weight they should be given; and the reviewability of the various actors' public policy decisions.

Member States' interests *can* be considered under Article 81(3) EC, although probably within the Article 2 EC limits. The first question I want to deal with here is whether Member States' interests are best considered under Article 81(1) or (3) EC. Monti, relying on his conclusion that national issues could not be considered within Article 81(3), suggests the use of a rule of reason mechanism under Article 81(1) for Member States' interests, providing *Wouters* as an example of the Community Courts' reasoning in this area.[41]

The European Parliament and the Council believe that Member States' objectives, such as culture, should be considered within Article 81(3) EC.[42] Chapter 6 explained why mere-balancing is best done under Article 81(3) EC;[43] this reasoning applies to both national and Community interests. However, there is an additional reason why this conclusion is even more appropriate for Member States' interests, from a Community perspective. Only considering restrictions of competition and Member States' interests under Article 81(1) EC may give them disproportionate weight, where Community policies are also affected. Imagine an agreement that restricts competition, undermines environmental policy and yet improves cultural awareness within the meaning of Article 151 EC. All of these objectives could be balanced under Article 81(3) EC to establish the optimal outcome. However, if Member State interests (culture) can be raised in Article 81(1), where this provision is not infringed, the environmental impact cannot be considered, as, according to Monti, it is only relevant in Article 81(3). This moves the pendulum too far in favour of Member States' interests at the expense of important Community policies, ignoring the Treaty's structure.[44] For these reasons, I think that both Member State and Community objectives should be considered under Article 81(3) EC.

The second problem that I want to cover here is who should decide what weight to assign to Member State interests within Article 81. Two cases should be considered: where the Treaty specifically defines the weight to be assigned to a particular objective; and where the Treaty does not define the weight to be assigned. This last point can be split into two parts, depending upon whether or not the relevant Member State clarifies what weight it believes should be assigned to its objective.

---

[39]   See Chs 2, 4.

[40]   ibid, for a demonstration of several Community public interests; and Ch 3, Section 3.2 showed that national interests are also relevant in Art 81(3) EC.

[41]   Monti (2007) 110–13 and Monti (2002) 1086–88.

[42]   Ch 2, Section 3.2.1.

[43]   Ch 6, Section 3.2.

[44]   This conclusion is not altered by Reg 1/2003, recital 9 and art 3(3): '*Without prejudice to general principles and other provisions of Community law*, paras 1 and 2 do not … preclude the application of provisions of national law that predominantly pursue an objective different from that pursued by Arts 81 and 82 of the Treaty.' (emphasis added). This is secondary legislation and is expressly without prejudice to other provisions of Community law. In any event it is intended to cover a different situation: see, eg Kingston (2001) 342 and Wesseling (1999) 429, 430.

Before entering into the debate, it should be underlined that it is desirable, on legitimacy and legal certainty grounds, for the competent national and Community authorities to assign the weight of public policy goals in advance. For this there must be political and administrative co-ordination and negotiation.[45]

Where the Treaty explicitly sets out the appropriate weight to be assigned to the objective, the position is relatively straightforward. Take the example of public health, this is an area in which, within the limits set by Community law, the Member States retain full competence.[46] Article 152(1) EC demands that 'A high level of human health protection shall be ensured in the definition and implementation of all Community policies and activities.'

Chapter 2 explained why public health issues, where relevant, must be considered in Article 81(3).[47] When performing the Article 81(3) balance, the decision-maker is also bound to give public health the weight ascribed to it in the Treaty, in this case, a high level of protection.[48] Once the weight for all relevant objectives has been established, the decision-maker must combine them to decide the case.

The Treaty rarely defines the weight to be assigned to public policy goals (and specifying a 'high level of protection' is still ambiguous). Consider national policies, such as the security of the energy supply, their weight is not defined in the Treaty. Where a diagonal clash arises between this objective and competition,[49] the decision-maker should be sensitive to the Member States' arguments on the importance of their goals. There are two problems: establishing what weight the Member States give these objectives; and, deciding who should have the final say about this weight, the Member States or the specific decision-maker seized of the case.

It should often be possible for the decision-maker to establish what the Member State concerned thinks its objective's weight should be. This is because the Member State can intervene directly in the matter and articulate the weight that it thinks is appropriate for this goal. Where the relevant Member State decides not to intervene, the decision-maker can invite the Member State to do so. If it does not intervene, then the decision-maker should use its discretion as to what weight to give the national interest.

To my mind, the decision-maker should be bound by the Member States' assigned weight; although the Community Courts would have the ultimate say.[50] This is similar to the issues raised in the Article 28/30 balance.[51] The ECJ discussed this point in cases such as *Henn and Darby*. There, two UK statutes forbade the importation of some types of pornography, which they saw as obscene. The ECJ held:

---

[45]   Schmid (2000) 161 and Deckert (2000) 181. Co-ordination is also possible in specific cases, post Reg 1/2003. The Commission can take Art 81 decisions still, preventing the Member States' authorities from acting, Reg 1/2003, art 10. Where this happens, Member States are still consulted through the Advisory Committee, Commission, *Co-operation Guidelines – NCAs*, s 4.1.1. Even where a Member State's competition authority retains control of a matter, the Commission, as well as other Member States, can discuss the case with them, Commission, *Co-operation Guidelines – NCAs*, s 4.1.2. See also Monti (2004) 408–10.

[46]   Mortelmans (2001) s 6.1.2.3.

[47]   Ch 2, Sections 2 and 3.

[48]   Although there are still quantitative issues to be resolved even here, see Ch 8, Section 3.1.

[49]   See Ch 4, Section 2.7.

[50]   Rodríguez Iglesias and Baquero Cruz (2003) 73, write that the ECJ is '… the final arbiter of the division of powers between the Community and the Member States.' See also, Handoll (1994) 240.

[51]   The issue of a possible public/private divide in the Treaty is discussed in Ch 2, Section 3.1.

In principle, it is for each Member State to determine in accordance with its own scale of values and in the form selected by it the requirements of public morality in its own territory.[52]

This shifts the weight very much in favour of Member States' interests.[53] In the absence of harmonised rules at the Community level,[54] recourse to Article 30 can entail the application of different standards in different Member States, as a result of different national judgments, and different factual circumstances.[55]

Nevertheless, the Community Courts do not completely relinquish control and insist on having the final say on where the balance lies in the free movement of goods provisions. Ultimately, it is for the Community Courts to decide whether or not derogation is justified. In *Campus Oil*, the ECJ held that Article 30's purpose:

> [I]s not to reserve certain matters to the exclusive jurisdiction of the Member States; it merely allows national legislation to derogate from the principle of the free movement of goods to the extent to which this is and remains justified in order to achieve the objectives set out in the article.[56]

A similar point should lie from the derogation of the undistorted competition principle. The Member States should have a limited input into the conditions of competition that they desire on their territory. In the *Wouters* Case, Member State and Community interests were balanced under Article 81(1) EC.[57] Chapter 3 noted that, in that case, the ECJ readily accepted the national assessment of the appropriate balance between competition and the Member State interest.[58] It also accepted that some Member States could legitimately have stricter rules than others.[59] Nevertheless, the ECJ seems to reserve the right to hold that the balance has gone too far through its use of the proportionality test. True, the Community Courts have been more reluctant to interfere in the Article 81(3) balance. Nevertheless, while they would leave the decision-maker a large discretion, they would probably intervene where important Community and Member State interests conflicted within Article 81(3) EC, if the weight that had been assigned was clearly wrong.[60]

Note that, in relation to balancing under Article 81(3), one Member State's interests may affect other Member States' interests. This is because Article 81 only applies where trade between Member States is appreciably affected. This may undermine the balance that the second state seeks to strike as well as restricting both Member States' ability to achieve the goals they seek.[61] Where such a clash takes place, it is for the decision-maker to try to take account of these 'externalities' in its decision.[62]

---

[52]   Case 34/79 *Regina v Henn and Darby*, para 15.
[53]   Schmid (2000) 164.
[54]   Case 72/83 *Campus Oil Limited v Minister for Industry and Energy* para 27.
[55]   See, eg Wyatt and Dashwood (2006) 616–18. See also, Case 94/83, *Albert Heijn* para 16.
[56]   Case 72/83 *Campus Oil v Minister for Industry* para 32. See also, Case 121/85 *Conegate Ltd. v Commissioners of Customs and Excise* paras 15–17; Mortelmans (2001) 622, 635, 637 and O'Loughlin (2003) 62–69.
[57]   Although I argue that this mere-balancing should now only occur in Art 81(3) EC.
[58]   Forrester (2005) 279, 280 and Siragusa (2005) 585, 586. By this I mean the prevailing perception in the Netherlands with respect to the legal profession, Gilliams (2005) 323.
[59]   Discussed in Forrester (2005) 280. Wesseling (1998) 485, refers to the subsidiarity principle in relation to this too, Art 5 EC.
[60]   The Member States may be unhappy about such interference, but they can always add new policy-linking clauses (and specific expressions of an objective's weight) in the next Treaty amendment, to the extent that they think that the right balance is not being achieved. These clauses are desirable as they improve clarity.
[61]   Gual (1995) 41. The same can be said of Art 28 EC.
[62]   I do not mean by this that one should look to the interest of the Community as a whole, as is done in the implementation of Art 87(3) EC, see Case 730/79 *Philip Morris v Commission* paras 24–26; Case C-301/87 *France*

Commission decision, *Ford/Volkswagen,* is an example of how clashes can arise. The joint venture was supposed to create about 15,000 jobs in one of the Community's poorest regions.[63] In the appeal to the CFI, the applicant argued that:

> [T]he project coincides with the closure of several industrial sites in Europe and merely amounts to a transfer of employment from areas where unemployment is high and labour is costly to an area where there is less unemployment and labour is cheaper, so that the joint venture cannot be regarded as contributing to the 'economic and social cohesion' of the Community.[64]

The Commission was bound, if it took account of employment considerations in the decision, to balance the interests of two Member States (Germany and Portugal) when applying Article 81(3) EC.[65]

In conclusion, in cases of diagonal conflict, the Member States' interests, where ascertainable, cannot just be ignored. It is preferable to take account of them in Article 81(3) EC. There is precedent for doing so. The easiest case is where there are policy-linking clauses and the Treaty expressly assigns the weight that certain objectives must be given. The additional clarity provided by such clauses means that, where possible, more should be provided for in other areas of Member State interest. The context can change the weight; here the decision-maker should pay particular attention to the arguments of the Member States. Even where there are no policy-linking clauses, the Member States' balance should be followed if this is ascertainable. However, the benefits to one Member State must not unduly affect another Member State. Where this is the case the decision-maker must take the interests of the others into account in its balancing too.[66] Where the importance that a Member State assigns to a particular goal is unclear then the decision-maker should have discretion about what weight to give it in the balance. In all situations, the Community Courts remain the ultimate arbiters on whether derogation is justified. Given the political sensitivity of diagonal conflicts, the decision-maker should take special care to discuss such cases with all relevant Member States. Indeed, this sort of (highly political) matter is precisely the type which the Commission might reserve for itself, see above.

The final point to consider is the different enforceability of public policy considerations, depending upon who the decision-maker is and the origin of the policy in question. Regulation 1/2003 essentially relies on three types of 'body' for the enforcement of Article 81, the Commission and Member States' competition authorities and courts.[67] In addition,

---

v Commission paras 49–51 and Case C-278/95P, *Siemens v Commission* para 35. It is individual Member State's interests that are important. However, where these undermine other Member States' interests, these must also be taken into account in the balance.

[63]   Commission decision, *Ford/Volkswagen,* para 36.

[64]   ibid, para 89.

[65]   Although it is debatable whether the Commission actually balanced in this way, because, as Ch 2, Section 2.3.1 explained, the CFI found that the Commission's decision was not informed by employment considerations; but even if this were true, the decision provides a good example of how such problems might arise. Note that the Commission argued that no link had been proven between the closure of the German factories and the opening of the Setúbal project, the *Matra* Case para 96.

[66]   It must also be seen to do this. It will be tempting for Member States' courts and competition authorities to, eg, take more account of the effect of an agreement on employment within the jurisdiction of their State, as opposed to that within other Member States, or the Community as a whole. Such acts, or the perception of them, may also lead to tit-for-tat strategies. If a Portuguese court had decided the Commission decision, *Ford/ Volkswagen* matter there may have been such a perception. eg, Jones reports that the *Bundeskartellamt* wanted to prohibit the arrangement, Jones (2004) 27. The Commission must be ready to intervene where bias seems likely. Bellamy suggests referring such cases to the Commission as an independent arbiter, Ehlermann (2001) 271.

[67]   Reg 1/2003, arts 4–6.

the public policy considerations have three different origins. These are the policy-linking clauses, other Treaty aims and objectives, and the Member States' public policy goals. I examine each body in relation to each of these policy sources.

The decision-maker has a lot of discretion in the application of Article 81(3) EC.[68] Having said that, it is important that this discretion, combined with the potentially wide remit of Article 81(3)'s first test, does not mean that there is no control:

> The judicial review of the assessment undertaken in the exercise of this discretion is … limited to ascertaining whether the procedural rules have been complied with, whether proper reasons have been provided, whether the facts have been accurately stated and whether there has been a manifest error of appraisal or misuse of powers …[69]

First, consider the Commission's application of Article 81(3) EC. It must take account of the Treaty objectives supported by one of the policy-linking clauses, for example, the environment, in its decisions. The policy-linking clauses create mandatory obligations,[70] which the Commission is bound to respect.[71] If the Commission clearly did not consider environmental issues, where they were relevant to its decision, then anyone with standing[72] could appeal to the Community Courts, as this would likely be a manifest error of appraisal.[73] The Commission's wide discretion under Article 81(3) means that the Community Courts would be unlikely to interfere with the weight that the Commission attributed to each objective, however.[74] In conclusion, the Commission *must* consider the policy-linking clauses' objectives when it conducts the balance. However, because of the enormous discretion it is given, the Commission can probably effectively elect *what weight to give them.*[75]

For Treaty objectives without a policy-linking clause the position is different. It would be extremely hard to show that specific objectives should be considered, even when it seems clear they would contribute to, for example, the Article 2 aims. In effect, this means that while the Commission *should* consider relevant public policy goals (and it could be challenged for not doing so),[76] pragmatically it will have a lot of *discretion* about whether or not to consider them in a particular case.[77] The same position occurs in relation to the

---

[68]   See the text around Ch 2, n 257.

[69]   Ritter and Braun (2005) 139.

[70]   Art 6, eg, says 'Environmental protection requirements *must be* integrated …' (emphasis added). Although some question the justiciability of these clauses, Lane (1993) 957, 972, 978.

[71]   Art 211 EC says '… the Commission shall: ensure that the provisions of this Treaty … are applied …' See also, Ch 2, Section 3.2.

[72]   See Kerse and Khan (2005) ch 8.

[73]   See Ch 2, Section 3.2.

[74]   Case C-284/95 *Safety Hi-Tech Srl v S & T Srl*, para 37, says there must be a 'manifest error of appraisal'. It was also the implication from the *Échirolles* Case para 25, see Ch 2, Section 2.2. See also, Bailey (2004) 1328; Wesseling (2001) 372; Cooke (2000) 62; Grimeaud (2000) 216, 217; Whelan (1999) 50; Bär and Kraemer (1998) 318, 319 and Evans (1981) 434–36. This is particularly true of policy-linking clauses such as Art 151 (culture), Psychogiopoulou (2006) 585. It is possible that, where a high level of protection is demanded (such as Art 152(1) (public health)), the Community Courts would be more likely to intervene if they thought that the objective had been given insufficient weight in the balance. See the discussion in Dhondt (2003) 147, 148.

[75]   It may be different where the policy-linking clause relates to a Member State interest, see above.

[76]   Environmental issues were considered before the policy-linking clause was added to the Treaty, see, eg McGillivray and Holder (2001) 152–54.

[77]   Although, in Case C-180/96 R *UK v Commission* para 63, the ECJ referred to Art 3(1)(p) on public health. One might argue that this was to show that the Commission should consider health issues in its Common

consideration of Member State public policy goals, which are not protected by a policy-linking clause. In fact, the Commission has even more discretion where there is no policy-linking clause.[78]

Where the enforcer is a Member State's competition authority the position is probably similar, although the reasoning is a little more complex. As regards the policy-linking clauses, most are not directed at the Member States. Nevertheless, one can probably argue that they should take Treaty objectives into account in their decisions. First, they have the Article 10 duty of co-operation. Secondly, Regulation 1/2003 stresses the need for consistency in the application of the competition rules[79] and the Commission will be bound by the policy-linking clauses in its decisions, see above. Temple Lang explains this by saying that, in such circumstances, the Member States are acting as agents or delegates of the Community in implementing its policies.[80] Whatever the motivation, the same logic should apply when the Member States' competition authorities apply Community competition policy through Article 81 EC. This means that the Member States' competition authorities probably should consider the objectives protected through the policy-linking clauses. However, as long as they do this, it is unlikely that, on appeal,[81] the Community Courts would change the balance they actually arrive at.[82] The same applies to Treaty objectives not protected by a policy-linking clause. However, as with the Commission, the difficulty of establishing that such a policy should have been considered means that, in fact, there is a large discretion for the decision-maker to ignore the issue. As regards the Member States' competition authorities' application of Member State objectives, the position is probably the same as it was for the Commission. The Community Courts would be even less likely to interfere in the balance where the policy in question was that of the Member State represented by the competition authority taking the decision;[83] they might intervene more readily where the policy is that of another Member State.

Finally, both points raised above in relation to the need for consistency from the Member States' competition authorities should also apply to judgments of the Member States' courts.[84] The argument in relation to consistency under Regulation 1/2003 is even more powerful.[85]

Agricultural Policy decisions. This might be one way of showing that certain objectives should have been considered. In that case the ECJ also referred to the policy-linking clause for health, which might have made a difference.

[78]   If the Commission does not exercise its discretion in a way that pleases the Member States, they can add more policy-linking clauses in later Treaty changes. In fact, recent Treaty amendments do just this.

[79]   Reg 1/2003, arts 3(1), (2), 16. If the Commission is bound to take account of policy-linking clauses then the Member State body should foresee this and do the same, to avoid a potential future conflict.

[80]   Temple Lang (1991). For similar ideas see Constantinesco (1985) 44.

[81]   In addition, most cases from the Member States' courts will come via Art 234 EC, where the ECJ does not apply the facts to the law.

[82]   Ehlermann suggests that one effect of modernisation might be that the Community Courts will look more closely at decisions in relation to Art 81(3) EC, Ehlermann (2000) 39 and Ehlermann and Atanasiu (2002) 74, 75. The Community Courts are unlikely to feel comfortable performing such an exercise, see Ritter and Braun (2005) 139 and the margin of discretion that the ECJ was prepared to allow in *Wouters* and *Meca Medina*.

[83]   This could lead to political tension if a Member States' own competition authority gives 'disproportionate' weight to a national policy consideration. A challenge might lie in extreme cases, but normally the weighting of such issues is for the decision-maker and will not be overturned, see above.

[84]   See, eg in relation to Art 10 EC, Lenaerts and Arts (1999), para 5–032.

[85]   Reg 1/2003, arts 3, 16(1).

3 THE SECOND TEST:
CONSUMERS' FAIR SHARE OF THE RESULTING BENEFIT[86]

The second Article 81(3) condition states that the agreement must allow '… consumers a fair share of the resulting benefit …' This provision raises three key issues: what is a 'benefit'?; how much of this consumers should get; and the definition of 'consumer'. I start by briefly examining the first two issues, but the focus is on the definition of 'consumer'.

In relation to the definition of 'benefit', the Commission now focuses on economic benefits.[87] However, there is widespread agreement that non-economic benefits are also relevant,[88] although only economic benefits are normally considered.[89] The Commission would probably say the same today,[90] remember that it has said that 'Goals pursued by other Treaty provisions can be taken into account to the extent that they can be subsumed under the four conditions of Article 81(3) …'[91]

The second issue is, how much of the resulting benefit consumers should get. The Treaty does not define a 'fair share' either.[92] The Commission has said:

> The concept of '*fair share*' implies that the pass-on of benefits must at least compensate consumers for any actual or likely negative impact caused to them by the restriction of competition found under Article 81(1).[93]

Even this is not obvious, one could argue that where, for example, an agreement would generate considerable environmental benefits, for society as a whole, it is *fair* that those that consume pay extra to achieve this.[94] Whatever is ultimately decided, it is hard to produce a precise definition in the abstract[95] and the decision-maker has a lot of discretion.[96] In the past, a fair share has been established relatively easily.[97]

These issues are important, but Section 3's focus is the definition of 'consumer' in Article 81(3). The concept of a 'consumer' in Article 81 EC is unclear. Perhaps as a result, the Commission has not defined it consistently. Starting with an analysis of the ordinary

---

[86]   Thanks to Heli Askola, Galina Cornelisse, Johanna Engstroem, Poul Noer, Assimakis Komninos, Tobias Witschke and Lorenzo Zucca for their comments on some different Treaty language versions.

[87]   Commission, *Article 81(3) Guidelines*, paras 83–104.

[88]   Whish (2008) 153–55, but note pp 155, 156; Cseres (2007) 161–64, as regards the past; Vedder (2003) 170–74; Monti (2002) 1075; Jans (2000) 280; Bouterse (1994) 28 and Jacobs (1993/2) 56.

[89]   For examples of when the Commission has considered non-economic objectives there, even, arguably, when economic benefits were not present, see Commission decisions, *Jahrhundertvertrag* and *VIK-GVSt*, para 32 and *International Energy Agency* (1994), para 6(b). It has said, eg, that the use of cleaner facilities will result in less air pollution, and consequently in direct and indirect benefits for consumers from reduced negative externalities, Commission decision, *Philips-Osram*, para 27. See also, Commission decisions, *KSB/Goulds/Lowera/ITT*, para 27; *REIMS II*, paras 77–85 and *CECED*, paras 47–57. In *CECED* Art 81(3)'s first and second tests are merged together, so it is difficult to know how important environmental issues were under each head.

[90]   For a contrary view see Cseres (2007) 164–66.

[91]   Commission, *Article 81(3) Guidelines*, para 42. See also para 89. Furthermore, it is the overall benefit that is relevant, there is no need for consumers to participate in all benefits, they must just be better off overall, Commission, *Article 81(3) Guidelines*, para 86 and Jacobs (1993/2) 56.

[92]   Lyons (2002) 1.

[93]   Commission, *Article 81(3) Guidelines*, para 85. See also, Lyons (2002) 1.

[94]   Although see Evans (1985) 102 in this regard.

[95]   Whish (2003) 156.

[96]   Jones and Sufrin (2001) 196.

[97]   See Cseres (2007) 161; Reich (1997) 133, and the references made there; Faull and Nikpay (1999), para 2.156 and Bourgoignie (1985a) 430.

meaning of 'consumer' and then considering this term in the light of the objectives and spirit of the Treaty, I examine the Commission's latest views and discuss the implications of this for balancing non-economic objectives within Article 81.

The *Oxford English Dictionary* defines 'consumer' as a purchaser of goods or services. It can be any purchaser, but there is an inference that the purchaser is '… an individual who buys goods and services for personal use rather than for manufacture, processing or resale.'[98] for the purposes of Section 3, 'private end-users'.

Many of the different language versions of the Treaty employ an equivalent word to 'consumer', implying that an agreement can only be exempted if it can be shown that a fair share of the resulting benefit goes to private end-users.[99] Other language versions utilise the more ambiguous term 'user', which could include private end-users, but also embraces those that will use these goods or services for manufacture, processing or resale, including firms that buy from the parties to the agreement.[100]

It may be helpful to illustrate the distinction with an example. Imagine that two companies, A and B, manufacture sulphuric acid. They set up a joint purchasing pool for sulphur. A and B sell all their sulphuric acid to C and D. C, a large multinational, uses all of its sulphuric acid in a further industrial process to make synthetic detergent. C sells the synthetic detergent directly to private end-users, E, in its factory shop. D is a wholesaler that sells all of its sulphuric acid to privately owned schools, F. Pupils, G, attend chemistry lessons at F, from whom they buy sulphuric acid for their experiments.

If A and B's agreement falls within Article 81(1) it will need an Article 81(3) exemption. For this to happen, amongst other things, consumers must get a fair share of the resulting benefit. We have seen that the consumers might be those that: (i) 'consume' the sulphuric acid, G (C is not using it in a private sense); or (ii) 'use' the sulphuric acid, even in a business sense, C, D, F and G. The English language version suggests the former; the French language version the latter.[101]

The Commission is not normally explicit about who the consumer is in Article 81(3). On the rare occasions that it is, the Commission has not been consistent.[102] Sometimes it:

– only considers the benefits of those that buy directly from the parties, whether or not they are end-users, in our example, C and D;[103]
– considers the benefits for the end-users of the relevant product:

---

[98]   Ammer and Ammer (1977).

[99]   This interpretation is supported by the Danish language version of the Treaty, '*forbrugerne*'; the Finnish language version, '*kuluttajat*'; the German language version, '*verbraucher*'; the Greek language version, '*katanalotes*'; as well as the Swedish language version, '*konsumenterna*'.

[100]   This is the implication of the Dutch language version, '*gebruikers*'; the French language version, '*utilisateurs*'; the Italian language version, '*utilazzatori*'; the Portuguese language version, '*utilizadores*'; and the Spanish language version, '*usuarios*'.

[101]   The definition could be widened even further by assessing the agreement's effects on those that 'consume' or 'use' products *derived from* the sulphuric acid too. In this case, E would be included too.

[102]   Except in one sense. In a vertical agreement, the buyer of the products covered by the agreement is normally one of the parties to the agreement (by definition). The Commission is not interested in any benefits the parties may get from the agreement in relation to this provision, see Commission decision, *P&I Clubs*, OJ 1985 L376/2 paras 40, 41 and Commission, *Article 81(3) Guidelines*, para 84.

[103]   Commission decisions, *Enichem/ICI*, paras 38, 39 and *Bayer/BP Chemicals*, OJ 1988 L150/34 paras 32–34.

- sometimes confining itself to an examination of the benefits for end-users, in our example, C and G;[104]
- often assessing the benefits to those downstream, between the parties to the agreement and the end-users, in our example, C, D, F and G;[105]

– considers the benefits for the 'consumers' of the products made with the relevant product, in our example, E. Here the Commission has confined itself to an examination of the benefits for the end-users of the derived product,[106] ignoring those higher up the distribution chain;

– combines these four approaches; and,[107]

– analyses the benefits to society as a whole.[108]

In 2004, the Commission helpfully sought to clarify its position:

> The concept of '*consumers*' encompasses all direct or indirect users of the products covered by the agreement, including producers that use the products as an input, wholesalers, retailers and final consumers, ie natural persons who are acting for purposes which can be regarded as outside their trade or profession. In other words, consumers within the meaning of Article 81(3) are the customers of the parties to the agreement and subsequent purchasers.[109]

This explains that 'consumers' includes all direct and indirect users of the products covered by the agreement. Some ambiguity remains, in relation to whether a fair share of the benefit must accrue to the customers of the parties to the agreement *as well as* subsequent purchasers,[110] ie must there be a fair share of the benefit to all those downstream.[111] However, the Commission has also said 'The decisive factor is the overall impact on consumers of the products within the relevant market and not the impact on individual members of this group of consumers …'[112] The emphasis on consumers *within the relevant market* might support the idea that only the buyers from the party must benefit, but this seems contrary to the preceding citation.[113]

To sum up so far, the different language versions of Article 81(3) introduce ambiguity and the Commission's application of this provision has been inconsistent. Commission

---

[104] Commission decisions, *SPCA – Kali und Salz*, 5; *Kali und Salz/Kali Chemie* 25, 26; *Beecham/Parke, Davis*, para 38; *Vimpoltu*, para 49; *Synthetic Fibres*, paras 39–41 and *LH/SAS*, paras 74, 75.

[105] Commission decisions, *Uniform Eurocheques*, para 38; *ARG/Unipart*, para 41; *Eurocheque: Helsinki Agreement*, paras 67–70 and *FRUBO*, 21.

[106] Commission decision, *Film purchases by German television stations*, para 54, and possibly also Commission decision, *Bayer/Gist-Brocades*, para 2.

[107] Commission decisions, *MasterCard*, para 693; *Rennet*, para 30; *National Sulphuric Acid Association*, para 47; *Rockwell/Iveco*, para 9; *Schlegel*, para 20; *Ivoclar*, para 23; *Rich Products/Jus-rol*, para 42; *BBC Brown Boveri*, para 24; *Cekacan*, para 45 and *GEAE/P&W*, paras 81, 82.

[108] Commission decisions, *Continental/Michelin*, para 27; *KSB/Goulds/Lowera/ITT*, para 27; *Philips – Osram*, para 27; *P&I Clubs*, OJ 1999 L125/12 para 108 and *CECED*, paras 47–57.

[109] Commission, *Article 81(3) Guidelines*, para 84.

[110] This appears to be contrary to the CFI's judgment in *Glaxo*, paras 244, 258, 267, 273, although, see, eg para 259. This judgment is currently on appeal to the ECJ, in part on this issue, see Joined Cases C-501/06 etc. *GlaxoSmithKline Services v Commission*.

[111] Also, 'direct and indirect' may either include users of derived products, in our example E, or direct and indirect purchasers of the specific product. Kjølbye (2004) 575, suggests the latter. The Commission, *Article 81(3) Guidelines* are unclear on this point too.

[112] Commission, *Article 81(3) Guidelines*, para 87, see also paras 43, 89, 103, 104.

[113] Alternatively, it may refer to the situation where the parties themselves supply into different relevant markets? Also note that Commission, *Article 81(3) Guidelines*, para 90 states '… if the restrictive effects of an agreement are relatively limited and the efficiencies are substantial it is likely that a fair share of the cost savings will be passed on to consumers.' This might imply that we need only look at the parties' customers.

Article 81(3) Guidelines seek to impose order, but they do not. They seem to merge both the French and English language versions. In so doing the Commission may have introduced a twist. 'Consumers' are defined as *all* (direct and indirect) users of the products covered by the agreement. This may mean that in each market downstream of the parties to the agreement, the consumers must obtain (or perhaps all downstream markets must collectively obtain) a fair share of the agreement's resulting benefit.

The first principle of interpretation is to look at the ordinary meaning of the word in its context and in light of the Treaty objectives.[114] Predicting how the Community Courts will react to the Commission's 'clarification' is difficult because all the language versions of the Treaty are authentic, Article 314 EC. It cannot be assumed that the Community Courts will adopt the meaning indicated by the majority of the texts. In *Elefanten Schuh v Jacqmain*,[115] the ECJ followed the French and Irish texts of Article 18 of the *EC Brussels Convention*, ignoring the wording of the Danish, Dutch, English, German and Italian texts. The ECJ explained that it had followed the French and Irish texts because they '... were more in keeping with the objectives and spirit of the Convention.'[116] This is the teleological approach to Treaty interpretation so often emphasised by the Community Courts. It will only help us here if I can determine what the Community Courts believe Article 81(3)'s *telos* to be. In this respect, it may be helpful to analyse the effect that the various interpretations might have on the relevant actors.

At first sight, the 'French version' is unsatisfactory. In effect, it means that those downstream of the parties to the agreement are considered more worthy of surplus than those upstream. In many cases this will simply mean favouring downstream undertakings at the expense of those above them; and, it is unclear why one would want to favour such firms in and of themselves.[117] Furthermore, it would be both difficult and expensive to assess *every* downstream market.

Alternatively, in light of the environmental policy-linking clause, Article 6 EC, Jans suggests looking at the benefits to society as a whole, as opposed to consumers in particular.[118] However, Monti argues that construing the provision in this way is problematic, because it collapses Article 81(3)'s first and second tests.[119] An additional problem is which society is important?[120]

The Commission has certainly caused a lot of confusion here. Not only have its decisions considered societal benefits under Article 81(3)'s second test, its notices also

---

[114] Case 53/81 *Levin v Staatssecretaris van Justitie* para 9.

[115] Case 150/80 *Elefanten Schuh v Pierre Jacqmain* paras 12–17.

[116] ibid, para 14. The ECJ looks at how many language versions of the Treaty say 'X', but this is only to support what on other grounds seems the best interpretation, Jacobs (2003) 304.

[117] One suggestion is that a core aim of EC competition law is to protect market participants' economic freedom, Monti (2007) 99. However, the CFI held in the *Glaxo* Case, para 273, that the legitimacy of a wealth transfer from producer to intermediary is not in itself of interest to competition law, which is concerned only with its impact on the welfare of the final consumer. The *Glaxo* Case is now on appeal, see references in n 110 above.

[118] Jans (2000) 280, 281. Jacobs (1993/2) 57, discusses a similar concept.

[119] Monti (2002) 1076, 1077. See also Heimler and Fattori (1998) 599; Tesauro (1998) 223 and Evans (1985) 103, 104, 113.

[120] What happens if the relevant geographic market partially covers several Member States and even non-Member States, for example?

speak of societal benefits.[121] Furthermore, some of the Commission's decisions actually merge its analysis of Article 81(3)'s first and second tests.[122]

Monti's critique seems to focus on the wording of Article 81(3)'s second test. This merely says that '… consumers [must get] a fair share of the resulting benefit …' It does not state that these must be the consumers of the products in question. This may be acceptable on a purely (English) reading of the text; however, such an interpretation would be in direct contradiction with the French, Italian, Portuguese and Spanish texts.[123] These languages all refer to *the users*. This is more specific than the English text and seems to exclude the generalisation of the term to society as a whole.[124]

Another approach is that of Vedder. He distinguishes between economic and non-economic benefits, arguing that:

> Only with regard to the economic benefits of an agreement … is closer scrutiny in the form of the determination of an individual fair share called for. This is inherent in the purpose of the requirement of establishing a fair share for consumers, which … is to ascertain that only advantages that not only benefit the parties themselves are exempted. Environmental benefits, by their very nature, cannot be kept for oneself. Economic benefits, on the contrary, may very well not be passed on to consumers.[125]

This is similar to Jans' argument, although Vedder adds a kind of teleological point too. He says that, unlike economic ones, non-economic benefits cannot be reserved to the parties. As a result, there is no need to analyse the pass-on of non-economic benefits.

There is some logic in this position.[126] However, the core of Vedder's point is that the second test ensures that not only the parties benefit from the agreement. But, as we have already seen, the French language version seems to require something more, that a specific group (users) must benefit too. Secondly, the Commission does not distinguish between economic and non-economic benefits when it refers to societal benefits (nor does the Treaty[127]). Indeed, it has expressly referred to societal benefits in relation to economic efficiencies:

---

[121] Commission, *Article 81(3) Guidelines*, para 85. True, these comments come after a discussion of consumers, but why are societal benefits mentioned if they are not relevant?

[122] Commission decisions, *Visa International – MIF*, paras 74–95 and *CECED*, paras 47–57.

[123] The French text says '… *tout en réservant aux utilisateurs une partie équitable …*'; the Italian text says '… *pur riservando agli utilizzatori una congrua parte …*'; the Portuguese text says '… *contanto que aos utilizadores se reserve uma parte equitativa …*' and the Spanish text says '… *y reserven al mismo tiempo a los usarios una participación equitativa …*'

[124] Although, relying on the French text, Commentaire Mégret (1997), para 222, adopts a similar position to Jans, '… *à notre avis, la notion d'utilisateur doit être entendue comme comprenant toute personne autre que les parties à l'entente.*' This view is based on Commission decision, *P&I Clubs*, OJ 1985 L376/2 where the Commission said that it was not enough that just the parties benefited. However, in that decision the Commission did not look to benefits for society as a whole. As para 41 it said '… it must be shown that persons other than the insured themselves, *namely transport users who are their customers, and the final consumers, also benefit from the agreement in question.* (emphasis added)' In the same para Commentaire Mégret (1997) also seeks to rely on the *Metro I* Case para 48. But here the ECJ expressly refers to the consumer benefit of improved supplies, which I do not think can be understood as society as a whole, but rather users.

[125] Vedder (2003) 173.

[126] That said, it is unlikely that Art 81(3) was originally designed with non-economic objectives in mind; which makes one wonder why the second test was originally inserted.

[127] See the *Consten and Grundig* Case, 339 and the *Glaxo* Case para 280.

[S]ociety as a whole benefits where the efficiencies lead either to fewer resources being used to produce the output consumed or to the production of more valuable products and thus to a more efficient allocation of resources.[128]

Furthermore, Vedder's suggestion ignores the fact that consumers need not benefit from every type of benefit, but must just get a fair share of the *overall* benefit, see above. It may be that an agreement generates some economic benefits and a lot of environmental benefits. Where this is the case, and the parties reserve all the economic benefits to themselves, Vedder's method would not be able to assess whether consumers got a fair share overall. The Commission (implicitly) seems to accept this point.[129] In addition, where an agreement only generated non-economic gains, according to Vedder, Article 81(3)'s second test would be irrelevant. The Community Courts could read his interpretation into the provision, but I do not think they would readily do so.

To return to the Commission's preferred definition of consumers, defined as both direct and indirect users, see above, the assessment will have to be made on many markets, especially if users of derived products are also considered. As a result, the group of relevant consumers could become extensive. In this case, it may be that references to examining the overall benefits to society are merely shorthand for a detailed analysis of consumers on each and every relevant market. Although I prefer the English definition of consumer, to that implied by the French language version of the Treaty, use of this shorthand would sit comfortably with my desire to avoid a partial equilibrium analysis.[130] However, the Commission has not embraced this shorthand; as we have seen, it may insist that one assess the overall benefits *on each relevant market.*[131]

There are some possible alternative definitions. It might be advantageous, for example, to interpret 'consumers' in Article 81(3) EC as private end-users of the goods or services covered by the agreement, in our example G.[132] This would be in line with, amongst others, the English and German versions of the Treaty. The Preamble tells us that the essential objective of the Member States' Treaty efforts is '... the constant improvement of the living and working conditions of their peoples ...' Article 2 EC talks of '... the raising of the standard of living and quality of life ... ' Ensuring that private end-users benefit from anti-competitive agreements would help promote this end.[133]

Other justifications can be found in the Treaty for this approach. The English language version, for example, uses the same word for 'consumer' in Article 81(3), as is used in Article 153 EC, in relation to 'consumer protection' (essentially private end-user).[134] This occurs in other language versions too,[135] although not in all of them.[136] Perhaps the

---

[128]   *Article 81(3) Guidelines*, para 85.

[129]   Ch 4, Section 2.3 and Ch 8, Section 4 show it attempting to quantify the *extent* of environmental benefits in Commission decision, *CECED*, for example.

[130]   See Ch 6, Section 3.

[131]   Commission, *Article 81(3) Guidelines*, paras 43, 89, 103, 104.

[132]   I may choose to include within this definition private end-users of derivative products too, in my example E. This is discussed later in the text. In the interim, I do not include these end-users in my definition of consumers.

[133]   Although, depending upon the relevant geographic market, some non-EU private end-users might also benefit.

[134]   See, eg Council Directive, *On unfair terms in consumer contracts* (2005), art 2(a), which restricts the notion of consumers to natural persons who are acting outside their trade, business, craft or profession. Thanks to Giorgio Monti for this point. See also Cseres (2007) 131.

[135]   This is the case in the Danish, English, Finnish, German, Greek and Swedish texts.

[136]   The Dutch, French, Italian, Portuguese and Spanish texts all use a different term in relation to those considered worthy of consumer protection in Art 153 EC.

Danish, English, Finnish, German, Greek and Swedish language versions of the Treaty implicitly carry within them the idea that a 'consumer', as used in Article 81(3) EC, is someone who needs protection. The definition of consumer protection in Article 153 EC is wide enough to include consumers' economic interests. Article 153(1) reads:

> In order to promote the interests of consumers and to ensure a high level of consumer protection, the Community shall contribute to protecting the health, safety *and economic interests of consumers*, as well as to promoting their right to information, education and to organise themselves in order to safeguard their interests.[137] (emphasis added)

Defining 'consumer' in this way would also give weight to Article 153(2) EC, which states 'Consumer protection requirements shall be taken into account in defining and implementing other Community policies and activities.'

Interpreting the word 'consumers' in Article 81(3) to mean that private end-users should get a fair share of the agreement's resulting benefit should appeal to the Commission. Former Commissioner Monti has said that this contributes '… to an image of the European Union as a project not only of politicians, or for the benefit of business, but as a project for the people.'[138] This interpretation of 'consumer' also receives support from the Community Courts. In relation to Article 82, for example, the ECJ differentiates between customers and consumers:

> Article 86 [now Article 82] prohibits any abuse by an undertaking of a dominant position . . . The dominant position thus referred to relates to a position of economic strength enjoyed by an undertaking which enables it to prevent effective competition being maintained on the relevant market by affording it the power to behave to an appreciable extent independently of its competitors, its *customers and ultimately of the consumers.* (emphasis added)[139]

If Article 81(3)'s second test is to be read as a consumer protection provision,[140] we must define exactly who needs protection. It seems coherent with the Treaty Preamble and Article 2 EC to adopt the same concept as that used in relation to 'consumer' in Article 153.[141] It is unclear why the Commission should intervene to protect other firms here, unless this would ultimately benefit private end users.[142]

---

[137]   Art 153(1) EC demonstrates why one might want a consumer protection interpretation of Art 81(3), even if Art 81(1) contains a consumer welfare standard. This is because the interests protected by consumer protection standards are often wider than those consumer welfare focuses on, see also Cseres (2007) 136. In addition, both consumer and competition policy can reinforce each other, Haracoglou (2006), s 3.

[138]   Mario Monti (2001a). See also Kroes (2008a); Kroes (2005) and Haracoglou (2006), s 4.2.

[139]   Case 85/76 *Hoffmann-La Roche v Commission* para 38. See also, the *Glaxo* Case para 171; the *Metro I* Case para 47; the *Matra* Case paras 120–25; Case T-30/89 *Hilti AG v Commission* para 90 and Case 27/76 *United Brands and United Brands Continentaal v Commission* para 65, *cf* Case 6/72 *Europemballage Corp and Continental Can Co v Commission*, para II.3. Thanks to Giorgio Monti for this argument.

In the French version of these judgments the ECJ uses yet another word '*consommateurs*'. Also, in the *Pavlov* Case the ECJ refers to *final* consumers (although this may be a literal translation from the French 'utilisateur final'), para 81. This undermines the weight of this point somewhat.

[140]   Monti (2002) 1075–77, suggests it already is. See also, Commission decision, *VW*, para 189, when discussing the possibility of an individual exemption of an agreement, the Commission said that this could not be contemplated. The agreement had not been notified and 'The export ban/restriction is in serious contradiction with the objective of consumer protection which Art 85(3) [now Art 81(3)] makes an integral part of the Community's competition rules.'

[141]   This is also in line with my emphasis on benefiting citizens, Ch 1, Section 2.1.

[142]   Economic freedom, if relevant, can be considered in Art 81(3)'s first test.

Most of the actors in our example are established companies acting in the course of their business, so they would be unlikely to be considered 'consumers' in this sense. The only exception to this is G, who is a private individual.[143] Therefore, if we interpret 'consumer' in this way, we must assess whether or not G (and possibly E, if we decide to include consumers of derived products) gets a fair share of the resulting benefit.

Some imply that reading Article 81(3)'s second test as a consumer protection provision would be inappropriate, because, so the argument goes, competition and consumer law have different goals.[144] I disagree with this implication though; while the goals of these two disciplines may not perfectly overlap, there are many Commission and CFI statements that make it clear that Community competition law is there for the benefit of private end-users.[145] One might also argue that reliance on Article 153 EC in order to define 'consumer' within Article 81(3), is misleading; when the Treaty was adopted in 1957 it did not embrace the concept of consumer protection.[146] Therefore, so the argument goes, one cannot read this concept into Article 81(3)'s *telos*. However, this misconstrues the Community Courts' teleological approach; the Community Courts interpret the Treaty in light of its objectives, *as they see them today*.[147]

However, inserting the consumer protection notion into Article 81(3)'s second test creates two major problems. First, particularly in horizontal agreements that fall within Article 81, the parties will rarely sell directly to 'consumers'. We would need to examine every level of trade between the parties and the consumers to ensure that competition exists there too. If fierce competition does not exist in *all* downstream levels, even if there is perfect competition at the parties' level, then it is unlikely that the surplus that the agreement creates will be passed right down the supply chain. As a result, private end-users may not get a fair share of the benefit. Assessing all downstream levels would be an enormous task.[148] It is also unfair on the parties[149] and reduces welfare for society as a whole. This is because, in effect, even agreements in fiercely competitive markets that create large benefits under Article 81(3)'s first test may breach Article 81(3) if competition is not fierce in all downstream markets. This, in turn, reduces the parties' ability to compete with their rivals on the merits. It also undermines the efficient allocation of resources and increases firms' incentives to vertically integrate. Such distorted incentives are probably inefficient and costly to society.

---

[143]   For ease of reference, I repeat the original example relied on here. Imagine that two companies, A and B, manufacture sulphuric acid. They set up a joint purchasing pool for sulphur. A and B sell all their sulphuric acid to C and D. C, a large multinational, uses all of its sulphuric acid in a further industrial process to make synthetic detergent. C sells the synthetic detergent directly to private end-users, E, in its factory shop. D is a wholesaler that sells all of its sulphuric acid to privately owned schools, F. Pupils, G, attend chemistry lessons at F, from whom they buy sulphuric acid for their experiments.

[144]   Cseres (2007) 133.

[145]   See the cases in n 139 above, particularly the *Glaxo* Case; Mario Monti (2001a) and Kroes (2008a).

[146]   This is, in fact, debatable, Evans (1981) 425, notes that when the consumer protection initiative started in the 1970s the Community institutions '… were quick to point out that the promotion of consumer interests had been implicit in their earlier work, especially the implementation of competition policy.'

[147]   See Ch 6, Section 2.2.1.

[148]   In some of its decisions, the Commission implies that it has carried out such an assessment in downstream markets. See, eg Commission decisions, *SABA*, para 43; *National Sulphuric Acid Association*, para 47; *SABA's EEC distribution system* 50; *Yves Rocher*, paras 61, 62; *Pronuptia*, para 35 and *EBU/Eurovision*, para 68. The ECJ obliquely refers to such an analysis in the *Metro I* Case para 47, although it did not impose it as a general requirement in all cases there.

[149]   Who cannot normally *ensure* that the benefits are passed down through markets where they might not even operate, Commentaire Mégret (1997), para 222 and Evans (1985) 101, 109.

This leads us to the second problem that incorporating a consumer protection notion into Article 81(3) creates. Many goods and services do not have consumers, (private end-users), or have very few (as opposed to 'consumers' of derived products); think, for example, of large commercial aircraft. For such products and services one could either ignore the second Article 81(3) provision; or, consider the effects on the consumers of the derived products, in our example E. The latter would be preferable, the Community Courts will not ignore Treaty provisions lightly. But, if these 'derived consumers' are included then the assessment becomes extremely complex. Manufacturers often sell to hundreds, if not thousands, of customers. There may be millions of derived consumers. It would be very difficult for the decision-maker, and impossible for private parties, to assess whether all these groups of derived consumers got a fair share of the resulting benefit.

One could infer the necessary consumer benefits merely by checking that these were passed on to the customers of the parties to the agreement, if vigorous competition exists at all levels of production and distribution between the parties to the agreement[150] and the 'consumers' (derived or not). However, assessing this could still be Herculean.

The conclusion so far is that there are good reasons, from a political and teleological perspective, to interpret 'consumer' within Article 81(3) EC, as a private end-user. However, refusing exemption unless *private end-users* get a fair share of an agreement's resulting benefit complicates the analysis immensely and may often mean that beneficial agreements (in Community terms) will not be allowed. This is unfair on the parties, as it will undermine their ability to compete on the merits and reduces society's welfare.

However, there may be a way of focusing on benefits to private end users, ie achieving these consumer protection goals, while avoiding these complexities. Interpreting consumers as private end-users was not the only possibility. The French word '*utilisateur*' also includes those that buy from the parties to the agreement. I said above that, at first sight, this did not seem satisfactory.[151] In fact, when one considers the issue in more detail, the benefits of a 'refined French approach' become clearer. Imagine that every level of manufacturing and distribution below the parties to the agreement is competitive. Remember too that competitive pressures will normally ensure that cost-savings (or other benefits) are passed on by way of lower prices, etc. This means that as long as one can ensure that a fair share of the benefits created by the agreement *are passed on to the parties' customers*, then these benefits should be passed on, right down the supply chain, to the private end-users.[152] To the extent that there is insufficient competition at every level beneath the parties to the agreement, the competition authorities should intervene to improve this, rather than outlaw beneficial agreements generated by undertakings competing on the merits upstream.[153]

---

[150] Commission, *Vertical Guidelines*, para 136 and Commission, *Horizontal Guidelines*, para 34, which say 'Generally the transmission of the benefits to consumers will depend on the intensity of competition on the relevant market. Competitive pressures will normally ensure that cost-savings are passed on by way of lower prices or that companies have an incentive to bring new products to the market as quickly as possible.' See also, Commission, *Article 81(3) Guidelines*, para 96.

[151] See the text around n 117 above.

[152] EAGCP Report (2005) 8.

[153] The exception to this is where the effects of the commercial conduct on intermediate purchasers are different to those on private end-users. This is quite rare, but exceptions can be found; see, eg the *Glaxo* Case and Cseres (2007) 131, 132, 159, 160.

Pelkmans criticises this suggestion. He believes that Article 81(3) demands that certain direct benefits, as opposed to merely indirect efficiency ones, be passed on to consumers.[154] However, he does not explain or justify this view; which is hard to understand because Article 81(3) does not distinguish between the types of benefits involved; nor do the Community Courts or the Commission, in their application of this provision. Perhaps the idea is similar to that of Evans, when he notes that:

> [W]hile the benefit for intermediaries in the economic process lies in profitability and the benefit for consumers as members of the public lies in the broader notion of consumer satisfaction, the Commission does not appear to recognise such a distinction.[155]

The private end-user might get consumer satisfaction from, for example, a certain amount of choice in relation to the products in question. This would increase marketing and distribution costs and so, Evans seems to assume, that, for example, it conflicts with the intermediaries' profitability and would be ignored in an assessment of their benefits. However, this need not always be the case. In a competitive market, the intermediaries should be receptive to consumer demand. If consumers value increased choice enough to pay for it then, in theory, the intermediaries would take account of this, and the two concepts would no longer conflict. Pelkmans is right in that direct consumer benefits should *also* be relevant here, but I see no reason why the provision should relate exclusively to them.

As a result, it certainly seems to be *acceptable*, to deem Article 81(3)'s second condition to be fulfilled where it can be shown that a fair share of the resulting benefits are passed on to private end-users. However, for the reasons outlined above, it should not be *necessary* to show that this group receives a fair share of the resulting benefit. Where all downstream markets are efficient, one can normally achieve the consumer protection aim by ensuring that the parties to the agreement pass a fair share of their agreement's benefit on *to their customers.* One does not normally need to look any further, even if they are not private end-users. Even if not all downstream markets are competitive (so that these benefits are not, in fact, passed down to private end-users), then the best strategy is to ensure that these markets become competitive. It is not to refuse exemption for an otherwise acceptable agreement in the upstream market.

It is hard to justify Article 81(3)'s second test on anything other than consumer protection grounds. I have suggested a practicable mechanism for the assessment of this objective, ie the transfer of benefits to the parties' direct customers. In my view, this is how Article 81(3)'s second objective should be interpreted.

Consumer protection is an important Treaty objective. It should be considered within Article 81.[156] Chapter 2 argued that the Commission and the Community Courts have widened Article 81(3)'s first test to a public interest balancing exercise. This would likely include consumer protection, particularly in light of Article 153(2)'s policy linking clause. The Commission may have already considered it there.[157] One might argue that this means

---

[154] Pelkmans (1985) 32, 33. See also Evans (1985) 109.
[155] Evans (1985) 105.
[156] Also, see the arguments of the Plaintiff, Case 249/85 *Albako Margarinefabrik v Bundesanstalt für landwirtschaftliche,* 2348 and Case C-376/92 *Metro SB-Großmärkte v Cartier,* see the Opinion of A-G Tesauro para 33, '… considerations relating to *consumer protection* … should not be unconnected with the interpretation of Art 85 [now Art 81] of the Treaty.'
[157] See Ch 4, Section 2.4.

that I am wrong to interpret both the first and second Article 81(3) tests as incorporating consumer protection. I disagree. First, in relation to Article 81(3)'s first test, I think it vital that consumer protection is considered there to ensure that the optimal balance is achieved. The insistence that Article 81(3)'s second test contain a consumer protection goal is another example of how a *détournement de pouvoir* can be avoided; even an optimal balance under Article 81(3)'s first test is insufficient unless the agreement also generates consumer benefits; otherwise, tools outside competition law must be used to achieve the public policy gains.

4 THE THIRD TEST: INDISPENSABILITY, ARTICLE 81(3)(a)

The indispensability test is an important limit on the balancing to be conducted within Article 81(3)'s first test. This section starts by explaining how this test limits the balance and then suggests a more radical way of interpreting the provision, which would further enhance the weight given to consumer welfare in Article 81, with all the benefits this brings.

Consideration of many Community and Member State interests is necessary within Article 81 EC. The best place for this is Article 81(3)'s first test. The fact that all relevant objectives can be openly considered there means that other provisions and definitions within Article 81 are less likely to be distorted. This should lead to a more open and transparent application of the provision.[158]

Nevertheless, such a wide balancing test in Article 81(3) EC demands an extensive and complex analysis. It could also provide ample scope for fundamentally undermining the market mechanism, depending upon how much 'weight' competition is given in the balance. While this possibility sometimes reflects the balance advocated within the Treaty, Sections 3 (consumers must get a fair share of the benefit) and 5 (Article 81(3)(b)) of this chapter examine Article 81(3) provisions that seem designed to limit the influence of the possibility of exemption.

The limit on the consideration of public policy goals discussed in Sections 3 and 5 is different from that advocated by my theoretical conclusion in Chapter 1. There I said that ignoring non-economic policy objectives when applying competition law can create significant benefits, in terms of enhanced legal certainty; which encourage firms to invest and innovate. That said, at a certain point the benefits that enhanced legal certainty brings may be outweighed by the importance of the policy goals it undermines. Even then, it may be better to focus on a pure welfare test in competition policy if these non-welfare goals can be adequately protected through other legislative tools that more efficiently promote them.[159]

Remember that Chapter 1 arrived at its conclusions in a legal vacuum. It did not take account of the various demands that the Treaty's structure or provisions make about the consideration of non-economic objectives within Article 81. Section 4 does this by analysing the third Article 81(3) 'limit', the 'indispensability test', agreements must not

---

[158]   See Ch 6, Section 3.
[159]   See Ch 1, Section 3.2.

'... impose on the undertakings concerned restrictions which are not indispensable to the attainment of these objectives.'[160] The indispensability test reminds us that although non-economic objectives can be weighed within Article 81(3), competition can only be undermined where this is indispensable.

Article 81(3)(a) EC embodies a three stage test. As a preliminary step, there must be a balancing exercise to assess which combination of objectives should be achieved by the agreement in question.[161] Then the decision-maker must ensure that:

> First, the restrictive agreement as such must be reasonably necessary in order to achieve the efficiencies. Secondly, the individual restrictions of competition that flow from the agreement must also be reasonably necessary for the attainment of the efficiencies.[162]

The indispensability test does not only apply to restrictions necessary in order to achieve efficiencies. Those needed in order to achieve non-economic objectives are relevant as well.[163]

There is general agreement that the Article 81(3)(a) test ensures that the agreement is indispensable, in the sense that without it *the parties* could not have attained the relevant objectives.[164] However, it is possible to further increase the importance of competition in Article 81(3)(a) EC, if one interprets the provision yet more restrictively. This should ensure more legal certainty, while respecting the Treaty's optimal balance and further avoiding a *détournement de pouvoir*. The economic theory of optimal intervention says that one can rank the efficiency of different policy instruments, according to the end to be achieved.[165] When considering whether or not a restriction of competition is indispensable, one could take this into account.[166] As a result, on the condition that Chapter 6's suggestions for Article 81(1) are accepted,[167] perhaps Article 81(3)(a) should be reinterpreted such that an agreement is only held to be indispensable if there is no other method (whether the parties could use it or not, ie this would include direct legislation, etc.) which is at least as effective for achieving the balance achieved by the agreement[168] and does not reduce welfare less than the agreement. This would allow us to ensure that the parties' intervention is as successful as possible, while at the same time reducing (presumably consumer) welfare losses to the bare minimum.[169]

---

[160] 'these objectives' refers back to those considered in Art 81(3)'s first two heads of exemption, see T-66/89 *Publishers Association v Commission* para 73 and Faull and Nikpay (1999), para 2.165.

[161] See Sections 2 and 3, above. The system of this paragraph is somewhat strained if the balancing is carried out again in the context of the first negative condition of Art 81(3) EC, see the Opinion of A-G Verloren van Themaat, the *VBVB/VBBB* Case, 88.

[162] Commission, *Article 81(3) Guidelines*, para 73.

[163] Vedder (2003) 178, 179; Commission, *Article 81(3) Guidelines*, para 42; the *VOTOB* matter, Commission, *RCP 1992*, points 177–86 and Jacobs (1993/2) 57.

[164] See eg van Gerven (2004) 431; Commission, *Article 81(3) Guidelines*, paras 75, 76; Vedder (2003) 175–81; Faull and Nikpay (2007), para 3.441; the *Matra* Case para 138; the Opinion of A-G Roemer in the *Consten and Grundig* Case, 374–77; Case 71/74, *Nederlandse Vereniging voor de Fruit v Commission* para 42 and Commission decisions, *Duro-Dyne – Europair*, 13; *Goodyear Italiana – Euram*, para 13; *Grundig's EC distribution system*, para 38; *Enichem/ICI*, paras 40–45; *Atlas*, para 56; *Exxon/Shell*, para 72 and *Pheonix/GlobalOne*, para 61.

[165] See Ch 1, Section 3.2.1.

[166] The need to achieve Treaty ends through the most efficient means, taking account of the costs of each 'solution', has been accepted by the Commission, SEC(92) 1986a 9, 10.

[167] Ch 6, Section 2.3.

[168] Art 81(3)'s first two tests are there to ensure that the balance the agreement achieves is an acceptable one.

[169] This seems in line with the recommendations in OECD (2006) 44.

Some Commission decisions hint that this has sometimes been the test applied. For example, Commission decision, *Aluminium imports from Eastern Europe*, dealt with an agreement to reduce imports of aluminium into the Community. In relation to whether or not the restrictions were indispensable the Commission said:

> Even if the protection of the western aluminium market from competitive perturbation were accepted as an improvement in production or distribution, or contributed to economic progress, the Brandeis arrangements [the agreements that the Commission was considering] were not indispensable for the achievement of that purpose.

> If EEC producers of aluminium had needed any protection from the competition offered by aluminium producers in eastern Europe, their proper course would have been to make an application to the public authorities entrusted by law with the regulation of trade.[170]

Note that this kind of a test is fundamentally different to the other 'limits', which are to be found within Article 81(3) EC. Those tests affected the balance achieved under Article 81(3)'s first test. This interpretation of Article 81(3)(a) is completely different because it places a *procedural* limit on the use of the Article 81(3) exemption. Thus, it does not deny the importance of the various Community and Member State objectives. Instead, it encourages all relevant actors to achieve these ends in as efficient a way as possible. Note too, that the proposal does not deny the role of undertakings in the achievement of non-economic objectives.

Sometimes the only, or most efficient, way of achieving a particular non-economic end is through agreements between undertakings. Chapter 1's discussion of corporate social responsibility underlines this point.

However, there is a weakness in redefining the test as I suggest. An important benefit of corporate social responsibility comes from encouraging firms to engage as moral actors.[171] This tendency will be reduced if the indispensability test is refined in the way this proposal suggests. Nevertheless, I believe that the proposal strikes the right balance as although it reduces undertakings' use of corporate social responsibility, it only does so to the extent that this is inefficient.[172]

If one is persuaded by the logic of my position, then the question remains of how one could implement such a system. The party relying on the Article 81(3) exemption must

---

[170] Commission decision, *Aluminium imports from Eastern Europe*, s 16.2.3. See also similar arguments in, Commission decisions, *United Reprocessors GmbH*, para III(3); *Grohe's distribution system*, para 24; *Ideal-Standard's distribution system*, para 24 and *Uniform Eurocheques*, paras 40, 42, 43. Furthermore, in a Press Release relating to book pricing agreements between publishers and booksellers in Germany and Austria the Commission said, in relation to a book-pricing scheme it had sent a statement of objections on 'The Commission takes the view that alternative mechanisms are available which are a great deal less objectionable from the point of view of competition policy: publishers and booksellers could contribute to a fund to support more demanding literary works; *targeted and selective direct aid could be given*; discounts could be quality-based rather than quantity-based; or indeed there could be a selective distribution system designed to encourage works with a strong cultural element.' (emphasis added), Press Release, IP/98/30.

[171] Ch 1, Section 3.2.1.

[172] The rule presented here also bears a passing resemblance to the subsidiarity test, see Art 5 EC. The subsidiarity test asks whether, in certain areas, an action is best taken by the Community or the Member States, Craig and de Búrca (2008) 103. 'In practical terms, subsidiarity means that, when exercising its powers, the Community must, where various equally effective options are available, choose the form of action or measure which leaves the Member States, individuals or businesses concerned the greatest degree of freedom.', *The subsidiarity principle*, (1992) Bulletin of the EC 10–122. However, my rule does not seek greater freedom for the actors, but more efficient mechanisms for achieving the relevant objectives. Sometimes these two coincide, but this will not always be the case.

demonstrate that the agreement fulfils Article 81(3)'s first two balancing tests. If this is the case, it (and the opposing party) must list the various ways of achieving the relevant objectives to the same extent as the agreement.[173] Exemption is only allowed where the parties have adopted the most efficient method for achieving the optimal balance.[174]

Imagine, for example, that an agreement reduces the environmental impact of washing machine use in the European Union by prohibiting all machines that belong to energy categories D–G of the relevant Commission directive.[175] One way of achieving this may be to allow all, or the majority, of undertakings in the relevant sector to agree to only produce washing machines better than or equal to this energy efficiency.[176] Alternatively, the Commission could have proposed environmental legislation prohibiting the sale of washing machines, belonging to energy categories D–G of the relevant Commission Directive. It, or the Member States, could also have introduced more fundamental reform aimed at internalising the environmental externalities.[177] Assuming that the second or third suggestions above would achieve the end in question, just as effectively as the first option, then, subject to what is said in the rest of this section, the indispensability test should have prevented the adoption of Commission decision, *CECED*. This is on the assumption that the restriction on competition used there is more welfare reducing than the other two methods suggested above.

In Commission decision, *Synthetic Fibres*, for example, the Commission had been asked previously whether it would exempt an agreement on restructuring within this industry and each time had refused. At the same time it contacted Member States, asking them to '… avoid aggravating the over-capacity problem by granting any form of State aid to the sector.'[178] It might also be possible for the Commission to suggest to Member States that they grant State aid, where this would be just as effective and have a less restrictive effect on competition.

Chapter 1 watered down this extreme efficiency rule, however. It suggested that there may still be times when the decision-maker, in its discretion, could legitimately allow a restriction of competition, even if this would not be the most efficient route to achieve the goals in question.[179] I argued that this might be the case where: (i) inclusion of certain factors in the price mechanism might not be possible, or at least not at the level that the Community demands;[180] and (ii) the relevant objectives have not been achieved to the level promised by the agreement, and allowing the restriction means that the relevant objectives could be achieved to this level more quickly than would otherwise be the case.[181]

---

[173] In Commission decision, *Olivetti/Canon*, para 56, the Commission refused to follow a less restrictive proposal because this did not achieve the agreement's benefits to the same extent.

[174] For an interesting discussion of comparability and how this might work see Commission, *Impact Assessment Guidelines* 39–44.

[175] Commission, *Directive on Energy Labelling of Household Washing Machines*, see Annex IV.

[176] See Commission decision, *CECED*, discussed in Chs 2, 4 and 8.

[177] See Hahn and Hester (1989).

[178] Commission decision, *Synthetic Fibres*, para 12.

[179] Ch 1, Section 3.

[180] Jans (2000) 271.

[181] See Ch 1, Section 3. The Commission or Member States may also be bound to act multi-laterally in certain areas and so until agreement can be generated between them the Commission might achieve its ends through voluntary agreements between undertakings, as suggested in, SEC(92) 1986a 6. This is already a principle within the indispensability test as currently interpreted, see Commission, *Article 81(3) Guidelines*, para 76.

Without the agreement one might have to wait for a sufficiently large gap in the legislative programme. Fundamental reform, such as internalising environmental externalities, could take years.[182]

The Commission may be tempted to seize such cases for itself, as it is permitted to do under Regulation 1/2003, and resort to this method of 'legislation', where it has a lot of control, rather than to using the normal routes, see Articles 250–252 EC. This it should not do otherwise its acts may be *ultra vires*. However, it might be that the Commission believes that while legislation is the best option, the objectives that require protection are important enough to require a temporary restriction on competition until the appropriate legislation is enacted. In such a case the right course of action might be to grant an Article 81(3) exemption until the relevant Institutions have time to legislate. Such a policy should lie within the discretion of the Commission. Nevertheless, it will have to consider whether:

(i) the inaction on the part of the Institutions is, in itself, a policy decision. In other words, the Institutions might have analysed the need for environmental protection legislation relating to the energy efficiency of washing machines. If they had decided that no such legislation was necessary because the appropriate level of protection had already been achieved, it would normally be wrong for the Commission to introduce such an exemption by this route;

(ii) the same would apply where the Community has legislated in an area and the Commission decides that a specific risk has not been adequately covered. In the *Verband* Case[183] there was already European legislation in place that sought to prevent firms from knowingly maintaining an imbalance between income and expenditure.[184] Unless it can be shown that either the specific problem at issue in a specific case is materially different from the issues that the legislation sought to deal with; or, that circumstances have materially changed since the legislation was passed; then it is not the place for the Community Courts or the Commission to substitute their will for that of the legislature.

This additional change introduces a type of moral hazard. If the Commission is able to 'legislate' in this way it may reduce the Member States' incentive, through the Council, to take common positions in certain areas, although under certain circumstances it might increase it too. Nevertheless, there will be occasions when it is still better to take this path, at least until longer term solutions can be found and agreed upon.

It should be noted that this interpretation of indispensability also helps simplify the balancing task in the first two of Article 81(3) EC tests. This is because where some of the objectives could be achieved more efficiently in another way they should not be considered within the basket of benefits (or cons) of the agreement.

To my mind, the 'indispensability test' should be amended in this way to restrict the impact of non-economic policy objectives upon competition policy. This should force the

---

[182] By way of example, an implementing regulation was not provided in sea transport for some 24 years. Commission reports suggest that the 'new' Member States will take some 11 years to implement some of the binding European environmental legislation, '11 years for EU laws', *The Law Society Gazette*, 14 October 2004.

[183] The *Verband* Case, 427.

[184] A-G Darmon argued for allowing a horizontal cartel seeking to make sure that the risk was more adequately covered than the European legislation demanded. Although, ultimately, he felt that the restrictions on competition went too far it seems clear from the case that if the agreement had related to the fixing of net premiums, rather than gross premiums, he would have recommended an exemption, ibid, 445–46.

decision-makers to focus on consumer welfare.[185] At the same time, public policy goals can be pursued to the extent that the Treaty demands via the Article 81 mechanism where this is the best/most efficient way of achieving them. It should be noted that this is a long way from arguing that Treaty objectives are/should be irrelevant to those implementing Article 81. Nor can it be said that in this way I am effectively giving consumer welfare too much weight in the balance. Rather than exclusively promoting that objective, I am promoting the development of an efficient market system, as a mechanism for wealth maximisation.

5 THE FOURTH TEST:
DO NOT ELIMINATE COMPETITION, ARTICLE 81(3)(b)

Agreements must not afford undertakings '… the possibility of eliminating competition in respect of a substantial part of the products in question.', Article 81(3)(b). This provision creates a hierarchy, by promoting one objective (competition) above all others in Article 81(3) analysis, at least to a limited degree. This section questions whether this limit might contradict the balance from Article 81(3)'s first test by promoting 'competition' too highly; and discusses the implications of this.

The concept of 'competition' under Article 81(3)(b) is unclear. A similar issue arose in Chapter 6, in relation to the definition of 'competition' under Article 81(1) EC.[186] Monti believes that it refers to economic freedom.[187] Many Commission decisions suggest that Monti might be right.[188]

I argued that 'competition' should be interpreted as injury to consumer welfare. One of the clearest examples of this interpretation is Commission decision, *IFPI 'Simulcasting'*. This decision deals with an agreement between collecting societies, which facilitated the grant of multi-territorial licences for simulcasting activity. The Commission found that the agreement encouraged competition between record producers' collecting societies, where there had been no competition before. This was because 'The collecting societies will be able to actually compete and to differentiate themselves in terms of efficiency, quality of service and commercial terms.'[189] The Commission added that the agreement also meant that, after an additional adaptation period, the competition between collecting societies would extend to pricing:

> Accordingly, the participating EEA [European Economic Area] societies will have to increase their efficiency as regards their administration costs in such a way as to be able to provide a 'one-stop' simulcasting license at the lowest cost possible to EEA users.[190]

---

[185]   This would not only be the Commission but also the Member States' courts and competition authorities. However, these are the sort of cases that the Commission may seize for itself, under Reg 1/2003.

[186]   Ch 6, Section 2.

[187]   Monti (2002) 1064.

[188]   See Commission decisions, *Rennet*, paras 32, 33; *Uniform Eurocheques*, para 43; *VIFKA*, paras 21–23; *Dutch Banks*, para 65; *IATA Passenger Agency Programme*, para 63; *IATA Cargo Agency Programme*, para 54; *Assurpol*, para 41; *Schöller Lebensmittel GmbH & Co. KG*, paras 130, 135 and *Stichting Baksteen*, para 39. Also see Joined Cases T-185/00, etc *Métropole Télévision v Commission* paras 63–86.

[189]   Commission decision, *IFPI 'Simulcasting'*, para 119.

[190]   ibid, para 120.

In the next paragraph the Commission emphasised that the increased transparency that the agreement would introduce would '… allow users (as well as members of the societies) to better assess the efficiency of each of the societies and have a better understanding of their management costs.'

In light of these (and other) factors the Commission said that the agreement would not eliminate competition for the purposes of Article 81(3)(b) EC. Prior to this decision, the Commission had not been so explicit in its language. That said, there is certainly the implication in many other cases, decisions and communications, that the word 'competition', as used in Article 81(3)(b) EC, refers to efficiency gains.[191] For example, Commission, *Article 81(3) Guidelines* emphasise the importance of rivalry to achieve long term efficiency gains:

> Ultimately the protection of rivalry and the competitive process is given priority over potentially pro-competitive efficiency gains which could result from restrictive agreements. The last condition of Article 81(3) recognises the fact that rivalry between undertakings is an essential driver of economic efficiency, including dynamic efficiencies in the shape of innovation. In other words, the ultimate aim of Article 81 is to protect the competitive process. When competition is eliminated the competitive process is brought to an end and short-term efficiency gains are outweighed by longer-term losses stemming *inter alia* from expenditures incurred by the incumbent to maintain its position (rent seeking), misallocation of resources, reduced innovation and higher prices.[192]

In conclusion, there is a lack of consistency from the Commission.[193] Sometimes it interprets Article 81(3)(b) as referring to economic freedom; increasingly, of late, it seems to refer to long term efficiency, achieved through a process of rivalry.[194]

One might question whether the hierarchy that Article 81(3)(b) introduces clashes with Article 81(3)'s first test. Chapter 6 argued that 'restriction of competition' should be interpreted as consumer welfare.[195] We have seen that the relevant factors under Article

---

[191] See, eg Commission decisions, *Bayerische Motoren Werke AG*, para 31; *SABA*, paras 47–50; *Bayer/Gist-Brocades*, para 4; *United Reprocessors GmbH*, para 4; *KEWA*, para 4; *Junghans*, para 37; *De Laval – Stork*, para 12; *Beecham/Parke, Davis*, para 45; *Langenscheidt/Hachette*, para 23; *Amersham Buchler*, para 14; *Rockwell/Iveco*, para 11; *Nuovo CEGAM*, para 25; *Synthetic Fibres*, paras 48–52; *Grundig's EEC distribution system*, paras 6, 7; *Optical Fibres*, paras 73–80; the *Metro II Case*, paras 40–47; *ENI/Montedison*, paras 39–41; *Yves Rocher*, paras 64, 65; *Boussois/Interpane*, para 20; *Enichem/ICI*, paras 46–50; *Olivetti/Canon*, para 58; *Bayer/BP Chemicals*, OJ 1988 L150/34 paras 38–41; *IVECO/FORD*, paras 37–40; *BBC Brown Boveri*, para 33; *Charles Jourdan*, para 42; *UIP*, paras 56–59; *Alcatel Espace/ANT Machrichtentechnik*, para 21; Commission, *RCP 1991* 42; *Yves Saint Laurent Parfums* 34; *Parfums Givenchy system of selective distribution*, paras 21, 22; *Ford/Volkswagen*, paras 37, 38; the *Matra Case*, paras 150–56, although note, para 155; Commission, *RCP 1993*, point 85(iv); *Exxon/Shell*, paras 79–82; *Pasteur Mérieux-Merck*, paras 95–101, 103, 110, 113; *Olivetti-Digital*, para 33; *Fujitsu AMD Semiconductor*, para 45; *Atlas*, paras 59–74; *Pheonix/GlobalOne*, paras 65–72; *Unisource*, paras 94–101; *Uniworld*, paras 83–85; *Van den Bergh Foods Limited*, paras 242–46; *Sicasov*, para 77; *TPS*, paras 135–38; *P&I Clubs (1999)*, paras 113–15; *P&O Stena Line*, paras 67–130, 135; *REIMS II*, para 90; *British Interactive Broadcasting/Open*, paras 168–86; *Eurovision (2000)*, paras 100–05; *SAS Maersk Air*, para 77(d); *DSD and Others*, paras 158–63, although there is a hint of economic freedom in paras 159, 163 and Commission, *Horizontal Guidelines*, para 134. See also Faull and Nikpay (2008), para 3.453.

[192] Commission, *Article 81(3) Guidelines*, para 105.

[193] Nor have the Community Courts clarified the matter; their judgments do not contain clear and consistent statements on this issue either.

[194] That is not to say that these concepts are not affected by other relevant objectives, see Vedder (2003) 181–85; Jans (2000) 283, 284 and Bouterse (1994) 22–25, 122–25.

[195] See Ch 6, Section 2.3.

81(1) are balanced against the restriction of competition under Article 81(3)'s first provision (ie the agreement's objective benefits). In the words of the ECJ, the:

> [I]mprovement [under Article 81(3)'s first test] must in particular show appreciable objective advantages of such a character as to compensate for the disadvantages which they cause in the field of competition [Article 81(1)].[196]

Imagine that, in the context of a specific agreement, Article 81(3)'s first test deems it worth restricting competition (consumer welfare) in order to achieve the promised public policy gains. Furthermore, imagine that the prospective Article 81(3) benefits were so important that application of the balance under this first test justified the elimination of competition. The outcome of this balance would be frustrated because it would 'fail' Article 81(3)(b). In other words, the fourth provision might undermine the assessment of the 'optimal balance' in Article 81(3)'s first test.

An inconsistency can arise between Article 81(3)'s first and fourth tests. It must be stressed that this is not because Article 81(3)'s first test is a public policy balance.[197] Only three factors are needed for inconsistency to arise: 'competition' under Article 81(1) and 81(3) EC must have the same meaning; the factors in Article 81(1) and those considered under Article 81(3)'s first test must be balanced against each other; and the outcome of Article 81(3)'s first test's balance must justify the elimination of competition.

The first two points are relatively uncontroversial. First, 'competition' probably has the same meaning[198] in both Article 81(1) and 81(3)(b) EC.[199] As a result, the resulting elimination of 'competition' (as defined under Article 81(3)(b)) must already have been considered within Article 81(3)'s first test. Secondly, the Commission and the Community Courts embrace a test where the factors in Article 81(1) and those considered under Article 81(3)'s first test are balanced against each other.[200]

The final point which is necessary to establish inconsistency was that the outcome of the balance (as applied by the decision-maker) must be that the objective introduced under Article 81(3)'s first test justifies the elimination of competition.

The question to consider is whether Article 81(3)(b) EC promotes competition too highly. In other words, does it accurately reflect the balance that the decision-maker considers appropriate under Article 81(3)? When the decision-maker decides the optimal balance there, it should consider whether or not the objective benefits justify (within the context of the Treaty's telos) the elimination of competition in respect of a substantial part of the products in question.[201] Presumably it would not decide this very often, but when it does, should the decision-maker's balance be undermined by Article 81(3)(b)?

However, even if, in a particular case, the 'optimal Treaty balance', as established under Article 81(3)'s first test, indicates that competition should be eliminated; it might still be the case that the 'optimal balance' *in relation to agreements between undertakings* should

---

[196]   The *Consten and Grundig* Case, 348.
[197]   Although, theoretically, inconsistency might be more likely where more factors are considered in Art 81(3)'s first test, such that those considered in Art 81(1) are more readily outweighed.
[198]   This would most likely occur because 'competition' has the same meaning within Art 81(1) EC. It would be unusual to interpret the same word in the same article in a different way.
[199]   See, eg Commission, *Horizontal Guidelines*, paras 36, 71, 105, 134, 155, 174, 175, 197 and Hildebrand (2002) 247.
[200]   Ch 2 explained that, while the first Art 81(3) test *allowed* for a balancing process, it does not *demand* one. It merely asks that there be some contribution to improving the production or distribution of goods, etc.
[201]   In other words, one could argue that there is no need for a separate Art 81(3)(b) test.

not eliminate competition. Such agreements significantly undermine the free market mechanism; the ECJ has held many times that agreements between undertakings should not completely undermine this important mechanism. In both the *Metro I* and the *Metro II Cases*,[202] for example, the ECJ held:

> The powers conferred upon the Commission under Article 85(3) [now Article 81(3)] show that the requirements for the maintenance of workable competition may be reconciled with the safeguarding of objectives of a different nature and that to this end certain restrictions on competition are permissible, provided that they are essential to the attainment of those objectives and that they do not result in the elimination of competition for a substantial part of the Common Market.[203]

Such a rule is a major limit. To my mind this sort of limit is entirely appropriate in a competition rule. Where the efforts to achieve public policy goals are so demanding that rivalry is eliminated (even though it can be restricted), then I think another policy tool should be used. Member States could still legislate here, for example.[204]

There is another benefit of Article 81(3)(b) EC and this is *procedural*. The balancing exercise which must be undertaken within Article 81(3)'s first test is complex and expensive.[205] The 'elimination of competition' test is relatively simple (and cheap).[206] As long as it accurately reflects the outer limits of the balancing exercise,[207] retention of the Article 81(3)(b) test could still be beneficial as a kind of quick 'first check'. If the agreement failed here, the expense of Article 81(3)'s first test could be avoided.

In conclusion, competition is an important Treaty objective. It is rarely in the public interest for this to be eliminated. As a result, Article 81(3)(b) EC has a role in providing a first quick check when exemption is being considered. Where an agreement eliminates competition it is unlikely that it will pass the first Article 81(3) test either. Article 81(3)(b)'s presence in such cases would make the proceedings cheaper, easier and more predictable than a general balance. Even if, in a specific case, the public policy balance would have justified the elimination of competition, such that Article 81(3)(b) undermines Article 81(3)'s first test, I think this is an acceptable price to pay, given the importance given in the Treaty to the market mechanism.[208]

---

[202] Paras 21 and 65 respectively. See also, the citation above of Case 6/72 *Europemballage Corporation and Continental Can Company v Commission* para 24.

[203] The Commission made the same point in a different way in the *VBVB/VBBB* Case, when it said, at p 39, that there '... are no grounds for attributing to the cultural factor any absolute priority over the rules of competition.' A-G Verloren van Themaat concurred, p 89.

[204] Möschel (1991) 12.

[205] The expense, complexity and lack of predictability of this process dramatically increase when many other objectives are considered, as we argued should take place in Section 2, above and Ch 6.

[206] There are difficulties with it due to the definition of the relevant market, etc. Nevertheless, it is simpler, cheaper and more predictable than a general balancing test.

[207] Even if this were not always the case, if it were nearly always so, such a per se rule might still be beneficial, see Ch 6.

[208] Indeed, the esteem that the Treaty, as interpreted by the Community Courts, holds for the market mechanism may mean that the outcome of Art 81(3)'s first test is never to eliminate competition, in which case there will be no conflict at all.

6 CONCLUSION

Non-economic objectives must be taken into account in Article 81 EC. I have suggested that their consideration be confined to Article 81(3). In my view, Article 81(1) of the Treaty should be a pure consumer welfare analysis.

While accepting that non-economic goals are relevant in Article 81(3), Commission, *Article 81(3) Guidelines* imply that they must contribute to consumer welfare and the guidelines offer no counsel on how such goals should be integrated. This issue is of prime importance given how often these objectives have been considered in the past, and the inconsistent ways in which this has been done.[209] In addition, since 1 May 2004, the Member States' courts and competition authorities need guidance too.

This guidance would involve explaining which non-economic objectives are relevant; defining each objective precisely;[210] and clarifying its weight. This is because, in Article 81(3)'s first test, these non-economic objectives must be weighed against the restriction of competition, established under Article 81(1) EC. Chapter 8 discusses the issue of weight in the balance; it also provides a framework for balancing which makes the process more predictable and easier for the relevant actors to apply.

Section 2 deals with two other issues in relation to Article 81(3)'s first test. The first matter is what sort of balancing test should occur there. Various non-economic goals have been considered and combined there; sometimes their aggregate weight was necessary to 'justify' the restriction of competition. I argue that whether an agreement *undermines* non-economic objectives should also be a relevant consideration in the Article 81(3) balance. Both aggregating public policy impacts and negative balancing should be used, where appropriate in Article 81(3)'s first test. This must be done in a more structured way. Secondly, many non-economic Community objectives are raised in Article 81(3) EC;[211] some of them had policy-linking clauses, some did not. Member State non-economic objectives are also relevant there, in cases of diagonal conflict. As in Article 30 EC, I suggested that, ultimately, it is for the Community Courts to decide whether the Member State objective has been given excessive weight in the balance.

This leaves Article 81(3)'s first test as a wide assessment. However, although many objectives must, theoretically, be considered there, their effect on welfare depends upon how much weight they are given in the balance. Furthermore, although an agreement frequently affects many non-economic objectives, these effects are often not appreciable, and thus might not be considered. Chapter 8 discusses the application of the appreciability concept in such cases.

How much competition can be restricted also depends on the importance placed on Article 81(3)'s other three tests. Article 81(3)'s second provision demands that consumers get a fair share of the agreement's resulting benefit. Section 3 suggested that the rule only makes sense where consumers are defined as private end-users of the relevant goods or services. However, it is inordinately difficult to assess whether such people get a fair share

---

[209]   See Part B and the Introduction to this book.
[210]   The Netherlands Dutch Ministry of Economic Affairs, *The Liberal Professions* 24, 49, 84 and Gual (1995) 21.
[211]   See Ch 2, Section 2 and Ch 4, Sections 2 and 3.

of the benefit. I showed that assessing the benefits for the parties' direct customers was usually sufficient, significantly facilitating the analysis.

Section 4 went on to argue that Article 81(3)(a) EC should be redefined. In order to take proper account of the concept of optimal intervention, mere-balancing should be restricted to the occasions when it is the most efficient way of achieving the end in question. This does not mean that non-economic objectives are unimportant. It is simply that, in order to preserve the market mechanism, which the Community considers important, one must keep market distortions to a minimum. This is as long as non-economic objectives can be achieved in alternative (and equally effective) ways.

Another implication of mere-balancing in Article 81(3) EC is that, at the very least, a more consistent approach to the definition of 'competition' in Article 81(3)(b) is needed, Section 5 focuses on this test, arguing that it is a useful shortcut to the full balance discussed in Section 2.

Considering all relevant non-economic objectives under Article 81(3) EC, both those of the Community and those of the Member States, has two main benefits. It is in line with my view of the Treaty, described in Chapter 2, of a wide range of interlinking, self-reinforcing and conflicting objectives, none of which are permanently prioritised, but which should be blended to achieve the optimal Community balance. The Community Courts also embrace this reading of the Treaty. Secondly, once public policy goals can be overtly considered then decision-makers will be under less pressure to distort other parts of the Article 81 analysis in order to achieve similar aims.[212] This should lead to more transparent reasoning and predictable definitions throughout Article 81.

Such a wide definition of the first condition imposes some costs. As already mentioned, it would be both politically and evidentially difficult to assess every single effect that an agreement has. This should not be exaggerated. In most cases only arguments relating to consumer welfare, and possibly those relating to market integration, will be raised. In most other cases only one or two objectives will be considered.[213] True, the number of non-economic objectives discussed will probably increase once it is clear that they are relevant. Nevertheless, in many cases these will not be appreciable, see Chapter 8. That is not to say that the balancing exercise itself is going to be easy. It will be especially difficult to ensure consistency in light of the many decision-makers that Regulation 1/2003 creates. As a result, Chapter 8 is dedicated to providing a framework for this balancing process.

---

[212]   In relation to how the definition of 'undertaking' is affected by non-economic objectives, see Townley (2007). For similar issues in relation to the definition of: a 'restriction of competition', see the *Albany* and *Wouters* Cases (respectively the Community objective of promoting certain collective labour agreements and the Member State objective of the administration of justice) Ch 2, Section 2.2; and, an 'effect on trade between Member States', see the *Leclerc* Case (the Member State objective of culture), discussed in Ch 2, Section 2.2.

[213]   Aleinikoff (1987) 977 *ff*, says courts often narrow down the issues they will consider in this kind of balancing exercise. He criticises this because he feels that this tendency can be at the expense of getting the right answer. Many other public bodies probably only base their decisions on a few underlying objectives too.

8

A Framework for Balancing in Article 81 EC

1 INTRODUCTION

Within Article 81, conflicts between objectives are, principally, resolved through balancing.[1] Given the significance of this method of dispute resolution, one would expect clear guidance about how to balance public policy goals there. None exists.[2] Some doubt that the provision of useful guidelines is possible.[3] Despite this pessimism, this chapter provides a framework for balancing Article 81's objectives.

The Commission now argues that Article 81's sole objective is to enhance consumer welfare and ensure an efficient allocation of resources; the CFI agrees.[4] If this were true then there would be less need for this framework. Yet, I have repeatedly shown that many other objectives should be (and are) considered in Article 81.[5]

---

[1] That is not to say that exclusion is irrelevant in Art 81, although it is quite rare, see Ch 2, Section 2.2.1. In addition, Art 81(3)(b), discussed in Ch 7, Section 5, states that the agreement must not afford the parties to it '... the possibility of eliminating competition ...' As a result, Art 81 contains within it a limited form of hierarchy, competition cannot be eliminated.

[2] The OECD found a similar position in many other countries, OECD (2003) 3, 10.

[3] Bourgeois and Demaret (1995) 110.

[4] See references in Ch 1, n 3.

[5] See Ch 2, Section 2 and Part B to this work. The Introduction shows how prevalent public policy considerations are in Art 81 decisions.

Guidance is desirable then, as it helps the decision-maker balance. This enhanced predictability should also create a more unified body of decisions, rather than a set of individual ad hoc and inconsistent measures. As a result, the underlying objectives are more likely to be realised.[6] Without such a system, the overall quality of competition law would be endangered.[7]

Defining the balance's objectives, as well as the rules on how to perform it, informs those doing the balance of *what* they are trying to achieve and *how* to do this.[8] This chapter shows how crucial guidelines are in this regard, by exposing many value judgments that are involved in Article 81's balance. Guidance is particularly important because many different courts and competition authorities can be called upon to perform this public policy balance. The Member States' courts and competition authorities, while bound to apply Articles 81 and 82 in their entirety,[9] cannot take decisions running counter to Commission decisions; Member State courts must even avoid giving decisions which conflict with a decision contemplated by the Commission.[10] For Member State bodies to replicate Commission decisions and achieve the 'right result' in a 'new' case, they need to know what the Commission is trying to achieve through its balance and what factors are relevant to it.[11] Also, to generate an acceptance of balancing, as well as to improve their capacity for this, decision-makers need to have the process explained and justified to them.[12] Greater understanding and acceptance of the balancing standard reduces arbitrariness and subjectivity, breeding a system of trust.[13]

Additionally, guidelines provide greater predictability (legal certainty) and transparency to undertakings, their advisers and other actors in the market place.[14] Since 1 May 2004 this is even more important. Article 81's prior notification system has been replaced by a system of direct applicability.[15] Undertakings can theoretically seek guidance on novel

---

[6]   See the Economic and Social Committee's *Opinion on the Twentieth Report on Competition Policy*, 236 of Commission, *RCP 1991*, point 2.1.2.9; COM(2001) 486 17–19 and Goldman (1998) 327.

[7]   Van den Bergh (2002) 35.

[8]   See Goldman (1998) 327 and Goldman and Barutciski (1998) 414.

[9]   Reg 1/2003, recital 4 and arts 3, 5, 6.

[10]   ibid, recital 22 and art 16.

[11]   D'Agostino (2003) 163–65. The Commission must be kept aware, in good time, of all Art 81 and 82 actions by the Member States' competition authorities and courts, Reg 1/2003, recital 21 and art 11(3); it can also appear before Member States' courts and competition authorities, Reg 1/2003, recital 21 and art 15(3) and Commission, *Co-operation Guidelines – National Courts*, paras 17–20, 31–35. These bodies can also send questions regarding the application of Arts 81 and 82 EC to the Commission, Reg 1/2003, recital 21 and arts 11(5), 15(1) and Commission, *Co-operation Guidelines – National Courts*, paras 27–30. In exceptional cases, where the public interest of the Community so requires, the Commission can also reserve a case to itself, Reg 1/2003, recitals 11, 14, 17 and arts 10, 11(6). That said, the previous system, where the Commission alone took Art 81(3) decisions, prevented it from concentrating its limited resources on curbing the most serious infringements, Reg 1/2003, recital 3. Public policy objectives (and thus balancing) are relevant in many cases. Unless the Member States' courts and competition authorities are given sufficient information about how to perform the balancing test, and are confident that they can do this correctly, then they will continue to refer (and arguably are bound to refer) many cases to the Commission/Community Courts. This may undermine the reform process itself, see Gyselen (2002) 79, 80, 85.

[12]   Miller and Rose (1993).

[13]   Porter (1995) ix, 90. This is particularly important if there are principal/agent relationships involved, Bamberg and Spreman (1989), perhaps like those created between the Commission and the Member State authorities by Reg 1/2003, see references in Ch 7, n 80.

[14]   D'Agostino (2003) 163; Goldman (1998) 327 and Korah (1998) 526. Ch 1, Section 3.2.1 explains why legal certainty is important.

[15]   Reg 1/2003, art 1.

questions from the Commission, but are no longer protected from fines.[16] More Article 81 decisions should also be taken under the new system.[17]

This chapter provides a framework for balancing. It does not stipulate precisely how to balance. National courts and competition authorities can use their own balancing procedures. However, to ensure the uniform application of Community competition law, they must implement Community legislation consistent with the general principles of Community law, such as clarity and certainty;[18] and in line with the results the Commission would achieve.[19] How they achieve this is largely up to them:

> In the absence of Community law provisions on procedures … related to the enforcement of EC competition rules by national courts, the latter apply national procedural law … However, the application of these national provisions must be compatible with the general principles of Community law.[20]

The framework I propose facilitates the predictability and consistency of this process. This chapter's minimum framework for balancing focuses on three areas. First, no balance can be properly conducted without defining what ultimate objective is being pursued. Section 2 argues that Article 81's meta-objective must be enunciated.[21] Secondly, due to the number, breadth and complexity of the objectives involved, explicitly defining the meta-objective (while necessary) may not sufficiently enhance clarity for those interpreting the competition provisions, at least in the short term. Guidance is also needed on which factors should affect the relevant objectives' weight when the balance is performed. Section 3 highlights features that the Commission currently considers when assessing restrictions of competition and discusses the adequacy of the Commission's approach when applied to non-economic goals. Finally, Section 4 asks how the disparate public policy objectives can be rationally balanced. Section 5 concludes.

A word of caution, I am seeking a more coherent, transparent system for Article 81; as such, legal certainty and the uniformity of Community competition law are important.[22] That said, each case is different; objectives clash and value judgments must be made about the optimal balance *in each case*. The Commission exercises discretion here; balancing is not a procedure leading to a precise and unavoidable outcome in every case.[23] The framework does not advocate a naïve, Benthamesque, felific calculus; but it is useful because it exposes factors, which may be relevant in specific cases.

Since 1 May 2004, the Member States' courts and competition authorities share this discretion. Their decisions will not always be precisely what the Commission (or the Council) would like. However, uniformity is not principally threatened by rogue judges but by the lack of transparency that shrouds balancing *as a process*. National authorities do

---

[16] Commission, *Guidance Letters Guidelines*, paras 5, 7. Considering the sensitivity of balancing objectives within Art 81, as well as the Commission's reluctance to explain this issue thus far, it is unlikely that the Commission will often answer such questions, Gyselen (2002) 79, 80.

[17] See Reg 1/2003, recital 3 and Lenaerts (2002) 18.

[18] See Arnull, Dashwood, Ross and Wyatt et al. (2006) ch 6.

[19] Reg 1/2003, recitals 21, 22 and art 16.

[20] Commission, *Co-operation Guidelines – National Courts*, para 10.

[21] The expressions 'meta-objective', 'ultimate aim', 'over-arching goal' and 'optimal objective', as well as combinations of these terms, are used synonymously in this chapter.

[22] Reg 1/2003, recitals 21, 22 and art 16.

[23] Alexy (2002) 100. See also pages 83, 105, 362–66, 383–85, 402; Goldman (1998) 327; Faull (1998) 509, 510 and Burton (1992) 59.

not know what the Commission would do in their place (as it denies the relevance of public policy objectives in Article 81[24]), so they cannot emulate it. Through appropriate notices, the Commission can guide the balancing process;[25] but legal balancing is not mathematics; the Commission cannot eliminate diverging opinions of these goals' relative values, or it could only do so by reducing the flexibility needed for balancing such disparate goals in myriad situations. Legal certainty is not the only value that legal systems espouse,[26] think of fairness and justice. The national decision-maker should be guided, but his (or her) hands should not be tied.

Happily, the Community is developing impact assessment tools; these should help me in my efforts to build a balancing framework. Typically, impact assessment considers the potential or actual impacts (positive and negative) of a regulatory measure in terms of the three pillars of sustainable development, namely, economic, social and environmental.[27] Impact assessments should improve the efficiency, effectiveness and coherence of the Community policy development process; identifying the likely positive and negative effects of proposed policy actions on different objectives, means that more informed judgments can be made in relation to proposed policy actions.[28] This bears some resemblance to the needs of the decision-maker when performing the Article 81 balance.[29] By identifying the likely positive and negative effects of an agreement on the relevant public policy objectives the decision-maker can make a more informed and transparent judgment about where the optimal balance lies.

2 DEFINING AN OVER-ARCHING OBJECTIVE

It is important to define the ultimate objective of the balance[30] so that those performing the balance know what they are trying to achieve.[31] It allows them to better determine which values should weigh positively/negatively in the balance; and, where there is a problem of limited resources, as may be the case for our purposes, decide how much of each value to allow in order to arrive at the 'best decision'. Secondly, defining overall guiding principles for decision-making helps create a unified body of decisions, rather than a set of individual ad hoc and inconsistent measures. Finally, defining a meta-objective provides greater predictability (legal certainty) and transparency to undertakings, their advisers and other actors in the market place.

Defining the optimal objective potentially has three disadvantages. First, it is very hard (both in fact and politically) to find one that incorporates all the relevant values according

---

[24] The Commission, *Horizontal Guidelines*, expressly apply only to economic considerations, para 10; see also Commission, *Article 81(3) Guidelines*, para 42 and Whish (2008) 155. Even more confusingly, Ch 2, Section 2.3 showed that despite what its guidelines say, the Commission often considers public policy criteria in its Art 81 decisions.

[25] Notices help clarify theory in practice, Baker and Wu (1998) and Vogelaar (1994) 544.

[26] Frazer (1990) 622, 623.

[27] Kirkpatrick and Parker (2007) 1.

[28] COM(2002) 276, 2 explains where the impetus for this came from.

[29] Impact assessment would not apply itself in competition decisions, see Commission, *Impact Assessment Guidelines* 6.

[30] See the Economic and Social Committee's *Opinion on the Twentieth Report on Competition Policy*, 236 of the Commission, *RCP 1991*, points 2.1.2.7–9.

[31] Bell (1983) 26, 27.

to the weight they should be given and yet is not meaninglessly wide. Some even argue that the definition of an over-arching goal is theoretically impossible. It certainly requires difficult political choices.

The monism/pluralism debate in political philosophy is relevant here. Monists believe that, in the event of a conflict between values, one can define an over-arching goal if the underlying values are compatible with each other. Pluralists disagree;[32] however, their assessment is contingent upon the values in dispute, ie it applies to fundamental, incommensurable, political values (eg liberty and the autonomy of the individual). If the values considered in Article 81 are incommensurable, balancing is not rationally possible there.[33] However, this point is not discussed further as the values considered in Article 81 are normally quantifiable;[34] to the extent that they are not, these problems are contingent on the pluralists' conception of such values. The Commission and the Community Courts evidently do not share this pluralist conception, as they advocate balancing.[35]

Secondly, if the decision-maker is forced to define the meta-objective, this may reduce his/her discretion in a concrete case, making challenges to the decision easier. I do not consider this a relevant disadvantage, as the limited discretion referred to here is really limited arbitrariness. Restricting this may be disadvantageous to the decision-maker seized of the matter; however, it benefits most other actors, as well as the Community competition system as a whole, through the greater predictability it engenders.

Thirdly, the definition of a meta-objective may create rigidity, making it difficult to incorporate values that were not part of the test when it was established, or to disregard values that are no longer considered important. The relevance of this factor can be overstated. Changes in values are not a daily occurrence. When values need to be added or subtracted the meta-objective can be changed to incorporate them. Expressly changing the meta-objective in this way should further enhance clarity.

As a result, defining the balance's objective is helpful. However, I am making an even stronger claim; without a meta-objective it is *impossible* to balance rationally. Peczenik correctly asserts that each principle, or value, can be a *prima facie* reason of action; but these values can collide. One needs meta-reasons to choose between them.[36]

The meta-objective defines, in a sense, the rules of the balancing game and is necessary for two reasons. First, without isolating the meta-objective one cannot know whether different objects or effects should be considered positively or negatively in the balance. For example, if one wants to know whether increasing employment is to be considered positively or negatively, one needs a meta-rule to tell us. One might say that increasing employment is positive because it provides a better quality of life;[37] and a better quality of life is important because it contributes to human dignity. One can continue this 'conversation' until one arrives at the meta-objective upon which all rational Article 81 judgments must be based. One might retort that the Treaty already explains whether specific values

---

[32]   For a summary see Dworkin (2001) and Lilla (2001).

[33]   See Zucca (2007), although note the contrary view of Lucy (1999) 153, 154.

[34]   See, eg Berlin (1990) 11–12. This problem may apply to the extent that fundamental rights are considered in our balance, and possibly even other values such as 'fairness'.

[35]   See Part B of this work.

[36]   Peczenik (1989) 75. See also, Lucy (1999) 154–56; Burton (1992) 51–54 and Brkić (1985) 44.

[37]   On the other hand, one could say it is negative because many find it unpleasant.

are positive or negative, in a Community context.[38] However, the Treaty does not do this for all objectives that are relevant in the Article 81 balance; for example, it does not even mention either economic freedom or efficiency.

Secondly, definition of a meta-objective is also imperative, as without it one cannot assign different weights to the values in the balance; this is necessary to solve conflicts through balancing. Imagine that, in a concrete case, employment comes at the expense of consumer welfare. Assume that both are to be considered positive values in our balance and that both cannot be fully achieved with our limited resources. Understanding the over-arching objective enables us to decide how much of each of these two entities is optimal, ie where the balance should lie between them. Sometimes the Treaty provides an insight into what weight should be assigned to certain values, Article 152(1) EC demanded a high level of protection, for example. However, it is unclear what a *high* level of protection means; in addition, the Treaty does not provide a weighting for all the values it mentions; nor does it define what happens, for example, when two objectives requiring a high level of protection clash. On top of this, not all relevant values are explicitly mentioned in the Treaty.

To this one might retort that courts perform balancing every day and rarely define a meta-objective. This is certainly true (the same can be said of academics[39]), although there are exceptions.[40] However, this does not mean that they do not rely on a meta-objective, just that it is not explicit. This may be due to the political controversy that such a definition would cause; and yet, unless it is explicitly (and correctly[41]) defined, the requisite balance will be neither predictable nor replicable for the relevant actors.

If a meta-objective is necessary, that does not mean that one is easy to define. It is hard to select an optimal objective that incorporates all relevant values according to the weight that should be given to them and yet is not so wide that it is meaningless. This, possibly combined with the sensitivity of defining this meta-objective,[42] is probably why, at times, the Institutions have avoided defining an underlying objective in abstract terms. In one case, Advocate-General Tesauro, when introducing Article 81(1), although his words seem to apply more generally to the whole of Article 81, said:

> In relation to the *ratio legis* of that provision, the Court has stated that the requirements of protection of competition pursued by it cannot be defined in abstract terms but must be seen in the specific context in which the conduct of the undertakings came about.[43]

---

[38]   The Treaty states what should be considered positively, 'A high level of human health protection shall be ensured', Art 152(1) EC, for example.

[39]   In her seminal article on the proportionality test De Búrca does not consider this issue, De Búrca (1993). Nor does Aleinikoff, in an equally influential article on balancing, Aleinikoff (1987).

[40]   This has been accepted in German Public Law, eg, see Limbach (2000) 158–61; Emiliou (1996) 32–34, 43, 57–59 and the references made there and Alexy (2002) 93, 94. Alexy hints at the need for a meta-objective at pages 107, 404, 405.

[41]   As I note above, the Commission's recent insistence that public policy is irrelevant in Art 81 does not reflect its own decisions or the Community Courts' case law, see references in n 24 above and so this meta-objective just creates greater confusion, rather than reducing it.

[42]   Bell (1983) 27.

[43]   Case C-250/92 *Gøttrup-Klim v Dansk Landbrugs*, 5654.

Advocate-General Tesauro is right that the balance is affected by the specific context of the agreement. However, this should not prevent the definition of an abstract objective. Even when one is balancing in the specific context of a case, a meta-objective is needed in order to guide the process.[44]

This all demands the definition of the meta-objective, however hard it may be. Some believe that consumer welfare should be the sole objective of the balance.[45] However, this meta-objective is too narrow; public policy objectives should be (and are) relevant in Article 81 cases.[46] The picture is further complicated because, as the EU moves away from a 'pure economic' community,[47] the factors that need to be taken into account within Article 81 include ever more public policy goals.[48] As a result, a clear, consistent, meta-objective has not emerged over time.

In order to take account of the burgeoning number of values, Article 81's underlying objectives have, at times, been defined very generally indeed. Some Community Court judgments aim at attaining the '… objectives of a single market between States.'[49] Others refer to '… the observance of the conditions of competition and unity of the market which are so essential to the Common Market …'[50] Achieving European unity has also been mentioned as a goal.[51] More generally, the ECJ has held that the competition rules aim '… to prevent competition from being distorted to the detriment of the public interest, individual undertakings and consumers.'[52] None of these definitions are very helpful in and of themselves, as they do not provide much content to, or guidance for, dealing with conflicts. Nor does taking the 'European social balance'[53] as Article 81's underlying objective provide the disciplined framework that is needed, because it is an illusive and largely undefined notion.[54] This argument need not be decisive, however. Over time, case law and Commission notices could flesh out these skeletal concepts.[55]

A good place to look for the meta-objective is the Treaty's Preamble. There, the High Contracting Parties state that '… the essential objective of their [the High Contracting

---

[44] Heimler (1998) 596.

[45] This is the view of the Commission and the CFI, eg, see Ch 1, n 3.

[46] Part B of this work shows that public policy goals are considered in Art 81; Ch 2, Section 2 and Ch 7, Section 2 argue that this is appropriate in the EU context.

[47] See, eg Streit and Mussler (1995).

[48] I discuss this transition, including the possible impact of the Lisbon Treaty, Ch 2, Section 2.1.

[49] The *Consten and Grundig* Case 341; Case 5/69 *Franz Völk v Vervaecke* paras 5, 7 and Case 1/71 *Société Anonyme Cadillon v Firma Höss* para 6. See also, Bredimas (1978) 91. Although, note the *Metro I* Case para 20, for example. Bouterse (1994) 3 criticises this as '… insufficient for any clarification of what exactly makes up the spirit of Community action – and thus of Art 85 [now Art 81] …'

[50] Case 40/70 *Sirena v Eda* para 10.

[51] See Opinion 1/91 *Opinion delivered pursuant to the second subpara of Article 228(1) of the Treaty*, paras 17, 18. Although Rasmussen argues that when Mr Robert Lecourt left the ECJ the other judges lost their over-riding allegiance to this goal, Rasmussen (1993) 3.

[52] Joined Cases 46/87, etc *Hoechst v Commission* para 25.

[53] This is implied in Case C-185/91 *Bundesanstalt für den Güterfernverkehr v Gebrüder Reiff*, in the Opinion of A-G Darmon, paras 23, 24. He also cites Fox (1986) 982.

[54] See in this regard, Commission, *RCP 1996* 7 and COM(96) 90 'Europe is built on a set of values shared by all its societies and combines the characteristics of democracy – human rights and institutions based on the rule of law – with those of an open economy underpinned by market forces, internal solidarity and cohesion.' On a similar point, cultural identity, see Amato (1999) 1, 9–15. See also, Jebsen and Stevens (1995–6) 450, 451, 460, discussing the objectives of Community competition policy more generally.

[55] Alexy (2002) 108.

Parties'] efforts [is] the constant improvement of the living and working conditions of their peoples ...' Similarly, if the Lisbon Treaty is accepted, the Preamble to the EU Treaty will say that the Member States are:

> DETERMINED to promote economic and social progress for their peoples, taking into account the principle of sustainable development and within the context of the accomplishment of the internal market and of reinforced cohesion and environmental protection, and to implement policies ensuring that advances in economic integration are accompanied by parallel progress in other fields ...[56]

To the extent that this accurately reflects the Treaty objectives as they are currently interpreted,[57] it may be a good objective, to be further clarified over time.[58]

That the Commission has not clearly and accurately defined Article 81's meta-objective (or even, until recently, attempted this) is troubling. Where the ultimate objectives remain undefined, balancing may be occurring in an intuitive, rather than a wholly reasoned, way.[59] This is unacceptable for a public body[60] and makes its decisions hard for others to predict and replicate. Even if each individual Commission decision were decided rationally and reflectively, the Commission's decision-making practice implies that there is no meta-objective that it is consistently trying to achieve. This suggests that decisions are taken on an ad hoc basis, as opposed to being part of an over-arching system.[61] Greater clarity in the underlying objectives pursued may lead to better quality decision-making as well as increased legal certainty.

The Commission might argue that it has an overall policy objective that it consistently applies in its case law. If this is correct then it is not obvious what it is.[62] This lack of clarity, and the enormous discretion that the Commission's balance is given by the Community Courts, means that even if the Commission is using a proper system it needs to explain more clearly what it is.[63] The difficulty for the Community Courts is that they have been led by the Treaty to allow the inclusion of various objectives within Article 81 analysis. However, because of the structure of their review of its Article 81 decisions (essentially a judicial review type process) they have been reluctant to intervene with the Commission's discretion and impose greater order.[64]

---

[56]   Arts 2 and 3 EU Treaty offer other suggestions. See also Commission, *Impact Assessment Guidelines*, Annex One, p 6.

[57]   This may need to be further refined; see, eg Arts 177 and 178 EC on development co-operation and Commission, *Impact Assessment Guidelines* 26, 28.

[58]   Many clarifications are needed; such as, the meta-objective should indicate the time-scale over which the benefits are sought and whether short-term sacrifices can be made for long or medium term gain, etc.

[59]   The idea that balancing takes place either arbitrarily or unreflectively is one of Habermas' main critiques of it as a process, see Habermas (1996) 259. See also, the reference to Schlink (2001) 445–65 in Alexy (2003b) 436.

[60]   Finnis (1997) 215, 216.

[61]   Think of the lack of clarity and consistency that Ch 4 pointed to in relation to various public policy goals. The Commission has been most explicit where market integration is involved in the balance, see, eg Commission, *Vertical Guidelines*, paras 49–55. But even here, the Commission's notices are indicative of a mechanical, as opposed to a rational, reasoned, process, see Ch 3, Section 2.1 and Ch 4, Section 2.2. They are of some help, but not much.

[62]   Whish (2001) 14. Whish (2008) 155 points out that the Commission has now embraced the sole consumer welfare goal. However, as I explained above, this is an unacceptable meta-objective in the Treaty context, see references in n 46 above.

[63]   Forrester (1998) 382.

[64]   As I have said already, since 1 May 2004 these problems are magnified. Decision-making devolves to national courts and competition authorities as well. The lack of clear guidance may lead to a disparate body of case law emerging from these various authorities, which will be hard to check.

A meta-objective must be defined in order for the balancing process to be clear, predictable and effective. It would also provide the decision-maker with guidance in difficult cases. The meta-objective needs to be both wide enough to include all relevant Treaty objectives and flexible enough to adapt to changes in these. The Lisbon Treaty, if adopted, suggests that such an objective might be to '... promote economic and social progress for their peoples, taking into account the principle of sustainable development and within the context of the accomplishment of the internal market and of reinforced cohesion and environmental protection, and to implement policies ensuring that advances in economic integration are accompanied by parallel progress in other fields ...' Due to the complexity of the underlying objective's constituent parts, such a formulation does not immediately, precisely and directly explain what the balance is. The Commission might have to rely on Notices and cases, to illustrate where the balance should be drawn in specific instances, in order to produce a more specific picture via induction that others can use in a meaningful way.

3 WEIGHT FOR THE RIGHT BALANCE

I have shown that both the Community's and Member States' public policy objectives, which contribute to the relevant ends, should be considered.[65]

Determining an objective's weight is difficult and controversial.[66] Explicitly defining a meta-objective may not sufficiently enhance clarity for those interpreting Article 81; due to the number, breadth and complexity of the goals involved, at least in the short term.

Further guidance may be needed on which factors affect the objectives' weight in the balance. Section 3.1 discusses how qualitative and quantitative aspects might impact upon this. Other factors can also be important; the two main ones are the *likelihood* that the objective will be achieved, Section 3.2, and, *when* the objective will be achieved, Section 3.3. Finally, Section 3.4 covers the appreciability doctrine, this simplifies the decision-makers' task by ensuring that objectives that only experience minimal impacts are ignored in the balance.

3.1 Qualitative and quantitative weight

According to Alexy, balancing can be broken down into three stages:

> The first stage is a matter of establishing the degree of non-satisfaction of, or detriment to, the first principle. This is followed by a second stage, in which the importance of satisfying the competing principle is established. Finally, the third stage answers the question of whether or not the importance of satisfying the competing principles justifies the detriment to, or non-satisfaction of, the first.[67]

In order to balance, one must be able to rationally determine how much each objective is infringed (and the competing one achieved), this is a quantitative assessment. There is also

---

[65]   Ch 4, Section 3 and Ch 7, Section 2.2.
[66]   Dworkin (1977) 26.
[67]   Alexy (2003a) 136. See also, Alexy (2002) 102.

a qualitative assessment of the importance of the infringement (or achievement) of the goal.[68] The qualitative and quantitative elements are then combined to ascertain each objective's weight in the balance; then the competing objectives must be weighed against each other. When doing this, reference must be made to the meta-objective.

The Community Courts and the Commission state that the legal, economic, political and social context should be taken into account when applying Article 81 EC.[69]

3.1.1 Qualitative weight

The qualitative assessment is trying to distil the objective's abstract importance. For example, human health may be more worthy of protection than cultural concerns. Similarly, within the same objective, certain types of damage may be worse than others.

Two things must be decided under this heading: should the objectives have different qualitative weights in the balance; and if so, what should these weights be.

As regards the first issue, the Treaty does not *expressly say* that the objectives should be assigned different qualitative weights. Indeed, some suggest that they should not.[70] However, the Treaty does refer to a 'high level of protection' in relation to some,[71] but not all,[72] objectives. The 'high' appellation must mean something;[73] environmental protection became a 'high' priority after the Treaty of Maastricht, before that, a high level was not demanded, for example.[74] These textual differences are hard to explain, except in relation to the qualitative weight that the objectives might be given in the balance.[75] Policy statements by the Commission, Council and European Parliament support the use of qualitative weight.[76] The ECJ may support this too.[77]

---

[68] See also, The World Bank and OECD (1999) 9 and Wathern (1988) 12, 13.

[69] Case T-168/01 *GlaxoSmithKline Services v Commission* para 110; Case T-61/89 *Dansk Pelsdyravlerforening v Commission* para 52; Case 45/85 *Verband der Sachversicherer v Commission* para 15 and Joined Cases 25 and 26/84 *Ford-Werke and Ford of Europe v Commission* paras 33, 34. See also, Frazer (1990) 622, 623; Wesseling (2000) 35; and Commission, *RCP 1992*, where the Commission says that competition policy cannot '... be pursued in isolation ... without reference to the legal, economic, political and social context.' point 13.

[70] Demetriou and Higgins (2003) 197 and Wasmeier (2001) 160, on the Art 2 EC heads.

[71] Art 127(2) EC demands that '... a high level of employment shall be taken into consideration in the formulation and implementation of Community policies and activities.' Also see Arts 152(1) (public health: '... a high level of human health protection shall be ensured ...'), 153(1), (2) (consumer protection '... ensure a high level ...') and 6 and 174(2) EC (environment '... aim at a high level ...').

[72] Art 151(4) EC merely says, '... cultural aspects shall be taken into account ...' See also, Arts 157 (industrial policy '... shall contribute to the achievement ... [without creating] ... a distortion of competition ...'), 159 (economic and social cohesion '... take into account ...'), 163(3) (R&D '... implemented in accordance with ...') and 178 (development co-operation '... take account ...').

[73] Loman, Mortelmans, Post and Watson (1992) 195, 196. Collège d'Europe (1998) 229, suggests that the practical effect of these 'high' labels appears to be minimal. Schmid (2000) 164, 165 and Monti (2002) 1075, disagree.

[74] On the importance of the Treaty's wording in strengthening environmental protection considerations: see McGillivray and Holder (2001), s IV, for example.

[75] See Krämer (2000) 6–9. Lenz (2000) 47–49, may disagree.

[76] The Commission has said that both qualitative and quantitative dimensions should be considered in Community policy impact assessments, eg, Commission, *Impact Assessment Guidelines* 26, 33, 34, 39–44. The Council and the European Parliament also imply that both qualitative and quantitative dimensions should be considered: see European Parliament and Council, *on the assessment of the effects of certain plans and programmes on the environment*, Annex II, for example.

[77] Case C-233/94, *Germany v European Parliament and Council*, where Germany argued that consumer protection required a high level of protection, which the directive at issue had not achieved. The ECJ held that '... although consumer protection is one of the objectives of the Community, it is clearly not the sole objective. As has already been stated, the Directive aims to promote the right of establishment and the freedom to provide

The Treaty and the Institutions imply that certain objectives should be given a high priority, and that others should not. If this level of priority can be 'captured' in the objectives' weight in the balance, then Article 81's weighing process would better reflect this preference. Achieving/undermining high priority objectives would count for more, so undertakings would be more likely to consider them in their agreements.[78]

It might be helpful to provide an illustration of how the different qualitative appellations might affect the objectives' weights. At the outset, one might choose to differentiate between at least two distinct levels: those where a high level of protection is demanded, and all the rest. This would produce the following bifurcation:

Qualitative weight	Policy (open lists)
High	Employment, public health, consumer protection, environment, competition
Not-high	Culture, economic and social cohesion, R&D, development co-operation[79]

These groups could be further sub-divided. One might ask, for example, whether the 'value' of public health's 'high' appellation, Article 152(1) EC, is the same as that in Article 174(2) (environment). This is unclear. There are strong similarities between these articles. The Treaty uses the same word (high) in them both. On the other hand, the public health language (*ensure* a high level of protection) seems stronger than that of environment (*aim at* a high level).[80] A similar split emerges in the 'not-high' band.

It may be that these textual differences do not reflect diverse priorities; but, on balance, a second sub-division along these lines probably better mirrors the Treaty's aims and wording. If this Treaty language signals a prioritisation then reflecting this in the objectives' qualitative weights is essential. Tentatively, I suggest the following:

Qualitative weight		Policy (open lists)
High	Heavy	Public health, consumer protection, competition
	Light	Employment, environment[81]
Not-high	Heavy	R&D
	Light	Culture, economic and social cohesion, development co-operation

services in the banking sector. Admittedly, there must be a high level of consumer protection *concomitantly with those freedoms*; however, no provision of the Treaty obliges the Community legislature to adopt the highest level of protection which can be found in a particular Member State.' (emphasis added), para 48. The different objectives must be balanced. The ECJ seems to imply that the 'high' appellation has a *relative*, as opposed to an *absolute*, weight.

[78] On the benefits of this see Ch 1, Section 3.2.1.

[79] Industrial policy is not included because of Art 157(3) EC. However, in Ch 4, Section 2.6, I noted that it is considered in Art 81 despite this provision.

[80] One might even argue that the words 'ensure that' indicate a hierarchical threshold, as was the case for 'eliminating competition' under Art 81(3)(b) EC. This point is not considered further here.

[81] One could justify the 'promotion' of environmental protection into the 'heavy' category on other grounds. For example, it is included as a principle in Art 6 EC, see Monti (2002) 1078 and Hession and Macrory (1998) 103; it is explicitly mentioned in Art 2 EC; and the Commission often emphasises its importance, eg, COM(2003) 338.

Further sub-divisions are also possible. For example, due to the breadth of many policy heads one might ask whether the whole objective should be given the same weight. Take consumer protection: Article 153(1) EC refers to protecting the '… health, safety and economic interests of consumers …' Without denying the importance of consumers' economic interests, their health and safety may be considered of greater consequence,[82] especially as this overlaps with the public health policy-linking clause in Article 152 EC. The Treaty provides some support for further sub-division; several articles expressly provide for prioritisation.[83] It is already Council and Commission practice to focus their initiatives on more precise goals in all areas.[84] This would be reinforced by reflecting the importance of these goals in their qualitative weight in Article 81's balance; which makes their achievement more likely.[85]

The discussion this far has revolved around whether the two basic categories ('high' and 'non-high') can be sub-divided. This seems possible. I suggest further sub-divisions, mainly for illustrative purposes. Even if these were agreed, there is a further problem. There is no real guidance on the *relative values (weights)* of the high and 'non-high' appellations in the Treaty or elsewhere. How much more important (weighty) are policies that require a high level of protection than those that do not? The same point can be expressed in relation to the further sub-divisions, how much weight does a 'High-Heavy' policy carry relative to a 'High-Light' one, for example?

This point is fundamental. All that I have discussed so far has been a tentative lexicographical or ordinal ranking. This gets us part of the way, but is insufficient for balancing. Even where only two objectives are balanced, an ordinal ranking does not provide conclusive help where the balance involves other dimensions to the ranked one;[86] which is the case in Article 81's balance, where the quantitative dimension is also relevant.[87] Furthermore, ordinal rankings cannot be used to order more than two objectives in the balance;[88] which can happen in Article 81 too.

The decision-maker must employ qualitative weights for the objectives *relative to* one another,[89] not just rank them. The Preamble and Article 2 EC might provide some guidance on these weights, but are not precise enough to resolve the matter,[90] particularly while Article 81's meta-objective remains undefined. To my knowledge, despite frequently balancing objectives (and accepting that the qualitative dimension is important), the Institutions' statements rarely explain what the objectives' relative weights are in general,

---

[82] A similar point could be made in relation to most other policy-linking clauses, see Arts 125 – employment; 151(1) and (2) – culture; 152(1) – public health; 157(1) – industry; 158 – economic and social cohesion; 163 and 164 – R&D; 174(1) – environmental protection; and 177 – development policy.

[83] See Arts 161 – economic and social cohesion; 166(1) – R&D; and 175(3) – environmental protection.

[84] See, eg Commission, *EU Consumer Policy Strategy 2007–2013*, s 3; Council, *On Community consumer policy strategy 2007–2013*, recital I and European Parliament and Council Decision, *Laying down the Sixth Community Environment Action Programme* (2002), art 1(4).

[85] See, eg COM(2002) 208 11 and COM(1999) 587, paras 17–24, 27.

[86] Knowing that A has a higher ranking than B, does not tell us whether A has a higher ranking than 2B.

[87] While incorporating qualitative weight within his formula, Alexy (2003b) 440, 446, Alexy sidesteps the issue of how it would apply in practice; his examples assume equal qualitative weight between rights. He is forced to do this as his triadic scale only produces an ordinal ranking.

[88] D'Agostino (2003) 7 and Adler and Posner (1999) 192.

[89] Unless, in a particular case, the qualitative weights can be ignored, see n 87 above.

[90] See, eg Commission, *Impact Assessment Guidelines*, Annex 2, p 6.

let alone provide their relative qualitative weights.[91] The Commission's decisions in this area, in particular, are opaque and unsatisfactory.[92]

Qualitative weights are only needed if objectives are ranked. Earlier, I used textual arguments to suggest that the Treaty ranks objectives. Yet, the Community Courts would probably place more emphasis on teleological arguments in this area.[93] So, while textual arguments provide some help, they cannot be relied upon entirely. However, there is some evidence that the ECJ pays heed to the 'high' and 'non-high' appellations, so ranking does seem appropriate.[94]

If ranking is appropriate, the relative qualitative weights must be established. This is not only extremely difficult, it is also controversial.[95]

Future Treaty changes should explicitly deal with the qualitative weight to be applied to each policy head, or at least allow the decision-makers to do this in concrete cases.[96] In the meantime, the qualitative weight to be attributed to those objectives not set out in the Treaty, as well as the relative and absolute weight of Treaty objectives, should both be refined and explained through the judgments and decisions of the Commission and the Community Courts.

Commission Notices would be particularly useful in resolving ambiguities in the short term. The Commission should clearly rank or weight the qualitative values.[97] To keep the political problems to a minimum, this system of values might be kept as simple as possible (at least at first), possibly having only two bands, for example, 'high' and 'not-high'. The Commission could reduce the lack of transparency through regular notices etc., which could reflect the priorities in its annual legislative and work plans, for example.

Until this has been done, the relevant Member State actors will not have the tools (or experience) to rationally provide different, relative, qualitative values for the objectives in the way the Commission would like. Obviously, judges (and national competition authorities) take political decisions too;[98] but their lack of experience; lack of clear authority on these issues; and, the fact that the 'wrong decision' may undermine the achievement of objectives here and in other areas[99] means that the Commission should provide more guidance. In a balance there is always a margin of discretion, but there is currently so little guidance that this discretion demands fundamental policy choices. As a result, until concrete guidance is given, the Member States' authorities should adopt an interim position. The best strategy would be for the decision-maker in a specific case to seek Commission help on qualitative issues before coming to a decision,[100] Regulation 1/2003,

---

[91] See Section 3.1.3. Even where a balance was arrived at I have found no explanation about what the qualitative weights are, see Commission, *Environmental State aid Guidelines*, Section E, for example.

[92] See Ch 4, Section 3, for example.

[93] See Ch 2, Section 2.2.

[94] See n 77 above, for example.

[95] For example, the Commission's most recent guidelines on consolidated impact assessments for economic, social and environmental factors do not assign concrete qualitative values, calling this a political decision, Commission, *Impact Assessment Guidelines* 39–44.

[96] Indeed it has been suggested that Art 3 EC should more clearly hierarchise the different Treaty objectives, Whish (1998) 462, 501 and Kirchner (1998) 515.

[97] See Forrester (1998) 382.

[98] Sturgess and Chubb (1988) ch 6.

[99] COM(2002) 208, s 3 and COM(2002) 276.

[100] The same applies to undertakings, but the Commission has already sought to reduce their power to do this, see Reg 1/2003, recital 3 and Commission, *Guidance Letters Guidelines*, paras 6–10.

articles 11(5) and 15(1) allow for this.[101] The quantity of potential references may lead to bottlenecks, however. If the Commission is not forthcoming then the national competition authorities might adopt a common position, either themselves, or through the Advisory Committee.[102] For example, they could assume that all objectives have the same qualitative weight. Then they could conduct the balance. If, after that, the result is ambiguous, then more weighty (high) objectives might be given decisive weight. Their decisions may be appealed to the Community Courts, this can only be beneficial, in terms of clarity, in the long term.

3.1.2 Quantitative weight

A determination of how much each relevant objective will be infringed/achieved is also relevant.[103] This is a quantitative assessment. For example, it should be relevant whether, in a particular case, the positive (or negative) environmental repercussions would be felt throughout the whole Community or in just a part of it.[104] It should also be relevant how long these effects will last.[105] These issues should be reflected in the balance.

3.1.3 Combining qualitative and quantitative weight

The next step is to combine the objective's qualitative and quantitative weights. More clarity is needed on how to do this. Multiplication is an appropriate methodology, in Article 81, as it accounts for the relative nature of the qualitative element.[106] This process must be performed in the light of Article 81's meta-objective and the factors outlined in Sections 3.2 to 3.4, below. Once each objective has been assigned a weight, these must be added or subtracted to decide the outcome of the balance, see Section 4, below.

3.2 Likelihood that objective will be achieved/harmed

Uncertainty is our constant companion and it impacts upon balancing. Imagine that the agreement *could* do significant harm to a relevant objective, but the *likelihood* of that harm occurring is small. Arguably, the decision-maker should account for certainty, or the lack of it, in the weight that this objective is assigned in the balance. This is because rational actors choose options that maximise their expected benefit.

Under Bayesian logic, the value of an objective in the balance should be its *expected* benefit (or harm); that is the benefit (or harm) if it occurs multiplied by the likelihood of the benefit (or harm) occurring.[107] We do not 'maximise' benefits under Article 81 EC, we evaluate whether the factors on one side of the balance out-weigh those on the other side. Nonetheless, the notion of expected benefit is relevant here too.[108]

---

[101]   The Commission might even take up the case itself, Reg 1/2003, recital 14 and art 10.
[102]   See, eg Reg 1/2003, recital 15 and Commission, *Co-operation Guidelines – NCAs*, paras 1, 43, 58.
[103]   See also Commission, *Impact Assessment Guidelines*, Annex 7.
[104]   For a similar issue in competition impacts, Commission, *Fining Guidelines (2006)*, paras 13–18.
[105]   ibid, para 24 and Commission, *Vertical Guidelines*, para 133.
[106]   Alexy (2003b) 440, 444.
[107]   This is an accepted part of decision theory, see, eg Schick (1997) 35.
[108]   See, eg Slote (1989).

The Commission discusses this issue in many policy areas;[109] including in relation to restrictions of competition. Where the object of an agreement is not to restrict competition, Article 81(1) should take account of actual effects on competition but it '... must also take account of the agreement's potential effects on competition ...'[110] The Commission has also said that the *likelihood* of, for example, each claimed efficiency under Article 81(3) must be substantiated.[111] Logically, the same should apply to the likelihood of achieving public policy objectives there too.

Alexy suggests that the 'likelihood factor' be incorporated through use of a sliding scale, meaning that the expected harm/benefit would be multiplied by the probability of achieving it.[112] In theory, this is the 'perfect' option as it produces the exact probability-weighted average of the benefit (or harm). In practice, the level of uncertainty is often too hard to predict.[113] Where it is disproportionate to calculate the probability of the relevant impact, approximations of probability can be used. To facilitate balancing, values need to be assigned for the different possibilities.[114] This is, somewhat, arbitrary, but at least it is relatively clear. Alexy tries to reduce the arbitrary nature of this exercise by assigning ratings (such as low, medium and high) to reflect the probability that a specific objective will be achieved (or harmed).[115] In this way, one can take account of the expected benefit (or harm), but reduce difficulties related to precise risk-quantification. The downside of this approach is that it is difficult to compare these values in the final stage of the balance.

The Commission has chosen a different strategy in Article 81. It simply ignores impacts unless the agreement has '... *likely* anti-competitive effects ...'[116] [117] (emphasis added). This formulation is easier to apply than Alexy's;[118] but, before embracing it, I want to consider whether it is appropriate for public policy balancing in Article 81.

In relation to some public policy objectives, only considering likely impacts is probably acceptable. Take development policy, promoted by Article 178 EC, for example, this provision says that:

> The Community shall take account of the objectives ...[of Community development policy] in the policies that it implements which are *likely* to affect developing countries. (emphasis added)

However, where we are not specifically told to ignore all but the likely effects then Alexy's three-part scale (such as low, medium and high) may be a better compromise. This is because the Commission's more convenient test (ignoring all but likely effects) may lead us to ignore (potentially) important outcomes simply because we cannot show a high level of probability that an agreement will cause them. Significant precision (and weight) is

---

[109]   eg Commission, *Impact Assessment Guidelines* 26, 33–36.

[110]   Case C-7/95 P, *John Deere v Commission* para 77 and, more generally, Goldman and Barutciski (1998) 415.

[111]   Commission, *Article 81(3) Guidelines*, para 51.

[112]   For a similar discussion in constitutional balancing, see Alexy (2003b) 446–48 and Alexy (2002) 414–22.

[113]   Alexy (2002) 417, '... empirical knowledge of this quality is practically never available.' Attempts to get round this problem can be found in Jeffrey (1983) and Sahlin (1990).

[114]   For example, these might be: certainty = 1, high risk = 0.75, medium risk = 0.5, low risk = 0.25.

[115]   See Alexy (2003b) 446–48 and Commission, *Impact Assessment Guidelines* 33–36.

[116]   Note that there is a link with the notion of appreciability, see Section 3.4, below.

[117]   In relation to Art 81(1) see Commission, *Article 81(3) Guidelines*, para 24. Later in the paragraph the Commission uses the alternative phrase '... with a reasonable degree of probability ...' The same guidelines discuss the Art 81(3) position at paras 55–58, the relevant efficiencies, eg, must be '... likely to materialise ...', para 56, and in relation to consumer benefits, refer to '... any actual or likely negative impact caused ...', para 85. See also, Joined Cases 142 and 156/84, *British American Tobacco Reynolds v Commission*, paras 57–59.

[118]   Although it is not clear what probability a 'likely' event must have, it must be reasonably high.

sacrificed for convenience. This could be particularly important where, even if it is not likely that it will occur, the outcome would be catastrophic if it did.

Furthermore, in relation to some objectives, ignoring all but the likely outcomes seems contrary to the Treaty. Environmental policy, for example, '… shall be based on the precautionary principle …'[119] This leaves open the question of how much certainty is needed;[120] but, the implication is that even where there is considerable uncertainty as to the *existence* of risks in relation to environmental protection, these risks (and potential benefits) should be weighed in the balance. Note that the Treaty says that the precautionary principle *shall* be taken into account.[121] As a result, only considering *likely* environmental risks probably infringes the Treaty in relation to the environment.[122]

Where uncertainty occurs, the weight these objectives are given in the balance should be less than it would have been if we were certain that the specific problems/benefits would arise. If possible, the probability should be calculated. Bayesian logic then suggests multiplying the objective's weight by the probability of achieving it. Where this is disproportionate, approximations of probability should be used; values need to be assigned for them. This is, somewhat, arbitrary, but at least it is relatively accurate and clear. To simplify the balance the Commission might continue to ignore objectives with a low, or even a medium risk, unless the precautionary principle applies to that objective.

3.3 Discounting for the future

An agreement's costs and benefits occur over time. Economic analysis and decision theory[123] tend to assume that a given unit of benefit today matters more if experienced now than if it occurs in the future. This is because people prefer their benefits now; and, if we invest capital, rather than consume it now, these resources should yield a higher level of consumption in a later period. Where the benefits of investment exceed the 'costs' of impatience, it is worth waiting before consuming.[124]

Discounting is the mechanism through which one finds the present value of future benefits and costs.[125] We should account for when the costs and benefits occur; so that their weight in the balance better reflects the harm/benefit that is caused.[126]

---

[119]   Art 174(2) EC. The Treaty does not define the precautionary principle, but the ECJ has interpreted it as follows 'Where there is uncertainty as to the existence … of risks … the institutions may take protective measures without having to wait until the reality … of those risks become fully apparent …', Case C-157/96, *The Queen v MAFF, ex p National Farmers' Union* para 63. See also COM(2000) 1.

[120]   Majone (2002) 91–95 and Scott and Vos (2002) 254–73, 283–86.

[121]   This is confirmed in the French ('*doivent être intégrées*'), Spanish ('*deberán integrarse*') and Italian ('*devono essere integrate*') versions of the Treaty, for example. Note though that use of the precautionary principle must be proportionate and based on the costs and benefits of action and lack of action, COM(2000) 1, 17–19.

[122]   The Treaty only mentions the precautionary principle in relation to environmental policy. However, the Commission wants to apply the principle in other areas too, COM(2000)1 2, 9, 22. See also, Majone (2002) 90, 95–98.

[123]   See, respectively, Broome (1999) ch 4 and Schick (1997) 64–68.

[124]   Pearce and Turner (1990) 213 and Broome (1999) 53–67.

[125]   Pearson (2000) 77, 78.

[126]   For more information on how discounting is used in Community impact assessments, see Commission, *Impact Assessment Guidelines*, Annex 12.

The Commission encourages discounting for efficiencies in Article 81's balance by saying that it is relevant *when* each one is achieved.[127] This allows the decision-maker to account for the value of the claimed efficiencies.[128]

An analogous process is justified in relation to public policy objectives. The predicted harm (or benefit) that arises as a result of the agreement should be discounted in the balance, depending upon when it occurs. Improvements in environmental protection or public health today are worth more than equivalent improvements tomorrow.[129]

However, specific problems arise in relation to some objectives. For example, depending upon the circumstances, increasing the discount rate can have an ambiguous effect on environmental protection.[130] On one hand, higher discount rates may encourage discrimination against future generations. If social costs occur well into the future and net social benefits occur in the near term,[131] high discount rates make the project more acceptable in the balance, think of global warming.[132] On the other hand, a low discount rate would discourage development projects that compete with existing environmentally benign land use. This may slow the depletion of natural resources.[133]

The Commission suggests that the '… discount rate applied must reflect the rate of inflation, if any, and lost interest as an indication of the lower value of future gains.'[134] The appropriate discount rate for non-monetary objectives is extremely difficult to quantify, involving economic theory, empirical observation and ethical choices.[135] Development of specific formulae for discounting each relevant objective is technical and controversial and goes beyond the scope of this work;[136] but the Commission needs to take a stance on the economic and ethical choices; develop guidelines of how it will discount in the balance (at least a range of values), and whether this is always appropriate.[137] One must be careful, otherwise considerable uncertainty may be generated; and yet, to ignore this effect could have serious consequences on resource allocation in the future in general, and sustainability in particular.[138]

---

[127] Commission, *Article 81(3) Guidelines*, para 51.

[128] ibid, para 55. A similar point is made in s 3.4 of the same guidelines, which discuss the 'fair share for consumers' test.

[129] Although it is normally harder to show future effects than more proximate ones.

[130] See Broome (1999), s 4.4.

[131] Special care is needed when comparing policies with different time horizons, see Commission, *Impact Assessment Guidelines*, Annex 12.

[132] For a discussion of this see *Degrees of Difference*, The Economist, 1 May 2004, p 80, and more generally see Pearce and Turner (1990) 217–24 and Pearson (2000) 86–94.

[133] The Commission suggests that goals involving long time horizons, such as climate change, may justify use of a lower discount rate, Commission, *Impact Assessment Guidelines*, Annex 12.

[134] Commission, *Article 81(3) Guidelines*, para 88.

[135] Pearson (2000) 77, 78. The discount rate is (potentially) different for each commodity. As it is different from monetary discounting, one does not overcome this problem by use of the common meter. For example, if one wants to value a future risk of environmental harm (at time T), it would not be appropriate to change the present day value of the environmental harm into monetary form (imagine it was worth £X) and then find the value of £X at T. This is because the valuation discounts for monetary and not environmental future risks.

[136] As regards the environment see, eg Pearce and Turner (1990) ch 14; Pearson (2000) ch 4; Broome (1999), s 4.6 and Lomborg (2004).

[137] Commission, *Impact Assessment Guidelines*, Annex 12, suggests a discount rate of 4%.

[138] Art 6 EC reads 'Environmental protection requirements must be integrated into the definition and implementation of the Community policies and activities referred to in Art 3, in particular with a view to promoting sustainable development.' Other public policy goals have similar principles, COM(2007) 642.

3.4 Appreciability

An agreement could impact upon many policy objectives. Some of these impacts may be large, but many would normally be small. In an ideal world, one would consider all of these (potential) effects in the Article 81 EC balance. However, this could be extremely difficult and expensive and, where the effects are likely to be small, the cost of calculating them might be disproportionate to the gains we achieve in approximating the meta-objective.

We saw above that one might ignore objectives that were *unlikely* to be achieved, unless the precautionary principle applied.[139] In addition, where an objective will be affected but is not relevant *to any important degree*, in a qualitative or a quantitative way, then the benefits of clarity, as well as the fact that decisions can be taken more easily, quickly and cheaply by ignoring this objective, may outweigh the benefits of perfection.[140] In other words, a second-best solution might be preferable.[141]

The Commission, with the support of the Community Courts,[142] already uses this type of limitation in relation to the Article 81(1) objective(s).[143] In its *De Minimis Notice* the Commission states that where the parties' aggregate market share is below a certain level,[144] it will not, normally,[145] find an appreciable restriction of competition. These market share screens seem designed to assess whether an agreement significantly contributes to closing off the markets at issue.[146] This is probably done to establish whether or not competition is significantly affected; it is a quantitative test. There may also be a qualitative element to the test. The Commission says that the market share screen does not apply to agreements containing certain hardcore restrictions, such as price-fixing and limiting output.[147] The *de minimis* doctrine can still apply where there are hardcore restraints,[148] it is just that its presence cannot be presumed where they are present and it may be harder to justify.[149]

Similar principles could be created for other public policy objectives (or certain aspects of them[150]) in Article 81(3) EC. The Commission could publish notices setting out both qualitative and quantitative tests. The qualitative element should define core areas of each policy objective; later Treaty amendments could incorporate these. Some objectives, particularly those where a high standard is demanded, will contain many such areas. For example, in relation to public health, all areas relating to life-saving techniques may be hardcore. Other objectives, such as culture, may contain none.

Once the Commission has defined these hardcore areas it must also establish a quantitative test. Insofar as an agreement impacts upon a non-hardcore part of a specific

---

[139] See Section 3.2, above.
[140] Kirkpatrick and Parker (2007) 4, 5.
[141] On the theory of second-best, see Ch 5, Section 4.
[142] Case 5/69 *Franz Völk v Vervaecke* paras 5, 7 and Case 22/71, *Béguelin v GL* para 16.
[143] More generally, the Commission points to this trade-off in its work on impact assessments too, Commission, *Impact Assessment Guidelines* 8, 33–36.
[144] *De Minimis Notice*, paras 7, 9.
[145] ibid, para 8.
[146] Case T-77/94, *Vereniging van Groothandelaren v Commission* para 140.
[147] *De Minimis Notice*, para 11.
[148] See, eg Case 5/69 *Franz Völk v Vervaecke* para 5, 7.
[149] Faull and Nikpay (2007), paras 3.158–3.161.
[150] eg, there may be three cultural issues, but one may be so much less important than the other two such that it can safely be ignored without significantly affecting the robustness of the balance.

objective then only appreciable effects on that aim will be considered in the balance. The Commission must define the appreciable concept in its guidance. For the sake of argument, in the area of environmental protection, the effects of CO_2 emissions might be non-hardcore. The Commission may then decide that an agreement that would lead to, for example, less than 20 tons of such emissions per year would be *de minimis*. It would then ignore environmental policy in the balance for agreements that caused annual emissions of less than 20 tons. Environmental policy would normally be a factor in the balance for agreements that created more pollution than this.

However, as with the *de minimis* concept as currently employed,[151] where an agreement went over this level (over 20 tons of emissions) it could still be *de minimis*, when placed in its legal and economic context. Alternatively, it might also be that, even where the effects under one or more public policy objectives were not appreciable, their cumulative effect might be such that, taken together, they should be weighed in the balance.[152] Furthermore, this concept should also apply in the area of hardcore restrictions as long as, taking into account the legal and economic context, the effect was in fact *de minimis*. Even if such an effect were found not to be *de minimis*, small non-hardcore public policy effects may not be given much weight in the balance.

If the Commission is to ensure the uniformity of Article 81 decisions it must explain what factors affect the objectives' weight in the balance. Section 3 has examined difficulties associated with ascertaining the qualitative and quantitative weight. It also looks at issues, such as discounting and the likelihood of achievement, which the Commission ought to account for, as well as explaining how to do this. Other factors, such as the irreversibility[153] and the duration[154] of the harm might also be considered. Finally, one might simplify the balance by ignoring non-appreciable objectives. There is still much work for the Commission to do. It would be helpful if it provided a practical balancing framework. In part this can be communicated via induction, but I believe that guidelines are more appropriate for such an important clarification.

4 COMPARING APPLES AND PEARS – A COMMON METER

There is a practical problem at the balance's core. Once we have calculated each objective's weight, we must weigh it in the balance with the others. This is the third step in Alexy's process.[155]

---

[151] See Cases C-215/96 and C-216/96, *Carlo Bagnasco and Others v Banca Popolare and Others* paras 34, 35.

[152] This point is similar to the effect which para 8 of the *De Minimis Notice* seeks to prevent. Cumulative impacts are considered in relation to environmental impact assessments, see, eg Commission, *A Handbook on Environmental Assessment* 50.

[153] See Commission, *Article 81(3) Guidelines*, para 45. This issue is mentioned in relation to impact assessments, Commission, *Impact Assessment Guidelines*, Annex 15.

[154] See Commission, *Impact Assessment Guidelines* 27.

[155] See Section 3.1, above.

Balancing involves summing the relevant objectives' weighted averages.[156] Summing is only possible if the relevant objectives can be substituted for one another (are comparable).[157] Absent substitutability one cannot establish which combination of objectives has the greatest weight; and so, one cannot assess which side of the balance should prevail.

This means that we have to assess whether the relevant objectives are substitutable. Some of them are, sometimes. Chapter 3 asked what market integration means, for example. The Commission[158] and the CFI[159] have said that it is there to achieve consumer welfare. It may be that market integration can be defined *in terms of* consumer welfare. That said, the Commission has not exclusively defined market integration in efficiency terms;[160] so, there may not always be substitutability between these goals. In any event, many other public policy objectives, such as culture and public health, are relevant in Article 81 EC.[161] Imagine a restrictive agreement that undermines public health and yet promotes culture. It might be argued that these objectives cannot be directly compared; if they are not directly substitutable then a rational balance will be hard to perform. One can directly compare 2 and 3, they are both natural numbers, and thus substitutable, (2<3). In contrast, one cannot directly establish whether 2 apples<3 pears. Apples and pears are not directly comparable; there is no direct rate of substitution.

Fortunately, comparability can also arise by means of an indirect scale.[162] Given a common meter (common denominator), such that 1 apple is equivalent to 3 bananas, and 1 pear is equivalent to 5 bananas, for example, then one can easily show that:

1 apple = 3 bananas   1 pear = 5 bananas
1 banana = 1/3 apple   1 banana = 1/5 pear
⇒ 1/5 pear = 1/3 apple
⇒ 1 apple = 3/5 pear
⇒ 2 apples = 6/5 pear
⇒ 2 apples<3 pears

The common denominator enables us to overcome the *direct* incommensurability problem. As a result, apples and pears become comparable through this indirect scale.

As Aleinikoff notes, the problem for balancing '… is the derivation of the scale needed to translate the value of interests into a common currency for comparison.'[163] If disparate factors, such as consumer welfare, culture and public health, are to be balanced against each other then one needs an indirect meter, into which they can be converted. Otherwise,

---

[156]   Accounting for their qualitative and quantitative aspects, Section 3, above and Schick (1997) 42.

[157]   Lucy (1999) 154–56; Schick (1997) 41–44 and D'Agostino (2003) 28.

[158]   Agreements which undermine market integration '… hold back the improvement in the economic efficiency of the Community's production structure …', Commission, *RCP 1992*, point 2.

[159]   Case T-168/01 *GlaxoSmithKline Services v Commission* esp paras 118, 273. This judgment is currently on appeal to the ECJ, in part on this issue, see Joined Cases C-501/06 etc *GlaxoSmithKline Services v Commission*. See also, the Opinion of A-G Trstenjak, Case C-209/07 *The Competition Authority v BIDS* para 56, supporting the CFI's judgment and Joined Cases C-468/06 to C-478/06 *Sot Lelos kai Sia EE and Others v GlaxoSmithKline* esp para 65, which seems to undermine it.

[160]   See Ch 3, Section 2.1 and Ch 4, Section 2.2.

[161]   See Ch 2, Section 2.

[162]   Johansson (1991) 111 and Wathern (1988) 14.

[163]   Aleinikoff (1987) 973, 976.

these objectives cannot be compared, as the Community Courts' interpretation of Article 81 demands, and balancing becomes impossible.

This means that we must select a common meter for the Article 81 balance. However, selecting (and using) a common meter is not a value-neutral exercise.[164] Therefore, it is vital that the Commission is explicit about *which* common meter it selects and *how* to convert different objectives into it. This will introduce more transparency (enhancing repeatability) into the decision-making process.

The indirect method of comparability allows us to assign a value for the amount of damage/benefit attained, both qualitatively and quantitatively. Using environmental protection as my example, I illustrate this process below. Once a comparable value has been established for all relevant objectives, the values can be added/subtracted, as appropriate, to ascertain which side of the balance is weightier.

How can one translate the environmental harm an agreement causes onto a common scale; or, what numerical value should one give X amount of environmental harm on the meter? Remember, harm has both a quantitative and a qualitative dimension.[165] Examining the quantitative dimension first, Article 174(2) EC explains that:

> Community policy on the environment … shall be based on … the principles that preventive action should be taken, that environmental damage should as a priority be rectified at source and that the polluter should pay.

Article 174(2) gives us a clue as to how to evaluate the quantitative aspect of environmental damage; the polluter should pay. One could assess, quantitatively, how much environmental damage has been/will be done and money could be the common meter.

Money would be a good meter.[166] It is readily divisible, and thus, flexible. Furthermore, the Community institutions, the Member States and undertakings are already familiar with using money for balancing. Member States, and the Community itself, must decide how much of the EU budget is to be spent on the different policy areas. Individuals are also used to balancing such disparate decisions as whether to buy oranges or medical insurance, houses or education, using the money they earn.[167]

A monetary meter is more easily applied to some Treaty objectives, such as environmental protection and consumer welfare, than to those such as economic and social cohesion, the effect of which can be hard to quantify in monetary terms. Objectives such as respect for human rights and public health may also be difficult to quantify in this way.[168] It is important that such goals are not ignored just because they may be hard to quantify in monetary terms.[169]

Note that environmental protection's conversion to the common meter is already riddled with value judgments. The polluter must pay, but is this the most effective/best/cheapest way to reduce environmental harm?[170] A second problem relates to what is meant

---

[164]   Espeland and Stevens (1998) 317, 323–32 and D'Agostino (2003) 9–14 and s 21.
[165]   As discussed in Section 3 above, it should also account for issues such as the likelihood of damage and when damage will occur, but I do not consider these issues here.
[166]   Commission, *Impact Assessment Guidelines* 26, 36 and Annex 11.
[167]   This familiarity with money could also be a disadvantage, however. One must ensure that this intimacy does not blind us to some of the assumptions that its use involves; see Commission decision, *CECED* (2000), discussed below.
[168]   Sunstein (1997) 235–38.
[169]   Commission, *Impact Assessment Guidelines* 36 and Annex 11.
[170]   Other suggestions can be found at Commission, *Impact Assessment Guidelines*, Annex 13.

by asking how much it would cost the polluter to sort out the environmental concern. Article 174(2) implicitly prioritises two alternative approaches to environmental harm. Rectifying the damage at source is a priority (Option A); alternatively, the polluter could clear up the environmental damage that has occurred (Option B). This complicates the analysis somewhat. Imagine that Option A costs £90 and Option B costs £50.[171] The Treaty ranks these options in order of preference, but it does not tell us *how much more preferable* Option A is than Option B.

For the purposes of this discussion, I assume that the best Community strategy, taking account of both price and the Treaty's ranking, is to rectify the environmental damage at source, Option A.[172] This means that I now have the quantitative assessment of the environmental damage caused by the agreement, £90. To establish the objective's weighted average, I must multiply £90 by the qualitative value of this environmental harm.[173] Determining the qualitative value is a complex and controversial exercise. The Commission may determine one figure, or there may be a function that describes an indifference curve between the two (or more) objectives. There are many methodologies that can be used to obtain this sort of information.[174] One is to articulate different levels of gravity of infringement, for each objective (qualitative issue). For example, there could be two categories of 'high' and 'non-high', reflecting the Treaty's own distinction.[175] Then, the qualitative and quantitative values must be combined.[176]

An alternative methodology is cost-benefit analysis. This collapses the qualitative and quantitative steps into one assessment.[177] By assessing people's 'willingness to pay',[178] cost-benefit analysis should automatically account for qualitative and quantitative weight, as well as discounting.[179] The same applies to pricing through the market. Some suggest that cost-benefit solutions (including internalising externalities) are the most appropriate means for valuing public policy objectives.[180] However, I am more cautious, because the qualitative values (implicitly) adopted are those of the individual. These might differ from the qualitative weight that the Treaty assigns; for example, due to a lack of information, different priorities, or externalities. The individual might also assess the importance of the

---

[171]   These assessments should take account of all appreciable direct and indirect costs. In relation to the four different environmental costs, see Johansson (1991) 114. As regards culture, see Snowball and Antrobus (2001) 755 *ff.*

[172]   No other objectives expressly incorporate the 'polluter pays' principle. The Commission could, as a starting point for the other objectives, compare the position with and without the agreement, a kind of 'the parties pay' principle. The cost of reducing the level of harm to its level before the agreement (or the cost of achieving the same improvement through other means) is the amount of quantitative harm/benefit provided by the agreement. This might price these objectives too highly. Another possibility would be to use cost-benefit analysis. A final suggestion would be to employ a form of the Neumann/Morgenstern technique, D'Agostino (2003) 97–99.

[173]   As discussed in Section 3.1.1, above, the qualitative figure is based upon an abstract value related to the importance of environmental protection, as explained by the Treaty's meta-objective. It *may* also take account of the specific type of environmental damage threatened by the agreement.

[174]   D'Agostino (2003) 99, 100 and Dasgupta (2001) C4-C13 and references made there. In relation to the environment, see, eg Sinden and Thampapillai (1995).

[175]   See Section 3.1.1, above, for issues that must be considered if this approach is adopted.

[176]   See Section 3.1.3, above. Once again split into different degrees of seriousness. For more accuracy a list of aggravating and attenuating factors could also be added, see, eg Commission, *Fining Guidelines.*

[177]   See Adler and Posner (1999) 197–204.

[178]   See, eg Commission, *Cost-benefit analysis of MSWs* 269.

[179]   See Broome (1999) 57.

[180]   See Gyselen (1994) 244.

impact of his/her decision on others differently than the Treaty.[181] For example, she might not take 'sufficient' account of the environmental damage that she creates for future generations when driving her car, as this will not affect her.[182] As a result, cost-benefit analysis might not always give the 'right' qualitative weight.[183]

There is very little evidence of the Commission using meters in its Article 81 analysis. I suggest using money as a meter. There are other alternatives. The meter might even change, depending upon the objectives at stake. The Commission must provide guidance on which common meter(s) to use and how to translate the objectives into them. One decision where the Commission embarks upon this process is Commission decision, *CECED*.[184] There, the Commission focused on the agreement's economic benefits to consumers. It argued that the increase in the purchase price for these environmentally friendly machines would be compensated for by savings on electricity bills.[185] The Commission added that there were also collective environmental benefits.[186] It highlighted Article 174 EC, and added 'Agreements like CECED's must yield economic benefits outweighing their costs and be compatible with competition rules…'[187] The Commission said that 'economic benefits' could include the costs of pollution.[188] It discussed the cost, to society, of avoiding the CO_2 and SO_2 emissions, which the increased energy efficiency would obviate and concluded that 'On the basis of reasonable assumptions, the benefits to society brought about by the CECED agreement appear to be more than seven times greater than the increased purchase costs of more energy-efficient washing machines.'[189] Taking its base point as what would have happened absent the agreement,[190] the Commission found that the environmental benefits to society were seven times greater due to the agreement. It concluded that the expected improvements to energy efficiency, the cost–benefit ratio of the standard and the return on investment for individual users, implied that the agreement would contribute significantly to technical and economic progress.[191] In conclusion, the Commission found that individual users' return on investment meant that, although the initial purchase price would rise, the lifetime cost of the machine would likely fall. It also found that the cost of avoiding the pollution that would arise if the

---

[181]   See, eg the Economic and Social Committee, *Comments on COM(1999) 543*, point 3.3. and Majone (2002) 101.

[182]   Broome (1999) 51. For example, in *The Sixth Environment Action Programme* (2001), para 1, the Commission says: 'A clean and healthy environment is part and parcel of the prosperity and quality of life that we desire for ourselves now *and for our children in the future*.' (emphasis added)

[183]   This is hinted at by Poiares Maduro (1999) 466, 470.

[184]   You will remember that this involved an agreement between CECED, a Brussels-based association comprising manufacturers of domestic appliances and national trade associations, and its members; companies comprising some 95% of the relevant market. The agreement concerned the domestic washing machines' market in the European Economic Area. The parties to the agreement bound themselves to cease producing and/or importing into the Community certain categories of washing machines on criteria relating to their energy efficiency, reducing consumer choice and technical diversity. For a more detailed description of the facts, see Ch 2, Section 2.3.2.

[185]   Commission decision, *CECED*, para 52.

[186]   The Commission followed a similar approach both in relation to the EACEM Agreement, see Commission, *RCP 1998*, point 130 and p 152, and in the Annex to COM(95) 689, where the Commission made a preliminary assessment of the costs and the benefits of technical measures to reduce CO_2 emissions from cars.

[187]   Commission decision, *CECED*, para 55.

[188]   See Ch 4, Section 2.3.2.

[189]   Commission decision, *CECED*, para 56.

[190]   As I suggest in n 172 above.

[191]   Commission decision, *CECED*, para 57.

agreement were not adopted would be seven times that of the increased purchase price of the more energy-efficient machines.

In order to compare the environmental improvements with the initial loss of consumer welfare, the Commission used a common meter. The meter it chose was money. However, while the Commission took account of the quantitative dimension of the benefit, it failed to consider the qualitative aspect.[192] Nor did it discuss whether preventative action was better than cleaning up the damage (Option A or B), so it did not account for this in the balance. Furthermore, it assumed that *all* environmental problems would be fixed *completely*; this prices environmental protection too highly.

Despite the problems highlighted above, I welcome the Commission's use of a meter, at this stage. First, its introduction is an extremely important step, creating greater transparency in the area. Secondly, a monetary meter, while not ideal, should be applicable to many of the Treaty objectives that are touched by agreements considered under Article 81. Nevertheless, the Commission must use the common meter more consistently and make provision for qualitative analysis too, where appropriate. It must also increase the clarity of its analysis. Furthermore, efforts need to be undertaken to produce a meter or meters in areas where the monetary meter developed above is deemed inappropriate.

5 CONCLUSION

Many objectives must be considered within Article 81. They often conflict. The Commission, supported by the Community Courts, normally resolves these conflicts through balancing. There is little or no explanation about how balancing should be performed. As a result, Article 81 decisions involving public policy are often less predictable for undertakings than they could be, nor are Commission decisions easily reproducible by the Member States' authorities. Guidance in this area would significantly contribute towards the effective enforcement of Article 81.

For this reason I proffer this framework. The Commission should produce *Guidelines on Weighing*, providing a framework for balancing, as well as training for decision-makers. These guidelines should allocate an abstract (qualitative) value for each relevant objective, or at least the important ones that are frequently cited. This would introduce a more mechanised approach to balancing; which, while remaining sensitive to the demands of the Treaty, should make the prediction of the balance, and, ultimately, decision-making, simpler.[193] These abstract values will be somewhat arbitrary. But the logic of the Treaty framework demands that they be assigned. Due to the political importance of setting such weights, the Member States may consider defining them in future Treaty amendments. In concrete cases, the qualitative dimension must be combined with the quantitative harm (or benefit) attained by the agreement. I demonstrated how this might be done in relation to environmental protection. Different rules may apply to other objectives and the Commission should clarify this procedure in relation to at least the major goals.

---

[192]   As noted above, n 87 above, this is only acceptable if the objectives being weighed have the same qualitative values. The Commission also ignores discounting and likelihood.
[193]   Espeland and Stevens (1998) 314.

The Commission must also explain which factors theoretically affect the objectives' weight in the balance. Likelihood of harm is relevant, as is discounting for the future. The Commission should explain how these concepts can be calculated and provide examples in relation to the important Article 81 objectives. It should also explain the relevance of appreciability and establish a common meter, or meters.

Finally, these guidelines should adopt a meta-objective. At first, this will probably be too general to provide much help. That said, it is still important and decision makers will refer to it when, after having allocated values to the relevant objectives in the case before them, they remain unsure about how specific conflicts should be decided. Over time, case law will help define the content of the meta-objective and increasingly decisions will be made relying directly upon it.

This chapter is not revolutionary; it is not intended to be. Rather, it has taken concepts that the Commission normally uses in the balance and asked how they will operate in relation to objectives such as public health and environmental protection. It has shown that: (i) the application of these concepts to the relevant objectives raises many difficult questions; and, (ii) it demands a plethora of value judgments.

I have not produced this list of issues in the belief that balancing can be reduced to a mathematical formula. Rather, it is hoped that by highlighting these factors, decision-makers will be encouraged to consider them when balancing; making their assessments more complete, transparent and reproducible.

Producing guidelines is not easy; but it is this difficulty that makes them necessary. Without them, the various decision-makers and undertakings must struggle with these issues alone. They are inexperienced in applying Article 81(3) EC. Without guidance they will soon become lost, rudderless ships in the night. Nor must they be allowed to shelter in their home ports of nationally influenced value judgments. The Commission must guide them out of this darkness, towards the light of the optimal Community balance's dawn.

Conclusion of Part C

Non-economic objectives can conflict with antitrust's economic goals. Chapter 2 argues that the Treaty and the Community Courts demand the consideration of several public policy goals in Article 81 EC. This is not lost on the Commission, which has often balanced non-economic objectives there too.

Part B examines public policy balancing in Article 81 in more detail. It uncovered two balancing mechanisms, market and mere-balancing; there is little order or consistency in which is used. Furthermore, sometimes the Community Courts balance in Article 81(1) EC, sometimes in Article 81(3), and sometimes they claim that they cannot balance within Article 81 at all. The Commission's guidelines now claim that public policy goals are irrelevant within Article 81, unless they raise efficiency benefits. This lack of coherence and transparency is problematic. Given the number of decision-makers post 1 May 2004, the problem is likely to get worse. Until a better framework (which chimes with the Community legal order) is found, many relevant goals are likely to be undermined.

In the light of these observations, Part C makes some proposals for how to consider non-economic objectives within Article 81 EC in a more coherent way. Certain elements must be at the heart of any proposed clarification. First and foremost, the proposed system must respect the Treaty, unless amendments are proposed; and the fundamental tenets of the Community Courts' case law. This means that decision-makers must be able to consider relevant public policy objectives within Article 81. Secondly, undertakings, decision-makers and consumers need more legal certainty in the balancing test and transparency in the way it is conducted. Thirdly, within this framework, the competition rules must be as efficient possible.[1] I also seek to take into account, to the extent allowed by the Treaty, Chapter 1's conclusions.

Chapter 6 proposes a consumer welfare test, as Article 81(1) EC's sole goal; arguing that while non-economic objectives must be considered within Article 81, this does not mean that they should be directly considered all of the time, ie within Article 81(1). To do so would create too much uncertainty and involve too much cost, for insufficient return. It also risks a *détournement de pouvoir*. In any event, Chapter 1 showed that a consumer welfare test often helps achieve non-economic objectives, in the long term. Having said that, it would not take account of all of these, nor could it be guaranteed to give them the weight that the Treaty demands. This should not be too prejudicial as most public policy objectives can normally be more efficiently promoted through other instruments. In any

---

[1] The Community is part of a global trading system. The Treaty's aims will more likely be achieved where the increasingly global nature of commerce is recognised. To this end, my proposals open the way for more convergence with US antitrust than we have seen in the past. Nevertheless, although the consideration of non-economic objectives reduces convergence (Ehlermann (1998) xi), the Treaty's imperative for this cannot be ignored.

event and to the extent that consumer welfare is appreciably undermined, Article 81(3) EC is there to ensure that, where necessary, relevant non-economic objectives can be taken into account in Article 81.

Chapter 7 deals with Article 81(3) EC, recommending that the first test there should involve a full balancing (ie considering the positive and negative effects) of Community public policy objectives. Relevant Member States' public policy objectives should also be considered in cases of diagonal conflict. Secondly, consideration of all appreciable public policy effects, even those outside the relevant market, should be possible. I also argue that Article 81(3)(a) should be re-interpreted to mean that the agreement must be indispensable; which, for my purposes would essentially mean that only where an objective could not be achieved by anyone in any way (to the appropriate level) more efficiently than by distorting competition would the agreement be exempted. This is not because non-economic objectives are unimportant; quite the contrary. However, this should preserve the market mechanism as the fundamental tool of wealth creation, because of its many advantages. At the same time, it will encourage the use of the most efficient tool to achieve relevant objectives; which might be through restrictions of competition, where necessary.

Finally, Chapter 8 provides a framework for balancing non-economic objectives within Article 81 EC, under Article 81(3)'s first test. The framework has not been produced with the idea that balancing can be reduced to a mathematical formula. However, by exposing various relevant factors that might be considered in the balance, I hope to help decision-makers focus upon several criteria that they might otherwise ignore. This should help them make their balancing more transparent and thus repeatable as well. Amongst other things, I discuss factors which could hypothetically affect an objective's weight in the balance. These include quantitative and qualitative aspects; the likelihood of harm; discounting for future effects; the appreciability of non-economic objectives; and an appropriate meta-objective for Article 81 balancing.

Given its leadership role in Article 81, I hope that the Commission will produce guidelines explaining how the balance would work in more detail. Producing these guidelines will not be easy; but this is precisely what makes them so necessary.

Conclusion

This book has considered public policy's place in Article 81 EC. It demonstrated that public policy concerns are relevant within that provision. It also suggested how and where they should be considered there.

There are three parts to this story. Part A asked whether antitrust laws should consider public policy objectives outside of economic welfare. It did this from two perspectives. Chapter 1 was a theoretical analysis in a legal vacuum, asking whether it is ever rational to consider non-economic objectives within competition policy. Chapter 2 changed the emphasis, examining the question within the context of a specific legal system, Community competition law's Article 81 EC. The Commission *Article 81(3) Guidelines* accept that public policy can be considered in Article 81;[1] however, they seriously restrict the impact of this by imposing a unitary consumer welfare goal:

> The objective of Article 81 is to protect competition on the market as a means of enhancing consumer welfare and of ensuring an efficient allocation of resources.[2]

Many influential Community competition scholars and practitioners would agree. An oft-cited reason is that public policy objectives are increasingly irrelevant in other jurisdictions' competition provisions—including those of the USA. By following a similar policy in the Community we could, so the argument goes, reduce costs for multinational firms. Furthermore, competition policy cannot do everything. Non-economic goals can normally be better achieved using other policy instruments.

Chapter 1 asked why competition policy might incorporate non-welfare objectives. This was relatively easy to answer. Competition laws often have a welfare objective. I showed that all welfare standards are value-laden and advocated the consumer welfare standard. However, I went on to demonstrate that a competition law's pursuit of consumer welfare can affect the achievement of other public policy objectives. I argued that allowing competition policy to take account of these interactions means that a better balance can be attained overall. Nevertheless, if public policy goals are incorporated into competition policy it is vital that their relevance is acknowledged upfront and the consideration of these goals must be as rational, transparent and open as possible.

Given this conclusion, a second issue arose, when should competition policy consider non-welfare objectives? While, it is difficult to agree abstract theoretical limits on when one should intervene in specific cases, I suggested some possible filters. Let us start with tests for when public policy issues should not be considered in the competition assessment. I suggest three. First, one should only balance public policy where there is a reduction in consumer welfare. In other words, only where there is a competition problem

---

[1] Commission, *Article 81(3) Guidelines*, para 42.
[2] ibid, para 13.

should one use competition law to achieve public policy goals. Secondly, where the agreement's qualitative and/or quantitative impact on public policy goals is not appreciable then it should be ignored. Finally, one might also be less open to public policy balancing where the legislator has recently intervened in the specific balance, or explicitly decided not to, because it thought the current balance was appropriate.

In other cases, where the legal context demands it, public policy balancing should take place. There, the entity performing the balancing exercise must consider, in the legal and economic context, the impact upon competition and weigh this against the impact upon other relevant public policy goal(s). However, one should be sceptical about any claimed public policy effects. I argued that these should either be costed in some way, or at the least be supported by some widely accepted theoretical model.

Having said that, Chapter 2 shows why these limits may not be appropriate in a Community competition law context. Both the structure of the Treaty and the presence of (an ever-increasing number of) policy-linking clauses create the possibility of conflicts in Community law. The Treaty normally prefers compromise (balancing) to resolve the conflicts, but sometimes it is silent. The Community Courts have had to fill the gaps. When the Community Courts construe particular Treaty articles they have regard to the framework of the Treaty as a whole, to its general principles and to the tasks and activities which the Treaty prescribes for the Community. In the vast majority of cases, including those related to Article 81, the Community Courts have also chosen compromise to resolve these conflicts. Article 81 (and competition policy as a whole) is not an end in itself but rather one of the instruments for achieving the Treaty's fundamental goals. Community competition provisions cannot be understood or applied without reference to this legal, economic, political and social context.

There is a growing tendency among Community competition specialists to treat their topic in a highly technical way, as distinct from Community law as a whole. This is inappropriate. Back in 1966 the ECJ held:

> Article 85 [now Article 81] as a whole should be read in the context of the provisions of the preamble to the Treaty which clarify it and reference should particularly be made to those relating to 'the elimination of barriers' and to 'fair competition' both of which are necessary for bringing about a single market.[3]

It is clear, then, that the Treaty's telos must inform Article 81's content; this was, in part, but not wholly, to do with eliminating barriers and ensuring fair competition. Since 1965, the Treaty (and our understanding of it) has deepened the need for policy coherence.[4] The gradual process of building an ever closer union amongst the peoples has pushed the Community into ever-wider policy fields. The signing of the Single European Act, the Maastricht Treaty and the Amsterdam Treaty (as well as the more recent Lisbon Treaty, which has yet to be implemented) have transformed the legal, economic, political and social context in which the Community now operates. It is no longer merely an economic community; it is much more than that. As a result, it is little surprise that the CFI has held that:

---

[3]   Case 32/65 *Italy v Council and Commission*, 405.
[4]   See the Presidency Conclusions, Lisbon European Council, 23 and 24 March 2000.

[I]n the context of an overall assessment, the Commission is entitled to base itself on considerations connected with the pursuit of the public interest in order to grant exemption under Article
85(3) [now Article 81(3)] of the Treaty.[5]

This notion has also received support from the European Parliament and the Council. The
Commission's position is more complex. Chapter 2 showed that it is creating a lot of
ambiguity by implying in its guidelines that public policy concerns are irrelevant in Article
81 decision-making and yet actually considering them in its Article 81 decisions. The
confusion that this contradictory stance engenders is unfortunate. In any event, the
Commission is not able to make such a policy change (to ignore relevant public policy
goals in Article 81) as it is bound by the Treaty and the Community Courts' judgments.

This conclusion is foundational. Most Community lawyers would readily accept it;
many Community competition lawyers would be surprised. What is clear is that the ability
to consider non-economic objectives within Article 81 can fundamentally alter that
provision's assessment; which could affect the agreement's status under Article 81(2) EC;
there are also fining, damages and reputational implications. For these reasons alone,
resolving the debate on how and where to consider public policy in the Community
competition rules is vital. However, there are additional reasons why answers are particularly keenly sought today, such as the Council debates on how competition is currently
given too much weight; the introduction of Regulation 1/2003 (and the risk of less legal
certainty and decentralisation); the EU's enlargement on 1 May 2004; and the potential
appointment at the end of 2009 of a Commissioner for Competition.

Once it is understood that non-economic objectives can be relevant in Article 81
decisions, many other queries arise. Part B asked three questions: how are public policy
objectives balanced in Article 81?; where does this happen?; and what are the limits of this
balance? Its findings are surprising. Non-economic objectives are balanced against the
restriction of competition in both Article 81(1) and (3), see Chapters 3 and 4, respectively
(I call this mere-balancing). There is no guidance, or apparent consistency, about when
one paragraph is more appropriate than the other. There is no explanation of what public
policy objectives might be considered relevant and why; in fact, the very consideration of
these objectives is often disguised or even denied. Nor are we told how much weight these
values should be given; even the appropriate balancing mechanism is unclear.

There is even confusion about what methodology to use to consider public policy goals,
Chapter 5 outlines a second method through which these goals are considered within the
consumer welfare analysis itself. Three avenues were highlighted. First, the Commission
seems to temper its consumer welfare goal for industrial policy purposes. The second
avenue was to weigh short-term allocative efficiency losses against potential long-term
allocative efficiency gains through encouraging R&D. Finally, I investigate the Commission's advocacy of the partial equilibrium framework; which affects the facility with which
public policy goals can be considered in Article 81.

---

[5] Joined Cases T-528/93, etc, *Métropole Télévision v Commission* para 118. However, this should be contrasted
with its more recent judgment in the *Glaxo* Case, which is currently on appeal, as well as later judgments by the
ECJ, see Ch 1, n 3.

There is much work to do and answers are urgently needed. To my mind, the mechanism that the Commission adopts when balancing is unclear and thus not repeatable by undertakings, their lawyers, or the Member States' courts and competition authorities. Furthermore, the limits of the balance are uncertain. Firm conclusions are hampered by the lack of formal, transparent, decisions; but, in fact, in Commission decisions, when public policy objectives are considered relevant, they always seem to tilt the balance in their favour, ie public policy 'wins'. This is not in line with either the Commission's recent policy statements or the perceived wisdom.

Some fault must be laid at the Commission's door here. However, others are also to blame. Community competition lawyers must consider all relevant objectives within their competition assessments, to do otherwise is a disservice to their clients. The Member States might have provided a clearer, more coherent, system for dealing with such conflicts in the Treaty; the relevant weight of the various objectives could have been discussed in more detail there. On top of this, the Community Courts should reach internal agreement on the relevance of public policy in Article 81 and where and how to consider non-economic goals there.[6] They should also explain this accord clearly. I believe that the current appeal from the CFI's judgment in the *Glaxo* Case presents the ECJ with an ideal opportunity to clarify many of these issues, in particular that a unitary consumer welfare goal is not an appropriate meta-objective for Article 81 EC.

In the light of Part B's observations, Part C makes some proposals for how to consider non-economic objectives within Article 81 EC in a more coherent way. Certain elements must be at the heart of any proposed clarification. First and foremost, the proposed system must respect the Treaty, unless amendments are proposed, and the fundamental tenets of the Community Courts' case law. This means that decision-makers must be able to consider relevant public policy objectives within Article 81. Secondly, undertakings, decision-makers and consumers need more legal certainty in the balancing test and transparency in the way it is conducted. Thirdly, within this framework, the competition rules must be as efficient possible. I also seek to take into account, to the extent allowed by the Treaty, Chapter 1's conclusions.

Chapter 6 proposes a consumer welfare test, as Article 81(1) EC's sole goal; arguing that while non-economic objectives must be considered within Article 81, this does not mean that they should be directly considered there all of the time, ie within Article 81(1). To do so would create too much uncertainty and involve too much cost, for insufficient return. It also risks a *détournement de pouvoir*. In any event, Chapter 1 showed that a consumer welfare test often helps achieve non-economic objectives, in the long term. Having said that, it would not take account of all of these, nor could it be guaranteed to give them the weight that the Treaty demands. This should not be too prejudicial as most public policy objectives can normally be more efficiently promoted through other instruments. In any event and to the extent that consumer welfare is appreciably undermined, Article 81(3) EC is there to ensure that, where necessary, relevant non-economic objectives can be taken into account in Article 81.

Chapter 7 deals with Article 81(3) EC, recommending that the first test there should involve a full balancing (ie considering the positive and negative effects) of Community

---

[6]   One can only assume that such agreement is lacking, compare the *Wouters* Case and the *Meca-Medina* Case, on the one hand, and Case T-112/99 *Métropole télévision (M6) and Others v Commission* paras 76, 77, on the other, see Ch 6.

public policy objectives. Relevant Member States' public policy objectives should also be considered in cases of diagonal conflict. Secondly, consideration of all appreciable public policy effects, even those outside the relevant market, should be possible. I also argue that Article 81(3)(a) should be re-interpreted to mean that the agreement must be indispensable; which, for my purposes would essentially mean that only where an objective could not be achieved by anyone in any way (to the appropriate level) more efficiently than by distorting competition would the agreement be exempted.

The Commission could then, once it arrives at a clear and consistent internal position, produce guidelines to clarify the scope of, at least the most important, objectives (including the definition of consumer welfare); and to explain why these objectives are pursued, so that it is clearer when conflicts arise between them. In addition, it could set out what considerations are relevant when balancing non-economic objectives under Article 81(3)'s first test; Chapter 8 provides a framework for this. The framework has not been produced with the idea that balancing can be reduced to a mathematical formula. However, by exposing various factors that might be considered in the balance, I hope to help decision-makers focus upon several criteria that they might otherwise ignore. This should help them make their balancing more transparent and thus repeatable as well. As Chapter 8 explains, this framework should include provision of a meta-objective; guidance on the qualitative weight of at least the commonly invoked public policy objectives, as well as rules for assessing their quantitative weight (including the relevance of how likely the cost or benefit is to arise, discounting for the future and appreciability); and, rules on how to convert each objective into a common meter. It would also be helpful if the Commission could provide a clear co-ordination mechanism between the decision-maker, the relevant Director-Generals in the Commission and any concerned Member States, when their interests, or those with which they deal, are appreciably affected by an agreement. It goes without saying that the Commission would have to keep all of its thinking in these areas up-to-date, so as to reflect the balance as it changes over time. These guidelines will be difficult to produce. However, it is this difficulty that drives the imperative for them.

The Member States might also contemplate, in the next Treaty revision, explaining which provisions, if any, justify the exclusion of the competition provisions;[7] providing guidance on the Treaty's meta-objective and explaining how public policy objectives should be balanced in general throughout the Treaty's operational provisions. More guidance from them on the qualitative weight to be assigned to objectives in case of conflict between them would also be useful. The Council might also consider amending Regulation 1/2003, if it is felt that Member States' courts (and possibly even Member States' competition authorities) are not suitable fora for the public policy balance that Article 81 demands.

Given that the Commission is unlikely to give public policy guidance in an area which it is publicly trying to distance itself from at the moment, more responsibility may fall on the Member States and the Community Courts to clarify the above issues in the short term. It is also encumbant upon Community competition lawyers to take account of public policy criteria in their competition work, where this would serve their clients' best interests.

Until this guidance is forthcoming, undertakings would be well advised to seek political support for any agreements that might appreciably undermine consumer welfare. Where

---

[7] Should the *Albany* Case be confirmed, for example?: see Ch 2.

the parties to an agreement act in accordance with a specific Community law, DG Competition is more willing to accept the relevance of non-economic objectives. While it is not necessary to have prior Community support in this way, it clearly helps. It is also beneficial to get another of the Commission's Directorate-Generals to support the agreement in question; in other matters the approval of one of the Member States may also have affected the outcome of the balance.

In the Introduction I cited Bork:

> Antitrust policy cannot be made rational until we are able to give a firm answer to one question: What is the point of the law—what are its goals? Everything else follows from the answer we give. Is the antitrust judge to be guided by one value or by several? If by several, how is he to decide cases where a conflict in values arises? Only when the issue of goals has been settled is it possible to frame a coherent body of substantive rules.[8]

In the European Union, competition policy is incorporated into the Community legal order's constitution. This has an important impact upon how the relevant provisions should be interpreted. The Treaty's structure, the policy-linking clauses, the Community Courts' judgments, statements of the Council, the European Parliament and countless Commission decisions all support the consideration of public policy objectives within Community competition policy.

As to how, where and the limits of this balancing, there is less agreement. Sauter has written:

> As a 'constitutional charter', the Treaty sets out the objectives, principles, policies and institutional provisions of the Community. As an international agreement, however, it did not aim to establish and justify a coherent and independent political structure before a critical polity, or even to resolve conflicts of laws. Successive Treaty amendments have produced only half-hearted attempts at revising its structure. Hence the Treaty does not clearly establish goals, principles and instruments at various levels in an explicit hierarchy of norms and legal acts, as a written constitution would usually do, and the priorities of the Community are difficult to discern. This gives rise to conflicts of interpretation which are repeated with each amendment of the Treaty.[9]

Although the Lisbon Treaty attempts a more thorough structural revision, it does not confront the main problems highlighted either. The 2004 procedural reforms of Articles 81 and 82 EC are predicated on the idea that the law is clear. In relation to the consideration of public policy within Article 81, I have shown that this is not the case.

This book has suggested how and where to consider public policy within Article 81 EC. The aim is to help establish a coherent framework of substantive rules. In so doing, I have sought to produce a structure that enhances the clarity and predictability of decision-making. At the same time, I wanted to reflect the weight that the Treaty gives to non-economic goals.

Even if all my recommendations were implemented, there would not be perfect transparency. Compromise is difficult and can never be entirely predictable. Public policy balancing is not mathematics, as Chapter 8 explains, every case is different and value judgements must be made about the optimal balance in each one. The presence of this

---

[8] Bork (1978) 50.
[9] Sauter (1998) 38.

discretion should be celebrated. Legal certainty is not the only value legal systems espouse. There is also justice and fairness. While I argue that decision-makers need much more guidance, their hands should not be tied.

There is much (difficult) work to do. I have suggested several tasks that could be undertaken by the Community Courts, the Commission, the Member States and Community competition lawyers in order to provide a minimum level of clarity in the area. Only once this is done can Community competition law legitimately claim to have come of age.

Annex

TABLE 1

| Year | Total Number of Article 81(3) Cases | Number of Article 81(3) Cases where: | | | |
| | | Market Integration considered decisive | | Other non-economic objectives considered decisive | |
		Number	%	Number	%
1993	3	0	0	2	67
1994	11	0	0	5	45
1995	1	0	0	0	0
1996	5	3	60	1	20
1997	2	0	0	0	0
1998	3	0	0	0	0
1999	12	1	8	2	17
2000	3	0	0	1	33
2001	5	0	0	1	20
2002	3	0	0	0	0
2003	3	1	33	0	0
2004	2	0	0	0	0
Total	53	5	9.4%	12	23%

TABLE 2

Year	Total Cases[1]		Total Cases where Non-Economic Treaty Objectives Considered, but not Decisive[2]				Total Cases where Non-Economic Treaty Objectives Considered and Decisive			
	Case only has Article 81(1) Analysis	Case with Article 81(3) Analysis	Market Integration		Objectives Considered outside of Market Integration		Market Integration		Objectives Considered outside of Market Integration	
			Article 81(1)	Article 81(3)	Article 81(1)	Article 81(3)	Article 81(1)	Article 81(3)	Article 81(1)	Article 81(3)
1993	2[3]	3[4]	0	0	0	0	1[5]	0	0	2[6]
1994	6[7]	11[8]	0	0	0	3[9]	3[10]	0	0	5[11]
1995	3[12]	1[13]	1[14]	0	0	0	1[15]	0	0	0
1996	4[16]	5[17]	0	0	1[18]	2[19]	2[20]	3[21]	0	1[22]
1997	0	2[23]	0	0	0	1[24]	2[25]	0	0	0
1998	4[26]	3[27]	0	0	0	0	2[28]	0	0	0
1999	4[29]	12[30]	1[31]	0	0	0	2[32]	1[33]	0	2[34]
2000	7[35]	3[36]	0	0	0	2[37]	3[38]	0	0	1[39]
2001	10[40]	5[41]	0	0	1[42]	0	5[43]	0	1[44]	1[45]
2002	8[46]	3[47]	0	1[48]	0	1[49]	8[50]	0	0	0
2003	1[51]	3[52]	0	0	0	0	1[53]	1[54]	0	0
2004	3[55]	2[56]	0	0	0	0	1[57]	0	0	0
TOTAL	52	53	2	1	2	9	31	5	1	12

[1] Only formal Reg 17 decisions reported in Official Journal are considered. I analyse all Commission decisions from 1993, until 1 May 2004.

[2] There is a double-counting problem in relation to 1996, 1997, 2000, 2001 and 2002. This is because, sometimes, the same decision has considered more than one non-economic objective and one has been decisive and the other(s) have not. In these instances, I have included the case under *both* columns. I have *not* done the same in the Introduction itself. There, I have only listed each decision once. Where the same decision involved consideration of a 'decisive' objective as well as a 'non-decisive' one, I have listed it as a 'decisive' objective.

[3] Commission decisions, *CNSD*, OJ 1993 L203/27 and *Zera/ Montedison*, OJ 1993 L272/28.

[4] Commission decisions, *EBU/Eurovision*, OJ 1993 L179/23; *Auditel*, OJ 1993 L206/50 (breached Art 81(3) on indispensability and elimination of competition grounds, no balance conducted) and *Grundig's EC distribution system*, OJ 1994 L20/15.

Table 2   323

⁵   Commission decision, *Zera/ Montedison*, OJ 1993 L272/28 (market integration, paras 98–113).

⁶   Commission decisions, *EBU/Eurovision*, OJ 1993 L179/23 (benefits to smaller members, and thus smaller countries, paras 59, 63, can show more of the event as can alternate between stations in a country, one station could not show all of the Olympics, para 60, facilitates market integration, para 61, funding of minority sports, paras 62, 63, cheaper production costs, paras 63, 65, better quality signal, para 64) and *Grundig's EC distribution system*, OJ 1994 L20/15 (not in the decision, but consumer protection seems important, see Ch 4).

⁷   Commission decisions, *PVC*, OJ 1994 L239/14; *Cartonboard*, OJ 1994 L243/1; *Cement*, OJ 1994 L343/1; *International Private Satellite Partners*, OJ 1994 L354/75; *Far Eastern Freight Conference*, OJ 1994 L378/17 and *Tretorn and Others*, OJ 1994 L378/45.

⁸   Commission decisions, *International Energy Agency*, OJ 1994 L68/35; *Stichting Baksteen*, OJ 1994 L131/15; *Exxon/ Shell*, OJ 1994 L144/20; *Bayer/ BP Chemicals*, OJ 1994 L174/34; *BT-MCI*, OJ 1994 L223/36; *Pasteur Mérieux-Merck*, OJ 1994 L309/1; *Olivetti-Digital*, OJ 1994 L309/24; *Fujitsu AMD Semiconductor*, OJ 1994 L341/66; *Asahi/ Saint-Gobain*, OJ 1994 L354/87; *Trans-Atlantic Agreement*, OJ 1994 L376/1 and *Philips-Osram*, OJ 1994 L378/37.

⁹   Commission decisions, *Pasteur Mérieux-Merck*, OJ 1994 L309/1 (public health may have been a factor, paras 84, 85, 87, 88); *Asahi/ Saint-Gobain*, OJ 1994 L354/87 (safety was an issue, para 24, as was industrial policy, paras 10, 25. Both of these could have been decisive but there are also economic efficiency arguments, which probably predominated, para 24) and *Philips-Osram*, OJ 1994 L378/37 (probably motivated by economic efficiency, but environmental protection also important, paras 25, 26).

¹⁰   Commission decisions, *Fujitsu AMD Semiconductor*, OJ 1994 L341/66 (market integration probably decisive, para 32, economic efficiency also important, paras 33–36); *Cement*, OJ 1994 L343/1 and *Tretorn and Others*, OJ 1994 L378/45 (market integration, paras 51–63).

¹¹   Commission decisions, *International Energy Agency*, OJ 1994 L68/35 (continuity of energy supply); *Stichting Baksteen*, OJ 1994 L131/15 (industrial policy, seems to be the main motivation, paras 18–26, also mentioned was that agreement allows for improved social conditions, including the redeployment of employees, para 27); *Exxon/ Shell*, OJ 1994 L144/20 (industrial policy, probably the main reason, para 67, also improves health and environment, para 68 and economic efficiency, para 69; *Bayer/ BP Chemicals*, OJ 1994 L174/34 (industrial policy, para 6) and *BT-MCI*, OJ 1994 L223/36 (industrial policy probably the main reason, para 53).

¹²   Commission decisions, *Coapi*, OJ 1995 L122/37 (unclear whether they applied Art 81(3) and found it was not fulfilled, but it seems as though no notification for an exemption was ever made, para 41); *PMI-DSV*, OJ 1995 L221/34 and *BASF Lacke+Farben AG, and Accinauto SA*, OJ 1995 L272/16.

¹³   Commission decision, *Stichting Certificatie Kraanverhuurbedrijf and the Federatie van Nederlandse Kraanverhuurbedrijven*, OJ 1995 L312/79.

¹⁴   Commission decision, *Stichting Certificatie Kraanverhuurbedrijf and the Federatie van Nederlandse Kraanverhuurbedrijven*, OJ 1995 L312/79 (market integration was an additional factor, para 26, but, the decision seems to have been adopted on economic efficiency/ freedom grounds, paras 20–30).

¹⁵   Commission decision, *BASF Lacke+Farben AG, and Accinauto SA*, OJ 1995 L272/16 (market integration, paras 89, 90).

¹⁶   Commission decisions, *ADALAT*, OJ 1996 L201/1; *Iridium*, OJ 1997 L16/87; *Ferry Operators – Currency surcharges*, OJ 1997 L26/23 and *Novalliance/ Systemform*, OJ 1997 L47/11.

¹⁷   Commission decisions, *LH/ SAS*, OJ 1996 L54/28; *Fenex*, OJ 1996 L181/28; *Banque Nationale de Paris – Dresdner Bank*, OJ 1996 L188/37; *Atlas*, OJ 1996 L239/23 and *Pheonix/ GlobalOne*, OJ 1996 L239/57.

¹⁸   Commission decision, *Banque Nationale de Paris – Dresdner Bank*, OJ 1996 L188/37 (industrial policy probably carried some weight, para 16).

¹⁹   Commission decisions, *Atlas*, OJ 1996 L239/23 (industrial policy had some influence, para 50, but economic efficiency/ freedom were the main motivators, paras 48–52) and *Pheonix/ GlobalOne*, OJ 1996 L239/57 (industrial policy probably had a mild influence, paras 57, 58).

²⁰   Commission decisions, *ADALAT*, OJ 1996 L201/1 (market integration was decisive, paras 189, 190) and *Novalliance/ Systemform*, OJ 1997 L47/11 (market integration was decisive, paras 54–60, 62, were also price-fixing problems, para 61).

21   Commission decisions, *Banque Nationale de Paris – Dresdner Bank*, OJ 1996 L188/37 (market integration was important and probably decisive for clearance, para 18); *Atlas*, OJ 1996 L239/23 (market integration was decisive, paras 38–40, 43) and *Phoenix/ GlobalOne*, OJ 1996 L239/57 (market integration seems to have been one of the decisive factors, paras 48, 52, 54).

22   Commission decision, *LH/ SAS*, OJ 1996 L54/28 (although not evident from the decision the basis of this case seems to have been industrial policy, see Commission, *RCP 1996*, 120–121).

23   Commission decisions, *Unisource*, OJ 1997 L318/1 and *Uniworld*, OJ 1997 L318/24.

24   Commission decision, *Unisource*, OJ 1997 L318/1 (industrial policy and regional policy may have contributed to the exemption, paras 86, although economic efficiency was probably the basis for the decision, paras 87–89).

25   Commission decisions, *Unisource*, OJ 1997 L318/1 (market integration decisive, paras 80, 83) and *Uniworld*, OJ 1997 L318/24 (market integration one of the decisive points, para 66).

26   Commission decisions, *VW*, OJ 1998 L124/60; *Pre-Insulated Pipe Cartel*, OJ 1999 L24/1; *British Sugar plc and Others*, OJ 1999 L76/1 and *Greek Ferries*, OJ 1999 L109/24.

27   Commission decisions, *Van den Bergh Foods Ltd*, OJ 1998 L246/1; *Sicasov*, OJ 1999 L4/27 and *Transatlantic Conference Agreement*, OJ 1999 L95/1.

28   Commission decisions, *VW*, OJ 1998 L124/60 (market integration, paras 130–145) and *Sicasov*, OJ 1999 L4/27 (market integration, paras 62–64).

29   Commission decisions, *Télécom Développement*, OJ 1999 L218/24; *Nederlandse Vereniging van Banken and Others*, OJ 1999 L271/28; *FEG and TU*, OJ 2000 L39/1 and *Seamless steel tubes*, OJ 2003 L140/1.

30   Commission decisions, *Whitbread*, OJ 1999 L88/26; *TPS*, OJ 1999 L90/6; *EPI code of conduct*, OJ 1999 L106/14; *P&I Clubs*, OJ 1999 L125/12; *P&O Stena Line*, OJ 1999 L163/61; *Bass*, OJ 1999 L186/1; *Scottish and Newcastle*, OJ 1999 L186/28; *Europe Asia Trades Agreement*, OJ 1999 L193/23; *Cégétel+ 4*, OJ 1999 L218/14; *REIMS II*, OJ 1999 L275/17; *British Interactive Broadcasting/ Open*, OJ 1999 L312/1 and *GEAE/ P&W*, OJ 2000 L58/16.

31   Commission decision, *FEG and TU*, OJ 2000 L39/1 (market integration may have had some impact, para 108, otherwise economic efficiency/ freedom prevails, paras 103–122).

32   Commission decisions, *Europe Asia Trades Agreement*, OJ 1999 L193/23 (market integration, paras 49, 50) and *Seamless steel tubes*, OJ 2003 L140/1 (market integration, paras 101–104, there was another point that just raised economic efficiency/ freedom points, paras 111, 112, but this formed another head of claim).

33   Commission decision, *REIMS II*, OJ 1999 L275/17 (improved market integration due to 'considerable improvements with regard to cross-border mail', paras 69–76).

34   Commission decisions, *EPI code of conduct*, OJ 1999 L106/14 (the only reason given for exemption is to allow an orderly transition from a changeover from a system of virtually total prohibition on advertising and on the supply of unsolicited services, as currently exists, to one of total freedom, involves a significant transformation of the framework within which professional representatives operate. If this changeover is made suddenly, there is a potential risk of confusion in the mind of the public such as might damage the image that professional representatives give to institutions participating in the administration of justice, para 46) and *GEAE/ P&W*, OJ 2000 L58/16 (environmental protection may have had some influence, albeit minor, para 79, the rest of the balance only discusses economic efficiency, paras 79, 80. However, the decisive part of this decision may well have been political. It was to develop an engine for Airbus and having a two engine choice would make the aircraft much more attractive to airlines, see, eg para 81 and Ch 2).

35   Commission decisions, *Inntrepreneur*, OJ 2000 L195/49; *Unisource*, OJ 2001 L52/30; *Nathan-Bricolux*, OJ 2001 L54/1; *Opel*, OJ 2001 L59/1; *Amino Acids*, OJ 2001 L152/24; *JCB*, OJ 2002 L69/1 and *Soda-ash – Solvay*, CFK, OJ 2003 L10/1.

36   Commission decisions, *Eurovision*, OJ 2000 L151/18; *CECED*, OJ 2000 L187/47 and *FETTCSA*, OJ 2000 L268/1.

37   Commission decisions, *CECED*, OJ 2000 L187/47 (environmental protection was certainly an issue, paras 47–57, but probably not decisive, see Ch 4) and *Nathan-Bricolux*, OJ 2001 L54/1 (market integration seems to have been the fundamental motivation, paras 72–85. Economic efficiency/ freedom was also important, paras 86–90, it is possible that improving education also had a small part to play, para 85, but this is debatable).

Table 2   325

38 Commission decisions, *Nathan-Bricolux*, OJ 2001 L54/1 (market integration seems to have been the fundamental motivation, paras 72–85. Economic efficiency/ freedom was also important, paras 86–90, it is possible that improving education also had a small part to play, para 85, but this is very debatable); *Opel*, OJ 2001 L59/1, paras 118–135 and *JCB*, OJ 2002 L69/1, paras 179–191.

39 Commission decision, *Eurovision*, OJ 2000 L151/18 (benefits to smaller members, and thus smaller countries, paras 85–87, can show more of the event as can alternate between stations in a country, one station could not show all of the Olympics, para 88, 89, cheaper production costs, paras 86 (note since 1993 no longer discussion of the better quality signal, aiding of minority sports, or market integration objectives)).

40 Commission decisions, *UEFA's broadcasting regulations*, OJ 2001 L171/12; *Eco-Emballages*, OJ 2001 L233/37; *Identrus*, OJ 2001 L249/12; *Visa International*, OJ 2001 L293/24; *Citric Acid*, OJ 2002 L239/18; *Luxembourg Brewers*, OJ 2002 L253/21; *Vitamins*, OJ 2003 L6/1; *Bank charges for exchanging euro-zone currencies – Germany*, OJ 2003 L15/1; *Zinc phosphate*, OJ 2003 L153/1 and *PO/ Interbrew and Alken-Maes*, OJ 2003 L200/1.

41 Commission decisions, *Volkswagen*, OJ 2001 L262/14; *SAS Maersk Air*, OJ 2001 L265/15; *Glaxo Wellcome and Others*, OJ 2001 L302/1; *DSD and Others*, OJ 2001 L319/1 and *Revised TACA*, OJ 2003 L26/53.

42 Commission decision, *Eco-Emballages*, OJ 2001 L233/37 (there may be a hint of environmental protection being considered in paras 80, 81, the main reasons seem to be economic efficiency/freedom though, paras 73–86).

43 Commission decisions, *Glaxo Wellcome and Others*, OJ 2001 L302/1 (market integration seems decisive, paras 124, 125 – note that this was decided under Art 81(3), but there market integration arguments were not in evidence); *Luxembourg Brewers*, OJ 2002 L253/21, paras 67–73 (although other factors considered too); *Vitamins*, OJ 2003 L6/1, para 589; *Zinc phosphate*, OJ 2003 L153/1, para 213 and *PO/ Interbrew and Alken-Maes*, OJ 2003 L200/1, para 262.

44 Commission decision, *DSD and Others*, OJ 2001 L319/1 (environmental protection may well have had a decisive effect on the Commission and how tolerant it was prepared to be of any potential restrictions in some area, paras 110–116, but economic efficiency/ freedom seem the general basis of the decision, paras 104–140).

45 Commission decision, *DSD and Others*, OJ 2001 L319/1 (environmental protection seems clearly to have been the basis of the exemption, paras 142–146, economic efficiency may have been an additional motivation for the Commission, para 145).

46 Commission decisions, *Graphite electrodes*, OJ 2002 L100/1; *Industrial and medical gases*, OJ 2003 L84/1; *Methionine*, OJ 2003 L255/1; *Omega – Nintendo*, OJ 2003 L255/33; *Mercedes-Benz*, OJ 2002 L257/1; *Methylglucamine*, OJ 2004 L38/18; *Austrian Banks – 'Lombard Club'*, OJ 2004 L56/1 and *Food flavour enhancers*, OJ 2004 L75/1.

47 Commission decisions, *AuA/ LH*, OJ 2002 L242/25; *Visa International – Multilateral Interchange Fee*, OJ 2002 L318/17 and *IFPI 'Simulcasting'*, OJ 2003 L107/58.

48 Commission decision, *IFPI 'Simulcasting'*, OJ 2003 L107/58 (market integration – increasing it – might have contributed to the exemption, para 90, although economic efficiency seems at the basis of the exemption, paras 84–92).

49 Commission decision, *AuA/ LH*, OJ 2002 L242/25, para 86 (hints that economic and social cohesion, or even market integration, might have had some influence, not very much though as not considered in detail here).

50 Commission decisions, *Graphite electrodes*, OJ 2002 L100/1, paras 108–110; *AuA/ LH*, OJ 2002 L242/25, paras 76–82; *Mercedes-Benz*, OJ 2002 L257/1; *Industrial and medical gases*, OJ 2003 L84/1, paras 354, 360; *Methionine*, OJ 2003 L255/1, paras 213–215; *Omega – Nintendo*, OJ 2003 L255/33, paras 331, 332; *Methylglucamine*, OJ 2004 L38/18, para 181 and *Food flavour enhancers*, OJ 2004 L75/1, para 172.

51 Commission decision, *French beef*, OJ 2003 L209/12.

52 Commission decisions, *UK Network Sharing Agreement*, OJ 2003 L200/59; *Joint selling of the commercial rights of the UEFA Champions League*, OJ 2003 L291/25 and *REIMS II renotification*, OJ 2004 L56/76.

53 Commission decision, *French beef*, OJ 2003 L209/12, para 126.

54 Commission decision, *REIMS II renotification*, OJ 2004 L56/76 (improved market integration due to 'considerable improvements with regard to cross-border mail', paras 111–117).

55   Commission decisions, *Carbonless paper*, OJ 2004 L115/1; *Electrical and mechanical carbon and graphite products*, OJ 2004 L125/45 and *Industrial tubes*, OJ 2004 L125/50.

56   Commission decisions, *T-Mobile Deutschland/O2 Germany: Network Sharing Rahmenvertrag*, OJ 2004 L75/32 and *ARGEV/ ARO*, OJ 2004 L75/59.

57   Commission decision, *Carbonless paper*, OJ 2004 L115/1, para 334.

Bibliography

A Smith (1976 Reprint) – Smith, A, *An Enquiry into the Nature and Causes of the Wealth of Nations*, Vol One (Chicago, University of Chicago Press, 1976)

Ackermann (1997) – Ackermann, T, 'Joined Cases C-319/93, C-40/94 and C-224/94, *Hendrik Evert Dijkstra and others v Friesland (Frico Domo) Coöperatie BA and others* (Full Court) Judgment of 12 December 1995, [1995] ECR I-4471; Case C-399/93 *HG Oude Luttikhuis and others v Verenigde Coöperatieve Melkindustrie Coberco BA* (Full Court) Judgment of 12 December 1995, [1995] ECR I-4515' (1997) *CMLRev* 695

—— **(1997a)** – Ackermann, T, *Article 85 Abs 1 EGV und die rule of reason* (Köln, Carl Heymanns Verlag, 1997)

Addy (1993) – Addy, G, 'International Co-ordination of Competition Policies' in Kantzenbach, E, Scharrer, H-E, and Waverman, L (eds), *Competition Policy in an Interdependent World Economy* (Baden-Baden, Nomos Verlagsgesellschaft, 1993)

Adler and Posner (1999) – Adler, M, and Posner, E, 'Rethinking Cost-Benefit Analysis' (1999) *Yale Law Journal* 165

Ahdar (2002) – Ahdar, R, 'Consumers, Redistribution of Income and the Purpose of Competition Law' (2002) *ECLR* 341

Akman (2007) – Akman, P, 'Searching for the Long-Lost Soul of Article 82 EC' (2007) CCP Working Paper 07–5, available at <http://www.ccp.uea.ac.uk/publicfiles/workingpapers/CCP07–5.pdf> accessed 30 April 2009

Albors-Llorens (2002) – Albors-Llorens, A, *EC Competition Law and Policy* (Devon, Willan Publishing, 2002)

Aleinikoff (1987) – Aleinikoff, A, 'Constitutional Law in the Age of Balancing' (1987) *Yale Law Journal* 943

Alexander (1973) – Alexander, W, *The EEC Rules of Competition* (London, Kluwer Harrap Handbooks, 1973)

Alexy (2002) – Alexy, R, *A Theory of Constitutional Rights* (Oxford, OUP, 2002)

—— **(2003a)** – Alexy, R, 'Constitutional Rights, Balancing, and Rationality' (2003) *Ratio Juris* 131

—— **(2003b)** – Alexy, R, 'On Balancing and Subsumption. A Structural Comparison' (2003) *Ratio Juris* 433

Amato (1997) – Amato, G, *Antitrust and the Bounds of Power* (Oxford, Hart Publishing, 1997)

—— **(1999)** – Amato, G, 'The Long-term Implications of EU Enlargement: culture and national identity' (1999) Robert Schuman Centre Policy Paper 99/1

Ammer and Ammer (1977) – Ammer, C, and Ammer, D, *Dictionary of Business and Economics* (New York, The Free Press, 1977)

Anderman (1998) – Anderman, S, *EC Competition Law and Intellectual Property Rights: the regulation of innovation* (Oxford, OUP, 1998)

Andries and Julien-Malvy (2008) – Andries, A, and Julien-Malvy, B, 'The CISAC Decision: creating competition between collecting societies for music rights' (2008) *Competition Policy Newsletter* (number 3)

Aquaro (2003) – Aquaro, G, 'Enhancing the Legal Protection of the European Consumer' (2003) *European Business Law Review* 405

Areeda (1992) – Areeda, P, 'Antitrust Law as Industrial Policy: Should Judges and Juries Make It?' in Jorde and Teece (1992)

Areeda and Hovenkamp (2000) – Areeda, P, and Hovenkamp, H, *I Antitrust Law* (New York, Aspen Law & Business, 2000)

Areeda and Turner (1978) – Areeda, P, and Turner, D, *I Antitrust Law* (Boston, Little, Brown and Co, 1978)

Areeda, Solow and Hovenkamp (1995) – Areeda, P, Solow, J, and Hovenkamp, H, *IIA Antitrust Law* (Boston, Little, Brown and Co, 1995)

Ariño (2004) – Ariño, M, 'Competition Law and Pluralism in European Digital Broadcasting: addressing the gaps' (2004) 54 *Communications and Strategies* 97

Armentano (1990) – Armentano, D, *Antitrust and Monopoly: anatomy of a policy failure*, 2nd edn (Holmes and Meier, New York, 1990)

Arnull (1999) – Arnull, A, *The European Union and its Court of Justice* (Oxford, OUP, 1999)

—— **(2006)** – Arnull, A, *The European Union and its Court of Justice*, 2nd edn (Oxford, OUP, 2006)

Arnull, Dashwood, Ross and Wyatt (2000) – Arnull, A, Dashwood, A, Ross, M, and Wyatt, D, *European Union Law*, 4th edn (London, Sweet & Maxwell, 2000)

Arnull, Dashwood, Ross and Wyatt et al (2006) – Arnull, A, Dashwood, A, Dougan, M, Ross, M, Spaventa, E, and Wyatt, D, *European Union Law*, 5th edn (London, Sweet & Maxwell, 2006)

Art (1994) – Art, J-Y, 'Rules Against Collusion Between Firms' in Nicolaides, P, and van der Klugt, A (eds), *The Competition Policy of the European Community* (Maastricht, European Institute of Public Administration, 1994)

Arthur (1988) – Arthur, T, 'Workable Antitrust Law: the statutory approach to antitrust' (1988) 62 *Tul L Rev* 1163

Aubry-Caillaud (1998) – Aubry-Caillaud, F, *La Libre Circulation des Marchandises Nouvelle Approche et Normalisation Européenne* (Paris, Pedone, 1998)

Auricchio (2001) – Auricchio, V, 'Services of General Economic Interest and the Application of EC Competition Law' (2001) *World Competition* 65

Averitt and Lande (1996–97) – Averitt, N, and Lande, R, 'Consumer Sovereignty: a unified theory of antitrust and consumer protection law' (1996–97) *Antitrust Law Journal* 713

B&C (2001) – Bellamy, C, and Child, G, *European Community Law of Competition*, Roth, P (ed) (London, Sweet & Maxwell, 2001)

—— **(2008)** – Bellamy, C, and Child, G, *European Community Law of Competition*, Roth, P, and Rose, V (eds) (London, Sweet & Maxwell, 2008)

Bailey (2004) – Bailey, D, 'Scope of Judicial Review under Article 81 EC' (2004) *CMLRev* 1327

Baker and Wu (1998) – Baker, S, and Wu, L, 'Applying the Market Definition Guidelines of the European Commission' (1998) *ECLR* 273

Baldock (1992) – Baldock, D, et al, *The Integration of Environmental Protection Requirements into the Definition and Implementation of other EC Policies* (London, Institute for European Environmental Policy, 1992)

Bamberg and Spreman (1989) – Bamberg, G, and Spreman, K (eds), *Agency Theory, Information and, Incentives* (Berlin, Springer Verlag, 1989)

Banks (1997) – Banks, D, 'Non-Competition Factors and their Future Relevance under European Merger Law' (1997) *ECLR* 182

Baquero Cruz (2002) – Baquero Cruz, J, *Between Competition and Free Movement* (Oxford, Hart Publishing, 2002)

Bär and Kraemer (1998) – Bär, S, and Kraemer, A, 'European Environmental Policy after Amsterdam' (1998) *Journal of Environmental Law* 315

Barack (1981) – Barack, B, *The Application of the Competition Rules (antitrust law) of the European Economic Community* (Antwerp, Kluwer, 1981)

Barents (1990) – Barents, R, 'The Community and the Unity of the Common Market' (1990) *German Yearbook of International Law* 9

Barnard (2008) – Barnard, C, 'Viking and Laval: an introduction' (2007–08) Vol 10 *The Cambridge Yearbook of European Legal Studies* 463

Baxter (1983) – Baxter, W, 'Responding to the Reaction: the draftsman's view' (1983) *Californian Law Review* 618

Beckmann (2001) – Beckmann, A, 'One Step Forward, Two Steps Back' (2001) *Central Europe Review*

Bell (1983) – Bell, J, *Policy Arguments in Judicial Decisions* (Oxford, Clarendon Press, 1983)

Bengoetxea (1993) – Bengoetxea, J, *The Legal Reasoning of the European Court of Justice* (Oxford, Clarendon Press, 1993)

Bengoetxea, MacCormick, and Moral Soriano (2001) – Bengoetxea, J, MacCormick, N, and Moral Soriano, L, 'Integration and Integrity in the Legal Reasoning of the European Court of Justice' in De Búrca, G, and Weiler, J (eds), *The European Court of Justice* (Oxford, OUP, 2001)

Bergès-Sennou (2002) – Bergès-Sennou, F, Loss, F, Malavolti, E, and Vergé, T, '*Modernisation de la politique communautaire de concurrence*' (2002) *Revue Economique* 53(3)

Berlin (1990) – Berlin, I, 'The Pursuit of the Ideal' in Hardy, H (ed), *The Crooked Timber of Humanity: chapters in the history of ideas* (London, John Murray, 1990)

Bhagwati (1971) – Bhagwati, J, 'Generalised Theory of Distortions and Welfare' in Bhagwati, J, Jones, R, Mundell, R, and Jaroslav, V (eds), *Trade, Balance of Payments and Growth* (Amsterdam, North-Holland Publishing Co, 1971)

Bird (2006) – Bird, C, *An Introduction to Political Philosophy* (Cambridge, CUP, 2006)

Bishop (2001) – Bishop, S, 'Modernisation of the Rules Implementing Articles 81 and 82' in Ehlermann (2001)

Bishop and Ridyard (2002) – Bishop, S, and Ridyard, D, 'EC Vertical Restraints Guidelines: Effects-Based or Per Se Policy?' (2002) *ECLR* 35

Bishop and Walker (2002) – Bishop, S, and Walker, M, *The Economics of EC Competition Law*, 2nd edn (London, Sweet & Maxwell, 2002)

Black (1997) – Black, O, 'Per Se Rules and Rules of Reason: what are they?' (1997) *ECLR* 145

Bobek (2008) – Bobek, M, 'On the Application of European Law in (Not Only) the Courts of the New Member States: "Don't Do as I Say?" ' (2007–08) Vol 10 *The Cambridge Yearbook of European Legal Studies* 1

Boch (2003) – Boch, C, 'Devolution and Community Law' in Hoskins and Robinson (2003)

Bolze (1995) – Bolze, C, 'Atteinte à la concurrence, affaire C-250/92 – *Gøttrup-Klim Grovvareforening and others v Dansk Landbrugs Grovvareselskab AmbA*, inédit au Recueil' (1995) *Revue Trimestrielle de Droit Commercial et de Droit Economique* 554

—— **(1996)** – Bolze, C, 'Droit des ententes (CJCE 12 déc 1995 aff C-319/93, C-40/94 and C-224/94, *Hendrik Evert Dijkstra ea/Friesland Coöperative BA* et CJCE aff. C-399/93 *HG Oude Luttikhuis ea/Verenigde Coöperatieve Melkindustrie Coberco BA*)' (1996) *Revue Trimestrielle de Commerciale et de Droit Economique* 582

Bork (1985) – Bork, R, 'The Role of the Courts in Applying Economics' (1985) *Antitrust Law Journal* 21

—— **(1993)** – Bork, R, *The Antitrust Paradox: A Policy at War with Itself* (New York, The Free Press, 1993)

Bos (1995) – Bos, P, 'Towards a Clear Distribution of Competence between EC and National Competition Authorities' (1995) *ECLR* 410

Bourgeois and Demaret (1995) – Bourgeois, J, and Demaret, P, 'The working of EC policies on competition, industry and trade: a legal analysis' in Buigues, Jacquemin and Sapir (1995)

Bourgoignie (1985) – Bourgoignie, T, 'Theoretical Framework and Introductory Remarks' in Goyens (1985)

—— **(1985a)** – Bourgoignie, T, 'Final Remarks' in Goyens (1985)

Bouterse (1994) – Bouterse, R, *Competition and Integration – what goals count?* (Kluwer Law and Taxation Publishers, Boston, 1994)

Bovis (2001) – Bovis, C, 'Transforming the Application of EC Competition Laws: the case of decentralisation' (2001) *European Business Law Review* 98

Brau and Carraro (2001) – Brau, R, and Carraro, C, 'Are Voluntary Agreements a Threat to Competition?' in Higley, Convery and Lévêque (2001)

Bredimas (1978) – Bredimas, A, *Methods of Interpretation and Community Law* (Amsterdam, North-Holland Publishing Co, 1978)

Bright (1995) – Bright, C, 'Deregulation of EC Competition Policy: rethinking Article 85(1)', (1994) Fordham Corporate Law Institute 505

Brittan (1992) – Brittan, L, 'European Competition Policy: Keeping the Playing Field Level' (1992) Centre for European Policy Studies, London

Brkić (1985) – Brkić, J, *Legal Reasoning: Semantic and Logical Analysis* (New York, Peter Lang Publishing, 1985)

Brodley (1987) – Brodley, J, 'The Economic Goals of Antitrust: efficiency, consumer welfare, and technological progress' (1987) 62 *NYU Law Review* 1020

Broome (1999) – Broome, J, *Ethics out of Economics* (Cambridge, CUP, 1999)

Buigues, Jacquemin and Sapir (1995) – Buigues, P, Jacquemin, A, and Sapir, A (eds), *European Policies on Competition, Trade and Industry: conflict and complementarities* (Aldershot, Edward Elgar, 1995)

—— **(1995a)** – Buigues, P, Jacquemin, A, and Sapir, A, 'Introduction: Complementarities and Conflicts in EC Microeconomic Policies' in Buigues, Jacquemin and Sapir (1995)

Burnside (2002) – Burnside, A, 'GE, Honey, I Sunk the Merger' (2002) *ECLR* 107

Burton (1992) – Burton, S, *Judging in Good Faith* (Cambridge, CUP, 1992)

Buttigieg (2005) – Buttigieg, E, 'Consumer Interests under the EC's Competition Rules on Collusive Practices' (2005) *European Business Law Review* 643

Calvani (2003) – Calvani, T, 'Devolution and Convergence in Competition Enforcement' (2003) *ECLR* 415

Cappelletti (1987) – Cappelletti, M, 'Is the European Court of Justice "Running Wild"?' (1987) 12 *EL Rev* 3

Carlton (2007) – Carlton, D, 'Does Antitrust Need to be Modernised?', US Department of Justice, Economic Analysis Group Discussion Paper, January 2007, EAG 07–3

Castañeda (1998) – Castañeda, G in Ehlermann (1998)

Chalmers (1995) – Chalmers, D, 'The Single Market: from prima donna to journeyman' in Shaw, J, and More, G (eds), *The New Legal Dynamics of European Union* (Oxford, Clarendon Press, 1995)

Chang and Choi (1988) – Chang, SJ, and Choi, U, 'Strategy, Structure and Performance of Korean Business Groups: A Transaction Cost Approach' (1988) *Journal of Industrial Economics* 141

Coarse (1960) – Coarse, R, 'The Problem of Social Cost' (1960) *Journal of Law and Economics* 1

Collège d'Europe (1998) – Glöckler, G, Junius, L, Scappucci, G, Usherwood, S, and Vassallo, J, *Guide to EU Policies* (London, Blackstone Press Ltd, 1998)

Comanor and Smiley (1975) – Comanor, W, and Smiley, R, 'Monopoly and the Distribution of Wealth' (1975) 85 *Quarterly Journal of Economics* 177

Commentaire Mégret (1992) – *Commentaire Mégret: le droit de la CEE*, Vol 8 (Brussels, edns de L'Université de Bruxelles, 1992)

—— **(1996)** – *Commentaire Mégret: le droit de la CE*, Vol 8, 2nd edn (Brussels, edns de L'Université de Bruxelles, 1996)

—— **(1997)** – *Commentaire Mégret: le droit de la CE*, Vol 4, 2nd edn (Brussels, edns de L'Université de Bruxelles, 1997)

—— **(1999)** – *Commentaire Mégret: Culture, santé, consommateurs, réseaux transeuropéens, recherche et développement technologique, environnement, énergie* (Brussels, edns de L'Université de Bruxelles, 1999)

Constantinesco (1985) – Constantinesco, V, 'Division of fields of competence between the Union and the Member States in the Draft Treaty establishing the European Union' in Bieber, R, Jacqué, J-P, and Weiler, J, *An Ever Closer Union* (1985) Commission of the European Communities in co-operation with the EUI, Luxembourg

Convery and Lévêque (2001) – Convery, F, and Lévêque, F, 'Applying Voluntary Approaches – some insights from research' in Higley, Convery and Lévêque (2001)

Cooke (2000) – Cooke, J, 'Changing Responsibilities and Relationships for Community and National Courts: the implications of the white paper' in *The Modernisation of European Competition Law: the next ten years* (Centre of European Legal Studies Occasional Paper No 4, Cambridge, 2000)

—— **(2004)** – Cooke, J, 'General Report' in Cahill, D (ed), *The Modernisation of EU Competition Law Enforcement in the European Union*, FIDE National Reports (Cambridge, CUP, 2004)

—— **(2006)** – Cooke, J, 'Vocation as Commodity' in Ehlermann (2006)

Cooter (1987) – Cooter, R, 'Liberty, Efficiency, and Law' (1987) *Law and Contemporary Problems* 141

Coppel and O'Neill (1992) – Coppel, J, and O'Neill, A, 'The European Court of Justice: taking rights seriously?' (1992) *CMLRev* 669

Corden (1974) – Corden, W, *Trade Policy and Economic Welfare* (Oxford, OUP, 1974)

Craig and de Búrca (1998) – Craig, P, and de Búrca, G, *EU Law: Text, Cases and Materials*, 2nd edn (Oxford, OUP, 1998)

—— **(2008)** – Craig, P, and de Búrca, G, *EU Law: text, cases and materials*, 4th edn (Oxford, OUP, 2008)

Crampton (1997) – Crampton, P, 'Alternative Approaches to Competition Law' (1997) *World Competition* 55

Craufurd Smith (2008) – Craufurd Smith, R, 'Balancing Culture and Competition: state support for film and television in European Community law', (2007–08) Vol 10 *The Cambridge Yearbook of European Legal Studies* 35

Cseres (2004) – Cseres, K, *Competition Law and Consumer Protection: A Love-hate Relationship* (PhD, University of Amsterdam, 2004)

—— **(2007)** – Cseres, K, 'The Controversies of the Consumer Welfare Standard' (2007) *The Competition Law Review* 121

Cucinotta, Pardolesi and Van den Bergh (2002) – Cucinotta, A, Pardolesi, R, and Van den Bergh, R, *Post-Chicago Developments in Antitrust Law* (Cheltenham, Edward Elgar, 2002)

Cunningham (2001) – Cunningham, C, 'In Defence of Member State Culture: the unrealised potential of Article 151(4) of the EC Treaty and the consequences for EC cultural policy' (2001) *Cornell International Law Journal* 119

D'Agostino (2003) – D'Agostino, F, *Incommensurability and Commensuration: The Common Denominator* (Hampshire, Ashgate, 2003)

Dabbah (2003) – Dabbah, M, *The Internationalisation of Antitrust Policy* (Cambridge, CUP, 2003)

Dasgupta (2001) – Dasgupta, P, 'Valuing Objects and Evaluating Policies in Imperfect Economies' (2001) *The Economic Journal* C1

Dashwood (2002) – Dashwood, A, 'The Draft EU Constitution – first impressions' (2002–03) *The Cambridge Yearbook of European Legal Studies* 395

—— **(2008)** – Dashwood, A, 'Viking and Laval: issues of horizontal direct effect' (2007–08) Vol 10 *The Cambridge Yearbook of European Legal Studies* 525

de Búrca (1993) – de Búrca, G, 'The Principle of Proportionality and its Application in EC Law' (1993) *Yearbook of European Law* 105

—— **(1995)** – de Búrca, G, 'The Language of Rights and European Integration' in Shaw, J, and More, G (eds), *The New Legal Dynamics of European Union* (Oxford, Clarendon Press, 1995)

de Jong (1990) – de Jong, H, 'Competition Policy in Europe: Stimulus, Nuisance, or Drawback?' in Groeneveld, K, and Maks, G (eds), *Economic Policy and the Market Process* (Amsterdam, North-Holland, 1990)

de Roux and Voillemot (1976) – de Roux, X, and Voillemot, D, *Le droit de la concurrence des communautés européennes*, 3ème édn (Paris, Juridictionnaires Joly, 1976)

de Wilmars (1986) – de Wilmars, M, 'Reflexions sur les Methodes d'Interpretation de la Cour de Justice des Communautes Européennes' (1986) *Cahiers de Droit Europeen* 5

Deacon (1995) – Deacon, D, 'Vertical Restraints under EU Competition Law: new directions' in (1995) Fordham Corporate Law Institute 139

Deards (2002) – Deards, E, 'Closed Shop versus One Stop Shop: the battle goes on' (2002) *European Law Review* 618

Deckert (2000) – Deckert, M, 'Some Preliminary Remarks on the Limitations of European Competition Law' (2000) *European Review of Private Law* 173

Demetriou and Higgins (2003) – Demetriou, M, and Higgins, I, 'Free Movement and the Environment: seeing the wood for the trees' in Hoskins and Robinson (2003)

Dhondt (2003) – Dhondt, N, *Integration of Environmental Protection into other EC Policies* (Groningen, Europa Law Publishing, 2003)

Dornbusch (1993) – Dornbusch, R, 'Introduction' in Dornbusch, R (ed), *Policymaking in the Open Economy: Concepts and Case Studies in Economic Performance* (Published for the World Bank, Oxford, OUP, 1993)

Drahos (2001) – Drahos, M, *Convergence of Competition Laws and Policies in the European Community* (The Hague, Kluwer Law International, 2001)

Duhamel and Townley (2003) – Duhamel, M, and Townley, P, 'An Effective and Enforceable Alternative to the Consumer Surplus Standard' (2003) *World Competition* 3

Dworkin (1977) – Dworkin, R, *Taking Rights Seriously* (London, Duckworth, 1977)

—— **(2001)** – Dworkin, R, 'Do Liberal Values Conflict?' in Dworkin, R, Lilla, M, and Silvers, R (eds), *The Legacy of Isaiah Berlin* (New York, New York Review of Books, 2001)

Easterbrook (1984) – Easterbrook, F, 'The Limits of Antitrust' (1984) *Texas Law Review* 1

—— **(1992)** – Easterbrook, F, 'Ignorance and Antitrust' in Jorde and Teece (1992)

Edward (1996) – Edward, D, 'Judicial Activism: Myth or Reality?' in Campbell, A, and Voyatzi, M (eds), *Legal Reasoning and Judicial Interpretation of European Law* (Trenton NJ, Trenton Publishing, 1996)

— **(2002)** – Edward, D, 'Competition and National Rule-Making' in von Bogdandy, A, Mavroidis, P, and Mény, Y, *European Integration and International Co-ordination: studies in transnational economic law in honour of Claus-Dieter Ehlermann* (The Hague, Kluwer Law International, 2002)

Ehlermann (1992) – Ehlermann, C-D, 'The Contribution of EC Competition Policy to the Single Market' (1992) *CMLRev* 257

—— **(1998)** – Ehlermann, C-D, and Laudati, L (eds), *European Competition Law Annual 1997: The Objectives of Competition Policy* (Oxford, Hart Publishing, 1998)

—— **(2000)** – Ehlermann, C-D, 'La Modernisation de la politique antitrust de la CE: une révolution juridique et culturelle' (2000) *Revue du Droit de l'Union Européenne* 13

—— **(2000a)** – Ehlermann, C-D, 'The Modernisation of EC Antitrust Policy' (2000) *CMLRev* 537

—— **(2001)** – Ehlermann, C-D, and Atanasiu, I (eds), *European Competition Law Annual 2000: The Modernisation of EC Antitrust Policy* (Oxford, Hart Publishing, 2001)

—— **(2006)** – Ehlermann, C-D, and Atanasiu, I (eds), *European Competition Law Annual 2004: The Relationship between Competition Law and (Liberal) Professions* (Oxford, Hart Publishing, 2006)

Ehlermann and Atanasiu (2002) – Ehlermann, C, and Atanasiu, I, 'The Modernisation of EC Antitrust Law: Consequences for the Future Role and Functions of the EC Courts' (2002) *ECLR* 72

Elhauge (2003) – Elhauge, E, 'Defining Better Monopolisation Standards' (2003–04) *Stanford Law Review* 253

Ellis (1963) – Ellis, J, 'Source Material for Article 85(1) of the EEC Treaty' (1963) 32 *Fordham Law Review* 247

Elmslie (2004) – Elmslie, B, 'Adam Smith and Non-Economic Objectives' (2004) *Review of International Economics* 689

Elzinga (1977) – Elzinga, K, 'The Goals of Antitrust: other than competition and efficiency what else counts?' (1977) *University of Pennsylvania Law Review* 1191

Emiliou (1996) – Emiliou, N, *The Principle of Proportionality in European Law* (London, Kluwer Law International, 1996)

Espeland and Stevens (1998) – Espeland, W, and Stevens, M, 'Commensuration as a Social Process' (1998) *Annual Review of Sociology* 313

Evans (1981) – Evans, A, 'European Competition Law and Consumers: the Article 81(3) exemption' (1981) *ECLR* 425

——— **(1983)** – Evans, A, 'Economic Policy and the Free Movement of Goods in EEC Law' (1983) *The International and Comparative Law Quarterly* 577

——— **(1985)** – Evans, A, 'Article 85(3) Exemption: the notion of "allowing consumers a fair share of the resulting benefit" ' in Goyens (1985)

Farrell and Katz (2006) – Farrell, J, and Katz, M, 'The Economics of Welfare Standards in Antitrust' (2006) *Competition Policy International* 3

Faull (1991) – Faull, J, 'The Enforcement of Competition Policy in the European Community: a mature system' in (1991) Fordham Corporate Law Institute 139

——— **(1998)** – Faull, J in Ehlermann (1998)

Faull and Nikpay (1999) – Faull, J, and Nikpay, A (eds), *The EC Law of Competition* (Oxford, OUP, 1999)

——— **(2007)** – Faull, J, and Nikpay, A (eds), *The EC Law of Competition*, 2nd edn (Oxford, OUP, 2007)

Fels and Edwards (1998) – Fels, A, and Edwards, G in Ehlermann (1998)

Fennelly (1997) – Fennelly, N, 'EC Competition Law – the millennium approaches' in (1997) Fordham Corporate Law Institute 243

——— **(1998)** – Fennelly, N, 'Preserving the Legal Coherence within the New Treaty: the ECJ after the Treaty of Amsterdam' (1998) *Maastricht Journal of European and Comparative Law* 185

Finnis (1997) – Finnis, J, 'Commensuration and Public Reason' in Chang, R (ed), *Incommensurability, Incomparability, and Practical Reason* (Cambridge MA, Harvard University Press, 1997)

Fisher and Lande (1983) – Fisher, A, and Lande, R, 'Efficiency Considerations in Merger Enforcement' (1983) *Californian Law Review* 1580

Fishwick (1993) – Fishwick, F, *Making Sense of Competition Policy* (London, Kogan Page, 1993)

Fleming (2002) – Fleming, H, 'Book Pricing in the European Union' (2002) *European Law Review* 747

Fletcher (2006) – Fletcher, A, 'The Liberal Professions – getting the regulatory balance right' in Ehlermann (2006)

Forrester (1994) – Forrester, I, 'Competition Structures for the 21st Century' in (1994) Fordham Corporate Law Institute 445

——— **(1998)** – Forrester, I in Ehlermann (1998)

——— **(2001)** – Forrester, I in Ehlermann (2001)

——— **(2006)** – Forrester, I, *Where Law Meets Competition: is Wouters like a Cassis de Dijon or a Platypus?* in Ehlermann (2006)

Forrester and Maclennan (2001) – Forrester, I, and Maclennan, J, 'EC Competition Law 1999–2000' (2001) *Yearbook of European Law* 365

——— **(2003)** – Forrester, I, and Maclennan, J, 'EC Competition Law 2001–2002' (2003) *Yearbook of European Law* 499

Forrester and Norall (1984) – Forrester, I, and Norall, C, 'The Laicisation of Community Law: Self-help and the Rule of reason: How Competition Law is and could be Applied' (1984) *CMLRev* 11

——— **(1993)** – Forrester, I, and Norall, C, 'Competition Law' (1993) *Yearbook of European Law* 427

Fox (1986) – Fox, E, 'Monopolization and Dominance in the US and the EC: efficiency, opportunity and "fairness" ' (1986) *Notre Dame Law Review* 981

—— **(1987)** – Fox, E, 'The Battle for the Soul of Antitrust' (1987) 75 *Californian International Law Review* 917

—— **(1998)** – Fox, E in Ehlermann (1998)

—— **(1998a)** – Fox, E, 'International Antitrust: against minimum rules; for cosmopolitan principles' (1998) *The Antitrust Bulletin* 5

—— **(2000)** – Fox, E, 'Equality, Discrimination, and Competition Law: lessons from and for South Africa and Indonesia' (2000) *Harvard International Law Journal* 579

—— **(2001)** – Fox, E in Ehlermann (2001)

Fox and Sullivan (1987) – Fox, E, and Sullivan, L, 'Antitrust-Retrospective and Prospective: where are we coming from? Where are we going?' (1987) 62 *New York University Law Review* 936

Frazer (1990) – Frazer, T, 'Competition Policy after 1992: The Next Step' (1990) *Modern Law Review* 609

Freeman (2000) – Freeman, J, 'Private Parties, Public Functions and the New Administrative Law' (2000) *Administrative Law Review* 813

Friedman (1962) – Friedman, M, *Capitalism and Freedom* (Chicago, University of Chicago Press, 1962)

Fukuyama (1992) – Fukuyama, F, *The End of History and the Last Man* (London, Penguin, 1992)

Fuller (1969) – Fuller, L, *The Morality of Law*, revised edn (New Haven, Yale University Press, 1969)

Furse (1996) – Furse, M, 'The Role of Competition Policy: a survey' (1996) *ECLR* 250

Gardner (2000) – Gardner, N, *A Guide to United Kingdom and European Union Competition Policy*, 3rd edn (London, Macmillan Press Ltd, 2000)

Gavalda and Parleani (2002) – Gavalda, C, and Parleani, G, *Droit des affaires de l'Union européenne*, 4ème édn (Paris, Litec, 2002)

Geradin (2006) – Geradin, D, 'Efficiency Claims in EC Competition Law and Sector-Specific Regulation' in Ullrich, H (ed), *The Evolution of European Competition Law: whose regulation, which competition?* (Cheltenham, Edward Elgar, 2006)

Gerber (1987) – Gerber, D, 'Law and the Abuse of Economic Power in Europe' (1987–88) *Tulane Law Review* 57

—— **(1994)** – Gerber, D, 'The Transformation of European Community Competition Law?' (1994) 35 *Harvard International Law Review* 97

—— **(1994a)** – Gerber, D, 'Constitutionalising the Economy: German Neo-liberalism, competition law and the 'new' Europe' (1994) *American Journal of Comparative Law* 25

—— **(1998)** – Gerber, D, *Law and Competition in Twentieth Century Europe: protecting Prometheus* (Oxford, Clarendon Press, 1998)

—— **(2001)** – Gerber, D, 'Modernising European Competition Law: a developmental perspective' (2001) *ECLR* 122

—— **(2008)** – Gerber, D, 'Two Forms of Modernisation in European Competition Law' (2008) *Fordham International Law Journal* 1235

Gilliams (2006) – Gilliams, H, 'Competition Law and Public Interest: do we need to change the law for the (liberal) professions?' in Ehlermann (2006)

Ginsburg (1991) – Ginsburg, D, 'The Goals of Antitrust Revisited – comment' (1991) JITE 24

Glatz (1985) – Glatz, H, 'Comments on the paper of Mr. Joerges' in Goyens (1985)

Goldman (1998) – Goldman, C in Ehlermann (1998)

Goldman and Barutciski (1998) – Goldman, C, and Barutciski, M in Ehlermann (1998)

Gonzalez-Díaz (1992) – Gonzalez-Díaz, F, 'Procedure' in Overbury, C (ed), *The EEC Merger Regulation* (London, Sweet & Maxwell, 1992)

Goyder (2003) – Goyder, D, *EC Competition Law*, 4th edn (Oxford, OUP, 2003)

Goyens (1985) – Goyens, M (ed), *EC Competition Policy and the Consumer Interest* (Centre de Droit de la Consommation, Cabay Bruylant, Louvain-Le-Neuve, 1985)

Graupner (1965) – Graupner, R, *The Rules of Competition in the European Economic Community: a study of the substantive law on a comparative basis* (The Hague, Martinus Nijhoff, 1965)

Graupner (2007) – Graupner, F, 'The Battle over the Role of European Competition Policy: now you see it, now you don't' (2007) *Competition Law Journal* 89

Green (1988) – Green, N, 'Article 85 in Perspective' (1988) *ECLR* 190

Grimeaud (2000) – Grimeaud, D, 'The Integration of Environmental Concerns into EC Policies: a genuine policy development?' (2000) *European Environmental Law Review* 207

Gual (1995) – Gual, J, 'The Three Common Policies: an economic analysis' in Buigues, Jacquemin and Sapir (1995)

Gustafsson (2000) – Gustafsson, M, 'Some Legal Implications Facing the Realisation of the Commission White Paper on Modernisation of EC Antitrust Procedure and the Role of National Courts in a Post-White Paper Era' (2000) 27(2) *Legal Issues of Economic Integration* 159

Gyselen (1984) – Gyselen, L, 'Vertical Restraints in the Distribution Process: Strength and Weakness of the Free Rider Rationale under EEC Competition Law' (1984) *CMLRev* 647

—— **(1994)** – Gyselen, L, 'The Emerging Interface between Competition Policy and Environmental Policy in the EC' in Cameron, J, Demaret, P, and Geradin, D, *Trade & the Environment: the search for balance*, Vol I (London, Cameron May, 1994)

—— **(2002)** – Gyselen, L, 'Morning Panel Discussion' in Stuyck and Gilliams (2002)

—— **(2002a)** – Gyselen, L, 'The Substantive Legality Test under Article 81(3) EC Treaty – revisited in the light of the Commission's modernisation initiative' in von Bogdandy, A, Mavroidis, P, and Mény, Y, *European Integration and International Co-ordination: Studies in Transnational Economic Law in Honour of Claus-Dieter Ehlermann* (London, Kluwer International, 2002)

—— **(2006)** – Gyselen, L, 'Anti-competitive State Action in the Area of Liberal Professions: an EU/US comparative law perspective' in Ehlermann (2006)

Habermas (1996) – Habermas, J, *Between Facts and Norms* (Cambridge MA, MIT Press, 1996)

Hahn and Hester (1989) – Hahn, R, and Hester, G, 'Where Did All the Markets Go? An Analysis of EPA's Emissions Trading Program' (1989) *Yale Journal on Regulation* 109

Handoll (1994) – Handoll, J, 'The Protection of National Interests in the European Union' (1994) *Irish Journal of European Law* 221

Haracoglou (2006) – Haracoglou, I, 'Competition law, Consumer Policy and the Retail Sector: the systems' relation and the effects of a strengthened consumer protection policy on competition law' (2006) *The Competition Law Review* 175

Hartley (1996) – Hartley, T, 'The European Court, Judicial Objectivity and the Constitution of the European Union' (1996) *LQR* 95

—— **(2004)** – Hartley, T, *European Union Law in a Global Context: text, cases and materials* (Cambridge, CUP, 2004)

Hawk (1987) – Hawk, B in (1987) Fordham Corporate Law Institute

—— **(1988)** – Hawk, B, 'The American (Anti-trust) Revolution: Lessons for the EEC' (1988) *ECLR* 53

—— **(1995)** – Hawk, B, 'System Failure: vertical restraints and EC competition law' (1995) *CMLRev* 973

—— **(1998)** – Hawk, B in Ehlermann (1998)

—— **(2001)** – Hawk, B in Ehlermann (2001)

Hawk and Denaeijer (2001) – Hawk, B, and Denaeijer, N in Ehlermann (2001)

Heimler (1998) – Heimler, A in Ehlermann (1998)

Heimler and Fattori (1998) – Heimler, A, and Fattori, P in Ehlermann (1998)

Henderson (2001) – Henderson, D, *Misguided Virtue: False Notions of Corporate Responsibility*, New Zealand Business Roundtable, June 2001

Hervouët (2008) – Hervouët, H, 'La Dérive de l'Union Européenne: de l'objectif de l'union entre les peuples à celui de la concurrence' (2008) *Revue du Marché Común et de l'Union Européenne* 9

Hession and Macrory (1998) – Hession, M, and Macrory, R, 'The Legal Duty of Environmental Integration: Commitment and Obligation or Enforceable Right?' in O''Riordan, T, and Voisey, H (eds), *The Transition to Sustainability: the politics of agenda 21 in Europe* (London, Earthscan, 1998)

Higley, Convery and Lévêque (2001) – Higley, C, Convery, F, and Lévêque, F, 'Voluntary Approaches: an introduction' in CAVA, International Policy Workshop on the Use of Voluntary Approaches, 1 February 2001, at the Centre Borchette, Brussels

Hildebrand (2002) – Hildebrand, D, *The Role of Economic Analysis in the EC Competition Rules: the European school*, 2nd edn (The Hague, Kluwer Law International, 2002)

—— **(2002a)** – Hildebrand, D, 'The European School in EC Competition Law' (2002) *World Competition* 3

Hirschl (2007) – Hirschl, R, *Towards Juristocracy: The Origins and Consequences of the New Constitutionalism* (Cambridge MA, Harvard University Press, 2007)

Holmes (1897) – Holmes, O, 'The Path of the Law' (1897) 10 *Harvard Law Review* 457

Holmes (2000) – Holmes, K, 'The EC White Paper on Modernisation' (2000) 23(4) *World Competition* 51

Hornsby (1987) – Hornsby, S, 'Competition Policy in the 80's: more policy less competition?' (1987) *European Law Review* 79

Hoskins and Robinson (2003) – Hoskins, M, and Robinson, W (eds), *A True European: Essays for Judge David Edward* (Oxford, Hart Publishing, 2003)

Houttuin (1994) – Houttuin, G, 'Exceptions' in Nicolaides, P, and van der Klugt, A (eds), *The Competition Policy of the European Community* (Maastricht, European Institute of Public Administration, 1994)

Hovenkamp (1986) – Hovenkamp, H, 'Chicago and its Alternatives' (1986) *Duke Law Journal* 1014

—— **(1998)** – Hovenkamp, H in Ehlermann (1998)

—— **(2002)** – Hovenkamp, H, 'The reckoning of post-Chicago antitrust' in Cucinotta, Pardolesi and Van den Bergh (2002)

Howe (1998) – Howe, M in Ehlermann (1998)

Idot (2001) – Idot, L, *A French Point of View on the Radical Decentralisation of the Implementation of Article 81(1) and (3)* in Ehlermann (2001)

—— **(2003)** – Idot, L, 'Le Nouveau Systèm Communautaire de Mise en Oeuvre des Articles 81 et 82 CE (Règlement 1/2003 et projets de texts d'application)' (2003) *Cahiers de Droit Européen* 283

Jacobs (1993/2) – Jacobs, R, 'EEC Competition Law and the Protection of the Environment' (1993/2) *Legal Issues of European Integration* 37

Jacobs (2003) – Jacobs, F, 'Approaches to Interpretation in a Plurilingual System' in Hoskins and Robinson (2003)

Jacquemin and de Jong (1977) – Jacquemin, A, and de Jong, H, *European Industrial Organisation* (London, The Macmillan Press Ltd, 1977)

Jans (2000) – Jans, J, *European Environmental Law*, 2nd edn (Groningen, Europa Law Publishing, 2000)

Jans and Vedder (2008) – Jans, J, and Vedder, H, *European Environmental Law*, 3rd edn (Groningen, Europa Law Publishing, 2008)

Jebsen and Stevens (1995–6) – Jebsen, P, and Stevens, R, 'Assumptions, Goals and Dominant Undertakings: the regulation of competition under Article 86 of the European Union' (1995–6) *Antitrust Law Journal* 443

Jeffrey (1983) – Jeffrey, R, *The Logic of Decision*, 2nd edn (Chicago, Chicago University Press, 1983)

Jenny (1993) – Jenny, F, 'Competition and Efficiency' in (1993) Fordham Corporate Law Institute 185

—— **(1998)** – Jenny, F in Ehlermann (1998)

—— **(2000)** – Jenny, F, 'Competition Law and Policy' in Hope, E (ed), *Competition Policy Analysis* (London, Routledge, 2000)

—— **(2001)** – Jenny, F, 'Regulation, Competition and the Professions' in Amato, G, and Laudati, L (eds), *The Anticompetitive Impact of Regulation* (Cheltenham, Edward Elgar, 2001)

Joerges (1997) – Joerges, C, 'The Market without the State? The 'Economic Constitution' of the European Community and the Rebirth of Regulatory Politics' (1997) European Integration Online Papers – <http://eiop.or.at/eiop/pdf/1997–019.pdf> accessed 30 April 2009

—— **(2002)** – Joerges, C, 'The Law in the Process of Constitutionalising Europe' (2002) EUI Working Paper LAW No 2002/4

Johansson (1991) – Johansson, P-O, 'Valuing Environmental Damage' in Helm, D (ed), *Economic Policy Towards the Environment* (Oxford, Blackwell Publishers, 1991)

Joliet (1967) – Joliet, R, *The Rule of Reason in Antitrust Law* (The Hague, Martinus Nijhoff, 1967)

Jones (2004) – Jones, C, *Foundations of Competition Policy in the EU and USA: conflict, convergence and beyond*, paper presented at the First Askola Workshop on Comparative Competition Law, *The Evolution of European Competition Law: whose regulation, which competition?*, EUI, Florence, 12 and 13 November 2004

Jones and Sufrin (2001) – Jones, A, and Sufrin, B, *EC Competition Law: text, cases and materials* (Oxford, OUP, 2001)

—— **(2008)** – Jones, A, and Sufrin, B, *EC Competition Law: text, cases and materials*, 3rd edn (Oxford, OUP, 2008)

Jorde and Teece (1992) – Jorde, T, and Teece, D, *Antitrust, Innovation and Competitiveness* (Oxford, OUP, 1992)

Joskow (2002) – Joskow, P, 'Transaction Cost Economics, Antitrust Rules, and Remedies' (2002) *The Journal of Law, Economics & Organization* 95

Kaczorowska (2000) – Kaczorowska, A, 'International Competition Law in the Context of Global Capitalism' (2000) *ECLR* 117

Kaplow (1992) – Kaplow, L, 'Rules versus Standards: an economic analysis' (1992) 42 *Duke Law Journal* 557

Kapteyn and VerLoren van Themaat (1998) – Kapteyn, P, and VerLoren van Themaat, P, 3rd edn (edited and revised by Gormley, L,) (London, Kluwer Law International, 1998)

Kennedy (1976) – Kennedy, D, 'Form and Substance in Private Law Adjudication' (1976) 89 *Harvard Law Review* 1685

Kerse (1994) – Kerse, C, *EC Antitrust Procedure*, 3rd edn (London, Sweet & Maxwell, 1994)

—— **(1998)** – Kerse, C, *EC Antitrust Procedure*, 4th edn (London, Sweet & Maxwell, 1998)

Kerse and Khan (2005) – Kerse, C, and Khan, N, *EC Antitrust Procedure*, 5th edn (London, Sweet & Maxwell, 2005)

Kingston (2001) – Kingston, S, 'A "New Division of Responsibilities" in the Proposed Regulation to Modernise the Rules Implementing Articles 81 and 82? A Warning Call' (2001) *ECLR* 340

Kirchner (1998) – Kirchner, C in Ehlermann (1998)

Kirkpatrick and Parker (2007) – Kirkpatrick, C, and Parker, D (eds), *Regulatory Impact Assessment: towards better regulation?* (Cheltenham, Edward Elgar, 2007)

Kjølbye (2004) – Kjølbye, L, 'The New Commission Guidelines on the Application of Article 81(3): an economic approach to Article 81' (2004) *ECLR* 566

Kolasky (2004) – Kolasky, W, 'What is Competition? A Comparison of US and European Perspectives' (2004) *The Antitrust Bulletin* 1

Komninos (2005) – Komninos, A, 'Non-competition Concerns: resolution of conflicts in the integrated Article 81 EC', The University of Oxford Centre for Competition Law and Policy, Working Paper (L) 08/05

—— **(2006)** – Komninos, A, 'Non-competition Concerns: resolution of conflicts in the integrated Article 81 EC' in Ehlermann (2006)

Korah (1981) – Korah, V, 'The Rise and Fall of Provisional Validity – the need for a rule of reason in EEC antitrust' (1981) *Northwestern Journal of International Law and Business* 320

—— (**1985**) – Korah, V, *Patent Licensing and EEC Competition Rules Regulation 2349/84* (Oxford, ESC Publishing Ltd, 1985)

—— (**1986**) – Korah, V, 'EEC Competition Policy – Legal Form or Economic Efficiency' (1986) *Current Legal Problems* 85

—— (**1987**) – Korah, V, 'Critical Comments on the Commission's Recent Decisions Exempting Joint Ventures to Exploit Research that Needs Further Development' (1987) *European Law Review* 18

—— (**1990**) – Korah, V, 'From Legal Form to Economic Efficiency – Article 85(1) of the EEC Treaty in contrast to US antitrust' (1990) *The Antitrust Bulletin* 1009

—— (**1997**) – Korah, V, *An Introductory Guide to EC Competition Law and Practice*, 6th edn (Oxford, Hart Publishing, 1997)

—— (**1998**) – Korah, V, 'The Future of Vertical Agreements under EC Competition Law' (1998) *ECLR* 506

—— (**2000**) – Korah, V, *An Introductory Guide to EC Competition Law and Practice*, 7th edn (Oxford, Hart Publishing, 2000)

—— (**2002**) – Korah, V, 'Rule of Reason: apparent inconsistency in the case law under Article 81' (2002) *Competition Law Insight* 24

—— (**2007**) – Korah, V, *An Introductory Guide to EC Competition Law and Practice*, 9th edn (Oxford, Hart Publishing, 2007)

Korah and O'Sullivan (2002) – Korah, V, and O'Sullivan, D, *Distribution Agreements under the EC Competition Rules* (Oxford, Hart Publishing, 2002)

Krämer (2000) – Krämer, L, *EC Environmental Law*, 4th edn (London, Sweet & Maxwell, 2000)

—— (**2003**) – Krämer, L, *EC Environmental Law*, 5th edn (London, Sweet & Maxwell, 2003)

—— (**2006**) – Krämer, L, *EC Environmental Law*, 6th edn (London, Sweet & Maxwell, 2006)

Kühn (1997) – Kühn, K-U, 'Germany' in Graham, E, and Richardson, J (eds), *Global Competition Policy* (Institute for International Economics, Washington DC 1997)

Kühn and Vives (1995) – Kühn, K-U, and Vives, X, 'Information Exchanges Among Firms and their Impacts on Competition' (1995) European Commission, Luxembourg

L'Heureux (1992) – L'Heureux, N, 'Effective Consumer Access to Justice: class actions' (1992) *Journal of Consumer Policy* 445

Lafuente (2002) – Lafuente, A, '*La Política de Competencia en Europa*' (2002) *Papeles de Economía Española* 151

Lane (1993) – Lane, R, 'New Community Competences under the Maastricht Treaty' (1993) *CMLRev* 939

Laudati (1998) – Laudati, L, 'Impact of Community Competition Law on Member State Competition Law' in Martin, S (ed), *Competition Policies in Europe* (Amsterdam, Elsevier Science BV, 1998)

Laussel and Montet (1995) – Laussel, D, and Montet, C, 'Discussion' in Buigues, Jacquemin and Sapir (1995)

Lehmann (2004) – Lehmann, M, 'Voluntary Environmental Agreements and Competition Policy' (2004) 28 *Environmental and Resource Economics* 435

Lenaerts (2002) – Lenaerts, K, 'Modernisation of the Application and Enforcement of European Competition Law – an introductory overview' in Stuyck and Gilliams (2002)

Lenaerts and Arts (1999) – Lenaerts, K, and Arts, D, *Procedural Law of the European Union* (London, Sweet & Maxwell, 1999)

Lenz (2000) – Lenz, M, *The Interplay between the Environment and Competition Law in the EU*, LLM Book (Florence, EUI, September 2000)

Lilla (2001) – Lilla, M, 'Wolves and Lambs' in Dworkin, R, Lilla, M, and Silvers, R (eds), *The Legacy of Isaiah Berlin* (New York, New York Review of Books, 2001)

Limbach (2000) – Limbach, J, 'The Protection of Human Rights in Germany' in Markesinis, B, *The Clifford Chance Millennium Lectures* (Oxford, Hart Publishing, 2000)

Lind and Muysert (2003) – Lind, R, and Muysert, P, 'Innovation and Competition Policy: challenges for the new millennium' (2003) *ECLR* 87

Lipsey and Lancaster (1956) – Lipsey, R, and Lancaster, K, 'The General Theory of Second Best' (1956–57) 24 *The Review of Economic Studies* 11

Lipsky (1998) – Lipsky, A in Ehlermann (1998)

Loman, Mortelmans, Post and Watson (1992) – Loman, A, Mortelmans, K, Post, H, and Watson, S, *Culture and Community Law: before and after Maastricht* (Deventer, Kluwer Law and Taxation Publishers, 1992)

Lomborg (2004) – Lomborg, B (ed), *Global Crises, Global Solutions* (Cambridge, CUP, 2004)

Lonbay (1996) – Lonbay, J (ed), *Enhancing the Legal Position of the European Consumer* (London, BIICL, 1996)

London (2003) – London, C, '*Concurrence et environnement: une entente écologiquement rationelle?*' (2003) *Revue Trimestrielle de Droit Européen* 267

Lovdahl Gormsen (2007) – Lovdahl Gormsen, L, 'The Conflict between Economic Freedom and Consumer Welfare in the Modernisation of Article 82 EC' (2007) *European Competition Journal* 329

Lowe (2004) – Lowe, P, 'Facing New Challenges for EU Competition Policy' in *The European Antitrust Review 2004* (Global Competition Review, London , 2004)

Lucy (1999) – Lucy, W, *Understanding and Explaining Adjudication* (Oxford, OUP, 1999)

Lugard and Hancher (2004) – Lugard, P, and Hancher, L, ' "Honey, I Shrank the Article" A Critical Assessment of the Commission's Notice on Article 81(3) of the EC Treaty' (2004) *ECLR* 410

Lukoff (1986) – Lukoff, F, 'European Competition Law and Distribution in the Motor Vehicle Industry: Commission Regulation 123/85 of 12 December 1984' (1986) *CMLRev* 841

Lutz (1989) – Lutz, F, 'Observations on the Problem of Monopolies' in Peacock and Willgerodt (1989a)

Lyons (2002) – Lyons, B, 'Could Politicians be more Right than Economists? A Theory of Merger Standards' (2002) <http://www.economics.adelaide.edu.au/workshops/doc/lyons.pdf> accessed 30 April 2009

Majone (2002) – Majone, G, 'The Precautionary Principle and its Policy Implications' (2002) *Journal of Common Market Studies* 89

Mancini and Keeling (1994) – Mancini, GF, and Keeling, GT, 'Democracy and the European Court of Justice' (1994) *Modern Law Review* 175

Manzini (2002) – Manzini, P, 'The European Rule of Reason – Crossing the Sea of Doubt' (2002) *ECLR* 392

—— **(2003)** – Manzini, P, '*Parafernali del giudizio antitrust: regola della ragionevolezza, restrizioni accessorie, divieto "per sè"*' (2003) *Giurisprudenza commerciale* 285/II

Marenco (1999) – Marenco, G, 'La notion de restriction de concurrence dans le cadre de l'interdiction des ententes' in *Mélanges en hommage à Michel Waelbroeck* (Bruylant, Brussels, 1999)

—— **(2001)** – Marenco, G in Ehlermann (2001)

Marques (2000) – Marques, I, *Política Industrial no Contexto Europeu: fundamentos, alcance e limites* (Lisbon, Centro de Informação Europeia Jacques Delors, 2000)

Marsden (2000) – Marsden, P, 'The Divide on Verticals' in Evenett, S, Lehmann, A, and Steil, B (eds), *Antitrust Goes Global: what future for transatlantic co-operation* (Washington DC, The Brookings Institution, 2000)

Marshall (1890) – Marshall, A, *Principles of Economics* (London, MacMillan, 1890)

Martínez-López (2000) – Martínez-López, M, 'Horizontal Agreements on Energy Efficiency of Appliances: a comparison between CECED and CEMEP' (2000) *Competition Policy Newsletter* (no 2)

—— **Martínez-López (2002)** – Martínez-López, M, 'Commission Confirms its Policy Line in Respect of Horizontal Agreements on Energy Efficiency of Domestic Appliances' (2002) *Competition Policy Newsletter* (no 1)

Martins (1996) – Martins, J, et al, 'Mark-up Pricing, Market Structure and the Business Cycle', *OECD Economic Studies* No 27, 1996/II

Massarotto (1997) – Massarotto, A, 'Integrating the Economic Dimension in EIA' in The Environmental Law Network International (ed), *International Environmental Impact Assessment: European and Comparative; Law and Practical Experience* (London, Cameron May, 1997)

Massey (1996) – Massey, P, 'Reform of EC Competition Law: substance, procedure and institutions' in (1996) Fordham Corporate Law Institute 91

Matte (1998) – Matte, F in Ehlermann (1998)

Mavroidis (1995) – Mavroidis, P, 'Discussion' in Buigues, Jacquemin and Sapir (1995)

McGillivray and Holder (2001) – McGillivray, D, and Holder, J, 'Locating EC Environmental Law' (2001) *Yearbook of European Law* 139

McGowan (2000) – McGowan, L, 'Safeguarding the Economic Constitution: the Commission and Competition Policy' in Nugent, N (ed), *At the Heart of the Union – Studies of the European Commission*, 2nd edn (Basingstoke, Macmillan, 2000)

McGowan and Wilks (1995) – McGowan, L, and Wilks, S, 'The First Supranational Policy in the European Union: Competition Policy' (1995) *European Journal of Political Research* 141

Mercier, Mach, Gilliéron and Affolter (1999) – Mercier, P, Mach, O, Gilliéron, H, and Affolter, S, *Grands principes du droit de la concurrence* (Brussels, Bruylant, 1999)

Mestmäcker (1994) – Mestmäcker, E-J, 'On the Legitimacy of European Law' (1994) *Rabels Zeitschrift für ausländisches und internationales Privatrecht* 615

—— **(2000)** – Mestmäcker, E-J, 'The EC Commission's Modernisation of Competition Policy: a challenge to the Community's constitutional order' (2000) *European Business Organisation Law Review* 401

—— **(2001)** – Mestmäcker, E-J, 'The Modernisation of EC Antitrust policy: constitutional change or administrative convenience' in Ehlermann (2001)

Michalowski and Woods (1999) – Michalowski, S, and Woods, L, *German Constitutional Law: the protection of civil liberties* (Aldershot, Dartmouth Publishing Co, 1999)

Miller and Rose (1993) – Miller, P, and Rose, N, 'Governing Economic Life' in Gane, M, and Johnson, T (eds), *Foucault's New Domains* (London, Routledge, 1993)

Mitchell and Simmons (1994) – Mitchell, W, and Simmons, R, *Beyond Politics: Markets, Welfare and the Failure of Bureaucracy* (Boulder, Westview Press, 1994)

Mohamed (2000) – Mohamed, S, 'National Interests Limiting EU Cross Border Bank Mergers' (2000) *ECLR* 248

Monti (2002) – Monti, G, 'Article 81 EC and Public Policy' (2002) *CMLRev* 1057

—— **(2004a)** – Monti, G, 'New Directions in EC Competition Law' in Tridimas, T, and Nebbia, P (eds), *European Union Law for the Twenty-first Century*, Vol II (Oxford, Hart Publishing, 2004)

—— **(2007)** – Monti, G, *EC Competition Law* (Cambridge, CUP, 2007)

Monti (2000) – Monti, M, 'European Competition for the 21st Century' in (2000) Fordham Corporate Law Institute 257

—— **(2004)** – Monti, M, 'EU Competition Policy After May 2004' in (2004) Fordham Corporate Law Institute 403

Mortelmans (2001) – Mortelmans, K, 'Towards Convergence in the Application of the Rules on Free Movement and on Competition' (2001) *CMLRev* 613

Mortelmans and Watson (1996) – Mortelmans, K, and Watson, S, *The Notion of Consumer in Community Law: A Lottery?* in Lonbay, J (ed), *Enhancing the Legal Position of the European Consumer* (London, BIICL, 1996)

Möschel (1989) – Möschel, W, 'Competition Policy from an Ordo Point of View' in Peacock, A and Willgerodt, H (eds), *German Neo-Liberals and the Social Market Economy* (London, Macmillan, 1989)

—— **(1991)** – Möschel, W, 'The Goals of Antitrust Revisited' (1991) JITE 7

Motta (2004) – Motta, M, *Competition Policy: Theory and Practice* (Cambridge, CUP, 2004)

Moussis (2000) – Moussis, N, *Guide to EU Policies*, 6th edn (Belgium, European Study Service, 2000)

—— **(2003)** – Moussis, N, *Access to European Union: Law, Economics, Policies*, 2th edn (Rixensart, European Study Service, 2003)

Murphy and Nagel (2002) – Murphy, L, and Nagel, T, *The Myth of Ownership: taxes and justice* (Oxford, OUP, 2002).

Nadeau (2003) – Nadeau, R, *The Wealth of Nature* (New York, Columbia University Press, 2003)

Nazerali and Cowan (1999) – Nazerali, J, and Cowan, D, 'Reforming EU Distribution Rules – has the Commission found vertical reality?' (1999) *ECLR* 159

Nazzini (2006) – Nazzini, R, 'Article 81 EC between Time Present and Time Past: a normative critique of "restriction of competition" in EU law' (2006) *CMLRev* 497

Neale and Goyder (1981) – Neale, A, and Goyder, D, *The Antitrust Laws of the USA*, 3rd edn (Cambridge, CUP, 1981)

Neumann (2001) – Neumann, M, *Competition Policy: History, Theory and Practice* (Cheltenham, Edward Elgar Publishing Ltd, 2001)

Neven (1998) – Neven, D in Ehlermann (1998)

Neven and Röller (2000) – Neven, D, and Röller, L-H, 'Consumer Surplus versus Welfare Standard in a Political Economy Model of Merger Control' (2000) *WZB Working Paper* FS IV 00–15

Neven, Papandropoulos and Seabright (1998) – Neven, D, Papandropoulos, P, and Seabright, P, *Trawling for Minnows* (Centre for Economic Policy Research, London, 1998)

Niedobitek (1997) – Niedobitek, M, *The Cultural Dimension in EC Law* (London, Kluwer Law International, 1997)

Niels and ten Kate (2004) – Niels, G, and ten Kate, A, 'Introduction: antitrust in the US and the EU – converging or diverging paths?' (2004) *The Antitrust Bulletin* 1

O'Loughlin (2003) – O'Loughlin, R, 'EC Competition Rules and Free Movement Rules: an examination of the parallels and their furtherance by the ECJ in the Wouters decision' (2003) *ECLR* 62

Odudu (2001) – Odudu, O, 'Interpreting Article 81(1): demonstrating restrictive effect' (2001) *European Law Review* 261

—— **(2002)** – Odudu, O, 'A New Economic Approach to Article 81(1)?' (2002) *European Law Review* 100

—— **(2002a)** – Odudu, O, 'Article 81(3), Discretion and Direct Effect' (2002) *ECLR* 17

—— **(2006)** – Odudu, O, *The Boundaries of EC Competition Law: the scope of Article 81* (Oxford, OUP, 2006)

Oliver (2003) – Oliver, P, *Free Movement of Goods in the European Community* (London, Sweet & Maxwell, 2003)

Ostry (1993) – Ostry, S, 'Beyond the Border: the new international policy arena' in Kantzenbach, E, Scharrer, H-E, and Waverman, L (eds), *Competition Policy in an Interdependent World Economy* (Baden-Baden, Nomos Verlagsgesellschaft, 1993)

Palgrave Dictionary of Economics (1998) – Newman, P (ed), *The New Palgrave Dictionary of Economics and the Law* (London, Macmillan Reference Ltd, 1998)

Peacock and Willgerodt (1989) – Peacock, A, and Willgerodt, H (eds), *German Neo-Liberals and the Social Market Economy* (London, Macmillan, 1989)

—— **(1989a)** – Peacock, A, and Willgerodt, H (eds), *Germany's Social Market Economy: origins and evolution* (London, Macmillan, 1989)

Pearce and Turner (1990) – Pearce, D, and Turner, K, *Economics of Natural Resources and the Environment* (Hemel Hempstead, Harvester Wheatsheaf, 1990)

Pearson (2000) – Pearson, C, *Economics and the Global Environment* (Cambridge, CUP, 2000)

Peczenik (1989) – Peczenik, A, *On Law and Reason* (London, Kluwer Academic Publishers, 1989)

Peeperkorn (2002) – Peeperkorn, L, 'EC Vertical Restraints Guidelines: Effects-Based or Per Se Policy? – a reply' (2002) *ECLR* 38

Pelkmans (1985) – Pelkmans, J, 'Consumer Interests in the EC Competition Regime: an economic perspective' in Goyens (1985)

Pera and Todino (1996) – Pera, A, and Todino, M, 'Enforcement of EC Competition Rules: need for a reform?' in (1996) Fordham Corporate Law Institute 125

Pescatore (1974) – Pescatore, P, *The Law of Integration* (Leiden, Sijthoff, 1974)

Petersmann (1991) – Petersmann, E-U, 'Constitutionalism, Constitutional Law and European Integration' (1991) *Aussenwirtschaft* 247

—— **(1995)** – Petersmann, E-U, 'Proposals for a New Constitution for the European Union: building blocks for a constitutional theory and constitutional law of the EU' (1995) *CMLRev* 1123

—— **(2003)** – Petersmann, E-U, 'Constitutional Economics, Human Rights and the Future of the WTO' (2003) *Aussenwirtschaft* 49

Petrakis, Sartzetakis, and Xepapadeas (1999) – Petrakis, E, Sartzetakis, E, and Xepapadeas, A (eds), *Environmental Regulation and Market Power* (Cheltenham, Edward Elgar Publishing Ltd, 1999)

Pitofsky (1998) – Pitofsky, R in Ehlermann (1998)

Poiares Maduro (1997) – Poiares Maduro, M, 'Reforming the Market or the State? Article 30 and the European Constitution: economic freedom and political rights' (1997) *European Law Journal* 55

—— **(1998)** – Poiares Maduro, M, *We the Court* (Oxford, Hart Publishing, 1998)

—— **(1999)** – Poiares Maduro, M, 'Striking the Elusive Balance between Economic Freedom and Social Rights in the EU' in Alston, P, *The EU and Human Rights* (Oxford, OUP, 1999)

Porter (1995) – Porter, T, *Trust in Numbers* (Princeton, Princeton University Press, 1995)

Porter (2001) – Porter, M, 'Competition and Antitrust: towards a productivity-based approach to evaluating mergers and joint ventures' (2001) *The Antitrust Bulletin* 919

Posner (1975) – Posner, R, 'The Social Costs of Monopoly and Regulation' (1975) *The Journal of Political Economy* 807

—— **(1998)** – Posner, R, *Economic Analysis of Law*, 5th edn (New York, Aspen Law and Business, 1998)

—— **(2001)** – Posner, R, *Antitrust Law*, 2nd edn (Chicago, University of Chicago Press, 2001)

Psychogiopoulou (2005) – Psychogiopoulou, E, 'EC Competition Law and Cultural Diversity: the case of the cinema, music and book publishing industries' (2005) *European Law Journal* 838

—— **(2006)** – Psychogiopoulou, E, 'The Cultural Mainstreaming Clause of Article 151(4) EC: protection and promotion of cultural diversity or hidden cultural agenda?' (2006) *European Law Journal* 575

Rasmussen (1986) – Rasmussen, H, *On Law and Policy in the European Court of Justice* (Dordrecht, Martinus Nijhoff Publishers, 1986)

—— **(1993)** – Rasmussen, H, *Towards a Normative Theory of Interpretation of Community Law* (Copenhagen, Copenhagen Political Studies Press, 1993)

Rawls (1999) – Rawls J, *A Theory of Justice*, revised edn (Oxford, OUP, 1999)

Rehbinder (1997) – Rehbinder, E, Jean Monnet Chair Paper RSC 97/45, 'Environmental Agreements: a new instrument for environmental policy' (Florence, EUI, 1997)

Reich (1997) – Reich, N, 'Competition Law and the Consumer' in Gormley, L (ed), *Current and Future Perspectives on EC Competition Law* (London, Kluwer, 1997)

Reich and Woodroffe (1994) – Reich, N, and Woodroffe, G (eds), *European Consumer Policy After Maastricht* (Dordrecht, Kluwer Academic Publishers, 1994)

Rey and Venit (2004) – Rey, P, and Venit, J, 'Parallel Trade and Pharmaceuticals: a policy in search of itself' (2004) *European Law Review* 153

Riley (1998) – Riley, A, 'Vertical Restraints: a revolution?' (1998) *ECLR* 483

Ritter and Braun (2005) – Ritter, L and Braun, D, *European Competition Law: a practitioner's guide*, 3rd edn (London, Kluwer Law International, 2005)

Ritter, Braun, and Rawlinson (2000) – Ritter, L, Braun, D, and Rawlinson, F, *European Competition Law: A Practitioner's Guide*, 2nd edn (London, Kluwer Law International, 2000)

Rivas and Stroud (2001) – Rivas, J, and Stroud, F, 'Developments in EC Competition Law in 1999/2000: an overview' (2001) *CMLRev* 935

Rodríguez Iglesias and Baquero Cruz (2003) – Rodríguez Iglesias, G, and Baquero Cruz, J, 'The Convention and the Court' in Hoskins and Robinson (2003)

Roessler (1993) – Roessler, F, 'The Constitutional Function of the Multilateral Trade Order' in Hilf, M, and Petersmann, E-U (eds), *National Constitutions and International Economic Law* (The Netherlands, Kluwer, 1993)

Rosenthal (1990) – Rosenthal, D, 'Competition Policy' in Hufbauer, G (ed), *Europe 1992: an American perspective* (Washington DC, The Brookings Institution, 1990)

Ross (1995) – Ross, A, 'Cultural Protection: a matter of Union citizenship or human rights?' in Neuwahl, N, and Ross, A (eds), *The European Union and Human Rights* (London, Martinus Nijhoff Publishers, 1995)

Ross (1996–97) – Ross, S, 'Afterword – Did the Canadian Parliament Really Permit Mergers that Exploit Canadian Consumers so the World can be More Efficient?' (1996–97) 65 *Antitrust Law Journal* 641

Roth (2006) – Roth, W-H, 'Strategic Competition Policy: a comment on EU competition policy' in Ullrich, H (ed), *The Evolution of European Competition Law: whose regulation, which competition?* (Cheltenham, Edward Elgar, 2006)

Rousseva (2006) – Rousseva, E, 'The Concept of "Objective Justification" of an Abuse of a Dominant Position: can it help to modernise the analysis under Article 82 EC?' (2006) *Competition Law Review* 27

Sahlin (1990) – Sahlin, N-E, *The Philosophy of FP Ramsey* (Cambridge, CUP, 1990)

Sanderson (1996–97) – Sanderson, M, 'Efficiency Analysis in Canadian Merger Cases' (1996–97) 65 *Antitrust Law Journal* 623

Sandmo (2000) – Sandmo, A, 'Towards a Competitive Society?' in Hope, E (ed), *Competition Policy Analysis* (London, Routledge, 2000)

Sauter (1997) – Sauter, W, *Competition Law and Industrial Policy in the EU* (Oxford, Clarendon Press, 1997)

—— **(1998)** – Sauter, W, 'The Economic Constitution of the European Union' (1998) *Columbia Journal of European Law* 27

Scalia (1989) – Scalia, A, 'The Rule of Law as a Law of Rules' (1989) University of *Chicago Law Review* 1175

Scarpa (2001) – Scarpa, C, 'The anticompetitive effects of minimum quality standards: the role of self-regulation' in Amato, G, and Laudati, L (eds), *The Anticompetitive Impact of Regulation* (Cheltenham, Edward Elgar, 2001)

Schaub (1996) – Schaub, A, 'European Competition Policy in a Changing Economic Environment' in (1996) Fordham Corporate Law Institute 71

—— **(1998)** – Schaub, A in Ehlermann (1998)

—— **(2001)** – Schaub, A in Ehlermann (2001)

—— **(2002)** – Schaub, A, 'Continued Focus on Reform: Recent Developments in EC Competition Policy' in (2002) Fordham Corporate Law Institute 31

Scherer (1987) – Scherer, F, 'Antitrust, Efficiency, and Progress' (1987) 62 *NYU Law Review* 998

—— **(1992)** – Scherer, F, 'Schumpeter and Plausible Capitalism' (1992) *Journal of Economic Literature* 1416

—— **(1992a)** – Scherer, F, 'Antitrust: ideology or economics?' (1992) *Critical Review* 497

Scherer and Ross (1990) – Scherer, F, and Ross, D, *Industrial Market Structure and Economic Performance*, 3rd edn (Boston, Houghton Mifflin, 1990)

Schick (1997) – Schick, F, *Making Choices: A Recasting of Decision Theory* (Cambridge, CUP, 1997)

Schlink (2001) – Schlink, B, 'Der Grundsatz der Verhältnismäßigkeit' in Badura, P, and Dreier, H (eds), *Festschrift 50 Jahre Bundesverfassungsgericht* (Tübingen, Mohr Siebeck, 2001)

Schmid (2000) – Schmid, C, 'Diagonal Competence Conflicts between European Competition Law and National Regulation – a conflict of laws reconstruction of the dispute on book price fixing' (2000) *European Review of Private Law* 155

Scholz and Stähler (1999) – Scholz, C, and Stähler, F, *Unilateral Environmental Policy and International Competitiveness* (Kiler Studien 299 (Tübingen, Mohr Siebeck, 1999)

Schroeder (1997) – Schroeder, D, 'The Green Paper on Vertical Restraints: beware of market share thresholds' (1997) *ECLR* 340

Schröter (1987) – Schröter, H, 'Antitrust Analysis under Article 85(1) and (3)' in (1987) Fordham Corporate Law Institute 645

Schumpeter (1942) – Schumpeter, J, *Capitalism, Socialism and Democracy* (London, Allen and Unwin, 1942)

Schweitzer (2007) – Schweitzer, H, 'Competition Law and Public Policy: reconsidering an uneasy relationship. The example of Article 81', *EUI Working Papers, Law* 2007/30

Scott and Vos (2002) – Scott, J, and Vos, E, 'The Juridification of Uncertainty: Observations on the Ambivalence of the Precautionary Principle within the EU and the WTO' in Dehousse, R, and Joerges, C (eds), *Good Governance in Europe's Integrated Market* (Oxford, OUP, 2002)

Semmelmann (2008) – Semmelmann, C, 'The Future Role of Non-competition Goals in the Interpretation of Article 81 EC' (2008) 1 *Global Antitrust Review* 15

Sen (2002) – Sen, A, *Rationality and Freedom* (Cambridge MA, The Belknap Press of Harvard University Press, 2002)

Shelkoplyas (2003) – Shelkoplyas, N, *The Application of EC Law in Arbitration Proceedings* (Groningen, Europa Law Publishing, 2003)

Shenefield (2004) – Shenefield, J, 'Coherence or Confusion: the future of the global antitrust conversation' (2004) *The Antitrust Bulletin* 385

Shepherd (1990) – Shepherd, W, *The Economics of Industrial Organisation*, 3rd edn (Englewood Cliffs, NJ, Prentice Hall, 1990)

Shyam Khemani (2002) – Shyam Khemani, R, 'Application of Competition Law: Exemptions and Exceptions' (2002) UNCTAD/DITC/CLP/Misc.25

Simms, Kjell and Potts (2005) – Simms, A, Kjell, P, and Potts, R, *Clone Town Britain: the survey results on the bland state of the nation* (London, New Economics Foundation, 2005)

Sinden and Thampapillai (1995) – Sinden, J, and Thampapillai, D, *Introduction to Benefit-Cost Analysis* (Melbourne, Longman, 1995)

Siragusa (1997) – Siragusa, M, 'Rethinking Article 85: Problems and Challenges in the Design and enforcement of the EC competition rules' in (1997) Fordham Corporate Law Institute 525

—— **(1998)** – Siragusa, M in Ehlermann (1998)

—— **(2005)** – Siragusa, M, 'Critical Remarks on the Commission's Legal Analysis in its Report on Competition in Professional Services' in Ehlermann (2006)

Slot (2004) – Slot, P, 'A View from the Mountain: 40 years of developments in EC competition law' (2004) *CMLRev* 443

Slot and van der Woude (1988) – Slot, P, and van der Woude, M (eds), *Exploiting the Internal Market: co-operation and competition toward 1992* (Deventer, Kluwer Law and Taxation Publishers, 1988)

Slote (1989) – Slote, M, *Beyond Optimizing* (Cambridge MA, Harvard University Press, 1989)

Slynn (1985) – Slynn, G, 'EEC Competition Law from the Perspective of the Court of Justice' in (1985) Fordham Corporate Law Institute 383

Smit and Herzog (1976) – Smit, H, and Herzog, P (eds), *Columbia Law School Project on European Legal Institutions: the law of the European Economic Community*, Vol 2 (New York, M Bender, 1976)

Snell (2002) – Snell, J, *Goods and Services in EC Law* (Oxford, OUP, 2002)

Snowball and Antrobus (2001) – Snowball, J, and Antrobus, G, 'Measuring the Value of the Arts to Society' (2001) *The South African Journal of Economics* 752

Snyder (1990) – Snyder, F, *New Directions in European Community Law* (London, Weidenfeld & Nicolson, 1990)

Souty (2003) – Souty, F, *Le droit et la politique de la concurrence de l'Union européenne*, 3ème édn (Paris, Montchrestien, 2003)

Sporman (1968) – Sporman, K, *Kontouren einer Europäischen Wettbewerbspolitik* (Aussenwirtschafts-dienst des Betriebsberaters, 1968)

Srinivasan (1996) – Srinivasan, T, 'The Generalised Theory of Distortions and Welfare Two Decades Later' in Feenstra, R, Grossman, G, and Irwin, D (eds), *The Political Economy of Trade Policy* (Cambridge MA, The MIT Press, 1996)

Stigler (1985) – Stigler, G, 'The Origin of the Sherman Act' (1985) 14 *Journal of Legal Studies* 1

Streit and Mussler (1995) – Streit, M, and Mussler, W, 'The Economic Constitution of the European Community: from "Rome" to "Maastricht" ' (1995) *European Law Journal* 5

Sturgess and Chubb (1988) – Sturgess, G, and Chubb, P, *Judging the World: law and politics in the world's leading courts* (London, Butterworths, 1988)

Stuyck (2000) – Stuyck, J, 'European Consumer Law after the Treaty of Amsterdam: consumer policy in or beyond the internal market?' (2000) *CMLRev* 367

Stuyck and Gilliams (2002) – Stuyck, J, and Gilliams, H (eds), *Modernisation of European Competition Law* (Antwerp, Intersentia, 2002)

Subiotto and Snelders (2003) – Subiotto, R, and Snelders, R (eds), *Antitrust Developments in Europe 2002* (The Hague, Kluwer Law International, 2003)

Sufrin (2006) – Sufrin, B, 'The Evolution of Article 81(3) of the EC Treaty' (2006) 51 *Antitrust Bulletin* 915

Sullivan and Grimes (2000) – Sullivan, L, and Grimes, W, *The Law of Antitrust: an integrated handbook* (St Paul, Minn, West Group, 2000)

Sunstein (1997) – Sunstein, C, 'Incommensurability and Kinds of Valuation: some applications in law' in Chang, R (ed), *Incommensurability, Incomparability, and Practical Reason* (Cambridge MA, Harvard University Press, 1997)

Temple Lang (1991) – Temple Lang, J, 'The Sphere in Which Member States are Obliged to Comply with the General Principles of Community Fundamental Rights Principles' (1991) *Legal Issues of European Integration* 23

—— **(1996)** – Temple Lang, J, 'European Community Antitrust Law: innovation markets and high technology industries' in (1996) Fordham Corporate Law Institute 519

Tesauro (1998) – Tesauro, G in (1998) Fordham Corporate Law Institute 221

The World Bank and OECD (1999) – The World Bank and OECD, *A Framework for the Design and Implementation of Competition Law and Policy* (The World Bank and OECD, 1999)

Tirole (1988) – Tirole, J, *The Theory of Industrial Organisation* (London, The MIT Press, 1988)

Tizzano (1998) – Tizzano, A in Ehlermann (1998)

Toggenburg (2003) – Toggenburg, G, 'Cultural Diversity at the Background of the European Debate on Values – an introduction' in Palermo, F, and Toggenburg, G (eds), *European Constitutional Values and Cultural Diversity* (European Academy, Bolzano, 2003)

Townley (2002) – Townley, C, 'Some Possible Objectives of Competition Law from the Economic Theory Perspective' (2002) *EUI, mimeo*

—— **(2004)** – Townley, C, 'The Liner Shipping Block Exemptions in European Law: has the tide turned?' (2004) *World Competition* 107

—— **(2007)** – Townley, C, 'The Concept of an Undertaking: the boundaries of the corporation – a discussion of agency, employees and subsidiaries' in Amato, G, and Ehlermann, C-D (eds), *EC Competition Law: a critical assessment* (Oxford, Hart Publishing, 2007)

—— **(2008)** – Townley, C, 'Is anything more Important than Consumer Welfare (in Article 81 EC)?: reflections of a Community lawyer' (2007–08) Vol 10 *The Cambridge Yearbook of European Legal Studies* 345

Trebilcock (1975) – Trebilcock, M, 'Winners and Losers in the Modern Regulatory System: must the consumer always lose?' (1975) 13 *Osgoode Hall Law Journal* 619

Tridimas (1999) – Tridimas, T, *The General Principles of EC Law* (Oxford, OUP, 1999)

Tunney (2001) – Tunney, J, 'Is the Emerging Legal Concept of Culture the Cuckoo's Egg in the EU Competition Law Nest?' (2001) *ECLR* 173

Uitermark (1996) – Uitermark, P, 'The Concept of Competition' in van Mourik, A (ed), *Developments in European Competition Policy* (The Netherlands, EIPA, 1996)

Ullrich (1996) – Ullrich, H, 'Harmonisation within the European Union' (1996) *ECLR* 178

van den Bergh (1995) – van den Bergh, R, 'Modern Industrial Organisation versus Old-fashioned European Competition Law' (1995) *ECLR* 75

—— **(2002)** – van den Bergh, R, 'The Difficult Reception of Economic Analysis in European Competition Law' in Cucinotta, Pardolesi and Van den Bergh (2002)

van den Bergh and Camesasca (2000) – van den Bergh, R, and Camesasca, P, 'Irreconcilable Principles? The Court of Justice Exempts Collective Labour Agreements from the Wrath of Antitrust' (2000) *European Law Review* 492

—— **(2001)** – Van den Bergh, R, and Camesasca, P, *European Competition Law and Economics: a comparative perspective* (Groningen/Oxford, Intersentia/Hart, 2001)

van der Esch (1980) – van der Esch, B, 'EEC Competition Rules: Basic Principles and Policy Aims' (1980) *Legal Issues of Economic Integration* 75

—— **(1991)** – van der Esch, B, 'The Principles of Interpretation Applied by the Court of Justice of the European Communities and their Relevance for the Scope of the EEC Competition Rules' in (1991) Fordham Corporate Law Institute 223

van der Woude (2002) – van der Woude, M, 'National Courts and the Draft Regulation on the Application of Articles 81 and 82 EC' in Stuyck and Gilliams (2002)

van Empel (1988) – van Empel, M, 'European Competition Rules – effective implementation' in Slot and van der Woude (1988)

van Gerven (2004) – van Gerven, G, 'The Application of Article 81 in the New Europe' in (2004) Fordham Corporate Law Institute 415

van Miert (1997) – van Miert, K, *The Importance of Competition Policy for the Future of European Integration* (Foundation Paul-Henri Spaak, Brussels, 1997)

—— **(1999)** – van Miert, K, 'European Competition Policy: a retrospective and prospects for the future' in (1999) Fordham Corporate Law Institute 1

Vedder (2003) – Vedder, H, *Competition Law and Environmental Protection in Europe: towards sustainability?* (Groningen, Europa Law Publishing, 2003)

Venit (1986) – Venit, J, 'Pronuptia: ancillary restraints – or unholy alliances' (1986) *European Law Review* 213

—— **(1998)** – Venit, J in Ehlermann (1998)

—— **(2001)** – Venit, J in Ehlermann (2001)

—— **(2003)** – Venit, J, 'Brave New World: the modernisation and decentralisation of enforcement under Articles 81 and 82 of the EC Treaty' (2003) *CMLRev* 545

Verhoef and Nijkamp (2003) – Verhoef, E, and Nijkamp, P, 'The Adoption of Energy Efficiency Enhancing Technologies. Market Performance and Policy Strategies in Case of Heterogeneous Firms' (2003) *Economic Modelling* 839

Verouden (2003) – Verouden, V, 'Vertical Agreements and Article 81(1) EC: the evolving role of economic analysis' (2003) *Antitrust Law Journal* 525

Verstrynge (1984) – Verstrynge, J-F, 'Current Antitrust Policy Issues in the EEC: some reflections on the second generation of competition policy' in (1984) Fordham Corporate Law Institute 673

—— **(1988)** – Verstrynge, J-F, 'The System of EEC Competition Rules' in Slot and van der Woude (1988)

Vickers (2003a) – Vickers, J, 'Competition Economics and Policy' (2003) *ECLR* 95

Videras (2002) – Videras, J, 'Voluntary Environmental Programmes as a Collusive Mechanism: incentives, design and welfare effects' (2002) Working Paper 02/05, Hamilton College <http://academics.hamilton.edu/economics/home/Workpap/02_05.pdf> accessed 30 April 2009

Viscusi, Vernon and Harrington (2000) – Viscusi, W, Vernon, J, and Harrington, J, *Economics of Regulation and Antitrust*, 3rd edn (England, The MIT Press, 2000)

Vogel (1997) – Vogel, L, '*Cronique de droit de la concurrence*' (1997) *Revue du marché commun* 130

Vogelaar (1994) – Vogelaar, F, 'Towards an Improved Integration of EC Environmental Policy and EC Competition Policy: an interim report' in (1994) Fordham Corporate Law Institute 529

von Weizsäcker (1980) – von Weizsäcker, C, *Barriers to Entry: a theoretical treatment* (Berlin, Springer Verlag, 1980)

Vossestein (2002) – Vossestein, A, 'Case C-35/99, Arduino, Judgment of 19 February 2000, Full Court; Case C-309/99, *Wouters et al v Algemene Raad van de Nederlandse Orde van Advocaten*, judgment of 19 February 2002, Full Court; not yet reported' (2002) *CMLRev* 841

Waelbroeck (1987) – Waelbroeck, M, 'Competition, Integration and Economic Efficiency in the EEC from the Point of View of the Private Firm' in Michigan Law Review Association (ed), *The Art of Governance: Festschrift zu Ehren von Eric Stein (Michigan Law Review Assn)* (Baden-Baden, Nomos Verlagsgesellschaft, 1987)

—— **(1987a)** – Waelbroeck, M, 'Antitrust Analysis under Article 85(1) and Article 85(3)' in (1987) Fordham Corporate Law Institute 693

Waelbroeck (2004) – Waelbroeck, D, *Vertical Agreements: 4 years of liberalisation by Regulation 2790/99 after 40 years of legal (block) regulation*, paper presented at the First Askola Workshop on Comparative Competition Law, *The Evolution of European Competition Law: whose regulation, which competition?*, EUI, Florence, 12 and 13 November 2004

Wasmeier (2001) – Wasmeier, M, 'The Integration of Environmental Protection as a General Rule for Interpreting Community Law' (2001) *CMLRev* 159

Wathelet (2003) – Wathelet, M, '*Du concept de l'effet direct à celui de l'invocabilité au regard de la jurisprudence récente de la Cour de justice*' in Hoskins and Robinson (2003)

Wathern (1988) – Wathern, P, 'An Introductory Guide to EIA' in Wathern, P (ed), *Environmental Impact Assessment: Theory and Practice* (London, Unwin Hyman, 1988)

Weatherill (1997) – Weatherill, S, *EC Consumer Law and Policy* (London, Longman, 1997)

—— **(2006)** – Weatherill, S, 'Anti-doping Re-visited – the demise of the rule of "purely sporting interest" ' (2006) *ECLR* 645

Weatherill and Beaumont (1999) – Weatherill, S, and Beaumont, P, *EU Law*, 2nd edn (London, Penguin, 1999)

Weiler (1991) – Weiler, J, 'The Transformation of Europe' (1991) *Yale Law Journal* 2403

—— **(1997)** – Weiler, J, 'The Reformation of European Constitutionalism' (1997) *Journal of Common Market Studies* 97

Weiler and Lockhart (1995) – Weiler J, and Lockhart, N, ' "Taking Rights Seriously" Seriously: the European Court of Justice and its Fundamental Rights Jurisprudence – Part II' (1995) *CMLRev* 579

Wesseling (1997) – Wesseling, R, 'Subsidiarity in Community Antitrust Law: setting the right agenda' (1997) *European Law Review* 35

—— **(1998)** – Wesseling, R in Ehlermann (1998)

—— **(1999)** – Wesseling, R, 'The Commission White Paper on Modernisation of EC Antitrust Law: unspoken consequences and incomplete treatment of alternative options' (1999) *ECLR* 420

—— **(1999a)** – Wesseling, R, *Constitutional Developments in EC Antitrust Law: the transformation of Community antitrust law and its implications* (PhD Book, Florence, EUI, 1999)

—— **(2000)** – Wesseling, R, *The Modernisation of EC Antitrust Law* (Oxford, Hart Publishing, 2000)

—— **(2001)** – Wesseling, R, 'The Draft Regulation Modernising the Competition Rules: the Commission is married to one idea' (2001) 26 *European Law Review* 357

Whelan (1999) – Whelan, A, 'Fundamental Principles of EU Environmental Law' (1999) *Irish Journal of European Law* 37

Whish (1998) – Whish, R in Ehlermann (1998)

—— **(2000)** – Whish, R, 'Regulation 2790/99: The Commission's "New Style" Block Exemption for Vertical agreements' (2000) *CMLRev* 887

—— **(2001)** – Whish, R, *Competition Law*, 4th edn (London, Butterworths, 2001)

—— **(2003)** – Whish, R, *Competition Law*, 5th edn (London, LexisNexis UK, 2003)

—— **(2008)** – Whish, R, *Competition Law*, 6th edn (London, LexisNexis UK, 2008)

Whish and Sufrin (1987) – Whish, R, and Sufrin, B, 'Article 85 and the Rule of Reason' (1987) *Yearbook of European Law* 1

—— **(2000)** – Whish, R, and Sufrin, B, 'Community Competition Law: Notification and Individual Exemption – Goodbye to All That' in Hayton, D (ed), *Law's Future(s): British legal developments in the 21st century* (Oxford, Hart Publishing, 2000)

Wilks (1996) – Wilks, S, 'Options for Reform of European Competition Policy' in van Mourik, A (ed), *Developments in European Competition Policy* (Maastricht, European Institute of Public Administration, 1996)

Williams (1989) – Williams, P, 'Why Regulate for Competition?' in James, M (ed), *Regulating for Competition?: trade practices policy in a changing economy* (NSW, The Centre for Independent Studies Ltd, 1989)

Williamson (1968) – Williamson, O, 'Economies as an Antitrust Defence: the welfare trade-offs' (1968) *The American Economic Review* 18

—— **(1969)** – Williamson, O, 'Allocative Efficiency and the Limits of Antitrust' (1969b) 59 *The American Economic Review* 105

—— **(1977)** – Williamson, O, 'Economies as an Antitrust Defence Revisited' (1977) 125 *U Pa L Rev* 699

Willimsky (1997) – Willimsky, S, 'The Concept(s) of Competition' (1997) *European Competition Law Review* 54

Wils (2002) – Wils, W, *The Optimal Enforcement of EC Antitrust Law* (London, Kluwer Law International, 2002)

—— **(2004)** – Wils, W, 'Community Report' in Cahill, D (ed), *The Modernisation of EU Competition Law Enforcement in the European Union*, FIDE National Reports (Cambridge, CUP, 2004)

Winter (2003) – Winter, G, 'Environmental Principles in Community Law' in Hans, JH (ed) *The European Communities and the Future of European Environmental Law* (Groningen, Europa Law Publishing, 2003)

Wißmann (2000) – Wißmann, T, 'Decentralised Enforcement of EC Competition Law and the New Policy on Cartels' (2000) *World Competition* 123

Wit, Davidson and Dings (2003) – Wit, R, Davidson, M, and Dings, J, 'Meeting External Costs in the Aviation Industry', CE, August 2003, <http://www.cfit.gov.uk/docs/2003/aec/research/pdf/aec.pdf> accessed 30 April 2009

Wolf (1998) – Wolf, D in Ehlermann (1998)

Woods and Scholes (1997) – Woods, L, and Scholes, J, 'Broadcasting: the creation of a European culture or the limits of the internal market?' (1997) *Yearbook of European Law* 47

Wyatt and Dashwood (1993) – Wyatt, D, and Dashwood, A, *European Community Law*, 3rd edn (London, Sweet & Maxwell, 1993)

—— **(2006)** – Wyatt, D, and Dashwood, A, *European Community Law*, 5th edn (London, Sweet & Maxwell, 2006)

Zäch (2008) – Zäch, R, 'More Economic Approach and Constitutional Law', 3rd ASCOLA Conference, organised by the University of Zurich, 5 and 6 September 2008

Zucca (2007) – Zucca, L, *Constitutional Dilemmas* (Oxford, OUP, 2007)

Zuleeg (1997) – Zuleeg, M, 'The European Constitution under Constitutional Constraints: the German scenario' (1997) *European Law Review* 19

SPEECHES

Cremona (2008) – Cremona, M, *Understanding the EU Reform Treaty*, Centre of European Law, King's College London, 8 Feb 2008

Freeman (2008) – Freeman, P, *Is Competition Everything?*, Law Society European Group, Law Society, 21 July 2008

Kroes (2005) – Kroes, N, *European Competition Policy – delivering better markets and better choices*, speech for the European Consumer and Competition Day, London, 15 September 2005

—— **(2007)** – Kroes, N, *European Competition Policy in a Changing World and Globalised Economy: Fundamentals, New Objectives and Challenges Ahead*, speech for the GCLC/ College of Europe Conference on '50 Years of EC Competition Law', Brussels, 5 June 2007

—— **(2007a)** – Kroes, N, *What Competition has Done for Europe's Citizens in the Wake of Globalisation*, speech for the GCLC/ College of Europe Conference on '*Libéralisme vs Protectionisme: pour une Europe ouverte mais pas offerte*', Paris, 30 June 2007

—— **(2008)** – Kroes, N, *Competitiveness – The Common Goal of Competition and Industrial Policies*, speech for the Aspen Institute, Paris, 18 April 2008

——**(2008a)** – Kroes, N, *Consumers at the Heart of EU Competition Policy*, speech for the BEUC Dinner, Strasbourg, 22 April 2008

Lowe (2007) – Lowe, P, *Consumer Welfare and Efficiency – new guiding principles of competition policy?*, speech for 13th International Conference on Competition and 14th European Competition Day, Munich, 27 March 2007

Mario Monti (2001) – Monti, M, *Antitrust in the US and Europe: a History of convergence*, speech for the General Counsel Roundtable American Bar Association (Washington DC), 14 November 2001

—— **(2001a)** – Mario, M, *Content, Competition and Consumers: Innovation and Choice*, European Competition Day, Stockholm, 11 June 2001

—— **(2002)** – Monti, M, *EC Competition Policy*, speech for the Fordham Annual Conference on International Antitrust and Policy (New York), 31 October 2002

—— **(2002a)** – Monti, M, *Priorities for EU Competition Policy*, at the Hellenic Competition Commission, *EU Competition Law and Policy: developments and priorities*, Athens, 19 April 2002

—— **(2003)** – Monti, M, *EU competition policy after May 2004*, speech for the Fordham Annual Conference on International Antitrust Law and Policy (New York), 24 October 2003

—— **(2003a)** – Monti, M, *The New Shape of European Competition Policy*, speech for the Inaugural Symposium of the Competition Policy Research Centre (Tokyo), 20 November 2003

—— **(2004)** – Monti, M, *Comments to the Speech Given by Hew Pate*, Assistant Attorney General, US Department of Justice, at the Conference, *Antitrust in a Transatlantic Context* (Brussels), 7 June 2004

Pons (2001) – Pons, J-F, *European Competition Policy for the Recycling Markets*, Pro Europe International Congress, Madrid, 20 September 2001

van Miert (1993) – van Miert, K, *Competition Policy in the 1990's*, speech for the Royal Institute of International Affairs (Chatham House, London), 11 May 1993, cited in Sauter (1997), page 120

Vickers (2003) – Vickers, J, *Competition Economics*, at the Royal Economic Society annual public lecture, London, 4 December 2003

Wood (1999) – Wood, D, *High Tides, Low Tides: The Scope of the Conference Group Exemption*, EMLO 1999, The Royal Society of Arts, London, 29 January 1999

NEWSPAPER ARTICLES

11 years for EU laws, The Law Society Gazette (London 14 October 2004)

Agence Europe (21 January 2004)

Agence Europe (10 November 1978)

Bravura Nonsense, The Economist (London 22 May 2004)

Bulletin Quotidien Europe, No 8627 (21 January 2004)

Colin Mayer, Financial Times (London 28 August 2002)

Creating European Business Champions, The Economist (London 22 May 2004)

Debating the Minimum Wage, The Economist (London 1 February 2001)

Degrees of Difference, The Economist (London 1 May 2004)

Digging Deep, The Economist (London 8 August 2002)

How Divided Europe Came Together, BBC News, 23 March 2007 <http://news.bbc.co.uk/1/hi/world/europe/6483585.stm> accessed 30 April 2009

La difficile émergence de l'entreprise européenne, Le Monde (Paris 7 July 2004)

M Barroso a été officiellement nommé président de la Commission européenne, Le Monde (Paris 29 June 2004)

Sarkozy modifie le projet de Traité, Le Soir (27 June 2007)

Strategic Caring, The Economist (London 3 October 2002)

Index

Introductory Note

References such as '138–9' indicate (not necessarily continuous) discussion of a topic across a range of pages. Wherever possible in the case of topics with many references, these have either been divided into sub-topics or only the most significant discussions of the topic are listed. Because the entire volume is about Article 81 EC and public policy, the use of these terms (and certain others occurring throughout the work) as an entry point has been minimized. Information will be found under the corresponding detailed topics.

343.240721

TOW

#534241